A Traitor's Kiss

A Traitor's Kiss

The Life of Richard Brinsley Sheridan, 1751–1816

FINTAN O'TOOLE

FARRAR, STRAUS AND GIROUX

New York

Farrar, Straus and Giroux
19 Union Square West, New York 10003

Printed in the United States of America
First published in 1997 by Granta Books, United Kingdom
First American edition, 1998

Library of Congress Cataloging-in-Publication Data
O'Toole, Fintan, 1958–
A traitor's kiss : the life of Richard Brinsley Sheridan, 1751–1816 / Fintan O'Toole. — 1st American ed.
p. cm.
"First published in 1997 by Granta Books, United Kingdom"—T.p. verso.
Includes bibliographical references and index.
ISBN 0-374-27931-4 (alk. paper)
1. Sheridan, Richard Brinsley, 1751–1816—Biography. 2. Dramatists, English—18th century—Biography. 3. Theatrical managers—Great Britain—Biography. 4. Legislators—Great Britain—Biography. I. Title.
PR3683.086 1998
822'.6—dc21 98-23261

Acknowledgements

"Recollect," wrote Lord Byron to Sheridan's first official biographer Thomas Moore, "that he was an Irishman and a clever fellow." No one could forget that he was a clever fellow, but since Moore's, there has been no Irish biography of Sheridan. He came, over time, to be seen as a colourful flaw in the pattern of public life in eighteenth-century England. And because he never quite fit the frame of English history, he became an impossibly contradictory figure. This book is an attempt to suggest that Sheridan looks contradictory because he lived in two different places—a real England and a passionately imagined Ireland—at the same time.

In undertaking that task, I owe a considerable debt to Conor Cruise O'Brien for his book on Edmund Burke, *The Great Melody*, which both suggested the way an Irish life could affect English politics in the eighteenth century and provided a political grain to go against.

I am extremely grateful, too, for more direct assistance from Caitriona Crowe and her colleagues at the Irish National Archives in Dublin; to Dr. Pat Donlon and the staff of the National Library of Ireland; to Colm Tóibín for his comments on the manuscript; to Michael Collinge of Collinge and Clark booksellers; to Dr. Luke Gibbons, Dr. Kevin Whelan, Professor Kevin Barry, Professor Terence Brown, Professor Brian Cosgrove, Antony Farrell of Lilliput Press, Derek Johns, and Dermot Bolger.

Conor Brady, the editor of the *Irish Times*, has been extraordinarily tolerant of my waywardness in the day job, as have Paddy

Woodworth, Victoria White, Sean Flynn, Peter Murtagh, Patsy Murphy and all my colleagues. The enormous contributions to this book of Neil Belton, Emma Sinclair-Webb, Becky Hardie, and Elisabeth Sifton will, I hope and pray, never be given their due. And for the vastness of their support and the paucity of their complaints, I owe to Clare Connell, Samuel O'Toole and Fionn O'Toole a great debt of gratitude and love.

For Clare Connell,
with love

Contents

Preface to the American Edition

About fifteen years after his death, Richard Brinsley Sheridan spoke to a young black boy in Baltimore. Frederick Douglass, then a house slave around twelve years old, had persuaded some white boys to teach him to read. He had heard his white friends talk of a schoolbook from which they were learning to recite. With fifty cents he had earned from blacking boots, he bought the book and spent every spare moment absorbed in its pages. There he found one of Sheridan's great rhetorical arguments on behalf of the oppressed Catholics of his native Ireland. As Douglass put it in his autobiography, "I met with one of Sheridan's mighty speeches on and in behalf of Catholic emancipation. These were choice documents to me. I read them over and over again with unabated interest. They gave tongue to interesting thoughts of my own soul, which had frequently flashed through my mind, and died away for want of utterance . . . What I got from Sheridan was a bold denunciation of slavery and a powerful vindication of human rights."

In a country Sheridan had never visited and in a mind he could scarcely have imagined, his words unleashed strong emotions. For Frederick Douglass they engendered feelings of consolation, but also of deep discontent. They brought the torment of understanding that his own enslavement was not the natural order of things but a willed, created condition. "I would at times feel that learning to read had been a curse rather than a blessing . . . In moments of agony, I envied my fellow-slaves for their stupidity. I have often wished myself a beast. I preferred the condition of the meanest reptile to my own. Any thing, no matter what, to get rid of thinking!"

That Sheridan's political rhetoric could have such immediate force in early-nineteenth-century America may now seem implausible. He is remembered on this side of the Atlantic as the writer of two delightfully artificial comedies that continue to hold a place on the American stage—*The Rivals* and *The School for Scandal*. Those plays keep his name alive. But their world—brittle, powdered, playful, ostensibly trivial—seems impossibly remote from war and revolution, from slavery and human rights, from the epic matter of history.

Yet the connection between the Sheridan who makes us laugh in the theatre and the Sheridan who could engender rage in the heart of a slave is real and deep. It reaches across the Atlantic from Ireland and Britain to the United States. And it goes both ways. Events in America had a crucial impact on Sheridan's political attitudes and alignments. He, in turn, influenced post-revolutionary American culture in its formative phase.

Sheridan's relationship to America is, moreover, germane to any attempt to understand his achievements. For one thing, Sheridan belongs to the era of emerging modernity and not to that of fading feudalism. Yet it is not unusual to hear Sheridan's plays spoken of as a late flowering of Restoration drama, as if he belonged in the culture of the mid-seventeenth century rather than that of the late eighteenth. To remember that he was known and admired in revolutionary America, that he had a place with the newest aspects of the New World, is to dispel that illusion. When we think of George Washington laughing his way through a performance of *The School for Scandal*, Sheridan's life makes far more sense than when we mistakenly imagine him a contemporary of the Restoration wits. If Sheridan had really been a culturally backward figure, his appeal in revolutionary America would be incomprehensible, but if one accepts his modernity and that appeal is comprehended, his place in his own times is obvious and secure.

Second, we must understand that Frederick Douglass's angry, agonised reaction to Sheridan's speeches was entirely appropriate. Though the enduring allure of his plays may distract attention from his politics, Sheridan always saw himself as a political figure first, a man of the theatre second. Theatrical success was, for him, a means to a political end, and his politics were, essentially, radical. One of his finest moments, his powerful participation in the attempt to render the governor-general of India, Warren Hastings, accountable for his abuses of power, was also an important moment in the development of the ideals of universal human rights and of international law.

Lastly, the American connection to Sheridan reminds us that his life was shaped not just by art and by politics but also by fame. To remember that his name was carried across the then vast expanse of the Atlantic Ocean is to recall that he was not only a politician and a playwright but a celebrity. What makes him such a modern figure is that he helped to manufacture an image for himself, to manipulate art and life, fact and invention, into a richly ambiguous persona. To understand him at all one must bear in mind that he was, in a very modern way, known for his romantic adventures before he was known as a playwright or politician, and, afterwards, as a man whose personality was itself the site of political contest. There is no greater proof of this than the way he obtained a foothold in the American imagination even before his plays were performed in the colonies.

It is but a small exaggeration to say that America pushed Sheridan into politics while Sheridan reconciled America to theatre. The American Revolution coincided with Sheridan's emergence as a public figure and shaped his consciousness in the most profound ways. He was passionately committed to the revolutionary cause, and many of his earliest political writings were in its defence. The divisions which the War of Independence created in British politics and society opened up a fissure through which he inserted himself into British public life.

After his death, there were rumours that, when he entered the House of Commons in 1780, he was offered a great deal of money by the Americans to act as their advocate. (According to his first biographer, Thomas Moore, he refused the money but assured the Americans they would always have his support.) The story itself is improbable, but that it was widely believed is testament to the degree to which Sheridan was then identified with the colonies' revolt against Britain. He even played a small part in the politics of America's formal breach with the British monarchy. As deputy Minister for Foreign Affairs in 1782, he argued, without success, that the mother country should recognise American independence as a right rather than concede it in negotiations.

But if America helped to shape Sheridan, he had some effect of his own on its post-revolutionary culture. Even before his own plays were composed, his father's works on language and speech were reasonably well known among the American intelligentsia—the young Thomas Jefferson, for instance, assiduously studied Thomas Sheridan's writings on rhetoric and public speaking. Then, by the late 1770s, Richard's plays, though not yet produced in America, were sufficiently famous for political satires based on them to be comprehensible to American audiences. In 1778, a pro-revolutionary publisher in Philadelphia reprinted, from the London edition of 1776, a squib based on *The Duenna*, Sheridan's successful comic opera; it was called *The Political Duenna, A Comic Opera in Three Acts as it is Performed by the Servants of His Britannic Majesty, with Lord North's Recantation*. The following year, also in Philadelphia, a reprint of an English satire based on *The School for Scandal* appeared. These were evidence, as George Nettleton put it, that already in America Sheridan's "dramatic titles and medium had a popular appeal worth exploiting in the field of contemporary political satire."*

The war and the revolution, however, made production of the plays themselves a rather complicated affair. In 1774, the Continental Congress had adopted a resolution that "exhibitions of shews, plays and other expensive diversions and entertainments" be discouraged. The exigencies of the times, coupled with a strong strain of Puritan distaste for the theatre, had virtually cleared the stage. But over the next decade, Sheridan's dramas did gradually seep into American culture. And in a sense they were the vehicle by which theatre as a form established itself as a legitimate activity in the new United States. One of the founding conceits of a specifically American drama, indeed, was the seductive power of *The School for Scandal* to insinuate itself into stern republican consciousness.

One reminder of the turmoil of the times in which Sheridan wrote his delightful comedies is that they owed their earliest appearances in the New World to refugees and invaders. The first American productions of his work were not in the United States but in Kingston, Jamaica, for after the Continental Congress' prohibition of theatre, the main professional theatre company, the American Company of Comedians, under the direction of Lewis Hallam the Younger, had taken refuge there. Hallam had copies of Sheridan's texts with him: the company presented *The Duenna* in Kingston in November

*George H. Nettleton, "Sheridan's Introduction to the American Stage," Modern Language Association of America Publications, March 1950, pp. 163–82.

1779, followed by *The Rivals* in June 1780 and *The School for Scandal* in May 1781.

Sheridan was brought to the American mainland, by contrast, on the tails of the Redcoats. Ironically for a writer who was openly on the side of the revolutionaries, his fame was spread by the very forces whose mission in America he passionately opposed. The British commander General John Burgoyne was both a playwright and a member of the same Whig circles as Sheridan. In Boston during the opening winter of the war, he encouraged his officers to form a company of "Military Thespians." This example was followed in New York, where British forces under Sir Henry Clinton literally occupied the stage until their evacuation in 1783. On April 21, 1778, just three years after its London premiere, Clinton's Thespians produced *The Rivals* at the John Street Theatre (renamed the Theatre Royal for the duration of the occupation), advertising it as "never before performed in America." It was presumably well received, since it was repeated on April 27 and revived in 1781. On April 15, 1782, the Thespians brought their final New York season to a climax with the first mainland production of *The School for Scandal*, again advertised as "never performed here." They repeated it a week later. The text was probably a copy of a garbled, pirated edition printed in Dublin: almost simultaneously, a reprint of this Dublin edition appeared in Philadelphia. These very early performances made Sheridan virtually unique as a living playwright whose work was being performed simultaneously on both sides of the Atlantic.

The quirk of history that brought Sheridan to the eastern seaboard of continental America as an amusement for the enforcers of King George's will was in a way emblematic of his career as both insider and outlaw. And it certainly did his reputation in America no harm. With the winding down of the war, his plays began to establish themselves in the independent republic. As early as February 1784 *The School for Scandal* was given a professional production in Baltimore by Dennis Ryan's company. The following year, the American Company returned from Jamaican exile and brought its Sheridan repertoire with it. (There is some evidence that the leaders of the company were in touch with Sheridan himself. In 1786 *The School for Scandal* was published in New York and advertised as "from a manuscript copy in the possession of John Henry Esq., joint manager of the American Company, given him by the Author." Since Henry also produced in New York an apparently accurate reproduction of

Sheridan's pantomime *Robinson Crusoe or Harlequin Friday*, it seems certain that he had visited Sheridan at Drury Lane Theatre in London and had been received sympathetically.) It was probably with Sheridan's approval that the American Company, in its first New York season from November 1785 to summer 1786, presented both *The School for Scandal* and *The Rivals*. In October 1786, it opened a new theatre in Richmond, Virginia, with *The School for Scandal*, which also had other productions that season in Maryland and South Carolina.

The American Company, in fact, deployed Sheridan's fame as a weapon in the struggle to establish theatre as a respectable activity against the deep-seated Puritan disdain for illusion and luxury. By July 1787, having honed its Sheridan repertoire in many American cities, the company smuggled it into Philadelphia. The performance of plays was still illegal there, so "a Concert" was held, a discreet but not very subtly coded advertisement in the local press proclaiming: "Between the Parts of the Concert will be introduced a comic LECTURE in five parts on the PERNICIOUS VICE OF SCANDAL. By particular desire—The original prologue to the SCHOOL FOR SCANDAL, Written by R. B. Sheridan, esquire, Author of The Duenna, Rivals, Critic, etc." Sheridan probably did not know about this use of his work to circumvent Pennsylvania law, but there can be little doubt that the idea that a play whose villain is a self-righteous hypocrite became a wicked entertainment advertised as a lecture on vice would have appealed to his sense of humour.

These early productions of Sheridan's plays were important in re-establishing the theatre itself in post-revolutionary America. As President, George Washington lent his prestige to this process, attending performances of *The School for Scandal* in New York. That this was still a rather daring act is evidenced by the reaction of Senator William Maclay, whom Washington brought to one such performance and who was, as the historian James Flexner has put it, "horrified that the chief magistrate should countenance the exposure of 'ladies of character and virtue' to such an 'indecent representation.' "*

So striking, indeed, was the power of the play to overcome Puritan resistance to the theatre that precisely such a triumph is actually woven into the play that inaugurated a self-consciously independent

*James T. Flexner, *George Washington and the New Nation, 1783–93* (New York and Boston, 1970), p. 210.

American drama, Royall Tyler's *The Contrast*. Tyler, a Bostonian who had served as an American staff officer during the Revolution, visited New York in March 1787. There he made his first visit to a regular theatre, to see *The School for Scandal* at the John Street Theatre. Within weeks, he had written *The Contrast*, which became the first comedy by an American author to be produced on the New York professional stage. His play nationalised and explicitly politicised Sheridan's original, re-working the contrast between Charles and Joseph Surface as an opposition of honest Yankee heroism to foppish Anglicised decadence—successfully exposing the latent political content of Sheridan's apparently artificial comedy. Joseph becomes the two-faced Billy Dimple, a slippery lover of all things English, ashamed of his American nationality; Charles becomes the all-American hero Colonel Manly, a brusque, honest warrior and Billy's rival for the hand of the fair heroine. Thus, at one remove, Sheridan contributed to one of the earliest cultural formulations of a specifically American self-image.

The Contrast, in turn, spurred the first professional American playwright, William Dunlap, generally regarded as "the father of American drama," to write *his* first play. Dunlap was already a devotee of Sheridan's, having seen both *The School for Scandal* and *The Critic* in their original productions at Drury Lane while he was studying in London.

Tyler not only was inspired by Sheridan, however, but also paid homage to him as the man whose work seduced suspicious Yankees back to the theatre. In a remarkable passage in *The Contrast*, the theatre is described as it might appear to someone entirely ignorant of its conventions, almost as a Native American might describe the first sighting of a Spanish galleon. The plain American yeoman Jonathan, wandering in New York, is seduced into a playhouse on the promise that he is emphatically not about to witness one of those devilish plays that the preachers had warned against. He is sitting in his seat when, as he says, "they lifted up a great green cloth and let us look right into the next neighbour's house."* It is a performance of *The School for Scandal*. In an intertwining of performance, role, and reality that is also typical of Sheridan's place in the culture of his time, Jonathan was played, in the first production of *The Contrast*,

*Royall Tyler, *The Contrast*, in Richard Moody (ed.), *Dramas from the American Theatre 1762–1909* (Cleveland and New York, 1966), pp. 47 ff.

by Thomas Wignell, who had also played Joseph Surface in the production of *The School for Scandal* that Tyler had seen—and, in the play, Jonathan witnesses—in New York. The surreal humour of this double vision reached its heights when Jonathan, played by Wignell, describes Joseph played by Wignell:

> There was one youngster they called Mr. Joseph; he talked as sober and as pious as a minister; but like some ministers that I know, he was a sly tike in his heart for all that. He was going to ask a young woman to spark it with him and—the Lord have mercy on my soul!—she was another man's wife.

Eventually Jonathan, suspecting that he has been misled into watching a sinful play, discovers he has been watching "the School for Scandalization—The School for Scandalization!—Oh! ho! No wonder you New York folks are so cute at it, when you go to school to learn it."

Sheridan's presence in early American culture tended to involve such confusions of reality and theatre. One of the strangest, most poignant encounters between European and Native Americans involved his work. On March 6, 1786, the American Company's production of *Robinson Crusoe or Harlequin Friday* was performed in New York "for the entertainment of the Indian Chiefs of the Oneida nation, now in this city." Probably devised by Elizabeth Sheridan with assistance from her husband, this pantomime seems, from surviving accounts, to have been itself a strange fantasy of meetings between European travellers and New World natives. The first half follows the outline of Daniel Defoe's novel. But in the second, set in Spain, Crusoe disappears back to England, leaving the black man Friday—played by one of the first black-face performers to appear on the American stage—in the arms of a white Columbine. The lovers are rescued from various distresses by a black magician and transported back to the island, where "the Piece concludes with a Grand Dance of Savages."* What the Oneida chiefs made of these dancing savages and fantasies of interracial love can never be recovered from such a curious historical moment. In white culture,

*See Cecil Price (ed.), *The Dramatic Works of Richard Brinsley Sheridan*, Oxford University Press, 1973, II, 784–86.

though, this momentary encounter may well be one of the first collisions of idealised images of the Noble Savage with the actual process of white dispossession of the Indians.

Sheridan's work continued to influence American culture's ambiguous attitudes toward the continent's original inhabitants—the impact in America of his last play, *Pizarro*, with its heroic Indians resisting European conquest, continued to be refracted throughout the nineteenth century in such popular plays as John Augustus Stone's 1829 *Metamora or The Last of the Wampanoags*. *Pizarro* also appealed to African-Americans: Ira Aldridge, the first black actor to earn an international reputation in straight drama, made his debut with the black African Company at the age of fifteen, when, in 1822, he played Rolla, the Inca hero, in *Pizarro* at New York's African Grove Theater. Again, as with the Oneida watching *Robinson Crusoe*, the meaning of such performances cannot be recovered. But the idea of a black Rolla inspiring his people to throw off the European yoke in pre–Civil War America is tantalising. That the words in his mouth were Sheridan's is another reminder of how politically complex and ambiguous a force he remained until well into the nineteenth century.

Gradually, though, in the United States as in Britain, Sheridan was absorbed into the comfortable realm of established classics. Shaped and adapted to the needs of the repertory companies, his work lost its edge of danger. Augustin Daly, the dominant American theatre manager of the last quarter of the nineteenth century, did his own versions of Sheridan's plays, allowing Ada Rehan to become a reportedly spectacular Mrs. Malaprop. In the 1881–82 season, Joseph Jefferson adapted *The Rivals* for a production at the Union Square Theatre in New York, cutting out the Julia-Faulkland subplot and emphasising his own role of Bob Acres and that of Mrs. Malaprop, played in her most famous role by Louisa Lane, grandmother of the Barrymore theatrical clan. It toured extensively, playing to packed houses.

The American tendency to re-invent Sheridan was not confined to his plays. The confusion of theatre and reality that often surrounded Sheridan's image reached its height in America in 1893 and 1894, with Paul E. Potter's successful romantic comedy *Sheridan; or The Maid of Bath*, a play that opened at the Lyceum Theatre in New York in August 1893, with Sheridan played by the rising star and "young comedian" E. H. Sothern.* In an author's note, Potter deliberately fused Sheridan's own plays and his early life: "Sheridan's comedies are admitted to have been drawn from life; hence, the purpose of this play is to introduce some of his originals." To confuse art and life further, Potter wove together two aspects of Sheridan's life that were actually separated in time—his romance with Elizabeth Linley, culminating in the duels he fought with her would-be seducer, Captain Mathews, and the writing and first production of *The Rivals*. Theatrical figures whom Sheridan did not become involved with until after his marriage to Elizabeth—David Garrick and Michael Kelly—were introduced alongside versions of protagonists in his romantic adventures: Mathews; Elizabeth's father, Thomas Linley; and "Mr Barnett of Castle Magillicuddy, Ireland."

Potter's play opens with Sheridan's introduction to and acceptance by the circle of the Linleys. It then has him wrongly disgraced on account of his efforts to protect Elizabeth from Mathews. He writes *The Rivals* and endures agonies of desperation because of the failure of its first performance. The tension leads him to denounce Mathews publicly, and Mathews in turn challenges him to a duel. The young hero then fights Mathews, and forces him to confess the truth, restoring Sheridan in the eyes of the Linleys and smoothing the way to marriage; at the same time, the re-worked version of *The Rivals* is staged by Garrick and is a great hit. Life and art blend completely into a perfect triumph. In the process, Sheridan's messy biography had been organised into a prototype for the Hollywood biopic, in which perseverance and romance triumph over adversity and injustice.

Potter's play marked the final transformation of Sheridan in America into a colorful but harmless figure, remote from history, revolution, slavery, and rage. His plays continued to hold the American stage, especially in the 1930s and 1940s. In 1931, Ethel Barrymore's performance as Lady Teazle in *The School for Scandal* was one of the events of the season. In 1942, an all-star production of *The Rivals* ran for fifty-four performances on Broadway. In 1946, the Old Vic Theatre from London brought its double bill of *Oedipus Rex* and *The Critic*, with Laurence Olivier playing both Oedipus and Mr. Puff, to New York.

*See the Robinson Locke Collection of Dramatic Scrapbooks, New York Public Library for the Performing Arts, NAFR, v. 435, p. 47.

But by then, if Sheridan the man existed at all in the American public imagination, it was almost certainly as an archetypal Regency rake. The main American biography of him, Oscar Sherwin's *Uncorking Old Sherry*, published in 1960, did little to deepen or correct that impression. The prevailing critical view of his plays, meanwhile, was that they were a pleasant throwback or, as Eric Bentley put it, "a pale ghost of the earlier variety" of comedy exemplified by Congreve and Molière. In this view, Sheridan's relationship to his own times did not really matter because, in the creation of everything important about him—the plays themselves—he was not *of* his own times. His plays were "uncharacteristic of their age, not only in their genius, but in their adherence to [an] earlier formula."*

This book is an attempt to put some flesh on the pale ghost, to suggest that Sheridan, far from being uncharacteristic of his age, was a vivid and vital presence in the culture of his time, both as a writer and as a politician. It tries to locate him in a time of upheaval, to see him as a public man animated by three revolutions, the American, the French, and, in his soured hopes, the Irish. It makes an effort to see him in the light of the ways he defined himself—as an Irishman, as an enemy of oppression, as a child of the Enlightenment, as a consummate conspirator, and, in the midst of all these things, as a man of the theatre. If, at the end of it, the reader no longer finds it strange that such a man as Frederick Douglass could have been so moved by Sheridan's words, the book will have done its job.

New York
May 1988

*Eric Bentley, *The Playwright as Thinker* (New York, 1946), pp. 105, 161.

Once in a showery summer, sick of war,
I strode the roads that slanted to Kilmore.

John Hewitt, "Townland of Peace" (1944)

A Traitor's Kiss

Chapter 1

BLOODY CHARACTERS

The madman was, they said, a very acute scholar who had cracked his brain with too much study.[1] Though Catholic and Irish as well as mad, he was allowed, as he went begging along the hills and lakes of West Cavan, into the houses of the Protestant Bishop of Kilmore, William Bedell, and of his ministers, among them a native Irish convert called Donnchadh O Sioradain.[2] That autumn of 1641, the madman passed the spot on the road, near the houses of both the bishop and his nemesis, Edmund O'Reilly, chief of the most powerful clan in the county, where strange insects, the length of a man's finger, had riddled the ground with holes and stripped it bare of any green thing. And in the houses he visited, there were curious multitudes of rats, so bold that they ran under the very tables in daylight to steal crumbs and bones. The old Irishwomen said that the rats were a sign of war. And after the calamity descended on them, even the God-fearing Protestants would come to believe, too, that the insects had been its "forerunning tokens."

The crazy scholar, when in the houses of the bishop or his ministers, would address them in deranged Latin. If he could get his hands on a piece of paper or a book, he would write curious, disjointed sentences. And so, that autumn, when his broken words and illogical sentences were portents of disaster, the reverend gentleman paid no notice to the vital information they contained. Walking up and down in a minister's house, sighing and, contrary to his normally merry kind of madness, looking grief-sticken, he repeated over and over the words "Where is King Charles now?" He took out an old almanac, all scribbled over with his crazed characters, and wrote, "We doubt not of France and Spain in this action."[3]

Afterwards, when Edmund O'Reilly led the natives in a fierce uprising against the colonists, when the madman's words were "put together and commented upon by the rebellion in bloudy characters," the men of God would realise that the madman had passed through houses where conspirators had been discussing their plot against the English. He had carried in his scattered wits intelligence that could have saved many lives. Soon, through blood and chaos would a madman's shattered sentences be translated into stark raving sense.

The nineteenth-century historian W.E.H. Lecky, writing his great treatise on the eighteenth century, felt it necessary to begin with the insurrection of 1641. And he did so with good reason, for in the words of Roy Foster, "What people thought happened in that bloody autumn conditioned events and attitudes in Ireland for generations to come."[4] Lurid and exaggerated reports of events that were in any case horrifying enough in themselves were driven into the Protestant consciousness, where they remained as a warning against Catholic treachery and an encouragement to hard-faced repression, most immediately in Oliver Cromwell's ferocious campaign against Irish resistance in 1649 and 1650. In 1662, the Irish Parliament declared that the first day of the rebellion should be "kept and celebrated as an anniversary holy day in this kingdom for ever." John Wesley was chilled to the bone by the blood-curdling accounts of the rising circulating in the middle of the eighteenth century. Sir John Temple's carefully selective book on the massacres, written in 1646, was still being published in a new edition just six years before the death of Richard Brinsley Sheridan in 1816. Even then it continued to provide one of the main arguments for the maintenance of repressive laws against Catholics.[5]

And just as that day in October 1641 changed forever the fate of Ireland, so, more intimately, did it shape the destiny of one branch of the O'Sheridan family in Cavan.

In the houses the madman visited in those days before the great rebellion of 1641, men were engaged in an effort of translation much more momentous but no less doomed. The bishop's house in Kilmore, a remote settlement nestling amidst the woods, bogs, and drumlins—"little hills rising in the forms of hogs' backs"[6]—of a pleasant, rolling landscape, was occupied by William Bedell, the son of an Essex yeoman, who had been sent to Ireland as Provost of

Trinity College, Dublin, and then been made Bishop of Kilmore in 1629.

Less than a mile away, at Drumcor, in a small farmhouse by the side of Lough Oughter, lived Donnchadh O Sioradain. O Sioradain was a native and a Gaelic-speaker, but a convert to Protestantism. He seems to have been orphaned at an early age, educated as a Protestant by a local English minister, and married to an Englishwoman called Foster. Bedell took a special liking to him and valued him for his "good conversation and skill in the Irish language." The bishop made O Sioradain a minister, and granted him a living in the parish of Killesher. But O Sioradain was still very much an Irishman, close to his people and his family, who were, after the O'Reillys, the most "numerous and potent" in Cavan.

That O Sioradain's skill in the Irish language was valued by Bedell is not as surprising as it might seem, for Bedell himself was a virtually unique figure, an English Protestant divine who believed it his business to bring light to the native Irish, to come as a missionary rather than a conquerer. While most English bishops in colonised Ireland looked to their native flocks for the spoils of conquest, Bedell genuinely believed himself their humble servant. Granted two dioceses, Kilmore and Ardagh, he gave up the latter, hoping to set an example of humility to his fellow bishops. Explaining his action, he wrote to his friend Samuel Ward in Cambridge that it was the fault of the Protestants that the native Irish preferred to stay loyal to their Catholic priests: "The Popish clergy is double to us in number, and having the advantage of the [Irish] toung, of the love of the people, of our extortions upon them, of the very inborne hatred of subdued people to their conquerors, they hold them still in blindness and superstition, our selves being the cheefest impediments to the worke that we pretend to set forward."[7]

Bedell set in train one of the most poignant enterprises in Irish cultural history, the translation of the Old Testament into Irish. He learned the language himself, "taking to his assistance one Mr King and Mr Dennis Sheridan, both Irishmen and clergymen and excellently skilled in the language of their own country, whose office it was to translate the English version into Irish."[8] Every day, at one o'clock in the church of Kilmore, Bedell had his deacon, Owen O'Sheridan, another of the O'Sheridan converts, read in Irish from the Book of Common Prayer "for the benefit of those he had brought from popery but understood not the English tongue."[9]

Bedell's translations were not just instruments of conversion. They also placed in the hands of the Irish poor, for the first time ever, comprehensible texts of the Scriptures, which in fact continued to be used in Catholic Masses as late as the 1970s. He also engaged the local Catholic priests and scholars in theological argument, treating them with respect and affection, in the process converting a number of them. Among them, and "the learnedst of them" was "my loving brother Cohonaght O'Sheridan," to whom he wrote in Latin with "the desired effect."[10] At least three of the O'Sheridans around Kilmore—Donnchadh, Owen, and Cohonaght—therefore became Protestant clergymen.

Through Bedell, the O'Sheridans had become involved in one of the bravest, oddest, and most potentially far-reaching enterprises in Irish history: the attempt to found, in the drumlins of Cavan, a Gaelic Protestantism, to escape the identification of Catholic and Irish, Protestant and British, that would bedevil that history for centuries. It was a noble project, but a doomed one. Bedell was under constant pressure from his own religious and political superiors, who looked with suspicion on his respectful attitude to the Irish Catholics. And, shortly after the madman's disjointed warnings, the Irish Catholics put an end to his mission by rising up in a rebellion that would shape for centuries the sectarian contours of Irish history.

The rebellion reflected the complex nature of religious and political power in Ireland at the time. The Protestant reformation had made little progress in Ireland: the vast majority of both the Gaelic Irish and of the descendants of early settlers (the so-called old English) were still Catholic. But the newer English and Scottish settlers were Protestant, and their increasing power placed new strains on the loyalty of the old English. So long as Charles I, with his policy of relative religious tolerance, remained in control in England, those strains could be contained. But when, from 1640 onwards, his power was threatened by the militantly Protestant Parliament, the old English and the Gaelic Irish began to look to their mutual interests as Catholics. Charles I, realising that they could be of considerable use in his struggle with Parliament, encouraged the arming of the Gaelic Irish in Ulster. When they rose against the Protestant settlers in October 1641, therefore, they did so in the name of the King. After a few weeks, the old English Catholics joined them, and a clear identification between religion and politics began to take shape in Ireland. In what gradually became a civil war between Catholics and

Protestants, William Bedell's attempts to blur the distinctions between Gaelic and Protestant were doomed to failure. Instead he and his allies among the Sheridans became footnotes in a long saga of atrocity and counter-atrocity as war set up a ten-year reign in Ireland.

Beginning on 23 October 1641, the Irish chieftains of Ulster launched concerted attacks on the English and Scottish settlers, killing perhaps two thousand of them. In Cavan, Edward O'Reilly was more moderate, sacking some houses but for the most part merely urging the settlers to leave. After a fortnight, though, crowds of refugees, most of them destitute and half-naked, began to arrive at Bedell's house in Kilmore, where they were given shelter. Bedell himself was unmolested, the rebels telling him that "he should be the last Englishman that should be put out of Ireland."[11]

So well trusted was Bedell, indeed, that the rebels asked him to draw up a statement of their grievances for delivery to the Lords Justices of Ireland. It was a markedly more minimal set of demands than those set out in statements in other parts of the country, playing down religious issues and concentrating on threats to land titles, the depredations of the government and, significantly, a residual loyalty to the King.[12] For some time, Bedell managed to maintain an uneasy peace with the O'Reillys, protecting as best he could the miserable refugees now under his care, and refusing offers of safe passage to Dublin. Donnchadh O'Sheridan, "being Irish, and of a name and family powerfull in that countrey, was exempted from the violence which the protestants sadly suffered from the Irish."[13]

When eventually the rebels decided to evict Bedell from the bishop's house and install his Catholic rival, the bishop was imprisoned over Christmas in the dismal Cloughoughter Castle, built on a rock in the lake. O'Sheridan, however, helped to persuade Edmund O'Reilly to release him. Bedell chose to move with his family to O'Sheridan's house nearby, which was already a sanctuary "to as many distress'd English as it could contain." According to Bedell's son, O'Sheridan's influence with his own clan was still so strong that "all the chief of the name, Sheridons, out of their love to their kinsman and the bishop now sojourning with him, did often express and promise their utmost endeavours, to the hazard of their lives, to secure them and the house from any violence whatever." O'Sheridan, who was on good terms with the Catholic bishop, even managed to retrieve from the bishop's house Bedell's treasured Hebrew manuscript Bible.

In January, though, there was an outbreak of fever in O'Sheridan's overcrowded house, and Bedell himself was infected. After a few days, the bishop who had laboured to put the right words on his faith, to translate a Protestant sensibility into Gaelic terms, was so ill that "he could neither command his mind nor yet his tongue, either to conceive or express what he intended and desired." In O'Sheridan's house, the great effort at articulation that was Bedell's doomed mission fell silent. When he was dead, O'Sheridan went to the Catholic bishop to ask that Bedell be buried beside his wife in Kilmore churchyard. The bishop replied that "the churchyard was no more to be polluted with heretick's bodies."[14] O'Sheridan appealed to O'Reilly, who overruled his bishop and allowed Bedell a place in the soil of Cavan.

Bedell had asked in his will to be buried without pomp, but on the day of his funeral, 9 February 1642, large numbers of O'Sheridans arrived at their kinsman's house to accompany the coffin on the short walk to the churchyard. Some of the O'Sheridan chiefs even insisted that they be bearers. And, when the cortège passed the house of Edmund O'Reilly, he and his son Mullmore, together with their followers, some armed with muskets, some beating drums, joined the procession. When they reached the grave, Mullmore O'Reilly told Bedell's family "that they might use what prayers, or what form of burial, they pleased; none should interrupt them." When the Protestant service was finished, the rebels fired a volley over the grave and cried out "Requiescat in pace, ultimus Anglorum"—"May the last of the Englishmen rest in peace."

It was a strange and tantalising moment. An English Protestant divine, in the midst of an elemental war of nationality and religion, recognised as being at once alien and native. In thinking it right that this "heretick" should be laid to rest among them, according to his own heretical ceremonies, the Cavan rebels acknowledged for a moment the possibility that the rigour of fixed divisions of English and Irish, Catholic and Protestant, might somehow be eluded. But this moment of acknowledgement was, of course, a death not a birth. It marked the end of Bedell's great enterprise and the beginning of a darker, clearer history.

After Bedell's funeral, his family and the surviving refugees stayed at O'Sheridan's house until the middle of June, "marvellously sanctuaryed in the midst of their enemyes." Then, under a truce with the rebels, 1,200 Protestants, some of them chewing on the leather hides that had been used to furnish their huts, some pregnant, some carrying two children on their backs, set out on a long march towards Dublin. Two thousand rebels accompanied them as far as Drogheda as a "lyfe-guard." From Dublin, Bedell's family sailed back to England.

O'Sheridan, of course, stayed behind. He preserved the manuscript of the translation of the New Testament into Gaelic, and later passed it to the Bishop of Meath, Dr. Henry Jones.[15] With the defeat of the rebellion by Cromwell, he returned to his parish at Killesher, where he lived "to a great yet vigorous old age."[16] But, in the aftermath of rebellion, war, and savage repression, he could no longer be a middle man, a go-between, a Gaelic Protestant. Cavan, in common with the rest of the country, was depopulated and devastated, nearly half its land confiscated for Cromwellian settlers. Catholics, who had held nearly 60 percent of Irish land in 1641, held just 9 percent in 1660.[17] There was no middle ground between Catholicism and Protestantism left to occupy, just a choice between Catholic poverty and ignominy on the one hand and Protestant respectability on the other.

Detached from the Gaelic tribe by Bedell's promise of intellectual liberation, Donnchadh O'Sheridan, now known as Dennis Sheridan, was left with no other possibility than a firm identification with Protestant civility. He and his English wife had five sons, each of whom adopted careers in the power structures of the official Church and of the state itself. Two became senior army officers, one a Commissioner for the Irish Revenue, and two became bishops in the Church of Ireland. Patrick Sheridan served as Bishop of Cloyne from 1679 to 1682. Dennis's youngest son, William, succeeded to Bedell's old office as Bishop of Kilmore and Ardagh in 1681.[18]

Even such a spectacularly successful transition from Gaelic Irish to pillar of Protestantism, however, could not obscure the political and religious contradictions of the Sheridans' position. In 1688, when the Catholic James II was dethroned by William of Orange in the Glorious Revolution, only one bishop of the Church of Ireland, William Sheridan of Kilmore, refused to take the Oath of Supremacy and Allegiance to the new Protestant monarchy. In 1691, after the Williamite forces had completed their victory over James in Ireland, Dennis Sheridan's youngest son was ignominiously removed from his bishopric as a traitor. A decade later, we glimpse him, in a description by Archbishop King, as "exceeding poor and crazy."[19] Right to the end of his life, though, he continued to sign himself "William

Kilmore,"[20] as he does in what is probably his last letter to his doctor: "I tell you I shall be no longer a false prophet, for I am now dying. Therefore, I desire that you should come to see me before I dye." Even as they made their way in the world, the shadows of madness, poverty, and treason would always follow the descendants of Dennis Sheridan.

Chapter 2

THE GODFATHER

At the end of January 1752, when Richard Brinsley Sheridan was an infant, the *Dublin Journal* carried as its leading item of local news the information that his father, Thomas Sheridan Esquire, manager of the Theatre Royal at Smock Alley, was planning to stage a benefit play to raise money for a memorial to "that glorious Patriot and great Genius, the late Jonathan Swift."[1] The proposal was not surprising. Swift was Thomas Sheridan's godfather and the closest friend of his father, Dr. Thomas Sheridan. Thomas Sheridan regarded him, as he wrote in his *Life of the Rev. Dr. Jonathan Swift*, as the most beneficent influence on his life.

If the proposal for a monument to Swift was appropriate, though, it was also fruitless. Sheridan's benefit performance attracted a full house and raised the impressive sum of £101. But hardly anyone turned up to a meeting organised to appoint trustees to handle the money, and the monument, in the event, was never built. Six years later, Thomas Sheridan was still defending himself from the imputation that the money had been raised under false pretences.

But the imputation, taken either literally or metaphorically, was unjust. Thomas Sheridan was no swindler. And, albeit accidentally, he did help to perpetuate, through his son Richard, the legacy of Jonathan Swift. It was an inheritance of linguistic attitudes, of ways to use words to keep afloat in the dangerous cross-currents of loyalty and betrayal that swept the shores of Irish Protestant radicalism.

Dr. Thomas Sheridan was a clergyman and schoolmaster passionately interested in language, theatre, and mathematics. He was, in

Swift's words to Sheridan himself, "of a weak constitution, in an employment precarious and tiresome, loaden with children, *cum uxore neque leni neque commoda*, a man of intent and abstracted thinking, enslaved by Mathematiks and complaint of the world."[2] But for all that, Swift found in this odd man twenty years his junior one of the few people in Ireland with whom he could talk and work.

Swift once described himself stealing away from a card party to write to Dr. Thomas "like a lover writing to his mistress," and there was indeed something almost sexual in their linguistic relationship. The pair exchanged verses and riddles, ranging from mock-panegyrics to low insults. In the game, Swift expected the younger man to remain within unspoken boundaries of deference. But Dr. Thomas continually crossed those borders. In his verse essay on wit, *To Mr Delany*, Swift talks directly of his friend's tendency to transgress. Sheridan is, he writes, a man

> Who full of humour, fire and wit,
> Not allways judges what is fit;
> But loves to take prodigious rounds,
> And sometimes walks beyond his bounds.

To Mr Delany was written, indeed, in order to be passed on to Sheridan to show him the error of his ways. It is a subtle attempt to school the schoolmaster. But Swift was also fascinated by and attracted to Dr. Thomas's anarchic use of language, his promiscuous and sometimes surreal punning. The years of Swift's most intense friendship with Sheridan are also the years of *Gulliver's Travels*, *The Drapier's Letters*, and *A Modest Proposal*, the years, in other words, of Swift's own most resolute transgression of the boundaries of what should be said in public. While trying to curb Sheridan's tongue, Swift learned to loosen his own.

Language and its boundaries were the very soul of the relationship. There is no doubt that the tension in Swift's writing between a desire for order and a tendency to anarchy reflects the deep ambivalence of Swift's position between Ireland and England. As Irvin Ehrenpreis put it, "An ambivalence underlay his wavering between two nations, and found expression in his style: the English vocabulary, the Irish mockery; English restraint, Irish exuberance; English scepticism, Irish fantasy."[3] And this ambiguity had political connotations, especially in a society like that of Ireland in the eighteenth century, where the forms of words in oaths of allegiance were of pivotal significance for the separation of the Protestant political community from the great Catholic mass of people who were excluded from it. The great drama of Swift's writings—the contradiction between a rage for social order on the one hand and the unstable language in which it is expressed on the other—was also played out in his attitude, by turns censorious and encouraging, to Dr. Thomas Sheridan's dangerous way with words. Swift gave his friend the nickname "Tom Punsiby," marking him as the personification of linguistic ambiguity.

That ambivalence, at once political and linguistic, was woven into the texture of the relationship. Swift's friendship with Dr. Thomas Sheridan brought him into sustained contact with linguistic instability and diversity. Some of that diversity—Sheridan's great mastery of Greek and Latin—was acceptably classical. But some of it, too, was dangerously Irish. Through Sheridan, Swift had his most sustained contact with the Gaelic Irish during his long stay at Dr. Thomas's house in Quilca, County Cavan.

He stayed there for long periods in the 1720s, when William Bedell's project of a Gaelic Protestantism was being revived. Bishop Wetenhall of Kilmore was supporting the programme of the rector of Belturbet, John Richardson, to print versions of the New Testament, the catechism, and the Book of Common Prayer in Irish.[4] Swift knew Richardson—he met him in London in 1711 and dismissed him as a crank[5]—and later became very friendly with his brother, William.

But he also had much more direct contact with Gaelic culture. He refers, during a visit in 1722, to "blind harpers" at Quilca: Turlough O'Carolan, born near Nobber, a few miles to the east, was at the height of his fame. Swift himself translated *O'Rourke's Feast*, a Gaelic song to which Carolan had put music, around this time. Again, though on much more modest a scale than a century earlier, the Sheridans in Cavan found themselves at the site of an extraordinary confluence of cultures. Dr. Thomas Sheridan refers, in a poem, to Swift enjoying the conversation of "Irish Teagues" (Catholics) at Quilca and even to his learning to "gabble" in Gaelic:

> Instead of Bolingbroke and Anna
> Shane Tunelly and Bryan Granna;
> Oxford and Ormonde he supplies

In every Irish Teague he spies,
So far forgetting his old station,
He seems to like their conversation.
Conforming to the tattered rabble,
He learns their Irish tongue to gabble.

Gulliver's Travels, much of which was written and revised at Quilca, uses some words derived from Gaelic—like the "luhimuhs" (derived from *luc*, mouse in Irish, and *mus*, mouse in Latin) that the Yahoos eat, or the land of Traldragdrubb or Trildrogdrib, which Gulliver visits on the voyage to Laputa and whose name may be derived from the Irish words *triall, droch* and *drib*—slave, evil and dirt—referring to the fact that those received by its king have to crawl up to the throne, licking the dirt from the floor on the way.[6] We know that Dr. Thomas read at least some of *Gulliver's Travels* in manuscript because Swift, in a letter to him from Quilca in September 1725, refers without explanation to "my description of Yahoes."[7] While it cannot be said with any certainty that Sheridan had any part in suggesting these Gaelic references, there remains the poignant possibility that these hidden traces of another culture in one of the great books of the English language owe their existence to the peculiar displacement of the Sheridans.

In any case, Swift's relationship to the Sheridans produced a perfect parable on the treachery of language in a time of political uncertainty. In May 1725, as a direct result of lobbying by Swift, Dr. Thomas Sheridan was appointed by the Lord Lieutenant, John Cartaret, to the living of Rincurran in County Cork. Swift was delighted with his friend's good fortune and plied him with stern advice about how to behave. He knew Sheridan to be playful and impetuous, one, as he put it, whose "thoughts are sudden, and the most unreasonable always come uppermost." He urged his protégé to wise up, to look out for himself, and to seize his opportunity for comfort and status. "Pray," he wrote, "act like a man of this world."

Some of what Swift meant by acting like a man of this world is obvious enough. Swift's letters to Sheridan on the subject are full of sound and detailed economic advice about how to keep an eye on the tithes and make sure that the theoretical value of the living was translated into actual cash. But much of it, too, is about language or, more precisely, about how to deploy language as a political weapon for securing advantage. On 28 June 1725, Swift wrote to Sheridan from Quilca: "If you are under the Bishop of Cork, he is a capricious gentleman; but you must flatter him monstrously upon his learning and his writings." Much more importantly, though, Swift added instructions about taking oaths of allegiance:

> Take the Oaths heartily to the Powers that be, and remember that Party was not made for depending Puppies. I forgot one principal thing—to take care of going regularly thro' all the Forms of Oaths and Inductions, for the least wrong step will put you to the trouble of repassing your patent, or voiding your Living.[8]

The meaning of these warnings is obvious enough. Thomas Sheridan, as Swift knew, was, as a descendant of William Sheridan, the only Irish Protestant bishop to refuse to take the Oath of Allegiance to William and Mary in 1688, suspected of being a closet Jacobite.[9] Swift's warning that impoverished pups like Sheridan could not afford the luxury of political allegiance came from the heart, since he had suffered for his own suspected affection for the Jacobite cause. And indeed, the next day, on 29 June, Swift underscored the point in another letter, this time adding the endorsement of Stella: "But Mrs Johnson and I go further and say you must needs observe all grave Forms for the want of which both you and I have suffered."[10]

From the death of Queen Anne onwards Swift had been accused from time to time of being a Jacobite, and as late as 1730, five years after these letters to Thomas Sheridan, he was still being publicly derided as a "Jacobite libeller."[11] The charge is almost certainly misplaced, but many of Swift's political associates were Jacobites. Bolingbroke, Ormond, and Ford fled to the court of the Pretender, James III, in 1713, and Francis Atterbury, in a trial which is referred to in a number of passages in *Gulliver's Travels*, was found guilty of conspiring to restore the House of Stuart and banished in 1723. Not for nothing does Gulliver in Lilliput learn that his friendly and innocent associations with the ambassadors from Blefescu have made him a suspicious character: "I had a Whisper from a certain Person that *Flimnap* and *Bolgolam* had represented my Intercourse with those Ambassadors as a mark of Disaffection, from which I am sure my Heart was wholly free."[12] The danger of being suspected as a Jacobite was certainly fresh in Swift's mind at the time he wrote these letters to Sheridan warning him to take the oaths to the powers that be.

It was a warning that would have a profound effect on the careers of three generations of Sheridans—Dr. Thomas, his son Thomas, and his grandson Richard Brinsley Sheridan. In Swift's sanction for outward show and inner allegiance, for a theatrical language of loyalty counterpointed with a private language of disloyalty, is to be found, perhaps, the root of the extraordinary political and theatrical balancing act which Richard Brinsley Sheridan came close to pulling off sixty years later.

What Swift was advising Dr. Thomas Sheridan about was how to exploit the gap between political feelings and political expression, how to flirt with treason while proclaiming loyalty. A passage in the fourth of *The Drapier's Letters*, Swift's brilliant polemic against the British government's proposals to foist debased coinage on Ireland, issued less than a year before these letters to Sheridan, offers a superb example. It simultaneously protests fierce loyalty to the Hanoverian crown and raises the spectre of Jacobite rebellion:

> I am so far from depending upon the People of England, that if they should ever rebel against my Sovereign (which God forbid) I would be ready at the first Command from his Majesty to take Arms against them; as some of my countrymen did against theirs at Preston. And if such a Rebellion should prove so successful as to fix the Pretender on the Throne of England; I would venture to transgress that Statute so far as to lose every Drop of my Blood, to hinder him from being King of Ireland.

These sentences are simultaneously treasonous and excessively loyal. They seem to be passionately pro-Hanoverian, yet they provoke the unthinkable thought that a Stuart might again rule in England. And they also imagine the possibility of a King of England who was not King of Ireland, a legal impossibility amounting to treason which Richard Brinsley Sheridan would, in time, try to make a reality.

In his warnings to his friend about the need for outward shows of loyalty to the powers that be, Swift almost certainly had *The Drapier's Letters* in mind. There is a good deal of evidence that Dr. Thomas Sheridan had a hand in the *Letters*. His appointment to the living in Cork was opposed by the English party in Dublin politics, who saw Sheridan as a confederate of the Drapier. One of them, the lawyer John Pocklington, wrote to a friend that "Mr Sheridan, a schoolmaster in town and second to Swift in the battle about the halfpence, has got a living, which last is surprising to all here." On 31 August 1725, Swift wrote to the Reverend John Worrall cancelling plans for "An Humble Address to both Houses of Parliament," which was part of the Drapier campaign. This projected pamphlet became redundant when the patent was surrendered. Swift wrote to Worrall, "Since Wood's patent is cancelled, it will by no means be convenient to have the paper printed, as I suppose you and Jack Grattan and *Sherridan* [sic] will agree; therefore if it be with the printer, I would have it taken back and the press broke."[13] This certainly suggests that Sheridan contributed to the *Letters*, either as a co-author or at least as an editor and co-conspirator. However well-founded the suspicions of Jacobitism may have been in Sheridan's case, it is clear that he had at least participated in Swift's ambigious interplay of treason and loyalty in *The Drapier's Letters*.

Sheridan went down to take up his living and was invited to give a sermon in Cork city on Sunday, 1 August, the anniversary of the accession of George I. According to his son's *Life of Swift*, Sheridan forgot about the sermon, until he was summoned by a messenger with an urgent reminder that his congregation was waiting. "He dressed himself with all speed, and of the two sermons he had brought with him, took the first that came into his hand, without looking into it."[14] Of all the texts in Holy Scripture, the chosen sermon happened to be on Matthew, Chapter 6, Verse 34: "Take therefore no thought for the morrow: for the morrow shall take thought of the things of itself. Sufficient unto the day is the evil thereof." In the congregation was a fierce Whig, probably Richard Tighe, an MP and Privy Counsellor, who immediately raised the alarm in Dublin Castle.[15] The "evil" of the day was assumed to be the accession of the Hanoverians. Sheridan's choice of text was heard as a Jacobite protest. As Swift wrote:

> It happened to be the first of August; and the first of August happened that year to light upon a Sunday: And it happened that the Doctor's text was in these words; sufficient unto the day is the evil thereof; and lastly it happened that some one person of the congregation, whose loyalty made him watchful upon every appearance of danger to his majesty's person and government, when service was over, gave the alarm; and by the zeal of one of no very

> large dimensions of body or mind, such a clamour was raised that we in Dublin could apprehend no less than an invasion by the Pretender who must be landed in the south.

There ended the glorious clerical career of Dr. Thomas Sheridan, destroyed by the untrustworthiness of language in a society where the governance of the tongue was the price of preferment. Swift wrote ruefully to Sheridan: "It is safer for a man's Interest to blaspheme God, than to be of a Party out of Power, or even to be thought so. And since that was the case, how could you imagine that all Mouths would not open when you were received, and in some manner preferred, by the Government . . ."[16] The choice of text for the sermon, he wrote later, was a fatal slip of the tongue. Whig enemies of Swift had "dinned the words Tory and Jacobite into his Excellency's Ears, and therefore your text etc. was only made use of as an opportunity."[17] The moral of the story was that words needed to be watched, that language, especially if it hinted at treason, was treacherous.

It is a lesson that was well learned by the Sheridans. Thomas Sheridan's son, Thomas, became obsessed with language and speech and, as one of the first compilers of an English dictionary, with the need to standardise and define, to anchor words in solid and immutable meanings. His grandson Richard Brinsley Sheridan, on the other hand, learned to exploit words, to master the tongue. By turning the ambiguity of language into a weapon and by reinforcing it with the power of theatricality, he would learn Swift's great trick of making words powerful by speaking them from behind the mask of an assumed persona. In that sense, his work as a playwright and as a politician would become the monument to Swift's memory that his father never managed to build.

Chapter 3

NO ONE ELSE TO LOVE

At first, he was given the name of his dead brother, so that ghosts hovered at his baptism. His parents decided to call him Thomas, the name of his father, his father's father, and of an illustrious forebear who had been King James II's private secretary. In the Sheridan family, to be called Thomas was a mark of great expectation. But in his case, the honour had been intended for someone else—for his parents' first child, who had died the previous year at the age of three. He himself was a substitute, and not much care was taken over his name—he may or may not have been given Butler as a third name. A later family tradition suggested as much, but he himself never used it.[1] In the baptismal register of St. Mary's Church in Dublin, he is listed simply as "Thos. Brinsley."

Nor did anyone bother to record the date on which, at 12 Dorset Street, on the then fashionable north side of Dublin, he was born. His sister Alicia, three years his junior, wrote many years later that he was born in September 1751. All we know for certain is that Thomas Brinsley Sheridan was baptised on 4 November, and that his parents, each of whom had a brother called Richard, changed their minds and started to call him by that name instead. From the very start, the spoken word mattered more than the written. Richard Brinsley Sheridan came into the world as a figure of speech, an improvised identity.

Such carelessness about names is all the more striking because both his parents lived for words. Thomas was an actor, sometime playwright, and obsessive theorist of language, elocution, and rhetoric.

His mother, born Frances Chamberlaine, was a superb writer, whose love of words was in direct proportion to the difficulty she had in acquiring them. Her father, a Church of Ireland clergyman, had regarded writing as "perfectly superfluous" in female education and had tried to prevent her from learning to read. But her brothers had subverted these paternal prohibitions, and by the age of fifteen she was writing sermons and novels.

Frances was a formidable and strong-willed woman. Once, travelling in a stage-coach, she sat silent a long time while a young man chattered away, showing off his wit and style. Noticing the silence at last, he simpered, "A'nt I a most egregious coxcomb?" A deaf old man beside him said "Um?" Frances leaned forward, and bawled into his ear: "The gentleman, Sir, is a great coxcomb: he thinks we don't observe it, and he wants to tell us of it."[2]

It was her directness that brought her to Thomas Sheridan's attention. In 1743, when she was nineteen, she wrote and published a poem defending him in a furious controversy that had followed a very theatrical dispute between him and a fellow actor, Theophilus Cibber. They met, and were married four years later. Richard was their second surviving son, his elder brother Charles having been born a year earlier and baptised on 23 July 1750.

The house in Dorset Street was modest and elegant at the same time, a solid four-storey building in a newly developed part of Dublin, respectable but not ostentatious, indicative of success tempered by prudence. Thomas Sheridan was at the height of his popularity as manager of Smock Alley, the unrivalled "Monarch of the Stage," ascending with apparent confidence towards honour and prosperity. The year of Richard's birth was one of the most admired and most profitable in the theatre's history. The Duke of Dorset, an enthusiastic patron of the theatre, returned as Lord Lieutenant and, in the first months of Richard's life, visited Smock Alley almost every week, lending it both glamour and government approval. One of the greatest actresses of the day, Peg Woofington, had also returned to Dublin from London and played the full season at Smock Alley to audiences rapt with awe. In the forty nights on which she played leading roles, the theatre took in an unprecedented £4,000 at the box office.

With both government favour and public popularity on his side, Thomas seemed at last to have transformed theatre into a respectable profession, both morally serious and financially lucrative. He had become a considerable personage, employing about eighty people, and managing a business worth £9,000 a year. The Sheridans were far from rich, but there seemed to be every reason to suppose that they might with patience, and without the least display of threatening brashness, become so. By the time Richard was eighteen months old, his father was already thinking of his future, imagining him as a small-time Cavan squire. In April 1753, he was reported to have bought 800 acres of bogland around Quilca, "all of which by theatrical art, and Smock Alley chemistry, is to be transformed into fine arable land, to be an establishment for his younger children."[3]

But Thomas's transition from denizen of the dodgy world of theatre to member of an enlightened, cultivated, smoothly progressive Protestant middle class was never likely to be easy in the uncertain circumstances of Ireland. Just as he was laying plans for his son's future, Dublin politics were toppling into a crisis that would soon engulf him. Both he and the political system found that prosperity could be as dangerous as adversity. In 1754, the Irish treasury, at a time of economic boom, reported a surplus. The issue of whether the King had the power of consent over the use of this surplus became a test case for the Patriot opposition in the Irish Parliament, and Irish politics divided into a country party, which opposed the King's right to consent, and a court party, led by Dublin Castle, which supported it. Dissident office holders were dismissed, and eventually the Irish Parliament itself was prorogued.

Thomas Sheridan was sucked into this conflict by his very success in attracting the patronage of the Lord Lieutenant and his circle. In 1752, he had established a dining club, the Beefsteake Club, as a kind of support group for the theatre, made up of between thirty or forty men (Peg Woofington was the only woman) which met each week for dinner. Most were Ascendancy figures, and among them was the Lord Lieutenant's son, Lord George Sackville, after whom Thomas and Frances named their own short-lived son Sackville, born in early 1754. Although Sheridan's private political sympathies almost certainly lay on the Patriot side, his associations with Sackville and the Castle created the opposite impression among the public.

This might not have mattered had it not been for a choice of play almost as disastrous as the choice of sermon made by his father many years before in Cork. The play, an adaptation of Voltaire's *Mahomet: The Imposter*, had been decided on in 1753, before the political crisis had erupted. But it had been delayed, and opened on 2 February

1754, the very day that saw the announcement of the suspension of the Irish Parliament.[4] The opening-night audience, mostly made up of members of the country party, broke into applause when West Digges, the actor playing Alcanor, the defender of the city and of the people's liberty, delivered a speech in which the gods were called on to "crush, crush these vipers / Who, singled out by the community / To guard their rights, shall, for a grasp of ore, / Or paltry office, sell them to the foe." At the insistence of the audience, the speech was repeated to continuing applause, and the audience reacted with equal enthusiasm to similar sentiments throughout the play.

Even though this event made Thomas Sheridan a focus for the political debate that was raging, he decided to give the play a second staging, on 2 March. Before it, he warned his actors that their duty was to the characters they were playing and that the repetition of passages from the play at the insistence of the audience was a betrayal of the freedom of the stage and the rights of actors. He failed, however, to give his cast sufficiently clear instructions about how to behave if and when the audience chose to use the play as the vehicle for a political protest.

When Digges delivered the first inflammatory speech, the audience called for an encore. But Digges stepped out of character and announced that, much as he would like to comply with their request, "his Compliance would be greatly injurious to him," clearly implying that Sheridan had ordered him not to do so. The audience then called out for Sheridan himself, who refused to come forward and, fearing for his safety, instead left the theatre. The audience stayed for an hour, calling for Sheridan and refusing to be mollified by Digges's belated announcement that the latter had "laid him under no Injunction not to repeat the Speech." When Sheridan failed to appear, the audience began the methodical destruction of the theatre, throwing stones and bottles onto the stage, smashing the seating, slashing the curtain and scenery, and trying to set fire to part of the backstage area. The riot continued for six hours, but its consequences, for Thomas and Frances Sheridan and their children, were to last well into the nineteenth century. Instead of rising inexorably towards comfort and honour in their own city, Thomas and Frances were to spend the rest of their days as unsettled people, wandering between three countries as exiles struggling to find a place for themselves. Instead of becoming the squire of a pleasant estate in Cavan, their son Richard would have to make his own way in the world.

A week after the riot, Thomas Sheridan announced that he had "entirely quitted the Stage, and will no more be concerned in the direction of it." By May, he had sub-let the theatre, and after a summer spent at Quilca, he left for London in September, to be joined a little later by Frances and Charles. Richard and his sister Alicia (known in the family as Lissy) were left behind in Dublin, in the care of a nurse. At the age of three, therefore, Richard was separated from both his parents and from his older brother. The next eight years were what must have seemed to a little boy a series of expulsions from and re-admittances to the bosom of the family. They were with him again in Dublin from October 1756 to the summer of 1758, then away again for another year. In September 1759, Richard was allowed to join his family in London, but in January 1762 he was sent to boarding school at Harrow. In all, between the ages of three and eighteen, he spent just four and a half years living with either of his parents.

He seems to have been neglected physically as well as emotionally during his parents' first absence. On her return to Dublin in 1756, after Thomas had agreed, with deep misgivings, to resume the management of Smock Alley, Frances found both him and Lissy to be frail and unwell, and wrote to Samuel Richardson that "the joy of seeing them again has been embittered by the illness of my two youngest children: they have both had fevers, and are but now recovering." She moved the family for a few months to Glasnevin, then a village on the outskirts of Dublin, in the hope of improving their health.[5] Over the next year and a half, Richard was again the object of his mother's care and his father's teaching—Frances wrote to Samuel Richardson that Thomas was "instructing his boys."[6] The family even managed to spend the summer of 1757 together at Quilca.

But this stable home life was built on the shifting foundations of theatrical fortune. Thomas, who was still embittered by the trauma of the riot, was unable to repeat the success of previous years. He had also become increasingly obsessed with theories of education. However, when his dual plan of reforming Irish education and turning Smock Alley and the rival stage at Crow Street into something like a national theatre company came to nothing, he was left with debts of £7,000, including a heavy mortgage on Quilca. He and Frances, who was pregnant, left Dublin again for London, taking Charles with them, but leaving Richard and Lissy with their nurse in Dublin. As Lissy remembered many years later, "neither he nor I were very happy, but we were fondly attached to each other. We had no one else to love."[7]

While the family settled first in Covent Garden and then in Windsor, Richard started school in Dublin, in a small academy that had just been established in Grafton Street by Samuel Whyte, the illegitimate son of Frances's uncle. He and Lissy moved into Whyte's house, but their nurse whom, as Frances put it in a letter to Whyte, "they have been so long used to," stayed with them "to dress them, wash for them and mend their clothes."[8] Frances fretted over them, asking Whyte, "Keep me alive in their remembrance. I have all a mother's anxiety about them, and long to have them over with me." But Richard was left with Whyte for nearly eighteen months. It is clear that he did not thrive. He suffered "long and frequent absences" from school through illness. When, in August 1759, he and Lissy were sent for, and at last joined their parents, now living in Windsor, Frances found him slow and backward.

From the time he left Dublin in 1759 until his death in 1816, Richard Brinsley Sheridan never set foot in Ireland again. But neither did he ever regard himself as anything other than Irish. His younger contemporary, the Duke of Wellington, who, like him, was born in Dublin but made his entire career in England, remarked on being described as an Irishman that "being born in a stable does not make a man a horse." But Sheridan, to a degree that would be utterly baffling even to some of those closest to him, remained obsessed with Ireland. However unhappy his life in Dublin had been, he continued to regard it as the capital of his country.

When he rejoined his family in Windsor, young Richard found that, in his absence, his older brother, Charles, who had always been kept with their parents, had become his father's unassailable favourite. "My father's affections," as Lissy wrote, "were fixed on his eldest son [Charles] and on my sister," Anne Elizabeth, known in the family as Betsy, who was nearly a year old. Frances spent much of the time teaching both boys herself, paying particular attention to English, but Thomas had decided that Charles would pick up the fallen standard of the family's hopes and plant it on the highest peaks of honour.

He already had plans for Charles to become a great orator, and in February 1762, he had him recite in public for the first time, giving a speech from Milton's *Paradise Lost* as a demonstration of the success of the courses in rhetoric which he was then attempting to sell. According to Frances, in a letter to Sam Whyte, Thomas had trained the boy so well that he "acquitted himself in such a manner as astonished everybody." Accordingly, therefore, he was to perform in public again on Thomas's next course and to be made "in a very little time . . . complete in his own art."[9] Richard, however, showed no such promise. Samuel Parr, who taught him at Harrow, hinted that this may have been the source of his father's relative lack of interest in him: "I know not whether Tom Sheridan found Richard tractable in the art of speaking, and upon such a subject, indolence or indifference would have been resented by the father as crimes quite inexpiable."[10]

In the minds of his parents, Richard was already consigned to the role of brother of the more famous Charles. While attention, admiration, and affection were to be lavished on Charles, it is clear that Thomas and Frances had decided that Richard would have to look out for himself. Frances wrote to Samuel Whyte of her younger son, "As he probably may fall into a bustling life, we have a mind to accustom him early to shift for himself."[11] In January 1762, therefore, at the age of eleven, he was again placed outside the inner circle of the family and sent as a boarder to the public school at Harrow, run by his father's friend Robert Sumner. The two men had become friendly while Thomas was living in Windsor and Sumner was teaching at nearby Eton.

Thomas's relative indifference towards Richard is all the more striking because he was, at the same time, acting as a mentor to a young Scotsman, James Boswell, then twenty-one years old. The two had met in Edinburgh in the summer of 1761, when Boswell attended a series of lectures on English elocution which Thomas had delivered. Thomas offered himself as a guide and Boswell addressed him as "My Mentor! My Socrates!," asking him to "direct my heedless steps." Thomas lent Boswell money to pay his gambling debts and entered him as a law student at the Inner Temple in London.

In November 1762, James Boswell found in the Sheridans' London home, from which Richard had been exiled, "a good table, ease and hospitality, and useful and agreeable conversation."[12] It is obvious from Boswell's diaries that Sheridan willingly offered himself as a father-figure, giving advice, encouragement, and even money. Nevertheless, even such obvious affection could not blunt his tendency to sarcasm and tactlessness. When Boswell wrote a prologue to Frances's play *The Discovery* and was dreaming of having his lines resound in David Garrick's voice through Drury Lane, Thomas squashed him. He pointed out its many faults with what Boswell called "an insolent bitterness and clumsy ridicule that hurt me much, and when I answered them, bore down my words with a boisterous vociferation."[13]

Thomas, it seems, was all too willing to be a father-figure, but only to a protégé worthy of his paternalistic patronage. The problem with his second son was that he showed no signs of being worthy. If Richard had any illusions about his importance in the family, they were cruelly dispelled in September 1764, when Thomas and Frances left England for France, taking Charles and the two girls with them, but leaving him behind. Thomas had visited Richard at Harrow a few weeks earlier and presumably told him that the family was planning to leave England without him. Thomas had narrowly escaped arrest at the behest of his creditors on a visit to Dublin and was afraid that he would be pursued to London. At the same time, Frances's health was poor, and it was believed that a change of air might do her good. The family therefore slipped quietly out of London and took ship at Dover. In France, they settled in a "commodious cottage" on the banks of the Loire, in the suburbs of Blois.

Each of them was occupied with a literary project. Thomas worked on a dictionary and a grammar of the English language.[14] Frances, meanwhile, wrote a two-volume follow-up to her hugely successful novel, *Memoirs of Miss Sidney Biddulph*. The first two volumes of this epistolary epic had been published in Dublin and London in 1761, with the encouragement of Samuel Richardson, to whom it was dedicated. And it had been something of a sensation, selling out its first edition in three months, earning wide acclaim and being translated into French by the Abbé Prevost. Its heroine was a kind of female Job—a righteous woman enduring an endless series of afflictions. For the new middle-class readership her combination of extreme suffering and exemplary fortitude, of the eighteenth-century cult of deep feeling with the traditional Christian virtues, was overwhelming. Boswell accurately noted that "what it teaches is impressed upon the mind by a series of as deep distress as can affect humanity, in the amiable and pious heroine who goes to her grave unrelieved, but resigned."[15]

Yet precisely because it was such a peculiar mixture of traditional morality and the new sensibility, the novel also tended to subvert its own precepts. At every point, Sidney insists on the virtues of female obedience, piety, and sexual control. But there is also a strain of bitter resentment at the willingness of others (especially men) to take advantage of her meekness. She does what she is told, but comes to realise that "I am treated like a baby, that knows not what is fit for it to choose or to reject." She holds firmly to her faith, but most of the religious people around her are heartless hypocrites. She is sexually fastidious, but her inability to talk about or deal with the sexual conduct of others leads her to disaster. In all of these ambivalences, Frances Sheridan was revealing the nature of her times and, perhaps, of her own life.

At school back in England, Richard was no longer the sickly and dull child he had been in Dublin, but neither was he doing much to challenge his parents' belief that Charles was the family's great hope for the future. According to an account of Richard's schooldays published in 1788, "He seemed better than most boys to measure his strength, and know how to accomplish his desires."[16] But, as he himself told Thomas Creevey many years later, at Harrow he "never had any scholastic fame while he was there, nor did he appear to have formed any friendships."[17] The only friends we know of are Nathaniel Brassey Halhed, with whom he worked on a translation from Theocritus and formed a lasting attachment, and an Irish boy, Thomas Quin, from County Kildare, who was with him for only the first year.

Richard was poorly dressed and he may have been teased because his father was a mere actor. Lord Holland, who knew Sheridan well in later life, wrote in 1816 that at Harrow he "was slighted by the master and tormented by the boys, as a poor player's son. I have heard him relate with tears in his eyes that he never met with kindness at school but from Dr. Parr."[18] One of the stories told about him in later life was that at Harrow he was scorned by the son of an eminent physician because of his father's occupation, and replied, "'Tis true my father lives by pleasing people, but yours lives by killing them."[19]

At schoolwork, he appeared gifted but lazy and rather detached. "He could have done anything he would, but would have done nothing if he could." His worst subject was Latin verse, which required effort and discipline; his best was English prose, in which he had been given a good grounding by his mother. Samuel Parr, who sometimes taught him, found him "not only slovenly in construing but unusually defective in his Greek grammar" and "inferior to many of his school fellows in the ordinary business of a school."[20] The only scholastic achievement for which he was given any credit at the time was his impressive delivery of one of Mark Antony's speeches from *Julius Caesar*. He seems to have done the minimum amount of work necessary to avoid corporal punishment. As Parr put it, "his industry was just sufficient to protect him from disgrace."

If he does not seem to have been bullied or ill-treated at school, he was undoubtedly miserable. He was left without money, with very little contact with his family, and often with nowhere to go during the school holidays. Even before the family left for France, visits from his father seem to have been rare—Samuel Parr never saw father and son together, and Lissy remembered seeing Richard only when he was allowed home for holidays. After his parents left England, he was largely dependent on his mother's brother, Richard, a surgeon in London. His first surviving words were written to Richard Chamberlaine in March 1765, complaining of being left at Harrow for the Easter holidays and of his single suit of clothes being so worn out that "I am almost asham'd to wear them on a Sunday," and pleading for news of his family, who had not written to him or to the headmaster Sumner for a long time: "if you have had a letter lately I should be obliged to you would [you] let me know how they are, and when they come to England for I long to see them."[21] Small wonder that he told Thomas Creevey years later that he was "a very low-spirited boy, much given to crying when alone, and he attributed this very much to being neglected by his father, to his being left without money, and often not taken home at regular holidays."[22]

Something of what Richard felt as a child, of what made him cry when alone, can be gathered from his attitudes in later life. For the rest of his days, he was afraid of the dark and full of odd fears and superstitions. When he had children of his own, he worried incessantly about them, so much so that Charles Grey advised him to put his son in a glass case. He hated his children to be left in the care of servants, even for a day or two.[23] And, in his work as a playwright and orator, the deepest wellspring of feeling was an idealised vision of family life in which the bond between parent and child was elevated to an almost religious status.

In his most famous speech, at the trial of Warren Hastings in 1788, the highest pitch of emotion and outrage was reserved for the accusation that the British had turned the begum of Oudh's son against his mother. He excoriated "those who could ridicule the respective attachment of a mother and a son; who could prohibit the reverence of the son to the mother; who could deny to maternal debility the protection which filial tenderness should afford." And he placed the relationship between parent and child at the very core of politics and civilisation:

> Filial piety! It is the primal bond of society. It is that instinctive principle which, panting for its proper good, soothes, unbidden, each sense and sensibility of man. It now quivers on every lip. It now beams from every eye. It is that gratitude which, softening under the sense of recollected good, is eager to own the vast, countless debt it never alas! can pay, for so many long years of unceasing solicitudes, honourable self-denials, life preserving cares. It is that part of our practice where duty drops its awe, where reverence refines into love . . . Pre-existing, paramount over all, whether moral law or human rule, few arguments can increase, and none can diminish, it. It is the sacrament of our nature; not only the duty but the indulgence of man. It is his first great privilege. It is among his last most enduring delights.[24]

This hymn to mother-love has all the rapture of an impossible dream, all the obsessive insistence of a vision hopelessly pursued. It is a cherished fantasy. As a child, he often had no one to soothe his sensibilities. He had no long years of unceasing solicitude, just episodes of familial warmth long enough to add the pain of loss to his even more frequent episodes of loneliness. What beamed from his eye were not tears of gratitude but the bitter tears of a boy "much given to crying when alone." And what he did have of his mother's love was soon taken away.

At the beginning of August 1766, when Richard was fourteen, his father wrote to Samuel Whyte with the good news that, after nearly two years of peace in the French countryside, Frances had been restored to "a perfect good state of health, a blessing she had not known for ten years before."[25] The following month, on 26 September, she died "almost suddenly" at Blois, aged just forty-two, after a short illness. She had had an "intermitting fever" but with no serious symptoms until the day before her death "when she was suddenly deprived of her senses." An autopsy found that "all the noble parts were attacked, and any one of four internal maladies must have proved mortal."[26]

Nobody went to Harrow to tell Richard in person what had happened to his mother, whom he had not seen for two years. He was told of her death by the headmaster, Robert Sumner. A week later, he had still not heard from his father, and wrote to his uncle Richard to ask when he would be home: "I have wrote to Riley, who, with your orders, will make me a suit of Black." This short note is eloquent in its tight-lipped economy. There is no expression of feeling, no desire for sympathy, no warmth, just as little acknowledgement of the "melancholy knews [sic] of my poor mother's death" as is possible. "You will excuse the shortness of my letter," he tells his uncle, "as the subject is disagreeable," and adds in a heartbreaking postscript, "I must also have a new hat with a crape and black stokins and buckles. I should be glad of them on saturday."[27]

He had to cope with grief on his own. For two years after his mother's death, the family remained dispersed, with Thomas moving between England and Ireland, the other children in the care of a Protestant family in France, and Richard at Harrow, where he remained until after his sixteenth birthday. He left with little in the way of either academic distinction or fond memories and later declined to send either of his own sons to the school. He took with him an imperfect command of Greek and Latin, almost no French, and, as yet, no great depth of learning. The most useful knowledge he had gained may have been a grasp of numbers, which would serve him well in his political career—he left behind at Harrow six notebooks filled with mathematical calculations.[28]

He had, however, learned what his mother had believed he would need to know—how to shift for himself. The isolation and the loneliness had taught him that he could not take his relationship to others and the world for granted. Whatever he wanted, he would have to make for himself. If he wanted love, he would have to dazzle for it. If he wanted money, he would have to discover some alchemy that could turn into gold his own base prospects as the unfavoured second son of a poor player. If he wanted power, he would have to be watchful and clever, to play subtle games, to turn every opportunity to advantage. For the moment, his one asset was the freedom that was the obverse side of neglect. Owing little to his father and with only a tantalising memory for a mother, he was free to conceive of himself.

Chapter 4

THE LANGUAGE OF TRUTH

By the time the family was at last reunited in London under the same roof, briefly in Chelsea, and then in Frith Street, off Soho Square, Sheridan was seventeen. Lissy, seeing her brother for the first time in four years, found him

> handsome, not merely in the eyes of a partial sister, but generally agreed to be so. His cheeks had the glow of health, his eyes, the finest in the world, the brilliancy of genius as soft and tender as an affectionate heart could render them, the same playful fancy, the same innoxious wit that was shown afterwards in his writings, cheered and delighted the family circle. I admired, I almost adored him.[1]

That his father, who spent most of 1769 and 1770 with his children in London, acting at the Haymarket Theatre and giving "Attic Evenings" where his own recitations of poetry were interspersed with songs, showed no such inclination to deify his son was now, however, no longer entirely a burden on Richard's self-confidence. There may have been a notion of putting Richard on the stage,[2] but nothing came of it, and he was left, for now, largely to his own devices, apart from lessons in rhetoric and grammar given by his father. His friend Henry Angelo, who was taught by Thomas at around the same time, has left an account of the experience in his *Reminiscences*:

> With the elder Sheridan, all was pomposity and impatience. He had a trick of hemming, to clear his throat, and, as I was not apt, he urged me on with—Hem-hem heiugh-em, boy, you mumble like a bee in a tar-bottle; why do you not catch your tone from me?—Heugh-heium—exalt your voice—up with it. *Caesar sends health to Cato.* Cannot you deliver your words, hem-hemm-heiugh-m-m-m, with a perspicuous pronunciation, Sir?

These lessons in oratory were supplemented by classes in mathematics and Latin given by Lewis Ker, "an Irish gentleman."[3] But these were hardly onerous, and with his father making no obvious effort to send him to university or find him a job, Richard had time on his hands.

Along with the adoration of his little sister, Richard also found warmth and friendship at the home of Elizabeth Johnson, the Irish wife of a famous swordsman and horseman, Domenick Angelo. In return for Thomas's previous kindness to the Angelos' son Henry, Richard was taken under their wing. Domenick Angelo taught him to fence and to ride, giving him at least some of the accomplishments of a gentleman. He was a frequent guest at dinner in the Angelos' house in Hanover Square. At their table he was able to try out his developing wit, to relax into the role of an engaging conversationalist.

And he had an increasing amount to talk about. In later years, in conversation with Thomas Creevey, Sheridan "dwelt upon the two years he spent [in Soho] as those in which he acquired all the reading and learning he had upon any subject."[4] And much of the knowledge he was acquiring concerned politics. For while his father was pursuing his high-minded schemes for the reform of language and rhetoric, Richard was absorbed by a much more direct and dangerous demonstration of rhetorical power. The two years after he left Harrow, the years in which he did his real learning, were those in which English politics were dominated by Philip Francis's coruscating polemics against the government of Lord Grafton, the "Letters of Junius," published anonymously in the *Public Advertiser* between January 1769 and January 1772.

This was the period when British radicalism was beginning to take fire, poked into life by increasing unease about the American colonies on the one hand and the growing threat of royal despotism on the other. The radical hero John Wilkes, who had been prosecuted in 1763 for libelling the King, was ejected from the House of Commons and re-elected three times. In this context, the anonymous Junius Letters renewed the power of political invective by forging a language in which, without resort to open treason, even the King could be addressed with a kind of contemptuous hauteur:

> Sir, It is the misfortune of your life, and originally the cause of every reproach and distress which has attended your government, that you should never have been acquainted with the language of truth, until you heard it in the complaints of your people. It is not, however, too late to correct the error of your education. We are still inclined to make an indulgent allowance for the pernicious lessons you received in your youth . . .[5]

The young Sheridan was so excited by the Junius Letters that he himself wrote to the *Public Advertiser* in imitation of his hero. But he added a twist of his own, turning his letter into a facetious satire, purporting to be a defence of Grafton against his accusers. And this satiric touch is, of course, that of Swift, whom he had almost certainly been reading (the complete works were in his father's library).[6] The method of Sheridan's letter is that of Swift's *A Modest Proposal*—the making of a case so grotesque that it supports the opposing point of view. In this, his first effort at an intervention in politics, Sheridan silently calls the spirit of his father's godfather, and of his own grandfather, to his aid. For his letter, inspired as it so obviously is by Junius, is also an attempt to recall *The Drapier's Letters* to which Dr. Thomas Sheridan had lent a hand. In a sense, he is reaching back a generation, skipping his father's obsessive pursuit of linguistic purity and returning to the sharp, instrumental use of words to change the world.

At first sight, there may seem to be a contradiction between the Jacobite tinge to Sheridan's political ancestry and the radical Whiggism to which he was now attaching himself. But by the time Sheridan became conscious of public life, the vestiges of Jacobitism had become, paradoxically, a few stray threads in the banners of the radical Whigs. Rather paradoxically, Tory blue became the colour of Wilkes's supporters.[7] The *Public Advertiser*, which published the Junius Letters, also published Jacobite propaganda. Later, a number of prominent former Jacobites, including Sir Thomas Gascoigne, Francis Plowden, and Joseph Ritson, became adherents of the radical

Whig Charles James Fox. Sir Francis Burdett's family had come out for Bonny Prince Charlie in 1745. The apparent conservatism of Jacobitism, its hankering after an increasingly mythic utopia in the past, was not really out of tune with the language and sentiments of the radicals. As Paul Kleber Monod puts it, "The illusion that a 'golden age' might have existed at some time in the past fascinated radicals . . . The old promises of unity and moral regeneration continued to appeal to the imaginations of English radicals even after the Stuart cause collapsed."[8]

The unlikely link between Jacobitism and Wilkes had, significantly for Sheridan, an Irish dimension. Irish strikers in London in 1768 supported Wilkes, but they were also connected to the Whiteboy rural secret societies back home, many of whom had sworn oaths to Charles Edward Stuart. "Irish support for Wilkes," as Monod puts it, "originated in the same rebellious spirit that animated the Whiteboys, and both may have owed their impetus to Jacobitism."[9] In attaching himself to the cause of Wilkes, Sheridan could connect himself at one and the same time to his own Irish past and to a vibrant English present.

His letter to the *Public Advertiser* was probably prompted by a reference by Junius on 30 May 1769 to the possibility of Grafton's ending up like Charles I and being beheaded. Sheridan framed his "reply" as one written by a supporter of Grafton's arguing why his "patron" should not lose his head. Seeing the Duke's severed head, he writes, the public might "begin in their hearts to pity him, and from the fickleness so common to human nature, perhaps by way of compensation acquit him of part of his crimes."[10]

He goes on, with rather more effective Swiftian irony, to demonstrate that the alleged faults in Grafton's character are really "virtues a little misapplied." To the charge that Grafton consorted with "low and mean people," he replies that this is merely "Christian humility only carried to a little excess. Did the saviour of mankind assort with sinners and publicans and who shall dare to blame one of his followers for following his example?" Far from being unreliable, as Junius had alleged, Grafton had, when Wilkes returned from exile in France the previous year, been seen to keep an appointment with his mistress Nancy Parsons. And far from fawning on the King, "he has fronted him with his whore—is this ambition?"

Though very much a trial piece, the letter is significant precisely for what Sheridan is trying out. For he is testing in it two things that will be critical to his later achievements. The first is a special kind of political ventriloquism, in which he appears to take on the voice, and the arguments, of his opponents, only to say the opposite of what they had intended. Much of his rhetoric over the next forty-five years will depend on the perfection of this device. And the second, related trick that is being tested here is the old Drapier's one of getting away with treason. Behind it is Sheridan's early insight into the way the instability of language, the bane of his father and grandfather, can be exploited to one's own advantage.

The connection between his own family's history of tripping over words on the one hand and the subversive possibilities of language in the unstable politics of his own time was probably made for Sheridan by his reading of one of the great works of the French Enlightenment's assault on arbitrary power, Montesquieu's *De l'esprit des lois* (*The Spirit of the Laws*). That Sheridan was reading it at this time is certain: he quoted extensively from Thomas Nugent's English translation in another letter he wrote to the *Public Advertiser* in October 1769.

In *De l'esprit des lois*, Montesquieu makes a connection between the uncertainty of language, especially of the spoken word, and the difficulty of proving the crime of treason:

> Words do not constitute an overt act; they remain in the realm of ideas. Taken on their own, and divorced from the tone in which they are spoken, they generally signify nothing. Often, the same spoken words can have different meanings; the meaning depends on their connection to other things. Sometimes silence says more than any words could do. Since nothing is more ambiguous than all this, how can it be made into the crime of high treason? Wherever such a law is established, not only liberty itself, but even the shadow of liberty, is no more.[11]

How to take such liberties was the lesson that Sheridan was learning from his reading of Swift and of Junius. What this passage in Montesquieu may have suggested to him is that the spoken word could be even more fruitfully ambiguous than the written, and that there might, after all, be something in his father's obsession with speech that he could use for his own purposes.

His second letter to the *Public Advertiser* could almost, indeed, have been written by his father. It is a reply to a genuine defence of

Grafton (his own satiric defence had not been published) by Novus.[12] But instead of making any substantial political arguments, Sheridan mocks the writer's style and use of language, his clichés and pomposities. Although this letter was published at considerable length, its effect is underwhelming, displaying the writer's grasp of grammar to better effect than his grasp of politics. But this, too, may be an exercise in ventriloquism—it is hard not to hear in its hectoring tone and pedantic superiority the voice of Thomas Sheridan lecturing his recalcitrant son on the proprieties of grammar and diction.

Having tried out his father's voice, he returned to his own, writing another attack on Novus, but this time attempting to deal with political, rather than stylistic, issues. His own politics were formed by the Enlightenment "principles of true liberty"—the rule of law over arbitrary power. But in order to begin to make anything of them, he had first to free himself from the arbitrary power of his father. For Thomas, determined to demonstrate the efficacy of his own educational methods, had decided to give up the theatre and to establish his own school. Both his sons had a place in his plans. As Thomas Creevey reported many years later, "At the end of this time, his father determined to open a kind of academy at Bath—the masters or instructors to be Sheridan the father, his eldest son Charles, and our Sheridan, who was to be *rhetorical usher*."[13] An usher, at the time, was a teacher's assistant. Richard's status, in other words, would be not much more elevated than that of a servant. This nightmarish fate, trapped as a menial figure of speech inside his father's linguistic obsessions, a verb to Thomas's and Charles's nouns, was intended for him on the family's move to Bath in the autumn of 1770.

Chapter 5

LIKE SONS OF ONE FATHER

The academy at Bath was to be the culmination of Thomas Sheridan's long struggle to reform English society by reforming English speech. He had always wanted to be a teacher, and had been deflected into the theatre only by a remark made to him by Jonathan Swift, his godfather and hero, while a student at Trinity College, Dublin. The conversation had reportedly been (with Swift asking the questions): "Do they teach you English? No. Do they teach you how to speak? No. Then, said he, then they teach you *Nothing*."[1] From this, Thomas had conceived the belief that the reform of speaking was the route to the promised land of the eighteenth-century Enlightenment, the virtuous society. As he wrote in his book *British Education: Or, The Source of the Disorders of Great Britain*, published in 1756, when Richard was four, the ancient republics of Greece and Rome were founded on oratory: "Their end was liberty; liberty could not subsist without virtue, nor be maintained without wisdom and knowledge; and wisdom and knowledge unless communicated with force and perspicuity, were useless to the state . . ."[2]

These were times when many powerful people worried that the government of the tongue had a slim majority. The surge of interest in language itself in the second half of the eighteenth century was prompted by a deep unease about the slippery, unstable nature of something so essential to social and political order. Lord Chesterfield, reviewing Samuel Johnson's *Dictionary* in *The World*, remarked:

> It must be owned that our language is, at present, in a state of anarchy, and hitherto, perhaps, it may not have been the worse for it . . . The time for discrimination seems to be now come. Toleration, adoption, and naturalisation have run their lengths. Good order and authority are now necessary. But where shall we find them, and at the same time the obedience due to them? We must have recourse to the old Roman expedient in times of confusion and chuse a dictator.[3]

Likewise Lord Monboddo, in his *Of the Origin and Progress of Language* (1773–92), warned that as a fragile creation language needed constant maintenance, "and if that is but a little remitted, down the stream we go to our natural state of ignorance and barbarity." A stability of signs, shared definitions and regularities of grammar, might at once reflect and help to constitute a well-ordered political state.

Conversely, a language that was always breaking into double-meanings might threaten to undo the state itself. The late eighteenth century was also of course a great time for parody and literary forgery. At the heart of parody is the realisation that language itself is infinitely malleable, that there is no indissoluble link between author and text, and, even more disturbingly, that language can be shaped to any political purpose. The *Probationary Odes*, published in 1785, in which poets supposedly competed for the vacant laureateship using the familiar forms "to record the virtue of the Stuarts or to immortalise the talents of a Brunswick," makes this explicit. Likewise, the great prose work of the time, Laurence Sterne's *Life and Opinions of Tristram Shandy*, is one in which the narrator assumes arbitrary powers, not merely indulging in the pleasures of manipulation, of frustrated expectation, of perverse digression, but always reminding the reader of just how capricious he is being. Forgeries, too, are exemplary of the linguistic vulnerability that characterised the age: Macpherson's *Ossian* poems, Chatterton's pretence that his own poems were written by a fifteenth-century monk, and Ireland's Shakespeare forgery, in which Richard Brinsley Sheridan himself would play a part. In all of them, literary history itself is unstable, open to inventions and interventions.

For Thomas Sheridan, the way out of these problems lay not with the written word but with the spoken. And this belief was itself a legacy of his family's complex relationship to language, pulled between Gaelic and English, between an oral culture and a written one. For while Protestantism in general tended to favour the written word of the Bible over the spoken word of inherited tradition, the Sheridan brand of Gaelic Protestantism was slow to distance itself from an oral culture. Preaching in Dublin in 1686, Richard Brinsley's ancestor William Sheridan explained the written Bible almost as a necessary evil. God had his law written down, he said, "lest this rule might be forgotten or corrupted in tract of time by a bare oral Tradition of it, from age to age, he committed it to Writing; *for though the Word spoken be more efficatious*, yet the Word written is more durable: therefore it was that Moses was commanded to write the moral law into two Tables." He even suggested that "if we were so well assured of the truth of it," oral tradition could have "the same Authority with Scripture; for until the means of salvation was fully perfected, and the Scripture committed to Writing, Tradition was the Rule: for St Paul bids Timothy to take heed to all that he had received, either by word or writing."[4] Describing St. Paul, William Sheridan could almost be his grand-nephew Thomas: "Two things are required in a Preacher, to be able to Exhort with wholesome Doctrine and to confute Gain-sayers; the one requires Rhetorick, the other Logick. We cannot have a better precedent for this than Saint Paul; whom for his admirable Elocution the Infidels took for Mercury, their God of Eloquence, come down from Heaven."

One of the things that helped Thomas Sheridan to reconcile the oral and written word, a Gaelic culture and a British allegiance, was James Macpherson's spectacularly successful forgery, *Fingal, an Ancient Epic Poem in Six Books: together with several other poems, composed by Ossian the son of Fingal, translated from the Gaelic language*, published in 1762, when Richard was starting at Harrow. Both Thomas and Frances were devotees of Ossian. Thomas told James Boswell in February 1763 that he

> preferred [Ossian] to all the poets in the world, and thought he excelled Homer in the Sublime and Virgil in the Pathetic. He said Mrs Sheridan and he had fixed it as the standard of feeling, made it like a thermometer by which they could judge the warmth of everybody's heart; and that they calculated beforehand in what degree all their acquaintances would feel them, which answered exactly.

The *Ossian* poems, Thomas believed, "give us great light into the history of mankind. We could not imagine that such sentiments of delicacy as well as generosity could have existed in the breasts of rude, uncultivated people."[5]

It is not difficult to understand this enthusiasm. The *Ossian* poems appealed not only to the cult of sensibility in which Thomas and Frances were acolytes, but for Thomas especially they had a very particular meaning. They were part of a cultural project that tried, with astonishing success, to reorder the historic relationship of Irish and British cultures. And for Thomas, they offered at least a partial solution to the puzzle of the Sheridans' contradictory origins in Gaelic Ireland on the one hand and British Protestantism on the other. For what Ossian seemed to promise was a reinvention of history in which Gaelic and British were no longer opposed categories of religion, culture, and nationality.

If Gaelic were to be naturalised within a British context, it was important that the link between Scottish Gaelic culture and Ireland be broken. The reality—that Gaelic culture in Scotland was an obvious off-shoot of Irish culture—could not be comprehended within a putative British Celticism. What James Macpherson did, therefore, was to invent the idea that there was a Gaelic culture in Scotland (and therefore in Britain) that owed nothing to Ireland. He picked up Irish ballads in Scotland, wrote an "epic" in which he transferred their whole scenario from Ireland to Scotland and then dismissed the genuine Irish ballads as a mere debased reflection of these Scottish "originals." His collaborator, the Reverend John Macpherson, then wrote a *Critical Dissertation* on the Ossian poems, placing Gaelic-speaking Celts in Scotland four centuries before their actual arrival, and explaining genuine Irish literature as having been stolen from the innocent Scots.[6]

The effect of these audacious forgeries was to present a whole new version of the Gaelic past, in which the wild and fantastic impulse was tempered to British notions of classical civility. There is no doubt that Thomas Sheridan partly responded as he did to the Ossian forgeries because they offered a high-flown version of his own Gaelic past. But, more than that, the forgeries had the effect of nullifying the opposition of Gaelic and British, of wild Catholic on the one hand and civilised Protestant on the other. They seemed to lend the weight of antiquity and romance to the Gaelic Protestantism that was his odd inheritance from history. And they seemed to make the

Gaelic past of the Sheridans itself respectable. In a sense, Macpherson achieved through mendacity what William Bedell's heroic integrity had never achieved—an imaginative reconciliation of Protestant and British with Gaelic and Celtic.

Thomas Sheridan developed a great enthusiasm for Scotland, which he imagined as a laboratory for his linguistic experiments. If he could teach Scots to speak "proper" English, he could help them belong to the virtuous British society that he so desired. By making himself the instrument for the transformation of Scots into Britons, he was exploiting his own ambiguous position, turning his Irish Protestantism into a bridge over which ambitious Scots could pass to reach a successful state of "Britishness."

The comedy of Thomas Sheridan's position as an Irishman teaching proper English speech—mocked by Johnson as the equivalent of "burning a farthing candle at Dover to shew light at Calais"[7]—is apparent in the description by his Scottish protégé, James Boswell, of Sheridan's instruction of "Mr Alexander Wedderburn, whose sister was married to Sir Harry Erskine, an intimate friend of Lord Bute, who was the favourite of the King":

> Though it was too late in life for a Caledonian to acquire the genuine English cadence, yet so successful were Mr Wedderburn's instructors, and his own unabating endeavours, that he got rid of the coarse part of his Scotch accent, retaining only as much of the "native woodnote wild" as to mark his country . . . he by degrees formed a mode of speaking, to which Englishmen do not deny the praise of elegance. Hence his distinguished oratory, which he exerted in his own country as an advocate in the Court of Session, and a ruling elder of the Kirk, has had its fame and ample reward in much higher spheres.

Wedderburn transformed himself with Sheridan's help into "Lord Loughborough at London," later Chief Justice and Lord Chancellor, a change Boswell regarded as "almost like one of the metamorphoses in Ovid."[8] So highly regarded were Thomas's elocutionary services to the Scottish nation that he was awarded the freedom of the city of Edinburgh in July 1761. In England, too, he had powerful supporters: both Oxford and Cambridge awarded him honorary MA degrees. The following year, Lord Bute, then effectively Prime Minister, obtained a government pension of £200 a year for him. Bute understood the political significance for an emergent Britain of an attempt to fix and standardise a new British language, underlined by Thomas in his *Dissertation on the causes of the Difficulties which occur in learning the English Tongue*:

> The consequence of teaching children by one method, and one uniform system of rules, would be an uniformity of pronunciation in all so instructed. Thus might the rising generation, born and bred in different Countries, and Counties, no longer have a variety of dialects, but as subjects of one King, like sons of one father, have one common tongue.[9]

Thomas twice attempted to set up an academy to teach his system of elocution and rhetoric, once in Dublin in 1758, and again in Edinburgh four years later. But each attempt failed. By 1770, he felt himself ready to try again, this time in Bath, where back in 1763 he had staged his "Attic Evenings" with great success.

Chapter 6

THE BEGINNING OF HAPPINESS

Bath was a kind of petrified irony, a beautiful and elegant town that owed its fortune to disease and the fear of death. It had grown up around the fashionable practice of "taking the waters" for their curative properties, but by the time the Sheridans moved there, this had become a mere excuse for idle pleasures. Daniel Defoe called Bath "the resort of the sound rather than the sick" and Horace Walpole remarked that people "went there well and returned home cured." For those who came to preserve rather than to regain health, the vague reminder of illness merely confirmed their own vitality.

Even in the eighteenth century, this holiday atmosphere induced a marked slackening of social distinctions. Bath etiquette, enforced by the master of ceremonies, Beau Nash, and his successor, Samuel Derrick, decreed that all should obey the same rules. No swords were to be worn, and the dancing was to be commenced, not, as elsewhere, by those of most senior rank, but in strict rotation. The new rich, anxious to display their wealth, mingled with the new poor, hoping to rescue their fortunes by an advantageous match. In *Humphrey Clinker*, Tobias Smollett described the human flotsam that washed around the pump-room:

> . . . clerks and factors from the East Indies, loaded with the spoil of plundered provinces; planters, negro-drivers, and hucksters, from our American plantations, enriched they know not how; agents, commissaries, who have fattened, in two successive wars,

> on the blood of the nation; usurers, brokers, and jobbers of every kind; men of low birth and no breeding . . . suddenly translated into a state of affluence, unknown to former ages.

It is easy to see why Thomas Sheridan chose Bath as the location for his academy. Nowhere else in England were the borders of polite society so permeable, and he imagined himself manning the linguistic check-points, conducting elocutionary rites of passage. The services he had performed for ambitious Scots like James Boswell, knocking the edges off their accents and making them easy on upper-class English ears, would now be on offer to other kinds of *arriviste*. But it is hard to imagine a place in which his second son's ambitions were less likely to be successfully confined to the exalted station of rhetorical usher in his father's academy.

A letter to Mrs. Angelo written by Richard from Bath shortly after the family settled there in September 1770 shows him in playful, almost giddy spirits, trying out on her some of the modes of address that he had earlier tried on the *Public Advertiser*. Asked by his father to send the family's regard to the Angelos, he turns a necessity of politeness into a comic display of mock-political ventriloquism, composing the letter as a humble address from the people to the monarch:

> May it please your Majesty,
>
> At a meeting of the Sheridanian society, in Parlour assembled, the following resolutions (amongst many others of great importance) were determined on, and I appointed to give your Majesty information of them.
>
> Thomas Sheridan in the chair. RBS. Sec.
>
> 1. Resolved—that we are all alive. This pass'd nem. com.
>
> 2. Resolved—that her majesty be acquainted thereof.
>
> 3. Resolved—that RBS be honoured with that commission.
>
> Therefore I take the first opportunity of remitting to your Majesty these important, and interesting particulars, in obedience both to the resolution of the society and, (what are still more binding) your Majesty's commands. But as it has been the fashion for Address-bearers to have a little conversation with Majesty at the presentation of them; I must beg leave to take advantage of the precedent, and assume the same liberty.[1]

And he was already testing the artistic potential of this kind of literary burlesque. From the summer of 1770 onwards, Sheridan began to correspond regularly with Nathaniel Halhed, his old friend from Harrow, now a student at Oxford. Together, the two began to experiment with writing. Unlike Sheridan, Halhed was a brilliant linguist and classical scholar, who afterwards became one of the most important figures in eighteenth-century Orientalism and one of the first scholars to identify the common roots in Sanskrit of Persian, Arabic, Greek, and Latin. His interest in classical themes was reflected in the choice of subject matter for their collaborations, with the first effort being a burlesque of the Amphitryon myth, already the basis for plays by Plautus, Molière, and Dryden.[2] Halhed sent his text to Sheridan, who reworked it, cutting, adding, and placing the action in a radically different frame.

Sheridan's version of the play, called *Jupiter* in some of their letters and *Ixion* in others, is now lost, except for an extract in Thomas Moore's biography. But there is enough of it to see not simply that Sheridan was already a better dramatist than Halhed but that he was working from radically different assumptions about language. For while Halhed's text was lively and well-written, Sheridan already had a highly developed sense of theatre. While Halhed was drawing on a scholarly knowledge of past myths, Sheridan was creating a present tense for the action. In a device he would later use to brilliant effect in *The Critic*, he framed Halhed's play within a rehearsal conducted by the "author" of the play, Simile, a forerunner of the latter play's Mr. Puff:

> Draw up the curtain and (*looking at his book*) enter Sir Richard Ixion,—but stay—zounds, Sir Richard ought to over-hear Jupiter and his wife quarreling,—but, never mind,—these accidents have spoiled the division of my piece.—So enter Sir Richard, and look as cunning as if you had overheard them.[3]

Already, for Sheridan, the meaning of words depends on the actions and intentions that surround them, not on roots in the past.

The fascination of the collaboration between Sheridan and Halhed, indeed, lies not in the quality of the work they produced, but in the fact that their different approaches to language would, in less than twenty years, lead to their engagement on opposite sides in one of the great political conflicts of the day—the impeachment of Warren Hastings, governor-general of India. Sheridan's understanding of words as weapons would reach its height in his rhetorical assaults on Hastings. Halhed's sense of language as a force to be analysed and controlled would make him the protégé of the same governor-general, who employed him to translate and codify Indian legal texts. Halhed would repay that support by weighing in on his protector's side, publishing pamphlets in defence of Hastings against the charges of Edmund Burke and Sheridan.

Apart from its immediate interest in self-conscious theatricality (suggested almost certainly by Garrick's contemporary play *A Peep behind the Curtain* and Buckingham's older *The Rehearsal*), the other striking feature of Sheridan's scenario for *Jupiter* is that it seems to hint at a comic send-up of his father's grand scheme for creating a unified British language from the Irish, English, and Scots dialects. Simile, the author, appears to be English, as does the theatre manager. A third speaker, O'Cul[ligan?], is clearly Irish, and a fourth, Macd[onald?], is Scottish.* But instead of blending into a synthetic harmony, their voices are heard in a burlesque babel.

Adding to the impression of a deliberate parody of his father's projects and a rebellion against his own intended place in them are two further hints. One is that the theatre manager is called Monopoly—as manager of Smock Alley in Dublin, Thomas had run a passionate and contentious campaign to secure a monopoly for his theatre. The other is that, in a fragment which seems to represent a further development of Richard's idea of a rehearsal play, there is a merciless parody of Thomas's belief that the stage must be an arena for moral reformation:

> S[imile?]: No, sir, it ever was my opinion that the stage should be a place of rational entertainment; instead of which, I am very sorry to say, most people go there for their diversion: accordingly, I have forced my comedy so that it is no laughing, giggling piece of work. He must be a very light man that shall discompose his muscles from the beginning to the end.
>
> M[acdonald?]: But don't you think it may be too grave?
>
> S: O never fear; and as for hissing, mon, they might as well hiss the common prayer-book: for there is the viciousness of vice and the virtuousness of virtue in every third line.

*The names of the speakers, apart from Simile, survive only in abbreviated forms.

The need for a rational and morally uplifting theatre was at the heart of his father's career and writings, in which he insisted time and again on "the importance of the stage towards forming the Morals and Taste, particularly of the people of this country . . ."[4] And "the well reading of the common prayer" was another of his obsessions. What is more, these notions of his father's were now, as Thomas's plans for his academy took shape, of immediate concern to Richard.

In December 1770, an advertisement in the *Bath Chronicle* informed its readers that Thomas Sheridan had established "an Academy for the regular instruction of Young Gentlemen in the art of reading and reciting and Grammatical Knowledge of the English tongue," and that he would "receive the commands of any ladies and gentlemen at Bowers' in Kingsmead Street."

The commands, however, never arrived. The idea that an Irishman could provide a passage into Engish society may have made sense in Scotland, or even in Dublin, but in Bath it was merely risible. As Richard told Creevey many years later, "The whole concern was presently laughed off the stage, and then Sheridan described his happiness as beginning. He danced with all the women at Bath, wrote sonnets and verses in praise of some, satires and lampoons upon others, and in a very short time became the established wit and fashion of the place."[5]

The collapse of Thomas's scheme for an academy freed Richard to begin his own life. It is clear that he was already hoping to make his living as a writer. Halhed and he hoped to sell *Jupiter*, and, as Halhed put it, "The thoughts of £200 shared between us are enough to bring tears into one's eyes."[6] Sheridan suggested that they should send it to the playwright and manager of the Haymarket Theatre, Samuel Foote. This was not done until well into 1771—Halhed wrote to Sheridan that he was "very tardy"—but by the time Halhed left for India, Foote was clearly considering a production.

In the meantime, Sheridan was also working with Halhed on a translation and rendering into verse of the *Love Epistles* of Aristaenatus, an obscure Greek writer. This, again, was Halhed's idea, and again he was prepared to defer to Sheridan's opinions of his work. He sent "my Aristaenatus"—obviously a more or less finished text—to Bath in November 1770 asking his friend to "add and correct whatever you like, for I have some time had full belief and confidence that every correction of yours would be an *emendation*, and every addition a new perfection." The work was published in August 1771, with the initials H.S. at the end of the preface, suggesting that it was a joint effort by Halhed and Sheridan. This was rather generous on Halhed's part, considering that the bulk of the work was his, but he clearly felt that Sheridan's work as editor, contributor, and reviser entitled him to be regarded as co-author.

Though not especially interesting in itself, the Aristaenatus book was important for Sheridan as an opportunity to study and practise the language of love, to learn an erotic rhetoric that his father never taught him. Moving around Bath, going to the balls and teas, hanging around the pump-room, he was to find a use for words of seduction as well as for words of persuasion. And he was finding that each could be allied to the other. Around the same time as he was working with Halhed, he wrote his first successful poem, "Clio's Protest," addressed to one of the beauties of Bath, Mrs. Margaret Fordyce.

In "The Bath Picture, or a Slight Sketch of its Beauties," Miles Peter Andrews had found no more to say about her than that she had a "dimpling sweet smile." Sheridan took this as his cue for a reply that was part public satire, part critical essay, part seductive display, and all an advertisement for himself:

> And could you really discover,
> In gazing those sweet beauties over,
> No other charm, no winning grace,
> Adorning either mind or face,
> But one poor dimple, to express
> The quintessence of loveliness?

His best lines were in his conclusion, calling on Andrews to mend his ways:

> And first, leave panegyric, pray;
> Your genius does not lead that way:
> You write with ease to show your breeding;
> But easy writing's damn hard reading.
> —Henceforward Satire guide your pen;
> But spare the women—lash the men.

This was as much a declaration of intent as a piece of unsolicited advice, and from Halhed's letters it is obvious that Sheridan was trying to live up to it, proposing a collection of epigrams, a compendium of "Crazy Tales," even a dissertation on pastoral poetry, ancient and modern. And he was also planning to launch his own periodical, to be called *Hernan's Miscellany*. This was on his mind from the time he moved to Bath: on 30 October 1770, Lewis Ker, who had taught him Latin and mathematics in London, wrote to him referring to "your intended periodical paper."[7] Ker, evidently at Richard's request, had made enquiries about the feasibility of selling a weekly paper on the lines of *The Tatler*. He got the agreement of a publisher, who wanted, however, to be indemnified against commercial failure, and suggested that a sale of a thousand copies at threepence each would yield a profit of £5.

Richard wrote a draft first issue himself. Again, he instinctively approached writing as an act of ventriloquism, following the Swiftian tactic of inventing a character, an eccentric old codger, Fred Hernan, through whom he could speak. But from the whimsical tone, his immediate model is more probably Sterne's *Tristram Shandy*, the final volume of which had been published the previous year: "*I will sit down and write for the good of the People*—for (said I to myself pulling off my spectacles, and drinking the remainder of my six pen'worth) it cannot be but people must be sick of these same rascally Politics." In an especially Shandyesque touch, Hernan looks up his commonplace book before beginning to write, only to find that he had decided to write for the people before, but "coming home and finding my fire out, and my maid gone abroad, was obliged to defer the execution of my plan to another opportunity . . . 'Good Heavens!,' said I, 'How great events depend upon little circumstances.' "[8]

Nothing, however, came of *Hernan's Miscellany*. By June, Lewis Ker was writing to Sheridan, teasing him with charges of laziness: "How it comes to pass that you are ever in appearance indolent without being really so I cannot conjecture; for I find you have some excuse always ready . . ." But the failure of the project probably had more to do with poverty than indolence. Neither Richard nor Halhed was in a position to raise the money to indemnify a printer against loss. It may well be that Sheridan decided that, in any case, a £5 profit on a thousand copies was hardly worth the effort. By 16 April 1771, Halhed was writing that "[I am] horribly vexed with you for giving up all thoughts of Mr Hernan. All I objected to was the *title*, the plan I approved, and still approve and I make no doubt it would conduce to the recompense of its authors, much more than *Aristaenatus* or even *Jupiter*, god as he is . . . I see no reason why we should defer to the winter a project big with so much expectation . . ."

Halhed's disappointment was rooted in the fact that the failure to make any money from literary schemes left him with no good reason to refuse the plum job of writer with the East India Company, which his father had secured for him. By the early summer of 1771, he had decided to take the job. But his decision also forced a choice on Sheridan. Writing to Sheridan on 29 July, after his own decision to go to India, Halhed urged his friend to go with him: "I think, Dick, the best thing you can do is to accompany me. Your abilities cannot fail to distinguish you in a place where wit is of great recommendation, and where such qualifications as yours must place you in a most exalted sphere."[9]

It appears from Halhed's letter that he was in a position to get Sheridan into the East India Company, and that a job was on offer. And such a job was a virtual guarantee of wealth, an invitation to share the spoils of conquest. Every day in Bath, Richard would have seen and met nouveau riche adventurers who had done their time in India and were now gentlemen of leisure. For a young Irishman of twenty, with no money, no professional qualifications, an irascible father, and a more favoured older brother, it ought to have been an offer he could not refuse, especially as he would have his closest friend with him. He had few other friends to leave behind—as he wrote to his father a few months later, "the relying on *acquaintances*, or *seeking* of friendships is a fault which I think I shall always have prudence enough to avoid."[10] But there was one thing keeping him in Bath, pulling his life, and his politics, in a direction directly opposite to Halhed's. He was in love with Elizabeth Linley.

Chapter 7

THE LANGUAGE OF LOVE

Thomas Sheridan had known the Linley family since his first stay in Bath in 1764, and had "rendered some service to Mr Linley, at that time in very narrow circumstances." Because, when they met, Thomas Linley was a struggling and impoverished musician, Thomas Sheridan continued to think of the family as his social inferiors, an attitude that was to have an important bearing on subsequent events. Sheridan was a state pensioner, a man who had published books on education and language, not a mere actor but a respected theatre manager. Linley was a musician he hired from time to time to take part in his Attic Evenings. The relationship was, in effect, that of employer to employee. And Thomas Linley's eldest daughter, Elizabeth (commonly known as Eliza),* was one of the employee's assets.

As an apprentice indentured to her father until she came of age, Eliza's physical beauty and marvellous soprano voice were at the service of her master. As a little girl, she had stood appealingly at the entrance to the pump-room in Bath, selling tickets for her father's benefit concerts. By the age of eight, she could, according to the painter Ozias Humphry, who lodged with the family, sing all the songs from *The Beggar's Opera* and other operettas.[1] She had her father's high forehead, sensuous lips, and large, limpid eyes, but her mass of dark hair and porcelain fragility gave her an appealing soft-

*She was often called Betsy within her own family, but to avoid confusion with Sheridan's sister Betsy, she is here referred to throughout as Eliza.

ness that was bound to attract attention when, at the age of eleven or twelve, she began performing on stage with her father and her brother Thomas.

Almost from the moment she began to perform in public, she was transformed into a virtual icon. She was not yet fourteen when Thomas Gainsborough painted her for the first time in a highly sexualised image of a child-woman, innocent and seductive at the same time. The tension in his picture between her self-conscious poise and inviting décolletage on the one hand and her unfinished and immature face on the other created a way of seeing Elizabeth Linley that would persist throughout her life, not least in Gainsborough's continuing series of portraits: he painted her at least three times more and made clay models of her head, none of which survives.

Thomas Sheridan was quick to spot Eliza's commercial potential. In the early part of 1769, then just fifteen but already the principal singer in Bath concerts, she sang for one of his Attic Entertainments in London. When the Sheridans moved to Bath the following year, Thomas Linley invited the whole family to a "small musical party"[2] at the fine house which he had been able to buy largely as a result of his daughter's success. Here, Richard met Elizabeth for the first time. In spite of Thomas Sheridan's snobbish desire that his children should not "cultivate too great an intimacy" with the Linleys, the young people in both families were "much pleased with each other."

It was not Richard, at first, who fell in love with Eliza but his brother, Charles, who became "strongly attached" to her. So too did Richard's friend Halhed, still an undergraduate at Oxford, who, under cover of his genuine passion for music, had become acquainted with the Linleys. Watching and listening to Eliza as she rehearsed for a concert, Halhed was, as he wrote to Richard, "annihilated with wonder."[3] Richard seems at first to have been content with the role of go-between, passing messages from Halhed to Eliza. Whatever attraction there may have been between the pair was unlikely to go very far however: Halhed was already planning to leave for India.

At all events, Eliza was not free to follow her own affections. By the early months of 1771, she had attracted another suitor, Walter Long, a Wiltshire squire who had accumulated both years and wealth. The disparity between Eliza and him encouraged a subsequent exaggeration of Long's age, which was almost certainly nearer forty-five than sixty. Eliza became the subject of a commercial transaction between him and Thomas Linley. Long "stipulated that within a day or two of the intended marriage, that the young Lady should retire to his Seat, and promise not to be seen at Bath or in London for the space of two years."[4] In return for the loss of income that this would entail for Thomas Linley, Long was to pay him £1,000.

Shortly before the marriage was to take place, however, Long broke off the engagement. The *London Magazine* suggested a year later that Eliza had absolutely refused to consent to the match and Alicia Sheridan stated much later that Eliza had written to Long begging him to call off the match without making her father angry with her. When Long did so, however, Thomas Linley threatened him with a lawsuit. Long, either from generosity towards Eliza or from a desire to avoid scandal, settled £3,000 on her and also allowed her to keep diamonds worth about £1,000 which he had given her. If his largesse was motivated by the latter consideration, though, this gesture could not have been more spectacularly futile. Samuel Foote, the playwright to whom Richard and Halhed had sent *Jupiter*, visited Bath, picked up all the gossip about the affair, and turned it with speed and skill into a comedy, *The Maid of Bath*, produced at the Haymarket in London on 26 June 1771.

The play, in which her identity was covered only with the diaphanous alias of Kitty Linnet, completed Eliza's transformation into a public icon. In it, Long was depicted as Solomon Flint, a sixty-year-old miser who tries to persuade Kitty to spend the night with him at his lodgings with a false promise of marriage. Foote deliberately blurred the borders between truth and fiction, having one of the characters threaten to set "Maister Foote the play-actor" on Flint and "bring the filthy loon on the stage." And the depiction of Eliza was equally ambivalent. On the one hand, her defiance of Flint's attacks on her honour seemed to vindicate the rights of female performers to control their own bodies and private lives. On the other, the play itself, more or less openly exposing Eliza's personal business to the public gaze, was a subtler attack on that very right.

As well as this unfair caricature of Long, though, the play also included a character called "Major Racket," possibly intended as a version of another of the men with designs on Eliza, Captain Thomas Mathews. Mathews was rather typical of Bath's pleasure-seeking habitués. Though he was the grandson of an admiral and the son of an army major, he was not a professional soldier but held a commission in the militia. He had estates in both Wales and Ireland, but spent most of his time in Bath, and much of it playing cards. He was regarded as one of the finest whist players in England, and wrote the standard book on the game.

The fact that Mathews was married did not prevent him from battening on Eliza. He began to pay attention to her when she was still little more than a child, and at first she seems to have regarded him as a charming friend. As time went on, however, she became more alarmed at his attempts to seduce her. Mathews threatened at times to commit suicide if she would not listen to him, at others to blacken her name around the town. She was terrified of telling her father what was going on, not only because she had given Mathews some encouragement but because she feared her father might challenge Mathews to a duel. She confided instead in her closest female friends—Lissy and Betsy Sheridan. Lissy, in turn, spoke to Richard, who was on good terms with Mathews. And by entering into intimate conversation with her brother on the subject, Lissy unwittingly invited a startling confession: he, too, was in love with Eliza.

Richard went to see Mathews, and had some apparent success in persuading him to leave Eliza alone. But this involvement in her private affairs also gave him the opportunity to place his own relationship with Eliza on a footing of conspiratorial, if not yet romantic, intimacy. Eliza, for her part, had decided to escape from Mathews and from her father "by retiring to a Convent in France, meaning to indemnify her father by giving up a part of the money settled upon her by Long." Lissy offered her letters of introduction to friends she had made while living in France, and Richard, seizing the opportunity, offered to accompany her in the role of gallant protector.

Eliza may well have been naïve enough to believe that she could escape the consequences of her fame by a dramatic flight to France, but Sheridan surely knew better. That knowledge does much to explain his rather sudden confession to Lissy that he was in love with Eliza—who had been entirely ignorant of his passion. Nothing in his previous behaviour had suggested that he was lovestruck. On the contrary, he had acted as a go-between for Halhed, who showed no signs of suspecting that his messenger might be planning to usurp him. It is true, of course, that nothing inspires love so much as evidence that the loved one is already an object of overwhelming desire for others. Eliza had, as well as beauty, extraordinary musical talent, an acute intelligence, considerable strength of character, and the aura of fame. Even so, it is hard to avoid the conclusion that Richard's sudden declaration of love for Eliza may not have been entirely divorced from his feelings of rivalry with his brother.

Charles had been deeply in love with Eliza since they had first met. But he had been too timid, and too calculating, to do anything about it. He was, as he afterwards wrote to his uncle Richard Chamberlaine, "conscious to myself that I was indulging a passion which could only make me acquainted with the pains of love, but never taste its sweets."[5] He was afraid of provoking his father's displeasure and losing the position of favourite which he had always enjoyed. So he moved out of Bath to live in a house in the countryside, getting Betsy to deliver a formal farewell to Eliza.

Now Richard had an opportunity to prove himself a better man than his brother. By boldness and spirit, he would attain what Charles could not: Eliza's love. In doing so, he could also take for himself some of the fame that she was so anxious to be rid of—to elope with the "Maid of Bath" was to be an actor in a real-life sequel to a popular drama. And he could, at the same time, break free from his father.

Essential to all that happened is the fact that Thomas Sheridan was absent. He had been in Dublin since the autumn of 1771, acting at Crow Street, and lobbying Parliament for a new theatre monopoly. When the crisis broke, he was in the middle of a Shakespeare season and his plans for re-establishing himself in the city with a new patent were at a critical juncture, so he was unable to return to Bath until 1 June. His absence allowed his son to make a dramatic declaration of independence that would establish him once and for all as a public figure in his own right.

Once the decision to elope was made, Richard showed the qualities that were to mark his subsequent career—an extraordinary capacity to seize the moment, a genius for improvisation, and powers of persuasion that bordered on the miraculous. He was, at this time, penniless and dependent, yet he managed to organise what was then a considerable expedition from Bath to Lille, and to borrow enough money to finance it.

On the night of 18 March, he called at the Linley house with a sedan-chair. He left a letter for Thomas Linley explaining his actions and describing Mathews's conduct. He then had Eliza carried to a carriage that was waiting for them on the London Road. They reached London the next day and made their way to the home in

Lower Thames Street of Sheridan's friend Simon Ewart and his father, John Ewart, a brandy merchant who traded through Dunkirk. They also called at the home in Holborn of Francis Field, an oil merchant, afterwards godfather to Charles Lamb, probably to secure introductions to some of his contacts in France.[6]

The self-consciously melodramatic nature of the escapade is suggested by the fact that Ewart was told that Eliza was an heiress called "Miss Harlow," casting her as the archetypal persecuted virgin, Clarissa Harlow, created by Sheridan's mother's friend Samuel Richardson in his famous novel.[7] John Ewart was certainly persuaded by the subterfuge. He lent Sheridan money, and also arranged passage on one of his ships sailing from London to Dunkirk.[8]

On the voyage, though, what had been a romantic adventure took a very serious turn when Eliza fell ill. A rough passage, combined with the stress of realising the enormity of the step she had taken, exposed the underlying frailty of Eliza's health. For all her beauty and commanding presence, she was almost certainly suffering from the tuberculosis that would mark the rest of her life. She became so ill that Sheridan actually thought she might die. And with that thought came the realisation that his feelings for her were much more profound than either her glamour or his need for the world's notice could make them. As he wrote twenty years later, at another moment of truth in their relationship, he "then loved her so that had she died as I once thought she would in the Passage I should assuredly have plunged with her body to the Grave."[9] There can be little doubt but that, at this moment of crisis, Sheridan must have told Eliza what his feelings for her really were, throwing off the disguise of guardian angel and revealing himself as yet another all-too-human claimant on her love.

They stayed for some days at Dunkirk with another merchant, one Paul Possell, and his wife, to whom John Ewart had given them an introduction: as late as 27 March, Ewart was still writing to them there. Even in France, however, Eliza could not escape unwanted male attention. According to Samuel Rogers, Sheridan later told him that one night he and Eliza visited a theatre where "two French officers stared a good deal at his 'wife' and Sheridan not knowing a word of French could do nothing but put his arms akimbo and look bluff and defying at them, which they, not knowing a word of English, could only reply to by the very same attitude and look."[10]

From Dunkirk, Sheridan and Eliza made their way towards Lille, where Eliza was, according to her plan, to be lodged in a convent. Before they got there, however, Sheridan proposed to Eliza. He told her that after all that had happened she could not reappear in England except as his wife. If it is unlikely that Eliza was unprepared for this proposal, which was an essential element of the plot in which they had chosen to entangle themselves, it is certain that Sheridan had been thinking several steps ahead. He had taken the trouble to get the name of a priest known to be willing to marry eloping English couples. They were, accordingly, married "at a village not far from Calais."[11]

The marriage was clearly a Catholic one, and this willingness to use the services of the church which Sheridan's ancestors had deserted is remarkable. Both he and Eliza would presumably have been aware, however, that the ceremony was not legally binding, since neither had yet reached the age of majority. Nor was the marriage consummated. The *Dublin Journal* reported in July that "nothing criminal passed between Mr Sheridan and the Maid of Bath, in their late Tour of France, that Mr Sheridan . . . at every place they put up requested the Land-lady's Company, and took care to have Miss Linley constantly provided with a Female Bedfellow." And it is clear from later correspondence between them that Sheridan and Eliza did not sleep together in France, even after their marriage. For both of them, indeed, the ceremony was probably more a protection against the possibility of sexual scandal than a licence for the beginning of a sexual relationship.

Their relaxed attitude to Catholicism was further underlined when Eliza took a place in a convent in Lille, probably that of the Ursulines, in early April.[12] She was taken ill again, however, and attended to by an English physician, one Dr. Dolman, who took her into his own house to care for her. It was there that her father, who had traced her whereabouts from letters sent to Bath, found her a few days later. He apparently accepted Sheridan's explanation for their flight and blamed Mathews for the entire episode, but he insisted that Eliza return to England to fulfil some singing engagements, promising that she could go back to the convent afterwards. The three of them began the journey home the following day.

Thomas Linley's anxiety to get his daughter back to Bath was partly motivated by financial considerations, but partly also by the need to "put an end to the many wicked suggestions which the malice of his Enemys have propagated."[13] For the elopement had caused a predictable sensation, flooding the town with gossip and rumour. On the morning that Sheridan and Eliza's disappearance had been discovered, Captain Mathews visited the Sheridans' house several times, apparently full of remorse, uttering "Oaths and Curses upon himself and his past life."[14] It is clear that the town blamed Mathews for what had happened, and that Mathews initially accepted this verdict, promising to leave Bath and never return.

On one of his visits to the Sheridan house, however, Mathews met Charles, who had returned from his rural exile "violently agitated" by the news of his brother's daring attempt to win the affection of the woman he himself loved. In talking to Mathews, Charles "unguardedly dropped some expressions of displeasure at his brother's conduct." These helped to convince Mathews that he himself was the injured party. This attitude hardened when he learned of the contents of the explanatory letter that Richard had left for Thomas Linley, exposing Mathews as the villain of the piece.

Mathews began to write letters to Sheridan in France, containing "several most abusive threats." Sheridan wrote back to Mathews from France on or around 7 April, saying that "he would never sleep in England 'till *he* had thank'd him as he deserved."[15] But before the letter can have reached Bath, Mathews's resentment at the opprobrium being heaped on him around the town had broken out in print. On 9 April, the following advertisement appeared in the *Bath Chronicle*:

> Mr Richard S[heridan] having attempted, in a letter left behind him for that purpose, to account for his scandalous method of running away from this place, by insinuations derogating from my character, and that of a young lady, innocent as far as relates to me, or my knowledge, since which he has neither taken any notice of letters, or even informed his own family of the place where he has hid himself; I cannot longer think he deserves the treatment of a gentleman, than in this public method to post him as a L[iar], and a treacherous S[coundrel].
>
> And as I am convinced there have been many malevolent incendiaries concerned in the propagation of this infamous lie, if any of them, unprotected by age, *infirmities*, or profession, will dare to acknowledge the part they have acted, and affirm *to* me what they have said *of* me, they may depend upon receiving the proper reward of their villainy, in the most public manner. The world will

be candid enough to judge properly (I make no doubt) of any private abuse on this subject for the future; as nobody can defend himself from an accusation he is ignorant of.

Thomas Mathews

Shortly after the publication of this aggressive statement—effectively a challenge to a duel—Mathews left Bath for London, where he took a room at 24 Crutched Friars, a house belonging to one John Coughlin.

Nearly three weeks after this public challenge appeared in print, Sheridan, Eliza, and Thomas Linley landed back in England, and Sheridan started towards London to confront Mathews. They stopped overnight at Canterbury, but Sheridan, according to himself, stayed awake so that he could keep his promise not to sleep a night in England until he had given Mathews his just deserts. At nine o'clock the following evening, 29 April, he arrived in London and met Simon Ewart, the friend whose father had helped him and Eliza on their way to France. Ewart informed him of Mathews's advertisement, and also said that Mathews had told him to warn Sheridan "not even to come in his way without a sword, as he could not answer for the consequence." Ewart told Sheridan where Mathews was to be found, and Sheridan "provided himself with pistols."

At about half-past midnight, Sheridan arrived at Coughlin's house looking for Mathews. He was initially given the excuse that the key to the front door had been lost, suggesting that Mathews's public bravado had turned to private alarm. At one point Mathews came down to the door and assured Sheridan he would be let in, but then disappeared back to bed. Eventually, after an hour and a half, Sheridan was admitted.

Instead of confronting Sheridan as he had threatened, however, Mathews was emollient. He addressed him as his "dear friend" and forced him to sit down. He then kept Sheridan until seven in the morning, assuring him that he meant no harm and that the advertisement, which Sheridan had not yet seen, was nothing more than an "inquiry about him, put in with the sanction of his family." He convinced Sheridan that "his enmity ought to be directed solely against his brother [Charles], and another gentleman at Bath."

Nothing could be more indicative of the fraught state of the relationship between Richard and Charles than the former's apparent willingness to be persuaded of this by Mathews. Having agreed that Mathews would merely make a mild retraction of the advertisement in the *Bath Chronicle*, he left. He picked up Eliza and Thomas Linley, who had stayed overnight in a hotel, and travelled to Bath. Once there, he went to the printers of the *Bath Chronicle* and got a copy of the edition that carried Mathews's advertisement. He then went to Kingsmead Street and confronted Charles. There was a loud and heated argument between them, but Charles seems eventually to have convinced his brother that he was blameless and to have offered to accompany him back to Mathews in London.

Three hours after arriving in Bath, Sheridan, now with Charles in tow, had departed again. They left confusion and distress behind them. Their sisters, knowing only that the brothers had quarrelled loudly and then disappeared, feared that they might themselves have fought a duel. Eliza, who did not know that her new husband had left Bath, collapsed in fainting fits at the news, and a doctor had to be called.

Back in London, the brothers went to the house of Thomas Brereton, a friend of the family. From there, Sheridan sent a message to Mathews, challenging him to meet him for a duel at Hyde Park. At six in the evening, Mathews arrived with a Captain Knight as his second, but after objections to the suitability of the ground from Mathews, both sides became concerned that they might be seen by a nearby officer of the guard. The antagonists and their seconds (Sheridan's was Simon Ewart) then went to an inn in Piccadilly, The Hercules' Pillars, to wait until the park was clear of onlookers. When they returned to the park, however, Mathews again objected that they might be seen. They adjourned to the Bedford Coffee House in Covent Garden, whose owner suspected what was going on and asked them to leave. They then went on to the Castle Tavern on the corner of Bedford Street and Henrietta Street.

It was here, by candlelight, that the duel finally took place. After a few passes, Sheridan got the point of his sword against Mathews's chest, and had caught Mathews's wrist with his free hand. With his adversary at his mercy he demanded that he should sign an apology to be published in the *Bath Chronicle*. Mathews's second, Captain Knight, took Sheridan's arm, crying, "Don't kill him." Mathews called out, "I beg my life," two or three times. When Sheridan backed off, however, Mathews refused to sign the apology, and claimed that Knight's intervention had saved Sheridan rather than himself. Sheridan, in anger, demanded that Mathews either give him his sword or set to again.

When Mathews released his sword, Sheridan broke it in two and flung the hilt into a corner of the room, a breach of the etiquette of duelling which, Mathews claimed, released him from his obligation to apologise. When he was offered another sword to continue the fight, however, Mathews refused it and, "with much altercation and much ill grace," wrote out an apology dictated by Sheridan and signed it.

The brothers returned to Bath the following day, and Mathews's apology was printed in the *Bath Chronicle* on 7 May:

> Being convinced that the expressions I made use of to Mr Sheridan's disadvantage were the effects of passion and misrepresentation, I retract what I have said to that gentleman's disadvantage, and particularly beg his pardon for my advertisement in the *Bath Chronicle*.
>
> Th: Mathews.

That should have been the end of the affair, and it seemed for a while that calm would now follow the storm. Thomas Sheridan returned to Bath from Dublin, where the elopement had been regarded as such sensational news that Crow Street Theatre had advertised a play with "music composed by Mr Lindley of Bath" to be performed at the beginning of June. While the father was "well enough reconciled to the part [his son] had taken in the affair,"[16] he was not, of course, aware of the marriage, nor did his son inform him of it. Most of Thomas Sheridan's attention was devoted in any case to his beloved Charles, for whom he had secured an appointment as secretary to the British legation in Sweden. Soon both Thomas and Charles were in London, making arrangements for taking up the appointment, leaving Sheridan to his own devices.

Richard Sheridan certainly took advantage of this freedom to enjoy some secret trysts with Eliza, who was now declaring that "I love you to Distraction, and that I would prefer you and Beggary before any other Man with a throne," in the Spring Gardens in Bath. In spite of the suspicious supervision of her parents, their relationship now became, by degrees, intensely sexual, and Elizabeth was conscious of her own physical awakening. In a letter to him soon after their return to England, she wrote, "I am sure we had more real happiness in those few moments of Stolen Bliss than we should have received had we went formerly to bed together. Don't you think me an impudent girl. I am sure you must. I often wonder at my own Assurance but I don't know how it is you have brought me to it by Degrees till I declare I can't perceive the Harm till after it is done."[17]

Soon, however, this appearance of a happy ending to the escapade was to be undermined by the return of unfinished business. Mathews was back in Bath and giving his own account of what had happened. He claimed that he had agreed to the apology "as a point of generosity" and only after Sheridan had ceased to demand it. He denied that he had begged his life and claimed that Sheridan had broken his sword without warning, after he had laid it on the table. Sheridan regarded this as a breach of the agreement made at the conclusion of the duel: that Sheridan would not humiliate Mathews by letting it be known that he had broken his sword so long as Mathews did not misrepresent what had happened between them. In retaliation, Sheridan then told "several gentlemen" about the breaking of Mathews's sword.

This, in turn, placed Mathews in a position where he had either to get Sheridan to agree to his version of events or to lose all face as a man who had not merely been humiliated in a duel but then lied about it. He sent letters filled with "scurrilous abuse" to Sheridan. He also drew up a written account of his version of the duel, authenticated by his second, Captain Knight. At the end of June, Sheridan was presented with this statement by William Barnett, a friend of Mathews, and asked to sign it. His refusal to do so made another duel inevitable. Soon afterwards, Barnett delivered Mathews's challenge to Lissy, telling her that it was an "invitation for her brother."

They met on Kingsdown, four miles from Bath, at dawn next morning. Prince Hoare, who was in Bath at the time, claimed in 1804 that Sheridan and Mathews were "both in liquor when they fought . . . having sat up all night drinking."[18] Mathews himself told Lord John Townshend many years later that Sheridan was indeed drunk when this second duel took place, and that he "could have killed him with the greatest ease."[19] What is claimed to be Mathews's account of the duel, given to "many now resident in Bath who remember to have heard him repeat his tale in a consistent manner," and published after his death, repeats the allegation.

It claims that Sheridan invited Mathews to drink with him on the night before the duel,

> that Sheridan remained at table drinking claret until the time of appointment; that when he quitted it, he walked up Milsom Street, and observing Captain Mathews's chaise waiting at the door to take him to the spot, he reeled into it himself, and insisted upon his seconds following his example; he then desired the driver to proceed to the ground, which Mathews could not have reached in time had not the carriage of Captain Paumier [Sheridan's second —"a very young man and quite new to such affairs"] taken him there. He found Sheridan in a state of high excitement from potations deep.[20]

Sheridan may well have been drunk, for if the first duel was high melodrama, the second had more than an element of black farce. Mathews wanted to use pistols, but Sheridan insisted on swords.[21] He rushed at Mathews and tried to grab his sword, as he had done in the London fight. But Mathews stabbed at him, and may have wounded him slightly on the upper body. Sheridan then either stumbled or was tripped by Mathews and fell over, dragging Mathews with him. In this wild mêlée, both their swords were broken. Mathews got on top of Sheridan and stabbed him several times in the neck and face with the hilt of his sword, which still had about six inches of jagged-edged blade on it. Sheridan, for his part, gave Mathews a slight wound in the stomach with what was left of his own sword.

Rather poignantly, in the midst of this fracas, a locket that Sheridan had round his neck, containing a picture of Eliza, was torn off and left lying on the blood-stained ground.[22] Both men were screaming "horrid curses" so loudly that their seconds—Barnett for Mathews and Paumier for Sheridan—had difficulty hearing each other. Paumier added to the cacophony by calling out, "Oh, he is killed, he is killed!" Before the seconds could do anything, however, Mathews managed to get hold of the much sharper point of his sword and to stab Sheridan in the stomach with it. Seeing this, Paumier and Barnett asked Sheridan to beg for his life. Sheridan refused to do so, crying out, "No, by God, I won't." Mathews may have stabbed him again in the neck before the seconds intervened to disarm them both. Mathews rushed off in his chaise for London, apparently believing that he had "done for" Sheridan.

On this at least, Sheridan was inclined to agree with him. He believed that he was dying, and for decades afterwards the thoughts that went through his head in these moments would remain vividly present for him.[23] He was carried to a nearby cottage for some water, then to a local inn, the White Hart. There, the five flesh wounds he had sustained were dressed almost immediately by two surgeons, Ditcher and Sharpe. This prompt attention saved him from the infection that would have posed a more serious threat to his life than any of the damage that Mathews had actually done. Although reports of his death soon reached as far as Dublin, it was obvious even to his fretful sisters, whom the surgeons allowed to bring him home the next day, that he would recover.

Chapter 8

GENTLEMEN AND PLAYERS

Why did Sheridan risk his life with Mathews a second time? Even by the code of honour that regulated duels, he could have refused a second contest without losing face, since he had already proved himself in single combat. He had everything to lose and little to gain. As Charles wrote to him from London when he heard of the second fight, "You risked everything where you had nothing to gain, to give your antagonist the thing he wished, a chance for recovering his reputation. Your courage was past dispute: he wanted to get rid of the contemptible opinion he was held in, and you were good-natured enough to let him do it at your expense."[1] If Sheridan did indeed sit up all night drinking before the duel, his need for Dutch courage suggests that far from being carefree and careless, he was deeply apprehensive about the likely outcome.

To understand why he nevertheless risked his life is to begin to understand Sheridan himself, and to appreciate the enormity of the social gulf which he saw the urgent need to cross. At one level, of course, Sheridan's motivation in the whole saga is obvious enough. Duels were a rather extreme form of male display. As V. G. Kiernan puts it, fighting a duel made a man appear as "woman's natural guardian, protector, possessor."[2] The sheer drama of his encounters with Mathews not only constituted a claim on Eliza but brushed aside as mere details the very real obstacles to their marriage posed by his father's disapproval and her father's unwillingness to lose his main economic asset. But while the first duel can be explained as an inevitable consequence of his courtship of Eliza, the second, fought after he and she had become lovers, cannot.

For what really drove Sheridan to such extremes is the challenge implicit in the words of Mathews's first advertisement in the *Bath Chronicle*: "I cannot longer think he deserves the treatment of a gentleman." To deserve the treatment of a gentleman, it was necessary to be recognised as a gentleman. And without that recognition, Sheridan had no chance at all of fulfilling any of his ambitions to be a public man. If he was to beat the system, he had first to be able to enter it. "Gentleman" was the password for entry, but it was a word whose meaning was becoming obscure. With the emergence of a new middle class, it was no longer easy to say who was and who was not a gentleman. But one sure way of proving one's right to the title was by showing a willingness to risk death in order to defend it.

It is not accidental that Sheridan's duels with Mathews were part of a general revival of duelling in the last three decades of the eighteenth century. The rise of an ambitious middle class was making social distinction increasingly difficult to enforce by mere codes of dress and manners. And Sheridan himself was a case in point: after the training he had received from Domenick Angelo in London and from his father, he could ride, fence, and speak like a gentleman, even though he was in reality nothing but an actor's son. He was living proof that gentility was no longer an obvious and unquestionable quality. Like all uncertain things, it needed to be tested.

For a few decades at the end of the eighteenth and the beginning of the nineteenth centuries, before middle-class values themselves gained ascendancy, the acid test of gentility was that gentlemen had the right to kill each other, and in so doing to stand outside any social contract binding on the common man. In a world where politics was still the property of gentlemen, the dangerous ritual of the duel of honour was a rite of passage into the world of public affairs.

It is worth remembering that, during their long night in Crutched Friars, Mathews actually managed to deflect Sheridan's anger. It was only when he saw the text of Mathews's *Bath Chronicle* advertisement that Sheridan became implacably determined to fight. To understand fully the vehemence of this reaction to a claim that he was not a gentleman, it is necessary to remember what awful visions such a claim conjured up in his family. A quarter of a century before Sheridan fought Mathews, his father, then also in his twenties, had to go through his own trial by combat in order to establish himself as a "gentleman." And that trial, like Richard's, had been rooted in the ambiguity of the woman performer, whose appearance in public left her open to association with the most established kind of public woman—the prostitute.

On the night of 19 January 1747, Thomas Sheridan was playing the title role in John Vanbrugh's *Aesop* at Smock Alley in Dublin.[3] The play was well under way when a drunken young Trinity College student from Galway, Edward Kelly, climbed out of the pit, onto the stage, and through to the green room. He found one of the actresses, Mrs. Dyer, and attempted to rape her, putting his hands up her petticoats, trying to pry her legs apart with his knee and telling her, as Mrs. Dyer afterwards put it with considerable delicacy, that he "would do what her husband, Mr. Dyer, had done to her, using the obscene expression." Another of the actresses, George Anne Bellamy, rescued Mrs. Dyer, and the two of them managed to lock themselves in a dressing room. Kelly then attacked one of the dressers, Ann Banford, even though she was visibly pregnant.

By now, the screams of the women and the abusive curses of Kelly had carried onto the stage, where Thomas Sheridan stopped the play. He went back to the green room, confronted Kelly, and had him taken away by the guard who did regular duty at the stage door. No sooner had the play restarted, however, than Kelly reappeared in the pit, having escaped from his guard. Along with a volley of abuse, Kelly hurled an orange at the stage and hit Thomas on the face. Thomas stopped the play again, stepped out of character, and began to remonstrate with Kelly and his friends. When Kelly continued to insult him, he replied, "I am as good a Gentleman as you are." This single sentence—soon improved by repute to "I am as good a Gentleman as any in the House"—became the focus of both a riot and a political controversy that kept Dublin in an uproar for weeks.

After the play had finished, Kelly followed Thomas backstage, demanding an apology. Thomas replied that he would apologise to no one below the royal family. Kelly then started to abuse him again, using, significantly, both the words that Mathews was to direct at Richard twenty-five years later: "liar" and "scoundrel." Eventually,

Thomas lost his temper, set about Kelly with a heavy oak stick that he was carrying as a prop for the Aesop character, and broke his nose.

Kelly's friends were outraged that a mere player had not merely claimed in public to be a gentleman but actually struck a young man who was entitled to that description. Their outrage was not without sanction in the attitudes of the time. In *Rosalind: or An Apology for the Life of a Theatrical Lady*, published in Dublin in 1759, it is made clear both that actors are the social equivalent of servants and that, like servants, they have no right to a private life:

> Actors are servants of the Public, and as such ought to be considered. They are our Stewards, and when they faithfully discharge the Duties of their offices, we respect and reward them; if they neglect them, we punish and despise them.
>
> If then they receive our Wages, they are accountable to us for their conduct; and not only that Part of it which relates to their immediately acting in the Province assigned them by us, for our service and amusement, but in their private behaviour when our Business has been transacted. Good servants of any kind, whether Butlers, Stewards, or Foot-men, Housemaids, Chamber-maids or Cooks, have no right to withdraw themselves from their respective Masters, and act in an unbecoming manner when their Master's business is finished; nor has an Actor a right, on his quitting the *small* stage for the entertainment of his master, to act on the *great one* with Indiscretion, Folly, or Vice; for in both respects their masters are injured, and themselves receive no service, but rather lasting Opprobrium, and justly merited Dishonour.[4]

Thinking along these lines, Kelly's friends banded together under the title of "the Gentlemen." Two nights later, they started a riot in the theatre when it was announced that Thomas Sheridan, taking the advice of his friends, would not appear on stage. They invaded the backstage area, beat up a tailor, and ransacked the place looking for Sheridan. Failing to find him, they went to his house but, finding it under guard, dispersed.

Sheridan then closed the theatre for two and a half weeks, officially for repairs. He tried to make peace with Kelly's party, but was told that he would have to make a public apology. To do so would be to accept that he was not a gentleman, that actresses were fair game for rape, and that the theatre should remain a low profession, closely allied to prostitution. This he refused to do. Instead, he went to law, and had seven of his antagonists, including Kelly himself, indicted for riot.

Before the case could come to trial, however, Thomas reopened the theatre with himself in the title role in *Richard II*. His appearance was greeted with cries of "a Submission, a Submission, Submission, off, off, off." He replied that he was ready to apologise, if the "Voice of the Publick" thought he should. One of his supporters in the audience, Dr. Charles Lucas, then called for a show of hands of those who were for "preserving the Decency and Freedom of the Stage." "The Gentlemen," seeing that the numbers were overwhelmingly against them, retired, but even as they did so they threatened that Thomas Sheridan was "never to be permitted, on any Account, to perform again, and those who took his part were doomed to Destruction." To underline this latter prophecy, Lucas was assaulted on the street shortly afterwards.

Two nights later, thirty armed "Gentlemen" occupied the front rows in the theatre and, when Thomas appeared on stage, ordered him off. After he withdrew, insults were traded between "the Gentlemen" and other members of the audience, mostly students at Trinity College. The following morning, a thousand students, some of them armed, attacked the lodgings of three "Gentlemen" leaders—a Mr. Martin, a Captain Fitzgerald, and John Brown of Neale, County Mayo.

This last name hints at one of the deeper undercurrents to the riot. For Brown had been one of those attacked and ridiculed by Swift in *The Drapier's Letters* for supporting the introduction of copper coinage to Ireland. Thomas's father, Dr. Thomas, who had, as we have seen, a hand in the *Letters*, referred to him in 1733 as "Half-Penny Brown" and told Thomas Carte that he "would not be acquainted with him because of an unlucky character given him by the Drapier."[5] There can be little doubt that enmity towards the father motivated Brown's hostility towards the son. The attack on Sheridan's claims to gentility was an attack on the whole family.

Both Brown and Martin were forced by the Trinity students to apologise on their knees, and further humiliated by having cold water poured over their heads. After this, Kelly himself came to the college voluntarily, though obviously in fear of serious reprisals, and made a public apology. The sheer size of the armed mob of students, though, so alarmed the authorities that the Lords Justices ordered all the city's theatres to close for three weeks.

The riots came to an end with a court case in which Sheridan and Kelly sued each other for assault. It was widely assumed that no jury would take the side of an actor against a gentleman. Kelly's lawyer told the jury: "I have often seen a Gentleman Soldier, and a Gentleman Taylor; but I have never seen a Gentleman Player." At this Thomas rose, bowed modestly, and said, "Sir, I hope you see one now." His display of calm dignity had the desired effect: the jury acquitted him and found both Kelly and Brown guilty of assault. Kelly, moreover, received a serious sentence: a fine of £500 and a month's imprisonment.

This outcome was, of course, a triumph for Thomas. But if he had arrived at a pleasant place, the journey towards it had been gruelling. The affair as a whole had been a disaster. Because of the closure of the theatre and the effect of the disturbances on audience numbers, he lost £1,000 on the season. And although his honour—his status as a gentleman—had been upheld, it had also been called into question in the most direct and public way imaginable. The whole point of status is that, like sanity, it operates as a working assumption. To question it is, in itself, to devalue it.

Nor did Thomas's vindication actually settle the question of whether actors could be gentlemen. His case, as he stated it in three pamphlets published in Dublin during the disturbances, was decidedly ambivalent, made as it was on his own behalf and not that of the profession as a whole. He claimed merely that "tho' the Profession of an Actor does not entitle a Man to the Name of a Gentleman, yet neither can it take it from him if he had it before." And in fact, the underlying attitude to the social status of performers remained unaltered by Thomas's victory. Well into the nineteenth century, it would continue to place invisible but impenetrable barriers in the way of his son Richard.

Richard would certainly have been well aware of what his father had had to go through in order to defend his right to be recognised as a gentleman. Mathews's public declaration that he did not deserve "the treatment of a gentleman" was much more than a mere personal insult. It threatened both to undo what his parents had achieved in the past and to undermine his own future. Conversely, it gave him the opportunity to step out of the paternal shadow by proving himself at least his father's equal.

Even though it had been in reality a sordid and wildly undignified affair, the second duel was quickly transformed into an epic conflict, with the drunken and defeated Sheridan as its hero and the victorious Mathews as the villain. Thomas Sheridan, in spite of his anger with his son, believed that Mathews, were he to appear on the streets of Bath by day, "would be stoned to death by the populace."[6] The man who lived in the cottage on Kingsdown where the wounded Sheridan had first been carried had a large cut stone placed on the spot where the combatants had stabbed at each other. On it, he displayed the locket that had been pulled from around Sheridan's neck, a button from his coatsleeve, and the two broken swords.[7]

And not only was the duel itself transformed into a memorable public event, but so too was Eliza's reaction to it. The news of the second encounter, along with reports that Richard was at death's door, was printed in all the newspapers, but Thomas Linley kept it from Eliza, so that she would fulfil an engagement to sing at Oxford. As she sang, the audience, made up mostly of students, was aware that events that deeply concerned her were taking place offstage. And in this knowledge, she, too, was transformed, her status as potentially "available" woman giving way to the more dignified role of tragic wife. As Lissy Sheridan subsequently wrote, "Her ignorance of the duel and its consequences . . . known to every person, and her beauty, joined to the effect of her truly enchanting powers could not fail to excite a degree of sympathy in youthful and susceptible minds when they thought of the heavy calamity that hung over her."[8] After the concert, she was told what had happened, and in her agitation she blurted out that she had a right to see Richard because she was his wife. What might have been in other circumstances a scandalous revelation was now, in the public mind, a romantic twist in a gripping real-life melodrama.

And by the end of the play, Richard and Eliza had changed places. She had moved from the public arena to the private, from the dangerous status of public woman to the protected sphere of faithful wife. He had moved in the opposite direction, from private obscurity as a lesser member of his father's household to fame and glamour as a man who had paid in blood and valour the price of entry into society. She had become private property—that of her young husband. He, on the other hand, had captured for himself a place in the public mind.

Chapter 9

THE GREAT GATE OF POWER

A few months after the second duel, when he had fully recovered from his wounds, Sheridan wrote to Thomas Grenville, an aristocratic pupil of his father's with whom he had formed a deep friendship. Since late August 1772 he had been staying at Waltham Abbey, Essex, with family friends, Edward Parker and his wife. He had been sent there by his father, to keep him away from Eliza, from Mathews, and from trouble. He was supposed to be studying law books before entering as a student at the Middle Temple, having given his father "solemn assurances of his determined application to the study of the law." He had managed, in spite of all the evidence to the contrary, to persuade him that, after the wild adventures of the previous months, he was about to settle down to a respectable and studious life.

It was a brazen deception, for nothing could have been further from his mind than the pursuit of a dutiful and respectable professional career. He now saw himself as a man who had moved beyond the ordinary. He had passed through the refining fires of two duels. He had diced with death and won. He had been reborn as a gentleman. In his own mind at least, he had confounded the ordained social order of eighteenth-century England. When Grenville used, in a letter to Sheridan, the phrase "the spheres in which God has placed us," his friend took the opportunity of a reply to state his own credo. Having made the beginnings of a life for himself, he saw no reason why he should not go on to make his own world, why, instead of remaining in a fixed orbit, he should not blaze his own trail across the sky:

> I shall one of these days learnedly confute the idea that God could ever have intended individuals to fill up any particular Stations in which accidents of birth or fortune may have flung them. The Track of a Comet is as regular to the eye of God as the orbit of a Planet. *The Station* in which it has pleas'd God to place us, (or whatever the words are) is not properly interpreted. And as God very often pleases to let down great folks from the elevated Stations which they might claim as their Birth-right, there can be no reason for us to suppose that he does not mean that others should ascend.[1]

He was himself one of these "others," and he was imagining his ascent. His plan was to make himself a man of the world, to learn French and Italian, to spend the summer of 1773 in France with his father and to "see as much abroad as I could," all, obviously, in preparation for a career in public life. He was apparently studying a wide range of subjects: his own son Charles later remembered having "six copybooks, each filled with notes and references to mathematics, geography, history, Latin, and other studies carefully written" by his father at Waltham Abbey.[2] He was spending his evenings with "a very ingenious Man," a penniless local autodidact who was teaching him "Mechanics, Mensuration, Astronomy etc." In his head, he was already an Elizabethan gentleman (like, perhaps, Sir Philip Sidney, whose *Arcadia* he was reading with rapture and delight), a well-travelled polymath, speaking many languages and able to interpret the heavens and understand the movements of the earth beneath them. And he was able, of course, to exercise power in the public world.

Sidney's *Arcadia*, indeed, was to be a crucial influence. For not only was its author the very model of a public man in whom literary and political pursuits were fused in a single quest but the book itself provided Sheridan with an important literary model. In recommending it to Grenville, he confessed, "I had much rather view the Characters of Life as I would wish they *were* than as they *are*: therefore I hate Novels, and love Romances."[3] This preference would be essential to his work as a writer—his interest was in creating not realist reflections of what he called "Vicious and corrupt Society" but a kind of utopia on stage where wishes might meet actualities. And *Arcadia* itself showed him a way to do it. In it, romance is not incompatible with politics. Sidney brought all the trappings of romantic adventure—intrepid princes finding their mates, disguises, narrow escapes, duels—to what was still a deeply and immediately political story, an allegory, in fact, on the dangers of absolute monarchy. The language of love was intertwined with the language of truth in *Arcadia*; the erotic was continuous with the political. This was exactly what Sheridan would soon try to do in his plays.

Writing, for him, was never meant to be an end in itself; even while reading and scribbling, he was hoping for an entry into the political world. An acquaintance of his father's, Lord George Townshend, had just left the Lord Lieutenancy of Ireland to become Master-General of the Ordnance and had promised to "do something handsome" for him. If this meant a desirable diplomatic posting he would certainly take it up, but he had high expectations, and if Townshend's offer were merely that "I am to be sent God knows where in a prenticeship to some Minister, I shall beg to be excused."[4] Nothing came of any of these plans. He never learned French, never mind Italian. He never again left Britain. And the handsome something promised by Townshend never materialised.

It is nevertheless clear that he considered himself, at the age of twenty-one, destined not merely for an elevated station but for public office. He had no time for the pious belief that virtue was to be found only in the private domain:

> It has been an everlasting Fashion to declaim against the Pursuits of Ambition, and the expectation of Happiness in the scenes of publick Life. Yet, may we not with some justice attempt to prove, that there is to be found there a surer Foundation to build on, than in any [of] the most captivating roads of private, and comparitively, solitary Enjoyments.—Envy is the attendant on Greatness.—A Prince's smiles are not to be depended on—The association of men in Power is full of Jealousy and Distrust—The voice of the People is inconstant.—True—But does malice never reach a private Station? are the smiles of Friendship never deceitful? Do we never meet with ill-will from our Companions—and does the syren voice of Love never turn to Discord?[5]

His would be a public life and a legal training would be merely "the great Gate of Power." This sense of destiny came from imagining himself, not as the impoverished second son of an actor, but as an archetypal heroic lover: "Amo ergo sum," he wrote to Grenville, I love therefore I am.[6] For romantic heroes, practicalities like money, social position, and a distinct lack of prospects are incidental obstacles. Eliza had told him in a letter that she would live with him even without a proper, public marriage, and implied that their passion placed them outside normal social conventions:

> Yet though I despize the ties that govern Vulgar Souls; yet I must look sometimes towards a time when I hope it will be in my dear Horatio's Power at least to make me his in every sence of the Word, not as a thing of any consequence should I then be my own Mistress. Without Connection I would live with you in any situation and in any place but as it is We must submit till Fortune puts it [in] our Power to be happy our own Way.[7]

Away from her in Waltham, he was able to feel the exquisite torments of the separated lover: "When I see a pair blest in peace and in each other Let me say 'why am I shut out from this forever?' and 'tis torture. Let me sit in a beautiful scene, I exclaim—'what would her presence make this?' and 'tis worse than a wilderness. Let me hear musick and singing—'I cannot hear her sing and play,' and the notes become the shrieks of the Damned."[8] Small wonder that he preferred, at this time, enobling romances like Sidney's *Arcadia* to the novels of Fielding or Smollett, whose realism might appeal to Vulgar Souls.

And this self-image was sustained by rumours that reached him from Bath: Mathews was said to be back there and to have bullied Sheridan's second, Paumier, into signing a disparaging statement. For a week in December 1772, he was contemplating the prospect of yet another duel, and working up the rhetoric of melodramatic outrage: "I shall seek the bottom of this treachery and if I do not revenge it may I live to *deserve* it."[9] And even when the rumours turned out to have been wildly exaggerated, there was no sign of public interest in his love life dying away. That autumn, the *London Magazine* published a long, detailed, and relatively well-informed account of his adventures with Eliza, hinting at the truth that they might already be married: "Whether they are married or not, their respective parents have since that time been very industrious in keeping them separate." As late as March 1773, when Eliza sang in London, she attracted huge crowds, among them King George III and the royal family, partly, as the *Westminster Magazine* put it, as a result of her natural talent, and partly because of "the fortuitous occurrence of remarkable incidents in her Life."[10] According to Fanny Burney, the town "has rung of no other name this month." She noted, too, that her lover "a Mr Sheridan," was "very well spoken of."

The persona he was now creating for himself was, indeed, shaped precisely by the strange intermingling of the public and the private, the intimate and the open, in everything that happened between himself, Eliza, and Mathews. He was making, in the relative solitude of Waltham Abbey, the personality that he would carry with him into the extraordinary career of the next forty years. What distinguished it was the absence of a clear separation between private relations and public performances, between sex and friendship on the one hand and politics and power on the other. He was discovering, in these months, that private life could be constructed as a political conspiracy and that public life could be conducted through personal engagements.

Already he was consciously converting his erotic passions and familial affections into political thoughts: his feelings for Eliza were translated into a demand that women in general should be respected. Thinking probably of Mathews's conduct towards Eliza, of his threats to blacken her name if she refused his advances, and of her bonded servitude to her father, he wrote a long essay on women's education. It was likely that he was thinking, too, of his own mother, whose father had tried to prevent her from learning to read and write. Through a political tract, addressed to the Queen, he was paying a kind of homage to the two absent women who had shaped his life. He attacked those who held that nature had decreed female subjection: "When Man is scarce better than a brute, he shews his degeneracy by his treatment of Women, but I will advance that with every ray of Reason that breaks in upon his Mind, his respect for Women increases."[11] To him, nature was a terrain of equality and love, not of brutal domination. That he had almost certainly been reading Rousseau is suggested by the manner in which he chose to rapturously evoke the love of the Noble Savage for his mate: "The wild Huron shall become Gentle as his weary Rein-deer to the object of Love, He shall present to her the spoil of his Bow on his knee, he shall watch the scene where she sleeps, with reward, he shall rob the Birds for feather for her hair, and dive for Pearl for her Neck, her Look shall be his Law, and her Beauties his worship—This is Nature."

Men, he wrote, had acquired power only through "chance and animal strength." They "ought to blush to think how many genteel souls suffer thro the pangs of Poverty, the insult of Dependence." The poorer daughters of clergymen and army officers were left as "the lawful Prey to libertines, and the Path they tread is so thorny and so few can possibly get through with Credit, that it is regard[ed] as Presumptive Proof of Sin to be in it." And therefore, he proposed, the King should establish a sheltered university for women, where they would be taught astronomy, history, languages, literature, dancing, embroidery, and, for those with talent, music, poetry, and drawing. This academy for distressed gentlewomen would inspire the establishment of similar institutions in all major towns and for all classes of women. The man fortunate enough to marry the paragon of virtue, intelligence, and refinement who would emerge from these institutions would have to be "more careful of his Conduct." Soon, it would be the fashion for men everywhere to be "wise and virtuous, to be brave and honourable."

And as well as causing him to indulge in political good thoughts, his erotic entanglement also forced him to develop less worthy but no less essential political skills. The exigencies of his situation with Eliza gave him a thorough grounding in private deviousness. In the months after the second duel, his life was awash with conspiracies, secret assignations, intimate deceptions. Solemnly promising his father that he need "never again have the smallest uneasiness" about his relationship with Eliza, because he had "extricated myself" from it,[12] he would slip away to meet her whenever he could. While assuring his father that he had mended his profligate ways and proclaiming himself converted to "Prudence and all the Cardinal Virtues," he also succeeded in getting him to pay bills under false pretences. He would write frank letters to his sisters—"never *shew* my Letters to *any* one"—while composing others "in a Style" meant for official family consumption.

Thomas had originally proposed to send him and his sisters to France, but then, when he discovered that he was still seeing Eliza secretly and was therefore not a fit person to be left in charge of young women, decided to send Richard alone to Yorkshire, since "all the Counties in the Neighbourhood of London were within the magic Circle of a certain Enchantress."[13] Eventually, Thomas took the girls with him to Dublin and left Richard in Essex on the strict condition that he did not try to see Eliza. She, for her part, told Richard "[My father] would Soonner follow me to the Grave than see me Married to you as you would Ruin me and yourself in a short time by your Extravagence."[14]

Sheridan did, at first, make an effort to keep his promises to his father and cut off all communication with Eliza. He convinced himself that their relationship was doomed. He stopped sending her letters and told Grenville, "I am determined not to write;—not from the conviction of the necessity of such a determination, but I cannot break my solemn Promise."[15] She responded with furious accusations of betrayal: "For God's sake Sheridan do not endeavour to plunge me again into Misery. Consider the situation I am in, Consider how much your Persisting to refuse my Letters will distress me. I cannot, never will be yours. Reason, Honnor everything forbids it—this is no sudden Resolution, but the consequence of cool deliberate reflection."[16]

Eliza seems to have convinced herself, indeed, that Sheridan was refusing to write to her or to accept her letters because his affections now lay elsewhere. She wrote, "When I tell you I have lately had some Conversation with Mrs L and Miss C-y you will not suppose I will be again deceived." This Mrs. L is almost certainly Mrs. Mary Lyster, a surgeon's wife who lived near Waltham Abbey and who also wrote him some cryptic letters at this time, exclaiming in one of them, "Would that I had taken a flight from this during your stay! It would have saved me much pain and by it I should have escaped the jealousy of your best-beloved."[17] Mrs. Lyster went to see Eliza to try to assure her that there was nothing untoward in her relations with Sheridan, but Eliza was not convinced. She wrote indignantly to him, "Mrs L's assurance led her to suppose that she could make me believe she was entirely innocent in regard to you, and that she never entertained a thought of you but as a friend. I was a good deal surprised at her endeavouring to vindicate her conduct to me, but her behaviour only heightened the contempt I before felt for her . . ." Miss C-y is impossible to identify, but it is obvious from Eliza's reference in a letter to Sheridan to "the violence of her love for you" that she, too, was greatly taken by the romantic hero. In her case at least, it is clear that the feelings were not reciprocated.

And to thicken the plot still further, Sheridan, for his part, concluded that Eliza was going to marry someone else—"*Your friend*, Sir T[homas] Clarges," he wrote to Thomas Grenville in December 1772, "is going to be married to or run away with Miss L."[18] Clarges, who was the same age as Sheridan, was indeed in correspondence with Eliza at this time, though she insisted to Sheridan, "I am incapable of loving any man," and through Grenville, he denied the rumour.

It was probably the very violence of Eliza's accusations and the alarming rumours that she was to marry someone else that forced Sheridan to give up his resolution of keeping his promise to his father. No details of their reconciliation survive from contemporary documents. What is clear, though, is that rumours of their marriage in France, already hinted at in public, were acquiring a strange air of authority. On 26 March, the London correspondent of the *Bath Chronicle* reported, "It is now publicly said that Mr Richard Sheridan is actually married to Miss Linley, and has been for some time."

In early April, the *Bath Chronicle* published a letter addressed to "Adorable Creature" by a man who signs himself "G—R" and declares that he "has it ever to lament that the laws will not permit me to offer you my hand." He offers, instead, his heart and his fortune, and asks her to give his messenger "Lady A———" permission for him to throw himself at her feet. Her answer was also published: "You lament the laws will not permit you to offer me your hand. I lament it too, my lord, but on a different principle—to convince your dissipated heart that I have a soul capable of *refusing* a coronet when the owner is not the object of my affection—despising it when the offer of an unworthy possessor."

The odd thing about both these letters is that they were sent to the *Bath Chronicle* with a covering letter explaining that they had passed between "Lord Grosvenor" and "the celebrated English syren Miss L—y." This covering letter was signed "Horatio"—Sheridan's own code name in his poems and love letters to Eliza. It seems that he himself concocted them, probably in order to convince Thomas Linley that his daughter's reputation was again in imminent danger and that another married Lothario, a second Mathews, was attempting to prey on her. By then sending them to the same newspaper that had published Mathews's original challenge to Sheridan, he was raising the possibility of yet another cycle of sensations. If so, the manoeuvre was a brilliant success. Even before the letters actually appeared in print, Thomas Linley suddenly dropped his opposition to the relationship and signed the register after the wedding of Elizabeth Ann Linley and Richard Brinsley Sheridan at Marylebone Church on Marylebone High Street in London on 13 April 1773. Afterwards there was a dinner at the Star and Garter inn on Richmond Hill, and in the evening the couple were left, according to the *Morning Chronicle*, "at a gentleman's house in Mitcham." The venue of the wedding (London rather than Bath), the fact that it was not announced beforehand, and the fact that it took place the day after Eliza had sung at a benefit concert in the Haymarket Theatre suggest that it was arranged quite suddenly.

So too does the fact that just a week before the wedding, Sheridan had finally entered as a law student at the Middle Temple, an odd thing to do if he intended to set up house with Eliza at the same time. And he made no effort to reconcile his father, who was still acting in Ireland, to the marriage. Thomas Sheridan was so outraged by the news that he wrote to Charles a week after the wedding telling him, "I consider myself now as having no Son but *you* and therefore my anxiety about you is the greater . . . Your sisters know of no other brother, and would therefore naturally expect an increase of attention."[19] His ex-son told Thomas Linley that he had been "prepared for" this reaction, and got him to write to his father on his behalf. But Thomas Sheridan was implacable and the breach would not be healed for many years.

Instead of settling down to study law, Sheridan retired with Eliza to a rustic cottage in East Burnham in Buckinghamshire. The only money they had was £1,000 that Walter Long had settled on Eliza. (The rest of this settlement went to Thomas Linley in compensation for the loss of his daughter's earnings.) Sheridan joked in a letter to Grenville about Eliza's magical singing making carrots and cabbages spring from the ground, but added that "whatever effect her Voice might have upon the Sheep on the Common, The Mutton still obstinately continued stationary at the Butchers." He was, however, "absolutely and perfectly happy."[20] But this was an idyllic interlude, not a happy ending. He had not the slightest intention of leading a quiet life. By February 1774, he and Eliza had moved back into London, where they bought a small house in Orchard Street, off Portman Square, and he was preparing himself for a public career by reading and writing.

In a long attack on Lord Chesterfield's recently—and posthumously—published *Letters to His Son*, an aristocrat's manual for success in the world, stressing the virtues of good breeding, manners and style, Sheridan objected to the idea that it was necessary for a young man to be constantly busy:

> "Hurry," he says, "from play to study; never be doing nothing." —I say "Frequently be unemployed; sit and think." *There are on every subject but a few leading and fixed ideas; their tracks may be traced by your own genius, as well as by reading:*—a man of deep thought, who shall have accustomed himself to support or attack all he has read, will soon find nothing new:—thought is exercise, and the mind like the body must not be wearied.[21]

This, for the moment, was what he was doing—thinking through his own ideas. And in his thoughts, the personal and the political—authority in the family and in the world—were intertwined. In his attack on Chesterfield, he was, in large measure, attacking his own father. He complained about the "selfish vanity of the father" in seeking "praise for his own mode of education," a condemnation at least as applicable to Thomas Sheridan as to Lord Chesterfield. And his resentment at the way his father had held up his brother, Charles, as the model for him to follow burned through his apparently abstract disagreement with Chesterfield: "Emulation is a dangerous passion to encourage, in some points, in young men; it is so linked with envy:—if you breed your son with reproach for not surpassing his school-fellows, he will hate those who are before him." In any case, he wrote, it was not that sons had a duty to their fathers, but the other way around. "The obligation of birth" was "nothing." In his own case at least this was true: he had no one but himself and Eliza to thank for the fact that, instead of being a minor functionary in his father's academy in Bath, he was now married to one of the most beautiful and sought-after women in England and had, moreover, the confidence to believe that his own genius could trace the tracks of any important idea. After a period of fruitful unemployment, he fully intended to put that genius to work.

If the previous two years of his life had been a romantic play, the scene that the audience might imagine after the curtain had come down would be that of himself and Eliza living together—talking, thinking, and playing music. After elopement, duels, intrigues, parental opposition, and a falling out, the happy couple settled in domestic bliss, eating plainly but feasting on each other. But, for Sheridan, all those events had been real, and he now imagined a brilliant beginning, not a happy end, contemplating not a life of secluded bliss but a great public career which would see the world turned upside down. Thus far he had been a mere actor in the drama; it was now time to become the author.

Chapter 10

BEASTLY PIMPING ACTORS

In March 1795, George Canning, then a young friend and political opponent of Sheridan's, later Prime Minister of Great Britain, was invited to join Lord Boringdon at Saltram, a mansion in the West Country. He would have liked to go, but it was out of the question. He declined the invitation but was ashamed to explain his reason for doing so. His mother divided her time between Exeter and Plymouth, both near to Saltram. While Canning would have been happy to visit her "if it could be done quietly and without much observation," he was, as he explained to his uncle and aunt, terrified that she might "come some fine day to visit me at Saltram, and that, you know, under all circumstances, would be rather inconvenient and distressing."[1]

Canning's mother, Mary Ann Costello, was not a madwoman, a murderer, or a prostitute. But she was an Irish actress and that, for a talented young man trying to make his way in English political life, was bad enough for him to fear that, as her child, he would be considered unfit for public office. Canning's dread of being associated with his mother's profession gives some idea of the difficulty that faced Richard Sheridan after his marriage to Eliza in his ambition to assume public office. Even without the stigma of having theatrical origins, he knew that there were only five ways for someone of low social status and without a fortune to attain a political career. He could make money in trade, usually by securing government contracts. He could become a war profiteer. He could join the East India Company and come home with his pockets full of loot. He could marry a wealthy landed heiress. Or he could work his way up through the legal profession and eventually leap the narrow chasm that separated a leading barrister from a Member of Parliament. Neither of the first two routes was a real option for Sheridan, who had already succeeded in running up debts and would eventually acquire a magnificent carelessness with money. And he had already, by the age of twenty-three, closed off the other three avenues. He had declined to go to India with Halhed. He had abandoned his plans to become a lawyer. And he had married a woman who was far from being a landed heiress.

Eliza could, of course, have earned more than enough to keep them both in some style. At the time of their marriage she was at the height of her success, and the demand for her to sing at concerts, choir festivals, university convocations, and elaborate church services was virtually limitless. Shortly after their marriage Sheridan was offered £2,000 a year for seven years if she would sing for one promoter. The composer Samuel Arnold offered £3,000 for twenty concerts. The Prime Minister, Lord North, implored him to allow her to sing at the convocation of Oxford University, of which he was Chancellor, and told him that he would "look upon it as the highest compliment."[2] The Earl of Coventry invited both of them to stay with him while Eliza sang at a choir festival in Worcester, of which he was Steward. The King himself had been reported as telling Eliza, just three days before the wedding, when she performed at Buckingham Palace, that he had "never in his life heard so fine a voice."

But there were two reasons why Eliza could not go on performing. One was that she herself hated being on public display and had been determined to stop performing once she was no longer her father's indentured servant. And the other was that, had she done so, Sheridan would have risked death with Mathews for nothing. A gentleman did not allow his wife to sing for money. A gentleman did not have a wife who, as a public performer, was assumed to be available to her public. And it was impossible to be a public man without being, in the first place, a gentleman. He could only move onto the public stage if Eliza moved off it.

Conversely, however, a young man without a fortune who valued his own and his wife's honour above the prospect of obtaining one was, unquestionably, a gentleman. After she fulfilled the engagements which had already been contracted—Oxford in July and Worcester in September—Eliza never sang for money again. For the first of her final paid appearances she was announced as "the celebrated Mrs Sheridan." For the second, her fee was a £100 note. On the Sunday afterwards, she ostentatiously placed it on the plate for the church collection. The magnificence of the gesture made the Sheridans a topic of conversation in all the best places. On 17 April 1775, the painter Sir Joshua Reynolds and the writers Dr. Samuel Johnson and James Boswell discussed them over dinner in Twickenham:

> We talked of a young gentleman's marriage with an eminent singer, and his determination that she should no longer sing in publick, though . . . her talent would be liberally rewarded, so as to make her a good fortune. It was questioned whether the young gentleman who had not a shilling in the world, but was blest with very uncommon talents, was not foolishly delicate, or foolishly proud . . . Johnson, with all the high spirit of a Roman senator, exclaimed "He resolved wisely and nobly, to be sure. He is a brave man. Would not a gentleman be disgraced by having his wife sing publickly for hire? No, Sir, there can be no doubt here. I know not if I should not *prepare* myself for a publick singer, as readily as let my wife be one."[3]

Had Sheridan been able to listen in, the use of the word "gentleman" three times in a few sentences about him would have delighted him even more than the tributes to his bravery, wisdom, and nobility.

Yet if he would not live on Eliza's earnings, how was he to make money for them both, if not by entering into the very field where the status of a gentleman would be most vulnerable: the theatre? It was the road to success most obviously open to him. He had been steeped in it almost from birth. Both his father and his mother had written plays. His father was still, in spite of everything, a famous and respected actor whose earnings from the stage had paid for the clothes on his back and the food on his table. He himself had already shown, in collaborating with Halhed on *Ixion*, a natural gift for dramatic dialogue and action. Yet ambivalence about the theatre was also a part of his inheritance. His father had a low opinion of his own achievements as an actor. He had told James Boswell that even if he were acknowledged to be the best actor in the world, "I would not choose that it should be remembered. I would have it erased out of the anecdotes of my life. Acting is a poor thing in the present state of the stage. For my own part, I engaged in it merely as a step to something greater, a just notion of eloquence."[4] The theatre for Thomas was a means to an end, the platform from which he would reform language, politics, and society.

Similarly, the deep anxiety about the moral status of women who performed in public that made Richard Sheridan so adamant that his wife's career had to end was matched by a general hostility to the theatre. In 1775, when his father-in-law, Thomas Linley, told him that Eliza's sister Mary had been offered work at Drury Lane by the great actor David Garrick, Sheridan wrote him an extraordinary letter. He declared that he had always had an "instinctive abhorrence" of the stage as "the greatest Nursery of Vice and Misery on the Face of the Earth." Were Mary to accept Garrick's offer, he thundered, she would become "the unblushing Object of a Licentious gaping croud," the "Creature of a mercenary Manager, The Servant of the Town, and a licens'd mark for Libertinism . . . a Topick for illiberal News-Paper Criticism and Scandal." She would be forced to

> . . . represent all the different modifications of love before a mix'd Assembly of Rakes, Whores, Lords, and Blackguards in Succession!—to play the Coquet, the Wanton, to retail loose innuendos in Comedy, or glow with warm Descriptions in Tragedy; and in both to be haul'd about, squeez'd and kiss'd by beastly pimping Actors! . . . everything around them is unchaste—their Studies are Lessons of Vice and Passion.—Like Wretches who work in unwhol[e]some Mines, their senses are corrupted in the operation of their Trade.[5]

The virulence of this wild tirade shows just how raw Sheridan's nerves really were. And there can be little doubt that the lurid violence of his language was provoked by fear of losing the credit he had gained by Eliza's withdrawal from public performance. Eliza, he told her father, had "married a Man from whom she could derive no consequence either thro' Birth, Fortune or Connections, yet I will venture to assert that she now stands in the Estimation and Respect of the World, far above what any Man of fifty times my advantages could have raised her to—had he taken her from behind the Scenes of Drury-Lane Playhouse." He stressed in the same letter, "No Gentleman of Character and Fortune ever yet took a Wife from behind the Scenes of a Theatre," and he might have added that no gentleman had a sister-in-law on the stage either. If Mary were to become an actress, he would again be allied to the unclean trade. He feared that in all likelihood she would marry an actor, that her younger sisters would follow in her footsteps, and that soon he would find himself not just the son of an actor but kith and kin to an entire tribe of thespians. Vehemently though he denied that this prospect provided the motivation for his outburst—"If you imagine that my earnest Prejudice on this Point is in the least assisted by any selfish Pride that so near Relations should be in a Profession which I think so ill of—you will do me the greatest Injustice"—the frantic urgency of his language belied his denials.

And yet, in spite of all these turbulent feelings about the theatre, it was his only weapon. He was caught between irreconcilable needs—to escape from the stigma of his theatrical connections and to attain a public success which only the theatre could bring him. Sometime in the summer of 1774, when he started to write a play, he found that there was a way to deal with the profound contradictions of his situation. Such contradictions could not be reconciled, they could not be evaded, but it might be possible to do what his father's godfather, Jonathan Swift, had done. Swift had discovered that awkward realities which could not be denied, could be exaggerated; they could not be diminished in the hope that they would become invisible, but they could be inflated to the point where they became almost blindingly obvious. This is what Sheridan did in his play *The Rivals*. He had announced almost casually to Thomas Linley, in November 1774, that a play of his would be in rehearsal at Covent Garden within a few days, even though, eight weeks previously, he had written only a scene or two. And, he added, Thomas Harris, the manager of Covent Garden, had assured him that "the least shilling I shall get (if it succeeds) will be six hundred pounds."[6]

What he had before him when he sat down to write were the materials of his own life. He had a mother and a father. One was dead, and the other regarded *him* as dead. But both had left pieces of themselves—books and plays—that could not be taken from him. And he had a story, made up of the extraordinary things that had happened to him over the last two years. Bits of this story had been taken from him, too—in Samuel Foote's *The Maid of Bath*, in the scandals and rumours, the newspaper advertisements and gossip, in the enthralled audience watching Eliza as she sang while, unknown to her, reports of Sheridan's death circulated. But that public knowledge merely gave him the opportunity to play with perceptions, to inflate everything that people thought they knew about him into a huge, hysterical burlesque. Instead of inventing a story and pretending it was real, he could present his own reality as if it were an invention.

In this, he seems to have had not only Eliza's full support but her active assistance. After the play had opened, her sister Mary wrote to her, "I know you have been very busy writing for Sheridan—I don't mean *copying*, but *composing*:—it's true, indeed;—you must not contradict me when I say you wrote the much-admired epilogue to The Rivals . . . What makes it certain is, that my *father* guessed it was *yours* the first time he saw it praised in the paper."[7] Whether she actually wrote any of the text or not, though, the play belonged as much to her as to him—it was their affair, and her fame, that had made it possible.

It is no accident that *The Rivals*, like the Sheridans' life at the time, starts where any ordinary romantic drama would end. The young lovers, Lydia Languish and Jack Absolute, have already met, courted, fallen in love, and agreed to marry. Nothing stands in their way: in fact Jack's tyrannical father "wants to *force* me to marry the very girl I am plotting to run away with." Sir Anthony Absolute, for his part, is infuriated, not by the usual disobedience of his errant son, but by the latter's meek acceptance of his commands. Lydia is already "so rich she feeds her parrot with small pearls," so neither love nor money should be a problem.

All the complications of the plot hinge on a mere caprice. Lydia will not marry Jack if she thinks he is wealthy, so he has to pretend to be a penniless ensign. And if she elopes with him, as her fantasy demands, she will lose her fortune. From the very beginning, all the trappings of the romantic love story that Sheridan and Eliza had really lived through—elopements, duels, secret messages, painful misunderstandings, assumed identities—are the mad exaggerations of a young woman's fancy. His own recent history becomes an impossible pantomime. The reality of his life as a penniless, unqualified, Irish actor's son, famous only for his involvement in some romantic but vaguely disreputable scrapes, is expanded into a gigantic joke and then explodes in a burst of laughter. And within this fantastical contrivance, his own theatrical origins are not evaded but flaunted to bring extra zest to the comedy. His mother's plays and novels, his father's plays and linguistic theories, are all placed before the audience in the protected space of a brilliantly absurd comedy. There is one character, Faulkland, whose name and mentality are taken directly from the same character in his mother's hugely successful novel, *Memoirs of Miss Sidney Biddulph*: his "ideas of love, honour, generosity, and gratitude, are so refined, that no hero in romance ever went beyond him." There is another, Sir Lucius O'Trigger, who is reminiscent of his father's creation Captain O'Blunder, in a farce of the same name. Then there is a borrowing from his mother's life: her father's attempts to prevent her from learning to read. In *The Rivals* Sir Anthony Absolute complains that Lydia's notions are "the natural consequence of teaching girls to read.—Had I a thousand daughters, by Heaven! I'd as soon have them taught the black art as their alphabet."[8] There are numerous borrowings from his mother's unfinished play *A Journey to Bath*, which, according to his sister, was "put into my brother Richard's hands by my father at Bath, when we were resident there."[9] And there is, in the memorable Mrs. Malaprop, a character who is both a borrowing from his mother and a satire on his father's obsessions.

In *A Journey to Bath*, Mrs. Tryfort is a crude version of Mrs. Malaprop, whose words continually approach but never quite arrive at meaning. Described by one of the other characters as being "fondest of hard words, which without *miscalling*, she always takes care to misapply" (almost exactly the words used about Mrs. Malaprop), she has lines like "Dear Sir, you needn't incommode yourself . . . ," "Miss's mind is in the greatest agility about it," and "Nobody can be embelished that has not been abroad, you know. Oh, if you were to hear him describe contagious countries as I have done . . . He is a perfect map of geography." But to make Mrs. Malaprop, Sheridan added a vicious twist to his mother's gentle satire. Mrs. Tryfort is a figure entirely compatible with Thomas Sheridan's obsessions—an example of what happens when the proper use of language is neglected. Mrs. Malaprop, on the other hand, is the illegitimate offspring of an imagined coupling between Mrs. Tryfort and Thomas Sheridan. She is at one and the same time an example of bad language and a pedant. In one of the most brilliant passages of the play, she simultaneously demands a Thomas Sheridanesque attention to propriety in the spoken word and unwittingly flaunts the ignorance she complains of. It begins with a direct echo of Mrs. Tryfort and then slips into an indirect satire on the man who proposed to make his son a rhetorical usher in an academy of speech:

> I would have her instructed in geography that she might know something of the contagious countries; but above all, Sir Anthony, she should be a mistress of orthodoxy, that she might not mis-spell, and mis-pronounce words so shamefully as girls usually do; and likewise that she might reprehend the true meaning of what she is saying—This, Sir Anthony is what I would have a woman know;—and I don't think there is a superstitious article in it.[10]

There were, in this, elements both of revenge on his father and of a gleeful escape from the rhetorical academy. By making Mrs. Malaprop both his father's worst nightmare and a satire on his father at his worst, Sheridan at once acknowledged and defused his own antecedents. Whereas most of the references to his mother's work—except the obvious and rather flattering borrowing of Faulkland—had merely private resonances, the butt of jokes on orthography and pronunciation, especially in a play set in Bath, would have been obvious to at least a section of the audience. And most of Mrs. Malaprop's more spectacular mistakes not merely are misuses of language but are actually *about* language. The words they misapply themselves refer to the act of reading and the act of speaking. *Illegible* for ineligible; *conjunctions* for injunctions; *delusions* for allusions; *oracular tongue* for vernacular tongue; a *nice derangement of epitaphs* for a nice arrangement of epithets; and that most literary of beasts, the *allegory on the banks of the Nile*, all belong to the kind of self-conscious analysis of language that Thomas Sheridan practised. And the point about Mrs. Malaprop is not that she is careless about her speech but that she is obsessively self-conscious about words. In her nice derangement of language there is a hint that too much concern with the niceties of language can derange the mind.

At a less directly personal level, Sheridan also made theatricality itself a part of the joyous joke. He was writing for an audience that was steeped in the comedies of Shakespeare, Jonson, the Restoration, and the early eighteenth century. In the 1770s, the two licensed theatres in London, Covent Garden and Drury Lane, staged about thirty comedies from the traditional repertoire each season. The repertoire, being so static, provided a stock of communal references, and it was safe for a playwright to assume that the audience would recognise conventional types and situations. *The Rivals* is a self-conscious compendium of such theatrical clichés, and part of its delight for the audience of the time lay precisely in the recognition of burlesque versions of familiar plots and devices.

The characters, the complications, the relationships are all taken from frequently performed plays. Lydia and Jack—a young woman who will lose a portion of her fortune if she marries without the consent of her aunt, and a young man who wants the girl *and* the money—are versions of Millamant and Mirabel in William Congreve's *The Way of the World*. Lydia is also remarkably close to the eponymous heroine of George Colman's *Polly Honeycombe*, which had been recently revived. Sir Anthony Absolute, lusting after his son's bride-to-be, is a slightly less disreputable Sir Sampson Legend from Congreve's *Love for Love*. Bob Acres is a first cousin of Oliver Goldsmith's Tony Lumpkin from *She Stoops to Conquer*, and Mrs. Malaprop is clearly related to Mrs. Hardcastle in the same play. Sir Lucius O'Trigger is a descendant, not just of Thomas Sheridan's Captain O'Blunder, but of a whole tribe of blustering stage Irishmen, chief among them Major O'Flaherty in Richard Cumberland's *The West Indian*. As for the plot, many of its main elements were familiar from David Garrick's *Miss in her Teens*, George Colman's *The Deuce is in Him*, and *Polly Honeycombe*. In some cases, these correspondences were underlined by casting—John Quick, who created the role of Bob Acres, had recently played Tony Lumpkin; Jane Green, who played Mrs. Malaprop, had created Mrs. Hardcastle. But Sheridan's general intention was not to parody any specific play but to make *The Rivals* at one level an ironic travesty of theatre itself. He was constructing a context in which he could at one and the same time exploit the theatre and declare a kind of knowing distance from it.

If *The Rivals* had merely done this, of course, it could not have been one of the great comedies of the century. The satiric exaggerations both of his own theatrical associations and of theatre in general were much more than a clever exercise in form. Their point was to allow him to create a brilliantly funny burlesque of his own story. Within the insistent artifice of the play, he could give a new comic life to almost everything that had happened to him in the previous two years.

Some of the glances at his own life in the play are purely private.

His collaboration with Nathaniel Halhed on a play about Jupiter's amorous intrigues receives a nod near the start with Fag's pronouncement that "Love . . . has been a masquerader ever since the days of Jupiter." When Jack Absolute mentions a song beginning "Go, gentle Gales!," there is a public echo of a poem by Alexander Pope, but also a private memory of the fact that Halhed had sent him an attempt at a "pastoral" beginning with the same words, when they were working together on the *Love Epistles*.

But mostly the assumption was that almost everything about the author was common knowledge. Even the prologue of the play seemed to assume that the audience would know that he had been registered as a law student at the Middle Temple. It was presented as a dialogue between a serjeant-at-law and an attorney, and as a mock-appeal on behalf of the author before the audience as jury. In a copy of the prologue in Sheridan's own hand, which, from the review in the *Public Ledger*, was clearly used on the first night, there are still more specific references to "a Student erring from the Temple's Bounds."[11] The insertion of his own history into the drama was signalled from the start, so that the audience could have no doubt that in the play's tale of elopements, duels, and romantic complications in Bath, he was making a show of himself.

Bath itself was vividly evoked. Specific references were made to real people and recognisable places in the town—Lewis Bull and William Frederick, both booksellers; James Cox, who exhibited mechanical toys in the Spring Gardens; the new Assembly Rooms, where Sheridan had danced; the Spring Gardens, where he had his secret trysts with Eliza; the fields behind the Sheridans' own house on Kingsmead Street. And it was the setting for people and events that drew very obviously on his own adventures. Eliza's singing was recalled in Bob Acres's rapturous description of Julia—"so sweet a voice—so expert at her Harpsicord—such a mistress of flat and sharp, squallante, rumblante, and quiverante . . . Odds Minnums and Crotchets! how she did chirrup at Mrs Piano's Concert."[12] The importunities of Long and Mathews were recalled in her surfeit of suitors. Sheridan's own intervention as her saviour was alluded to in Jack's promise to "rescue her from undeserved persecution and, with a licensed warmth plead for my reward." Their daring elopement, and its transformation into a journalistic sensation, were travestied in Lydia's fantasies of being spirited away in the dead of night: "so becoming a disguise!—so amiable a ladder of Ropes!—Conscious

Moon—four horses—Scotch parson—with such surprise to Mrs Malaprop—and such paragraphs in the News-papers!"

Their secret meetings in the Spring Gardens were also given a rapturous but hilariously bathetic reprise by Lydia:

> How mortifying, to remember the dear delicious shifts I used to be put to, to gain half a minute's conversation with this fellow!—How often have I stole forth, in the coldest night in January, and found him in the garden, stuck like a dripping statue!—There he would kneel to me in the snow, and sneeze and cough so pathetically! he shivering with cold, and I with apprehension! and while the freezing blast numb'd our joints, how warmly would he press me to pity his flame, and glow with mutual ardour!—Ah, Julia! that was something like being in love.[13]

Sheridan's difficulties with his father were echoed in the relationship between Jack Absolute and Sir Anthony Absolute. His determination to prefer love to money in forgoing the fortune that Eliza might have earned was also turned to comic purpose. Jack plays up to Lydia's romantic notions—"By Heav'n I would fling all goods of fortune from me with a prodigal hand to enjoy the scene where I might clasp my Lydia to my bosom, and say, the world affords no smile to me—but here—(*Embracing her*)." Lydia swoons over "how charming will poverty be with him!"[14]

Caricatures of himself could be spotted in each of the four younger male characters. As an Irish adventurer on the make, he shared much with Sir Lucius O'Trigger. As a social outsider trying to impress himself on Bath, he resembled Bob Acres. Elements of his experiences as a lover who had been embroiled in misunderstandings and jealousies could be discerned in the fretful Faulkland. And Jack Absolute brought to his courtship of Eliza the same peculiar combination of intrepid romance and cold calculation that had allowed him to seize his chance with Eliza. Above all, the most deadly serious aspect of his adventures—the duels—was transformed into pure comedy. The two duels he fought with Mathews became, in the delicious absurdities of the plot, two simultaneous challenges to fight two different opponents. The fierce contests of honour and social standing, the rituals of insult, challenge, and acceptance, were reduced to Sir Lucius's contention that there is no point in seeking a cause for a duel—"the quarrel is a very pretty quarrel as it stands

—we should only spoil it, by trying to explain it." The profound import of words like "liar" and "scoundrel" in Mathews's advertisement in the *Bath Chronicle* was replaced by Bob Acres's desperate attempt to avoid being offended:

> *Acres*: . . . 'tisn't that I mind the word Coward—*Coward* may be said in a joke.—But if you had call'd me a *Poltroon*, Odds Daggers and Balls!
> *Sir Lucius*: Well, Sir?
> *Acres*:—I should have thought you a very ill-bred man.

So many, indeed, were the allusions to the real events of Bath two years before that there were serious fears that the play itself might provoke a renewal of the animosity. William Barnett (sometimes called William Barnard), who was Mathews's second in the duel of July 1772, and who delivered the challenge to Sheridan's sister Lissy, was an Irishman, and rumours spread that Sir Lucius O'Trigger was based on him. Shortly after the opening of *The Rivals*, the *Morning Post* criticised "Mr B—d" for his attempt to "create a prejudice against the performance by every mode that malevolence could suggest." On the day of the opening, *The Gazeteer* carried what looked like a denial inspired by Sheridan himself: "It having been reported, that the story of the new comedy of The Rivals was not an entirely fictitious one, we have authority to assert, that such a report is entirely void of foundation, and that there is not the slightest local or personal allusion whatever throughout the piece." The claim was so far-fetched as to suggest a degree of panic.

Town and Country magazine reported shortly afterwards on the sources of such fears: "It was believed by the friends of the author that it would meet with opposition from a certain quarter, as it was thought by many to have a close connexion with a certain affair at Bath, in which the celebrated Miss Linley (now Mrs Sheridan) was the subject of rivalship . . ."[15] And there was certainly an organised claque on the opening night. The *Public Ledger* reported that there had been hissing from a section of the audience, and the *Morning Chronicle* that "a little malice from one corner of the gallery . . . shewed itself too early to produce any effect." Sheridan himself, in a preface to the first published edition of the play, remarked, "As some part of the attack on the Piece was begun too early to pass for the sentence of *Judgement*, which is ever tardy in condemning, it has been suggested to me, that much of the disapprobation must have arisen from virulence of Malice . . ."[16]

Yet such was Sheridan's tendency to make reality seem fantastic and to lace fancies with intimations of the actual that the play also risked precisely the opposite accusation of being not real enough. On the opening night, the play was threatened, not by the disruption from Barnett that Sheridan had feared, but by the audience's feeling that in places it was not so much burlesque as grotesque. The linguistic anarchy of Mrs. Malaprop had been pushed too far, taking the word-play into dangerous areas of sexual double entendre. Sir Anthony Absolute's lust for his prospective daughter-in-law was so heavily marked that it seemed genuinely disturbing rather than scabrously satirical. And, most ironically, Sheridan's joke on himself as an Irish adventurer in the character of Sir Lucius O'Trigger was interpreted by the opening night audience as a heavy-handed attack on the Irish in general. These last two problems were, moreover, exacerbated by poor performances from John Lee, who was thought crude as Sir Lucius, and Ned Shuter, who seemed not to know Sir Anthony's lines. And there were simpler problems—the play was too long, there were too many complications in the plot, and some of the puns were merely bad.

But while all these faults were alluded to in the first reviews, their largely negative tone owed more to a feeling of being wrong-footed, of being unable to understand quite what the author was up to. The *London Packet* complained: "The characters are not only larger than life but are rather awkwardly placed. The diction is an odd mixture of the elegant and the absurd." The *Morning Chronicle* was worried that Sheridan's characters were not "faithfully copied from nature," and found the acting of Sir Lucius "so far from giving the manners of our brave and worthy neighbours, that it scarce equals the picture of a *respectable* Hotentot . . ." The *Public Ledger* reckoned that the plot was "outré, and one of the Characters . . . an absolute exotic in the wilds of nature."

This feeling that the young playwright was unleashing the absurd and the exotic went hand-in-hand with an equally strong, and utterly contradictory, feeling that the characters and the plot were all familiar from other established plays in the repertoire. How could a play be at once so outlandish and so conventional, so outrageous and so commonplace? The answer, which the initial reviewers could not quite put their finger on, was that Sheridan, as he had proposed to

Thomas Grenville eighteen months before, had turned the world on its head. A world turned upside down still looks like the same world, and the theatrical clichés that Sheridan had appropriated were meant precisely to look familiar. But the perspective is different. The world of *The Rivals* is one which is being turned head-over-heels.

Gentlemen are no longer wearing wigs: in the first scene, a coachman worries about what the world will come to when such signs of decorum are abandoned. "Odd's life!—when I heard how the lawyers and doctors had took to their own hair, I thought how 'twould go next . . ." Rich young women are neglecting the sermons and manuals of moral improvement that ought to be their literary diet and are instead obsessed with sentimental novels. Lydia's library seethes with sex and sensibility. Among the novels she is said to be reading are French works like Treyssac de Vergy's *The Mistakes of the Heart*, steeped in Rousseau's disturbing doctrines of natural emotions, and a translation of a "thoroughly indecent romance," Paul Scarron's *L'Adultère Innocente*.[17] French fashions are also tormenting country squires like Bob Acres—the backbone of solid old England—making them unsteady on their feet:

> . . . these outlandish heathen Allemandes and Cotillions are quite beyond me!—I shall never prosper at 'em, that's sure—mine are true-born English legs—they don't understand their curst French lingo!—the *Pas* this, and *Pas* that, and *Pas* t'other—damn me, my feet don't like to be called Paws! No 'tis certain I have most Antigallican Toes![18]

Sexuality is threatening the orderly commerce of upper-class marriage: Lydia cannot bear to be a "mere Smithfield bargain." Worse, she is beginning to imagine that poverty might be glamorous. Bath is so full of adventurers, its class hierarchies so vulnerable, that Jack Absolute not only can maintain two different identities throughout the play—as himself and as Lydia's fantasy man, Beverley—but can belong to two different classes, his own landed squirearchy and Ensign Beverley's lower orders. And language itself, the signifier of order and meaning, has become, on Mrs. Malaprop's lips, deranged.

This, of course, was the point of the play for Sheridan himself. It placed his own story, his own public persona, firmly in the context of a changing social order. But it did so in a way that was to typify his approach as a public man—it appropriated old forms and gave them a new content, disguising the novel as the familiar. And this is why it was so confusing for its initial reviewers, why they could not make up their minds whether it amounted to outrageous innovation or a rehash of old clichés.

Sheridan told Thomas Creevey many years later that, after the disaster of the opening night, Eliza was "delighted." It seems, if Creevey's account is true, that she had grown tired of poverty and may also have regretted her earlier determination to give up her own career. "I always knew," she told Richard, "it was impossible you should make anything by writing plays; so now there is nothing for it but my beginning to sing publickly again, and we shall have as much money as we like."[19] But with the decisiveness and furious energy which he could always muster in times of crisis, Sheridan set about rescuing the play. The manager, Thomas Harris, agreed to withdraw it after the first night. The newspapers were told that it had been "withdrawn for the present, to undergo some severe prunings, trimmings, and patchings, before its second performance." John Lee was replaced as Sir Lucius by Lawrence Clinch, an old friend of the family. And, in ten days, Sheridan rewrote the play, pointing up Sir Lucius's respectability, toning down Sir Anthony's lasciviousness, removing many of the puns and double entendres, substantially shortening the running time.

When *The Rivals* reopened on 28 January, the whole tone of its reception was different, so much so, indeed, that it is difficult to account for the change merely by reference to Sheridan's editing of his text and the recasting of one character. It was almost as though the play had had a delayed impact, as if a break had been needed for its originality to sink in. The reviews were by no means ecstatic, but critics now saw "great and various improvements" and "many evident traits of literary genius." The great David Garrick, the era's dominant actor and now manager and part-owner of Drury Lane Theatre, was reported to have muttered early in the performance, "I see this play will creep," and then to have said at the end, "I see this play will run." The *Morning Post* pictured Sheridan as a budding hero who, "Hercules-like, even *in the cradle of genius*, tore the serpents asunder by the vigour of his mind, and baulked the cankered malice of his foes."

And Sheridan himself seems to have helped this process of rehabilitation along with a trick that he may have learned in his intrigues with Eliza—the planting of an article in the newspaper. A pseudonymous "Aristarchus," later identified as Sheridan himself, announced in the *Morning Chronicle* that the play, "which from some levities and want of experience was near being crushed the first night," will now "certainly stand foremost in the list of modern comedies." He defended the author from accusations of anti-Irish prejudice in the character of Sir Lucius, proclaiming that, in Clinch's portrayal, it was now "the genteelest Irishman we have on the stage, and there are some true Hibernian touches (which passed unnoticed before) but which now appeared admirably characteristic."[20] If the device of hiding behind a pseudonym was deceptive, it was, like the play itself, a disguise that revealed some truths. *The Rivals* would indeed stand foremost in the list of the comedies of its time. Some true Hibernian touches had gone into its making. And through it, at last, a very genteel Irishman had walked onto the stage of public life.

Chapter 11

ONE LEG AT BOSTON

The success of *The Rivals* in no way took Sheridan's mind off politics. As he was writing it, the most profound challenge to the order of British politics—the incipient revolution in the American colonies—was under way. And just after the success of the play's second coming at Covent Garden, the first shots in the long-threatened war between Britain and the Americans were fired. For most people in England, the war was initially experienced as a terrible domestic division, the first sudden and obvious crack in what had seemed to be the stable edifice of British politics since the days of the final Jacobite uprising of 1745. When the government tried to orchestrate addresses of support for the war from every part of Britain, many counties, towns, and cities responded with petitions for peace. In the context of an emerging anti-government response to the war, Sheridan knew at once which side he was on.

His views were not expressed publicly until early in 1776, when *The General Fast: A Lyric Ode*, a mocking and flagrantly seditious response to the government's call for a day of fasting and prayer for the success of the war, was published. Addressed "To the King" and published as being "by the author of *The Duenna*" (the play Sheridan wrote after *The Rivals*), the verses were prefaced with a rather brazen dedication to King George III: "The idea, Sire, of conquering a people, in arms and arts confessedly our equals, in every virtue undoubtedly our superiors, savours too much of folly, or something worse than folly, to have been promulgated by any genius less than those very contemptible [men] which at present surround and disgrace the Throne." The verse itself was a stark defiance of the order for fasting and prayer:

> Courtiers, forgive the rhyming past,
> I'll tell how *I* mean to fast,
> And sanctify the day:
> So God protect me, as I mean,
> With heart all pure, and conscience clean,
> To *feast*,—and not to pray.
> Or, if I pray, my vows shall be
> That every child of Liberty
> May hail its parent's name;
> And every foe, and every slave,
> And ev'ry all-submissive knave,
> May glory in his shame.

Appended to the ode was a suggested prayer "proper to be used on the approaching fast":

> O God, most Gracious, grant, we most humbly beseech Thee, success and freedom, and all the glorious consequences of that freedom, to our fellow-men, our brethren in America. And may that people, apparently a chosen race, be able, through all future ages, to afford an asylum to wretches who, oppressed by the hand of power, and trodden to the dust by the pride and insolence of unfeeling Despots, may be obliged, in assertion of the general rights of humanity, to seek such an asylum during their short and uncertain pilgrimage in this, Thy lower world. We pray also, O God, for the protection of our King and his family, and all his faithful subjects.[1]

The final protestation of loyalty did little to blunt the seditious edge of the piece. Earlier, however, Sheridan had worked on another intervention in the debate about America which was not, in the event, published. In 1775, Dr. Samuel Johnson, his father's old rival and enemy, published a pamphlet against the Americans called *Taxation No Tyranny: An Answer to the Resolutions and Address of the American Congress*. It was, as Johnson's faithful friend James Boswell admitted, not only "written at the desire of those who were then in power"[2] but actually edited and revised by government officials. Sheridan immediately wrote a reply, of which only some drafts of individual passages survive. He accused Johnson—rightly in this case—of prostituting himself for the government pension he had been granted and paying "the miserable quit-rent of an annual pamphlet." He was particularly enraged by Johnson's slighting references to Montesquieu, whom he himself admired so much, in his claim that the American Congress had "extracted a position from the fanciful Montesquieu that, *in a free State, every man, being a free agent, ought to be concerned in his own Government.*" Such insults, Sheridan wrote, were rich coming from a political beggar "who writes on the subject merely because he has been rewarded." Johnson claimed in the pamphlet, "As all are born the subjects of some state or other, we may be said to have been all born consenting to some system of government." Sheridan responded: "This is the most slavish doctrine that ever was inculcated. If by our birth we gave a tacit bond for our acquiescence in that form of government under which we were born, there would never have been an alteration of the first modes of government—no Revolution in England."

What is most striking, however, is that Sheridan's pro-Americanism was linked in his own mind to his personal revolution, his declaration of independence from his father. The political question engaged him so profoundly because, at one level, he could imagine George III as Thomas Sheridan, George Washington as himself. America, in his rhetoric, had grown up, come of age, and should now be free to lead its own life. "When a colony is of age, [there is] a Parallel between Father and Son." Just as he did not consider himself bound to his father by ties of birth, neither should the colonists be stuck with the system of government they were born under. But if he could forge a connection between his own experience and the situation of America, could the analogy not work in the other direction? Could his political opinions not also allow him to reflect on his personal identity? What state, what form of government was he himself born into? Was it Britain or Ireland? And if colonies grow up and strike out on their own, what of Ireland?

Sheridan had never been back to Ireland, and had now spent more of his life outside the island than on it. It is true that he had always been comfortable in Irish company: from his friends at Harrow, to Elizabeth Angelo in Soho, to the small Irish community in Bath—one letter of 1772 to his father in Dublin sends the best wishes of "all the Irish here." From references in his letters to "the Dublin papers" it seems likely that the family subscribed to some of the Irish newspapers and kept in touch with local news, which would, of course, also have been supplied in letters from their many relations in Dublin and Cavan. With his own polished speech, though, he had not been above teasing his Irish friends over their use of such distinctive constructions as "I am after doing it" for "I have just done it." When he was nineteen, he sent a message to his old schoolfriend Thomas Quin ("a certain Hibernian in your house") through Mrs. Angelo, wishing that he might "like a true Irishman . . . write me word whether he is after being set out or no . . ."[3]

With an English public-school education and an English wife, with the habits, manners, and probably the accent of an English gentleman, he could very easily have forgotten—and made others forget—that he was Irish. His deepest connections to Ireland, through the ties of family, were at this moment weaker than they would ever be. His father had cut off all communication with him, his mother was dead, his sisters were in Ireland, and his brother Charles was in Sweden at his diplomatic posting. He was, moreover, inventing a public self in which it was in his interests to distance himself as far as possible from the misfortune of having been born an Irish actor's son. And yet he chose this precise moment to declare his allegiance to Ireland.

Ireland was on his mind, ironically, because of Sir Lucius O'Trigger. When *The Rivals* was published he used a preface to declare a personal interest in the representation of the Irish on stage, and to disavow any suggestion of an intentional slur on his fellow countrymen. He went so far as to declare his gratitude to those English people who had taken offence on Ireland's behalf:

> It is not without pleasure that I catch at an opportunity of justifying myself from the charge of intending any national reflection in the character of Sir Lucius O'Trigger. If any Gentlemen opposed the Piece from that idea, I thank them sincerely for their opposition; and if the condemnation of this Comedy (however misconceived the provocation) could have added one spark to the decaying flame of national attachment to the country supposed to be reflected on, I should have been happy in its fate; and might have boasted, that it had done more real service in its failure, than the successful morality of a thousand stage-novels will ever effect.[4]

In the middle of April 1775, just as the American war was starting, he pushed his own identification with Ireland further forward. Lawrence Clinch, who had taken over the role of Sir Lucius and helped to rescue *The Rivals*, was in financial trouble. In gratitude for his help and affection for an old family friend, Sheridan offered to write a small farce for a benefit performance at Covent Garden to raise money for Clinch. Reportedly in two days, he turned out *St Patrick's Day*. As a farce, *St Patrick's Day* did not have Sheridan's name on it, but it was widely known that he was the author. The *Morning Post*, for instance, described it on the day after the opening as "said to be written by Mr Sheridan, Junior." And as well as writing the play, Sheridan was also dramatising himself, creating a different context in which to be seen.

The piece was a slight but very effective exercise in traditional *comedia dell'arte* knockabout, featuring the usual elements: a handsome and intrepid young man, a winsome young woman all too willing to fall into his arms, her sour old father who tries to stop them, and a good-natured apothecary who assists in the inevitable triumph of youth over age. It was interesting, though, for two reasons. One was Sheridan's reflection, even in such a light-hearted bagatelle, of the atmosphere of the American war. The hero was a lieutenant, and the piece was saturated with the atmosphere of a society under arms. The deep divisions over the war were reflected in the tensions between soldiers and civilians, from the opening scene, in which some of his men complain of having been barred from taverns in the town.

In the next scene, Sheridan inserted a scathing attack on the local militias, whose patriotic displays of military heroism were so far removed from the reality of war. Lauretta, the object of the lieutenant's desire, is urged by her mother to choose instead a suitor from among the local ranks of the toy soldiery: "Lieutenant Plough—or Captain Haycock—or Major Dray, the Brewer . . ." She replies in disgust: "Psha! Mama! you know I hate the Militia—officers indeed!—a set of Dunghill cocks with spurs on—Heroes scratch'd off a church door—Clowns in Military masquerade—wearing the Dress without supporting the Character . . ."

Sheridan was careful to contrast this cheap militarism with the more honest, but even less romantic, reality of the American war. Lauretta's ideal is a "bold, upright, noble Youth,—who makes love one day, and has his head shot off the next . . ." Her mother fills in the gory details behind this heroic cypher: "O barbarous! to want a husband, who may wed you in the morning, and be sent the Lord knows where, before Night.—Then in a Twelve month, perhaps, to have him come home like a Colossus, with one leg at Boston, and the other in Chelsea Hospital . . . No, give me a husband who knows where his limbs are . . ."[5] The image of British power as a Colossus with one foot on either side of the Atlantic Ocean was given a vivid, violent, and decidedly anti-heroic twist.

The second significant thing about the farce was that it was precisely in this context of the American war that Sheridan chose to introduce his first positive and defiant image of Irish nationality.

The piece took its title from the Irish national day, and opened with the entrance of several soldiers with the Irish national emblem—the shamrock, traditionally worn on St. Patrick's Day—in their hats. There was no intrinsic reason for these images of Irish pride, which are irrelevant to the plot. They acted instead to reinforce the Irishness of the play's hero, Lieutenant O'Connor.

O'Connor was played by Lawrence Clinch, who had, of course, just been playing Sir Lucius in *The Rivals*. For the Covent Garden audience at the time, the point could not have been obscure. If Sir Lucius, even in his revised form, had been a stage Irishman—an irascible, prickly adventurer on the make—O'Connor was another kind of Irish adventurer, also out to win the hand and the fortune of an English lady, but now with the whole force of the play on his side. He is young, handsome, dashing, well-educated, resourceful, and sure to outsmart his loved one's father, the sour old English Justice of the Peace, Credulous.

St Patrick's Day has, in fact, a range of Irish characters. As well as O'Connor and his corporal, Flint, there is a stock drunken Irishman whom the regiment tries to recruit. The play shows him in friendly company with an English blacksmith, however, and he is no more the butt of the comedy than a series of English bumpkins. And then there is Credulous's wife with the Irish name Bridget, whose constant arguments with her husband are presumably intended to explain the former's hatred of the Irish. At the end of the play, it is Irish pride that is vindicated. Credulous declares that O'Connor is "the two things in the world I hate most"—"an Irishman and an officer." Marriage to his daughter therefore goes hand-in-hand with the condition: "Foreswear your Country, and quit the Army," to which O'Connor responds by threatening to "pull your nose" for insulting Ireland. In the end, having outwitted the Englishman, he gets the girl.

It would be wrong to equate the national pride with which *St Patrick's Day* is suffused with modern-day notions of Irish nationalism. Sheridan's Irishness was Protestant, and like Irish Protestants in general he had no hankering after a restoration of the old Gaelic order of the O'Sheridans before Bedell. It is striking that in the play the Irish soldiers who set off to celebrate St. Patrick's Day with shamrocks in their hats are first required to "parade round the Market Cross, for the honour of King William." William of Orange was the Protestant King who, in the 1690s, had defeated both Irish Catholicism and the pretensions to absolutism of James II, ushering in the civil liberties and limited monarchy that Sheridan had no desire to roll back. But it was precisely for this Protestant, colonial Ireland that the American Revolution was so disturbing. If the lesson of America for Sheridan was that colonies grow up and grow away from their imperial father, the parallels with Ireland were all too obvious. "We are in water colour," said one member of the Irish Parliament, "what they are in fresco." It was this kind of parallel that encouraged Sheridan to see himself, and increasingly to present himself, as Irish. A deep connection was being made between his sense of nationality and his political radicalism.

He followed up *St Patrick's Day* almost immediately with a new play for Covent Garden, a comic opera called *The Duenna*. The subversive potential of musical theatre had been demonstrated fifty years before by John Gay's *The Beggar's Opera*, in which a ferocious satire on the ruling classes had floated on the innocent airs of melodic ballads. And in the ferment of Europe of the 1770s and 1780s, Mozart's operatic version of Beaumarchais's *The Marriage of Figaro* would exploit the free political spaces that could open up behind a façade of beautiful sound.

Sheridan anticipated Mozart with *The Duenna*, and if the connection between them seems fanciful, it should be remembered that, through the Linleys, they inhabited the same world. When Sheridan and Eliza were first married, they stayed for a short time in Marylebone with the Italian contrabassist Stefano Storace, who was a friend of the Linleys. Storace's daughter Anna went on to become the original Susanna in *The Marriage of Figaro*. Eliza's brother, Tom, who wrote much of the music for *The Duenna*, was, when he studied in Florence, a close friend of Mozart. And Sheridan's Irish friend, the tenor Michael Kelly, created the roles of Don Basilio and Don Curzio in *The Marriage of Figaro*. *The Duenna* may not be an opera of the same standing as any of Mozart's work, but in the sense that it springs from the culture of the Enlightenment it shares a common origin.

And, as in *The Marriage of Figaro*, the apparently conventional surface of *The Duenna* belies a subversive intent. Both titles, indeed, give the game away: Figaro is a servant who gets his name in the title because he is the driving force behind the plot. Likewise, Sheridan's duenna—the word means a kind of governess, usually an older woman set to guard the virginity of a girl—not only orchestrates the action of the opera but uses it to climb above her station. At one level *The Duenna* is a playing out of Sheridan's contention to Thomas Grenville that social hierarchies are not fixed and that, just as some of the great must fall, others must rise from obscurity. Behind its pleasant parade of young people falling in love and winning out against parental tyranny, *The Duenna* has another story in which the eponymous Margaret, a middle-aged, ugly, and impecunious woman, outwits her master, adopts the identity of her rich and beautiful mistress, and tricks a greedy merchant into marrying her.

The Duenna, moreover, was not just *about* someone of low social standing ascending by virtue of her wits, but also itself a part of such a story. As he was writing it, Sheridan was already planning to turn himself from a penniless adventurer into a man of power and property. Eliza was pregnant again after a miscarriage in November 1774, and this baby seemed likely to come to term. *The Rivals* had run for a very respectable sixteen performances and probably brought in the hoped-for £600, but it had not yet established a place for itself in the lucrative ranks of frequently revived classics. Sheridan needed money for more than the obvious reasons of having a family and a house in London to support: he was already planning to build his own empire. David Garrick, the owner of Drury Lane Theatre, was talking of selling up and Sheridan was thinking of buying in. But for this he needed capital, and *The Duenna* was intended from the start as his way to get it. Like the duenna herself, he knew that the humble could, with boldness, wit, and invention, arrange events so as to turn the established order of things on its head.

It was appropriate in this context that the play should build so openly on the achievements of his marriage. In September 1775, Eliza's father, Thomas Linley, wrote to a friend that he was assisting

Sheridan in writing an opera and explained the motive: "It is a matter of absolute necessity that he should endeavour to get money by this means, as he will not be prevailed upon to let his wife sing."[6] *The Duenna* was to be a family affair—Eliza helping to write the songs, her father and her brother, Tom, composing the music.

For Sheridan, there must have been a certain glee in the involvement of his father-in-law in a comic opera whose main action centred, yet again, on the triumph of the young over the old and hinged on two young women eloping from the houses of their tyrannical fathers. One of the heroines of the play, Louisa, is being forced by her father to marry a rich, older man—strikingly reminiscent of Linley's original plan that Eliza marry Walter Long. Louisa, like Eliza, takes refuge in a convent. And, of course, in the end, the young lovers force the obstinate father to accept the inevitability of their marriage.

Just as he had done in writing *The Rivals*, Sheridan also borrowed from his mother's unpublished manuscripts a literary context into which these parallels with his own experience could be sewn. Frances Sheridan had written, when she was just fifteen, a two-volume novel, *Eugenia and Adelaide*, suffused with the atmosphere of an imagined Mediterranean. There is no direct evidence that Sheridan had a copy of this work at the time, though later, in 1791, he almost certainly helped organise its publication in London. (It is also striking that his sister Lissy herself adapted it as a comic opera some years later.) There are a number of parallels between play and novel: the convent, the duenna, the names Clara and Ferdinand, love scenes in gardens, complications of identity, and a happy ending marked by a double marriage.[7]

Because of the speed with which he wrote *The Duenna*, which has an extraordinarily intricate plot, it seems likely, moreover, that Sheridan was working from the text of a farce which he had already drafted. Many years later, he indicated that he had written it at Waltham Abbey before his marriage. Even if this was the case, however, there is no doubt that he now rewrote it completely with a very specific production and very particular performers in mind. The need for a commercial success was uppermost in Sheridan's mind, and he devoted a great deal of attention not just to casting the piece but to tailoring the text he had written to the capacities of the singers. For instance, the Italian tenor Michael Leoni, whom he wanted in the play, had a heavy accent, which made it impossible for him to speak long or complex lines of dialogue. So Sheridan cut most of the speeches he had intended to give to his character (Don Carlos) and changed dialogue into songs.

Even with the songs themselves, though, he had very clear ideas of his own. He told Thomas Linley, for instance, that Leoni "sings nothing well but in a plaintive or pastoral style; and his voice is such as appears to me to be always hurt by too much accompaniment. I have observed, too, that he never gets so much applause as when he makes a cadence. Therefore my idea is, that he should make a flourish as 'Shall I grieve thee?' and return to 'Gentle maid,' and so sing that part of the tune again."[8] This same concern for applause was lavished, too, on the brilliant plotting, in which Sheridan performed deft variations on the traditional themes of the Spanish intrigue play, managing simultaneously to satirise and to perfect its conventions. In a stylised and entirely unrealistic Seville, the usual "Spanish" elements of deception, disguise, and romance were combined with rare virtuosity in a story of two interlocking elopements. Sheridan constructed an artifice at once complex and clear in which all the intricacies of the plot were driven by a single mechanism and all folded perfectly into a single resolution. If the uncertainties that attended *The Rivals* had suggested a writer still coming to terms with the stage, Sheridan was now, less than a year later, in total control of his materials, deploying them with a calculating confidence in his ability to dazzle an audience into submission.

But the commercial imperatives did not entirely overwhelm the political content. At the time he was rewriting *The Duenna* there was a public controversy over a revival of Dryden's play *The Spanish Fryar*, which attacked the hypocrisy of Catholic monks, who were shown as being, behind the disguise of their robes, venal and greedy. It was reported that the Spanish ambassador to London had applied to the censor, the Lord Chamberlain, to have a proposed revival of Dryden's play at the Haymarket Theatre banned. The application was refused, and the production went ahead, but Sheridan included in *The Duenna* a scene that seems to be a deliberate echo of Dryden's play.

The scene is all the more striking because it is largely unnecessary to the plot. The lovers go to get a priest to marry them. They find an assembly of monks, stuffing themselves with cake and wine, and drinking the health of all the prettiest nuns they know. When one of the monks remarks, "Don Juan Corduba has left an hundred ducats to remember him in our masses," another replies, "Has he! let them be paid to our wine merchant, and we'll remember him in our cups, which will do just as well."[9] This scene has generally been read as a typical piece of anti-Catholic propaganda, a very rare example of Sheridan pandering to Protestant prejudice. Such a reading is not entirely wrong: having declared his Irish identity, Sheridan was making it clear that being Irish and being Catholic were not the same thing, and that his patriotism should not be confused with popery. The urge to include the scene may well have been precipitated too by the knowledge that it touched on one aspect of his own story—the fact that he and Eliza were married in France by a Catholic priest and that she had stayed in a Catholic convent—which was most open to misunderstanding. He may have felt such a gesture to be all the more necessary because many of the ballads he had sent to Thomas Linley to be adapted for the score were Irish or Scottish tunes. There was, for instance, "Banna's Banks," which in the original retained signs of its Gaelic origins:

> They sung their little tales of love,
> They sung them o'er and o'er,
> Ah, gra mo chroi, mo chailin og,
> Mo Molly a stor.

Indirect as these musical allusions to Ireland undoubtedly were, coming so soon after *St Patrick's Day* they kept at least some hints of his Irish identity before the Covent Garden audience.

But, if the scene with the monks was an anti-Catholic gesture, it was, in the context of the play, far too ambiguous to serve as propaganda. In the first place, though it had no function in the plot, it had a critical function in the play's underlying exploration of identity. *The Duenna* is all about appearances and disguises: the plot depends on the fact that Louisa and her duenna swap identities, so that the rich suitor chosen by the tyrannical father ends up paying court to the governess. To make identities even less certain, Louisa's friend Clara also elopes and pretends to be Louisa. The religious satire is part of this play on the untrustworthiness of appearances. Louisa at one point remarks to her lover, Antonio, that "in religion, as in friendship, they who profess most are ever the least sincere." The attack on Catholic hypocrisy is, moreover, Sheridan's way of balancing another prejudice which the play seems to pander to: anti-

Semitism. For the man whom Louisa's father wants her to marry, the butt of all the jokes, is a Jew named Isaac Mendoza. As with the anti-Catholicism of the scene with the monks, there can be little doubt that in the character of Mendoza Sheridan was taking a stock type from a long tradition of English drama which had more recently appeared, too, in novels like Daniel Defoe's *Roxana* and Tobias Smollett's *Roderick Random*, and in plays like Charles Macklin's *Love à la Mode*. In *The Duenna*, however, the religious caricatures have to be seen in relation to each other, as complementary images of Christian and Jewish hypocrites.

Aside from the fact that the principal singer, Leoni, was himself Jewish, and that Sheridan agreed there should be no performances on the Jewish Sabbath, so that Leoni would be free to sing in the synagogue, there is some evidence that Sheridan deliberately sought to avoid giving an anti-Semitic message. In the first place, Isaac, although ugly and easily fooled, is also by far the most engaging figure in the play and in many ways the star part. He is greedy and self-deluding but very far from sinister, and the comedy of the character lies precisely in the fact that he is not the great Machiavellian schemer that a typically anti-Semitic portrayal might make him. In the second place, Sheridan seems to have taken a conscious decision to play down his Jewishness. In a surviving fragment of an early draft of the play, Isaac had a Jewish sidekick, Moses, and their joint presence would have enhanced the feeling that they were meant to represent Jews in general. In the final version, Moses was replaced with a Spaniard, Don Carlos. This change was also in keeping with the other critical dimension that Sheridan added: the fact that Isaac is not a practising Jew but a convert to Christianity, a man who, for monetary gain and social success, has discarded his true identity.

To understand Sheridan's intentions, it is necessary merely to recall the crux of *St Patrick's Day*, where O'Connor proudly refuses Credulous's demand to "Foreswear your Country." These words recur in *The Duenna* and they set the context in which Isaac is to be understood. Near the beginning of the play, Louisa and her brother Ferdinand are arguing with their father about Isaac's suitability as a son-in-law. Don Jerome asks for their objections to Isaac:

Ferdinand: He is a Portugueze in the first place.
Don Jerome: No such thing, boy, he has forsworn his country.
Louisa: He is a Jew.

Don Jerome: Another mistake: he has been a christian these six weeks.
Ferdinand: Ay, he left his old religion for an estate, and has not had time to get a new one.
Louisa: But stands like a dead wall between church and synagogue, or like the blank leaves between the Old and New Testament.[10]

Isaac is contemptible, in other words, not because he is a Jew, but because he is *not* a Jew. Like the monks who pretend to be holy but are really venal, he is a Jew who pretends to be a Christian. Their Christian hypocrisy balances his Jewish apostasy. O'Connor is a hero because he will not abandon his identity for love or money. Isaac is the obverse of O'Connor—a man who is easily fooled because he is neither one thing nor the other. The audience is given to understand that the worst thing about him is his willingness to take as a compliment what O'Connor would have taken as a terrible insult: that he has successfully disguised his origins. When the duenna tells him that he looks "so little like a Jew and so much like a gentleman!," he is thrilled. And that pleasure at what he takes to be a successful denial of his identity is what, in Sheridan's scheme of things, damns him.

Whatever the play was saying to its audience, it is clear what Sheridan was saying to himself: that he would not become a blank page between two testaments; that he would not, like Isaac, forget where he had come from. He would not wish to look like a gentleman at the cost of not looking like an Irishman. He would rise towards power and wealth, but not by becoming a hypocrite. When his mocking lyric ode *The General Fast* was published as "by the author of *The Duenna*," the gap between the gorgeous comic opera and the fierce denunciation of the American war was not as great as it might have seemed.

He needed, however, just such a warning to himself about the dangers of losing one's self in the pursuit of riches, for *The Duenna* was a phenomenal success. It needed to be: four days before the opening, Eliza gave birth to their son. Given the ubiquity of the name in both the Linley and Sheridan families, the child was inevitably named Tom. But if fatherhood increased Sheridan's anxiety for his own new progeny, *The Duenna* too emerged into a welcoming world. The *Morning Chronicle*, in spite of some nit-picking, declared Sheridan to be in possession of "a fertile imagination, great ability and real genius." *Lloyd's Evening Post* praised Sheridan for having "revived the honour of the drama, by boldly rescuing the stage from that state of lethargy and melancholy madness" into which the pre-eminence of wordy tragedies had plunged it. More important, after its opening on 21 November 1775, it ran for an unprecedented seventy-five nights at Covent Garden.

Even before the opening, negotiations were under way with David Garrick for the purchase of his controlling share of Drury Lane. Garrick had written to Thomas Linley at about the end of October, asking whether he could raise £35,000 to buy out his half share in the theatre. Linley himself had accumulated a sizeable sum from his own and Eliza's earnings—about £6,000 worth of property, mostly in Bath—and was able to raise a share of the capital. Sheridan, as Linley told Garrick, was then "more than ever sure of making good his share of the money. How this is possible, I no more know than I do how Subsidies are raised in Saturn."[11] Sheridan's optimism, though, was obviously based on his sense that *The Duenna* would be a success. When events justified that confidence, he determined to seize the opportunity and take control of Drury Lane.

He was optimistic, too, about the prospects for a reconciliation with his father, who had returned to London. With the sensational success of the opera, indeed, the city itself seemed to be staging a grand reconciliation of the Linleys and the Sheridans. Not only were the two families united in *The Duenna* but both of Sheridan's parents were on display. In January 1776, Frances's play *The Discovery* was revived by Garrick at Drury Lane, less as a rival attraction to *The Duenna* than as a tribute to its author. Garrick himself played the main character, paying Sheridan an implicit but very public compliment and signalling the advent of his own successor as the dominant figure in the London theatre. Thomas, meanwhile, had returned, to some acclaim, to act at Covent Garden for the first time in fourteen years. For a time it was impossible to go to either of the two patent theatres in London without encountering the Sheridans.

But Thomas Sheridan did not allow this deluge of public esteem to soften his anger. He was disgusted by Garrick's use of his late wife's play and refused to allow his daughters to go to it. Sheridan had, at around the end of October, predicted to his father-in-law, "I think it will not be many days before we are reconciled," but Thomas Linley was sceptical and told Garrick that Sheridan "wrote me word some time back that he should be reconciled to his Father in a few days, but I fancy that was Apocryphal." Linley was partly right—only in the last acts of plays did hard-hearted fathers suddenly throw off their bitterness and embrace their erring offspring.

Nevertheless, even Thomas Sheridan could hardly ignore the fact that the son he no longer had was about to take over Drury Lane. He had long believed that Garrick had deliberately kept him off the Drury Lane stage, and as is so often the case, a feeling of exclusion whetted his desire to gain entry. By December 1775, negotiations between his son, Thomas Linley, and Garrick were well advanced. Simon Ewart, who had helped Sheridan and Eliza in their flight to France, was initially involved in the consortium, but dropped out and was replaced by a fashionable "man-midwife," Dr. James Ford.

Between them, the three had to raise £35,000 for Garrick's half share. The other half was held by Willoughby Lacy, a young man who had inherited it from his father, and there was talk of his either buying Garrick's share himself or selling his own to Linley and Sheridan. By 11 January 1776, however, Lacy had definitely decided neither to buy nor to sell, and the way was clear for the purchase of Garrick's share.[12] Sheridan, moreover, had persuaded Lacy to be in effect a silent partner, entrusting everything to himself: "He has an opinion of me," Sheridan told Thomas Linley, "and is very willing to let the whole burthen and responsibility be taken off his Shoulders."[13]

Around this time, too, Thomas Sheridan agreed, if not to be reconciled to his son, at least to help with the theatre. It was something of a surrender: "My father," as Sheridan wrote to Linley, "offers his services on our own terms."[14] Those terms were clear enough: he was to help with the management of the theatre for a year but "only to give me what advantage he can from his experience." It was an uneasy and, as it happened, an unstable truce. Sheridan had not triumphed so completely over his father's opposition only to return to being again an unfavoured child. If Thomas Sheridan came into Drury Lane it was to be as a guest on his son's territory.

To secure his share of the property, Sheridan needed to raise £10,000. He borrowed £7,700 of this from Dr. Ford, on the security of his portion of the patent. Of the remaining £2,300, he raised £1,000 in mortgages, and presumably put up the rest from his earnings for *The Duenna*. By the middle of January 1776, he was the part-owner and effective controller of one of Europe's great theatres, with 2,300 seats. Just a month earlier, when the opera was gathering pace for its extraordinary run, he had been so hard up that he had had to borrow £200 from Garrick.[15] Then, he had simply been a twenty-five-year-old man of no property, hoping to earn a living with his pen; now, in the heart of London, he had secured his own domain, a physical presence in the city, a public space in which to operate. For the next thirty-five years, he would both hold that space and try to expand it.

Chapter 12

LIGHT ENTERTAINMENT

In the theatre, the dimming of the lights signals a beginning and an end—the play is about to start, the crowd is about to disappear. While the lights are on, the gathering watches itself, talks, gawks, nods, waves. The darkness descends to mark the separation, not merely of the stage from the auditorium, but of the members of the public one from another. Each watches the play as an individual, cocooned in darkness, wrapped up in private thoughts and feelings. No one in the auditorium is to acknowledge the presence of anyone else. The only interlocutors are on the stage. The assembled public ceases to be a crowd and becomes an audience.

In the theatre that Sheridan occupied, there was no such moment. When the prompter's bell had rung three times and the orchestra had struck up some music, the green baize curtain rose, revealing behind the proscenium arch the footlights and the scenery. But the hundreds of candles in the huge chandeliers that illuminated the crowd were not, could not, be dimmed. They stayed alight, so much so that a constant fear for those watching the play was a drip of hot wax down the back of the neck, and a constant disturbance was the operation of the candle-trimmers and snuffers. Not only, indeed, was it not dark in the auditorium, it was far brighter than in virtually any other night-time place. For people used to the half-light of oil lamps or single candles, the theatre, while the play was in progress, was awash with radiance. The public could, and did, still see itself, watch its own reactions, mutter, wave, hiss, applaud, shout, cry. The audience, in other words, began and remained a crowd.

It gathered at some time between a quarter to five and a quarter to six, depending on the length of daylight, with anything up to 2,300 people pushing to get through the doors and down the narrow corridors to the seats. Once inside, the crowd separated itself into a working model of society: the gentry paying five shillings for the boxes, the middle classes three shillings for a place in one of the nine or ten rows of backless benches that made up the pit, tradesmen and artisans two for the lower gallery, labourers and servants one for the upper. Except for those who had bought boxes, all had to push towards the appropriate corridor, pay the price, and get a metal token, which in turn was handed over at the doorway leading to the seats. This was a common experience: each week from a London population of 750,000 in the 1770s about 12,000 went to the theatre.

But within this formal display of rank there was movement and disorder. Like a gathering on the street, the theatre crowd shifted and changed. A night's entertainment was generally made up of the main play (a five-act comedy or tragedy, or a three-act musical comedy like *The Duenna*), followed by an afterpiece, which could be a pantomime, a farce, or a two-act comedy. About two-thirds of the way through the main piece, all unsold seats were knocked down to half price, so there was another influx of people. Often, too, members of the gentry who had begun their dinners at a later hour arrived midway through the performance, dismissed the servants who had been holding their seats in the boxes for them, and sat down to see and be seen.

The idea that one went to the theatre to be looked at as well as to look was more than a glib cliché. To many people, being in the sight of others at the theatre was not so different to being in the sight of God. Adam Smith, in *The Theory of Moral Sentiments*, published when Sheridan was eight years old, maintained that to be moral we must imagine what an "impartial spectator" would think of our behaviour and then act accordingly. The theatre was the place where people were expected to be impartial spectators of each other and of the plays on stage. But that detachment could break at any moment into the fierce passion of the partisan. Because the line between the actors and the crowd was thin, it was possible to cross it altogether. "In a great and populous City," wrote Benjamin Victor in his *History of the Theatres of London*, published in 1761, "the gay and wanton Young Men are, indeed, the constant visitors to a Theatre . . . they can hiss and laugh, and talk loud, and become by that means, Actors themselves."

This absence of an absolute distinction between the actors and the crowd reflected the sense in which they belonged, within the walls of the theatre, to the same world. Because so much of the repertoire was familiar, some moments in many plays were anticipated by actors and spectators alike. The actor would move down to the front and centre of the stage, and deliver the lines, full frontal to the crowd. The crowd would respond to this direct appeal for attention with either hoots and hisses or tears and wails.

But this emotionalism in the crowd was combined with a sense of critical distance. Different sections of the crowd interacted with the stage in distinctive ways. Sheridan's fellow Irishman and fellow playwright Oliver Goldsmith, adopting the character of a Chinese visitor writing home, categorised the various attitudes of those waiting for the show to begin. In the upper gallery, where the people were poorest, they regarded themselves as "masters of ceremonies. It was they who called for the music, indulging every noisy freedom, and testifying all the insolence of beggary in exaltation." In the lower gallery, where the crowd was made up mostly of out-of-town folk come for an unaccustomed treat, "they were chiefly employed during this period of expectation in eating oranges, reading the story of the play, or making assignations." But in the pit, occupied by the respectable regulars, the crowd "seemed to consider themselves as judges of the merit of the poet and the performers; they were assembled partly to be amused and partly to shew their taste; appearing to labour under that restraint which an affectation of superior discernment generally produces . . . they assumed the right of being censors because there was none to contradict their pretensions . . ."[1]

And at times their reaction became violent. Drury Lane was wrecked by riots in 1743, 1750, 1755, 1770, and 1776. In September 1791, while the old Drury Lane was being rebuilt, Sheridan moved his company temporarily to the King's Theatre and raised prices. On the opening night, the crowd demanded an explanation, and Sheridan's manager, John Philip Kemble, had to come forward and justify the rises. The crowd was not irrational: Kemble's explanation was listened to and accepted. Yet the threat of trouble was always there: the following year, there was a riot when Covent Garden put up its prices.

In times of political tumult, such riots seemed to those in power like harbingers of other, greater upheavals. In 1809, Sheridan's last year of real control at Drury Lane, price riots at Covent Garden, carried on over sixty-seven nights, turned into one of the greatest outbreaks of organised chaos for many decades. Sheridan's long-time political adversary William Windham saw in the challenge to the authority of theatre managers a challenge to the authority of the state: "I am more alive, I suppose, to this defeat of the managers, because I see it as a rehearsal of what is meant for higher performers; the managers being the government; the new prices the taxes . . . it seems to me to present but too sure a presage of the fate of the country . . ."[2] Such a leap from events within a theatre to events within a nation was made possible by a habit of mind. The underlying expectation of theatre in Sheridan's times was not that it might reflect on politics but that it was a form of politics. A letter to the editor of the *Constitutional Review* in 1809 made the point that "theatres in a country under a monarchical form of government can never be considered as private property, but as a great national concern; as a powerful political engine, as a wheel without which the remainder of the state machinery would be incomplete: in fact they form an absolutely constituent part of our political system."[3]

Because the holders of the two patents were royal servants, it was possible to regard the theatres themselves as, both figuratively and literally, public spaces. Figuratively, the idea was used, for example, during the Covent Garden price riots of 1809, when one anonymous pamphleteer wrote, "The legitimate British theatre . . . resembles our invaluable constitution. It has, from time immemorial, been fairly open to all classes of the public, in their several ranks and degrees . . ."[4] More literally, another pamphleteer denied that Sheridan and Thomas Harris, as the holders of the patents for Drury Lane and Covent Garden, *owned*, in any modern sense, the theatres themselves: "It seems almost an abuse of the sacred term *property*, to apply it to so complex, and contingent a tenure as that of the patentees. They may possibly have an indisputable title to the ground, on which the boxes are built; but the boxes themselves, *as places of theatrical exhibition*, they hold, as it were, in trust."[5] All through Sheridan's period of control of Drury Lane, those engaged in theatrical controversies were apt to quote, to the same effect, Charles Churchill's long poem on the theatre, *The Rosciad*, written in 1761:

The stage I choose—a subject fair and free,
'Tis yours—'tis mine—'tis public property
All common exhibitions open be,
For praise or censure to the common eye.

Because it was such a public space, the theatre could not be other than political. It related to politics first of all in a direct way: through law and regulation. When Sheridan bought into Drury Lane, he acquired a direct relationship with the King, for Drury Lane and Covent Garden were the "theatres royal," operating under licence from the King a duopoly of straight drama during the "season," which ran from the autumn until the early summer. And plays were subject to state censorship: under the Licensing Act of 1737, every play had to be licensed by the Lord Chamberlain. The theatre owner's status as a servant of the King, in theory at least, together with the necessity of avoiding censorship, forced a theatre manager to think politically.

The theatre was political, too, in a more direct sense. Especially after Sheridan took control of Drury Lane, it and Covent Garden, the two patent theatres within yards of each other, were seen as reflections of the political divisions within Parliament. Drury Lane was regarded as the opposition's theatre; Covent Garden, especially in the long period after 1783 when William Pitt the Younger was Prime Minister, as the government's. Sheridan became more and more closely identified with the radical Whig faction of Charles James Fox; Covent Garden's Thomas Harris was the man who paid off friendly journalists on behalf of the government, and then a close friend of Pitt's treasury secretary, George Rose. And this division was reflected in the pattern of the King's attendance at his royal theatres: he attended Covent Garden about seven times a year but was a rare visitor to Drury Lane.

There was a third, more nebulous, but no less important link between the theatre and politics: the fact that, for the elite in the boxes, the theatre was an arena for both aristocratic and sexual display. Montesquieu, whom Sheridan admired so greatly, had claimed that a Persian arriving unprepared at the Comédie Française in Paris would not have been able to guess who was on stage and who was watching. In London, too, the elite came to show itself to itself and to the crowd. Goldsmith described the denizens of the boxes thus:

> The rest of the audience came merely for their own amusement; these rather to furnish out a part of the entertainment themselves. I could not avoid considering them as acting a part in a dumb shew, not a curtesy, or nod, that was not the result of art; not a look nor a smile that was not designed for murder. Gentlemen and ladies ogled each other through spectacles; for my companion observed, that blindness was of late become fashionable; all affected indifference and ease, while their hearts at the same time burned for conquest.[6]

Performance, in other words, was not simply the prerogative of actors. As Sheridan himself became part of the elite, the theatre was a place where his friends could act and where he himself could burn for conquest. In taking control of Drury Lane, he placed himself at a crossroads where culture and politics, money and sex, the real and the imaginary, met and mingled.

When Sheridan bought into the patent in 1776, it was on the understanding that, although at one-seventh his share of the ownership was relatively small, his would be the guiding hand. He was the apostolic successor to David Garrick as the guardian of the theatre's place in the city, the culture, and the nation. And within little over a year, that role was secured when he, Linley, and Ford bought out the other half of the patent from Willoughby Lacy. This involved him in further financial complications, as did his almost simultaneous plan for an opera house at the King's Theatre in Haymarket, which he bought in October 1778 in conjunction with Thomas Harris of Covent Garden, but sold again in 1781. For the public, Drury Lane was Sheridan's theatre, especially after he had his new plays performed there and brought both *The Rivals* and *The Duenna* into its repertoire. For Sheridan himself, the theatre was the centre of a network of connections. It was a weather vane for the public mood: to stay in business he had to be sensitive to the temper of the times. It gave him a very special kind of access to the intellectual climate: this was a time when poets and generals, agitators and office-holders wrote plays, and most of them ended up on Sheridan's desk. It even connected him to the past: he rewrote John Vanbrugh's *The Relapse* as *A Trip to Scarborough*; he quietly amended other Restoration plays; and he provided prologues for the occasional revival.

He had under him a community, a business, and a small empire.

The community which looked to him for its livelihood included forty-eight actors, thirty-seven actresses, eighteen adult dancers, two child dancers, thirty dressers, fourteen door-keepers, seven box-keepers, four lobby-keepers and messengers, two numberers, one candle woman, three box inspectors, seven office-keepers, and two pensioners. There were porters, fruit sellers, sweepers, carpenters, prompters, set-builders, musicians, treasurers. The business involved not merely the choice and casting of plays but such critical questions as the need for new performers to provide their own white silk stockings, the fining of chorus members who turned up late, the issuing of demands that buff gloves and hats should be returned immediately to the wardrobe, and the problem of dressers pinching left-over candles from the dressing rooms. And the empire above all depended on the unstable, shifting, and often ungovernable crowd that passed through the theatre doors six nights a week, eight months a year. It could not be ruled, but it could be amazed, enthralled, distracted, or disturbed. On stage, the assumptions that controlled the political climate could be tested and modified. The light of everyday realities could be refracted through strange prisms.

Chapter 13

BRINGING THE HOUSE DOWN

Frederic Reynolds, twelve years old, thought he was going to die. He was walking down the narrow passage between Vinegar Yard and Bridges Street at nine o'clock on a May evening in 1777 when he heard a terrible noise above his head. The sudden, tremendous rumble made him sure that Drury Lane Theatre, which formed one side of the passage, was collapsing and that he was going to be killed. He covered his head with his hands and ran for his life, but "found the next morning that the noise did not arise from the *falling* of the house, but from the *falling* of the screen in the fourth act; so violent and so tumultuous were the applause and laughter."[1] He had passed by the opening night of Sheridan's new play, *The School for Scandal*.

Well into the nineteenth century, having seen the play in its early days was something to boast of, as if it had a meaning then which could never quite be recaptured. Great critics were apt to go misty-eyed at the memory. William Hazlitt, reviewing a production in 1815, asked, "Why can we not always be young, and seeing *The School for Scandal*? . . . What would we not give to see it once more, as it was then acted, and with the same feelings with which we saw it then?" Charles Lamb in 1822 wrote, "Amidst the mortifying circumstances attendant upon growing old, it is something to have seen *The School for Scandal* in its glory." What they longed for was not simply to see the play—for it was still being revived continually—but to have seen it *then*, at that moment between the American Revolution and the French when a new world seemed to be in the making and that play somehow a part of it.

What had caused the noise of delight mingled with terror that Frederic Reynolds had heard? On stage a screen had been dashed down and there, cowering behind it, was the scandalmonger Lady Teazle, her duplicitous relationship with the hypocrite Joseph Surface exposed to the full view of both her husband and the audience. What Joseph Surface called "my Politics"—scheming, double-dealing, injustice—had been stripped naked and exposed to the scrutiny of all under the light of the chandeliers. And the analogy with politics in the broader sense was made unmistakably plain to the audience with barbed references to Benjamin Hopkins, opponent of the radical hero John Wilkes in a struggle for the office of chamberlain of the City of London. If in the play the feckless Charles Surface, rather than his apparently upright brother Joseph, could emerge as the triumphant hero, then so too could Wilkes the good-hearted rake be a fit hero for the people.

Yet those echoes of contemporary politics hardly explain the explosive impact of such a simple if ingenious piece of stage business as the knocking over of a screen. Why should the exposure of hypocrisy, the revelation of what might lie behind a smooth personal surface, be so tumultuous? Why should a play with a consistently light touch, in which wit and laughter keep pain and despair at bay, have seemed so morally serious? Why does it matter that the trivial intrigues of an inconsequential cabal are exposed? Because the play's concerns—reputation and reality, appearance and emotion—were vital not just to private behaviour but to political life. The idea of reputation was at the heart of the Enlightenment's attempts to understand what, in the late eighteenth century, it meant to be modern. In fact it was a specifically *modern* concern, arising from the emergence of a phenomenon that had not been experienced before, namely urban life on a large scale. Big cities like Paris and London threatened the moral intimacy of the old regime. Previously when people had remained within their allotted circles in life, those who met them could know who and what they were. If you knew *what* someone was—a peasant, a tradesman, a lawyer, an aristocrat—you knew *who* they were. And until recently you could have told what someone was by looking at them: their clothes, their movements, their manners, their speech gave them away. But in the bustling, open life of the city, this was no longer possible. The new city was too diffuse. It was too full of strangers and social climbers.

This new social reality was in Sheridan's very bones. His father's life continued to be devoted to the removal of that very obvious marker of a man's place in the world: the way he spoke. Thomas Sheridan's system of standardised speech could transform the Scottish lawyer Alexander Wedderburn into the British Lord Chancellor Loughborough. His son's life to date had been an even more dazzling demonstration of the uncertainty of the city. At the age of twenty-five, a nobody from nowhere had taken control of an institution that was woven into the very life of the city and the political culture of the times. How, in such a world, could you trust appearances?

Moving about the theatres, cafés, and salons, a man (and the concern was essentially with the male-dominated world of politics and business) met too many strangers for comfort. How could one hope to know whether the stranger so encountered was sincere? How could he be judged if not by repute? Jean-Jacques Rousseau expressed this best: "In a big city, full of scheming, idle people without religion or principle . . . each [man,] easily hiding his conduct from the public eye, shows himself only by his reputation."[2]

Both Rousseau and another of the French *philosophes*, Denis Diderot, saw this problem, moreover, in explicitly theatrical terms: in the big city, people became actors. And good actors can manufacture emotions. They can put on with absolute conviction the outward signs of feelings that are not, in fact, present in their hearts. When Diderot saw David Garrick, who gave some private performances in Paris in the 1760s, he was both enthralled and disturbed:

> Garrick will put his head between two folding doors, and in the course of five or six seconds his expression will change successively from wild delight to temperate pleasure, from this to tranquillity, from tranquillity to surprise, from surprise to blank astonishment, from that to sorrow, from sorrow to the air of one overwhelmed, from that to fright, from fright to horror, from horror to despair, and thence he will go up again to the point from which he started. Can his soul have experienced all these feelings, and played this kind of scale in concert with his face?[3]

Sheridan had now taken on Garrick's mantle at Drury Lane: he had become directly associated with one of the most visible sites of this cultural disturbance. The abstract concerns of the *philosophes* were in Sheridan himself concrete and tangible. As both a social incomer and a creator of magnificent theatrical illusions, he could almost be said to embody the problem of trust and reputation in the big city. He had already, in *The Rivals*, presented his own adventures in the context of an emerging modern culture. And he had shown that culture to be one in which the old certainties were giving way to a new cult of romanticism, whose shrines were the Rousseauesque novels that Lydia Languish was devouring. Now, in *The School for Scandal*, he dealt much more directly with the culture itself. He placed his comedy firmly along the fault-lines of the new world by focusing on theatricality, reputation, and, above all, sensibility.

Perhaps the single most important notion in mid-eighteenth-century culture was what the French called *sensibilité* and the English sentiment or sensibility: the capacity for intense and authentic feeling. Against the cold and mannered formality of the old regime, the idea of sensibility placed the veneration of all that was natural: love, friendship, genuine emotion. It became acceptable to cry in public, to wear lockets emblazoned with the picture of a loved one, to grieve, to respond to a stirring speech with rapture. The notion of sensibility linked everything from fashion to politics. The body was a natural object; clothes should, therefore, conform to its lines, and wigs seemed ridiculous. The theatre should be about feelings, not just words; the brittle wit of Restoration drama must, therefore, give way to ponderous tragedies and sentimental comedies. And, above all, politics must be, not a maintenance of inherited forms of government, but the expression of public morality. Virtue held society together, and only those who had it could rule. And how was virtue to be known except by the authenticity of feelings?

These were precisely the problems Sheridan began to grapple with in the writing of *The School for Scandal*. He began, though, not with that play but with the theatre itself. The tentative reconciliation with his father had proved to be predictably evanescent, and Thomas Sheridan withdrew from any role in the new management's first season in autumn 1776. But Sheridan's own extraordinary success and the fact that he had become a man of substance soothed the almost hysterical fears about the degeneracy of the theatre that he had expressed to his father-in-law the previous year. To prepare the ground for *The School for Scandal*, he began his management of Drury Lane with what was in effect a rejection of his own tirade against theatre as a form of sexual pollution. He mounted an extraordinary sequence of Restoration plays, dominated by the work of William Congreve. Because Congreve was subsequently restored as a great figure in the theatrical canon, it is easy to miss the significance of Sheridan's decision to stage three of his four comedies in his first Drury Lane season. For in the new climate of sensibility, Congreve had become a symbol of all that was most disgusting about the theatre. Instead of deep and sincere feeling, his plays were concerned with brilliant surfaces. Instead of heartfelt sentiments, their characters employed sharp and savage wit. Instead of familial virtue, they offered frank and often cruel sexual conduct. By the 1770s, Congreve's plays were considered impossible to stage in a public theatre.

In 1770, for instance, a writer in *The Dramatic Censor* claimed that in Congreve's plays "a most abominable vein of licentiousness runs through the whole; virtue reluctantly peeps in, while vice with brazen front bolts forward unblushing, unrestrained . . ." When Garrick staged *Love for Love* the following year, the *Theatrical Review* pronounced that it was "the wish of Humanity, and of Virtue, that this Play was consigned to oblivion." Likewise *The Way of the World* was declared "scarcely fit to be exhibited at this time, when the public virtue of the age has so commendably laid the Stage under restrictions."[4]

In the first six weeks of his first season at Drury Lane, however, Sheridan staged three Congreve plays—*The Old Batchelor*, *Love for Love*, and *The Way of the World*—and then mounted his own adaptation of another Restoration comedy, John Vanbrugh's *The Relapse*, retitled *A Trip to Scarborough*. The latter was substantially bowdlerised, but the Congreve plays were performed with only minor excisions. Sheridan himself wrote a prologue for them, ridiculing the demand that they should be shorn of obscenities:

> What! shall they lop and lop Will Congreve's page,
> They'd better send him to the Opera Stage.[5]

This defiance was no mere gesture. The presentation of a series of plays regarded as incompatible with the finer feelings of the new age was an implicit defence of the theatre itself, and an implicit criticism of one version of the cult of sensibility. Sensibility had begun, in the writings of Rousseau and Diderot, as an aspect of the Enlightenment critique of the old regime. By 1777, when *The School for Scandal* was written, though, it had become the almost universal language of European culture. In France, Marie Antoinette dressed up as a shepherdess and had a "rustic village" built for her at Versailles where she could indulge the honest simplicities of authentic existence. In England, George III presented himself as a simple family man—Farmer George, frugal, good-hearted, happiest in his garden. And, as the exclusion of Congreve from the stage had shown, sensibility had tipped over into prudishness.

Sheridan probably intended the Congreve plays immediately to precede *The School for Scandal*, which he seems to have intended to finish well before it was finally produced. On New Year's Eve, 1775, he told Thomas Linley that he would have a new "two-act comedy" in rehearsal at Covent Garden within a week.[6] He had been working on drafts of two plays, one called *The Slanderers* and the other *The Teazles*, both of which eventually became ingredients for *The School*. Neither of them was in fact produced in the new year of 1776, almost certainly because negotiations with Garrick over Drury Lane were then reaching a conclusion and it would have made little sense for Sheridan to have given a new play to the rival theatre. The delay was in fact fortuitous, for it allowed Sheridan to begin to weave the two drafts into one five-act play. Even so, his new comedy was widely expected in early 1777—it was almost unheard of for a new play to be produced late in the season, which closed at the end of May. In the event, it was not finished until well into April, and the direct link with the Congreve plays was broken.

The School for Scandal would nevertheless make more explicitly and more profoundly the point Sheridan had implied in his staging of the Congreve plays: that the cult of sensibility was abused when it became a front for prudery and hypocrisy. It would do so by turning on its head the received idea that society was virtuous and the stage corrupt. Sheridan would show that the world of "fact"—the world as it appeared in the newspapers—was full of lies, while the inventions of the theatre could reveal a kind of truth. *The School for Scandal* was not therefore an attack on sensibility but a reclamation of its meaning. It played out a comic game in which everyone—the old and the young, the innocent and the corrupt, the sincere and the hypocritical—tried to claim ownership of the word "sentiment." And it dramatised Rousseau's concerns about life in the big city, where people could assume a language and a manner and be taken at their word, where to know people by reputation was not to know them at all. The very first exchange of the play revealed a world of linguistic deceptions:

Lady Sneerwell: The Paragraphs you say, Mr Snake, were all inserted?

Snake: They were Madam—and as I copied them myself in a feign'd Hand there can be no suspicion whence they came.

The newspapers are manipulated, handwriting is forged. Words are weapons and slander is an art form: Snake praises Lady Sneerwell's "delicacy of Hint—and mellowness of sneer."[7] Rumours run wild. Language runs amok. A young lady at a party mentions that her cousin's sheep has had twins. Within days, everyone is certain that the cousin has had a boy and a girl, and within a week "there were People who could name the Father, and the Farm House where the Babies were put out to Nurse." Reputations are so untrustworthy that even a bad name might be a fraud: Snake, when he does a good deed, begs people to keep it quiet because "I have nothing but my Infamy to depend on! and if it were once known that I had been betray'd into an honest Action I should lose every Friend I have in the world." Within this nexus of deceit and confusion, how can anyone tell a "Sentimental Knave" from "a *man of Sentiment*"—the two descriptions of Joseph Surface that are given at the same time in the first scene? The words "sentiment" and "sentimental" run through the play like a vivid stain, always attached to the people who, from the privileged viewpoint of the audience, are patently corrupt. Lady Sneerwell tells Joseph, "I'll go and Plot mischief and you shall study Sentiments—" The hapless Sir Peter Teazle announces that "there is nothing in the world so noble as a man of Sentiment!" Joseph himself tells the audience that instead of "the silver ore of pure Charity" he prefers to use "the sentimental French Plate."

The sentimental style is mocked at every turn. Charles Surface's great-aunt Deborah is, in her portrait, posed as "a Shepherdess feeding her flock," and in offering to sell the picture for five pounds ten shillings, Charles quips that "the Sheep are worth the Money." Joseph Surface indulges in the fashionable style of overstated emotions. Though dreading the arrival of his uncle Oliver, he declares himself "rejoiced to hear" of his arrival and unable to "express the sensations I feel at the thought of seeing him!" Joseph's "charitable Sentiments" are such that he has "as much speculative Benevolence as any private Gentleman in the Kingdom—tho' He is seldom so sensual as to indulge himself in the Exercise of it."

Yet it would be a mistake to conclude from all this that Sheridan was attacking the cult of sensibility. It is important to remember that his mother had been a friend and devotee of the great English practitioner of the sentimental novel, Samuel Richardson, and that her own novel, *Memoirs of Miss Sidney Biddulph*, had exemplified the sentimental aesthetic so thoroughly that Samuel Johnson had told her, "I know not, Madame, that you have a right, upon moral principles, to make your readers suffer so much."[8] And in writing *The School for Scandal* Sheridan paid his mother's memory a private compliment in naming the central characters Surface after a family in her unperformed comedy, *A Journey to Bath*.

If this was a nod to family history, the depiction of the Surface brothers was a very obvious wink at the relationship between himself and Charles. At one level, indeed, the contest over the meaning of sensibility is played out as a rivalry between brothers for the family's literary inheritance. The older Surface brother, Joseph, has projected himself as a man of sentiment, just as Charles Sheridan had been the obedient son. The younger, rather confusingly called Charles, is, like Sheridan himself, wayward and reckless but genuinely goodhearted. The brother with the good reputation is a cynical schemer while the brother with the bad name is, as Rowley puts it in the play, the real "Credit to his Family." This contest for the Sheridan inheritance is given wickedly comic expression in the fourth act, where the impecunious Charles is preparing to sell the Surface family portraits and heirlooms. He pulls out an old parchment with the family tree on it and reads, "*Richard heir to Thomas*—our genealogy in full!" It is a private gag, but the joke is on his brother, Charles, not himself: Thomas Sheridan's son and heir is being elbowed aside.

Again, as in *The Rivals*, Sheridan also played with more public aspects of his own life. The main subplot, centred on the awkward marriage of old Sir Peter Teazle to his young wife, echoed the affair of Eliza and Walter Long. More obviously, Sheridan had fun recalling and parodying the wild rumours that circulated at the time of his duels with Mathews. In the last act of the play, the gossips work themselves into a frenzy over a duel that has not taken place:

Sir Benjamin: . . . they began to fight with Swords—
Crabtree: With Pistols—Nephew—I have it from undoubted authority.—

Mrs Candour: Too true indeed Ma'am and Sir Peter's Dangerously wounded—
Sir Benjamin: By a Thrust in Seconde—quite thro' his left side.
Crabtree: By a Bullet lodged in the Thorax—

The relevance of all this to Sheridan's own story was unmistakable. But, unlike in *The Rivals*, he now extended the allegory into the political realm. As well as being versions of himself and Charles, the Surface brothers are also images of John Wilkes and Benjamin Hopkins, whose contest for the office of chamberlain of the City of London dramatised the deep divisions within British society over the American war. With British arms apparently in the ascendant, supporters of the American cause were broadly unpopular, and Wilkes, as the most potent and controversial of them, was being attacked as a bad character. Wilkes was notoriously and openly promiscuous and dissolute, a philanderer, a drinker, even a pornographer. His opponent, Benjamin Hopkins, on the other hand, was a respectable man—a banker and merchant. In showing that the man with a bad name is really good-hearted while the man with a good name is really a hypocrite, *The School for Scandal* had a direct relevance to contemporary politics.

The link between Sheridan's own life and the contest between Wilkes and Hopkins was provided by a money-lender, Jacob Nathan Moses.[9] Sheridan owed him £2,000, a debt he had probably taken over from Willoughby Lacy as part of the deal for his share of Drury Lane. Lacy's situation as a decent young man in debt to a money-lender may have provided Sheridan with the idea of having Charles Surface in debt to a money-lender called Moses. What is interesting, though, is what Sheridan did with that inspiration. He politicised it by making Moses merely the agent for a shadowy Christian, in whom contemporary audiences would be sure to see Hopkins. This was immediately apparent at the time. Sheridan, as the law required, submitted the play to the state censor, the Lord Chamberlain. On the night before it was due to open, he was told by the prompter that a licence had been refused because of references in the play to the contest between Wilkes and Hopkins. In the context of the time, it was obvious that the play's attack on hypocrisy was also an attack on Hopkins. For just at that moment, Parliament was debating an Annuity Bill, meant to control unscrupulous bankers who lent money to under-age clients on the security of future inheritances. The Wilkes faction accused Hopkins of being just such a usurer. The contrast they wanted to present was between Wilkes, the good-hearted and open rake, and Hopkins, the respectable man whose morality was a front for fraudulent business. Hopkins was accused of lending money on inequitable terms to a sixteen-year-old, and a correspondent with *The Gazeteer* described him as "our Christian Shylock." Rumours spread that Moses, the Jewish money-lender in *The School for Scandal*, was a satiric portrait of Hopkins. The play, as Sheridan later told the House of Commons, was therefore accused of being "a factious and seditious opposition to a court candidate."[10] Sheridan went to the Lord Chamberlain, the Earl of Hertford, and persuaded him that a scene involving Moses lending money to the under-age Charles Surface was "a matter of general satire, and not of personal obloquy or ridicule."[11] Hertford "laughed at the affair" and gave the licence.

Sheridan's persuasive powers were remarkable, because Hertford's initial misgivings were in fact well founded. The play's attack on Hopkins was actually quite strong. The campaign against unscrupulous money-lenders, culminating in the passage of the Annuity Bill just after the opening night of the play, drew on naked anti-Semitism, with "the Jewish tribe" accused of being "unconscionable and rapacious."[12] At first sight, the figure of Moses seems to fall into line with this bigotry. But in fact, Sheridan was at pains to make Moses a relatively benign front for a Christian "Gentleman from the city." He managed at one and the same time to make amends for the Jewish stereotype in *The Duenna* and to attack Hopkins by blaming Christians, not Jews, for the fleecing of the young.

Moses is actually quite a sympathetic character. Far from being a cynical manipulator of Charles's foolishness, he is said to have "done everything in his power to bring your nephew to a proper sense of his Extravagence."[13] Moses is not the cause of Charles's ruin: "He was ruin'd before he came to me for Assistance." Furthermore, he is merely a broker for the real lender who is not a Jew: "The principal is Christian."[14] While the rumour that Moses was meant to be Hopkins was clearly inaccurate, there is indeed a subtler attack on Hopkins—subtle enough to make the refusal of a licence unsustainable. Sheridan's political sophistication was in fact remarkable. At the same time he managed to distance himself from the anti-Semitism of the Annuity Bill campaign, to get in a telling blow against Hopkins, and to preserve his play from any sustainable accusation of political sedition.

This directly political dimension to the play explains the explosive effect of the screen scene in which hypocrisy is exposed. Joseph Surface lures Lady Teazle to his library. Her husband—to whom Joseph is a moral paragon—arrives, and she is hidden behind a screen. Charles Surface then comes on the scene and, after the audience has been teased with thrilling delays, throws down the screen to reveal not just Lady Teazle but a world of hypocrisy. In that single action, a whole array of cultural and political values, ranging from the immediate context of the play to the political struggle in the city of London to the American war, seems to be overthrown.

Sheridan was careful, though, to balance the unmasking of the man of sentiment with an example of genuine sensibility. While she is behind the screen, Lady Teazle in a sense becomes an audience herself. She is present but unacknowledged. She acquires what the real audience out in the auditorium has had all along: a privileged knowledge of the reality behind the illusions. She hears her despised husband, who does not know she is listening, talk of her with tenderness and affection and tell Joseph Surface of the arrangements he has made for her financial comfort in the event of his death. As the audience to this small episode, she is moved and transformed. She steps forward from behind the dashed-down screen as a figure of truth to speak the real language of sensibility. She tells her husband that "the tenderness you express'd for me when I am sure you could not think I was a witness to it, has penetrated to my Heart . . ." Her experience of watching what has happened on stage has taught her the true meaning of sentimental virtue. She has, as she says, "recover'd her Senses," a word that has a double meaning here. The wisdom of the senses, what she has seen and heard, has been united with the power of reason, to achieve the ideal balance of enlightened virtue. She owes this transformation to the theatre, which now appears not as a source of illusions but as a revelation of the truth.

This triumph of theatre was itself assured by a cast that was generally regarded as the strongest of the period: Thomas King as Sir Peter, Frances Abington as Lady Teazle, John Palmer as Joseph Surface, William Smith as Charles. And even though it was staged so late in the season (the first performance being on 8 May 1777), it was an astounding success. "The genius of Mr Sheridan," declared *The Gazeteer*, ". . . has happily restored the English drama to those rays of glory, of which it was long shorn by a tedious set of contemptible scribblers." The *London Evening Post* announced: "Under this poetical St George, we may expect to see the *Dragon* of *mere sentimental drama* entirely subdued . . ."

The response of the audience, however, was one of delight mingled with disturbance. David Garrick, a most authoritative judge, noted in the *St James Chronicle* that the play had produced not only "Bursts of Laughter but an uncommon Agitation of Spirit in the Audience." That agitation was created by the play's political resonance, and by an understanding that behind its glittering comedy lay a serious intervention in the affairs of the great world beyond the stage. Not for nothing did an anonymous author soon publish another version of *The School for Scandal*, reworked as an explicit satire on the conduct of the American war with the same characters recast as King George III; his Prime Minister, Lord North; and the other members of the government. It was no coincidence either that the original version of *The School for Scandal* became George Washington's favourite play. The screen behind which Lady Teazle is hidden is, as the dialogue makes clear, "hung . . . with Maps." As it comes crashing down, so too does the outline of the known world attached to its unstable surface.

Chapter 14

ALL THE RAGE

After the triumphant opening of *The School for Scandal*, Sheridan went on the town. Years later, he told Lord Byron that after the opening night "he was knocked down and put into the watch-house for making a row in the street, and being found intoxicated by the watchmen." For a man of twenty-six who had in the previous three years married one of the most beautiful women in England, fathered a healthy child, taken control of a great theatre, and written three of the most successful plays of the century, it was an understandable indulgence. But not a typical one, for by now most of his revelling was conducted in more salubrious surroundings. If he was drunk it was much more likely to be within the private domain of an aristocratic club than out on the public streets. Over six nights in the fortnight after the opening he spent nearly £7 on port, rum, claret, and food at Brooks's.

Brooks's was one of London's two most exclusive clubs, and the preserve of a self-conscious political and social elite. Within its walls, the wealthy could eat, drink, gamble, and talk "more freely than was compatible with the publicity of a coffee-house."[1] And the talk was often of politics. Brooks's was a kind of sanctuary for the younger members of the Whig oligarchy, and especially for those who gathered around the young radical politician Charles James Fox. Sheridan was not yet a member, but his frequent presence there was a mark of his acceptance into high society. That process had begun as early as 1775, when Sheridan and Eliza met Georgiana Cavendish, the Duchess of Devonshire, who had called to see Sir Joshua Reynolds, working on a portrait of Eliza as St. Cecilia, the patron saint of music. At first, the Duchess was reluctant to invite the Sheridans, an actor's son and his wife, to her husband's London mansion, Devonshire House. However, as Sheridan's success increased, he acquired a glamour equal to Eliza's, and between them they were irresistible to anyone who wanted to be regarded as fashionable. Georgiana was in any case perfectly capable of appreciating Sheridan's talents as a writer. She was then eighteen, tall, elegant, and charismatic, but also well-read and highly intelligent. She had been married for two years to the dull duke, and was already becoming bored. Her intellectual energy found an outlet first in the writing of a novel, then in making herself the centre of that section of aristocratic society most susceptible to a vague but potent radicalism in which the paternalism of a secure elite was leavened with the yeast of Enlightenment ideals. She knew her Rousseau. She was, in common with much of the Whig oligarchy, opposed to the American war. And she was adept at exercising the only kind of political power then open to women: that of transforming parties and soirées into a nexus for factional discussion and partisan encounter.

Such a transformation was possible because of both the intimacy of the British aristocratic elite and its hold over the political realm. In continental Europe at this time, the nobility comprised between 1 and 2 percent of the population. In Britain, it accounted for 0.001 percent of the population. Every ruling cabinet was drawn from amongst its members. Between 1782 and 1820, the period which encompassed Sheridan's political career, sixty-five individuals held cabinet office. Forty-three were peers, and a further fourteen the sons of peers. Only six could be regarded as non-aristocrats, and of these only one, William Windham, could be regarded as ever having been, like Sheridan, a Foxite Whig. The oligarchy controlled, of course, one-half of the Parliament, the House of Lords. But it also had effective control over the theoretically more democratic House of Commons. Well into the nineteenth century, three-quarters of the members of the Commons were landed gentry.[2] In the 1770s, a fifth of its members were actually the sons of peers. Many parliamentary consituencies had tiny electorates, and were directly under the control of one or other of the great landed families. To pursue the political career he had been planning all along, Sheridan had to make connections with at least some of these grandees.

Sheridan could never have been a true Whig, even if he had

wanted to be. Fundamental to the Whig self-image was the idea that the survival of liberty and of constitutional balance depended on the leadership in government of men whose breeding, wealth, and property would ensure their independence from the blandishments of the crown. Their very nobility would oblige them to descend into politics as a public duty, untainted by ambition, scornful of bribery or flattery. Political freedom, in other words, depended on the leadership of aristocrats. Sheridan wasn't one of them. Edmund Burke himself made this explicit in 1792, when he showed, accurately, that Sheridan's support for the French Revolution was inconsistent with membership of the Whig party, which he described as "an aristocratic party . . . a party, in its composition and its principles, connected with the solid, permanent long possessed property of the country."[3] Even Fox, for all his radicalism, continued to "think both property and rank of great importance in this country in a party view."[4] In 1799, he wrote that he could not "help feeling every day more and more that in this country at least an aristocratic party is absolutely necessary for the preservation of liberty."

Sheridan's conception of himself and of his political career could not have been more different. He told the House of Commons in 1804 that he would "call on the humblest peasant to defend his son's title to the great seal of England." He saw in the English constitution the possibility of a social order in which "no sullen line of demarkation separates and cuts off the several orders from each other." And fortunately for him, the ramparts surrounding political power were not impregnable. First, the ruling class was divided. The political power of the Whig oligarchy had been firmly established in 1714, when the Protestant landed gentry had installed the Elector of Hanover as King George I of England, and the following year, when a Jacobite rising created the opportunity for a witch-hunt against that part of the old aristocracy (called Tories) suspected of sympathy with the deposed Stuart dynasty. The Tories were excluded from office under both George I and George II, but then, in the 1760s, George III displaced the mighty Whig families from the power they took to be theirs by right, and brought in the Tories. Having monopolised the great offices of state for decades, families like the Devonshires, who had come to regard political power as personal property, found themselves excluded from government. Their resentment fuelled a willingness to resort to anti-monarchical rhetoric.

Second, the grandees could not operate in isolation from public opinion. The political system was not, except in the vaguest sense, democratic. Nor was it autocratic. In 92 of the 314 constituencies, the right to vote belonged to all men with freehold property valued at 40 shillings a year. Thus most counties had electorates of between 3,000 and 4,000 men, with Yorkshire having 20,000 voters. In other cases, only those who paid poor rates could vote, but with a rising middle class this could still produce relatively large electorates (for example, up to 12,000 people could vote in Westminster). Even in areas where the electorate was very small—in some cases, for instance, only the self-appointed corporation could vote—it could often be very jealous of its independence and of local rights. And with a thriving and relatively free press supported by high levels of literacy, political debate could not be private property.

Between them, the factionalism of the elite itself and the importance of public opinion meant that the grandees needed to have talented campaigners and politicians on their side. And in the crises of the 1770s, the fact that the King's Prime Minister, Lord North, was opposed to Wilkes and in favour of the American war encouraged some of the oligarchs to identify with Wilkes's radical demands for the limitation of royal power and to look with sympathy on the American cause. The old Whiggery began to break up into a right and a left wing. The latter was under the patronage of Charles Wentworth, Marquis of Rockingham, but its two most brilliant figures were Charles James Fox, its finest parliamentary orator, and Edmund Burke, who acted as its ideologue and propagandist. By the time of *The School for Scandal* Sheridan knew them both. If he had not done so before, he certainly met Burke by March 1777, when Samuel Johnson invited him to join the Literary Club over which he presided at the Turk's Head Tavern and of which Burke was a prominent member. Sheridan had also, sometime in 1776, met Fox at a dinner given by Lord John Townshend, after which Fox told his host that Sheridan's wit infinitely surpassed that of anyone else he knew. The admiration was mutual: Sheridan, for his part, told Townshend next day that he could not say whether he was more impressed by Fox's "commanding superiority of talents and universal knowledge, or his playful fancy, artless manners, and benevolence of heart, which shewed itself in every word he uttered."[5]

With Burke providing the intellectual ammunition, Fox was then leading the assault in Parliament on the American war, and Sheridan would have been attracted to him on that ground alone. But Fox was also personally congenial. Although he was, as the second son of Lord Holland, a member of the landed elite, he was also a colourful, exciting, and immensely impressive man. He was an accomplished classical scholar and historian, a superb orator, and a brave politician. Fat and often deliberately slovenly—he gave up the bright colours of the dandy and adopted the buff and blue of the American Revolutionary Army—he combined with his radical rhetoric the aristocratic hauteur of a man who assumed that gambling, drinking, and sexual adventure were privileges of the elite. He was less than two years older than Sheridan and treated him, moreover, as an equal. His conduct made him almost a caricature of the new man of the Enlightenment, carrying informality so far as to spit on the floor with alarming frequency and to receive visitors in his filthy night-gown. By the time Sheridan met Fox he had already gathered his own following in the House of Commons, defined by opposition to the American war, resistance to the extension of royal power, and sympathy towards demands for a more democratic Parliament.

Sheridan responded with enthusiasm to both sides of Fox's persona: the parliamentary radical and the warm-hearted rake. He was not yet able to join Fox in one of his domains, the House of Commons, but he was a frequent guest at the other, Brooks's. In four months either side of the opening of *The School for Scandal*, in fact, Sheridan spent about £25 at Brooks's. In March, he visited on two evenings, paying for three bottles of old port on each occasion. In April, while *The School for Scandal* was in rehearsal, he was there on three nights, paying for six bottles of port or Madeira.[6] On 9 June, he obviously entertained a small party of friends, paying for turbot, beef, mutton, tongue, chicken, lamb, eggs, and goose, at a cost of over £7 in one evening. He was back the following night, ordering four bottles of wine. On 16 June, he had a huge party, ordering seven dozen bottles of port as well as ice-cream, oranges, strawberries, pistachios, almonds, and raisins, at a cost of over £8. Three nights later, he ordered a bottle of brandy and, on 22 June, two bottles of Madeira.

Eating and drinking were, in such surroundings, excuses for talking. In the Literary Club, at Brooks's, at Devonshire House, Sheridan was drawing up verbal contracts, making connections by making conversation. Theodore Zeldin has noted, "So long as success in life depended on military strength, or noble birth, or having a patron to protect one, 'to converse' was understood to mean 'to live with, to frequent, to belong to the circle of someone powerful,' with no need for speech beyond proclaiming one's loyalty."[7] Slowly, under the influence of the salons organised in the cities of Europe by wealthy women like the Duchess of Devonshire, the term acquired a new meaning of elegant but informal self-expression. One way to understand Sheridan at this point in his life is to reflect that, in his early career, "to converse" retains vestiges of this earlier meaning while signifying on the surface a dazzling expression of its later one. In the salons of the ladies of the Whig aristocracy, at Brooks's, or in the Turk's Head, he was conversing in both senses. He was speaking his mind, sharing his thoughts, exercising his wit, expressing his personality. But he was also, between the lines, finding patrons to promote him, entering a circle, proclaiming his loyalty.

There was, for him, an almost sexual intensity in these friendships. When he was twenty-two, he had written to Thomas Grenville that he believed there could be an instant attraction between men as powerful as that between men and women:

> As We really find in *Love* frequent proofs of what the Novelists call *sudden sympathy*, I confess I have an opinion of the same in *Friendship*, and I believe the youngest Man's experience will furnish him with instances of his having felt a strong disposition towards a friendship with a man upon the very commencement perhaps of their acquaintance . . . For my Part, I confess myself an admirer of those times when the ties of *Friendship* as well as *Love* could with some safety be formed at the first instigation of our Hearts. It is what we call the *Civilisation* of Society that has destroyed this, by making a *Fashion* of *Professions*; and still more the *Corruption* that follow'd it, which has so far blunted all the nobler feelings of Man, that the test of Time and Services is become necessary to *apologise* for any mutual confidence, or *disinterested* regard.[8]

This sudden sympathy is what Sheridan felt for Fox. But the comparison he had made between friendship and love worked both ways. Within the intimate circles of Whig society, it was not unusual for one to tip over into the other. To the grandees, one of the privileges of aristocracy was sexual freedom, and one of the marks of good breeding was a disdain for both jealousy and middle-class morality. The Duchess of Devonshire, for instance, learned to live with the fact that her friend Lady Elizabeth Foster was also her husband's lover and would bear him children. And live with it is precisely what she did, since the three of them inhabited Devonshire House together. As he crossed the boundaries of conventional morality and entered this world, Sheridan took on its most intimate values.

In the late summer or early autumn of 1777, Sheridan sent a bound manuscript of *The School for Scandal* to Frances Ann Crewe with a verse dedication which, when he saw it again in old age, reminded him "what an ardent romantic Blockhead nature made me!"[9] Even then, however, he recalled the recipient as "the Handsomest of the set." Frances Crewe, the only daughter of Frances Greville, whose "Ode to Indifference" was immensely popular in the late eighteenth century, was indeed beautiful as well as being witty and intellectual. She had also been married for over two years to John Crewe, a minor aristocrat. Fanny Burney, after her first meeting with the Sheridans, noted that Eliza's beauty was unequalled by anyone's "except by Mrs Crewe's."

In the verses he sent to her, called "A Portrait," Sheridan not only praised "the Peril of her Lips," the "mild Irresolution of her Eyes," "the Mercy of her Smiles," and her wit and talent, but claimed her as "my Inspirer—and my *Model*—CREWE!" The verses, moreover, were a peculiarly public form of love letter, for they were passed around Sheridan's circle of friends. Garrick had a copy in early August. He gave them to Lord Camden, who showed them to Fox and reported back to Garrick that Fox "admires Sheridan's verses, and agrees with me in marking him the first genius of these times."[10] The combination of sexual seduction, linguistic delight, and coterie gossip is indicative of the kind of world in which Sheridan now moved. Adding a further dimension to this intertwining of sex and language was the fact that in Sheridan's developing relationship with Mrs. Crewe there was also a kind of textual ménage à trois involving Eliza as well. In 1775, Sheridan wrote to Eliza and described a ball given by Mrs. Crewe, praising the famous beauties who attended. Eliza, in return, sent him a poem, "Laura to Silvio," in which Sheridan is a young poet, Silvio, undecided which of many beauties to praise in verse. Among them is Frances Crewe, whom Eliza called Amoret:

> With gentle step and hesitating grace,
> Unconscious of her power, the fair one came;
> If while he view'd the glories of her face
> Poor Silvio doubted—who shall dare to blame?

Sheridan, in writing "A Portrait" for Frances Crewe as the dedication to the copy of *The School for Scandal* he sent her two years later, alluded directly to Eliza's poem:

> Come, gentle Amoret (for 'neath that name,
> In worthier verse is sung thy beauty's fame) . . .

Eliza certainly knew of the affair. As she wrote to her friend Mehitabel Canning, wife of Stratford Canning, a prominent Foxite: "S. is in Town—and so is Mrs. Crewe—*I* am in the country and so is Mr. *Crewe*—a very convenient arrangement is it not?" But she seems to have tolerated it, and even to have accepted it as a sign that they had moved into the elite. She and Mrs. Crewe remained on good terms, and she stayed quite frequently with Sheridan at Crewe Hall. And even to those who were aware of Sheridan's attachment to Frances Crewe, the bond between himself and Eliza did not seem any the weaker. Fanny Burney, meeting them both for the first time in 1779, noted that "he evidently adores her; and she as evidently idolises him."[11]

It may be, though, that there was a certain strain in their sexual relationship. Eliza's delicacy of health was already apparent, and it was affected by pregnancy. Before Tom was born she had at least one miscarriage, and just before the opening of *The School for Scandal* she gave birth to a still-born child. In June 1774, her father had warned Sheridan of her "seminal weakness" and warned him that "you must absolutely keep from her, for every time you touch her, you drive a Nail in her Coffin."[12] It is quite possible that in the aftermath of the still-birth, they ceased to have a sexual relationship for a time—certainly she did not become pregnant again for many years. If this is so, it may have been a factor not only in Sheridan's affair with Mrs. Crewe but also in Eliza's apparent willingness to tolerate it. The affair lasted, almost certainly, from the late 1770s until the mid-1780s. By November 1788, it was over. Sheridan's sister Betsy wrote to Dublin that "Mrs Crewe, among other lovers (favour'd ones I mean) has had our brother in her train. As his fame and consequence in life have increased, her charms have diminished, and passion no longer the tie between them, his affection, esteem and attentions return'd to their proper channel."[13]

Even if Sheridan was learning to live like an aristocrat, though, he was thinking like a democrat, and by the end of 1777 was actively involved in the Foxite campaigns against the American war. Just after the New Year of 1778, for instance, William Windham, a Foxite whom Sheridan had first met in Bath in 1771, was writing to him from Norfolk giving him full details of attempts to oppose a government effort to raise subscriptions for the war effort. Likewise, from March to June 1779, Sheridan was heavily involved with *The Englishman*, a twice-weekly paper to which Windham and probably Fox also contributed. It was aimed, as Sheridan put it in one anonymous piece, at "the middling class of people who, notwithstanding the contempt which gentlemen of certain principles affect to hold them in, have ever had, and ever will have in times of actual peril, a deciding voice for removal and punishment of incapable or unprincipled ministers." The paper was dominated by attacks on the government's conduct in the American war: Sheridan's most passionate contribution was a polemic against the Minister for War, Lord George Germaine, who was, he wrote, fighting "a war wherein no success can furnish matter of triumph to a good mind."

His alliance with Fox and the friendship of the Duchess of Devonshire placed Sheridan within the ambit of the oligarchy, but his real feelings towards the aristocracy were not always apparent. When David Garrick died in January 1779, Sheridan was chief mourner at his funeral and wrote a monody to his memory, which was performed at Drury Lane in March. (It was also, interestingly, printed over three columns on the front page of the *Independent Chronicle* in Boston, suggesting Sheridan's popularity in revolutionary America.) It was published with a dedication from Sheridan to "the Right Honourable Countess Spencer . . . with great deference." Years later, however, Lord Byron was with Sheridan when he took up a copy of the monody and noticed the dedication. "On seeing it he flew into a rage—exclaimed 'that it must be a forgery—that he had never dedicated anything of his to such a damned canting bitch etc etc' and so went on for half an hour abusing his own dedication or at least the object of it."[14] This was, of course, a later reaction, but from a letter that Sheridan wrote at the time of the monody it is clear that he found the task of writing the dedication a painful one and that he consigned a more fulsome verse tribute to the countess to the fire.[15] Sycophancy did not sit easily with him.

There was in any case a much more serious barrier to Sheridan's absorption by the Whig grandees: his sense of being Irish. Most of the great oligarchic families—the Rockinghams and the Devonshires included—had large estates in Ireland. In 1773, the British government proposed a tax on absentee landlords, owners who did not live on their estates. This was, obviously, against the interests of the grandees, and the Whig leader, Rockingham, was especially active in opposing the tax. The contrasting reactions of Sheridan and Edmund Burke to the controversy reveal a great deal about their respective relationships to the elite. The contrast is significant because Burke and Sheridan shared so much. Both were Dubliners. Both had been born into middle-class Protestant families with roots in Gaelic Ireland. Both were Irishmen making their way in England and writers making their way in politics. But Burke's progress in public life had depended on aristocratic patronage: he entered Parliament as Rockingham's private secretary and, at this time, held a seat which was essentially in the gift of the oligarchs. And when the tax on absentees was proposed, he placed his magnificent talents for polemic and oratory entirely at Rockingham's disposal, writing and speaking against the tax, which was, in 1774, withdrawn.

Sheridan, however, was in a much stronger position than Burke in his dealings with the Whig magnates. Through the theatre, he had acquired a fame and a position of his own. And he saw no reason to subordinate the interests of Ireland to the economic interests of the leaders of the political faction to which he was becoming allied. In his most considerable early political tract, an unpublished *Essay on Absentees* written at some time in the mid-1770s, he attacked those who owned land in Ireland but lived in England. Rather ironically, given its subject, Sheridan adopted in the essay the voice of an Irishman living in Ireland and addressing his fellow countrymen. The assumed audience was "we in Ireland," suggesting that his intention was to publish the piece in Dublin. The essay was written entirely from the point of view of Irish interests and attacked not just absentee landlords but also the effect on the propertyless poor of the restrictions on Irish trade and industry imposed by Britain. He complained that absentee landlords preferred to have as few tenants as possible and to give their land over to the raising of sheep, "whose produce we are not allowed a market for when manufactured, while we want art, honesty and encouragement to fit it for home consumption. Thus the indolent extravagence of the lord becomes subservient to the interests of a few mercenary graziers." Sheridan went on to set the wealth of individuals against the poverty of the nation:

> . . . had we in Ireland power to export our manufactured silks, stuffs and woollens, we should be assured that it would be our interest to import and cultivate their materials. But as this is not the case, the gain of individuals is no proof that the nation is benefited by such commerce. For instance, the exportation of unwrought wool may be very advantageous to the dealer, and through his hands bring money or a beneficial return of commodities into the kingdom; but trace the ill effects of depopulating such tracts of land as are necessary for the support of flocks to supply this branch, and number those who are deprived of support and employment by it, and so become a dead weight on the community—we shall find that the nation in fact will be the poorer for this apparent advantage. This would be remedied were we allowed to export it manufactured, because the husbandman might get his bread as a manufacturer.[16]

Sheridan then defended the idea of a tax on absentees. And it is striking that this political polemic was intertwined with both a passionate rehearsal of the doctrine of sensibility and an insistence on the power of the senses over the power of reason, of theatre over writing. Even if, he wrote, both the owners and the managers of absentee estates were assumed to be benevolent, no written appeal on behalf of the tenants by the agent to the landlord could have much effect.

> Can we expect any great exertion of pathetic eloquence to proceed from the [agent] to palliate any deficiency of the tenants?—or, if there were, do we not know how much lighter an impression is made by distresses related to us than by those which are *occulis subjecta fidelibus*? The heart, the seat of charity and compassion, is more accessible to the senses than the understanding. Many, who would be unmoved by any address to the latter, would melt into charity at the eloquent persuasion of silent sorrow. When he *sees* the widow's tear, and hears the orphan's sigh everyone will act

> with a sudden uniform rectitude because he acts from the divine impulse of "free love dealt equally to all."

This is arguably the most revealing passage in Sheridan's writings. As a critical definition of his underlying political motives, it is rooted in a concern not just for Ireland but for the Ireland of the masses, the predominantly Catholic tenantry. The idea of love dealt equally to all is, in the Irish context, not just a pretty sentiment but, for a system based on an inequality between Protestants and Catholics, a dangerously subversive doctrine. The passage represents, too, a reconciliation between Sheridan's politics and his achievements in the theatre. If moral and political justice arises from what is seen and heard, then the persuasive powers of performance need not be the mere tricks of charlatans. The actor, and by extension the orator, can make the audience not merely think the truth but feel it. By affecting the senses, he can also affect the heart, stirring the compassion and charity that, like a true Enlightenment man, Sheridan assumes to be locked within it, awaiting liberation.

In the *Essay on Absentees*, Sheridan was making his identification with Ireland central to his emerging public persona. It had become the link between his theatre and his politics, and was, crucially, the area of psychological reserve that would prevent him from being absorbed into the elite. Over the next decade, in the wake of its loss of prestige and public confidence in the disaster of the American war, the oligarchy would become increasingly conscious of the need to preserve its power by being seen to incorporate into its ranks a few landless men of obvious ability. Their intention, as Linda Colley has put it, was "not so much to make the upper ranks of the British polity easily accessible to talent, as to admit in a controlled fashion a number of truly exceptional men for the sake of efficiency and for the sake, too, of preserving the existing order. Outstanding talent and remarkable achievement were used like yeast. Absorbing a limited amount helped the dough of hereditary peers and younger sons to rise in the public estimation."[17]

At almost any time over the next thirty years, Sheridan, the most conspicuously talented member of the middle class, could have been absorbed into the upper ranks of the ruling class. On numerous occasions, that choice would be presented to him in the most explicit terms. His contemporaries would never really understand why a player's son who had gone to such lengths to establish himself as a gentleman did not wish to go further and join the gentry. He could, after all, ride and fence, he could talk like a gentleman, he dressed beautifully in well-cut and tasteful clothes, he was supremely clubbable, he could be a convincing lover of aristocratic ladies. But, because of his identification with Ireland, he could not and would not surrender his whole self to the world in which he now moved. Even while he worked his way into the heart of the elite, a part of him would always belong on the outside.

Chapter 15

THEATRICAL POLITICS

With Sheridan putting most of his energies into the cultivation of social and political connections, Drury Lane soon ran into trouble. The *Morning Chronicle* described the acting company as "like ships without a pilot," and after the glories of *The School for Scandal* the standard repertoire seemed thin and uninviting. By the autumn of 1778, when it was reported that for the first time in the theatre's history the name of the opening play had not yet been announced two days before the start of the season, it was clear that Sheridan would have to either devote himself more fully to the management or bring in his father at last. His tense relationship with his father had been given an oblique public expression in 1777. In spite of public enmity between Thomas Sheridan and Samuel Johnson, Richard paid an overt and even more public compliment to Johnson in his prologue to Richard Savage's play *Sir Thomas Overbury* when it was performed at Covent Garden, referring to Savage's fame being "fix'd by the hand that bid our language live."[1] Not only was this high praise of his father's enemy, but it also implicitly dismissed Thomas Sheridan's claim to pre-eminence over Johnson as a compiler of dictionaries and an authority on language.

His own inexperience as a manager nevertheless argued strongly for a healing of the rift. He had always intended that Thomas would help him to run Drury Lane, and he now decided to bring him in. From an angry letter written later by Thomas Sheridan it seems that the delay in taking this course of action was caused by Richard's continuing reluctance to have his father on show in the theatre as an actor. As Thomas complained, "When by extreme ill conduct, they [the owners of Drury Lane] were threatened with ruin, he agreed to put the management into my hands upon condition that I should not appear as a performer, and in this he got his brother to join him with such earnestness, that merely to gratify him I acquiesced."[2] Preparing as he was for an entrance into public life, Sheridan was still sensitive about his father's status.

Yet even when Thomas Sheridan agreed to stop acting and took on the role of manager, the relationship was not easy. He continued to be irascible and officious, earning the Linleys' title of "Old Surly Boots." In November 1778, when he was preparing a production of Voltaire's *Mahomet* with the young John Bannister in one of the principal roles, David Garrick, who had played the part, offered to help. Richard asked him to attend a rehearsal, probably forgetting that his father, too, had played the role when the play had sparked off the disastrous riot in Dublin twenty-four years before. Thomas evidently sent Garrick an insulting message through Bannister, causing Garrick to write to Richard in dignified but evidently hurt tones:

> I imagined (foolishly indeed) my attending Bannister's rehearsal of the part I once played . . . might have assisted the cause, without giving the least offence. I love my ease too well to be thought an interloper, and I should not have been impertinent enough to have attended any rehearsal, had not you, Sir, in a very particular manner desired me. However, upon no consideration will I ever interfere again in this business, nor be liable to receive such another message as was brought me this evening by young Bannister.[3]

To Sheridan's great embarrassment, this incident was widely reported, and exaggerated versions of the row spread as far as Dublin.

While his father's prickliness might have been forgivable had his management been successful, business at the theatre in fact grew steadily worse. The actors' company remained demoralised, and Richard himself was embroiled in a row when he tried to prevent them from taking the front seats in the boxes when they were off stage. Audiences were becoming increasingly rowdy, and there were reports of bottles being thrown at the stage. An arrangement between Drury Lane and Covent Garden allowing each theatre to borrow the other's performers came under sustained attack in the press. And worst of all, box-office receipts were down. The income for the 1778–

79 season, Thomas's first as manager, was £4,000 lower than the previous season.

The most obvious way to retrieve the situation was with a new Sheridan play. As he had done before, he chose to create it from the materials of his own embarrassments and entanglements. Rehearsals had given him grief, so the new play would be about a rehearsal. Letters to the newspapers had complained about the use of a foreign designer, the great French scenic painter Philippe Jacques de Loutherbourg, whom Garrick had brought to Drury Lane in 1772, so Loutherbourg's designs would be at the heart of the piece. Drury Lane had been a factory for gossip and rumour, so one of the new play's central characters would be a theatre groupie who skips the news of politics and war in the morning papers to get to the theatrical tittle-tattle. There had been murmurs that Sheridan, as a playwright himself, was using his position as manager to steal from his rivals, so another central character would complain about the manager of Drury Lane in just such terms.

In all of this, Sheridan would simultaneously satirise his own profession and defy his critics. But he would also reflect his position as a man in transition between theatre and politics. He decided to bring three disparate strands into the new play. One was the theatrical complications that were plaguing him; a second, the proven success of Loutherbourg's spectacles in attracting an audience; and the third was politics. Sheridan chose to focus on the general panic that had seized the country in the summer of 1779, when fears of invasion by Spain and France reached fever pitch, and on the rhetoric of English patriotism which it generated.

In *The Camp*, a light afterpiece which he had written in October 1778, probably in collaboration with Richard Tickell and General John Burgoyne, the British general whom the Americans had forced to surrender at Saratoga in 1777, he had already combined a gentle satire on the military preparations with some theatrical in-jokes. *The Camp* was also dominated by the designs of Philippe de Loutherbourg, whom Sheridan had sent to sketch the military bivouac at Coxheath. Within the play itself, Sheridan had included an Irish painter, O'Daub, sent by "the Managers of Drury Lane Theatre" to make sketches of the encampment as "a kind of Deputy Superintendent under Mr. Leatherbag the great painter." This device allowed for self-referential jokes:

Gauge: And what—are they going to bring the Camp on the Stage?
O'Daub: You have it—Cox-heath by Candle light my Jewel![4]

Though little more than a bagatelle, *The Camp* had run for fifty-seven performances as an afterpiece, and brought in much-needed revenue. It was not surprising that Sheridan was inclined to repeat the trick on a larger scale with what was to be his last comedy, *The Critic*. Into it he poured all the vexations of the previous season, alchemically transformed into pure hilarity.

In *The Critic* Sheridan went further than ever before in blurring the boundaries between the stage and the world, between theatre and politics. In the opening dialogue he has Dangle reading the newspapers, full of wars and rumours of wars, but impatient to get to what is really important: theatre. "Pshaw!—Nothing but about the fleet and the nation!—and I hate all politics but theatrical politics."[5] And in what followed, he placed theatre and politics side-by-side, so that they could contaminate and subvert each other. The playwright, Puff, explains that he writes what purport to be factual reports for the newspapers, making the external, political world seem like an invention. And conversely, the rehearsals for Puff's play are acted out before the audience, complete with interruptions and commentaries, so that the illusion of theatre is undercut by mundane realities. As usual, there were also political allusions in the playing that are not evident in the text. Two days after the first performance, for instance, the silent Lord Burleigh in Puff's play—"his part is to *think*"—was identified by the *Morning Post* as representing the Prime Minister, Lord North.

Sheridan himself, if not physically present on stage, hovered around the play. Early on, Sir Fretful Plagiary, modelled on Richard Cumberland, whose tragedy, *The Battle of Hastings*, was one of the first productions of Sheridan's management, remarks that he would "never send a play" to Drury Lane. He whispers to Sneer, who responds with "*Writes himself!*—I know he does—"

Sir Fretful: I say nothing—I take away no man's merit—am hurt at no man's good fortune—I say nothing—But this I will say —through all my knowledge of life, I have observed—that there is not a passion so strongly rooted in the human heart as

> envy! . . . Besides—I can tell you it is not always so safe to leave a play in the hands of those who write themselves.[6]

This skit on Cumberland itself derived from an incident during a performance of *The School for Scandal*. Cumberland's children had pestered their father to take them to see it, but such was his jealousy that whenever they laughed he pinched them, saying, according to the composer Michael Kelly, " 'What are you laughing at my dear little folks? You should not laugh, my angels; there is nothing to laugh at.'—And then, in an under tone, 'Keep still, you little dunces.' " Sheridan, when he was told of this, remarked that it was very ungrateful of Cumberland to have been displeased with his children for laughing at his comedy, "For I went the other night to see *his* tragedy and laughed at it from beginning to end."[7]

There was also in *The Critic* a private joke, probably not obvious to anyone but Eliza and himself. Puff offers as a further example of his art the "Puff Preliminary," in which a love affair is incited by planting in the papers a warning against it.

> Sir FLIMSY GOSSIMER wishes to be well with Lady FANNY FETE—He applies to me—I open trenches for him with a paragraph in the *Morning Post*.—It is recommended to the beautiful and accomplished Lady F four stars F dash E to be on her guard against that dangerous character, Sir F dash G; who, however pleasing and insinuating his manners may be, is certainly not remarkable for the *constancy of his attachments!*—in Italics . . .[8]

Six years before, Sheridan himself, as we have seen, had planted in the *Bath Chronicle* a letter addressed to "Adorable Creature" by a man who signed himself "G—R." It, too, was intended to advance an affair—his own with Eliza—under the guise of warning against a dangerous character. Yet again, Sheridan was playing with incidents from his own story.

That, though, was the only in-joke. If the audience had any doubts that Sheridan was playing with his own public image and reputation, he dispelled them in a moment of extraordinary theatrical exuberance. The audience knew of course that Sheridan was the author of the play they were seeing and that the designs were by Loutherbourg. Puff was played by Thomas King, Dangle by James Dodd, and Sneer by John Palmer. And each of the three actors was on stage when King, as Puff, gave an example of his prowess at puffing plays:

> . . . the day before it is to be performed, I write an account of the manner in which it was received—I have the plot from the author,—and only add—Characters strongly drawn—highly coloured—hand of a master—fund of genuine humour—mine of invention—neat dialogue—attic salt! Then for the performances —Mr DODD was astonishingly great in the character of SIR HARRY! That universal and judicious actor Mr PALMER perhaps never appeared to more advantage than in the COLONEL;—but it is not in the power of language to do justice to Mr KING!—Indeed he more than merited those repeated bursts of applause which he drew from a most brilliant and judicious audience! As to the scenery—The miraculous power of Mr DE LOUTHERBOURG's pencil are universally acknowledged!—In short, we are at a loss which to admire most,—the unrivalled genius of the author, the great attention and liberality of the managers—the wonderful abilities of the painter, or the incredible exertions of all the performers![9]

Elsewhere in the play, the prompter in the rehearsal is named as "Mr HOPKINS," identifying him as the actual prompter, William Hopkins. Time and again, the audience was required to use a kind of triple vision, watching people pretending to be characters making references to their real selves. In the rehearsal scenes, the play finds itself in a hall of mirrors: when the actors step out of their roles to comment on what is happening, they are first characters in Puff's play, *The Spanish Armada*, second, the actors playing those characters, and third the actors playing the actors playing the characters.

The audience itself, "brilliant and judicious," was included in this circle of satire. As the playwright and composer Charles Dibdin noted in 1788, this was "the first instance . . . where an audience have quietly sat down and consented to be laughed at by an author."[10] All through the play, in fact, the audience was being teased. Its judiciousness was questioned by Puff's remark that "the number of those who go thro' the fatigue of judging for themselves is very small indeed!" Its taste was mocked by a barbed if self-effacing reference to Sheridan's need to clean up the plays of Congreve and Vanbrugh: "No double-entendre, no smart innuendo admitted; even Vanbrugh and Congreve obliged to undergo a bungling reformation." Its willingness to accept the illusions of theatre was mocked in Sneer's snide running commentary on the rehearsals of Puff's ludicrous tragedy. When Sir Walter Raleigh and Sir Christopher Hatton give laboured descriptions of the background to the Spanish Armada ("PHILIP you know is proud IBERIA's king!"), the audience is reminded that it has just sat through some very bad theatre:

> *Dangle*:—Mr Puff, as he *knows* all this, why does Sir Walter go on telling him?
>
> *Puff*: But the audience are not supposed to know any thing of the matter, are they?
>
> *Sneer*: True, but I think you manage ill: for there certainly appears no reason why Sir Walter should be so communicative.
>
> *Puff*: Fore Gad now, that is one of the most ungrateful observations I ever heard—for the less inducement he has to tell all this, the more I think you ought to be oblig'd to him; for I'm sure you'd know nothing of the matter without it.[11]

The forms and conventions, the inner workings of the theatrical machine were laid bare, and the audience invited to wonder at its own credulity. How, Sheridan asked his paying customers, could they be so uncritical as to accept all the clichéd devices by which playwrights advanced their plots? When, for instance, two spies in Puff's play overhear Sir Walter making plans, Sneer interrupts to ask why, since they were plainly visible, they were not noticed. Puff indignantly replies: "O lud, Sir, if people who want to listen, or overhear, were not always connived at in a Tragedy, there would be no carrying on any plot in the world."[12] The connivance, of course, happens in the auditorium as well as on the stage.

This gentle but insistent needling of the audience was, at one level, no more than a daring theatrical joke. But, as always with Sheridan, it had a political dimension. Deep down, the games of appearance and reality in *The Critic* were very much a product of the philosophical scepticism of John Locke and George Berkeley. Like Laurence Sterne's *Tristram Shandy*, whose tone and method it so closely resembles, the play in its hilarious confusions of the real and the illusory could be both a parody and a comic demonstration of Berkeley's belief that material reality is just an idea in the mind of the beholder. It is, as well as everything else, a play about perception, and, following Berkeley, it advances the notion that to be is to be perceived. In all likelihood Sheridan was aware of the philosophical debates focusing on the nature of knowledge and perception. Certainly John Locke's works were in the house when he was growing up (his father quoted extensively from them in his tracts on education), and Sheridan himself made occasional references to Locke in his speeches.

But in *The Critic* the point was political, not abstractly philosophical. For as well as making the audience laugh, Sheridan was also asking it to think. By showing it how illusions worked, by reminding it that the actors were only playing, by underlining the performance *as a performance*, he was also inviting scepticism of patriotic appeals. Roughly speaking, the first two acts of the piece warn the viewers not to believe everything they might read in the newspapers or might see on the stage. The third, at the end, tests the value of the lesson by staging a spectacular and lavish patriotic procession. After the wonderful burlesque of *The Spanish Armada*, itself a devastating mockery of English heroic history, Puff announces, "Now then for my magnificence!—my battle!—my noise!—and my procession!" The ham-fisted epic of Puff's rehearsal melts into a stunning demonstration of true stagecraft, with all of Loutherbourg's special effects deployed in a lavish patriotic spectacle, with trumpets and cannon, fleets in battle, the Spanish ships destroyed by fire-boats, the orchestra playing "Rule Britannia," and the rivers of England in triumphal procession. After the parody comes the real thing. Having been teased about its brilliance and judiciousness, the audience was being asked to see through the kind of appeals to war-mongering euphoria that were, and would continue to be, so central to conservative politics.

Sheridan clearly took a long time to get this daring last scene right in his own mind. According to the composer Michael Kelly, it had not been written two days before the opening. Thomas Linley organised a night rehearsal during which the stage-manager, Thomas King, informed Sheridan that he had "something particular to communicate" and asked him to step into the green room. When he got there, Sheridan found a table with pens, ink, and paper on it, a fire in the grate, two bottles of claret, and a dish of anchovy sandwiches. King immediately stepped outside and locked the door behind him. Linley and the other patentee, Dr. Ford, then told him through the door that he would not be let out until he had written the final scene. Sheridan "took this decided measure in good part; he ate the anchovies, finished the claret, wrote the scene, and laughed heartily at the ingenuity of the contrivance."

The fact that he had finished the play so late was evidently well known at the time. On the opening night of *The Critic*, two men gazing at the bill outside Drury Lane wondered why the title had not been spelt *Critick*. A passing prompter's boy explained: "Lord, sir, that was owing to a joke of my Master's who meant to intimate by his short spelling that the Piece was not *finished* when the bills were printed." As was so often the case, Sheridan really finished the play after the opening night, cutting twenty minutes from a playing time that had been generally regarded as excessive.[13]

In spite of its swipes at newspapers, the play was reasonably well received by the critics, and was popular with audiences for many decades to come. But even on the opening night, the very prominent presence of the Duchess of Devonshire in Sheridan's party, leading the "claps all the evening," was itself a signal that Sheridan's theatrical career was shading ever further into politics. Every aspect of Sheridan's public life so far—the elopement, the duel, his Irish nationality, and now his management of Drury Lane—had been cannibalised for his plays, and there was little left for him to use. It was time to move more fully into public life as the politician he had long intended to become.

He could never escape the theatre, however, for it was both his livelihood and his family inheritance. Both he and his father were still bound up in Drury Lane. In spite of—indeed, in some senses, because of—the success of *The Critic*, Drury Lane continued to decline under Thomas Sheridan's management. The paradox of the play was that it jeered at precisely the kind of plays that his father was putting on in Sheridan's own theatre. After the devastating burlesque of *The Critic*, Thomas Sheridan's programme of hackneyed standards and mediocre tragedies seemed even more out of touch, and the gross income for the 1779–80 season dropped by a further £3,000, making for an overall decline of £7,000 in the two years of his management. It was inevitable that Thomas would have to step down. By 19 November 1780, he was complaining to Charles, "Dick has taken the reins into his own hands these three weeks past and has plaid the Devil." He was bitterly hurt, and relations sank to a new low. Eliza stopped bringing Tom to see his grandfather. Thomas retreated into a sulk of injured pride, expecting an apology before he would see his son at all.[14]

For most of the next eight years, Sheridan continued to be estranged from his father. In the autumn of 1784, when Thomas and Betsy returned to London from a period in Dublin during which they had also fallen out with Charles, Sheridan seemed anxious that "all would be made up." But when Eliza and her sister called, Thomas would not see them. He was now, in his own mind, at one with "old Lear," suffering the ingratitude not of two daughters but of two sons, bitten, as he imagined himself to be, by the serpent's tooth of "the infamous behaviour of one son, and the total neglect and utter disappointment of all my hopes in the other . . ."[15] By June the following the year, Betsy was convinced that "no human power can change his heart in that respect."

Even though he moved away from his father and to some extent from Drury Lane itself, Sheridan's theatrical achievements were to continue as a vibrant presence beneath his political career. Though he stopped writing plays, he did not stop talking to his audiences from the stage. Of the twelve mainpiece plays most frequently staged in England between 1776 and 1800, four were by Shakespeare and two—*The Duenna* and *The School for Scandal*—were by Sheridan.[16] With *The Critic* holding its place as one of the most frequently performed afterpieces, Sheridan the playwright continued to occupy a central place in British cultural life.

Chapter 16

A PUBLIC MAN

To those who recognised Sheridan's extraordinary achievements as a playwright, he was primarily a man of the theatre and his move into politics was considered a tragic diversion. But, as we have seen, this was never the way he saw himself. His desire to be a public man on the political stage came first. The theatre was both a means to that end and itself a form of public power. Moving in political circles, fired by political ideals, and deeply entangled in the political world through his work at Drury Lane, he was already a kind of politician. The journey from Drury Lane to the House of Commons at Westminster via Devonshire House and Brooks's would be a short one.

The Westminster Parliament was, at this time, not just a site of political conflicts but also the subject of political campaigns. From the beginnings of Sheridan's conscious political life, when John Wilkes was conducting his agitation against the King, parliamentary reform had been the great rallying-cry of the radicals. In March 1776, while Sheridan was taking over Drury Lane, Wilkes had introduced in the House of Commons the first parliamentary motion for reform calling for "a just and equal representation of the people." By the following year, when the government's mishandling of the American war was adding an epic dimension to domestic conflicts, the radicals had succeeded in capturing for themselves the ideas of "reform" and "reformation," words that had, in an exclusively Protestant political culture, a very special resonance. Resentment at the high taxation imposed to pay for the war allowed the reformers to link together the American cause, the huge cost of government sinecures and placemen, and the encroachment of royal power on the liberties of British subjects, and to propose the creation of a representative and responsive parliament as a cure for all three.

This movement for electoral reform gave Sheridan the opportunity to prove himself in politics. On 2 February 1780, he had himself appointed to the Westminster Committee, established by "a general assembly of the inhabitants of Westminster" to promote a petition for electoral reform, and to "prepare the plan of an association on legal and constitutional grounds" to agitate for it. Fox was in the chair, and at the first meeting in the King's Arms Tavern in Palace Yard, Sheridan was joined by twenty others, including John Wilkes, John Burgoyne, and Colonel Richard Fitzpatrick, a friend of both Fox and Sheridan.[1] He attended the committee meetings assiduously, being present at all the weekly meetings in February and March. At the meeting on 26 February, he was appointed, along with Fox and Fitzpatrick, to a sub-committee of nine mandated to coordinate the campaign with a similar committee established in the City of London. On 15 March, he was appointed to a sub-committee of seven "to enquire into the state of the representation of this country," in other words, to draw up the manifesto for the reform campaign. This committee met on Friday, 17 March, and Sheridan took the chair. He elaborated an erudite and passionate argument for annually elected parliaments and a wide franchise. In what was to become a typical rhetorical manoeuvre, he painted the future in terms of the past, arguing that a democratic parliament would be a restoration, not a revolution. Citing legal precedents going back to the Glorious Revolution of 1688 he claimed that "new parliaments to be holden once in every year were the ancient usage and declared to be the hereditary and indefeasible right of the People of England." He drew, notably, on the concept of the Third Estate: "The longer a parliament were to last, the more valuable to Corruptors would be the purchase; and that all the reasons that had been given for long parliaments might be given for making them perpetual, which would be an absolute subversion of the third 'estate.' "

His report (the manuscript bears his signature) also argued for a massively widened franchise, claiming that "nearly twelve hundred thousand" of the five million inhabitants of England and Wales would be entitled to vote if the electorate had remained as it was under Henry VI, whereas "no more than two hundred and fourteen thousand are at present admitted to vote." The committee thanked him for his "very intelligent report" and decided to print it and send it to all the other reform committees that had sprung up around the country. Sheridan was to remain one of the key organisers of the association. On 3 April, he was one of just three members (Fox and Fitzpatrick being the others) appointed to "prepare the plan of an association," one of the basic aims of the committee. On 25 April he was appointed to a committee "to enquire into the expenses incurred by this Committee, the subscriptions necessary to defray the same etc." He was now a central figure in the campaign for democratic reform. A seat in Parliament was obviously the next step.

Already, though, Sheridan's political opponents were beginning to define him as Irish. When he was chairing the sub-committee on electoral reform, a satire, "An Epistle from Joseph Surface Esq. to Richard Brinsley Sheridan," included the line "Hail, Irish chairman, Ireland too all hail."[2] Sir Horace Walpole, referring to Sheridan in a letter to the Countess of Ossory the following year, noted, "Your Milesians have hearts as unsteady as the equator; they have always an ecliptic that crosses their heads and gives them a devious motion."[3] His championing of democracy together with his need to appear as much more than another devious Irish adventurer argued strongly that, rather than use his connections to get himself a seat in the pocket of some Whig oligarch, he should seek election for a seat with a relatively broad franchise. This was in itself a considerable challenge: both Fox and William Pitt, who was to be Sheridan's main antagonist throughout most of his political career, first entered Parliament as the representatives of pocket boroughs.

The Parliament elected in 1774 was dissolved on 1 September 1780. Lord North's administration, though it could still command a comfortable majority for the prosecution of the American war, had been losing authority since March, when it was defeated on a motion of Edmund Burke's seeking to limit government sinecures. In April, John Dunning's famous motion "that the influence of the Crown has increased, is increasing and ought to be diminished" was carried by a majority of eighteen votes. North's authority was further diminished by the anti-Catholic Gordon Riots in June, after which he began to explore the alternatives of a coalition with Rockingham or a dissolution of Parliament.

The Rockingham faction was taken by surprise at the announcement of the dissolution. Sheridan quickly explored various avenues into Parliament, looking into the possibilities of contesting Wootton Bassett, Honiton, and Westbury. But at Devonshire House, Lady Cork suggested that she would give him a letter of introduction to her brother Edward Monckton, who was one of the MPs for Stafford. Up to the first week in September, when he installed himself in Stafford, Sheridan was still pursuing Honiton, a rotten borough, almost certainly as a fallback in case of failure.

Sheridan's candidacy for Stafford owed a great deal to aristocratic patronage. Lord Spencer had interests in the town, and the Duchess of Devonshire also gave Sheridan a letter of introduction to the Spencer retainers. As he afterwards wrote rather obsequiously to her, there were some who required "no other motive to support anyone who appeared honoured with Your Grace's recommendation."[4] But Stafford was relatively democratic, having about 320 electors, most of them tradesmen. Sheridan paid for his own campaign at a cost of about £2,000, paying 250 burgesses £5 each (an illegal but entirely accepted practice), treating voters to beer and meals, and subscribing to charities. The huge expenditure was necessary because his opponents could draw on £1,500 from the government's election fund as well as on their own resources, but in making it he bought not just votes but independence from aristocratic control. He himself had, besides, some semblance of patronage to dispense. Captain Rees Howell Gronow, who was elected for Stafford in 1832, "heard from some very old men amongst my constituents the singular history of the canvas of Sheridan for this immaculate borough."[5] According to him, many voters assumed that since Sheridan was a great man with "unbounded influence" and the control of a theatre, he ought to be able to provide jobs in return for votes.

> One had a son who had a great dramatic talent, another was an admirable scene-painter, others had cousins and nephews who would make excellent door-keepers, lamp-lighters, check-takers, or box-openers; there were tailors, *coiffeurs*, and decorators, who could dress with inimitable effect, the *dramatis personae*. Sheridan listened with his usual bland smile to every request, and complied with them all . . .

He did draw significant support from working-class electors and, according to one hostile account, was notable for "the freedom with which he could enter into the humours of the lowest part of the community."[6] But not all this support was mercenary. After his first day's canvassing in Stafford, Sheridan was approached at his headquarters by a deputation of the working men's committee, headed by Richard Grimshaw, a blacksmith. They had come to interrogate the candidate about his political principles, wishing "to judge a little for ourselves, before we give our vote."[7] Sheridan greeted them with a speech in which he declared that the working classes were "the bone, the sinew, and sterling wealth of the country," and declared himself a "bold and uncompromising advocate of popular rights." But the working men wanted specific guarantees, not abstract blandishments.

Grimshaw put a series of questions to him, telling him that "we know there's something wrong som'were, and we wants to find out its whereabouts, so that we may correct it; and this we can only do by our representative in parliament—cause why? our wives and children want the labour of our hands to keep 'em going, and we ha' no time to spend in politics." Would Sheridan oppose the American war? He would. Would he oppose Lord North, "the poor man's oppressor and the foe of freedom"? He would. Would he oppose taxes on working men? Taxes on labour, Sheridan assured them, were "a great national evil," and where taxation was necessary, it should fall on "those whom your labour has enriched." Would he agree to limit the working day to ten hours, and make employers pay for extra hours when work needed to be done? Ten hours, said Sheridan, was a very modest demand—he himself felt that eight hours a day should be the maximum.

But there was, significantly, one demand that Sheridan would not agree to. Grimshaw asked him to stand up for "liberty of conscience and no Popery." This was a question with a particularly potent undertow. The Gordon Riots the previous June had been triggered by the passage of the Catholic Relief Act, repealing some of the civil disabilities imposed on Catholics by the penal laws. The chapels of Catholic ambassadors had been burned down, Newgate prison destroyed, and the Houses of Parliament threatened by a huge crowd estimated at 60,000 people. And much of the violence had been directed at the opposition, which had strongly supported the act. Edmund Burke, in particular, had been fingered as an Irish Jesuit and threatened with death. Devonshire House had been attacked. Fox and his friend Fitzpatrick had sat with muskets ready to defend Lord

Rockingham's house. So the question was one to which Sheridan, had he been politic, might have given a pusillanimous answer.

He said that he had no difficulty with liberty of conscience. But his refusal to feed anti-Catholic prejudice, though tactfully expressed, was firm. He was, he said, a member of the Protestant Episcopal Church and would "strenuously uphold" his faith. But as a believer in liberty of conscience he would also "yield to every man the same right who may dissent from me in Christian doctrine." Any vote of his on a question of religion would be "in perfect accordance with that conscience which you yourselves claim to exercise, as your inherent right."

Though evidently uncertain about this answer, the working men's committee was enthusiastic about all the others, and their influence on a closely contested election may indeed have been decisive. The Tory candidates had a narrow lead after the first day's polling and maintained it for most of the second. Shortly after two o'clock, with just two hours of polling left and the Tories forty-nine votes ahead, the sound of a drum was heard, and Grimshaw appeared, leading the working men towards the hustings. By three o'clock, Sheridan and Monckton were twenty-three votes ahead, and by four, when the polls closed, Sheridan was a Member of Parliament.

His victory was all the brighter because, outside London, where the opposition came close to a clean sweep, radicals actually lost ground in the provincial cities. Edmund Burke lost his seat in Bristol, largely because of anti-Catholic and anti-Irish feelings, and there were similar Whig losses in Nottingham, Newcastle, and Worcester, though in terms of parliamentary numbers they were offset by gains for the opposition in the county boroughs.

At the conclusion of the poll, Sheridan made a rousing speech to the electors, said to have "done him great credit as an orator."[8] Its content was probably similar to an address to his supporters published a few days later in the *Morning Chronicle*. In it, he seemed at pains to emphasise that his victory depended, not on aristocratic interests, but on a free electorate: "You have now made it appear that you are *the masters of your own rights*, and that you are determined to hold them in your own hands, and to keep your Borough free."[9] This sense that the election had marked the liberation of the borough from aristocratic control was evidently shared by many of Sheridan's supporters, who proposed that 12 September, the day of the election, should thereafter be marked by an annual dinner as "the Day of our deliverance from Slavery."[10] Sheridan told Thomas Creevey a quarter of a century later that the happiest time of his life was that evening after dinner when he sneaked away from the celebrations to be by himself, contemplating the great future that he was sure now lay before him. He had become, at the age of twenty-nine, what he had most wanted to be: a public man.

According to Gronow's informants, however, there was trouble after the election when constituents attempted to call in the promises of jobs at Drury Lane so freely dispensed during the canvass and found them empty. An angry delegation from Stafford arrived at his house in London. Sensing the mood, Sheridan went into action, calling up all his reserves of memory and charm. He walked quietly up to each individual and started to ask questions. Did the jam that Mrs. Grundy was making when last he saw her prove to be delicious? Was Miss Grundy's playing of Steibelt's "Storm" on the piano as spellbinding as ever? How was the younger Miss Grundy getting on with her lessons in velvet painting? Has master Tommy had his vaccinations from Dr. Squill?

> To each the great man had something to say which seemed calculated to soothe the irritation of the hearer, and to prevent him from uttering a word of blame. Each man saw before him the most fascinating individual in the kingdom fixing upon him his dark flashing eye, and addressing him in persuasive accents, with the blandest smile. Sheridan moved through the admiring circle with graceful step, no one venturing to stop him; and as he reached the door he turned round, made an enchanting bow, and having entered the carriage, kissed his hand gracefully to his surrounding friends, and loudly told the coachman to drive to Carlton House.

(This last claim is clearly inaccurate; Carlton House, afterwards one of Sheridan's haunts, was not yet the residence of the Prince of Wales.)

In any case, as soon as his triumph had been secured at Stafford, Sheridan returned to London to canvass for Fox in the continuing election campaign for Westminster. The King had put up £8,000 to get him out, but Sheridan was confident that Fox would win, and his predictions were accurate. When Sheridan took his seat in Parliament for the first time, it was Fox who introduced him, just as a few days earlier he had proposed him for full membership of Brooks's. It is clear that Sheridan was regarded as a substantial catch for the Foxites. When he spoke for the first time, against a petition to have him and Monckton barred from taking their seats (a very common political manoeuvre of the time), he was "heard with particular attention, the House being uncommonly still while he was speaking." Sir Nathaniel Wraxall, a Member of Parliament, wrote: "Even while pronouncing the few sentences which he uttered, the fame of the author of *The Duenna*, *The School for Scandal* and *The Critic* was already so well established as to secure him the greatest attention." He was sneered at by Richard Rigby, Paymaster of the Forces in North's administration, but according to the *Public Advertiser*, "The retort of Mr Sheridan that 'Mr Rigby never had a serious Idea in his life, except for his own Interest,' was so pointed and well-sent that it made [a] deep Impression . . . and even raised the callous Cuticle of the bronzed figure to whom it was directed."[11] Clearly, Sheridan was not overawed by his new surroundings.

He waited until March 1781, however, to make his first really substantial speech, and it was, significantly, on the consequences of the Gordon Riots. Even more significantly, his concern was not only with the riots themselves but with the declaration of martial law that had been used to quell them. He tried to place himself in the middle, between a violent anti-Catholic mob on the one side and an overweening state on the other. He attacked the competence of the Westminster magistrates, calling them "men of tried inability and convicted depravity."[12] (His attack proved effective; he was himself appointed a magistrate of Westminster shortly afterwards.) Their weakness, and that of the police, had given the government the excuse to resort to the "unconstitutional" measure of martial law. He attacked the House of Lords for having praised the King's forbearance in not taking control of government in the midst of the crisis:

> What! was it in His Majesty's power, at that moment, to have trampled on the liberties of the country, and to have introduced military government in the place of the present constitution? Was that the crisis when this might have been established, when the minds of the people were lost in terror and confusion? No, that was not the moment of danger; the crisis was after the interference of the military power, when the chief justice of England said, that it was legal; and asserted that the military acted not as soldiers

> but as citizens; and when this declaration was not objected to by a specific resolution of parliament . . .[13]

He had begun to establish the style which so many of his political interventions would assume over the next three decades. He would, always and habitually, see public liberties as being endangered, not so much by riot and rebellion as by the state itself.

Chapter 17

DREAMS OF EMPTY FAME

Like many successful Irishmen in London, Sheridan dreaded the prospect of his poor relations crossing the Irish Sea to feast on the crumbs of his success. In April 1783, his Dublin connections were expecting him to find them places in the new Irish administration of Lord Derby: "I know Dick is intimate with Lord Derby."[1] The following November, his father wrote to his sister Alicia, in Dublin, warning her to be careful about recommending impecunious cousins to Richard: "If he finds that his poor relations, according to the Irish custom, are to look to him for support, he will soon turn his face against them. You know how great his vanity is, and how much it would mortify him to have any nearly allied to him in blood settled in low station here."[2] As with an invading army that scores extraordinary successes, the very rapidity of his advance exposed his rear. He was vulnerable to counter-attack. Having an Irish actor for a father was one thing, but being associated with a tribe of penniless adventurers was quite another.

And yet, instead of distancing himself from Ireland, he allowed his native country to dominate the early years of his political career. That career really began to take shape in November 1781, when news reached London that the Americans had defeated the British forces at Yorktown and forced them to surrender. In February 1782, the government was defeated in the House of Commons on a motion to end the American war. Lord North, who had attempted to resign as Prime Minister after the defeat at Saratoga in 1777, now finally managed to do so and left office on 20 March. The King had no choice but to call in the Marquis of Rockingham, under whose patronage the Foxites operated. Because of the parliamentary arithmetic, however, Rockingham could govern only in concert with the slippery Lord Shelburne, the holder of vast Irish estates, who led his own Whig faction and who was loathed by Burke and deeply distrusted by Sheridan.

Fox and Lord Shelburne became joint Secretaries of State: the former for the Northern (foreign affairs) Office, the latter for the Southern (home) Office. Sheridan, less than two years in Parliament, became under-secretary of state for the Northern Office, effectively Fox's deputy minister for foreign affairs. He entered an administration which had taken office on the understanding that there would be no royal veto over American independence, and with a broad if vague commitment to parliamentary reform, but which was united on little else. Shelburne was determined to use his own closeness to the King to challenge Rockingham for the real leadership of the government.

Tensions between the Foxite and Shelburne factions of the new administration would be felt in virtually every area of its operation, but for Sheridan the sharpest point of conflict was Ireland. Officially, Ireland was none of his business: it came under Shelburne's area of responsibility, not Fox's. But unofficially, it was at the heart of his concerns. The American war had conjured up tantalising visions for Protestant Ireland. If colonies across the Atlantic could take on a life of their own and eventually assert their independence, what about colonies across the Irish Sea? The Americans themselves made the connection early on. The writings of Irish Protestant Patriots like Swift, Charles Lucas, and Henry Flood were often quoted in American revolutionary pamphlets. In Ireland itself, ironically, it was the formation of volunteer corps to defend the country in the absence of the regular troops, who were fighting the Americans, that gave a critical impetus to popular and parliamentary demands for independence. When, in 1778, moves to lift restrictions on Irish trade were stymied by opposition from English merchants, economic self-interest gave a solid base to the political rhetoric of Patriot leaders like Henry Grattan. In November 1779, on King William's birthday, the Dublin Volunteers assembled outside the Irish Houses of Parliament in College Green with placards on their cannon reading "Free trade or else." The following month, Lord North, fearing the potential consequences of armed disaffection in Ireland on top of the American war, capitulated to their demands.

What was most disturbing about the Volunteers, though, was the fact that their movement threatened to break the bounds of Protestant politics, and to acknowledge in the public realm the presence in Ireland of the Catholic majority. Though officially confined to Protestants, the Volunteer corps in many parts of Ireland silently allowed many Catholics to join. And, even more seriously, the ideas they and their parliamentary supporters began to employ in their quarrels with England also carried dangerous messages for Catholics.

For a while the victory on free trade seemed to take the sting out of political radicalism in Ireland, but the imminence of American independence revived the issues of representation and reform. A convention of the Volunteers at Dungannon in February 1782 renewed the demand for Ireland to have legislative independence. The Chief Secretary for Ireland, William Eden, believed that there was no choice but to compromise and proposed that the Declaratory Act, which gave the Westminster Parliament the right to legislate for Ireland, should be repealed. Lord North, however, stood out against change. By the time he fell from power and Sheridan came into office, the agitation for at the very least a more equal relationship between Ireland and Britain was at fever pitch and, with the Irish Parliament due to reconvene on 16 April, there was little time to work out a coherent response. Both personally and as a member of the government, Sheridan had to take a stand.

It is likely that from an early age, Sheridan would have been taught to look upon the Patriot leader Henry Grattan with deep admiration, even though at first sight his rhetoric of Irish patriotism might seem at odds with Thomas Sheridan's project of creating a unified British culture. In general, Thomas Sheridan's politics were monarchist and imperial. James Boswell records a debate between him and Benjamin Victor, in which the latter argued for a republic but Thomas "stood up for monarchy." But he was also devoted to the ideal of an enlightened, civilised Ireland, and in Irish politics he was a devoted supporter of Grattan, who in his eyes not only had the inestimable advantage of being a great orator, but seemed to embody a kind of Irish Protestant civic virtue. "My Father," Betsy Sheridan noted in her journal, "is deeply interested in whatever relates to his Hero Grattan."[3] In November 1783, when Grattan was ill, Thomas wrote to Alicia of his "great anxiety for the fate of Grattan. I look upon his life to be of more importance not only to Ireland but to the general interests of the British Empire than that of any one man living."[4]

This family faith was now especially useful, for it allowed Sheridan to draw on his most obvious resource when it came to Irish politics: his brother. Charles was a member of the Irish Parliament and had a successful practice as a lawyer, but he was also ambitious. As soon as Richard came into office, Charles was asking for a government position. Sheridan assured him that "mon Frère is not likely to be forgotten,"[5] and Charles was soon appointed under-secretary for military affairs in the Irish government. Sheridan knew his elder brother well enough to know that he was not animated by deep political principles. If he had been in any doubt about his brother's motives, Charles's letter to him looking for an appointment would have put him straight, for in it he imparted advice that revealed his own thinking on the purposes of political office with absolute clarity: "As you may now be in a situation in which you may obtain some substantial advantage for yourself, for God's sake improve the opportunity to the utmost, and don't let dreams of empty fame (of which you have enough in conscience) carry you away from your solid interests." As if this crass attitude to politics was not enough, there was also the fact that their younger sister, Betsy, who had to live in Charles's household in Dublin, was being treated like a poor relation. By now, even Thomas Sheridan, for whom Charles had been a golden boy, was bitterly disillusioned with him. He wrote to his other daughter, Alicia, that Charles was "devoid of every principle of common justice and humanity . . . The whole of his conduct for more than a year past has given me deep concern. The vanities of the world have laid hold of him and he has put himself under the guidance of a blind ambition. I no longer expect to see in life such a Charles as my fond and partial fancy had figured out to me."[6]

But in spite of all this, and of their long-standing rivalry, Sheridan had another motive for helping his brother: he intended to use Charles as a conduit for information and as a co-conspirator. Over the coming years, Charles would be his eyes and ears in Dublin. In 1783, the Lord Lieutenant in Dublin, Earl Temple, mentioned to his brother in London "the pleasant private interchange of the two Sheridans which you may possibly trace in London as I do here."[7] That interchange was evident even before Richard was elected to Parliament. Charles wrote two pamphlets in support of the Irish Patriot cause. The first, published in 1779 and highly inflected with the Enlightenment ideals of Locke and Montesquieu, argued that since government derives its power from the community that established it, no British government could have lawful power in Ireland.[8] In this, the pamphlet was the nearest the Patriot movement came to what might be called outright nationalism. And it is likely that Richard at the very least approved of its contents. It echoed almost word for word some of his own arguments in his draft papers on America. In the latter, for instance, the claim that Britain had a right to America by right of conquest was countered with the argument that, in that case, America must belong to the descendants of the conquerors themselves, the colonists. In Charles's pamphlet, the same rhetorical device is used: he points out that if a right of conquest were to be claimed in relation to Ireland it would belong to the Irish Ascendancy, not to Britain. Such similarities suggest that the two brothers may have collaborated to some degree on the pamphlet.

Now, in 1782, Charles Sheridan anticipated that the Irish House of Commons, when it reconvened, would "certainly" pass a motion declaring total legislative independence, and told Richard so: "Read the resolutions of the Volunteers, and you will be enabled to form some idea of the spirit which at present pervades this country."[9] In fact, the crisis broke even before the Dublin Parliament reassembled. On 8 April, when the Westminster Parliament convened after the recess, William Eden, the outgoing Chief Secretary for Ireland, rose to submit the resignation of the viceroy, Lord Carlisle. He then unexpectedly put forward a motion to "repeal so much of the Act of George I as asserted a right to the king and parliament of Great Britain to make laws to bind the Kingdom of Ireland"—the famous "Sixth of George the First." The motion was sprung without warning on the new administration, and Eden's motive was almost certainly to cause as much trouble for the government as possible. In spite of shouts for him to withdraw the motion, he refused to do so, and threatened to go back to Dublin to tell the Irish Parliament that the question was being evaded by the new administration.

Sheridan knew from his contacts with Charles in Dublin that a repeal of the Act was vital. Charles had written to him a few days earlier, "The sooner you repeal the Sixth of George I the better; for, believe me, nothing short of that can now preserve union and cordiality between the two countries." Sheridan told Charles that he believed that now was "the precise time" for repeal, and begged for news of what Henry Grattan and the *éminence grise* of the Patriot movement, Lord Charlemont, thought.[10] Eden's manoeuvre had therefore placed him in "rather an awkward situation."[11]

Just as the Speaker was about to put the motion, Sheridan stood up and reportedly declared that "he could not sit still and see a question of this importance rejected or evaded in the manner which it was likely to be." While deploring Eden's "extraordinary conduct," Sheridan nonetheless declared himself "an enemy to the principle of the declaratory law in question, which he had always regarded as a tyrannous usurpation in this country" and said that "if the motion was put he would vote for it."[12] The motion was promptly withdrawn. He had managed to buy some time for the administration while making his own principles clear. But he had also gone much further than the leaders of his own administration were prepared to go. Fox and Rockingham were prepared to repeal the Sixth of George I, but only when there was a new Anglo-Irish agreement in place, creating a "new system and new arrangement of connection between the two kingdoms." Legislative independence was to be conceded to Ireland not on principle but as part of a negotiated settlement. This was the brief which the cabinet gave on that very day to the new Lord Lieutenant, the Duke of Portland, and his Chief Secretary, Richard Fitzpatrick. Sheridan's description of the act as "a tyrannous usurpation" effectively conceded the justice of the Irish case even before negotiations could begin. He was, in the most dramatic fashion, declaring not just Ireland's independence but his own.

He now wrote to Charles asking him to use all his influence to get the Irish Parliament to adjourn for a short while so that he and Fox could work out an official line on Ireland. After convening on 16 April, the Irish Parliament did indeed adjourn for a week, but not before it had passed a motion of Grattan's calling for legislative independence.[13]

Shelburne, the minister officially responsible for Ireland, instructed Fitzpatrick in mid-April to take a firm line with the Patriots and, by "arguing and persevering," to ensure that concessions were kept to a minimum.[14] But the popular mood in Ireland was such that Portland began to fear, as he wrote to Fox, that unless Grattan's demands were acceded to, "government cannot exist here in its present shape" and Britain would have to "renounce all claims to this country." By 15 May, the cabinet had capitulated, and two days later the Sixth of George I, Poynings Law, and the Mutiny Act—the three pillars of direct British rule in Ireland—were repealed at Westminster.

Sheridan was delighted that "Ireland has got her rights."[15] But he also knew that Shelburne saw legislative independence as a concession, not a right, and that he remained determined to secure a "final adjustment" of the relationship between the two kingdoms in return. Shelburne wrote secretly to Portland in Dublin, setting out what this arrangement should entail: the Irish Parliament should recognise London as the "superintending power" on all matters and should agree to the economic integration of the two islands. Sheridan however, wrote privately to Fitzpatrick, criticising these despatches and more or less encouraging Fitzpatrick to ignore them: "It is impossible not to see a reserve and disingenuous management in them that cannot be very pleasing to you who are to act under them." Shelburne was implying that it was only Portland's warnings about the "State of Ireland" that had led to the concession of legislative independence, and for Sheridan, who saw it as a matter of Irish "rights," this was unacceptable. He urged Fitzpatrick, on Fox's authority, to stand up to Shelburne by "not *giving way* or *conceding in the least*" to his demands.[16]

Sheridan was by now convinced, in any case, that his misgivings about the alliance with Shelburne were well placed. He wrote to his long-standing friend Thomas Grenville, who had been sent by Fox to Paris to negotiate American independence with Benjamin Franklin, that Shelburne would probably try to thwart any treaty with the Americans. He confided, prophetically; "I grow suspicious of him in every respect, the more I see of every transaction of his."[17] As with Ireland, Sheridan felt that American independence should be recognised as a right, and not "conceded" in negotiations with the French, not least because this would deprive France of the opportunity to appear as the sole champion of American rights.

This same line was put forward by Fox at cabinet on 30 June, but defeated. The following day, Rockingham, who had been ill on and off since the formation of the administration, and seriously so for the previous week, died. With the King's encouragement, Shelburne proposed himself as Prime Minister; Fox and his colleagues withdrew from the government. Sheridan supported this decision to resign, telling Grenville that the choice facing Fox and the others was "whether, having lost their power, they ought to stay and lose their characters."[18] His dislike of Shelburne had become so strong that, in December, at the annual dinner of the reformist Society for Constitutional Information, of which he was a member, Sheridan argued publicly with the radical Horne Tooke over the latter's support for Shelburne.[19]

He and Fox therefore faced back into opposition but, as Sheridan put it, "woefully thinned and disconcerted, I fear," for only one other member of the cabinet, Lord John Cavendish, Chancellor of the Exchequer, followed them out of office. One consolation was that with Rockingham's death, Fox himself became the leader of the Whig faction in the House of Commons, placing Sheridan closer at least to the top of his own party.

Already, on Irish affairs, Sheridan had demonstrated his willingness to take an independent and more radical line than his friend and ally Fox. And very quickly he was forced to pit his own judgement against his leader's, for in the aftermath of the fall of the Rockingham administration, Fox made two disastrous mistakes. The first was in the choice of a titular head of the party, who had to be an established magnate. Fox offered the job to the plodding, and in time reactionary, Duke of Portland, who had been Lord Lieutenant in Ireland during their brief period of power. And the second was, in the short term, even more foolish. In February 1783, when Shelburne failed to have his peace treaty with France endorsed by Parliament, Fox entered into negotiations with the very man who had run the American war, Lord North, with a view to forming a coalition.

Sheridan opposed the idea. Lord John Russell told Thomas Moore in 1823 that Sheridan "walked about for several hours with Fox, trying to dissuade him from the coalition with Lord North, and that the conversation ended with Fox's saying, 'It is as fixed as the Hanover succession.' "[20] A year later, after the coalition had broken up, Sheridan himself told the House of Commons:

> When the idea of a coalition with the noble Lord [North] was first started, I confess that I advised my right honourable friend [Fox] not to accept of it; and my reason was this:—my right honourable friend had great popularity, which he might lose by a coalition; respectable friends, whom he might disgust; and prejudices of the strongest nature to combat . . . Mutual diffidence between men long accustomed to oppose one another might nat-

> urally be expected. The prejudices of the public all concurred to prevent this coalition. The middling class of people, for whom I have the highest respect, and to whom the House of Commons must look for support in every emergency, sooner than to the great, are certainly not the best to judge of nice and refined points of politics. Accustomed to judge of measures by men, I apprehend that they would give themselves no time to examine the principles, motives, and grounds of a coalition: but condemn it on its first appearance, merely because it is composed of men who had long been political enemies. On these grounds, full of apprehension for the character of my right honourable friend, I most certainly gave him my advice against a coalition.[21]

Sheridan insisted, nevertheless, that his confidence in Fox had not been shaken by the formation of a coalition with North, under the nominal leadership of the Duke of Portland, and he joined the government again, this time as joint Secretary to the Treasury, along with Edmund Burke's kinsman, Richard. The new government took office on 2 April 1783, and held together until December. During this short period, however, there were three key developments in Sheridan's public role, each of which was to resonate right through to the end of the century. One was the beginning of tension between himself and Edmund Burke. Another was the onset of his interest in the affairs of the East India Company and its ruler, Warren Hastings. And the third was the emergence as Prime Minister of William Pitt, the man against whom all Sheridan's political energies would be directed for the next twenty-three years.

Sheridan did not allow his membership in the government to quell his radical sympathies. Aside from the purely financial questions which related to his office, he supported a mild motion for parliamentary reform, which Lord North opposed, complaining only that it did not go far enough. He opposed a bill to allow for the arrest of persons found at night-time with "implements for breaking into houses." If it was passed, he said, "a ladder on a poor labourer's shoulder might be deemed such an implement; as might also a strong shoe, because with a strong shoe a man might possibly kick a door open." He added that the way to tackle crime was to begin with the police, "for until the police should be reformed, little reformation could be expected among the lower classes."[22]

Balanced between speaking for a government and remaining as

an independent voice for change, Sheridan seemed to have carved out a position for himself. He seemed, furthermore, to be increasingly challenging Edmund Burke for a place of authority within the Foxite ranks. Certainly the relationship between the two Irishmen was no longer that of elder statesman to young acolyte. On 2 May, when Burke as paymaster of the forces was attacked by the opposition for reappointing an official who had been removed on charges of corruption, he got to his feet "in a violent fit of passion . . . but he could proceed no further for his friend, Mr Sheridan, by this time had pulled him down to his seat, from a motive of friendship, lest his heat should betray him into some intemperate expressions that might offend the house."[23] Sir Nathaniel Wraxall, at this time a follower of Lord North, noted that Sheridan's air of command contrasted favourably with Burke's passion: "Sheridan, by a wonderful combination of almost all talents which can meet in man, under the control of unalterable equality of temper began already to compete with Burke in parliamentary estimation; and frequently obtained a more ready or patient hearing from the House. Every day, while it confirmed the ascendant which he had acquired, placed him higher among the most distinguished supports of Administration."[24]

There are certainly signs of tetchiness in a letter that Sheridan wrote to Burke around this time in response to a complaint from the latter that is now lost. In it, he protested that "nothing could mortify me more than to think that you can for a moment believe me such a coxcomb as to receive any advice or hint of any sort from you with any other feeling than the most serious and grateful Attention. I did not express what I meant last night or you would not think otherwise, which I am afraid by your Note you do."[25] Such misunderstandings imply, at least on Burke's part, the first stirrings of resentment.

The growing tension between Sheridan and Burke played a part in the one piece of real political business attempted by the government: the reform of the East India Company, the extraordinary semi-private enterprise which controlled Britain's Indian colonies. In 1781, Sir Philip Francis, author of the Junius Letters that had excited Sheridan as a teenager, returned from a period as a member of the Bengal Council in India with an implacable hatred of the governor-general, Warren Hastings, and began a campaign against him. This crusade was joined, with all the immense moral and intellectual force of which he was capable, by Edmund Burke, who began, through the parliamentary select committee on India, to investigate and report on charges of corruption and oppression against Hastings. Burke, in turn, persuaded Fox to make legislation on India the centrepiece of the government's legislative programme.

The two India Bills, drafted by Burke, aimed to prevent and punish abuses of power by the East India Company, to ensure the observance of Indian rights and customs, and to place the company under the supervision of seven commissioners and nine assistant commissioners, all to be appointed by Parliament. But this last measure seemed to place enormous patronage in the hands of the government of the day, making it easy for powerful company interests inside and outside Parliament to attack it as an attempt by Fox to undermine all chartered rights and to accuse him of seeking to establish himself as an Eastern potentate. The company's political agent, Major John Scott, was organising resistance to the bills, and on 7 November, a meeting of the proprietors (shareholders) sent a defiant message of support to Warren Hastings and urged him to stay on in India. When George III's political agent Charles Jenkinson made it clear that the King also opposed the bill, the scale of the challenge which the government faced became obvious. The chances of defeat, especially in the House of Lords, were very high.

Sheridan's attitude was, as he explained it sixteen months later, one which mixed principle and pragmatism.[26] He believed that the government had two options. One was to recall Hastings from India and "punish him exemplarily" for his crimes against the Indians. For this, he believed, there was neither enough time nor enough political support. The other was to bring in the India Bills, draw a line under the past, and ensure that no abuses occurred in the future. This, he believed, offered room for at least some attempt to cool the opposition of Hastings's supporters.

On the day the bills were introduced, therefore, and with Fox's approval, Sheridan met with one of Warren Hastings's supporters. This meeting was especially poignant since the supporter was none other than his old friend and co-author Nathaniel Halhed. Halhed had just returned from India, where he had become one of Hastings's most trusted lieutenants. Meeting him again in these circumstances, Sheridan must have been struck by the thought that he himself would, if he had accepted his friend's offer, have become a servant rather than a scourge of the East India Company. According to an account written many years later by the son of another of Hastings's closest allies in India, Halhed was "so guileless" that he believed that his old friend Sheridan could be persuaded that the charges against Hastings were baseless. He asked for a meeting and proceeded "with a heart overflowing with candour" to demonstrate to Sheridan that he was wrong. He was met, on the contrary, with "an artificial reserve and an evasive arrogance which at once closed the door to all negotiation. From that moment, Halhed and Sheridan never met or spoke with each other upon amicable terms."[27]

It is just as likely, however, that it was Sheridan who asked for the meeting. The government was seriously concerned about rumours that the French were offering to provide Hastings with troops so that he could break his connection with Britain and declare himself "the sovereign prince of Indostan."[28] Sheridan, therefore, asked Halhed to go to Hastings's agent, Major Scott, to ask "whether Mr Hastings would come home, if recalled." Scott subsequently claimed in the House of Commons that Sheridan had, through Halhed, offered Hastings immunity from prosecution in return for dropping his opposition to the bills. Sheridan challenged this claim and insisted that "there had not been the most distant idea of bartering with Mr Hastings for his support of the India bill." Halhed, moreover, supported Sheridan's account of the meeting, and Scott was forced to withdraw his claim and to assure the House that Halhed had "confirmed . . . every syllable which Mr Sheridan has uttered." Since Halhed and Sheridan's friendship had been destroyed by their differences on Hastings, this is powerful testimony. The imputation, made most recently by Conor Cruise O'Brien, that Sheridan had been trying to "buy off" Hastings and his friends is completely unfounded.[29]

In any case, Edmund Burke, who dominated the parliamentary select committee on India, scuppered all attempts to neutralise Hastings's supporters by releasing on the same day that the India Bill was published a report accusing Hastings of personal corruption. While Sheridan and Fox were prepared to mix principle and pragmatism in order to get a decent measure of control over the East India Company and to ensure the survival of the government, Burke was engaged on an epic moral crusade which he would pursue to the end of his life.

Once the bills went to the House of Commons, Sheridan gave them his full support. Little of his speech survives, but it was regarded at the time as a tour de force, combining close argument and brilliant raillery. Opposition speakers used quotations from Shakespeare, Milton, and the Book of Revelations to damn the bills. Sheridan, working from memory and a quick reading of the biblical passages, took up the allusions, "foiling each of them with their own weapons, and citing, with the most happy ease and correctness, passages from almost the same pages that controverted their quotations and told strongly for the bill. He quoted three more verses from the Revelations, by which he metamorphosed the beast with seven heads, with crowns on them, into seven angels, clothed in pure and white linen."[30]

The bills passed comfortably through the House of Commons and went on to the House of Lords, where the King had determined to ambush the government. He authorised Lord Temple to let it be known that "whoever voted for the India Bill was not only not his friend, but would be considered by him as an enemy." With this threat of banishment to the exterior darkness beyond the reaches of royal patronage, the India Bills were roundly defeated in the House of Lords on 17 December. The King, with rather indecent haste, demanded that Fox and North hand back their seals of office, and called in William Pitt to form a government. The speed of the transaction strongly suggested that Pitt must have been approached by the King even before the bills were defeated and that he was, in effect, plotting against his own government.

Sheridan, again in opposition after a second brief stay in office, believed with Fox that the manner of their dismissal was both treacherous and illegal. And this sense of outrage gradually began to resolve itself around the figure of Pitt, the beneficiary of the King's high-handed interference. When Pitt called an election, Sheridan's judgement as to how public opinion would regard the Fox-North coalition was depressingly vindicated: Fox's supporters were massacred at the polls. But Sheridan himself was comfortably returned from Stafford, and the fact that Pitt's government spent only £400 in trying to unseat him suggests that his position was assumed to be almost impregnable. With the scale of the defeat, and the fact that Pitt used every possible manoeuvre to try to prevent Fox from taking the seat he had won at Westminster, resentment of Pitt began to harden into a hatred that would be regularly re-fuelled over the coming years.

Sheridan also confronted the reality that he could do very little about the King's coup. His own ascent within Parliament had been astonishing. Within three years of taking his seat, he had forged an independent line on Ireland, established himself as an ally rather than a mere follower of Fox, begun to outstrip Burke in parliamentary eminence, and held office twice. There seemed, for a while, to be no limit to the power he might achieve. But, with the sudden defeat and collapse of the government, he had woken from those dreams of empty fame to the realisation that the power of the House of Commons itself was cruelly confined within limits set by the East India Company, the aristocracy, and, above all, the monarchy. It is not surprising that it was precisely at this time that he began to cultivate a relationship through which he might begin to undermine the royal prerogative from the inside.

Chapter 18

THE CATHOLIC QUEEN

When Sheridan first became his friend, George, Prince of Wales, the heir to the throne, was just twenty-one. Tall, handsome, and charming, he was not yet the corpulent figure he was later to become. He was markedly more intelligent than his father, a lively, sometimes witty conversationalist, and an avid reader. He was a good mimic and a fine singer, with a resonant baritone voice. More important, he was out of favour with his father and had drifted into the orbit of Devonshire House, where the attitudes to drinking, gambling, and sex were greatly to his liking. He and Fox were close enough to share mistresses—first the actress Perdita Robinson and then Fox's long-time lover, Elizabeth Armistead. Either at Devonshire House or at Brooks's, the Prince met Sheridan, who became, over time, one of his closest and most trusted friends.

The friendship was genuine enough. He and Sheridan's shared interest in drinking, music, literature, and practical jokes meant that they enjoyed each other's company. But the relationship was also innately and unavoidably political. The Prince developed, as part of his Oedipal revolt, a sincere attachment to the principles of Charles Fox, the politician his father most abhorred. He also had a more specific interest in politics: he enjoyed spending and he expected his political friends to help raise funds. As his twenty-first birthday approached, giving him the right to a separate establishment and his own household at Carlton House, Pall Mall, Fox came into office, and the Prince expected to be granted £100,000 a year. The King furiously opposed this, and for a time, the wrangling over the

Prince's income seemed likely to bring down the Fox-North coalition long before the India Bills did so. In the end, a compromise was reached, but the Prince's identification with the Foxites had been so solidified that he made a rare appearance at the House of Lords and for the first vote on the India Bills supported the government.

After the election that followed, the Prince even joined Fox's triumphal procession through Westminster, wearing the party colours, the buff and blue of the American Army. To the Foxites, routed by the King, all of this seemed to hold out the alluring prospect that they would, eventually, have their very own monarch. At Brooks's, bets were taken on how long it would be before the King died and his errant son succeeded to the throne. Paradoxically, the most democratic faction in the House of Commons acquired a special interest in the death of the monarch and the survival of the monarchy.

For Sheridan, after the terrible political defeats of late 1783 and early 1784, this hope would become a personal lodestar. Not just his party's prospects but his own ambitions became bound up with the whims of a callow, engaging, petulant, and utterly self-centred young man. For genuine as his developing friendship with the Prince undoubtedly was, it was also of great advantage in the struggle for pre-eminence within the Foxite ranks. Again, rather paradoxically, it increased his sense of independence from the Whig oligarchy. His personal hold over the Prince meant that he possessed the key to an asset they needed and so depended much less on the favour of the likes of the Duke of Portland, the party leader.

Within months of their meeting, Sheridan's friendship with the Prince was already leading to wild gossip. In September 1784, Sheridan was sent into a "very violent" fury by an attack on him in the *Morning Post* under the signature "Neptune" (probably a pseudonym for Captain Edward Thompson, a naval officer with a particular hatred for both Sheridan and the Prince), which "exposed him as a swindler and the Prince as a drunkard." Thompson claimed that the Prince gave Sheridan an "unlimited draught on his treasury" to bribe the printers to reveal the name of the author.[1]

Certainly time spent in the Prince's company was bound to enhance Sheridan's own growing reputation for dissolution and profligacy. The friendship widened the gap between Sheridan's political beliefs, which were those of the enlightened middle class, and his social behaviour, which was marked by all the indulgences that were most abhorrent to that stratum of society. For Eliza, who was evidently delighted by her husband's social success, it was taken for granted that intimacy with the Prince involved a willingness to indulge in the fashionable passion for gambling—and losing—small fortunes at the game of faro. Gambling was, for the Whig oligarchs, an obsession rather than an entertainment, the ultimate gesture of aristocratic disdain for mere money-grubbers. Fox, who ran his own gambling bank at Brooks's, had lost £140,000 before the age of twenty-five. The Duchess of Devonshire ran up huge debts at the faro table. At around this time, Eliza wrote to the manager of the Prince's household, Captain J. W. Payne: ". . . as this is my first attempt at an assembly, if I am sinning against the rules of etiquette pray excuse it, and in a proper manner inform the Prince that I mean to be at home on the 17th and 24th of this month and that I hope his Royal Highness will honor me by his company. There will be faro and all sorts of gambling . . ."[2]

For Sheridan himself, such aristocratic indulgences were embarrassingly at odds with the middle-class values which he upheld in public. He did not himself gamble on cards—though he was forever placing bets on the outcome of real events—and he had, in 1781, spoken in the House on "the vice of gaming." He attacked the government-sponsored lottery on the grounds that "it not only promotes the spirit of gambling among the lower orders of society, but by suspending all industrious pursuits, tends to introduce every kind of depravity." Now, just three years later, that spirit and its attendant depravities were being given free rein in his own house. And the charge of hypocrisy to which such contradictions laid him open would always be the price he would have to pay for whatever access to political power he acquired through the Prince. Towards the end of 1784, that relationship also began to draw him into the swampy terrain of his own ancestral past. In the oddest paradox of all, as Sheridan became more and more intimate with the heir to the British Protestant succession, so he also had to enter into unstable territory where Catholicism and treason loomed.

When Frances Sheridan had died in France in 1766, her husband, Thomas, even in his grief, had taken pains to ensure that their children were left in the care of good Protestants. Later, when Richard was in France with Eliza, he was not so particular about religion, getting a Catholic priest to marry him and allowing his wife to stay in a convent. He was, at least outwardly, an Anglican, but his attitude was close to that of his sister who, in a letter in 1797, put it to him,

"I am in moral and political notions a Protestant as well as in religion, and I admit it to be very possible that a person may be right who neither says nor does as I do." Richard's private beliefs tended towards agnosticism, and he later described his attitude to religious faith as one of "selfish incredulity" that was "not quite hardened" into outright atheism.[3]

This kind of loose religious affiliation was not that of the British state and, more particularly, of its monarchy, which essentially embodied the notion of an indissoluble link between Britishness and Protestantism. In the mid-1780s, however, this absolute assumption was fundamentally threatened in a way that it had not been since the Glorious Revolution of 1688. Richard Sheridan found himself close to the epicentre of what could have been a constitutional earthquake.

In 1784, the Prince of Wales fell in love with Mrs. Maria Fitzherbert, twice widowed and six years older than himself. There was nothing surprising or problematic about a young heir to the throne fawning on a more experienced woman. The problem was that Mrs. Fitzherbert not merely came from an old Roman Catholic family in the north of England but was awkwardly serious about her religion. For the Prince of Wales to keep a Catholic mistress would be a scandal well within the broad latitude allowed to royalty. But a good Catholic like Maria Fitzherbert would never consent to be a mistress. And for the heir to the throne to marry her would be not scandalous, not even intolerable, but illegal to the point of treason. Two keystones of the constitution—the Act of Settlement and the Royal Marriage Act—absolutely forbade it. At best, the Prince would have to give up his claim to the throne. At worst, the legitimacy of the Protestant monarchy could be called into question.

For Sheridan, this most awkward of entanglements had the effect of tightening his own hold over the Prince. Previously, the Prince had looked to Sheridan for friendship but to Fox for political guidance. Fox, however, made no secret of his fierce opposition to any marriage with Mrs. Fitzherbert, and the Prince decided to lie to his mentor, assuring him that "there not only is but never was any ground" for rumours that he would marry her.[4] Mrs. Fitzherbert, for her part, knew that Fox wanted her to be content with the role of mistress and hated him for it. The combined effect of his own breach of trust and of his beloved's influence weakened the bond between the Prince and Fox, and made Sheridan, a thirty-five-year-old Irish actor's son, the most trusted adviser to the heir to the British throne. It was a moment that would shape the rest of Sheridan's life, conjuring up a tantalising vision of great power always in sight and always out of reach.

Events came to a head on 15 December 1785, when, in the drawing room of Mrs. Fitzherbert's house, she and the Prince of Wales were married by a young, debt-ridden Anglican priest. The only others present were the bride's brother and uncle; the Prince wrote out a marriage certificate which he, his new wife, and the two witnesses signed. Almost at once, London was humming with rumours not only that the Prince had married a Catholic but that the ceremony had been performed by a Catholic priest. Soon the rumours were given both visible form and direct political content. In March 1786, the great political cartoonist James Gillray published a print in which the Prince and Mrs. Fitzherbert are being married in a French Catholic church. The priest is Edmund Burke, already established in cartoon iconography as an Irish Jesuit. The bride is being given away by Fox. The two witnesses are the Prince's crony George Hanger, a notorious rake and dandy, and Sheridan, who stands with a napkin under his arm and a bottle of wine in each of his coat pockets, presumably ready to serve the wedding feast. The print inevitably sold in very large numbers.

To avoid the stirrings of scandal and to enjoy his wedded bliss, the Prince withdrew to Brighton and made a passable stab at living a relatively frugal life. He cut himself off from all his London circle, with the exception of Sheridan, who visited him regularly. That he was now the only political contact the Prince retained, and that Mrs. Fitzherbert saw him as a friend and protector, make it certain not only that he knew all about the marriage but that, unlike Fox, he expressed no criticism of it. Rumours that the Prince had, beyond breaking the law, threatened the whole fabric of the British constitutional settlement might have continued unchallenged had it not been that the Prince had to make himself the subject of public debate, for he was, as usual, deep in debt. By the spring of 1787, it was no longer possible for him to lie low.

Since late 1786, the Prince had been trying to raise money, but the Whigs, including Sheridan, were reluctant to raise the subject in Parliament for fear of drawing attention to the embarrassing subject of his marriage to Mrs. Fitzherbert. Only with some difficulty had Sheridan managed to dissuade him from borrowing money in

France, a move that would certainly have been regarded by the English public as giving hostages to the old enemy. Eventually, the Prince went behind Sheridan's back and got an independent Member of Parliament, Alderman Nathaniel Newnham, to put his case to Parliament.

On 20 April 1787, Newnham gave notice that he intended to bring forward a motion on the "embarrassed state of affairs" of the Prince. At once, however, a Tory, John Rolle, rose to say that the Prince's position was "a question which went immediately to affect our constitution in Church and State." This was a clear signal that any discussion of the Prince's affairs could not be confined to money, and would also involve the threat of a constitutional crisis presented by his marriage to a Catholic. William Pitt, taking the cue, warned that if Newnham persisted with his motion, he would have no choice but to disclose "circumstances which I would otherwise think it my duty to conceal." With Fox absent, Sheridan decided to respond at once by calling Pitt's bluff. He said that Pitt's insinuations made it impossible for the Prince's friends to withdraw the motion. Pitt, realising that he might have gone too far, backed off and assured the House that the only circumstances to which he had been referring were the Prince's financial problems.

Sheridan knew that Rolle would almost certainly go further the next time, and that some kind of strategy for dealing with questions about the Prince's marriage would have to be put in place. His own chances of improving his position through his influence over the Prince would be ruined if, after all, his protégé were no longer heir to the throne. That night, he went to talk to the Prince at Carlton House. It was clear to them both that the marriage might have to be denied in public and that, if this became necessary, Mrs. Fitzherbert's silence was essential. The following day, Sheridan went to see her. Though he did not tell her directly that a public statement denying the marriage might become imperative, he urged her to be discreet at all costs. She was, in fact, already well aware of the danger she was in and assured Sheridan that she had no intention of breaking her silence. But she asked him to protect her, and he agreed to do so.[5]

The Prince, in the meantime, continued to lie to Fox, assuring him that no marriage had taken place. Armed with these assurances, Fox decided to put an end once and for all to the rumours, not only of the Prince's marriage, but of his own supposed attendance at the ceremony. On 30 April, he stood up in the House of Commons and denounced, almost certainly in good faith, the "monstrous report of a fact which has not the smallest degree of foundation" as "a low malicious falsehood." The short-term effect was a great triumph for the Whigs—Fox, surely, would not have dared make such violent assertions had the rumours been true. But it was a triumph that presaged utter disaster. If now the truth emerged, the Prince would be debarred from the throne, Fox would be exposed as a brazen liar, and all their mutual friends, most especially Sheridan, would be assumed to have been party to at best a gross deception of the nation, at worst a vile plot to subvert the Protestant state.

Mrs. Fitzherbert was outraged. The Prince found her in "an agony of tears" next morning, and she later raged to Sir Philip Francis that Fox had "rolled me in the kennel like a street walker."[6] She even refused to see her husband, increasing the danger that she might make some kind of public comment or gesture. He, in turn, was "in tears, walking about the room and beating his head against the walls."[7] He confessed to the young Whig aristocrat Charles Grey that the marriage had in fact taken place, and asked Grey to say so in the House. Grey, however, refused. Yet somebody had to find a way to pacify Mrs. Fitzherbert without at the same time suggesting that Fox had lied to the House. "Sheridan," the Prince gasped, "must say something."

Rather bizarrely, Sheridan was the only person who could save the British state from a constitutional crisis. And such was his confidence in his own ability to deploy language with the infinite ambiguity required to satisfy Mrs. Fitzherbert's honour without admitting that the Prince of Wales had married a Papist that he immediately agreed to do so. On 4 May, when Newnham's motion came up, it was immediately withdrawn. Sheridan then rose and delivered a masterpiece of equivocation, full of careful mollifications and deft evasions, into which he slipped the requisite remark about Mrs. Fitzherbert:

> Whilst his Royal Highness's feelings had no doubt to be considered on this occasion, he must take the liberty of saying, however some might think it a subordinate consideration, that there was *another person* entitled in every delicate and honourable mind, to the same attention—one whom he would not otherwise venture to describe or allude to, but by saying it was a name which malice or igno-

> rance alone could attempt to injure, on whose conduct truth could fix no just reproach, and whose character claimed, and was entitled to, the truest and most general respect.[8]

As a statement of fact, this was highly disingenuous, but as a sleight of tongue it was brilliant. By slipping into the language of gallantry, by inveigling his listeners into imagining themselves as gentlemen charged with the protection of a lady's honour, he turned the occasion from a political contest into a sentimental drama. If it was indelicate even to mention the lady's name in public, who could dare to name her marital status? If only malice or ignorance could dare to injure her, who was going to stand up and claim the title? Logically, Sheridan's claim was ridiculous. If Mrs. Fitzherbert was not the Prince's wife, then she was his mistress and her character was not above reproach. If she was above reproach, then she was his wife, Fox had lied to the House, and the Prince could never be King. But Sheridan had smothered logic in sentiment.

And he got away with it, because the King and Pitt decided to pull back from the brink of a constitutional crisis and accept an overture for negotiations with the Prince about his debts. Just as the House was breaking up, Sheridan sent Pitt a note asking to see him, and then gave him a letter from the Prince. Pitt refused to discuss the business with Sheridan, but sent the letter directly to the King. The next morning, however, Sheridan arrived at Downing Street with another note from the Prince, asking for a meeting to discuss Pitt's remarks in the House. Pitt and his closest lieutenant, Henry Dundas, agreed to meet the Prince, who turned up with Sheridan. Pitt refused to discuss anything substantial in Sheridan's presence. As he informed the King, he "could enter on no business on which he was employed as your Majesty's servant . . . before any third person, and especially (without meaning any disregard to the gentleman alluded to) before one in habitual opposition to your Majesty's Government."[9] After preliminary discussions, both Sheridan and Dundas withdrew, leaving the Prince and Pitt to hammer out proposals for a deal, which was eventually concluded with the Prince getting £160,000 to pay off his debts, £60,000 to finish the reconstruction of his mansion at Carlton House, and an extra £10,000 a year from his father. Mrs. Fitzherbert was slowly reconciled to the Prince, and the subject of their marriage was allowed to slip to the back of the public mind.

His audacity had won Sheridan what he thought was a great prize, making him the most trusted confidant of the Prince of Wales and, above all, the link between the Foxite Whigs and their best hope of power. Fox himself and Charles Grey had let the Prince down in his hour of need. Sheridan had helped him out of an impossible bind. And, over time, his personal hold over the Prince became increasingly formidable. At a ball in May 1789, for instance, when the Prince got very drunk, Sheridan was asked to "get him away." As Eliza, who was present, described the scene to Betsy, Sheridan "went up to him but finding that he did not readily yield to persuasion, he pushed the bottle away from him saying '*You shall not* drink any more.' The Prince fired at the idea of control and said, 'Sheridan I love you better than anyone but *shall not* is what I can't put up with.' However . . . they got him away."[10] This struggle to control the Prince would be a feature of Sheridan's political life for the next twenty years. For his pains, he would be tormented with visions of power and with hopes that, because they were not entirely illusory, would remain agonisingly alive.

Chapter 19

A GREAT STIR ABOUT PADDY LAND

While the crisis over the Prince's marriage was still developing, Sheridan's strongest political concerns had been, again, with Ireland. Even after he had held office in two British governments, he was as passionately Irish as he had ever been. When, in 1785, he decided to campaign against Pitt's Irish policy, he took it up primarily as a personal cause as opposed to a party concern. As his sister Betsy wrote, in June, to Lissy in Dublin, "Dick is a very warm friend to the Irish, Mrs S[heridan] cannot conceive the violent attachment he has to that country, but from her I found he acts on this occasion from his own feelings, totally independent of any wish his party may have to harrass the Minister."[1]

Sheridan's obsessive interest in "this Irish Business" was indeed a source of puzzlement and sometimes annoyance to his wife, who wrote at this time, "Dick and I have eternal disputes about it for to say the truth he has a little too much of the blood of the O'Sheridans of County Cavan in him."[2] In another letter, she remarked that he was determined to attack Pitt's proposals for a settlement with Ireland "and to make a great stir about Paddy land." To her, Ireland was a strange and foreign place. Referring to reports on the activities of the Catholic secret societies in rural Munster, she told her Dublin in-laws, "I wish to God you could get a Bridge thrown over from Holyhead that I might get a peep at your wild White Boys and Right Boys that you live amongst."

Yet to her husband, Ireland was still a kind of homeland. He had, however, in losing the cooperation of his brother, Charles, during the 1782–83 crisis, lost one of his most useful assets. When the Fox-North coalition fell, Charles had clung to office in Dublin, believing, as he wrote to Richard, that "nothing could be so absurd as to attempt to extend the party distinctions which prevail on your side of the water to this."[3] Sheridan had told Charles that "you are all so void of principle in Ireland that you cannot enter into our situation." Charles had defended himself not by asserting that he had principles but by declaring that none were necessary: "There never can be hereafter in this country any such thing as party connections founded upon political principles; we have obtained all the great objects for which Ireland had contended for many years, and there does not now remain one national object of sufficient importance to unite men in the same pursuit."

His self-serving defence exposed a fundamental difference in the brothers' respective attitudes to Ireland. To Charles, it was obvious that "Irish politics" were the politics of the Anglican landed ascendancy. He explained to his brother the underlying reasons why party politics made little sense in Ireland:

> Two out of three millions are Roman Catholics—I believe the proportion is still larger—and two-thirds of the remainder are violent rank Presbyterians, who have always been, but most particularly of late, strongly averse to all government placed in the hands of members of the church of England; nine-tenths of the property, the landed property of the country I mean, is in the possession of the latter. You will readily conceive how much these circumstances must give persons of property in this kingdom a leaning towards government; how necessarily they must make them apprehensive for themselves, placed between such potent enemies; and how naturally it must make them look up to English government, in whatever hands it may be, for that strength and support which the smallness of numbers prevents their finding among themselves; and consequently you will equally perceive that those political or party principles, which create such serious differences among you in England, are matters of small importance to the persons of landed property in this country . . .[4]

For Richard, by contrast, Irish politics were already something more than the internal power struggles of an Anglican elite. But, like the Patriot movement to whom his ideas were addressed, he had not explicitly, or perhaps even implicitly, begun to conclude from the arguments he employed to advocate Irish independence that the political "community" represented by an independent Parliament should also include both Catholics and Presbyterians. From his *Essay on Absentees* onwards, he had, however, tried to approach questions like that of Irish free trade from the point of view of the tenant farmer in the cottage rather than that of the landowner in the mansion. What he meant when he talked of "Ireland" may not have been entirely clear, but it was certainly something more than just the Ascendancy.

Political differences were just one aspect of the split between the brothers, and there was also a good deal of personal bitterness within the family over Charles's treatment of Betsy, whose intended marriage was being held up by his refusal to release money owed to her. Around this time, Sheridan wrote Charles a stern letter on family business, to which, according to a surviving letter from Eliza, "he still expects an answer . . . which I am perfectly convinced he shall never receive." If Charles's politics were no laughing matter, it is clear that in his brother's circles, he and his wife were. Eliza told Lissy, "You have no notion how he is laughed at here for the ridiculous things he says about his Wife. A large party of them were talking over her *hidden beauties*, which they said Charles had sent over a description of to one of his correspondents—Good God!—Where is his delicacy?"[5] In 1786, Eliza wrote to Lissy of "poor Charles: I question after all his boasts if he will turn out so grand a husband as my poor Dick, that he holds so cheap—at least I should be sorry to make the experiment."

In politics, Charles had become, as Sheridan bluntly told him, "a Castle Tory."[6] He believed that, after the concession of legislative independence in 1782, nothing remained to be done, and became a defender of the establishment. As events unfolded in 1785, the brothers were for the first time openly engaged on opposite sides of a momentous political conflict. Richard brought to it not just his heightened confidence in his own political principles and abilities but all the deep-seated animosity of their relationship within the family. At stake was an attempt by Pitt to roll back the concession of legislative independence to Ireland. The implications of what had happened in 1782 were becoming clear: that Ireland had gained, in theory at least, something much closer to dominion status than mere Home Rule. Technically, Ireland could now, with the consent of the

King, not only regulate her internal affairs but also conduct her own foreign policy and impose her own customs tariffs, even against English goods. Ireland could trade with the colonies—except in the domain of the East India Company—without being bound by the Navigation Acts that were the cornerstone of British mercantile policy.

For the British government this was an alarming prospect, and Pitt was anxious to negotiate an agreement that would close off any prospect of such a radical breach. The deal he offered the Irish Parliament in February 1785 was that Ireland would enter on equal terms into a commercial union with Britain and in return would contribute to the upkeep of the imperial navy by handing over all the future surplus in its "hereditary revenue." Accountability for this expenditure would lie with the Westminster Parliament. Pitt's goal in all this was, as he put it, "making England and Ireland one country in effect, though for local concerns under distinct legislatures."[7] It was an aim that Sheridan was determined to thwart.

After some modification, eleven propositions containing this deal were passed by the Irish Parliament, with Henry Grattan's support and with only a small group of radical reformers led by Henry Flood and Isaac Corry putting up real resistance. Unhappy with the amendment, Pitt asked the Irish for a clearer commitment to contribute annually to the imperial effort, but he obtained only "conditional approbation" for the propositions at Westminster.

Sheridan, for the moment, held his peace. He was in the awkward position of opposing the Irish propositions from a point of view almost entirely opposite to that of Fox and the rest of the opposition. William Eden, with whom he had clashed over Ireland in 1782, was inciting hostility to the propositions. So were English mercantile interests, especially industrialists like Josiah Wedgwood and Matthew Boulton, who feared free trade with Ireland. To them, the propositions conceded too much equality to Ireland. To Sheridan, on the other hand, they tied Ireland too closely to England and threatened to roll back the gains of 1782. To most of the opposition, though, it did not matter on what grounds the Irish propositions were opposed, so long as the maximum embarrassment to Pitt could be caused in the process.

With virtually every manufacturing town in England raising petitions against the Irish resolutions, the House of Commons added new clauses placing restrictions on Irish trade, especially with the colonies. Among the additions was one stipulating that the Irish Parliament should ratify "all laws" enacted at Westminster regulating trade and navigation. No one paid much attention to this, and it elicited no adverse comment in the Irish Parliament when it was considered there at the beginning of May. But on 12 May, when the amended propositions were presented to Parliament in London, Sheridan pounced on it. He remarked of the new proposition, now numbered as the fourth, that "the purport of it was that [if] we did so and so, the Irish parliament was bound to do the same, which is, in effect legislating for both countries here."[8] The proposition, in other words, would effectively undo the legislative independence secured in 1782. Having spotted this opening, Sheridan set about using it to destroy the propositions.

Pitt realised almost immediately just how dangerous Sheridan's seizing of the initiative might be, and tried to undo the damage by adding an amendment to say that the Irish Parliament could, of course, discuss such laws before passing them. But it was too late. Fox, North, and Eden saw that Sheridan's line of attack was the one most likely to succeed, and swung in behind him. In one move Sheridan had not merely given himself an opening through which to thwart Pitt's efforts to make Ireland and England one country, but also ensured that the opposition attack would be launched on the grounds of Irish independence rather than of English commercial interests.

On 30 May, Sheridan spoke at great length on the Irish propositions, attacking both the idea that Ireland should be forced to contribute to the upkeep of the imperial navy and the new fourth proposition. He made it clear that he would resist any infringement of Ireland's "independence as a sovereign state." If he were a member of the Irish Parliament, he said, he would prefer to have it stated that all British laws were to be binding on Ireland than to have the "mockery" of pretending to debate laws when they had no power to alter them: "Where fetters were to be worn, it was a wretched ambition to contend for the distinction of fastening our own shackles."[9] The *our* was particularly telling.

Into the middle of the speech he inserted an extraordinary defence of the settlement of 1782. If commercial conditions had been applied to the grant of legislative independence, he said, "those patriotic spirits who were at that time leading the oppressed people of that insulted country to the attainment of their just rights, would have pointed to other modes of acquiring them;—would have called to them in the words of Camillus, *arma aptare ferro non auro patriam et libertatem recuperare*." To put on their armour and recover their country and their freedom by iron, not by gold: in other words, to take up arms against England. Behind the elegant classical allusion was more than a hint of sedition. For the implication was that if Irish rights were now taken away, armed resistance would be justified. He elaborated a metaphor of Ireland as a wild horse about to be tamed:

> . . . a new scheme of commercial arrangement is proposed to the Irish as a boon; and the surrender of their constitution is tacked to it as a mercantile regulation. Ireland, newly escaped from the harsh trammels and severe discipline, is treated like a high-mettled horse, hard to catch; and the Irish Secretary is to return to the field, soothing and coaxing him, with a sieve of provender in one hand, but with a bridle in the other, readying to slip over his head while he is snuffling at the food. But this political jockeyship, I am convinced, will not succeed.[10]

On 25 July 1785, Pitt informed the King that Sheridan, along with Fox, William Eden, and Lord Beauchamp, had that day opposed the royal address on the Irish commercial resolutions, using the "old arguments relative to the independence of Ireland," but that they had failed to press for a vote. The King expressed his delight at this and told Pitt that the address "must wipe away any real jealousies from the minds of the Irish."[11] It was a vain hope, for Sheridan was determined to stir up as much jealousy in Ireland as he possibly could.

Estranged as he was from Charles, Sheridan used his friend and political ally Stratford Canning, who was visiting Ireland, as a conduit for information and intrigue. As the Irish Parliament was preparing to debate the resolutions, he told Canning that "if they are treated with patience in Ireland you are a herd of Slows and Blockheads." He also, rather intriguingly, promised to send Canning "a *Ballad* for the Paddies," presumably of his own composition, and intended to help stir up opposition to the propositions. He referred Canning to his own cousin, Richard Sheridan, a staunch Whig member of the Irish Parliament, as a "sound man and true" with whom he could talk freely about "any confidential mischief."[12]

Just before the debate in Dublin, Sheridan wrote a short note to Charles—"that you will be surprised to receive"—telling him that if the resolutions were to be accepted in their present form, "I hope I shall never hear the name of Ireland again while I live." He presumably did not yet know that while his own speech of 30 May was being widely distributed in Dublin and "dispersed by the gross" in Munster,[13] his brother had become an active propagandist for the other side. His pamphlet *Free Thoughts on the Present Crisis* contended that if Pitt's proposals were rejected, the only alternatives were either a full political union with Britain or a complete separation. Britain's dominant role in the new arrangement would be justified, he argued, by its great place in world affairs and the generosity of its concessions. Sibling rivalry had become public contention.

However, Charles's efforts were ineffective, and public opposition to the propositions continued to mount. Some corps of the Volunteers defied the orders of their commander and passed angry resolutions denouncing them as "subversive of the recovered rights of Ireland." Most of the press began to adopt the same position. And, critically, Grattan, who had initially favoured the resolutions, changed tack and began to take Sheridan's line. That it was Sheridan's line is evident from his direct correspondence with Isaac Corry, the most vocal opponent of the propositions in the Irish Parliament. On 5 August, Corry replied to a now lost letter from Sheridan, giving him details of the campaign against the resolutions and telling him, "We hear astonishing accounts of *your* greatness in particular. Paddy will, I suppose, some *beau jour* be voting you another £50,000 [the sum which had recently been raised as a public subscription for Grattan], if you go on as you have done." Sheridan fed Corry with clauses of the government's draft bill, which he had obtained in London, and which enabled the parliamentary opposition to prepare their ammunition in advance.[14]

The propositions, consolidated as a commercial bill, were debated in the Irish Parliament on the night of 12 August, with Grattan making a speech described to Pitt by the Lord Lieutenant, Rutland, as being "a display of the most beautiful eloquence perhaps ever heard, but it was seditious and inflammatory to a degree hardly credible . . ." Grattan subsequently attacked the bill as inimical to legislative independence and as representing "an incipient and a creeping union, a virtual union, establishing one will in the general concerns of commerce and navigation, and reposing that will in the parliament of Great Britain."[15] On the vote to give the bill a first reading, the government had a majority of only seventeen, and several of those who voted in favour had indicated that they would later oppose the bill unless it was changed. Corry had told Sheridan that if the opposition mustered "anything like a hundred" votes, the bill would be dead; they managed 108. The best the government could do was to adjourn the debate for a month. But Pitt understood that the vote was "of the nature of a defeat," and the propositions were shelved indefinitely.

Corry acknowledged that much of the credit for Pitt's humiliating defeat should go to Sheridan. On the day of the vote, he wrote to "congratulate with you on 108 minority—against 127." A few days later, when the bill was shelved, he wrote, "I wish you joy a thousand times of our complete victory." It was Sheridan's perspicacity that had transformed a dull commercial treaty into an epic constitutional conflict, in which Irish independence could be vindicated. It was his speech which had helped to fuel the public and press campaigns against the measures in Ireland. And he had, through Canning and Corry, kept closely in touch with the details of the street and parliamentary opposition to Pitt's proposals. Without setting foot in his native country, he had achieved a brilliant political triumph. Having told Charles that if the propositions were accepted meekly he would not want to hear of Ireland again, the very opposite had now come true and Ireland became not just a passionate emotional attachment but a very real political territory whose name would seldom be far from his lips.

Chapter 20

A DAY IN THE LIFE

When Sheridan had to work intensively, he would get up at four in the morning, surround his desk with dozens of lit candles, and order a continual supply of toasted muffins.[1] But most days he woke about noon, often feeling fuzzy from the previous night's drinking. He had his breakfast in bed and stayed there until about two in the afternoon, making notes for the speeches he intended to make that night or attending to whatever theatre business he could not avoid. Often he did not bother to open his mail. His wife, referring to a letter that had been enclosed with one to her husband, complained to his sister, "Besides, you know Dick hardly ever reads his own letters: so that it [might] be in the bottomless pit for any good I am ever likely to reap by it."[2]

His son's tutor, William Smyth, saw his table covered with "manuscript plays, and pamphlets, and letters, and papers of every description . . . I could not help noticing that the letters were most of them unopened, and that some of them had coronets on the seal."[3] Sometimes the letters contained bank notes that he had urgently demanded from the treasurer of Drury Lane and then, having obtained the money somewhere else, simply forgotten. As for the heap of play manuscripts, John Philip Kemble, one of his managers at Drury Lane, referred to it as a "funeral pile."[4]

When he got up, he washed thoroughly and with the help of his manservant, George Edwards, dressed carefully in good well-cut clothes, and went towards the ante-room that separated him from the door to the street. Most days, it would be full of creditors, petitioners, theatrical or political acquaintances, and from long experience all of them knew that unless they could catch him before he reached the street, they would have no chance until the next day.[5] "A door opening above stairs," wrote one, "moved all the hopes below: but when he came down his hair was drest for the day, and his countenance for the occasion; and so cordial were his manners, his glance so masterly, and his address so captivating, that the people, for the most part, seemed to forget what they actually wanted, and went away, as if they had come only to look at him."[6]

The man who stepped out onto the street was of medium height, broad-shouldered, and well-built, giving the impression of being large but not fat. His face, though not very handsome, had an ambiguity which people found fascinating. "Even when I first knew him [early 1793]," wrote Smyth, "his forehead was very fine, and his eyes brilliant in the extreme. The lower part of his face was coarse, and not agreeable."[7] As he became more and more a public image, this contrast took on a mythic quality, seeming to be the outward sign of inner struggle between the divine and the demonic. Lord Byron said of him that "the upper part of Sheridan's face was that of a god—a forehead most expansive, an eye of peculiar brilliancy and fire; but below he shewed the satyr."[8]

This tendency in his contemporaries to indulge in physiognomy, to try to tell the construction of his mind by his face, was encouraged by the large patch of dry, sometimes inflamed, red skin that ran across his cheeks and nose. As early as October 1784, his sister Betsy noticed "a good deal of scurvy . . . in his face," and for the rest of his life it was to be one of his distinguishing features. In the accumulating iconography of cartoons and caricatures of him, this stripe was the mark of Cain, the physical signature of his dissolute life. It was assumed to be the result of heavy drinking. In fact, it was almost certainly the sign of a skin disease. In February 1805, his friend Lord Moira wrote to the Prince of Wales from Edinburgh: "Poor Sheridan is confined with a teazing erysipelas." This is a streptococcal infection that produces inflammation and a deep red colour on the skin, especially the face and the scalp—precisely the symptoms of Sheridan's condition.

But such an explanation was too mundane, and it was much more interesting to talk of "Sheridan's *Brandy* appearance."[9] Sheridan's red nose became the butt of many jokes. Lord Palmerston invented a riddle in 1806: Why would it be better to tumble half way down

Greenwich hill than have Sheridan's nose? Because half a roll is better than nob-red.[10] Thomas Moore, meeting Lissy in 1818, found her "the very image of Sheridan—having . . . all the light of his eyes without the illumination of his nose."[11] But, as in Moore's quip, Sheridan's eyes seemed to those who saw him to express the divine side of his nature. As a young man, according to Lissy, his eyes were "the finest in the world." Samuel Taylor Coleridge wrote in 1795 of how his "eye-beams dance." Henry Brougham, who saw him in his last years in Parliament, claimed that his eye was "singularly piercing" and that "it had the singularity of never winking."

As he walked down the street, Sheridan moved with a vigour rooted in bodily strength and mental confidence. He retained the bearing of the duellist, willing, if necessary, to confront his enemies physically. In July 1788, for instance, when Fox's Westminster election campaign took an especially violent turn, he was in the thick of things. A member of a gang of butcher's porters, supporting Fox's running-mate, Lord John Townshend, killed a sailor who was supporting the Tory Admiral Hood. The Bow Street magistrate, Sir Samson Wright, posted a platoon of soldiers in front of the Whig headquarters, the Shakespeare Tavern. Townshend, Fox, and Sheridan forced their way through them and went to Bow Street to confront Wright. According to Sheridan he told Wright to make the soldiers draw back, but Wright "sneeked behind a grenadier, crying 'drive them off.' " Sheridan, being "provoked a *little*, he did take the Fellow by the Collar and having dragged him forward gave him a shaking."[12]

Wherever he was going, he was nearly always late. He was, from an early age, fully aware of his reputation for being dilatory, and enjoyed playing on it. In his teens, scolding Betsy for being late in replying to a letter, he joked, "Do as I *say*, not as I *do*." Later, writing of his eventual reconciliation with his father, Eliza remarked that "if it depends on Dick's *punctuality*, I own I fear it, for in proportion as he has more business of consequence on his hands, his love of procrastination increases—he means well, however . . . and I hope the bad habits of his Youth will be therefore excus'd."[13]

When he arrived at a meeting, whether to deal with theatre business or to raise money, he would turn on his astonishing powers of persuasion. Prince Hoare told the artist Joseph Farington, "There is no way of combatting him but by being insensible to what he says, and never contesting by argument, only to adhere to the necessary demand." According to Hoare, the only person who could get the better of him was the actress Dorothea Jordan, "and of her he was afraid as a Mouse of a Cat." Even those who were utterly outraged by some act or neglect on his part soon fell under his spell. The actor John Philip Kemble, when manager of Drury Lane, fell out with Sheridan and, smouldering with anger, was determined to resign. At a meeting with Sheridan, remembered a witness to the scene, "The great actor now looked unutterable things, and occasionally emitted a *humming* sound, like that of a bee, and groaned in the spirit inwardly . . . A considerable time elapsed and frequent repetitions of the sound before mentioned occurred" before Kemble eventually stood up and let fly with a passionate comparison of himself to an eagle whose wings had been clipped and who would now fly free. Sheridan simply drew up a chair beside him, talked softly to him, and in two minutes had "resumed his old ascendancy."[14]

His son Tom's tutor, William Smyth, likewise remembered confronting Sheridan in a fury over his disruption of his son's education. He began the meeting with his mind set on resignation. He listed his complaints and insisted that "neither with proper prudence nor proper pride could I continue with him any longer." Sheridan listened with sympathetic nods until "I had tolerably well exhausted myself." He then began to talk, acknowledging the truth of all Smyth's complaints and explaining all his own difficulties in politics and the theatre.

> On topics of this kind he dwelt in a manner so earnest and plausible; he so soothed and flattered me, and described what would be the situation of himself and his son if I threw up my situation, in a manner to me at the time so affecting, that my indignation began to soften, my resolution to fail me. I began to hesitate in my answers; I knew not well what to say or to think; any powers of reasoning that I ever had, seemed, on some account or other, no longer fit to serve me; and, in short, though a little sullen, I stood at least silent; and at last, like the month of March in the calendar, I came into the room like a lion and went out like a lamb. I recovered myself a little as I went down the stairs. What a clever fellow this is, I thought to myself, as I went out of the door; and after a few paces down the street, I made one discovery more—what a fool I am.[15]

Most often, his powers of persuasion were needed to keep his precarious finances afloat. Because his name became a by-word for profligacy, Sheridan's achievements as a manager of money have seldom been given their due. The fact is that he had gone from being, in 1775, a young man with virtually no money, no property, and no prospect of inheritance to controlling a major business in Drury Lane and keeping up the appearance of a public man, complete with houses, servants, carriages, even estates. He spent a small fortune of his own money on politics—mostly on maintaining his Stafford seat—and earned almost nothing in return until very late in his political career, when the Duchy of Cornwall gave him an income.

There is no doubt that he could be extravagant and careless about money, largely because he genuinely didn't care for it in itself and saw it only as a means to an end. But the source of his debts was much deeper and much simpler than any personal foibles. Because he brought no money of his own to Drury Lane, his ownership was always dependent on mortgages. By having the theatre completely rebuilt and expanding its seating capacity, Sheridan in fact increased the annual income of Drury Lane very significantly, from £34,000 in Garrick's last season to between £50,000 and £60,000 by the end of the century. The problem was that the large-scale style of theatre that the new building demanded was fearfully expensive. The spectacular sets and extravagant effects (Colman's *Blue Beard* in 1798, for instance, cost £2,000 to mount) ate up more and more of the revenue generated at the box office. Under Garrick, about two-thirds of the theatre's expenditure went on actors' salaries. By 1800, only a third did so, with the rest going into design and spectacle. The result was that while income rose, profits fell.[16]

Far from being irresponsible in the management of the theatre, Sheridan's problem was that he took far too much personal responsibility. The root of his most serious difficulties lay in the rebuilding of Drury Lane in the early 1790s. When it was finished in 1794, the new theatre had cost £160,000 rather than the £80,000 that had been projected. Instead of spreading the debt among the shareholders, Sheridan took all of it on himself, setting off the endless series of borrowings, sales of boxes, fendings off of creditors and backers, and jugglings with income and expenditure that would plague him for most of the rest of his days. In the running of the theatre, he tended to switch between high artistic seriousness and, when money was tight, cynical commercial calculation. The great actress Sarah Siddons, whom his father always boasted of having discovered, remembered his intense interest in her performance as Lady Macbeth at Drury Lane. Just as she was waiting to go on in her first appearance in the part, he argued with her about whether or not Lady Macbeth should, in the sleepwalking scene, hold her candle while attempting to wash her hands. She stood her ground, but remarked, "My deference for Mr Sheridan's taste and judgment was, however, so great, that, had he proposed the alteration whilst it was possible for me to change my own plan I should have yielded to his suggestion . . ."[17]

By contrast, he was also capable of admitting at Drury Lane plays like Frederic Reynolds's after-piece *The Caravan or the Driver and his Dog*, performed by an actor, Charles Dignum, and, as the main attraction, by a dog called Carlo. One evening when Sheridan entered the green room he was confronted with a mournful Dignum, who told him, "Sir, there is no guarding against illness, it is truly lamentable to stop the run of a successful piece like this; but really—" "Really what?" came Sheridan's response. "I am so unwell that I cannot go on longer than tonight." "You! my good fellow, you terrified me; I thought you were going to say that the dog was taken ill."[18]

Early in the evening, when his theatrical and financial business were done, Sheridan made his way to the House of Commons, which then met in the cramped and often sweaty space of St. Stephen's Chapel. Often he was engaged in committee meetings, sometimes on tedious financial subjects. But when there was an important debate, he usually spoke in the House. Debates were dominated by a handful of leading orators—William Pitt, Henry Dundas, William Windham, Edmund Burke, Charles Fox, Charles Grey, Samuel Whitbread, and Sheridan. Its ordinary members were, as Byron put it, "not formidable *speakers* but very much so as an *audience*."[19] When he addressed this audience, Sheridan transformed himself as an actor does. Nathaniel Wraxall, a political opponent who watched him in the House all through these years, marvelled at the appearance of calm and control which formed a counterpoint to his often fierce words: "Nor did he, while thus chastening his adversary alter a muscle of his own countenance which, as well as his gestures, seemed to participate [in] and display the unalterable serenity of his intellectual formation." Keeping control of his face, he allowed "intellect, humour and gaiety" to "play about his lips when speaking" and they "operated with inconceivable attraction; for they anticipated, as it were, to the eye, the effect produced by his oratory to the ear, thus opening for him a sure way to the heart and the understanding."[20]

Where he got this utter self-possession, this uncanny ability to control every muscle of his face and every silent signal of his lips, is impossible to say. But it is hard not to trace it back to the experience of being a small boy on his own, sent to shift for himself in a foreign country. The child who, hearing of his mother's death, could write "I must also have a new hat with a crape and black stokins" for his mourning clothes, became the man who could keep up a front, who could calibrate his own gestures and expressions as a writer measures words, each deployed for the right effect. Just as in the theatre he was intensely aware of the visual as well as the aural, he knew in his own rhetorical performances that the semaphore of the body could be just as eloquent as the most sonorous turn of phrase.

This connection to his childhood could operate in both directions. If the self-control was that of a child who had been forced early into an adult awareness of how he must appear to others, there was also in his adult self a still unconsumed reservoir of childlike playfulness. Not only did he love practical jokes, but he could at times deploy them to political ends. On one occasion, at a party in a country house, Sheridan suggested that one of the guests, the Reverend Mr. O'Beirne, should ask for permission to preach at the village church the next day. When the clergyman protested that he had no sermon with him, Sheridan offered to write one. The next morning the clergyman found a manuscript by his bed-side with a sermon on "the abuse of riches." He duly preached it before a congregation which included the guests at the house, among them John Crewe, husband of Sheridan's erstwhile lover, and General John Burgoyne. Only months later, when O'Beirne noticed that the Crewes were treating him with distinct coldness, did he discover from Burgoyne that almost every line of the sermon was a veiled but easily recognisable attack on Crewe, who was known in the area for his mistreatment of the poor, and that this had been evident to everyone in the church except himself.[21]

This playfulness was brought to bear on Sheridan's political speech-making, which had for him the same combination of moral seriousness and sportive delight. He was acting in both senses of the word: both putting on a performance and trying to shape the world. And he didn't just become an actor; he became something like that actor he knew most intimately, his own father. His voice was rich and pleasant, but his normal speech was "rather slovenly," and at first even in Parliament it was thought to be "somewhat thick." But as he found his oratorical voice it became, like his father's, distinct and precise. His sister Betsy, watching him speak at the trial of Warren Hastings in 1789, was struck both by the resemblance—she called his manner "very like my father's, tho' not an imitation"—and by its irony.[22] In spite of all the unhappiness of their relationship, of all the hurt and mistrust between them, the son had after all inherited something from the father. There was, too, a deeper inheritance at work. The insistence of his ancestor William Sheridan that though the written word is more durable, "the Word spoken be more efficatious," shaped Richard's own mentality. Theatre and oratory were both forms in which speech took priority over writing, in which the living presence of the speaker imbued the words with meaning. And it is remarkable how little of his work was properly published while Sheridan was alive. Pirated editions of his plays and sometimes of his speeches abounded, but as he wrote towards the end of his life, "I never yet own'd or allow'd the printing of anything Play Poems or Speeches but two things to both which I put my name viz. The Critic and a Political Pamphlet on the affairs of India . . ."[23]

This reluctance to publish under his own name final, authorised versions of his texts seems almost pathological, since he lost a great deal of money by it. The text of his famous speech at the trial of Warren Hastings, for instance, could have earned him a small fortune. His failure to capitalise in this way has generally been attributed to mere indolence. But this is to miss an essential part of his nature. To him, as to his father and ancestors, the spoken version was the authentic one, the written one almost a translation into another language, in which much of the meaning would inevitably be lost. He always saw the original texts of his plays as mere templates for performance, to be altered and reshaped in the light of theatrical experience. And his attitude to his parliamentary speeches was the same. He practised a kind of verbal jazz. For big set-piece speeches he prepared meticulously, assembling facts and arguments with ferocious concentration and seriousness. But within this framework he left room for improvisation and response, for interaction with an audience that, like the one at Drury Lane, would very actively participate in his performance.

His voice was deep but mellifluous, and, just as important for his mostly English parliamentary audience, it was not, in the words of Wraxall, "accompanied by Burke's unpleasant Irish accent." Wraxall had said of Burke that "his Irish accent, which was as strong as if he had never quitted the banks of the Shannon, diminished to the ear the enchanting effect of his eloquence on the mind."[24] Sheridan, having spent his childhood in Ireland, probably retained some trace of Irish intonation, but it was certainly faint enough to be easy on English ears. And being easy on the ear was a critical aspect not just of his oratory but of his political strategy. The equanimity of his demeanour, the graceful self-control, the lulling voice, the unthreatening accent allowed him to say hard and startling things without giving his listeners time to arm their defences. And his rhetorical procedure was entirely in keeping with this device. He was careful always to speak *within* the accepted language of contemporary politics, to take the words and thoughts that were around and shape them into new meanings.[25] Everything that Sheridan did in his public career was about appropriating the given language. In his plays, he did not invent a new way of making theatre but transformed what was there through burlesque and parody. His political speeches followed the same logic. Fox, during a rare public debate between them in the House, remarked that Sheridan's ingenuity was such that he "could contrive to give an argument what turn he pleased." The turn, in fact, was his favourite manoeuvre.

In one of his first speeches, for instance, given on 26 February 1781 on an opposition motion to abolish some of the more outrageous abuses of royal patronage, he replied to an attack by John Courtenay on the opposition by taking two of Courtenay's similes and reversing their meaning. Courtenay had first described the opposition as being envious of those who basked in the sunshine of the court and desirous merely of taking their places. Sheridan took up this image of the sun and twisted it to his own purposes:

> He begged leave to remind the honourable gentleman that though the sun afforded a genial warmth, it also occasioned an intemperate heat, that tainted and infected everything it reflected on. That this excessive heat tended to corrupt as well as to cherish; to putrify as well as to animate; to dry and soak up the wholesome juices of the body politic; and to turn the whole of it into one mass of corruption. If those, therefore, who sat near him did not enjoy so

> genial a warmth as the honourable gentleman . . . he was certain they breathed a purer air, an air less infected and less corrupt.

Thus, staying within the bounds of Courtenay's own imagery, Sheridan transformed the monarch from a benign source of warmth and light to a polluter of politics radiating rottenness. And through this process of reversal, he managed to say something that he could not have said directly: that the King himself engendered corruption.

Later, when Burke and Sheridan had become bitter enemies as a result of their opposed reactions to the French Revolution, Burke argued against an opposition motion to put a wartime tax on government placemen and pensioners, on the grounds that it was the King's right to determine such payments. "Let any person reflect," said Burke, "whether he would give the same wages to his gamekeeper as to his footman, to his footman as to his groom." Instead of attacking the whole basis of Burke's analogy, Sheridan deftly adapted it. Burke, he said, "has put the case of a private family, and asked whether the master was not the proper judge in the distribution of reward; and if those rewards should be the same to all classes of his servants? I am ready to adopt the principle of his comparison, and to agree, that in both cases, those who pay are the proper judges of what should be paid."[26] Thus Burke's insufferable patrician metaphor was split open to reveal a subversive core: Sheridan managed to raise the question of who should be the master.

Charles Lamb remembered that when Jack Palmer played Joseph Surface in *The School for Scandal*, he used "two voices, both plausible, hypocritical and insinuating, but his secondary or supplemental voice still more decisively histrionic than his common one . . . the sentiments in Joseph Surface were thus marked out in a sort of italics to the audience . . ."[27] Sheridan's own speeches were also delivered in two voices, one straight and the other making use of a kind of audible italics in which he quoted the language and symbols of mid-eighteenth-century England for his own purposes. Instead of proposing alternative modes of understanding or feeling, he operated entirely within those that were given to him, but seized control of them and made them his own.

For most of his parliamentary career this oratory, on whatever subject, was a weapon against one man—the Prime Minister, William Pitt. In part, Sheridan and Pitt owed the depth of their mutual detestation to an awareness that each was a worthy enemy of the other. After Sheridan's death, the politician George Tierney told Thomas Moore that Pitt had "a very high idea" of Sheridan and thought him "a far greater man than Mr. Fox."[28] Three years before Pitt died, Sheridan wrote to his sometime lover Harriet Duncannon from the House of Commons that he had just heard "one of the most magnificent pieces of declamation that ever fell from that rascal Pitt's lips. Detesting the Dog as I do, I cannot withdraw this just tribute to the Scoundrel's talents. I could not help often lamenting in the course of his harangue, as I have frequently done before, what a pity it is that he has not a particle of honesty in him."[29]

When they first entered Parliament, Sheridan and Pitt were allies in the cause of parliamentary reform. But after the collapse of the Rockingham administration in 1782, when Pitt joined Shelburne's government, their enmity became deep and personal. The first and most famous clash was in February 1783, when Pitt taunted Sheridan in the House of Commons on his theatrical origins and connections. Listening to Sheridan's speeches, said Pitt, he admired

> . . . the elegant sallies of his thought, the gay effusions of his fancy, his dramatic turns and his epigrammatic points; and if they were reserved for their proper stage, they would, no doubt, receive what the Honourable Gentleman's abilities always did receive, the plaudits of his audience; and it would be his fortune "*sui plausu gaudere theatri*" [to rejoice in the applause of his own theatre]. But this is not the proper scene for the exhibition of those elegancies.

Sheridan replied that the House itself could judge the propriety and taste of Pitt's attack but that he himself was so "flattered and encouraged" by it that "if I ever again engage in the compositions he alludes to, I may be tempted to an act of presumption, to attempt an improvement on one of Ben Jonson's best characters, the character of the Angry Boy in *The Alchemist*."[30] The name "Angry Boy" stuck to Pitt for many years, and he did not again try to attack Sheridan for his theatrical connections.

But Sheridan's own attacks on Pitt were often deeply, if indirectly, personal. Pitt was not only unmarried but was famously chaste and was said to have no interest in women. While never openly accusing him of homosexuality, Sheridan teased him with the implication. In May 1785, for instance, he made a speech on Pitt's proposal for a tax on female servants for no apparent reason other than an inability to resist the opportunity it offered for a dig at Pitt's unmarried state. A tax on female servants, he suggested as "a bounty to bachelors and a penalty upon propagation . . . ought at least to be balanced with a tax on single men, who certainly were a description of persons less useful to the community than men who were married and had families."[31] Likewise, when Pitt arrived late in the House because he had been to see Sarah Siddons in *Venice Preserved*, Sheridan called out "*Jam redit est virgo!*" a quotation from Virgil: "The virgin has returned!" And in 1795, when Pitt berated him for his absence while on honeymoon after his second marriage, he replied that "it is unnecessary for me to state to the house the reasons which prevented my attendance, and were I to state them they most probably would be unintelligible to the right honourable gentleman."[32] Obliquely, he concealed crude innuendo in elegant allusion: He likened Pitt to the Duke of Buckingham, King James I's homosexual favourite, as a "minion of the crown," and compared him and his young supporter George Canning to Nisus and Euryalus, two warrior lovers from the *Aeneid*. He pictured Pitt and his friends holding "another Alexander's feast."

This implied contrast between Pitt and himself also built, more obviously, on the Joseph and Charles Surface dichotomy. Pitt, like Joseph, was "haughty and stiff-necked," cold, frigid, and unsociable. The implication that Sheridan's own unstable personal life, like Charles's, was the result of warm blood and an open heart, was of course entirely intentional. On at least one occasion, their clashes across the floor of the House came close to provoking physical violence. In March 1805, Sheridan took the opportunity of a motion he had proposed to reverse an increase in the size of the military to launch a fierce attack on Pitt for his treatment of Catholic emancipation. Pitt's eyes, according to Thomas Creevey, "started with defiance from their sockets and seemed to tell him if he advanced an atom further, he would have his life." Sheridan "left him a little alone, and tickled him about the greatness of his mind . . . and then he turned upon him again with redoubled fury . . . Never has it fallen to my lot to hear such words before in publick or in private used by man to man."[33] According to Henry Brougham, "they who witnessed the looks and gestures of the aggressor [Pitt] under the pitiless pelting of the tempest which he had provoked, represent it as certain that there were moments when he intended to fasten a personal quarrel upon the vehement and implacable declaimer."[34]

After the parliamentary sitting (and sometimes, if it was a late sitting, during it), Sheridan went to dine and drink, typically at Devonshire House, Carlton House, or Brooks's. This was an age of fierce drinking, and the political elite indulged more than most. Sir Gilbert Elliot told his wife in 1788, "Fox drinks what I would call a great deal . . . Sheridan excessively, and Grey more than any of them."[35] Pitt, too, drank copiously. Sheridan usually started on claret and then moved on to port. Sometimes he would drink all night: Eliza, in 1784, told Lissy in a letter, "Dick is in his Bed doing Penance for sitting up at Brooks's till seven this morning . . . disputing on the . . . truth of Christianity."[36] That Eliza worried about his drinking, and that he made resolutions to control it, is evident from a letter she wrote to him in 1790, referring to a binge of his with Lord John Townshend, the after-effects of which prevented him from giving a speech he had intended to make in Parliament:

> When you tell me how vexed and grieved you was at not being able to speak on Monday, on account of your making yourself so ill on Sunday, would you have me say drinking to that excess is *not an abominable habit*? And where I see *idletons* as Jack Townshend can overcome all your good, and strong resolutions, mustn't I think that London and its inhabitants and their ways *do* alter people whether they will or no?[37]

When seriously drunk, Sheridan could be "very quarrelsome and savage." Byron once described a dinner with him as "first silent, then talky, then argumentative, then inarticulate, and then drunk."[38] Most of his evenings, especially while he was still young, reached no further than the middle of the scale. The initial silence was important; he did not tend to dominate conversations but to move steadily into them. Nor was he a comic performer at the dinner table, for his conversation was at its most dazzling when he spoke on serious subjects. He did not himself laugh much, and, as Byron put it, "his humour or rather wit was always saturnine, and sometimes savage." He was not above amusing his companions by quoting lines from play manuscripts submitted to him by young hopefuls. Samuel Taylor Coleridge was once infuriated to hear that Sheridan had been quoting to "a large company at the house of a highly respectable Member of Parliament" a line from his tragedy *Osorio* as "Drip! drip!

drip! there's nothing here but dripping."[39] Coleridge insisted that the line was really "Drip! Drip! a ceaseless sound of water-drops," but in fact Sheridan's version did not do justice to the full horror of the original:

> Drip! drip! drip! drip!—in such a place as this
> It has nothing else to do but drip! drip! drip!
> I wish it had not dripp'd upon my torch.

At Brooks's, he did not take part in the obsessive gambling that preoccupied Fox and his circle, but he was, nevertheless, addicted to betting. For him, the game was not the abstract fall of cards on the table but the pitch and toss of history itself. Such was his faith in his own judgement of events that he was always ready to back it with money. In 1793 he placed two bets with General Fitzpatrick: 150 guineas that some measure of parliamentary reform would be passed within two years and fifty guineas that British troops would be sent to Holland within two months. At the same time, he bet two hundred guineas that Pitt would not be Prime Minister by March 1795 and two hundred guineas that the Duke of Portland would be at the head of an administration by March 1796. In 1794 Sheridan was responsible for eight bets running at Brooks's, on subjects which varied in importance from the question of the French armies having failed or succeeded in occupying Amsterdam, to the question of whether the shortest way from one house to another was by way of Sackville Street or Bond Street.[40]

By the time he got home, it was usually very late. If he was drunk, George Edwards would help him in. Edwards went in to tidy Sheridan's bedroom one morning and found the windows stuffed up with documents and bank-notes. He reckoned that his master had come in drunk and emptied his pockets, and that a high wind during the night had rattled the windows so that Sheridan, fumbling in the dark for something to stop the noise, had found the money and papers and used them.[41] As ever, his reliance on inspired improvisation had its price.

Chapter 21

A SPEAKING PICTURE

In 1790 Sir Elijah Impey, former Chief Justice of the Supreme Court in Calcutta and a close ally of Warren Hastings, governor-general of India, decided to contest the Stafford election in the hope of unseating Sheridan. He was a well-connected man with considerable financial resources to lavish on the contest. Sheridan responded with a simple theatrical spectacle. He had his supporters carry in their processions through the streets the effigy of a black man hanging from a gallows.[1] The image was as effective as it was eloquent, and almost immediately Impey withdrew from the contest. He knew what Sheridan knew, that this silent mannequin was charged with the most visceral emotions, that it had been given a powerful voice. That voice was Sheridan's and it had been provoked into speech by events that had begun thousands of miles from the English Midlands nine years previously.

In 1781 Chait Singh, Rajah of Benares and in effect a vassal of the East India Company, was, on the orders of Warren Hastings, and after bloody resistance, deposed. He had failed to pay the £50,000 which the governor-general had decided to levy on him as an involuntary contribution to the cost of the company's war against the French in India. He was also unfortunate enough to have had as his patron in the upper echelons of the company Sir Philip Francis, Hastings's bitterest enemy.

Warren Hastings had been in India since 1750, the year before Sheridan was born. He was, in his time, something of a liberal, trying to curb some of the more outrageous acts of rapacity by the company's employees and, through Sheridan's friend Halhed, had encouraged an interest in Bengali language and law. His comparative leniency had forced him, for a period in the mid-1760s, to resign and return to England. But when he resumed office in 1772 as governor (soon governor-general) he was a chastened man, determined to put his duty of making money for the company's shareholders before any other consideration. When Chait Singh caused trouble, Hastings decided to make an example of him and to fine him £500,000 for failure to pay his levy. This decision met with violent resistance, culminating in the crushing of Chait Singh and his followers.

With this done, Hastings turned his attention to the neighbouring but much larger territories of Oudh. These were ruled by a bitterly divided Shia Muslim family. The wazir, Asof-ud-Daula, was a weak ruler whose authority was being challenged by his brother, and whose mother—the Bahu begum, Sadr-ud-Din—and grandmother—the Burra begum, Sadr-un-Nisa—held him in contempt. The begums had large land holdings in eastern Oudh, adjoining Chait Singh's territories, and during the rebellion they had allowed Singh to draw recruits for his forces. They were also, more dubiously, accused by the company of inciting a revolt against the wazir (in effect against the company, whose pawn he was) in the districts of Bahriach and Gorakhpur. Hastings decided that they should be punished, and in September 1781 he signed a treaty with Asof-ud-Daula which included a provision allowing the seizure of the begums' lands. This was in breach of an earlier treaty, to which the company was a party, guaranteeing that the lands would not be interfered with. The begums resisted, and Hastings told the Chief Justice of the Supreme Court at Calcutta, Sir Elijah Impey, that they were in rebellion. In that case, suggested Impey, the Bahu begum's huge stores of treasure could lawfully be appropriated.

Hastings ordered Nathaniel Middleton, the company's resident at Lucknow, to take both the lands and the treasures. When Middleton, with a detachment of troops, took the begums' palace at Fyzabad, he wrote to Hastings to say that he was allowing some "temporary forebearance" in order to discover the whereabouts of the treasure. Hastings replied that negotiation would merely encourage resistance, threatening Middleton with the words "I shall hold you accountable in the case of failure."[2] The message was clear: the treasure was to be taken by any means necessary. On 25 January 1782, Middleton wrote to Hastings to inform him that although it had required "considerable address," he had seized the eunuchs in charge of the begums' treasury, Bihar Ali Khan and Jowar Ali Khan, and "by using some few severities with them" forced them to reveal the whereabouts of some of the treasure, worth £430,000. This was not, however, enough to satisfy Hastings. The eunuchs were moved to Lucknow, where they were starved and tortured until they revealed where more treasure was to be found. In all, property worth over half a million pounds was taken from the begums.

Sheridan's interest in all this stemmed from the fall of the Fox-North coalition and the defeat of Fox's India Bills. His concern, at first, was that the East India Company, through its wealth, influence, and closeness to the King, was itself becoming a new source of autocracy in Britain. In July 1784, when Pitt introduced his own India Bill, Sheridan warned the House of Commons,

> The India phalanx, those Swiss guards of Eastern peculation, had openly declared that they would overthrow the last administration; and, by doing so, teach another how to value and respect their friendship;—nay, these Eastern lords went so far as to declare that the depravity of this country was now arrived to such a pitch, that they could carry any point by money.

But his sympathy for India itself and his loathing for Hastings had also been engaged. In the same speech he "dwelt much on the rapacity, and other improper conduct of Mr Hastings."[3] This presumably included his offences against the begums of Oudh.

In January 1786, after Hastings had arrived back in England, his agent, Major Scott, challenged Edmund Burke on the floor of the House to bring forward the charges which he had long threatened. Burke took up the challenge, and seems at a meeting at the Duke of Portland's house to have secured the agreement of Fox, Sheridan, and their allies to a united opposition campaign to impeach Hastings. By the middle of February, Burke had begun the proceedings by moving for certain papers to be laid before the House. Interest was low, however, with the debates attracting small attendance. The only really encouraging sign for Burke was that Pitt, who might have been expected to throw his weight behind Hastings, was notably noncommittal, even though his right-hand man, Henry Dundas, was outspoken in defence of the governor-general.

In early March, however, Pitt opposed the release of some papers, and Sheridan made his first serious intervention in the debate on the impeachment proceedings, showing already a detailed grasp of some aspects of Hastings's conduct. In April Burke brought forward twenty-two charges against Hastings. The allegations spanned a period of almost a decade, from the conduct of the company's war against the Rohilla tribe in 1774, through the persecution of Chait Singh (known as the Benares charge), the awarding of corrupt contracts, the illegal acceptance of bribes and presents, and of course the treatment of the begums of Oudh. Sheridan was given responsibility for the begums charge, which was by far the strongest.

On 1 May Hastings himself was allowed to address the House of Commons in his defence. He came away feeling that he had "turned all minds to my own way" and believing that the whole business would, therefore, soon be dropped. Yet, for Hastings, his decision to give a detailed defence to each charge was to prove a terrible mistake. Sheridan's great strength as an orator was in appropriating the words of his enemies and transforming their meaning. By laying out his own narrative of events Hastings had given Sheridan precisely the ammunition he needed. It is noticeable that after Hastings's speech, Sheridan became much more deeply involved in the impeachment debates, speaking on India at regular intervals.

Burke lost the first vote—on a motion to impeach Hastings on the Rohilla charge—on 2 June, and since the government refused to support the charge, it was generally believed that the impeachment process would go no further. However, even in defeat there was some evidence that the independent country gentlemen who made up the centre ground in Parliament were beginning to turn against Hastings. And less than a fortnight later, on the Benares charge, Pitt expressed the view that the fine imposed on Chait Singh had been "exorbitant, unjust, and tyrannical." He allowed that charge to go forward, while explicitly refusing to commit himself to supporting a final vote for impeachment. The danger for the opposition was, however, that with Parliament going into recess, their momentum would soon dissipate.

In January 1787, when the new parliamentary session resumed, Sheridan began to take the initiative. He called Nathaniel Middleton, the resident at Lucknow, who had been Hastings's agent in the seizure of the begums' treasure, to give evidence before the House, and himself conducted most of the examination. Through the questioning, Sheridan established that a key part of Hastings's defence was untenable. Both to the East India Company's court of directors in 1782 and to the House of Commons in 1786, Hastings had justified the seizure of the treasure on the grounds that it was a punishment for the begums' refusal to hand over lands to the wazir. From an examination of the documents and from his cross-examination of Middleton, Sheridan was able to destroy this defence completely. He showed beyond any doubt that Hastings had authorised the seizure of the treasure *before* any attempt had been made to take possession of the lands.

Thus, even before Sheridan opened the debate on the charge, Hastings was forced to change his story. On the morning of the debate, in early February, Hastings had to issue a new defence, and to claim that the one he had delivered in the House the previous May had been written for him by Major Scott and by Middleton. He now claimed that between September and December 1781, he had received new information on the depth of the begums' involvement in stirring up rebellions against the company, which had led him to believe it was necessary to take the treasure as a punishment. This allowed Sheridan not only to exploit the contradictions between different versions of the events but to subject to scrutiny both the claim that the begums had fomented rebellion and the claim that Hastings had learned something new and significant about this after September 1781. He had the governor-general cornered, for if Hastings knew very little about the alleged subversive activities of the begums before September, then everything that happened later was entirely unjustifiable. If, on the other hand, he knew a great deal, then his new justification for the seizure of the treasures was a lie. In the detailed forensic work he had done in January, Sheridan had already won half the battle.

The begums' land and treasure had been taken for a very simple reason: the company wanted the money. But Hastings needed to construct a more high-flown motive, and he had sent Chief Justice Impey to collect affidavits showing that the begums had encouraged rebellion. Impey was called to give evidence before the House in January, and Sheridan found sufficient mistakes and contradictions in the affidavits to convince him that they were, in effect, concoctions. Thus Impey, too, was now forced to amend his evidence.

When, on 7 February, he rose to propose the Oudh charge, Sheridan occupied a commanding position. But he still had the huge task of transforming a mass of minute forensic detail into an epic drama.

In facing it, and a House of Commons packed with members, lords, and visitors, he spoke rapidly, clearly, and with supreme confidence, detailing without notes a vast amount of evidence. According to Wraxall, who was on Hastings's side, Sheridan "neither lost his temper, his memory, nor his judgement, throughout the whole performance." He began by confronting the belief that it was a waste of time for Parliament to be examining events that had taken place six years previously in a faraway place at a time when there were more pressing concerns to engage its attention.

> Is parliament mis-spending its time by inquiring into the oppressions practised on millions of unfortunate persons in India, and endeavouring to bring the daring delinquent who had been guilty of the most rapacious peculation, to exemplary and condign punishment? Is it a misuse of our function to be diligent in attempting, by the most effectual means, to wipe off the disgrace affixed to the British name in India, and to rescue the national character from lasting infamy?

Then, in his most triumphant act of appropriation, he announced that the main witness he would bring forward to support his charges of tyranny, oppression, corruption, and cruelty would be "one whom no man would venture to contradict—Warren Hastings himself." He took his audience on a guided tour through Hastings's evidence, using a close reading of the texts and a careful construction of chronological sequence to show that the real crime of the begums lay not in fomenting rebellion but in possessing the wealth that Hastings wanted: "Their treasure was their treason."

In his appropriation of Hastings's evidence, even non-events could be given a positive and powerful charge. Hastings maintained that he did not know the details of the methods Middleton used to torture the eunuchs. Even in accepting that Middleton had spared his master the minutiae, Sheridan conjured appalling visions: "He did not, perhaps, descend to the detail; he did not give him an account of the number of groans that were heaved; of the quantity of tears that were shed; of the weight of the fetters; or of the depth of the dungeons . . ." He also brought to bear the full weight of the powers of linguistic analysis learned from his father. Of Hastings's written self-defence he suggested that its defects of style pointed to defects of character. He painted him, in other words, as Joseph Surface:

> In his mind all is shuffling, ambiguous, dark, insidious, and little; all affected plainness, and actual dissimulation;—a heterogenous mass of contradictory qualities; with nothing great but his crimes; and even those contrasted by the littleness of his motives, which at once denote both his baseness and his meanness, and mark him for a traitor and a trickster. Nay, in his stile and writing there is the same mixture of vicious contrarieties;—the most grovelling ideas are conveyed in the most inflated language; giving mock consequence to low cavils, and uttering quibbles in heroics; so that his compositions disgust the mind's taste, as much as his actions excite the soul's abhorrence.

The brilliance of Sheridan's rhetoric lay not just in this turning of Hastings's evidence against himself but in its continual switching from the general to the particular, and from the epic to the mock-heroic. At one moment, he conjured up the teeming masses of India, the "oppressed multitudes"; at another he brought the whole saga down to the level of a single family, accusing Hastings of the "atrocious design of instigating a son against his mother" and of "sacrificing female dignity." At one moment, he was discoursing on the finer points of Muslim inheritance law; at another he was throwing out homely comparisons:

> Mr Hastings left Calcutta in 1781 and proceeded to Lucknow, as he said himself, with two great objects in his mind; namely, Benares and Oudh. What was the nature of these boasted resources?—that he should plunder one, or both,—the equitable alternative of a highwayman, who, in going forth in the evening, hesitates which of his resources to prefer—Bagshot, or Hounslow. In such a state of generous irresolution did Mr Hastings proceed to Benares and Oudh.

Likewise Impey, going about collecting affidavits to prove the begums' guilt, was "like an itinerant informer, with a pedlar's pack of garbled evidence and surreptitious affadavits." Impey had stated in his evidence that his tour of Oudh collecting affidavits was a kind of holiday. Sheridan picked up the image with superb sarcasm:

> Sir Elijah stated his desire of relaxing from the fatigues of office, and unbending his mind in a party of health and pleasure; yet

> wisely apprehending that very sudden relaxation might defeat its object, he contrived to mix some matters of business, to be interspersed with his amusements. He had therefore, in his little airing of nine hundred miles . . . escorted by an army, selected those very situations where insurrection subsisted, and rebellion was threatened . . . and passing through a wide region of distress and misery, explored a country that presented a speaking picture of hunger and of nakedness, in quest of objects best suited to his feelings, in anxious search of calamities most kindred to his invalid imagination.

He made devasting use of the contrast between the criminality of Hastings's behaviour on the one hand and his concern to dress it up in legalisms on the other:

> No sooner had Mr Hastings determined to invade the substance of justice, than he resolved to avail himself of her judicial forms; and accordingly dispatched a messenger to the chief justice of India, to assist him in perpetrating the violations he had projected. Sir Elijah having arrived, Mr Hastings, with much art, proposed a question of opinion, involving an unsubstantiated fact, in order to obtain even a surreptitious approbation of the measure he had predetermined to adopt. "The Begums being in actual rebellion, might not the nabob confiscate their property?" "Most undoubtedly" was the ready answer of the friendly judge.

And he tore Impey's affidavits to shreds. In the case of one witness who was able to "remember" events five years later which he had forgotten at the time, he remarked that there was evidently something "so relaxing in the climate of India and so affecting the memory as well as the nerves" that "men must return to their native air of England, to brace up the mind as well as the body, and have their memories, like their sinews, restrung."

Finally, after five and a half hours of cataloguing British shame, he concluded by holding out to his undoubtedly flattered audience a vision of British resurrection. If Hastings was the false man of sentiment, the Members of Parliament could be the real thing. Benevolence could enter their hearts and then be extended across thousands of miles to the Indian masses:

> You cannot behold the workings of the heart, the quivering lips, the trickling tears, the loud and yet tremulous joys of the millions whom your vote of this night will forever save from the cruelty of corrupted power. But though you cannot directly see the effect, is not the true enjoyment of your benevolence increased by the blessing being conferred unseen? Would not the omnipotence of Britain be demonstrated to the wonder of nations, by stretching its mighty arm across the deep, and saving by its *fiat* distant millions from destruction? And would the blessings of the people thus saved dissipate in empty air? No! if I may dare to use the figure,—we shall constitute Heaven itself our proxy, to receive for us the blessings of their pious gratitude, and the prayers of their thanksgiving.—It is with confidence, therefore, that I move you on this charge, "that Warren Hastings be impeached."[4]

The appeal was perfectly pitched, for the audience responded not as factional parliamentarians but as eighteenth-century men of sensibility. As soon as Sheridan sat down, the whole House, reportedly for the first time in its history, erupted in a tumult of cheering and applause. One member, Sir Gilbert Elliot, wrote to his wife next morning, with the speech "still vibrating on my brain":

> It is impossible to describe the feelings he excited. The *bone* rose repeatedly in my throat, and tears in my eyes—not of grief, but merely of strongly excited sensibility; so they were in Dudley Long's, who is not, I should think, particularly tearful. The conclusion, in which the whole force of his case was collected, and where his whole powers were employed to their utmost stretch, and indeed his own feelings wound to the utmost pitch, worked the House up into such a paroxysm of passionate enthusiasm on the subject, and of admiration for him, that the moment he sat down there was a universal shout, nay even clapping for half a second; every man was on the floor, and all his friends throwing themselves on his neck in raptures of joy and exultation. This account is not at all exaggerated and hardly does justice to, I daresay, the most remarkable scene ever exhibited, either there or in any other popular assembly.[5]

All the force of Romantic sensibility—tears, rapture, passion—had been unleashed on a parliamentary audience that had no defences against it. Sheridan had managed in Parliament to provoke the explosive response of an overwhelmed audience that had terrified Frederic Reynolds ten years earlier. Having brought down the house with the screen scene in *The School for Scandal*, he now brought the House down with his oratorical exposition of Hastings's perfidies. The enthusiasm went far beyond any notion of mere rational assent. The Earl of Chatham wrote the following day that it was "one of the most wonderful performances I ever heard, and almost the greatest imaginable exertion of the human mind."[6] Sir Philip Francis, whose Junius Letters had so influenced the young Sheridan, told the House the next day that he was still so overwrought that he could not do justice to the speech. He, too, resorted to the language of sensibility. Sheridan's was, he said, a triumph of the heart:

> I have always considered the human heart as the true source of human wisdom and folly as well as of virtue and vice . . . If this is true, the world would measure the virtues of [Sheridan] by his abilities; they would judge of the pure and copious fountain by the magnificence of the stream, and give him a higher and more honourable place than ever among the greatest of mankind.

John Wilkes, the old radical hero, now mellowing into hard reaction, voted against Sheridan on the motion, but confessed that he had been "dazzled with the brilliant eloquence and captivated with the beauty and variety of [Sheridan's] wit."[7]

Sir Horace Walpole wrote to the Countess of Ossory in the tones of a lonely sceptic confronted with universal belief in miracles:

> One heard everybody in the streets raving on the wonders of that speech; for my part I cannot believe it was so supernatural as they say—do you believe it was, Madam? . . . How should such a fellow as Sheridan, who has no diamonds to bestow, fascinate all the world?—Yet witchcraft, no doubt, there has been, for when did simple eloquence ever convince a majority? Mr Pitt and 174 other persons found Mr Hastings guilty last night . . . Well, at least there is a new crime, sorcery, to charge on the opposition.[8]

Pitt was indeed forced to put his weight behind the impeachment. Those who tried to speak for Hastings that night and the following day were shouted at, and the Pittite Daniel Pulteney wrote of "several of our own people clamouring at times with Sheridan from different parts of the House." Pitt sensed the mood. According to his supporter James Bland Burges, whom Pitt had deputed to speak in support of Hastings, he had intended to oppose the charge. But, the day after Sheridan's speech, Pitt described the Oudh charge as the one which "bore the strongest marks of criminality." That night, Sheridan's motion was carried by a huge majority, 175 votes to 68.

In Ireland, as news of Sheridan's extraordinary achievement spread, it was regarded as a national as well as a personal triumph. Charles told him that the speech would create "a new respect for the name of Irishman." Just as there had been few dry eyes in the House, there were also tears in Dublin: "I can solemnly declare to be a fact that I have, since the news reached us, seen good honest *Irish* pride, national pride I mean, bring tears into the eyes of many persons . . . who never saw you."[9] It may, indeed, have been about this time that Sheridan resolved to visit Ireland himself for the first time since his childhood: the following year Betsy mentioned that he was "by no means relinquishing his plan of visiting Ireland," implying that the intention—never fulfilled—had been formed for some time.[10] About the only person not to congratulate Sheridan on his speech was his father, who did, however, allow Lissy to tell his son that he was "gratified" and "truly pleased."

According to Hastings's agent, Major Scott, whose evidence must be treated with extreme caution, a translation of the speech was read to the begums of Oudh themselves in July at the palace in Fyzabad, and they were "so exceedingly callous as not to betray the slightest emotion of gratitude, though they expressed great remarks of astonishment on the occasion."[11]

The success of Sheridan's motion meant, nevertheless, that the impeachment of Hastings was now inevitable. Three more charges were carried by the House before, on 2 April, Sheridan himself put forward another, accusing Hastings of illegally accepting bribes and presents. The subject was, as Sheridan put it, "much colder and drier" than that of his last speech. He treated it without verbal pyrotechnics but with great clarity and force, laying out the case that Hastings had received bribes, notably one of £100,000 from the Wazir of Oudh in 1781, shortly before the seizure of the treasure, and another of the same amount from the same source in 1782. Again, he won the vote handsomely, and the following day, along with Fox, Burke, Windham, Grey, and others, he was appointed to a committee of the House charged with preparing the impeachment.

By the middle of May, Hastings was formally impeached by the House of Commons of "high crimes and misdemeanours," to be tried by the House of Lords. The Lords, in turn, set February 1788 for the beginning of the trial. For Sheridan, who was to prosecute the Oudh charge, that meant that a year after performing a miracle he would have to follow it up with another.

Chapter 22

THE RIGHTS OF MAN

The scarlet draperies on the walls of Westminster Hall, and the aura of pageant they were meant to create, could not keep out a cold and chilling dampness appropriate to a recitation of tortures and abuses. The trial of Warren Hastings opened at high noon on 13 February 1788. The doors were flung open and Edmund Burke entered at the head of the managers of the prosecution, a scroll in his hand and deep solemnity on his brow. Behind him came Fox, Sheridan, William Windham, Charles Grey, and the other prosecutors. They took their seats in their own special box. They were followed by the members of the House of Commons, who sat on the green benches which stretched along the left side of the hall. Then began a procession of clerks and lawyers, peers, bishops, and state officers in their coronation robes, the princes, and finally the chancellor, Lord Thurlow.

Warren Hastings was summoned, and after a delay of ten minutes, during which the tension became almost unbearable, he was brought into the court, a small, pale, and almost emaciated figure in a silk suit the colour of poppies. It was not necessary to be, like Fanny Burney, a partisan of Hastings to sense the importance of the moment. Burney described Hastings as "a man fallen from such height of power to a situation so humiliating—from the almost unlimited command of so large a part of the Eastern World to be cast at the feet of his enemies."[1] Having been a mighty potentate, Hastings had to sit, as he wrote, faced with "the common gazing stock of thousands of spectators—to see their attention riveted to an orator bellowing the grossest invectives, to hear their bursts of laughter, and even their claps as of theatrical applause."[2]

For Sheridan, satisfaction at this epic fall from grace was tempered by the knowledge that he had to face a trial of his own. He spoke briefly at the opening of the proceedings, but his main speech on the begums charge was set for early June, and he was faced with the almost impossible task of living up to the reputation he had gained by his Commons speech. He decided not to repeat any of the original speech, but he was slow to set about the huge task of writing a second one which could, without the advantage of surprise, make an impact similar to the first. At Crewe Hall, where he stayed in late January and early February with Eliza, who was recovering from the shock of her sister Mary's death, he was unable to concentrate his energies and confessed to Samuel Parr that he had been "a little idle" and was suffering "a truant's feeling about my India task."[3] To Burke, who was clearly alarmed by Sheridan's failure to attend meetings of the managers of the prosecution, he offered apologies and assurances that he would "work very hard afterwards."

He kept his promise. The new speech he began to write was full of high-flown eloquence and spectacular rhetoric, but it was also marked by what Sir Gilbert Elliot would call "acute and forcible and close reasoning." He organised the detail of the charge with both forensic acuity and exemplary clarity, ensuring that his more showy feats of language would support, rather than distract from, the truth of his accusations against Hastings. Eliza was "pestered with letters from morning till night to enquire when he is to speak and we continually hear of people coming from very distant Countys." This burden of expectation weighed heavily on Sheridan. He was "nervous and alarm'd at the wonderful expectations which everybody entertains of him . . . he feels how much of his name and future fortune depends perhaps on this event and is consequently at times uneasy . . ."[4] So much so, indeed, that when Alicia and Betsy wrote from Dublin to say that their father was ill, Elizabeth kept the news from Sheridan, fearing that "if I was at this time to acquaint him of his father's situation, it would terrify him and possibly prevent the exertion of those abilities on which so much depends."

He had good reason to be terrified. By 3 June, the first day of his speech, anticipation had given way to hysteria. Tickets for the hall were changing hands for as much as fifty guineas. The doors were to open at nine, though the business would not begin until noon, yet the crowds began to build up from six o'clock onwards, and by eight the New and Old Palace yards, leading to the hall, were packed with people. Many of them, "even women," as Sir Gilbert Elliot remarked in horror, "have slept at the coffee-houses adjoining Westminster Hall, that they may be sure of getting to the door in time." When the doors opened, there was a terrible crush. Many fashionable ladies lost their shoes in the mêlée, some going into the hall barefoot, others picking up other women's strays and sitting in the hall all day wearing one red and one yellow shoe.

Finally the show began. Sheridan rose to speak from the manager's box, with Burke on his left and Hastings in a separate box on his right, and declared the world's obligation to Burke for setting in motion "this embodied stand in favour of the rights of man against man's oppression."[5] At first, it seemed that Eliza's premonitions of disaster might come true. He was obviously nervous, and his voice failed to fill the echoing hall. At one point, he blanked out for a few terrifying moments before recovering his flow. But he gradually took control of himself and his audience, and at the end of the four and half hours for which he spoke on the first day, he had the audience, and Hastings's reputation, at his mercy with his charge that "the British government which ought to have been a blessing to the powers in India connected with it, had been a scourge to the natives, and the cause of desolation to the most flourishing provinces in Hindostan." The sceptical Walpole judged that Sheridan had not quite fulfilled the expectations that had been raised, yet added that the country was "not absolutely gone when history and eloquence throw out such shoots!" The more partisan Elliot admitted that the first day's speech had "imperfections and drawbacks" but still considered it "one of the very finest and most surprising exertions of genius I ever witnessed."

Sheridan continued the speech three days later, this time more confidently, displaying powers that Elliot judged "hardly to be conceived, and perhaps never equalled in their kind." He spoke mostly of the supposed rebellion of the begums and enjoyed himself by searching Impey's affidavits for evidence of it.

> In this rebellion, there is no soldier, neither horse nor foot: not a man is known fighting: no office-order survives, not an express is to be seen. This Great Rebellion, as notorious as *our Forty-Five*,

> passed away . . . *beginning* in nothing—and ending, no doubt, just as it began. If rebellion, my lords, can thus engender unseen, it is time for us to look about. What hitherto has been *dramatic* may become *historical*; Knightsbridge may at this moment be invested; and all that is left us, nothing—but the forlorn hope of being dealt with according to the statute—by the sound of the Riot Act, and the sight, if it can be, of another Elijah!

In more sombre tones, he satirised two of the commonplaces of British imperialism—the notion that British rule has a civilising effect and the idea that British mastery of other races is God's will. In the first place, he painted a daringly grim picture of the effects of British rule:

> Should a stranger survey the land formerly Sujah Dowlah's, and seek the cause of its calamity—plains unclothed and brown, villages depopulated and in ruins, temples unroofed and perishing, reservoirs broken down and dry—he would naturally ask what monstrous madness had ravaged thus, with wide-spread war—what desolating foreign foe—what disputed succession—what religious zeal—what fabled monster has stalked abroad? . . . the answer will be, if any answer dare be given, No, alas! not one of these things! . . . All this has been accomplished by the friendship, generosity and kindness of the English nation. They have embraced us with their protecting arms, and lo! we sink under the pressure of their support—we writhe under the grip of their pestiferous alliance!

And in the second place, he unmercifully lampooned Hastings's claim to the House of Commons that Providence had guided his actions. When, said Sheridan, a rajah accused Hastings of treachery,

> Providence so orders it that the Rajah has committed a *forgery* some years before; which, with some *friendly assistance*, proves a sufficient reason to remove out of the way so troublesome an acquaintance. If the company's affairs are deranged through the want of money, Providence ordains it so that the Begums, though *unconsciously*, fall into a rebellion, and give Mr Hastings an opportunity of seizing on their treasures! Thus the successes of Mr Hastings depended not on any positive merit in himself; it was to

the inspired *felonies*, the heaven-born *crimes* and the providential *treasons* of others that he was indebted for each success.

In such passages Sheridan began to extend the attack beyond Hastings and even beyond India and to come to grips with the basic assumptions that underlay the whole imperial project. But the strain was beginning to tell. After four hours of continual speaking, he stopped, "apparently exhausted." He resumed on the following Tuesday, but during the afternoon was taken ill. He asked for a break to see if some fresh air might revive him, but when it did not, the trial was adjourned. He spent that night "vomiting so severely as to make it doubtful whether he would be able to speak at all" the next day. These doubts were justified: the trial had to be postponed until Friday to allow Sheridan to recover.

When it resumed, Sheridan quickly returned to his attack on the reality of sacred British values in India:

> This was British justice! this was British humanity! Mr Hastings ensures to the allies of the company, in the strongest terms, their prosperity and his protection; the former he secures by sending an army to plunder them of their wealth and desolate their soil! His protection is fraught with a similar security; like that of a vulture to a lamb; grappling in its vitals! thirsting for its blood! scaring off each petty kite that hovers round; and then, with an insulting perversion of terms, calling sacrifice *protection!*

In assaulting the sacred symbols of British rule, Sheridan went so far as to reverse the meaning of the British flag itself. Dealing with the removal of the eunuchs from Fyzabad to the company's fortress at Srinagar, Sheridan picked up on the fact that the flag that flew over this second, more terrible, dungeon was the Union Jack:

> After being confined in Fyzabad—after being double-ironed at Lucknow—after being publicly scourged—now comes the climax, the threat that they will send them—where?—to Chunar Ghur . . . There where the British flag was flying, they were doomed to deeper dungeons, heavier chains and severer punishments;—there, where that flag was flying which was wont to cheer the depressed and to elate the subdued heart of misery, these venerable but unfortunate men were fated to encounter something *lower*

> than *perdition*, and something *blacker* than *despair!* . . . "We will send you from this place into custody purely British, and think what will be your situation then?" . . . They were both cruelly flogged, though one was about seventy years of age, to extort a confession of the buried wealth of the Begums! . . . "Tell us where are the remaining treasures . . . —it is only treachery to your immediate sovereigns:—and you will then be fit associates for the representatives of British faith and British justice in India!"

In conclusion he turned away from this "disgusting caricature" of justice and, giving full vent to the utopian strain that had been present in his thinking from his teenage years, launched into an impassioned evocation of the Enlightenment ideal:

> . . . the *real image—Justice!* I have now before me, august and pure, that abstract idea of all that would be perfect in the spirits and the aspirings of men; where the mind rises; where the heart expands; where the countenance is ever placid and benign; where her favourite attitude is—to stoop to the unfortunate; to hear their cry, and to help them; to rescue and relieve; to succour and to save!

Finally, with a dramatic "My Lords, I have done!," he swooned back into the arms of the waiting Burke. The historian Edward Gibbon, who was present on the last day of the speech to hear himself compared by Sheridan with Tacitus, wrote, "Sheridan at the close of his speech sank into Burke's arms;—a good actor; but I called this morning he is perfectly well." And indeed both Sheridan's friends and his enemies were aware of his performance at all times *as* a performance. Elliot described the crush of the crowd on the opening day of the speech as being "a rush as there is at the pit of the playhouse when Garrick plays *King Lear*." Ralph Broom, in his hostile satire on the trial, *The Letters of Simpkin the Second*, wrote of the reception by the audience of Sheridan's speech:

> The gallery folk, who, misled by the sport,
> Conceived 'twas a Play-House, instead of a Court;
> And thinking the Actor uncommonly good,
> They clapp'd, and cry'd "Bravo!" as loud as they could.

London audiences were, in fact, invited to make this connection for themselves. Covent Garden staged *The Duenna* while Sheridan was speaking at Westminster Hall, while his own Drury Lane put on *The School for Scandal*, implying that he himself did not mind if people saw a continuity between Sheridan the playwright and Sheridan the orator.

There was another, more profound sense in which this was a show. Even on the wave of optimism unleashed by his great Commons speech of the previous year, Sheridan must have known that this second astounding feat of oratory could not have a real effect. There were two chances of persuading the House of Lords, the very kernel of an entrenched oligarchy, to convict and punish a governor-general of Bengal for crimes against faraway people: fat and slim. It was, after all, Sheridan himself who, in his adaptation of the Vanbrugh play renamed *A Trip to Scarborough*, had a member of the House of Lords, Lord Foppington, when told that he is a "pillar of state," reply with the words "An ornamental pillar, Madam, for sooner than undergo any part of the burthen, rat me, but the whole building should fall to the ground."[6] And as events unfolded and the threat of revolution killed off the delicate buds of establishment radicalism, the trial of Hastings, long before its eventual conclusion in 1795, would come to seem an embarrassing anachronism, a throwback to a strange era when mere rhetoric could bring the House down. By then, anyone expressing outside Parliament the sentiments with which Sheridan had stunned its members in 1787 risked arrest and prosecution for treason. The prosecutors would become the prosecuted.

In the long perspective of history, the trial appears as a great moment in the history of international law. The ideas on which Sheridan relied—the universal nature of human rights and responsibilities—would not be fully elaborated until the twentieth century, but they were at least given powerful expression at the heart of an imperial power. Yet in the shorter perspective of the 1780s, they could only be, as Sheridan more or less acknowledged in his peroration, ideas of "what would be perfect." They expressed the preference he had admitted to Thomas Grenville sixteen years earlier, for viewing things "as I wish they *were* [rather] than as they *are*." They were, like a good piece of theatre, an exercise in attempting to answer the question "What if?"

Like all great public polemics, Sheridan's speech achieved its effect partly by means of an ingenious ambiguity. It was calculated to appeal simultaneously to monarchist conservatives and democratic radicals. On the one hand, he brought his ability to appropriate the rhetoric of the other side to new heights by exploiting his audience's sense of outrage at the desecration of hereditary power. Not the least of the ironies of the occasion, indeed, is that Sheridan's evocation of a royal household destroyed would, within two years, be turned back on him by Burke. The latter's lament for the destruction of the French royal family in *Reflections on the Revolution in France* owes a great deal to Sheridan's moving lamentations for the begums of Oudh. On the other hand, Sheridan tried to push this sympathy downwards into the mass of the "natives of Hindostan." The speech derived much of its power from its successful elision of the royal family and the Indian population in general.

It worked, too, because Sheridan brought his own deep-rooted concerns to bear on a world of which he had no direct knowledge or experience. In theory, the distance between Sheridan and India ought to have made his rhetoric artificial and ultimately bloodless. But in fact, he brought to the task in hand a range of both public and private obsessions that echo through his work both before and after the speech itself. His scornful dismissal of the "strange rebellion which was afterwards conjured up, and of which the existence and notoriety were equally a secret" looks back to the fabrications of *The School for Scandal* and forward to his great polemics of the 1790s against treason trials in Britain itself. His evocation of the sanctity of the zenana—the all-female compound in which the begums lived—violated by the company's intrusions, harked back to ideas for a sanctuary for single women he first voiced in 1772. And, most powerfully, his charge that Hastings had transgressed against nature by setting a son against his mother dredged up deep feelings of his own childhood longing for his mother's presence.

As his son was singing his hymn to "filial piety" at Westminster Hall, Thomas Sheridan was on the other side of the Irish Sea in Dublin. News of his illness with "dropsy and jaundice" was kept from Richard until after the speech, but by the time it was over he seemed to be recovering. He was well enough by 18 July to sail from Dublin, with the intention of consulting a particular doctor in London. When he got there, he found that all the talk was of his son. He dined with his old servant, William Thompson, who told him, "Sir, your son is the first Man in England—you will find every one of that opinion." After Thomas had gone to bed, Thompson insisted on acting out the peroration of the speech for Betsy: "Bad as the attempt must have been yet it convey'd some idea of the manner in which he spoke those words 'My Lords, I have done.' "[7]

The next day, when Betsy called at Bruton Street, she found her brother in an emotional state, preoccupied with thoughts of their father. "His eyes fill'd with tears and his voice choak'd. After embracing me very affectionately, he hurried out of the room. Mrs S. said he was *nervous* but would return soon which he did and then . . . he spoke very kindly of my Father." The day after, he and his father met and, as Betsy reported to Dublin, "All pass'd off very well—My Father a little stately at first but soon thoroughly cordial with his Son." For both of them, the triumph of the begums speech seems to have brought a realisation of how much, after all, they owed each other.

Thomas was anxious to go to a warm climate for the sake of his health, and decided on Lisbon. But he had got no farther than Margate when he became too ill to continue his journey. On 11 August, Sheridan arrived, bringing a doctor from London. His father "showed himself to be strongly impressed by his son's attention" and said "with considerable emotion," "Oh, Dick, I give you a great deal of trouble." The doctor who was present later said that Thomas Sheridan's manner seemed to imply "that his son had been less to blame than himself for any previous want of cordiality between them."[8]

After getting a few hours' sleep, Sheridan waited up with his father from three o'clock in the morning onwards. He stayed with him constantly for the next two days, until at last, on 14 August, Thomas Sheridan died. When he had breathed his last, his son closed his eyes. On discovering from Betsy that their father had expressed a wish to be buried in whatever parish he died, he arranged for the funeral at Margate, under the aisle of St. Peter's Church. Himself, his friend Richard Tickell, Thompson, and the doctor who had attended him were the only mourners.

It was, in one sense, fitting that this final reconciliation should take place in the aftermath of Sheridan's greatest oratorical triumph. The sensational impact of his two speeches on Hastings had been the ultimate vindication of his father's belief that public virtue could be upheld by public eloquence. And in spite of all the bitterness that had passed between them, Thomas Sheridan's obsession with the spoken word had undoubtedly contributed to his son's extraordinary ability to wield it as a weapon in the fight for human decency. In doing so, Richard had won a great personal victory. As a breathless Eliza wrote to Dublin,

> It is impossible . . . to convey to you the delight, the astonishment, the adoration, he has excited in the breasts of every class of people! Even party prejudice has been overcome by a display of genius, eloquence, and goodness which no one with anything like a heart about them, could have listened to without being the wiser and the better for the rest of their lives.[9]

But that triumph was also a burden. For even as he was denying that the begums had fomented one, Sheridan had also elaborated a rhetorical defence of armed rebellion. The cause of revolts, he said on the second day of the speech, was "that which Nature—the common parent—plants in the bosom of man." He continued:

> It grows with his growth! it strengthens with his strength! That feeling, which tells him, that man was never made to be the property of man; but that when through pride and insolence of power, one human creature dares to tyrannize over another, it is a power usurped, and resistance is a duty . . . Where there is injury will there not be resentment? Is not despair to be followed by courage? The God of battles pervades and penetrates the inmost spirit of man, and rousing him to shake off the burthen that is grevious, and the yoke that is galling; will reveal the law written in his heart, and the duties and privileges of his nature—the grand, universal compact of man with man! . . . that the rights of men must arm against man's oppression, for that indifference were treason to the human state; and patience, nothing less than blasphemy against the laws which govern the world.

This was dangerous talk, both because the events it sought to justify were attacks by colonial natives on British soldiers and because the appeal of the oratory was self-consciously universal, applying to all peoples in all circumstances. Whether he realised it or not, he was laying down principles which would within a year be on the lips of millions in France, in Ireland, and in Britain itself. He would be called on, sooner than he could have imagined, to show that he believed his own rhetoric.

Chapter 23

THE TONGUE SET FREE

The novelist Fanny Burney, keeper of the Queen's robes at the court of George III, spoke with the King one day in October 1788, or rather, as she put it, "I was the object to whom he spoke," for in those days George had begun to talk at people. He talked "in a manner so uncommon that a high fever alone could not account for it; a rapidity, a hoarseness of voice, a volubility, an earnestness—a vehemence rather—it startled me inexpressibly."[1] This encounter between a writer lost for words and a king unable to contain the flow of speech expresses well the state of England during the first episode of King George's madness. The barriers between thought and speech, between the private and the public, between the governance of the tongue and the governance of the realm, had collapsed.

It began with wet stockings and four pears, the King having, on 16 October, eaten the latter and refused to change the former. An attack of biliousness and pain that followed marked the onset of porphyria, a rare and then undiagnosed metabolic condition in which the nervous system is attacked by toxic chemicals, causing agony, nausea, paralysis, and delirium. But at the time the only word for the King's condition was madness. Words seemed to have taken on a life of their own: George was bewildered to find that having intended to say a certain prayer in the morning he was actually saying another one altogether.[2] Language and imagination, for a while, seemed to run riot at the heart of power. The borders between art and life, between the imaginary and the real, dissolved. The King could not stop talking, even though it was hard to hear him. On one occasion, he dictated from Cervantes and the Bible simultaneously to servants whose patience he rewarded by making them baronets and knights of the Holy Roman Empire. Fanny Burney reported him as "talking unceasingly; his voice was so lost in hoarseness and weakness, it was rendered inarticulate." The more he talked, the more inarticulate he became. He talked one day "for 19 hours without scarce any intermission." Meeting him accidentally in Kew Gardens, she found herself on the receiving end of a torrent of words. George still had "just such remains of his flightiness . . . as robbed him of all control over his speech." He repeated phrases and sentences over and over, uttered the word *no* "a hundred times in a breath." He gave her the entire life history of each of his page boys. He talked about Handel and ran through most of his oratorios, trying to sing them in a voice "so dreadfully hoarse that the sound was terrible."[3] He rummaged in his pockets for non-existent memorandums.

"I am nervous," he would cry. "I am not ill but I am nervous: if you would know what is the matter with me, I am nervous." He diagnosed himself because he sensed that his doctors would not tell him the truth: "I love Doctor Herberden best, for he has not told me a lie: Sir George has told me a lie—a white lie, he says, but I hate a white lie! If you will tell me a lie, let it be a black lie!"

Not only did the mad King begin to talk incessantly, pouring out an endless stream of language, much of it gloriously obscene, but he also played out absurd dramas, giving orders to non-existent people, imagining London flooded, and commanding his yacht to sail through the city, looking through a telescope and "seeing" Hanover, composing dispatches to foreign courts on imaginary causes, "elevating to the highest dignity . . . any occasional attendant." Power, literally, trembled. The great Lord Chancellor Thurlow, going in to see the King, "went into his presence with a tremor such as, before, he had been accustomed to inspire." George wrote down lists of the state officials he was going to sack and the new ones he was going to appoint, declaring: "I shall be much better served, and when once I get away, I shall rule with a rod of iron!" But this would-be tyrant was himself in need of firm rule. On 7 November he had risen in the middle of the night and refused to go back to bed until one of the equerries took him by the arm and led him away. "Here, then," wrote Earl Stanhope, "was the turning point. This was the precise moment when ceased the dominion of a Sovereign over his subjects and when began, on the contrary, the dominion of sound minds over an unsound one."[4]

With language gone astray and power deranged, Sheridan was in his element. The crisis exposed, ironically on its hundredth anniversary, the vulnerability of the British constitution established by the Glorious Revolution of 1688. It began to unfold just as Sheridan was involved with the Whig oligarchs in marking the anniversary, making for instance an "eloquent" speech at the Whig Club at the Crown and Anchor in the Strand, and proposing a subscription for a statue of King William. Yet at that very moment, there were reasons to believe that such a statue might be a memorial to a bygone era. The constitution was in chaos.

Parliament was prorogued until 20 November, but it would have to meet eventually because only the King could extend the period of suspension. Yet it could do no business until it was opened by the King or by a commission appointed by him. No regent could be designated except by Act of Parliament, and no such act could be valid without the King's consent. There were, as Pitt's cousin William Grenville wrote, "serious and difficult questions such as cannot even be discussed without shaking the security and tranquillity of the country."[5]

The vacuum created by the King's illness would have to be filled. If he died or if he was declared insane, the Prince of Wales would be either King or regent. And what then would this mean for Sheridan? In this crisis, his position as the most important link between the Prince and the political system ensured that he controlled one of the key approach roads on the path to power. Fox was away in Italy with his mistress Elizabeth Armistead for the first weeks of the crisis, not reaching England until 24 November, and even then he was tired and wracked with dysentery, leaving Sheridan free to work on the Prince. An anonymous ballad gave a sceptical view of his eminence:

> Poor Fox from Bologna was sent for in haste,
> And forc'd to forsake Betty Armstead the chaste;
> But when he arriv'd 'twas already too late,
> For *Dick* had usurp'd the first place in the State.
>
> Our Prince, with a view to improve this dull age,
> Has sought o'er all England for Counsellors sage,

And hopes by his choice to distinguish his reign,
Having chosen—the Manager of Drury Lane.[6]

The Prince's other important adviser was Loughborough, the former Lord Chancellor. But he, literally, owed his voice to Thomas Sheridan. In an earlier existence, he had been the Scot Alexander Wedderburn to whom Thomas had taught "a mode of speaking, to which Englishmen do not deny the praise of elegance." The younger Sheridan had little trouble exerting a similar influence over Loughborough, who told the Prince on 10 November that Sheridan's "judgement astonishes me as much as his extraordinary talents," and that he could add nothing to a long letter of advice that Sheridan had composed.[7]

As early as 6 November Sheridan was summoning the comptroller of the Prince's household, Captain J. W. Payne, to his house in Bruton Street; negotiating with Thurlow; and communicating urgently with the Prince, who was now at Windsor. Thurlow claimed that, on his visit to Windsor, he had advised the Prince to follow the instructions of the physicians and that the Prince had "appeared convinced," but that "after he saw Sheridan he adopted the contrary course."[8] On the night of 8 November, Payne wrote to Sheridan, enclosing a letter from the Prince, which contained full details of the King's state, arming him with the knowledge that at this unsettled moment was itself a form of power.

Sheridan was at the eye of the storm. The most precise—and accurate—details of what was happening at Windsor were being relayed to him at Bruton Street, and from there on to Dublin. Bruton Street was like a war room. Betsy, who was staying there, wrote to Dublin on 16 November remarking that since breakfast that day there had been "a constant Levee and the present situation of the king of course the only topic of conversation." Five days later, she reported the house "unsettled and uncomfortable . . . all confusion so that I literally can sometimes hardly find a place to sit down and write a line . . ." Sheridan had been gone since four in the morning to "a private conference. He is the head they all apply to now, and he will be if things turn out as we have reason to expect just what he chuzes."[9] (The conference was in fact a meeting with the Prince at Bagshot.) When he promised to spend a day with his family at Deepdene, in Dorking, which the Duke of Norfolk had lent them for the summer, he arrived very late at night, and was awoken at seven next morning with the news that Fox had arrived back from Italy and that he would have to go back to London immediately.

But this was the price of success. The Prince now had, as Betsy put it, "more esteem and friendship" for her brother "than for any Man in England." And this was not just the view of a doting sister: the Prince himself, speaking privately to the Duchess of Devonshire, "praised Sheridan very much and said that he has played his cards very well for he has devoted himself to a man who is not insensible to his merits." Payne sent Sheridan regular bulletins on the King's health ("The King last night about twelve o'clock . . . had a profuse stool") and told him, "Your advice will always be thankfully adopted."[10]

What Sheridan brought to the crisis was a democrat's keen sense of public opinion and a dramatist's feel for the importance of appearances. His immersion in an internal power struggle did not prevent him from seeing these extraordinary events as a drama which would have to play to different audiences—the political elite, Parliament, the press, the public. One of his first acts was to take control of the flow of information, first by keeping the details of the King's health out of the papers, and then by releasing selected facts. On 14 November, the *Morning Post* reported that "one of the leaders of the Opposition made use of all his influence to induce the Conductors of the Public Prints not to mention the illness of the King." That this leader was Sheridan is clear from a surviving letter of his written on 5 November to the editor of the *General Advertiser*: "I beg you will take care not to suffer anything whatever to be inserted in your paper respecting the State of the King's Health—it is the Prince's particular desire."[11]

He knew, however, that the effect of this would be merely to feed the wildest rumours, and indeed he told the Prince two days later that "the Town is full of Consternation and strange Reports—and these are increased by the silence of the Papers."[12] The rumours included one to the effect that Fox had poisoned the King and then gone to Italy to await the outcome. This was the time to release the grip: "The interdiction in the Papers should *in Part* be taken off. And a general line of intelligence . . . be permitted." One critical piece of information he had to control was the Prince's secret marriage to Mrs. Fitzherbert, the public revelation of which might have disastrous consequences for a regency. He devoted much effort to keeping Mrs. Fitzherbert calm and trying to reconcile her to Fox, and indeed to stopping the Prince from going into hysterics. Sheridan's authority was such that he could afford to display his irritation at the Prince's fears about his marriage to Mrs. Fitzherbert resurfacing, telling him that he had "the most womanish mind."

But the Prince's fears were not without foundation. There was now a widespread anxiety that not only was the country on the brink of civil war but if it came it would be in part a religious conflict. Anti-Catholic feeling was being stirred up, and Sheridan heard in late December that the ministers were planning to heighten religious tensions by forcing the Prince solemnly to declare that he had not contracted a Catholic marriage. Early in the New Year, the Duchess of Devonshire reported him on his way to a bookseller to suppress, presumably by paying off the publisher, a pamphlet which claimed that the Prince had no right to the throne because he had married a Catholic. He also went to John Rolle, the Tory who had raised the subject before, and asked him "in the Prince's name to desist from any enquiry about Mrs. Fitzherbert."[13] Rolle was not to be put off, however, and did raise the subject again in February 1789, when Sheridan produced another masterpiece of evasion, ridiculing his allegations without actually denying their truth.[14]

Information and intelligence were crucial to the power struggle, and every move was being observed. Lord Loughborough warned Payne: "I am sure His Royal Highness is very much watched . . . Expressions at table I am persuaded are very often collected and sent to some people."[15] Sheridan himself was certainly under official surveillance. A fragment of a spy's report survives in the papers of the Home Secretary, Thomas Townshend, Viscount Sydney.[16] The spy watched Sheridan from noon on 6 December until half past one the following morning:

> At twelve o'clock, Dr Ford and Kemble came and staid half an hour, at half after twelve Mr Wallace, attorney, Norfolk Street, came and stayed an hour. At Quarter before three o'clock Mr Sherriden went out on foot to Mr Wedgwood's in Greek Street, Soho, staid an hour and a half. From thence he went to Mrs Fitzherbert's staid half an hour, from thence to Mr Beckett's Pall Mall, staid a quarter of an hour, from thence to Brook's staid five minutes, from thence to Mr Fox's staid half an hour, from thence to the Duke of Devonshire's staid half an hour, from thence home staid a quarter of an hour, from thence he went to Mr Fox's to

dinner at half an hour after eight o'clock . . . Mr Sherriden there at half after one o'clock.

From the tone of the report, it is obvious that it was part of a surveillance mission which was already in progress and was expected to continue. And Sheridan probably knew he was being watched. In one note to the Prince's secretary he remarked that he would "send a man who will call on you very quietly, and without causing any Reports which the motion of a finger does at present."[17]

The skills of quiet deception and secret encounters learned during his courtship of Eliza were coming into their own. As well as being watched, he was also gathering his own information. He told the Prince that their enemies in the City of London, where Pitt had strong support, were already planning a response to the draft address to the nation which the Prince would deliver in the event of the King's death: "I have certain intelligence, that measures are *already taking place* to give a *particular complexion* to the address which would immediately come from the City of London in case of a certain event, and I suppose the same Game is preparing elsewhere."[18] He was able to report, not only that Pitt's supporters were planning a public meeting in Manchester, but that their plan to get it to pass an address of support for the Prime Minister would be thwarted.

His own game required a strict control of language, timing, and appearance—the opposites of the King's disordered tongue and dishevelled state. He suggested alterations to the Prince's proposed address to the nation, warning that "every syllable . . . will be canvass'd and all sort of *meaning* discovered in every syllable." Telling the Prince that his situation was "the most arduous, the most delicate, and difficult that can be conceived in the History of any country," he gave him detailed advice on every move in the psychological war against Pitt, who was desperately trying to keep control, first by trying to postpone a regency with the claim that the King would recover soon and, failing that, by making sure that any regency would not place the Prince in sole command. When the question of moving the King from Windsor to Kew arose, for instance, Sheridan warned the Prince to do nothing himself but to call a meeting of the cabinet and get them to make the decision, so as to place "responsibility where it ought to rest," in other words, to make sure that Pitt got the blame if anything went wrong.[19] And, above all, Sheridan was working to avoid a political arrangement that was being widely canvassed: a "unity" coalition between the Rockingham Whigs and Pitt. In one of a number of discussions with Sheridan around this time, Lord Thurlow, who was trying to keep in with both sides so as to save his own political skin whether or not the King recovered, "threw out to me a suspicion that Pitt and we should come together which I told him I thought utterly impossible for many reasons."[20] Sheridan's position in resisting such a move was greatly strengthened by the fact that, when at Windsor, the Prince had managed to get hold of his father's papers and to see that many of the more stinging rebukes he had received from the King over the previous few years had been drafted by Pitt. To Sheridan's evident delight, he heard the Prince abuse Pitt "like a Dog." But in the meantime, he continued to negotiate with Thurlow, believing that he could manipulate the Lord Chancellor's willingness to betray Pitt in return for a promise that he could retain his office in a new government. This scheme was distasteful to Fox, not least because he had already promised the lord chancellorship to Lord Loughborough, but as he wrote to Sheridan, "I have swallowed the pill—a most bitter one it is . . ."

Sheridan wormed his way so far into the intimacies of monarchical power that he was even writing letters from the royal family to the government. In one of history's more spectacular acts of ventriloquism, this self-made Irishman used the voice of the Prince of Wales, to address "his Majesty's confidential servants" (the cabinet) in tones of imperious command, informing them in a note he wrote in the early hours of the morning of 27 November that "the [royal] Family have received communications from the Physicians attending on his Majesty upon which The Prince must decline giving any opinion untill the whole of his Majesty's situation has been fully examined into by his Majesty['s] confidential Servants . . ."[21]

When it met on 20 November, Parliament had agreed merely to adjourn for fifteen days. When it met again on 4 December, it was becoming difficult to avoid some decision about a regency. The previous day, the King's physicians had been examined by the Privy Council, and all except Richard Warren, who was close to Fox and the Prince, agreed that King George was totally incapable at the moment but, given time, would probably recover. Warren was equivocal, suggesting that neither he nor anyone else had enough knowledge to say whether the King could recover at all. The report of the Privy Council was then laid before Parliament, which agreed, four days later, that each House would appoint its own committee to examine the physicians. The doctors became, as Burke said to Fox, "the men in power." And each side in the power struggle had its own physician: Warren for the opposition, Dr. Francis Willis for the government.

Sheridan was elected to the committee to examine the physicians, but he was also holding private discussions with Warren, making sure that he continued to give a pessimistic account of the King's prognosis. And he both harasssed Willis in the examinations and ridiculed him in the debates. On 16 January 1789, for instance, he attacked the inconsistency of Willis's claim on the one hand that the King's illness resulted from twenty-seven years of overwork, and on the other that his treatment had produced a marked improvement in a day:

> What must I think of Dr Willis when I hear him assert that his physic could in one day overcome the effects of seven and twenty years hard exercise, seven and twenty years study, and seven and twenty years abstinence? . . . Such assertions remind me of those nostrums which were to cure this and that malady and also disappointments in love and long sea voyages.[22]

Sheridan, with the astonishing concentration that he could summon up in periods of crisis, also set about making himself an expert on constitutional law and the precedents for a regency. The Duchess of Devonshire reported him spending "all day" at home on Sunday, 21 December, "studying precedents—Henry ye 6th, a whole Pile of [them]," but before he was out of bed, there came a message from the Prince "to beg to see him." Though first insisting that he was unwell and had taken medicine, within half an hour, as Betsy reported to Dublin, both the Prince and the Duke of York had arrived and were "both boring him and preventing him reading said papers."[23] When they finally left him alone, he complained of being ill and not properly prepared to speak in the debate on the regency next day. Yet all through the increasingly tortuous wranglings about the nature of, and limitations on, the regency that continued throughout January and February, he revelled in his position as the conductor of conspiracies, whispering in the Prince's ear, trying to entice Thurlow onto their side, attempting to loosen Pitt's still formidable grasp on power.

And then, all of a sudden, Fox, who was still unwell and was, moreover, inclined to listen to the oligarchs' suspicions about Sheridan, threw it all away with a single disastrous speech. While Sheridan was urging subtlety and caution, Fox blundered in to attack Pitt's proposals to make the regency subject to conditions to be laid down by Parliament with a high Tory tirade against limitations on royal power. He leaped headlong into the trap of arguing for the Prince of Wales's "right" to be regent and scorning the audacity of Parliament's apparent belief that it could interfere in that right. A delighted Pitt, famously remarking that he would "UnWhig the gentleman for the rest of his life," seized the opportunity to present himself as the defender of Parliament against monarchical arrogance. Pitt, adding a further dimension of drama to the crisis, had himself written at the age of thirteen a blank-verse tragedy in which a loyal minister defeats the intrigues of a conspirator who is trying to gain control of a regency. And he, like Sheridan, showed a dramatist's instinct for playing to the gallery. Sheridan tried to distance himself from Fox's folly by telling the House of Commons that the issue of the Prince's "right" should not have been raised, and he added that Pitt should not provoke "that claim to be asserted." Pitt brilliantly confounded him by interpreting his climb-down as a threat issued on behalf of the Prince. Sheridan leaped up to deny the suggestion, but the damage had been done.

He was furious with Fox. Not only did Fox's argument run against the grain of his own political ideals, but, with his acute consciousness of public opinion, he also realised that it would be viewed as a cynical betrayal of principles in the pursuit of power. At Devonshire House he attacked Fox, who replied that it was better to take the bull by the horns. "Yes," retorted Sheridan, "but you didn't have to drive the bull into the room first." According to the duchess, he was "out of spirits" over Fox's mistake, agreeing not to break openly with Fox's line but "very sorry that things are put out of ye course he put them in." In his own subsequent speeches, though, his divergence from his leader's tactics was obvious in the way he avoided the issue of the Prince's "right" to the regency by arguing that Pitt's real motive for placing restrictions on it was to limit the power of the "different body of men" that the Prince would inevitably ask to form a government. His own prospective place in that body was, however, a source of tension. As the reality of power came into view, it gave a sharp edge to relationships within the opposition, and animated the latent distrust of Sheridan among the aristocratic oligarchs. The Duke of Portland was offended by the close consultation between Sheridan and the Prince, and by January was declaring his determination "not to act with Mr Sheridan in council." Lady Elizabeth Foster reported that Charles Grey believed that Sheridan had deliberately insulted him in front of the Prince. Sheridan and Grey were believed to be rivals for the position of Chancellor of the Exchequer in the putative new government, though on 23 November, the Duchess of Devonshire, who was privy to all the internal gossip of the Whigs, noted in her diary,

> Sheridan might certainly be Chancellor of the Ex[chequer] if he chuses, but prefers reaching it by degrees and when he has prov'd his capability to ye public—he argued with Grey who would only accept the Chancellor of the Exchequer or Secretary of War. Grey says he will give way to Ld John [Cavendish], Charles Fox or Sheridan—but not to those Norfolks, Wyndhams and Pelhams. Sheridan wishes it to be a true Rockingham administration.[24]

Her belief that Sheridan wanted a less elevated position than Chancellor of the Exchequer is supported by the *Morning Post* of 28 November, which published a list of putative members of the new government, with Sheridan as treasurer of the navy. This is also in line with his refusal to seek personal advantage from his influence over the Prince. Both Betsy and Eliza were urging him to grab a sinecure, "any *Patent place* the regent may have to dispose of in Ireland," but his sister reported that his wife had told her that such was his "shyness of applying for any personal favour that tho' She knows the Regent would rejoice in the opportunity of providing for him, She has no hopes of his taking one Step in the business."[25] But his lack of greed did nothing to dampen the rivalries, and by 5 December, the duchess was noting, "Feuds between Grey and Sheridan worse than ever."

One factor in Sheridan's restrained attitude to the prospect of power in England was that he was keeping an eye on Ireland. Just before the crisis broke, he had been intending to go back to his native country for the first time since his childhood. Betsy reported in July 1788 that he was "by no means relinquishing his plans of visiting Ireland."[26] And now the political chaos threw up an intriguing possibility. His grandfather had, with Swift, played rhetorical games with the idea of the King of England not being the King of Ireland. That rhetorical notion now began to take on a certain reality. The Irish government supported Pitt's plan for a limited regency, and assumed that the Irish Parliament would follow the lead of Westminster. But the Irish opposition was attracted to the notion of having the Prince declared regent of Ireland in his own right, without Pitt's restrictions. Their main motive for doing so was to emphasise the standing of the Irish Parliament in its relations with the crown as a force separate from and equal to the British. And Sheridan did all he could to encourage the idea.

Towards the end of December his brother, Charles, who had been in the Irish government as under-secretary for military affairs since his defection from the opposition in the early 1780s, switched sides. He felt sufficiently confident of coming to power to boast to the Lord Lieutenant, the Marquis of Buckingham, that the days of the then Chief Secretary, William Grenville, were numbered. In anticipation of a change of government, Charles resigned from his office and started to use the words "we" and "us" in referring to his brother's political allies. His defection was a shock to the government: Buckingham was "more angry with me than with any other person who opposed him," Charles wrote to Sheridan. He began to work, with very considerable success, to get the Irish Parliament to offer the regency independently to the Prince. Given Charles's eye to the main chance, it is likely that he did this not out of any very profound sense of principle but rather on the promise of reward from his brother. As Betsy noted with her usual sharpness, Charles would have to be safe "in his own mind" before making any political move: "He would have taken due time to reflect before he resign'd."[27]

Sheridan was, through Betsy, supplying the Dublin Sheridans with that most precious of commodities: information. And when Charles gave a speech in the Irish House of Commons in February, arguing that the independence of the Irish Parliament would be undermined if it waited to see what Westminster was going to do, Sheridan had it published in London, and told Charles that "you have great credit with us."[28] That credit was all the greater when, in February, against the wishes of the government, the Irish Parliament voted to offer the regency of Ireland to the Prince.

Pitt and his supporters had meanwhile started a counter-attack against Sheridan's manipulation of public opinion by invading his own territory. On 26 December, a claque in the audience at Drury

Lane called loudly for "God Save the King," which was not usually played in the theatre. When it was sung, and the phrase "scatter his enemies" was reached, it was greeted with loud cheering and wild shouts. This anti-Sheridan demonstration gave the caricaturist Sayers the cue for a cartoon called "A Peep Behind the Curtain at Drury Lane," in which the audience in the pit is shouting "Play '*God Save the King*.' " Sheridan is peering out through a small gap in the curtain and hissing at the orchestra, "Damn'ee don't play '*God Save the King*.' "

Around the same time, Thomas Rowlandson published a cartoon entitled "Buff and Blue Loyalty," in which Sheridan and Dr. Willis face each other in two drawings, one entitled "Saturday" and the other "Sunday." On Saturday, Willis is being asked, "Doctor, how is your patient today?" and replies, "Rather worse, Sir." Sheridan, with a cunning and self-satisfied smile, says, "Ha-ha rare news." On Sunday, when the same question is put to him, Willis says, "Better, thank God," and Sheridan angrily shouts, "Damnation!"

On 12 January 1789, the pro-Pitt *Times* attacked him in a verse called "Queries Addressed to a Great Man's Great Man":

> Must Pitt from Honour's post retire
> He who so well has served the sire
> Give place to the Son's fav'rite Squire—
> Dic Sheridan
> Shall pseudo-patriot take the lead?
> Our Sovereign's foes to power succeed,
> Guilt at their heart—and at their head,
> Dic Sheridan
> And Britain her lost friends bewail
> Whilst faction laughs and cries—all hail
> Dic Sheridan.

And, as usual, Sheridan was vulnerable to slurs on his financial probity. The following day, placed prominently on the front page of *The Times*, was an advertisement calling on "such persons as have any demands on Richard Brinsley Sheridan" to proceed to the Shakespeare Tavern in Covent Garden, the Whigs' election headquarters, to have their financial demands checked prior to payment. Two days later, the paper admitted that this advert was "an imposition" and carried a statement from Sheridan that "if it is meant as humour, we are authorised to say the writer is a fool—and if seriously, then he is a fool and a libeller."

Rumours spread, too, that the Sheridans had been evicted from Bruton Street and had moved in with Mrs. Fitzherbert. That this was entirely untrue did not stop even the Archbishop of Canterbury, John Moore, from asserting it with the utmost confidence. He wrote on 16 January that Sheridan was

> . . . actually an intimate at Mrs Fitzherbert's now, with his wife. They took refuge there on being driven out of their own house by the bailiffs who are now in it. He is on all hands understood to be the prime favourite, and to be so sensible of it as modestly to pretend to a Cabinet place, which is firmly resisted by the Duke of Portland, who says they cannot both be in the same cabinet. Sheridan would willingly submit to be Chancellor of the Exchequer, but it is thought things are not yet ripe enough for the manager of Drury Lane to be manager of the House of Commons.[29]

These attacks were motivated not merely by a belief that Sheridan was the guiding hand behind the Prince's manoeuvres—successfully wooing, for instance, the Earl of Lonsdale, who controlled nine votes in Parliament, from Pitt's side to theirs—but by the knowledge that he was orchestrating the opposition press, especially the *Morning Herald*. Two days before the false advertisement, *The Times* had attacked him as the father of lies, referring to "the false and scurrilous paragraphs with which the Opposition prints are daily furnished by Mr Surface and his would-be witty associates."

Sheridan retained his hold over the Prince, however, and was given the task of composing the latter's magisterial reply to Pitt's offer of a conditional regency. Two drafts were prepared, one by Loughborough (which Sheridan found "all ice and snow"), the other by Burke ("all fire and tow"), and he then had to "make one out of Both."[30] He used this opportunity to put words into the Prince's mouth that were more pleasant to his own ears. Fox's doctrine that the Prince had a "right" to be regent was replaced by a more subtle contention that he should be regent unless the most obvious considerations of the "public utility" argued otherwise. The crown's powers were, he wrote, "a Trust for the Benefit of the People . . . and are sacred only as they are necessary to the Preservation of that Poise and Balance of the Constitution which Experience has proved to be the true Security of the Liberty of the Subject . . ."[31]

The letter had to be delivered on 2 January, but Sheridan had stayed "too late" at Devonshire House the previous night and was unable to get the final draft to Eliza, who was to copy it out in her much more elegant handwriting, until two in the afternoon.[32] It was late in the evening before he set off for Fox's house to show him the letter, wrapped against the bitter cold in a new fur-lined coat that the Prince had given him. A note he had written the previous day promising to be there at nine in the morning was pinned up above the mantelpiece. Fox abused him for the delay, and, as the duchess noted, "They have been boudeing [sulking with] each other all day." The row was settled two days later, but it was a sign that their friendship, after Fox's dreadful speech on the regency, would never be as easy as it had been before.

Sheridan's relations with Burke were also becoming strained. Burke resented Sheridan's rise to prominence at his own expense (he was himself a very marginal figure in the whole regency crisis) and in particular his rewriting of the Prince's reply to Pitt. Sheridan for his part was angered by Burke's behaviour when, on 6 January, he suggested his own amendment to a motion concerning the medical examination of the King. The motion was defeated because of Burke's mishandling, but Sheridan was blamed by the Whigs and was, according to the duchess, "very angry." And, around the same time, Grey and Sheridan were again privately accusing each other of treachery.

To make matters worse, Sheridan was literally faced down by the King's "mad-doctor," Francis Willis, whom he had teased so unmercifully in Parliament. In a January hearing of the committee examining the doctors, Sheridan tried to perplex Willis with "a long string of questions." But Willis, who was reputedly able to terrify the wildest of maniacs with his piercing gaze, remarked, "Pray, sir, before you begin, be so good as to snuff those candles that we may see clear, for I always like to see the face of the man I am speaking to." This, reportedly, so disconcerted Sheridan "that he could not get on in his examination, and for once in his life he was nonplussed."[33]

By the time the Regency Bill finally passed the House of Commons on 12 February, Pitt's brilliant delaying tactics were triumphantly vindicated. First Dr. Willis, and then even the opposition's pet physician, Warren, pronounced the King to be on the road to recovery. On the same day, Sheridan received a letter from Charles in Dublin informing him of the good news that the Irish Parliament had voted to declare the Prince regent of the kingdom of Ireland. It was, as Betsy noted without obvious regret, an "unlucky" move because any regency was now certain to be short and, on the King's full recovery, Charles would be dumped out of office again "without any compensation." (Being Charles, he in fact managed to wring a pension of £1,000 a year from the Irish government.) Sheridan sent him both congratulations on his part in the plot and condolences for his failure to receive the full reward for his sacrifice: "I wish you joy of your share of the good Deeds of Ireland—and I hope I may wish joy of no ill consequence following to yourself." His own demeanour at the news that all his schemes were coming to nothing was remarkably calm. By the end of the month, when it was completely clear that the King would be well enough to resume the throne, Betsy reported him "quite himself and Mrs Sheridan more cheerful than for many weeks past. The most disappointed faces are those who had least right to be sanguin."[34]

Just as the King's recovery was being announced, the delegates from the Irish Parliament sent to offer the Prince the regency of Ireland arrived in London. They were jeered and treated, as Betsy remarked, "like so many Indian chiefs," but Sheridan was ostentatiously kind to them, attending all their dinners and even arranging a dinner party for them at Bruton Street, to which he invited the Prince, Mrs. Fitzherbert, and the Duke of York. He also had the latter elected president of the London–Irish Benevolent Society of St. Patrick, with himself as vice-president, thus giving formal expression to both his Irish and his royal connections. However ludicrous the Irish delegates now seemed to London society, to him they suggested an intriguing set of possibilities. For the moment the Prince would not be King of Ireland, but having come so close to power this time, might he not be so in the near future? Might Sheridan not be able to use the ascendancy he had gained over him—which now extended to his writing the Prince's letters justifying his conduct during the crisis to both his mother and his father—to influence events in his own country? These possibilities, tantalisingly close to becoming actualities, would, from now on, never be far from his mind.

In the meantime, a loyal face had to be put on. When a grand ball was held at the Pantheon to celebrate the King's recovery, Sheridan's butler, Edwards, got the chance to earn some extra money as a waiter for the evening and Bruton Street was full of jokes about him being forced to wait on Pitt. Such was the atmosphere in the house, though, that the other servants considered Edwards "a kind of *Rat* for voluntarily engaging in the Service of the Enemy."[35] But his master had his own humble services to render. On 26 March Sheridan and the other Foxites had to go to Windsor for a reception to mark the King's recovery. "The Q[ueen]," noted Harriet Duncannon, "stood near the middle window with a small space round her, through which everybody pass'd one by one. She did not speak to any of the principal Opposition people, F[ox], S[heridan], T[ierney], G[rey], and very cold to the P[rince]s."[36] Two days later at Devonshire House, the Prince in a panic announced to his friends that "they mean to alter the succession and give it to the Duke of York." He begged Sheridan to talk to the duke on his behalf, insisting that he loved his brother too much and "felt too much hurt to do it himself." Sheridan listened for a long time, "allowed the truth of what he said," and agreed to go to Windsor the following day to talk to the duke, meanwhile urging the Prince to spend the following week at Oatlands, the Duke of York's residence, where he might get a chance to see the King. The Prince was now his principal political asset, and he had no intention of losing him.

Chapter 24

A HERO AND A HARLEQUIN

A row of nuns sat across the table, two of them in black veils, two in grey. They were playing out a line from *The Duenna* in which Louisa says that "to be sure, the character of a nun is a very becoming one—at a masquerade." Another woman, Mrs. Fitzherbert, wore a white dress and a black veil, but since she was actually a Catholic it was best not to flaunt it and she made sure that she did not resemble a nun too closely. A Highland chief (the Prince of Wales) sat between Eliza, dressed as a Gypsy, and Hecate, the queen of the witches, really the Duchess of Ancaster. Sheridan was wearing a domino, a loose cloak, with the upper part of his face masked. But one mask was not enough for him, and after supper he slipped away, put on another disguise, and moved around the room as an unknown man, plaguing people, speaking in strange voices, enjoying the thrill of impunity. Then he slipped off the second unofficial disguise and resumed the domino, pretending that he had just been to another table.[1]

In his private as well as his political life, Sheridan loved to play such games, indulging in disconcerting shifts of identity. At the Pavilion in Brighton, he dressed up as a policeman and arrested the Dowager Lady Sefton for unlawful gambling.[2] At a country house, when the women had disguised themselves and challenged the men to guess who was who, he challenged them to a return match and sent them upstairs. When they came down, they found their husbands dressed in Turkish costumes and were unable to guess their identities, until Sheridan came in and revealed that the Turkish figures were actually the housemaids.[3] At Crewe Hall, when the owner expressed a desire to meet his friend Joseph Richardson, he announced that he had invited him and that he would visit the next day. When he arrived, Richardson's language seemed disgustingly lewd and vulgar, his manners disturbingly odd. Only when the visitor had sufficiently unsettled his hosts did Sheridan reveal that he had in fact paid one of Crewe's tenants to impersonate Richardson.[4]

Now, at this masquerade in Mrs. Sturt's mansion in Hammersmith in mid-June 1789, he had reasons to indulge this love of deception. One of the grey-veiled nuns, Lady Harriet Duncannon, younger sister of the Duchess of Devonshire, was casting "many tender looks" across the table at him. To the watchful eye of his sister Betsy, he seemed to be ignoring them. His wife, Eliza, looked particularly beautiful in her Gypsy dress and was, moreover, the centre of attention. Some catch singers came to the table, and the Prince inveigled Eliza into joining him in a trio, giving this privileged audience a chance to hear once more her famous voice. Afterwards, Sheridan stayed with Eliza all evening, and people remarked that with such a partner it was no wonder he did so.

Betsy's joy at seeing Harriet Duncannon's tender looks unreturned was, however, unjustified. Not for the first or last time, appearances were deceptive. As Harriet's diary shows, Sheridan was seeing her very frequently: on the evenings of 25, 26, and 28 March, and on 9, 11, 12, and 15 April, for example. Harriet (Henrietta) Duncannon was, at this time, just past her twenty-eighth birthday and, if anything, more beautiful than her sister. Her long, elegant nose, large dark eyes, and dark hair set off a strong, lean face; she was tall, graceful, and a notably good dancer; she was also well-read and witty, and blessed with incisive intelligence and easy self-assurance. She was the wife of an Anglo-Irish magnate, John Ponsonby, Viscount Duncannon (in 1793 he became the third Earl of Bessborough and she was known as Lady Bessborough), whose estates in the south-east of Ireland had been acquired as a result of the Cromwellian wars. An unremarkable man, whose obsessions were playing cards and buying prints, he spent much of his time abroad. Sheridan wrote to her around this time, casting her as Eve, himself as the serpent, and using the babytalk that society ladies favoured with their lovers:

> I must bid *oo* good Night for by the Light passing to and fro near your room I hope you are going to bed, and to sleep happily, with a hundred little cherubs fanning their white wings over you in approbation of your goodness. Yours is the sweet untroubled sleep of purity . . . and yet and yet Beware! Milton will tell you that even in Paradise Serpents found their way to the ear of slumbering innocence.—Then to be sure poor Eve had no watchful guardian to pace up and down beneath her windows . . . And Adam I suppose was—at Brooke's!—"fye Mr. S"—I answer "fye fye Lord D[uncannon]. Tell him either to come with you or forbid your coming to a House so inhabited!" . . . I shall be gone before your Hazel eyes are open tomorrow.[5]

On 18 June, just days after the masquerade when Betsy had been so pleased to see her brother ignoring Harriet's tender glances, one of the "Ladies of Llangollen," Sarah Ponsonby, a close relation of Lord Duncannon's, heard that Sheridan and Lady Duncannon had been caught *in flagrante* and that Lord Duncannon was to institute divorce proceedings.[6]

Gossip about Sheridan's marriage had in fact been in circulation since the later stages of the regency crisis, when a general assault on his character had become a weapon in the power struggle. In January the famous dissenting minister, Richard Price, had mentioned in a letter to Lord Lansdowne "the loose and dissipated character" of the Prince's adherents, "particularly Sheridan."[7] In March, Eliza, though unwell, had been forced to attend society functions merely to counter rumours that Sheridan was locking her up, beating her, starving her, and using her "in every respect ill." In Sheridan's case, no reports were too salacious to be disbelieved. On the contrary, as Betsy noted, "the eagerness for scandal makes them wellcome."[8] The rumours were themselves untrue. Betsy, who was living with the Sheridans, described them as "infamous falsehoods," and Eliza herself assured her closest confidante, Mrs. Canning, that Sheridan never "used her ill."[9] But there was a bleak truth behind them, and the marriage, long under strain from Sheridan's neglect of Eliza, was approaching a breaking-point.

Sheridan's private affairs had public consequences. Another quarrel between him and Grey in early June nearly led to a duel, which would have had rather serious repercussions for the Whigs.[10] But just as he and Harriet were being found out, news of rather more momentous events in France, where the Third Estate of the States-General had proclaimed itself the National Assembly, was reaching London. Within a month the Bastille fell, and Fox wrote, famously, to Richard Fitzpatrick: "How much the greatest event it is that ever happened in the world! and how much the best! . . . all my prepossessions against French connections for this country will be at an end, and indeed most part of my European system of politics will be altered, if this revolution has the consequences that I expect."[11] Sheridan's initial reactions to the Revolution are not recorded, but they were undoubtedly those that he expressed a little later: "I never thought I should live to wish myself a Frenchman—but I would not hang the poor old foolish men."[12] He was, in other words, entirely on the side of the Revolution, and deeply envious of the historical fate that allowed middle-class intellectuals like himself in France to live out the implications of their convictions. His discomfort at the violence that accompanied their triumph did not stop him from sharing it. Everything in his intellectual background—the influence of Montesquieu and Rousseau, the deep distrust of royal power, the instinctive sympathy for the oppressed, the notion of a radical army that had remained with him from the triumphs of the Irish Volunteers, the relish for both democratic meetings and street politics—inclined him towards the same view of the Revolution as that which Fox so memorably expressed.

Edmund Burke, by contrast, was almost immediately sceptical of the Revolution. As early as August 1789, he was expressing that scepticism through theatrical metaphors: "Our thoughts of every thing at home are suspended, by our astonishment at the wonderful Spectacle which is exhibited in a neighbouring and rival Country—what Spectators, and what actors!"[13]

In the context of such political uncertainties, the state of the Sheridan marriage had grown beyond a domestic difficulty to become a threat to the stability of the Whig party. Lord Duncannon had decided not merely to seek a divorce from Harriet but also to sue Sheridan for criminal conversation with her, which would have made him, as Eliza put it, "an object of Ridicule and Abuse to all the World." The threat was taken with deadly seriousness: Harriet became physically ill. Sheridan, normally so confident in his ability to talk his way out of any corner, was "terribly frightened" at the prospect.[14]

Eliza, for her part, was being pursued by the Prince of Wales's younger brother, William, Duke of Clarence, and admitted that she was "not indifferent to his devoted attachment for me, and have thought more favourably of him still since I have had reason to make comparisons between his Conduct and S[heridan]'s." To her censorious friend Mrs. Canning, she insisted that "you may rely on the propriety of my Conduct in regard to him for many sakes," but it is obvious that she was tempted, more out of revenge than lust.

Such were the political resonances of Sheridan's private life that the Duke of Devonshire, who had been abroad, returned to manage the crisis by soothing Lord Duncannon's injured pride and getting him to withdraw his legal action against Sheridan. Charles Fox and the Prince of Wales also became involved, with the Prince trying to cool his brother's ardour for Eliza and Fox trying to convince her to forgive her husband. By now, as Betsy reported, "Dick never stays two days at a time with her."[15] Things were so bad that Eliza eventually decided to seek a formal separation. She wrote to Mrs. Canning from Crewe Hall in early 1790:

> S[heridan] and I shall most probably come to an amicable separation when I return to town. We have been sometime separated *in fact* as man and wife. The world, my dear Hetty, is a bad one and we are both victims of its Seductions. S. has involved himself by his Gallantries and cannot retreat. The Duplicity of his Conduct to me has hurt me more than anything else, and I confess to you that my Heart is entirely alienated from him, and I see no prospect of Happiness for either of us but in the Proposal I have made him of Parting . . . I will in future live by myself and to my own tastes.[16]

Eliza had been alienated not just by Sheridan's affair with Harriet Duncannon but by his refusal even to observe the etiquette of polite infidelity. Even while pleading for her forgiveness and swearing never to be unfaithful again, he was doing so under her very nose. At Crewe Hall, he was caught *in flagrante* with a governess, Miss Ford, "by the whole House, locked up with her in a bedchamber in an unfrequented part of the House." Not just the act itself, but "the apparent total want of feeling for me, of all sense of Honour, Delicacy, Propriety, considering the *Person*, the *Place*, and the *Time*," so enraged Eliza that she was on the verge of running away with the

Duke of Clarence even though, as she put it to Mrs. Canning, "I should have hung myself a week afterwards."

The rejected Clarence instead found solace in the arms of the actress Dorothea Jordan. Eliza meanwhile did not imagine for a moment that there was any real prospect of reforming Sheridan, and resigned herself to a marriage kept on track towards eventual domestic peace in old age only by a long line of parallel affairs: "We are both now descending the Hill pretty fast, and tho' we take different paths, perhaps we shall meet at the bottom at last, and then our Wanderings and Deviations may serve for Moralising in our Chimney Corner some twenty years hence." Once Lord Duncannon had dropped his suit, in late March 1790 he and Harriet left England for Brussels. Betsy Sheridan commented in a letter to Dublin, "Lady Duncannon is, thank God, gone to Bruxelles. I should not be sorry to hear that she was drown'd on her way thither."[17]

But while one source of instability was being dispatched to the Continent, another was moving in the opposite direction. The reverberations of events in France gave a British political system already weakened by the regency crisis a yet more violent shake. Within the Whig party, the tremors would open a gaping fissure, and the most prominent figures on either side of the gap would be two Irishmen, Sheridan and Burke. Once again, the borders between personality and politics revealed themselves as permeable. The personal relationship between Burke and the Sheridans had always been complex, and the complications had always been reflected in diverging conceptions of the theatre. On the one hand, the young Burke had been prominent amongst the Trinity students who supported Thomas Sheridan during the Kelly riots in Dublin in 1747. On the other, that support had quickly turned to hostility after Thomas rejected a play called *The Lawsuit* offered to him by Burke either as his own work or as the work of his friend Brennan.[18] By the end of that year Burke had begun to denounce Thomas's "arrogance and ignorance" and to run a public campaign to "reform" Smock Alley. For the first four months of 1748, Burke published a newsletter, *The Reformer*, largely devoted to attacking Thomas Sheridan's choice of plays and accusing him of pandering to the audience's taste for dancers, music, and spectacle. Burke objected to the licentiousness of Restoration plays, and to kissing on stage. More woundingly, he insulted Thomas's personal appearance, acting style, and literary taste, accusing him of being effeminate and ludicrous. His manner of dying on stage, wrote Burke, would "afford you the double Delight of a Hero and a Harlequin."[19]

For a man as thin-skinned as Thomas, such mockery was not easily forgotten, and there is little doubt that Richard would have grown up with an image of Burke as an inherited enemy instilled into him. This did not stop him from associating with Burke, first in the Literary Club that met for dinner at The Turk's Head in Soho once a week, and then, of course, in most of the political campaigns undertaken by the Foxites. Sheridan initially treated Burke as a respected elder; he once remarked, for instance, "I don't mean to flatter, but when posterity reads one of your speeches in Parliament, it will be difficult to believe that you took so much pains, knowing with certainty that it could produce no effect, that not one vote would be gained by it."[20]

The balance of the relationship may have tilted gradually in Sheridan's favour over the next decade, but until the regency crisis there was never any doubt that Burke carried more weight. Sheridan may have personally outshone Burke at the trial of Warren Hastings, but only in the way that a star soloist might distract attention from the conductor. Now Burke had reason to contrast the younger man's importance in the regency crisis with his own patently marginal role. Not only had Sheridan moved ahead of him in the political order but Burke also suspected that, having stolen the glory in the impeachment proceedings, Sheridan was now neglecting his duties as one of the managers of the trial. In March 1789, Burke wanted him to speak on the opening of another of the charges against Hastings —that of having accepted "presents"—but Sheridan confessed that although he had the prosecution of Hastings "as sincerely at heart as even you yourself," he had been so busy with "the Political occupations of the Winter" that he was as ignorant of the details of the "presents charge" as if he had never heard of it.[21]

These personal tensions were not, of course, the reason for the very different reactions of Burke and Sheridan to the French Revolution, but they ensured that those political and philosophical differences would culminate quickly and dramatically in a public rupture. From watching Sheridan during the regency crisis, Burke had concluded that he was dangerously ambitious and recklessly willing to upset the careful balance of the British constitution. He now believed that Sheridan had a strategy of aligning the Whigs with the reformers outside Parliament and of placing himself at the head of a radical popular front. And he feared that unless he himself intervened to divide Sheridan from Fox, the latter would be unable to resist this swing to the left.[22]

Once again, Burke was to use the theatre as the medium for his contest with a Sheridan. In his first book, *The Sublime and the Beautiful*, published in 1756, he had argued that the theatre had lost its impact when it moved from transforming the intellect to arousing the emotions. In the 1790s, that distrust of the emotional power of theatre became entangled with his opposition to Sheridan and to the French Revolution. In his last speech at the trial of Warren Hastings, delivered in 1794, after his own transformation into the intellectual fountain-head of reaction, Burke reversed the meaning of the screen scene in *The School for Scandal*. For Sheridan the falling of the screen had represented a moment of truth, an end to lies, duplicities, and conspiracies. Theatre exposed hypocrisy and broke the spell of mendacity. For Burke, theatre was itself a factory of lies. What was revealed when the screen fell was the foul machinery behind the pretty illusion:

> Now, my Lords, was there ever such a discovery made of the arcana of any public theatre? You see here, behind the ostensible scenery, all the crooked working of the machinery developed and laid open to the world. You now see by what secret movement the master of the mechanism has conducted the great Indian opera, —an opera of fraud, deceptions, and harlequin tricks. You have it all laid open before you. The ostensible scene is drawn aside; it has vanished from your sight. All the strutting signors, and all the soft signoras are gone; and instead of a brilliant spectacle of descending chariots, gods, goddesses, sun, moon, and stars, you have nothing to gaze on but sticks, wire, ropes and machinery. You find the appearance all false and fraudulent; and you see the whole trick at once.[23]

In this extended metaphor, theatricality in general is explicitly attacked, but a more specific reference is also made to Sheridan. To a late-eighteenth-century English audience, mention of an opera with strutting signors and soft signoras could point in but one direction: to Sheridan's *The Duenna*. Still in constant production, the play was published that same year. The astounded delight of the screen scene is gone, and now, in Burke's language, it is theatre itself that is the illusion that must be swept away.

On 9 February 1790, in the debate in Parliament on the Army Estimates, Burke made his first open attack on the French Revolution, describing the French as "the ablest architects of ruin that have hitherto existed in the world. In that very short space of time, they have pulled down to the ground their monarchy, their church, their nobility, their law, their revenue, their army, their navy, their commerce, their arts and their manufactures." And he explicitly criticised Fox, who had earlier in the debate applauded the conduct of the French Army, which, he said, in taking the side of the people had proved that "men, by becoming soldiers, did not cease to be citizens." With "a pain inexpressible," Burke chided Fox and reportedly declared that he "would part with his best friends and join with his worst enemies to . . . resist all violent exertions of the spirit of innovation." Making clear the real object of his attack, he condemned "cabals he thought were forming to make alterations under the idea of reforms in our constitution, and looking at Mr Sheridan gave it to be understood that he was the person."[24]

Fox was deeply shocked and rose to reply with, as he put it, "a concern of mind that it was almost impossible to describe." He launched himself into a passionate tribute to Burke, declaring that

> if I were to put all the political information which I had learned from books, all which I have gained from science, and all which any knowledge of the world and its affairs has taught me, into one scale, and the improvement which I have derived from my right honourable friend's instruction and conversation were placed in the other, I should be at a loss to decide to which to give the preference.

And instead of taking issue with Burke, he seemed to defer entirely to his judgement, insisting that he himself would never "lend himself to support any cabal or scheme formed in order to introduce any dangerous innovation into our excellent constitution." Burke triumphantly accepted Fox's "explanation" as an exculpation. And Fox, for his part, seemed willing to allow his deference to Burke to be understood as a recantation of his pro-revolutionary sentiments.

Sheridan, seeing at once the implications of this, stepped in to reopen the wound. His words were spontaneous and improvised, but the intention behind them was precisely calculated. If Burke's combination of emotional blackmail and political persuasion succeeded in forcing Fox to hold his tongue, the Whigs would slip into impotent collusion with reaction. But if, on the other hand, Burke himself could be goaded into declaring a breach with his former allies, Fox's followers would be forced to define themselves more clearly as democrats, and Sheridan's own position would be strengthened by the defection of his most eminent rival. Sheridan, with no time to think, had to seize the moment. He got to his feet "in a fury" and, in a typical act of rhetorical appropriation, turned what Burke had said of Fox's pro-revolutionary speech—that he did not wish his silence to be taken as approval for the views of his friends—back on Burke himself. He paid some warm compliments of his own to Burke, but insisted that "he differed decidedly from that right honourable gentleman in almost every word that he had uttered respecting the French Revolution."[25] It was, he said, incomprehensible that a man like Burke, who revered the English revolution, should oppose the French. Nor could he understand Burke's charge that the French had pulled down their laws, revenues, and industry. "What," he asked, "were their laws? The arbitrary mandates of capricious despotism. What their justice? The partial adjudications of venal magistrates. What their revenues? National bankruptcy . . . The public creditor had been defrauded; the manufacturer was out of employ; trade was languishing; famine clung upon the poor; despair on all." He agreed with Burke in abhorring the cruelties inflicted by the revolutionaries, but laid the blame for them on the *ancien regime*, "that accursed system of despotic government which had so deformed and corrupted human nature as to make its subjects capable of such acts." And he ridiculed Burke's belief that the French might have received a good constitution from the King: "What! Was it preparing for them in the camp of Marshal Broglio? or were they to search for it in the ruins of the Bastille?"

Burke, as Sheridan had no doubt hoped, was stung into replying. He regretted sincerely, he said, to cheers from the ministerial benches, "the inevitable necessity of now publicly declaring that henceforth his honorable friend and he were separated in politics." Sheridan's attack was not "what he ought to have expected in the moment of departed friendship." He accused Sheridan of making "a sacrifice of his friendship for the sake of catching some momentary popularity," and warned him that "all the applause for which he could hope from clubs was scarcely worth the sacrifice which he had chosen to make for so insignificant an acquisition."

Sheridan was later said to have "expressed some contrition for his conduct on the very evening the conversation passed."[26] But if he did so at all, it is most likely to have happened two nights after the debate and to have been merely a tactical act of contrition. Dennis O'Brien and others arranged a meeting between Burke and Sheridan, with both Portland and Fox in attendance, at Burlington House on the night of 11 February. It lasted from ten at night until three the next morning.[27] Its outcome was an agreement to contain the split by avoiding the subject of the French Revolution in the House of Commons.

Although Sheridan respected this agreement in the House, he had no intention of allowing Burke to set the political agenda. Instead, he publicly flaunted his support for exactly the kind of alliance between parliamentary reformers and extra-parliamentary radical societies that Burke had accused him of favouring. He accepted an invitation for members of the Whig Club to attend a monster reform banquet to celebrate the first anniversary of the fall of the Bastille on 14 July at the Crown and Anchor Tavern. The dinner, chaired by the radical Lord Stanhope, was attended by 652 "friends of liberty," among them members of the London Corresponding Society, the Society for Constitutional Information, and the dissenting congregation of Dr. Richard Price, whose sermons were soon to be the object of Burke's *Reflections on the French Revolution*.

The banquet began with an invocation of the Supreme Being, and a stone from the Bastille walls was symbolically placed on the table. Sheridan, acting in the name of the Whig Club, rose to propose a resolution:

> That this meeting does most cordially rejoice in the establishment and confirmation of liberty in France; and that it beholds with peculiar satisfaction the sentiments of amity and goodwill which appear to pervade the people of that country towards this kingdom, especially at a time when it is the manifest interest of both states that nothing should interrupt the harmony that at present subsists between them, and which is so essential for the freedom and happiness, not only of both nations, but of all mankind.

John Horne Tooke moved a cautious amendment to Sheridan's motion that "we feel equal satisfaction that the subjects of England by the virtuous exertions of their ancestors have not so arduous a task to perform as the French have had; but have only to maintain and improve the constitution which their ancestors transmitted to them." Sheridan was in no mood to be mealy-mouthed and actually opposed this amendment, but it was passed as a separate motion.[28]

Sheridan's resolution confirmed Burke's worst fears. For him, it proved that Sheridan was intent on undermining the unity of the Whig party in an effort to form a broader association of the "friends of liberty" with himself at its head. The resolution also had an impact in France. Lord Stanhope sent a copy of it to his friend the Duc de Rochefoucauld, with a request that it should be presented to the National Assembly as evidence that "soon we hope that men will cease to regard themselves under the odious aspects of tyrants and slaves, and that, following your example, they will look on each other as equals and learn to love one another as free men, friends, and brothers." The resolution evoked spontaneous congratulations from Jacobin clubs all over France.[29]

Sheridan's attempts to create a new alliance between Whig reform and popular support for the French Revolution was supported by Charles Grey, but Fox, in spite of his rhetoric, was more cautious. His enthusiasm for the Revolution had as much to do with his belief that it would weaken French competition with Britain as with his approval of its political principles. In March, when Henry Flood introduced the subject of reform in Parliament, Fox described it as a "sleeping question" on which the public was not yet ready for change.

If Fox was uneasy, the Duke of Portland, already leaning towards Burke's side, was furious at Sheridan's conduct. On 16 April Sheridan felt it necessary, in the course of a speech on tobacco duties, to insist—rather dishonestly—that he still enjoyed Portland's favour, and to deny "whispers or reports of jealousies among some of his dearest friends."[30] Many of these rumours were political, but some, as he said, had "fallen without mercy not only on his public conduct, but also on his private life." This time, however, the rumours had a solid foundation: Eliza, no less than her estranged husband, was making revolutionary connections of her own.

Chapter 25

NIGHT, SILENCE, SOLITUDE, AND THE SEA

In March 1814 at dinner in Samuel Rogers's house, the twenty-six-year-old Lord Byron sat listening to Sheridan talking of the great political upheavals of the 1790s: treason was in the air, Sheridan himself took the side of the seditious and the subversive, and Britain and Ireland were shaped by the twin forces of repression and resistance. Byron, though already an astoundingly successful poet, was overcome with feelings of jealousy and regret. For all his glamour and fame, listening to Sheridan made him feel that he had missed the best time to be alive. He lamented that at the time he had been but an infant: "If I had been a man," he wrote in his diary that night, "I would have made an English Lord Edward Fitzgerald."[1]

That Byron should fantasise about being an English version of Lord Edward Fitzgerald was not surprising. Fitzgerald was the epitome of the Romantic revolutionary, a handsome lover whose genuine political idealism added to his sexual allure, a golden youth who died a hero's death at the age of thirty-five, a scion of the aristocracy who took up the cause of egalitarianism and national independence. Byron lived out the identification with Fitzgerald that took root in his mind that night, and managed to die fighting for Greece at the same age that Fitzgerald died in the cause of Irish independence. What seems at first sight surprising, however, is the fact that Sheridan's memories provoked this fantasy. The Lord Edward Fitzgerald that Sheridan evoked so powerfully for Byron was none other than his own wife's lover.

Lord Edward was a younger son of the Duke of Leinster, and

thus a member of what was regarded as the first family of the Irish aristocracy. He was also a cousin of Charles James Fox, and the Sheridans had known him since 1784, when he helped the Foxites in the Westminster election. Back in London in 1791, after adventures in America and France, he was an open and enthusiastic supporter of the Revolution. Although his great-great-grandfather Charles I had been beheaded, he was not at all opposed to the decapitation of kings. He was a prominent member of the circle of democrats around the great radical pamphleteer Thomas Paine, and in 1792 the Marquis of Buckingham reported that he had "long before been mentioned to me as speaking the most direct treason."[2] By the summer of 1791, he and Eliza were lovers. It is obvious from one of her letters to Sheridan that he was beginning to be worried about their liaison. In a reply to a note of his, presumably hinting at his displeasure, she defended herself, referring specifically to Fitzgerald ("Lord F"), as well as to one of the Grenvilles who was also paying court to her:

> Whilst I live in the world and among people of the world, I own to you I have not courage to act differently from them. I mean no harm. I do none. My vanity is flattered, perhaps, by the attentions and preference which some men show towards me; but that is all. They *know* I care for nothing but *you*, and that I laugh to scorn anything that looks like sentiment or love. I feel naturally inclined to prefer the society of those who I think are partial to me. Lord F. and H. Grenville both appear to like me, that is to say as far as laughing and talking goes. As to anything serious, even if they were inclined to think of it, they know me too well to risk being turned into ridicule for the attempt. I never miss an opportunity of declaring my sentiments on the subject, and I am perfectly convinced they have no other views in seeking my society than that of amusing and being amused.[3]

But Fitzgerald was soon amusing her with more than laughing and talking. After she had visited East Burnham, where she and Sheridan had lived so happily when they were first married, she wrote to Mrs. Canning, "I wept so pitifully at the sight of all my old Haunts and the ways of Happiness and Innocence. But though I have tasted the forbidden fruit since that time, I have gained the knowledge of good and evil by it."[4] The forbidden fruit, surely, was

Fitzgerald. By the summer of 1791, she was not only sleeping with him but pregnant with his child. He described their relationship to his mother:

> When I look back on my conduct and see, loving her as I did—and God knows still do—how often I was near destroying my own happiness, I know I am not fit for marriage. She managed me, but I had no right to expect it then, or to expect to find it again. I am afraid I have given her very unhappy moments, but upon the whole, more happy ones or she would not have loved me.[5]

It is not hard to see why she was so attracted to him. He was young and well travelled, had beautiful eyes, and was besotted by her. For some years now she had been ready, at least in theory, to seek love and pleasure elsewhere. She and Sheridan were no longer sleeping together, and she was the object of other men's interest. In 1788 Betsy Sheridan reported that Eliza had told her that "she had converted Mrs Canning who was *uncommonly rigid* in her notions," and that Eliza now expected to persuade the righteous Betsy herself to stop "thinking differently in point of morals." But there is no evidence that before her relationship with Fitzgerald she had had other love affairs. The most powerful restraint on her sexuality was fear. She was at this time frequently ill and occasionally coughing up blood. As her father had warned Sheridan all those years before, pregnancy was likely to harm her delicate health. And in 1787 these anxieties had been deepened by the death from tuberculosis of her sister Mary. She must have known the risks that her relationship with Fitzgerald entailed, and her willingness to run them is a mark of her loneliness. With Mary dead and Betsy Sheridan, who had been an amiable companion for the previous few years, returned to Dublin to be married, she no longer had the close female companionship that had sustained her through Sheridan's early infidelities. In spite of promises to mend his ways, Sheridan was by now spending little time with her. Her affair with Fitzgerald probably began while Sheridan was with the Prince in Brighton. But even when he was in London, he was not much at home. William Godwin noted around this time, "Sheridan spends the night in gambling and dissipation." He had taken to breakfasting at the club in St. James's

Street owned by Louis Weltje, chef and confidant of the Prince of Wales; there he would feast "upon everything that was out of season to the amount of thirty pound per breakfast." According to Godwin, he ran up such huge debts with Weltje that he was arrested and the Prince had to intervene to sort things out and prevent a scandal.[6]

More serious, from the point of view of his relationship with Eliza, was that Harriet Duncannon's hasty departure for the Continent had not ended his infatuation with her. Unlike his affair with Mrs. Crewe, which had been conducted in the aristocratic spirit of amorous adventure, this one had turned, on his side at least, into a deep and abiding love. They were again in correspondence, and Sheridan expressed himself "happy and easy" at the news that she had recovered from illness. It was no longer possible for Eliza to see his infidelities as occasional aberrations. Harriet had, in effect, replaced her as the love of his life.

When it became known that Eliza was pregnant by Fitzgerald, Sheridan had the honesty to blame himself. Instead of assuming a distance from her, he moved closer, realising not only that her betrayal was a result of his own but that the consequences of her pregnancy might well be fatal. Her affair with Fitzgerald had undermined her last remaining friendship, that with Mehitabel Canning, who, contrary to what Eliza had told Betsy, had not been converted to aristocratic notions of sexual freedom. Sheridan, however, stepped in to heal the breach, first by arranging for Mrs. Arabella Bouverie, a mutual friend, to mediate, and then by writing to Mrs. Canning himself:

> I am confident you do not know what her situation is, or what effect may arise, and has indeed taken place on her mind, from the impression or apprehension that the Friend *she loved best in the world* appears, without explanation even, to be cooled and changed towards her . . . Pray forgive my writing to you thus, but convinced as I am that there is *no chance of saving her Life,* but by tranquillizing her mind, and knowing as I do and as I did hope you knew that God never form'd a better heart, and that she has no errors but what are the Faults of those whose conduct has created them in her against her nature, I feel it impossible for me not to own that the idea of unkindness or coldness towards her *from you* smote me most sensibly, as I see it does her to the soul.[7]

Almost as soon as Eliza became pregnant, the symptoms of tuberculosis reappeared. She was coughing blood. She was suffering, too, from the fevers and chills which seemed to be in the air of Isleworth that summer, and which also affected her husband. In mid-August *The Gazeteer* reported that Sheridan had been "confined for some days at Isleworth with a fever and sore throat which have prevailed this season very much in that neighbourhood." While he recovered, though, her illness lingered and she became weak and thin. The only consolation was that it provided an excuse for her to move out of Isleworth and to be with Fitzgerald: the need for a "change of air." As an army officer, he was stationed with his regiment in Portsmouth, and early in the New Year of 1792, she moved to nearby Southampton.

Fitzgerald, as he wrote to his mother in Ireland, intended to "go to see her whenever she lets me know she is arrived and that she can see me."[8] For him the affair had been much more than a passing diversion, and he believed that she returned his devotion. "During her illness at Southampton and in town," he wrote, "she must have seen how truly I loved her. Indeed she told [me] she did, and owned it almost made up to her for being so ill." He remarked "with what patience that angel bore her long illness and confinement, with what little repining."[9] But the affair was closer to a ménage à trois than to a conventional adulterous escapade. Sheridan spent some days at the end of January and the beginning of February 1792 with them in Southampton. He had to go back to London for political and theatre business, but returned in early March. What he saw of Eliza convinced him that she was dying. One night he went for a long walk on his own on the beach and thought about the past. As he wrote to Harriet, "Night Silence Solitude and the Sea combined will unhinge the cheerfulness of anyone, where there has been length of Life enough to bring regret in reflecting on many past scenes, and to offer slender hope in anticipating the future."[10] The sound of the sea reminded him of the voyage to France with Eliza after their elopement, when he had decided that, if she died on the passage, he would plunge into the grave after her. Now that she was really about to die, he could not work himself into such paroxysms of grief. The contrast between the passionate love he had felt then and the gloomy despair that was all he could muster now made him feel diminished. "What has the interval of my Life been, and what is left me—but misery from Memory and a horror of Ref[l]exion?"

At the end of March or the beginning of April, Eliza gave birth to a baby girl at Cromwell House, Brompton, in London. At the christening a month later she called her Mary, after her dead sister: the new life was at once a reminder of impending death. As Fitzgerald told his mother, she "encouraged all my dear thoughts about it. I had seen it in her arms, kissed, cried over it together. She wanted me to love it, had made me nurse it before her . . ." He saw the child as his way of capturing for himself Eliza's own early life, when he had not known her, thinking of "all the dear delights of seeing, as I had flattered myself, my dearest Betsy live, and tracing her through all her different stages of life, seeing her in her Youth, and fancying such had been her Mother before I knew her. In short, all the love of the Mother had centred in that child."

The mother, however, was dying. Although she showed signs of recovery after the birth, they didn't last long. She and Sheridan set out for the Hot Wells in Bristol, where the warm springs might have helped to restore her health. But he knew there was little hope. On the road to Bristol, he wrote to Harriet: "Many gloomy omens have told me our Hopes will be disappointed. I have been in long and great anxiety about her—flying from my Fears and yet hoping, one event safely over, that all would be well." They passed through the outskirts of Bath, she stretched out in one coach, he following her in his. When they came to Kingsdown, where he had fought his second duel with Mathews twenty years before, he stopped his coach and let her go on ahead. He walked over the down to the spot where they had fought, now marked by a large stone. He remembered lying there, thinking he was dying, and recalled all the promises he had made to himself then. "What an interval has passed since," he reflected, "and scarce one promise I made to my own soul have I attempted to fulfill." The sight of her carriage trundling along ahead of him wrung his heart. "My nerves are shook to pieces. The irregularity of all my Life and pursuits, the restless contriving Temper with which I have persevered in wrong Pursuits and Passions makes . . . reflexion worse to me than even to those who have acted worse."[11]

Edward Fitzgerald was not with them, but in Bristol they met up with his aunt, Lady Sarah Napier, who was herself nursing her sick husband, so that the sense of Eliza's belonging now to both her own family and to Fitzgerald's was kept alive. Mehitabel Canning was also with them, and she reported that Sheridan was doing everything he could "to soothe and comfort her." She was seeking comfort in religion, so he read her a sermon every night, and he kept up a brave face before her, reserving his gloom until after he had retired to bed. Alone, at night, he was sunk in feelings of horror, sleeping badly, tormenting himself with guilt, and expecting at any moment to be woken by some new crisis in her health. He found it especially difficult to restrain himself when one night she sat at the piano and played some music "with tears dropping on her thin arms," looking, as it struck him, "like a Shadow of her own Picture"—Joshua Reynolds's famous portrait of her as St. Cecilia sitting at the harpsichord. He decided to send for Tom, who was at school with his old friend Samuel Parr.

Throughout May and June, she swung between apparent recovery and relapse, and he remained with her, except for a few short visits to London on urgent theatre business, cut off from political events like the opening of negotiations between Pitt and the Duke of Portland that would lead, eventually, to a complete split in the Whig party. His only political communication was a letter written at Eliza's request to the resigning Lord Chancellor, Thurlow, asking a favour for her brother Ozias. In Sheridan's absence, Drury Lane was running into deep financial trouble, and at the beginning of June John Philip Kemble resigned the management of the theatre. But Sheridan was unable to deal with anything except Eliza's impending death, in anticipation of which Tom and her father came to Bristol. Her doctor, Andrew Bain, found Sheridan's "kindness to her, quite the devotedness of a lover."

During the last week in June, Eliza used what little strength she had to take her leave of her loved ones, seeing each of them in turn when the weakness of her once glorious voice, now almost gone, would permit. She told her father that instead of grieving he should be proud of her now when she really had something to boast of in the "perfect resignation with which she left a world that smiled on her." Sheridan would stay up all night with her. Around midnight on 28 June, Bain was called. When he arrived, Sheridan and Mrs. Canning were with Eliza in her bedroom. She asked them to go and had Bain lock the door behind them. Then she turned to him: "You have never deceived me. Tell me truly, shall I live over this night?" He felt her pulse, found it weak, and told her, "I recommend you to take some laudanum." She understood the import of his reply and took the laudanum (liquid opium), knowing that it would help her to take her leave.[12] When Sheridan was called back into the room and seemed about to weep, she told him, "Don't let me see so much kindness, for it will weaken my fortitude, I fear." She told him to go if he could not bear the sight, but if he could, to stay to the last. Then, grasping his hand, she gave a gentle shudder and died. Lady Sarah Napier wrote:

> His grief is very affecting, because quite free from ostentation, and his whole thought and conversation are recollections of all her wonderful, *good* mind. He dwells sadly on the idea that, if he had led a regular life suited to her cast of character she would not have died. And reproaches himself most cruelly for a thousand things—not that he ever used her *ill* as Mrs. C[anning] assures me he never did, but neglected her.[13]

Two years later, the sound of her sister singing in a voice that carried some resemblance to hers could still bring tears to his eyes.

By now, Eliza's illness and the cause of it had become subjects of public comment. Many years before at Oxford, the crowd, believing Sheridan dead, had watched her perform with a special rapture. Now her own death became a public spectacle. At Wells Cathedral, where she was buried, the crowds were so large that the carriage bearing her coffin could hardly get through the streets. The funeral was, as Sheridan remembered years later, "a gaudy parade and show from Bristol to Wells Cathedral, where all the mob, high and low, were in the church surveying and surrounding the vault."[14] The curiosity was not just undignified but, for the child, dangerous, suggesting as it did that Mary might have to face the world with the stigma of illegitimacy. Fitzgerald and Sheridan blamed each other for being indiscreet and allowing the story to spread, but otherwise they remained on good terms.[15] Both were anxious that rumour and scandal might blight the life of the new baby. Before Eliza died, she and Fitzgerald had been unsure whether Mary should be brought up as Sheridan's or as Fitzgerald's. The latter wrote to his mother,

> From the state of her mind she could not judge exactly what was best . . . she wished sometimes that I should have it, and at others that S[heridan] should have it, but that, at last, relying on Providence and all our loves for her and the dear baby, we should do what we thought best for it and her sake. It therefore comes to this—what is best for the child? I cannot deceive myself enough

> not to think it best for it to be S[heridan]'s . . . if once S[heridan] has adopted it, if he ever was not generous, which I am sure he is, his honour and all his family's will force them to behave kindly to it, and by their attention and fondness try to drown the story [of its parentage].[16]

Fitzgerald, after much agonising, agreed: "Accepting the opinion of the world, I have injured Sheridan. It is therefore me that ought to make atonement. I will do it by making every sacrifice of my own wishes, and doing what he wishes about the child . . . I will be a kind of guardian to it without its knowledge." The decision to have Mary baptised as a Sheridan and brought up by Mehitabel Canning was, for Fitzgerald, immensely painful:

> Owning it one's child, and not giving it one's name, is stamping it with what the *vile world* calls infamy; and then to have it bred up as a younger child, while it is older, may subject it to many unhappy moments. In short, upon the whole, I believe it is best for the dear little thing to be as it is, and better for the dear, dear, mother's sake . . . I am certain Sheridan will behave generously. I must be as cautious as him for the dear thing's sake. Any directions the dear angel has left he will, I am sure, fulfil with exactness—and what can I wish more than that her intentions should be fulfilled? Poor man, he has gone through a great deal. I feel for him thoroughly; he loved her and feels his loss. I love him for it.

Through this most intimate of entanglements, Sheridan and Fitzgerald had formed a bond of their own, and Mary was to remain the living embodiment not only of their mutual love for Eliza but of their own friendship.

As Tom's tutor, William Smyth, wrote, Mary was "a child of the most extraordinary beauty," eerily like her mother, and Sheridan clung to her as a promise that something good might be rescued from the wreckage of his marriage. Fitzgerald heard that "he has the child constantly with him. What a comfort it must be! His task is now a dreadful one. But yet I envy it him."[17] For three months, Sheridan kept Mary and Tom with him at Isleworth, and Mrs. Canning reported that "he cannot bear to be a moment" without the infant. Smyth noticed how devoted he was to her. A man who could be infinitely thoughtless, he nevertheless always remembered to bring "some cap or ribband or toy for this beautiful infant. And he would stand looking at it, and talking with the nurse, and endeavouring to engage its attention for the hour together, finding here the last image of her he had lost, to whose departed shade, I doubt not, he considered himself as making a grateful offering while he was thus hanging with affection over her child."[18]

But Mary was "small and delicate beyond imagination," as Mrs. Canning, who saw her every day, put it, and it was thought best to move her to the latter's house at Wanstead, east of London. On 23 October, a ball was arranged there for Tom and his friends. Sheridan came from town to be there and was in good spirits. Just as the dancing was about to start, though, the door of the ballroom flew open and Mrs. Canning came in crying, "Oh!, the child, the child is dying." Mary was having convulsions. Sheridan was frantic, and the look of horror on his face was one which William Smyth would never forget. A doctor arrived very quickly and there was some hope that Mary might survive. Just as the worst seemed to be over, a second bout of convulsions killed her. Sheridan was distraught. Smyth, who slept in the next room, heard him moaning pitifully that night. Tom was sent to talk to him, but he was inconsolable. He would go only as far as the bedroom where Mary lay, looking in death even more like Eliza. His friend Joseph Richardson came down from London to be with him, but for a long time Sheridan would talk to no one. After a day or two, he went downstairs and ordered that Mary be buried with Eliza in Wells Cathedral: "Where can the child be," he asked, "but in the bosom of its mother?" Finally, four or five days after Mary's death, Richardson managed to persuade Sheridan to return to London. Once there, he threw himself back into the public world, but, as Mrs. Canning noted, "he suffers deeply and secretly."

His private life, however, became even further entangled with Fitzgerald's. Late in 1791, he had met and become fascinated by two of the more interesting of the French exiles who were gathering in England. Madame Stéphanie-Felicité de Genlis was a devotee of Rousseau and a celebrated educational theorist and sentimental novelist. She was also the mistress of the Duc D'Orléans, a cousin of Louis XVI, who had adopted revolutionary ideas and styled himself Philippe Égalité. She was accompanied by her nineteen-year-old Pamela, widely assumed to be her daughter by Égalité, though in fact an English-born orphan originally called Nancy Sims. Even though they had fled the turmoil of the Revolution, they remained republicans and mixed with the English democrats. Sheridan met them at the house of the radical John Hurford Stone. For Sheridan, Pamela had a special attraction: she was strikingly like a younger Eliza. She had the same pale skin and high forehead, the same dark eyes and deep brown hair, pulled about her head in the close, revolutionary style.

Pamela and her mother, who was rumoured to carry a polished stone from the Bastille walls next to her breast, were shunned by respectable society because of their revolutionary associations. Horace Walpole referred to Madame de Genlis and Talleyrand as "Eve and the serpent," and trusted that "few would be disposed to taste their rotten apples." But Sheridan, for both political and personal reasons, was disposed to bite. After Eliza's death, mother and daughter went to stay at Isleworth, and arrived there by what was literally a strange route. Intending to return to France, they had set off for Dover, but found with a rising sense of alarm that they were being taken by odd roads and after a long time were nowhere near Dover. They panicked and ordered the coach back to London, where they drove to Sheridan's house. There the post-boys confessed that "an unknown gentleman" had persuaded them to drive around in this confusing meander, and Sheridan volunteered to take them to Dover himself, but he added that it would be a few days before he was free to do so. He then took them to Isleworth, where they remained as his guests for a month.

The suspicion that the whole escapade had been arranged by Sheridan is strengthened by Madame de Genlis's claim in her memoirs that he had, two days previously, declared his love for Pamela. He had asked for, and been promised, her hand in marriage. All this happened at around the same time as Mary's death, and it seems that Sheridan had dreams of finding in Pamela a substitute for the dead Eliza. He may even have arranged to follow her and Madame de Genlis to France. A letter of his written on 29 December to an unspecified correspondent says: "I must delay my coming to Paris, which I meant however to delay only to the present time when parliament will adjourn for three weeks." It also reveals that he was aware that letters to him from France were probably being opened by the state authorities: "That they have open'd here all Letters to us from France I have known for some time but there has been a fatality in their with[h]olding Letters which could answer no purpose to them. How inconsistent and unfeeling you must have thought me, and now when I hoped to have surprised you at Tournay, War and Public Folly are raising new Obstacles."[19] The reference to Tournai suggests very strongly that this letter was to Pamela or to her mother. The previous month, having been warned to leave Paris because of their royal connections, they had both moved to Tournai, near the border with Belgium.[20]

While they were travelling there, however, they were overtaken on the road by a man who now styled himself "le citoyen Eduoard Fitzgerald." He, too, had left England for Paris, where he had begun to discuss the idea of an Irish revolution with another radical exile from Ireland, Henry Sheares. While there, he had also seen Madame de Genlis and her ward at the opera and, like Sheridan, had been dumbfounded by Pamela's resemblance to Eliza. Again, like Sheridan, he now waylaid the pair on their journey, and proposed to Pamela. Sheridan's letters to her had almost certainly gone astray, and she may have assumed that he had lost interest or that he was merely amusing himself by asking her to marry him. Whatever her reasons, Pamela accepted Fitzgerald's proposal and they were married at Tournai. The witnesses, who could testify not just to a wedding but also to the extraordinary intermingling of revolution and royalty, included both Philippe Égalité, soon to die on the guillotine, and the future King of France, Louis Philippe. Shortly afterwards Fitzgerald and Pamela settled in Dublin and gradually wove themselves into the emerging Irish revolution.

In a strange way Fitzgerald may have done Sheridan a service by removing from before his eyes the fantasy of a new life with a new Eliza, thus allowing him to come to terms with his grief and shame. The relationship between the two men ceased to be personal and over time established itself as political. Through their courtships first of Eliza and then of Pamela, Fitzgerald had been like another version of Sheridan. Over the next five years he would also become a kind of political alter ego, expressing the same ideas in a different way: where one was "le citoyen Eduoard Fitzgerald," the other would become Citizen Sheridan. But while one would embrace more and more directly the role of traitor, the other would keep trying to juggle treason and loyalty, hoping that the speed of the hand would continue to deceive the eye.

Chapter 26

HERCULES AND THE HYDRA

In Karl Anton Hickel's monumental painting of William Pitt in the House of Commons declaring war on France, on 12 February 1793, the Prime Minister appears as a heroic figure, a modern Demosthenes rallying his nation with a call to arms. Hickel was an Austrian, and his own country was already at war with France, so the painting takes the rightness of Pitt's stance for granted. The sun streaming through the windows behind the Speaker's chair illuminates his face and upper body, placing him in an angelic light. Opposite him, on the opposition's front bench, the face of just one man—Sheridan—is completely in shadow. Fox has his eyes on Pitt, and his gaze is all attention. But beside him Sheridan is seen in profile, the left side of his face hidden by the head of Grey, to whom he has turned to whisper something. His left hand rests on his knee, his index finger raised as he points across the floor to Pitt, who is obviously the object of his dissenting murmurs. In this image, which was exhibited in the Haymarket in London throughout much of 1795, Sheridan is the shadowy conspirator on the edge of the nation's epic drama, muttering darkly through the hero's great oration.[1]

Around this time, too—probably in 1790—Lord Bristol commissioned a sculptor to execute "a colossal groupe of Hercules slaying the Hydra, but before the heads were finished he almost drove the sculptor mad by selecting for a model of Hercules's countenance that of Mr Pitt, and insisting on the Hydra being finished off into a triple likeness of Fox, North and Burke, which last he again cut off to make way for Sheridan."[2] These images of Sheridan as the enemy and main opponent of Pitt capture the epic nature of the struggle in which he was involved throughout the 1790s. This was the decade which set both British and Irish history in moulds that would endure for two centuries. In the years between the French Revolution of 1789 and the Act of Union between Britain and Ireland in 1800, decisions were made about the meaning of Irishness and of Britishness. On the one hand, the possibility of a new Irish identity which might transcend the sectarian divisions between Catholics and Protestants was tested. When it failed, an enduring conflict centering on religious and political allegiances was set in motion. On the other hand, Britain at the same time witnessed the gradual emergence of a new national identity—expansionist, imperial, and fuelled by military pride abroad and the entrenchment of the elite at home. In both cases, Sheridan was on the losing side. In this critical decade, he stood for an Ireland that did not come into being and against a Britain that did.

Though he supported the French Revolution, in the context of Britain he was not a revolutionary. There is nothing to suggest that at any time he favoured the violent overthrow of the British state. In April 1791 the radicals William Godwin and Thomas Holcroft wrote an open letter to Sheridan, advocating a revolution in Britain:

> Can you really think that the *new constitution of France is the most glorious fabric ever raised by human integrity since the creation of man* and yet believe that what is good there would be bad here? Does truth alter its nature by crossing the straits and become falsehood? Are men entitled to perfect equality in France and is it just to deprive them of it in England? . . . Six years only elapsed before the emancipation of America brought forth the Revolution in France . . . Will France, the most refined and considerable nation in the world remain six years without an imitator . . .[3]

It was a good question, but not one to which Sheridan was likely to give a simple answer. In January 1794 Sheridan's old friend William Windham, now Pitt's Minister for War, told Sir George Beaumont "that Fox is not a republican, but that in spirit Sheridan and Courtenay are."[4] Windham was right about Sheridan, but his description needs to be qualified by a sense of what the term meant in its context. He was republican in the loose, mid-century sense, which did not necessarily exclude the idea of a constitutional monarchy. In spite of

Montesquieu and Paine, most republican writers before the French Revolution continued to assume that some kind of limited monarchy would remain in a republic. John Adams, for instance, described the United States as a "monarchical republic" and thought that "the uncorrupted British constitution is nothing more or less than a republic in which the king is the first magistrate." This, essentially, is what Sheridan believed, and he expressed it in the same terms. In his speech in 1790 on the French Revolution, he expressed the hope that the King would "retain all the powers, dignities, and prerogatives becoming the first magistrate of so great a country."[5] It should be borne in mind that in this his thinking was in line with that of many of the French revolutionaries before the execution of King Louis XVI. The Abbé Sieyes argued that kings were needed "to save us from the peril of masters." Even Robespierre declared that the French constitution, as amended by the Revolution, offered the best of both worlds: "a Republic with a monarch."[6]

Sheridan was clearly attracted to the notion of an elected monarch, which had been on the fringes of British political thinking since Sir Thomas More's *Utopia* and the book that had so influenced him in his youth, Sir Philip Sidney's *Arcadia*. Even if Sheridan's republicanism hardened after the French Revolution, political conditions in Britain argued for an exploitation of, rather than an end to, the ambivalence inherent in this philosophical framework. Very few, even of the radicals, thought it wise to declare themselves openly as anti-monarchists. The Scottish radical Thomas Muir, for instance, was "for a monarchy under proper restrictions[, believing] that a republican form of government was for the best but that monarchy had been so long established in this country . . . it would be improper to alter it."[7] For Sheridan, of course, an additional and very weighty consideration was that there appeared to be an available candidate for the job of first magistrate of a putative democracy—his friend and confidant the Prince of Wales.

In any case, Sheridan, unlike Burke, was not dogmatic about forms of government. When the Burke-inspired clamour for "sound principles" helped to push Britain into war with revolutionary France, Sheridan, in reply to a speech in favour of the war by Lord Mornington, treated the House of Commons to a parable. A tradesman has a clock that keeps very good time but that has been made by a man who never learned the mechanical and scientific principles of measuring time. A neighbouring clockmaker encourages him to throw the clock out. The tradesman insists that the hands move round perfectly well, that it strikes the hour with a confident sound, that he winds it like any other clock, and that it tells the time perfectly. But the clockmaker replies that the clock has no right to work because it is not constructed on sound principles. He persuades the tradesman to buy at three times the price a clock that does not work half so well. "I wish," he said of Mornington's speech, "he could convince them that this revolutionary movement of theirs, which, however unskillfully and unmethodically put together, appears so strangely to answer their purpose, is an unworthy jumble of ignorance and chance; and that they would be much better off if they would take a regular constitution of his choosing."[8]

But to say that Sheridan was not a dogmatic republican and did not want to see a bloody English revolution is, in the context of the 1790s, to say very little. In the first place, to be a traitor in the climate of reaction which determined the political weather after 1792, it was not necessary to favour the violent overthrow of the state. It was necessary merely to favour democratic change, which Sheridan most emphatically did. He had huge sympathy with the demands of the popular radical societies, most notably the London Corresponding Society, which were agitating for precisely the kind of political reforms he himself had helped to formulate in the Westminster Association in 1780. And in the second place, Ireland was a very different matter. From the beginning of his political career, when the Irish Volunteers had threatened violence in support of Irish legislative independence, Sheridan had publicly countenanced the use of force to uphold "Irish rights." In the much more dangerous context of the 1790s he continued to do so. His support for radical reform in Britain and for potentially violent change in Ireland were between them more than enough to make him a traitor.

It needs to be remembered that at the beginning of the decade Sheridan was widely recognised as a figure of enormous political stature, and that it was far from fanciful to imagine that he might become Prime Minister. Early in 1792, on the margins of negotiations between the government and the opposition over the replacement of Thurlow by Loughborough as Lord Chancellor, the King was persuaded to ask Lord Shelburne, the astute operator with whom the Rockingham faction had formed a government in 1782 and who was now the Marquis of Landsdowne, for his views on the formation of a new administration. Landsdowne suggested that the best course would be for the King to attempt to break up the party system by trying to win over small groups and by securing a leader in the House of Commons, and he thought the new leader should be Sheridan. He would be enticed with a commitment to undertake large and generous measures of democratic reform. Nothing came of the idea, but the very fact that it was being canvassed at such a level is an extraordinary mark of Sheridan's standing.[9]

Yet Sheridan chose to throw his weight behind the increasingly beleaguered forces of democratic reform. Just a fortnight after Mary was born, he and Edward Fitzgerald had joined together in the Society of Friends of the People, a group formed on 11 April 1792 to oppose Burke's anti-revolutionary agitation within the Whig party and to compete with the new popular societies that had sprung up in the wake of the Revolution for the leadership of the radical reformist cause. Its aim was to secure through Parliament an unspecified measure of parliamentary reform: "to restore the freedom of Election and a more equal representation of the People in parliament"; and "to secure to the People a more frequent Exercise of their Right of electing their Representatives."[10] The organising committee included Charles Grey, Samuel Whitbread, Sir Philip Francis, and Sheridan, but not Fox, who was in fact somewhat embarrassed by its radicalism.

Sheridan's initial intention was for the Friends of the People to hold open the space for rational reform against the incursions of both reactionary and revolutionary forces. That he considered these forces to be largely indistinguishable because of the operation of *agents provocateurs* paid by the government to discredit the radicals by indulging in openly treasonous rhetoric is clear from a letter of his to a "Gentleman of . . . Political Integrity and steadiness of Principle" whom he was evidently recruiting into the Friends: "I need not say that at all meetings every precaution will be sought to prevent Hot men [generally spies of Government] promoting any violent expression or action, or anything not strictly conformable to the Laws even as they stand."[11] But as the laws became increasingly repressive, that intention would become more and more difficult to fulfil.

At their first general meeting on 26 April, the Friends adopted an address to the people, which Sheridan signed, in which they were careful to avoid the imputation that they were agitating for a violent revolution. Comparing England to France, they denied "the existence of any resemblance between the cases of the two Kingdoms; and we disclaim the necessity of resorting to similar remedies." They went on, however, to hint that violence might become inevitable in the future:

> We do not believe that, at this day, an absolute despotism in the hands of the executive power, would be endured in this country. But who can say to what conclusion the silent unresisted operation of abuses, incessantly acting and constantly increasing, may lead us hereafter; what habits it may gradually create, what power it may finally establish? The abuses of France were suffered to gather and accumulate, until nothing but an eruption could put an end to them . . . The inference from this comparison is at once so powerful and so obvious, that we know not by what argument to illustrate or enforce it.[12]

The effect of the foundation of the Friends of the People was to destroy once and for all the unity of the Whig party. It confirmed Burke's suspicions about Sheridan, and led him to break the uneasy silence that had been maintained since their very public split on the floor of the House. On 30 April Grey, with Sheridan's support, gave notice of his intention to introduce a motion for the reform of Parliament in the next session, and the Friends of the People simultaneously published its manifesto in several newspapers. The King considered it "the most daring outrage to a regular Government," but consoled himself with the thought that "if men are to be found willing to overturn the Constitution of this country, it is most providential they so early cast off the mask."[13] When Grey's motion was proposed, Burke lamented in the House that "there are in this country men who scruple not to enter into an alliance with a set in France of the worst traitors and regicides that have ever been heard of—the club of the Jacobins." Over the next few months the party split, with Burke, Windham, the Duke of Portland, and Earl Fitzwilliam moving towards an eventual alliance with Pitt.

Sheridan both supported Grey's motion—which, in an ominous sign of the coming repression, was crushed by 282 votes to 41—and argued for an inquiry into the representation in Parliament of the cities and towns of Scotland which had chosen him to present their petitions. His speech, described by the Tory John Rolle as "one of the most inflammatory, wicked and dangerous speeches he had ever heard," attacked the current "fashion to decry everything in the nature of reform" and claimed that the British constitution owed all its good qualities to enforced change: "We have, at this day, nothing in it that is beautiful, that had not been forced from tyrants, and taken from the usurpations of despotism."[14] Sheridan again praised the French Revolution, which ought, he insisted, to evoke "exultation and joy at the downfall of despotism in France, the greatest enemy England ever had." If, however, a repeat was to be avoided in England, "the thing for us to attend to is a rational and sober reformation of abuses." If this was not done, then "the spirit of enquiry excited among all classes of men" by the Revolution would be channelled in other directions.

Edward Fitzgerald had meanwhile returned with Pamela to Dublin, where a new organisation founded in Belfast in the late summer of 1791, the Society of United Irishmen, had established its headquarters. In December 1791, it had published its manifesto, declaring its aim of creating "an United Society of the Irish nation; to make all Irishmen Citizens—all Citizens Irishmen." Its leaders, Theobald Wolfe Tone, Thomas Russell, Napper Tandy, and Archibald Hamilton Rowan, were Protestants, but the word "all" had for them a special depth of meaning. It meant that their aim was to unite Catholics, Protestants, and Dissenters in an independent and democratic Ireland. As a mark of their radicalism, Thomas Paine, the greatest of revolutionary polemicists, was made an honorary member. Fitzgerald did not at first formally join the society, out of deference to his elder brother, the Duke of Leinster, but from the start he was a fellow-traveller.

The first formal contacts between the United Irishmen in Dublin and the Friends of the People in London were made on 26 October 1792. The United Irishmen, "impressed by the resemblance in the title, nature and destination of their respective institutions and acting under the fraternity of feeling which such a co-incidence naturally inspires,"[15] sent a formal address to the Friends, full of bold democratic rhetoric:

> The title which you bear is a glorious one: and we too are friends of the people. If we be asked "Who are the People?" . . . we answer "The multitude of human beings, the living mass of humanity associated to exist, to subsist, and to be happy." In them, and them only, we find the original of social authority, the measure of political value, and the pedestal of legitimate power.

The United Irishmen went on to explain their demands: an independent and democratic Irish Parliament in which "the *whole* people . . . free equal and entire" would be represented. They made an eloquent plea for the enfranchisement of Catholics: "the birth-right of millions, born and to be born, continue the spoils of war, and booty of conquest." And they hinted, already, at the willingness of the disenfranchised to follow revolutionary examples, not least that of the Irish Volunteers of the 1780s, whose campaigns Sheridan himself had done so much to encourage:

> Instructed by the late revolution in America; by the late revolution in Ireland; by the late revolution in France; hearing of all that has been done over the face of the globe for Liberty, and feeling all that can be suffered from the want of it; reading the Charter of Independence of Ireland and listening to the spirit-stirred voice of her great deliverer; actuated in fine by that imperishable spark in the bosom of man, which the servitude of a century may smother, but cannot extinguish, the Catholics of this country have been lessoned into Liberty; have learned to know their rights; to be sensible of their wrongs and to detail, by peaceable delegation their grievances, rather than endure without obedience.

The address concluded with a frank demand for Irish independence, coupled with an appeal that Sheridan, for one, could not resist:

> Look not upon Ireland with an eye of indifference. The period of Irish insignificance is passing fast away . . . As to any union between the Islands, believe us when we assert, that our union rests upon our mutual independence. We shall love each other, *if we be left to ourselves.* It is the union of minds which ought to bind these Nations together.

A month later, the Friends of the People sent a warm reply to the president of the Society of United Irishmen in Dublin:

> We cannot . . . delay expressing the pleasure we feel in finding so large a portion of our fellow-citizens entertaining sentiments so just, and expressing these sentiments with an energy that commands assent. Our endeavours must necessarily be confined to this Island, and can have no immediate relation to Ireland, which ever

> must possess a right to legislate for herself. Whether we shall give or take the example, our wishes will ever be earnest for your success.

This warmth towards an organisation which was openly declaring the need for Catholic emancipation was all the more striking since the most extreme anti-Catholics already regarded the Friends of the People as in any case a Papist front. Lord George Gordon, who had led the anti-Catholic riots of 1780, wrote an open letter to Baron de Alvensleben, the ambassador of Hanover, from Newgate prison. The demand for reform was, he warned, "only a plausible name assumed to impose on the public by the Jesuits and their tools." Adding the Prince of Wales's marriage to Mrs. Fitzherbert to Sheridan's leadership of the Friends of the People, he got the number of the beast:

> Can anything be more impudent than the Carlton House party bringing forward two professed Roman Catholics, Sir John Throckmorton as President of the Friends of the People at the Freemason's Tavern and Lord Petre as president of the Whig Club at the Crown and Anchor, Strand? This may tend, indeed, to feed the hopes of the apparent Roman Catholic connection at Carlton House but it must at the same time disgust all the Friends of the Constitution . . .[16]

While making connections with the Irish radicals, Sheridan was also keeping up contact with the powerful Girondin group in the French National Convention, and he intervened in its debates on the fate of King Louis XVI, who had been put on trial after an abortive attempt to flee the country. Sheridan was admired by the Girondin leader Jacques-Pierre Brissot, and his conduct received the rather unwelcome endorsement of the French National Convention. Early in January 1793 Brissot gave a pessimistic account of the state of public opinion in England, where "the most scandalous idolatry for royalty" had been displayed at the opening of Parliament:

> In the midst, however, of the terror, of the panic by which the public mind had been seized, Fox must be praised for having dared to urge the sending of an ambassador to France; Sheridan must be praised for having exculpated the [French] nation from the massacres which are merely the work of a few unprincipled

> men; and Erskine must be praised for having dared to defend Thomas Paine whose effigy was burned a little time after his works had been covered with incense. Notwithstanding the courage of these defenders of liberty . . . the triumph of the Ministry, I do not say over the revolutionists, but over the English nation which they have killed with their own hands . . . has been rendered complete.[17]

Needless to say, Pitt and his supporters ensured that these words of praise were translated and given wide circulation in England.

Sheridan, like Brissot and like Thomas Paine (who proposed in the National Convention that the King be sent to America, where he might be re-educated as a good citizen), opposed the royal execution. Fanny Burney noted on 20 December that Sheridan had said that the execution of the King of France would be "an act of injustice." He believed, as he told the House of Commons, that if the French were informed of the effect on British public opinion that the execution of the King would have "such a conviction might produce a considerable influence, I wish I could venture to say a successful effect, on the public mind in Paris, and throughout France."[18] He himself drew up a paper, calling for mercy for the King, which he sent to the National Convention through Madame de Genlis. The *Oracle* reported in January 1793 that "one of the strongest papers in favour of the unfortunate King of France was written by Mr Sheridan: it is said to have been translated by the elegant pen of Madame Sillery [better known as Madame de Genlis] and very much circulated by the Brissotins. Monsieur Sillery's speech on the subject did him the greatest honour." Sheridan proudly acknowledged his authorship in the House of Commons in March 1793 in a speech which earned a vote of thanks from a public meeting in Aldgate, for having "demonstrated to the confusion of Ministers, and the disgrace of their Municipal inquisitors, that they have artfully calumniated the People of this Country by imputing to them Treasons and Seditions by charges formed to varnish APOSTACY; to justify Oppression, and as a pretext to brand as TRAITORS those who would not be convicted as DESERTERS."[19]

The deserters in question were most of Fox's oligarchic followers, who were now switching to the government side. Sheridan's anger at their treachery gave a savage edge to the wit with which he mocked the willingness of Burke (who accepted a state pension) and others of his former allies to swap principles for "the dirty little traffic for lucre and emolument":

> The throne is in danger! we will support the throne!; but let us share the smiles of royalty. The order of nobility is in danger! I will fight for nobility, says the viscount, but my zeal would be much greater if I were made an earl. Rouse all the marquis within me, says the earl, and the peerage never turned forth a more undaunted champion in its cause than I shall prove. Stain my green riband blue, cries out the illustrious knight, and the fountain of honour will have a fast and faithful servant.[20]

Pitt, however, was not deflected by such jibes from his intention of showing Sheridan up as a treacherous ally of the French. In December, the cartoonist James Gillray, now in the pay of the government, published a drawing of a melodramatic scene in the House of Commons when Edmund Burke, having alleged that three thousand daggers had been manufactured for English revolutionaries, threw down a dagger and screamed, "This is what you are to gain by an alliance with France." In Gillray's drawing Fox and Sheridan shrink from the bloody dagger, Sheridan crying, "Charley, Charley, farewell to all our hopes of levelling monarchs! farewell to all hopes of paying off my debts by a general Bankruptcy! farewell to all hopes of plunder! in the moment of victory we are trapped and undone!"

Such accusations ceased to be funny in February 1793, when war was declared between Britain and France. Pitt and the government were aware that Sheridan was corresponding with France, and were watching for the opportunity of accusing him of consorting with the enemy. In March Sheridan noted that, as part of the gathering campaign of repression, letters were being opened by the government, "and I have no doubt," he later said, "that many of mine were among the number." Hints, he said, had been "thrown out in various channels, under the direction and encouragement of ministers, that I and others with whom I agree on public subjects held improper correspondence with other powers." He suspected, he said, that the government "kept copies of them, and various other letters, at the post office," and he challenged them to publish them.[21]

Just how serious the accusation of corresponding with French revolutionaries now was became clear in the autumn of 1793, when

Thomas Walker, president of the Manchester Constitutional Society, and six others were charged on the evidence of an informer with conspiring to overthrow the government with force of arms and with aiding French invasion. Walker and his friend Thomas Cooper had, as early as March 1792, been in correspondence with the Jacobin clubs in Paris and elsewhere, and Cooper had visited some of the clubs in France as a delegate from the Constitutional Society.[22] Walker was a friend of Thomas Paine, but he was also close both to Sheridan and to his most intimate personal allies, Sheridan's brother-in-law Richard Tickell and Joseph Richardson. In April 1792, after it had become known that Walker was in correspondence with the Jacobins, Sheridan had praised both Walker and Cooper in Parliament. He had said, in relation to his own willingness to put his name to a petition for parliamentary reform from Manchester, "One of the chief reasons that induced me to sign my name to the paper was seeing Mr Walker's name to the Manchester resolutions. Mr Walker is a very respectable character, a man of sense, character, and opulence. Mr Thomas Cooper, also, I have the pleasure to know." When Burke attacked Walker for corresponding with the Jacobin Club in Paris, Sheridan replied: "If I were furnished with [Burke's] speech, during the American war, in answer to some charges of having corresponded with the Americans, I dare say I should have a very good excuse set up."[23] Felix Vaughan, Walker's close ally and junior counsel at his trial, regarded Sheridan as "of all the Opposition . . . the stoutest,"[24] and if Sheridan was not himself on trial, he was certainly an interested party. With Walker on trial for treason, Sheridan continued to support him, and after the prosecution collapsed in April 1794 Walker's defence counsel, Thomas Erskine, asked him for proofs of the shorthand notes of his trial because he was to meet Sheridan, Fox, and Grey the following Monday, "when I mean to have some talk with them on that subject."[25]

Sheridan also threw himself into the cause of the first serious victims of the repression, the Scottish radicals Thomas Muir and the Reverend Thomas Fysche Palmer. Muir was, with Thomas Paine, an honorary member of the United Irishmen and the most important link between them and the Scottish branch of the Friends of the People.[26] In August 1793 Muir was sentenced to fourteen years' transportation to Botany Bay. The following month, Palmer, an English Unitarian ministering at Dundee, was given seven years' transportation. In each case the crime was "leasing making"—an extraordinarily vague Scottish common-law offence of speaking words which tended to incite discord between the King and his people.

Sheridan had strong connections to the Scottish reformers through his championing of the cause of Scottish representation. He visited Muir and Palmer in prison in Woolwich in December. As he subsequently told the House of Commons,

> I have seen them—seen them associated with convicts of the most worthless and despicable description; seen them, not indeed loaded with irons, but [with] these irons freshly taken off. I have seen them separated from one another; surely an unnecessary addition to their sufferings; thus wantonly depriving them of that last of all consolations, the society of affliction.[27]

He went to Pitt's Home Secretary, Dundas, to protest that their convictions were illegal and to demand their release. Dundas, according to William Godwin, told him that "he saw no great hardship in a man's being sent to Botany Bay."[28] He presented a petition to Parliament on Palmer's behalf, not asking for mercy but demanding justice. And he explicitly stated that violent resistance to such arbitrary proceedings would be justified:

> It is such a sentence that if it had taken place in England, I should not have been surprised that the country had risen up in arms to oppose it; and as little should I have been surprised if the attempt to introduce the law on which this sentence is founded, into this country, should have cost the head of that minister who should have dared so grossly to insult the principles of the British constitution.[29]

The severity of the repression, however, did nothing to make Sheridan break his connections with the radicals, either in Ireland or in England. At a meeting of the Friends of the People in April 1794 where Sheridan acted as chair, it was "unanimously resolved" to convey their "approbation" to the United Irishmen in Dublin and to "exhort them to persevere in their exertions to obtain justice for the people of Ireland."[30] On 3 December 1794, when the Catholic Committee—an association of Catholics agitating for emancipation —held a dinner in Dublin, a radical minority dined separately and drank toasts to Sheridan and Fox and the citizens of Belfast. This minority was the group most closely aligned with the United Irishmen.[31]

Through the Friends of the People, Sheridan also kept up contacts with the most radical of the extra-parliamentary reform societies, the London Corresponding Society. Its president, Thomas Hardy, whom Sheridan had described in Parliament as "an honest shoemaker," wrote to him in April 1794 deploring the government's campaign of repression and asking for the assistance of the Friends in assembling a "Convention of the Friends of Freedom, for the purpose of obtaining, in a legal and constitutional method, a full and effectual representation." Sheridan, through the Friends, declined to take part in such a convention on the grounds that it would "furnish the Enemies of Reform with the means of calumniating its Advocates." But he also assured Hardy that the Friends shared the London Corresponding Society's alarm "at the late extraordinary proceedings of Government, so ably detailed and so justly reprobated by your Society." And the Friends renewed "their assurances of good-will and desire of preserving a proper understanding and cordiality among all the Friends of Parliamentary Reform."[32]

This, together with his correspondence with France and his association with convicted traitors, was grounds enough in the current climate to precipitate his trial and imprisonment. In May 1794 Sheridan alleged in the House of Commons that "a great magistrate of the city of London" whom he refused to name had bet 120 guineas that when, as the government now proposed, habeas corpus was suspended, he would be sent to the Tower of London within two months.[33] It was a remarkable sign of the change in the political climate: two years after he had been seriously proposed as a potential Prime Minister, he was being spoken of as a potential felon. For the moment his public standing and parliamentary immunity protected him, but in the events that were about to unfold there was a real danger that neither would be enough.

Chapter 27

A SNAKE IN THE GRASS

Seventeen years after he had written *The School for Scandal*, one of Sheridan's characters came back to haunt him. Snake the journalist was in performance dressed in black so that he looked like a clergyman. To an informed audience this was a sneaky reference to both a previous theatrical character and its original. Samuel Foote had already caricatured a clergyman journalist in his play *The Capuchin* and had given him the name Dr. Viper. Both in the writing and especially in the performance, the model for the character was understood to be an Irishman, Dr. William Jackson, editor of the *Public Ledger* and a notorious spreader of salacious gossip. Sheridan, in turn, took over this theatrical version of Jackson for Snake, who was played in the same style.[1] Now, in a surreal entanglement of politics and theatre, Jackson not only came back into Sheridan's life but brought in his train a most dangerous scandal.

William Jackson was an unlikely revolutionary. He had been educated at Oxford University and ordained as a clergyman in the Church of Ireland. But he had then drifted into jobbing journalism in London as a prodigious hack writer. He became associated with both scandal and the theatre when he acted as confidant and secretary to the Duchess of Kingston in a famously lurid trial for bigamy before the House of Lords. In this role he wrote some blistering attacks on Samuel Foote, who struck back in *The Capuchin*.

In the political ferment of the early 1790s, Jackson had drifted into radical circles in London, and then moved on to Paris, where from the end of 1792 onwards a group of English and Irish exiles had been urging the declining Girondin regime to plan for an invasion of Britain or Ireland. It included, amongst others, Lord Edward Fitzgerald and Pamela, Thomas Paine, Thomas Muir, the Kerryman William Duckett, and John Hurford Stone, a former member, like Sheridan, of both the Society for Constitutional Information and the Revolution Society.

At the beginning of 1794 Stone and his friends, with the help of Nicholas Madgett, an Irishman who had taken over French intelligence operations aimed at the British Isles, persuaded the government to send an agent to England and Ireland to test support for a possible French invasion. The man chosen for the job was the Reverend William Jackson. He sailed from Hamburg and arrived at Hull on 26 February, posing as an American merchant and bearing letters of introduction from John Stone to his brother William, a Nonconformist coal merchant, and to Horne Tooke.[2] In the letter to his brother, John Stone identified the people whom Jackson was to consult with: the radicals Joseph Priestley, Horne Tooke, John Frost of the London Corresponding Society, and the Friends of the People—Sheridan, Grey, Lord Lauderdale, and Lauderdale's brother Major Thomas Maitland.[3]

From Hull, Jackson immediately made his way to the home in Oldford, Middlesex, of William Stone, who had already received another letter from his brother in Paris urging him to sell his house in Middlesex because "of the intention of the French to invade this country with their whole force."[4] Jackson, finding William Stone just about to depart for London, joined him in his coach. As they travelled, Stone asked about his brother, and Jackson took the opportunity to raise the topic of a French invasion. The French, he said, "entertained an opinion that if an attempt was made to invade this country, nine out of ten of the people in this country would join them." When Stone told him that the opposite was the case, Jackson urged him to write to this effect to his brother who was "so much respected with the people in power it might have a considerable effect in diverting them from their purpose."

How much William Stone knew about Jackson's real purpose as a French agent is not clear, but it was almost certainly more than he subsequently admitted. Even if he at first believed Jackson to be no more than an American merchant with news of his brother, it is very unlikely that his suspicions were not subsequently aroused. Jackson gave him addresses in Amsterdam and Hamburg to which he could safely send letters dealing with political subjects. He also told him that he was going to Ireland and would write to him under the name Popkins because he did not have a proper passport permitting him to enter England. Stone subsequently claimed that he believed this explanation, but he was then under suspicion of high treason and had every reason to portray himself as an innocent dupe. It is scarcely credible that a hard-headed, Nonconformist businessman would be so gullible as not to suspect that a man from Paris who was giving him secret addresses and a false name might be a spy.

But there is reason to believe that William Stone, far from being a dupe, was an active collaborator. He acknowledged that when he had written to his brother in Paris he had signed his name backwards—"Enots"—and that he had used the same stunningly ingenious code in writing to Jackson in Ireland.[5] Jackson's letters to him from Ireland contain transparently coded messages such as "the price and nature of the articles being entirely changed" and "if you have any letters from the family of Shields which regard their affairs in this country you cannot too soon inclose them to me as the assizes at Cork are about to commence." They indicate, too, an enthusiasm for the state of revolutionary opinion in Ireland—"the principles of the people with regard to trade, their opinion as to a change to be brought about by industry and co-operating exertion"—that he seems to assume will be shared by Stone. Stone also heard from Jackson that he had met with "warm persons" in Ireland—meaning, of course, members of the United Irishmen. Stone told the justice of the peace who examined him that these phrases "appeared to him quite enigmatical"—but Jackson was hardly writing deliberate gibberish to his most important contact in England.

William Stone may not have known all the details of Jackson's mission, but it is impossible to believe that he did not at least understand its general nature. Stone undertook to sound out some of the most radical opposition politicians on Jackson's behalf. According to him, "It occurred to me that the opinions of gentlemen who were known to be opposed to present measures" of war and repression "would have more influence" with the French. But it is rather more likely that the people who were approached were the ones who might be regarded as sympathetic to the French, and that the purpose of the exercise was to test their reactions to the invasion plan.

Shortly after Jackson's arrival, Stone met two opposition MPs, William Smith and Benjamin Vaughan, who knew John Stone as "the brother-in-law of one of my best and oldest friends." William Stone told Vaughan "how desirable it would be if a representation of the sentiments of the people of this country could be conveyed to France." Vaughan drew up a memorandum on the state of English opinion. This document did, indeed, seek to inform the French government of what was almost certainly the case—that an invasion would be counter-productive for the English radicals—but it did so in remarkably sympathetic tones. One passage in particular seemed to suggest that an English revolution was a matter of time and tactics, not of principle: "Terror pervades the Friends of Liberty who would soon show a different appearance if they were countenanced by a majority of the People, seeing that there are no regular troops in England but militia and a few cavalry, who are stationed near the coast only."[6]

Vaughan subsequently explained under questioning that his point had been that public sentiment rather than military repression was the most important obstacle for the radicals, and that it was for this reason that all notions of a French invasion were misconceived. Nevertheless, the document was deeply compromising. Its tone was that of friendly advice to fellow Friends of Liberty, rather than that of the outraged patriotic defiance that might be expected from legislators in a country threatened with invasion by an aggressive neighbour. And the passage in question did contain some information about the disposition of military forces, albeit of a kind that the French almost certainly knew already.

Stone was, in any case, anxious to show this document to Sheridan and to get his endorsement of its sentiments. He had his attorney, Richard Wilson, write a note "begging to be allowed to call upon him with Mr Stone."[7] Sheridan had, as he subsequently put it, "considerable knowledge" of Wilson: he was the auditor of the Drury Lane accounts. The two called at Sheridan's house the following morning, but did not get to see him. In the meantime, Stone had contacted two more of the targets listed by his brother, Lord Lauderdale and Major Maitland (a member of the Friends of the People), and arranged that they, too, would go to Sheridan's at noon the following day.

However, when Stone and Wilson arrived, Sheridan, who knew nothing of the appointment, was still in bed. They retired to Hudson's coffee house on Bond Street, where they met up with Lauderdale and Maitland and showed them Vaughan's paper. Stone and

Wilson then returned to Sheridan's house, and this time were admitted. They stayed with Sheridan for about twenty minutes. We have Sheridan's detailed account of what happened at this meeting, but it has to be treated with caution because it is the statement of a man being questioned as part of an investigation into a conspiracy to commit high treason.

Unknown to William Stone or to any of his contacts at this time, William Jackson was now himself under surveillance. Before he left London for Ireland, Jackson contacted an old friend, John Cockayne, a solicitor. Cockayne, however, contacted Pitt, who asked him to accompany Jackson to Ireland and report on his movements, which included meetings with the most prominent United Irishmen. On 26 April Jackson was arrested in Dublin, and on 3 May William Stone was arrested in London. For the government, these arrests seemed to provide an opportunity to revenge the particularly humiliating defeat at the hands of Sheridan's radical associates, when, shortly before Jackson's arrest, the treason trial of Thomas Walker and his associates collapsed after the evidence of the informer was shown to be perjured.

The Jackson affair was, for Pitt, an immediate opportunity to recover the momentum for repression that had been lost in the farce of Walker's trial, and perhaps to destroy his most potent political enemy. Sheridan was questioned by the Secretary of State's office on 8 May and by the Privy Council the following day. In political circles, this caused a sensation. George Canning noted that at the Hastings trial, "all the world were talking of Mr Stone's taking-up and of the examinations of Sheridan, Ld Lauderdale, Majr. Maitland, Mr Vaughan and W[illiam] Smith before the Cabinet."[8] What Sheridan told the Privy Council has to be read in the light of the danger he was now in, for Pitt's main interest in the prosecutions of Jackson and Stone lay in the possibility of incriminating Sheridan, easily the most important figure to have been touched by Jackson's mission. John Stone's letters and Jackson's dispatches to France, which had been intercepted by British agents in Hamburg, were sifted for evidence against him.[9] Even though Jackson was very obviously a French agent and a traitor, the government in London suggested to Dublin Castle that he be allowed to turn state's evidence if he would agree to incriminate others. The authorities in Dublin, indeed, were shocked by the extent to which Pitt was prepared to risk the effect on Irish public opinion that this might have. The Irish chancellor and attorney-general warned that "it would be thought, as is now insinuated, that Jackson was sent merely to entrap the others." But for Pitt the prize—at best the prospect of Sheridan facing charges of high treason, at worst a vast store of ammunition to fire at him across the floor of the House of Commons—was worth the risk.

Such was the danger that immediately after his interrogation by the Privy Council on the same day as Sheridan's, Benjamin Vaughan fled to France. But Sheridan remained remarkably calm. Vaughan had written a pamphlet under the pseudonym "The Calm Observer," and Sheridan now remarked, "I should be sorry if poor Vaughan was hanged, because it would sound so awkward when he was dangling in the air for people to say, 'There hangs the Calm Observer.' "[10] Though he understood that his own situation was no laughing matter, Sheridan assumed the demeanour of a man who had nothing to fear. In a sworn written statement he breezily informed the Privy Council that he would not have agreed to give any information about Stone unless summoned as a witness at a trial but for the fact that Stone himself had referred his inquisitors to Sheridan.[11]

He then gave his version of events. Stone had come to him, told him of the visit of "an American gentleman, a great friend of his brother's," and of his proposal to send a memorandum to the French on the state of opinion in England so as to dissuade them from their intention to invade. He had then read Vaughan's memorandum to him. Sheridan claimed that he had refused to comment on it but resolved "in my own mind to speak to Mr Vaughan respecting it," telling Stone that "tho' I did not doubt the goodness of his intentions it was a subject I would by no means meddle in and that he would do well to have nothing more to say to it." Stone, however, told his inquisitors that Sheridan did comment on the paper, to the effect that anything that could divert the French from an invasion "would be rendering a most essential service and he thought this step likely to do it."

Sheridan claimed that when Stone read him a letter from his brother in Paris, he expressed surprise at the carrying-on of such a correspondence. When Stone mentioned that the "American Gentleman" had gone "to Scotland or Ireland," he had, he said, taken the whole business much more seriously and warned him that "his

Friend whatever he profess'd to be seem'd very likely to get into [a] scrape." He also urged Stone to contact the government and to tell Home Secretary Dundas what he was up to.

Sheridan was careful not to incriminate either Stone or Vaughan in his statement to the Privy Council. He said that Stone did "not seem to consider his Brother's Friend at all as an agent from the French Government." He portrayed Stone as weak and foolish rather than devious or dangerous, insisting that he "appear'd really and zealously convinced that he was endeavouring at a Public Benefit." And he described how, when he met Vaughan at the House of Commons that evening and warned him that his paper was "liable to misconstruction," the latter had assured him that he had intended merely to be "serviceable to the Country."

It is likely that Sheridan was just as dismissive towards Stone as he claimed to be, though not necessarily for reasons he would want to admit to the likes of Pitt and Dundas. Sheridan was suspicious of Stone's approach and afterwards ticked Wilson off for "having introduced Stone to him upon any such business," asking how he "could think of bringing a man to me on such a foolish errand." To a man of Sheridan's intelligence and experience the approach of the brother of a well-known English revolutionary with tales of an American gentleman, a visit to Ireland, and a French invasion would have immediately suggested the possibility that all this was the work of an *agent provocateur* trying to entrap him.

When Jackson had arrived in Dublin, indeed, many of the United Irish leaders assumed that he was a government spy: Edward Fitzgerald refused to meet him, and Wolfe Tone was so suspicious that he had as little as possible to do with him. At their meeting after Jackson's arrest, the United Irishmen in Dublin "rejoiced that both Mr Jackson and Mr Cockayne are Englishmen and that it will appear to the World that they were probably sent by Mr Pitt as spies to this country."[12] That Sheridan, too, was keenly aware of the possibility of entrapment is obvious from a speech he made a few months later, attacking the government's use of spies and informers as a system creating sedition where it did not find it. His caution stood him in good stead. Even though he could be confident that Pitt and Dundas had nothing on him, he was still rather disingenuous in his sworn statement. He claimed that William Stone was "an entire stranger" to him, though this was almost certainly untrue: William Smith, in his statement, mentioned that he had met William Stone at meetings of the Friends of the People, of which Sheridan was chairman. And indeed in his statement Sheridan acknowledged, even while insisting that he had never seen or spoken to Stone before, that he "may have been in a room with him." He failed to mention an even more salient fact: that he had certainly met and corresponded with the instigator of Jackson's mission, William Stone's brother John, a far more dangerous traitor.

Sheridan in fact knew John Stone reasonably well: it was at dinner in Stone's house at the end of 1791 that he had met Madame de Genlis and Pamela.[13] Not only that, but they had remained in contact even after John Stone had joined the exiled radicals in Paris. Sheridan told the Privy Council that he had warned William Stone about writing to his brother in Paris and had claimed that if he were in office he would "think it my Duty to watch very narrowly any intercourse between Persons in this country and a Person in the situation which his Brother had chosen in France." According to Richard Wilson, "Mr Sheridan asked Stone if his letters to his brother at Paris or from his brother to him were not opened; Stone said they had not, he believed, though some he thought had never come to him. Mr Sheridan said he should have opened the letters if he had been in a public situation and had suspected the correspondence."

This description makes clear that Sheridan's queries were motivated more by anxiety than by high-minded censoriousness. And, in fact, Sheridan had good reason to worry about whether the authorities were opening letters to and from John Stone. Just eighteen months earlier, he himself had received, and almost certainly replied to, just such a letter.

John Stone's letter to Sheridan of November 1792 had informed him that Stone had blocked a proposal from the National Convention to confer honorary French citizenship on Sheridan and Fox, explaining that the convention was anxious to bestow "some mark of distinction on those who have stood forth in support of their cause, when its fate hung doubtful," but that he understood the honour would cause problems for Sheridan, "in the route which you have to take in the next session of Parliament, when the affairs of France must necessarily be often the subject of discussion." While others, including the anti-slavery campaigner William Wilberforce, had already been honoured in this way, no one, as Stone pointed out, was likely to believe that Wilberforce, now a supporter of Pitt's repression, had been seduced by the French, but some might well believe this of Sheridan. Stone reckoned that "that which is only a mark of gratitude for past services will be construed by malignity into a bribe of some sort for services yet to be rendered."[14] He therefore prevailed on Jacques-Pierre Brissot, who had chaired the committee that had proposed Sheridan's name, to delay the announcement of the honour, and in the meantime asked Sheridan whether or not he wanted it. Sheridan's reply is not extant, but he must have made one because the embarrassing honour was not bestowed.

Sheridan's statement also begged a rather obvious question. It is clear, since he raised this question directly with Stone, that he suspected William Jackson of being a French agent. He also claimed in the statement that he urged Stone to contact Dundas and tell him about Jackson. But he himself made no effort to alert the authorities to the presence of an enemy agent in volatile Ireland. Neither did he attempt to remove the passage about the Friends of Liberty and the disposition of the military from Vaughan's memorandum. He was guilty, at the very least, of withholding information about the activities of an enemy agent.

Fortunately for Sheridan, however, no incriminating references to him were found in the letters of John Stone and Jackson that had been seized by the authorities. Cockayne's evidence related only to Jackson's contacts in Ireland, and Vaughan had fled. And Sheridan's own coolness made it impossible to move against him without some substantial evidence that he had deliberately collaborated with the enemy. Much to Pitt's disappointment, the only possible prosecutions for high treason were those against William Stone, who was acquitted at his trial in January 1796, and William Jackson, who in April 1795 was tried in Dublin.

During his trial, Jackson, who had so often been linked in the newspapers with salacious gossip, now got his name in print as a revolutionary hero. His case was serialised in magazines, celebrated in the United Irishmen's newspaper the *Northern Star*, and argued over in pamphlets. He was found guilty of high treason, but the jury recommended mercy and sentence was postponed for a week. When the day came, and his lawyers were pleading for his life, he began to twitch and writhe, then collapsed in convulsions and died from the dose of arsenic he had put into his tea that morning. A few minutes before, when he was passing his lawyers on the way to the dock, he had whispered, "We have deceived the Senate"—the last words of Jaffeir, a conspirator who commits suicide on the scaffold in Thomas Otway's play *Venice Preserved*.

A few months later, in October, just as the new parliamentary session was about to open, Sheridan mounted *Venice Preserved* at Drury Lane, with John Philip Kemble as Jaffeir. From the government press, there was widespread criticism that the play was being staged in order to inspire rebellion, but Sheridan persisted. On 29 October, the day it was to have its third performance, stones and dirt were thrown at the carriage of the King on his way to and from the opening of Parliament. The Lord Chamberlain's licence for the play was withdrawn after that night's performance, and *Venice Preserved* was banned for seven years. The correspondence between theatre and reality had become dangerously close.

Chapter 28

CITIZEN SHERIDAN

On 5 January 1795 Sheridan rose in the House of Commons to put forward a motion to repeal the suspension of the Act of Habeas Corpus. His friend George Canning, who had now become a strong supporter of Pitt, considered the motion the most "foolish and ill-judged" thing Sheridan had done, since it was obvious to him and to "people in general" that the country was in great danger from radical democratic conspiracies. The suspension of the act was due for renewal on 1 February, and Canning believed that from a tactical point of view it would have made more sense to wait until then: "I believe that Fox and others of Opposition saw the subject exactly in this point of view, and were very earnest with Sheridan not to bring it forward. But he was determined to make a grand speech and nothing could dissuade him."[1]

But this was more than a grand gesture. The subject was one on which Sheridan was prepared to stake his entire political reputation. He would always regard his opposition to the suspension of habeas corpus as, he said, "the most meritorious part of his parliamentary conduct."[2] And this was a personal as well as a political mission. For if those who had suffered from the suspension of the act were guilty of treason, so was he: they had put forward the same ideas for which he had argued all his political life. This was a matter not of mere political advantage but of "conscience."

Sheridan wanted to speak out as soon as possible in order to celebrate the recent ignominious failure of a new round of trials on charges of high treason, this time of the leaders of the London Corresponding Society. He had attended these trials "from a principle of duty"[3] and on 20 November 1793 gave evidence in defence of one of the best-known defendants, the veteran democrat John Horne Tooke. Tooke was not one of Sheridan's friends, and the two had crossed swords after the Shelburne-Rockingham administration, and again in 1788, when Tooke was a supporter of Pitt and arguing against a regency.[4] But in giving evidence for him, Sheridan had been at pains to make Tooke look, if anything, more moderate than himself. He recalled the resolution which he had moved in 1790 before a "meeting to celebrate the establishment of liberty in France." Tooke, he said, had proposed an amendment to make it clear that the British constitution was not affected by the same corruptions of power that had made revolution in France inevitable, so as to avoid giving the impression of "a disposition to a revolution in this country." Sheridan gave evidence that he himself had objected to this amendment.[5] He was, in effect, inviting the government to ask whether, if Tooke was a traitor, he himself was not a greater one.

High treason, it had been argued, included not just explicit threats to the life of the King but all attacks on the constitution. Anyone advocating a republican form of government was effectively attempting to remove the King from power and was therefore treasonous. The intention of the government was to kill those against whom it could secure convictions: the attorney-general assured his ministerial colleagues that if the grand jury found against Horne Tooke, he would "undertake to hang him." Sheridan's evidence played an important part in securing Tooke's acquittal, and it had the added and particularly pleasing effect of humiliating Pitt into the bargain, for Tooke had boldy sub-poenaed Pitt as a defence witness. Acting as his own counsel, he asked Pitt to describe their meetings some years before when they were both opposing the government of Lord North. Pitt denied attending any such meetings. Tooke asked him to step down and called Sheridan to the witness box. He then asked him if he remembered political meetings attended by himself, Sheridan, and Pitt in the early 1780s. Sheridan gave a detailed description of several of them. Tooke then called Pitt back to the witness box, where he was forced to corroborate Sheridan's testimony. The jury not only acquitted Tooke in ten minutes but, to the applause of the crowds on the streets, marched with him to a coffee house.[6]

The very extremity of the government's charges discouraged English juries, composed mostly of members of the respectable middle class, from convicting the accused. Thomas Hardy's trial opened at the Old Bailey on 25 October 1794 and ended in his acquittal eight days later, after Sheridan had given evidence that Hardy's opinions were similar to his own. By December, a third defendant, John Thelwall, had also been acquitted. Around the same time, three other members of the London Corresponding Society were released without trial, having been charged on the word of a malicious informer with plotting to assassinate the King with a poison dart. The collapse of these show-trials probably prevented a much more general campaign against the democrats: Hardy had been told on good authority that 800 warrants against reformers (300 actually signed) were to be served immediately on his conviction.[7]

Sheridan's speech after the collapse of the trials was remarkable for the degree to which he identified himself with the democratic radicals of the London Corresponding Society and similar organisations throughout Britain. "When he recollected," he was reported to have said, "that his speaking and writing might have been instrumental in inducing those men to espouse the views which they had adopted, he could not separate his own cause from theirs." Considering that "those men" had been charged with high treason, this defiant statement of common cause, made explicitly on his own behalf and without the support of Fox and the opposition Whigs, was an act of personal and political witness. What is more, it was seen as such by the popular radicals. On the afternoon of 29 June 1795, the London Corresponding Society held a huge mass meeting in St. George's Fields, attended by a crowd estimated by government sources at 10,000 and by the Society at 100,000. On the morning of the meeting basket-loads of biscuits stamped "Freedom and plenty, or slavery and want" were distributed to the poor. Resolutions were passed demanding universal male suffrage and annual parliaments, denouncing the "cruel and unnecessary war," and calling on the government to "acknowledge the brave French republic and to obtain a speedy and lasting peace." Then there were votes of thanks to the lawyer Thomas Erskine for his defence of Hardy and Thelwall, and to Citizen Stanhope (a radical peer) and Citizen Sheridan for their proof that "the people had at least one honest man in each house of parliament."[8]

Sheridan took the opportunity of the failure of the treason trials to strike back against the government's campaign of repression. He attacked the whole idea of treason as it was being put forward by the government, claiming that if the attorney-general's logic were followed, "no man could, in my opinion, be safe." He pointed out that the sentiments of the societies were no more treasonous than the utterances of Burke and Lord Chatham on the American war in 1780, and wondered whether some "retrospective hanging" might not be called for. He implicitly placed the alleged conspirators, indeed, on a level above that of Pitt and Windham, since the former had been proven innocent of crimes, while the latter would be lucky to be acquitted on "the charge of levying war" and of conspiring "against the peace of the country."

As he had done with Burke in 1792, Sheridan went out of his way to invite the enmity of his old ally Windham, again trying to make sure that Fox's friendship with the apostates could not remain intact. Fox, he remarked, "clung to all those of whom he had been accustomed to think favourably," but he himself warned Windham that "he should henceforth meet him on the ground of fair and avowed hostility." Likewise, when he met Burke at the funeral of the painter Gainsborough in August, he declined the opportunity of patching up their personal relationship. That this determined animosity created tension between himself and Fox is clear from George Canning's description of Fox at this time "sitting almost alone on his bench, with none of the principal people of his party about him . . . It has been evident indeed throughout the session that [the] Opposition have not drawn well together—and that there must be some little differences of opinion amongst them which unhinge all their plans and operations. On the days when Grey is in the humour to debate, Fox is not—when they are, Sheridan is away."[9]

Sheridan was determined to fight Pitt tooth and nail. Revelling in the opportunity to avenge himself for the embarrassments of the Jackson affair the previous year, with vigorous wit he mocked the government's Committee of Secrecy, which drew up reports of wild conspiracies.[10] He implied that its members had been effectively bribed with peerages, and joked that many of them had been so alarmed by the evidence of conspiracies they had unearthed that they did not consider the House of Commons "a place of sufficient security and had taken refuge in the upper house. A coronet, the reward of their seasonable apprehensions, would, they thought, be most likely to secure the head of the owner from future danger." He excoriated the government's use of "the detestable evidence of spies":

> I will not say that there have been no instances of sedition; but I will affirm even that the evidence of these appears in so questionable a shape as ought to excite your suspicion. It is supported by a system of spies and informers, a system which has been carried to a greater extent under the present administration than in any former period in the history of the country . . . [T]he government which avails itself of such support does not exist for the happiness of the people. It is a system which is calculated to engender suspicion, and to beget hostility; it not only destroys all confidence between man and man, but between the governors and the governed; where it does not find sedition, it creates it.

This use of spies and informers showed the government to be incapable of communicating with the people through any other means. Sheridan set "the mass of the people," including "the slaving poor of the metropolis," against "stiff-necked" ministers, and identified himself with the former. Whereas before he had been careful to distinguish himself and the Friends of the People from the working-class radicals, his main concern now seemed to be precisely that he had been distanced from them by being identified too closely with the corrupt governing class. He may have been stung into this concern by the anonymous author of a pamphlet, *The Whig Club or A Sketch of the Manners of the Age*, published in 1794, who noted that Sheridan has "quit a path which must have led to honest fame and competence, to prostitute his talents to a faction, who, though they pretend to reject the pretensions of illustrious extraction, still are so much swayed by ancient prejudice, that they will never acknowledge the son of an actor as their leader, however superior may be his capacity." Sheridan's fate, the pamphleteer predicted, would be "to live forever the drudge of a party who distrust him while they employ him; who despise his obscure birth, while they avail themselves of his talents."[11]

Sheridan certainly moved towards apologising for his elite connections. Referring to the evidence of one of the London Corresponding Society's witnesses from Sheffield, he noted that they had declined to communicate with the Friends of the People because "they did not believe them to be honest; that there were several of them members of parliament; that they have some of them been in place [i.e., in office]; and that they conceived the ins and the outs, however they might vary in their professions, to be actuated by the same motives of [self-]interest." This was a perfect opportunity, if he had wanted one, for Sheridan to show how much he, as a Friend of the People in Parliament, differed from these dangerous plebeians. But on the contrary, he "felt rebuked and subdued by the answer." He meekly accepted the criticism as, if not justified in his own case, an understandable conclusion to draw from the corruption of high politics. And he came close to identifying his own principles with those of at least some members of the radical societies, telling Parliament that while they contained some "mischevious men intent on mischevious purposes," others were motivated by "that sort of enthusiasm which had actuated men of the purest minds."

It was, as the politically hostile Canning admitted, "a very brilliant speech." But the replies for the government from James Adair and William Windham, insisting on the need for continued repression, were much more in keeping with the feeling of the House, and Sheridan's motion was lost by 185 votes to 41. A few weeks later, the suspension of habeas corpus was continued by an even more emphatic majority—239 to 53. Now that the power of the elite was really threatened, mere eloquence could no longer sway the House, as it had done in the impeachment of Hastings. And the Hastings trial itself had at last come to its inevitable end. With Burke and Sheridan now bitter enemies in everything else but forced to act together in the prosecution, it had become something of an embarrassment. And whatever tiny chance there had been in 1788 that the House of Lords might convict Hastings had now, in these reactionary times when Hastings's accusers were being openly compared by the Archbishop of York to Marat and Robespierre, completely disappeared.[12]

In May 1794, right in the middle of his troubles with Jackson and Stone, the trial had landed back in Sheridan's lap. He arrived at his country house in Wanstead one day with a cartload of documents and told Tom's tutor, William Smyth, that he had to reply to Hastings's defence in two days' time. He had had the papers for six weeks, he said, but—"you know how I am plagued morning, noon and night"—had not had time to look at them. He managed to postpone the speech for three further days, locked himself away, and worked virtually without stopping. Yet even in these conditions, he managed to write what was, according to Canning, "by far the most brilliant and entertaining speech that I ever heard from him or any other person."[13] Smyth went to Westminster Hall to see him deliver it:

> When he came into the manager's box, he was in full dress, and his countenance had assumed an ashen colour that I had never before observed . . . He was evidently tried to the utmost—every nerve and faculty within him put into complete requisition . . . The voice was so fine, the manner so dignified and graceful, the flow of words so unembarrassed, the expressions sometimes so beautiful, the rapidity and fire of the eloquence sometimes so overpowering, the statements so clearly made, the appeals deduced from them so forcible, that the impression on my mind, as I sat under him in the manager's box, was quite that of listening to some being of a totally different nature from my own . . .

Sheridan turned on Hastings's defence counsel, Lord Ellenborough, who had wrongly accused him of deceiving a witness by showing him the wrong document. Smyth watched the lawyer under his fire: "I remember seeing him start up and tumble over his papers in a hurried manner; and though a more imperturbable and invincible front was never placed even under a lawyer's wig, I saw him soon change colour, and, evidently in a state of great confusion and distress, hide himself as well as he could in the bottom of his box and sit down."[14] Such brilliance, however, could achieve nothing now, and in March 1795, when the House of Lords finally delivered its verdict, Hastings was acquitted on all counts. On the begums of Oudh charge, just six of the twenty-nine peers who voted found him guilty.[15] If any further proof of the limits of mere parliamentary action were needed, this was it.

Sheridan was still, however, relying on contradictory forces in his fight against Pitt. One was mass popular radicalism. But the other was his continuing influence with the Prince of Wales. It was an uncomfortable alliance at the best of times, and the strain became palpable in June 1795, when the Prince's profligacy—he had run up astonishingly large debts of £630,000—created another crisis. In return for his agreement to ditch Mrs. Fitzherbert and marry a Protestant, Princess Caroline of Brunswick, Pitt agreed to bail him out. In a time of war, though, with extra taxes on everything, Pitt's proposals were massively unpopular, not least with the democratic radicals with whom Sheridan was aligning himself. He tried to solve the dilemma by suggesting that the Prince's debts should be paid, but from the sale of royal forests and crown lands and the abolition of sinecures. Thus they could "build the ease and dignity of the Prince on the ruins of idleness and corruption and not by the toil of the industrious poor." He also vehemently—and truthfully—denied that he himself had ever received "so much as the present of a horse or of a picture" from the Prince.[16] It was, noted Canning, "the strangest and most incongruous and unconstruable [speech] that ever fell from the mouth of man—toad[y]ing, republican, full of economy and of generosity, and in short a medley of sentiments irreconcilable in themselves, but which it was business to court the Prince and keep well with the people to reconcile."[17]

However, Sheridan's willingness to court the Prince did not prevent him from moving ever closer to open defiance of the King. On 29 October, two days after another huge mass meeting organised by the London Corresponding Society at the Copenhagen Tea House in Islington—the attendance, estimated at 150,000, made it at the time the largest political meeting ever held in Britain—King George, on his way to and from the opening of Parliament, was surrounded by large and decidedly hostile crowds demanding peace with France and the dismissal of Pitt. Stones and dirt were thrown at his carriage and in the Palace Yard one of its windows was broken, allegedly by a missile discharged from an air-gun.

After the King's address, Sheridan made remarks that were taken to be favourable to the rioters. Speaking with what Pitt described to the King as "great violence,"[18] he poured sarcasm on the King's speech. He reportedly declared himself surprised that the ministers could "have the front to put such words into the mouth of His Majesty; and they could suffer the King when he passed through his starving and oppressed, and sorry was he to hear, irritated and clamorous people, to come down to the house and express his satisfaction."[19] Sheridan subsequently said that when he made these remarks he was unaware that anything except "some indistinct clamours" had occurred, but the impression that he was on the side of the crowd was enhanced by his claim that the attacks on the King had been the work of *agents provocateurs* trying, in the aftermath of the collapse of the treason trials, to "revive the profitable trade of alarm."

Pitt seized on these incidents as an excuse for further repression. He and the government blamed the London Corresponding Society and the Islington mass meeting for the attacks on the King. On 9 November he brought to the Commons a "bill for better securing the King's person against treasonable and seditious practices and attempts." Sheridan again opposed it as a violation of the "fundamental principle of the bill of rights, the right of petitioning." He denied that the proceedings of the Islington meeting were "either treasonable or seditious" and again blamed government spies for the wilder handbills that had been distributed at it. He attacked the requirement that all meetings be attended by a magistrate on the basis that the magistrates in Westminster were "hired creatures, and agents of ministers, a despicable set of paid, pensioned place-hunters." And he asked, "As it is the nature of man always to resist oppression, how many magistrates will be wanted, in order to carry into effect this new system?"[20]

On 16 November, after the first reading of the Treason and Sedition Bills, Sheridan, along with Fox, spoke at a public meeting at Westminster Hall to take "the sense of the inhabitants of Westminster" against the bill. The meeting attracted such large crowds that it had to be moved to New Palace Yard, where a hustings was raised before the King's Arms tavern. Some of those present were "Crops and Democrats" (the former term being a reference to the fashion among revolutionaries for cropped hair).[21] The following day in Parliament Sheridan again spoke at length on the bills, and read a petition against them from the people of Bristol addressed to himself. He said that "with regard to the London Corresponding Society I cannot join in the clamour that had been raised against it."[22] There is at least some evidence to suggest, too, that he was actively colluding with some members of the London Corresponding Society. Sheridan exercised a degree of control over the *Morning Post*, which had been bought by the Prince during the regency crisis. A spy's report for June 1796 noted: "A Mr Sandford who writes for the *Morning Post* was employed by Mr Sheridan to write against the Government and a defence of Lord Fitzwilliam's [abortive reforming] administration in Ireland is one of the London Corresponding Society . . ."[23]

It is poignant to find Sheridan using the Prince's resources to encourage democratic radicals, but that is precisely the double game he was playing. And this tension between Sheridan the traitor and Sheridan the Prince's friend came to a head in the crisis over the Prince's disastrous second marriage. In April 1796, the Prince's wife, Caroline, to whom he had been married for just a year and who had just borne their first child, protested at being required to dine alone with a woman whom she described to her husband as "your mistress," Lady Jersey. By the end of May the dispute had reached the point where the Prince made a formal request to his father for a "final separation." In June, when the rupture had become a public scandal in which the Prince was almost universally regarded as the villain, Sheridan tried to take a hand. On 10 June, on his way to Southampton, he called on the Prince, who was staying near Winchester, and left a letter requesting a meeting, in order "to talk over with me the present circumstances, as I could not but suppose they must be uppermost in everybody's ideas." Sheridan stated that he would "rather . . . risk incurring your Royal Highness's displeasure by the appearance of intrusion than not to offer at this critical juncture in your royal Highness's *public* situation, the humble and sincere opinion of one who thinks he has the means of judging not incorrectly."[24]

Lord Moira was, however, already acting as a go-between in the negotiations between Caroline and her husband, and the Prince declined to see Sheridan:

> I will state to you with the greatest candour the real fact, and that is, that under present circumstances, my family in concert with myself have determin'd to avoid as much as possible all ministerial and even private discussion or interference. It is therefore that I feel myself under the unpleasant necessity of declining seeing you, were we even to talk upon indifferent matters. I am sure I need not add that, under any other circumstances or at any other moment, I should have been and always shall be very happy to see you as you pass by when you have nothing better to do.

This suggests that the King had warned his son to keep Sheridan out of the business, a suspicion that is strengthened by the speed with which the Prince then informed the King of Sheridan's letter and the earnestness with which he sought his father's approval: "I was much surpriz'd at this letter; however, I thought it right civilly to decline his visit, which I flatter myself will meet with your Majesty's approbation."[25] The Queen delivered the required pat on the head:

> The Kng. is very much surprized at Mr Scheridan's proposed visit, as he looks upon it quite in the light of impertinence, and he

> greatly approves of yr. having refused to see him. As a woman I hardly dare give my oppinion but to you I speak openly and am not afraid of telling you that I think he came to pump you in order to make things more public and perhaps to play against you with yr. own weapon. I am sure nobody ever can be safe with a man so totally void of principle as he is, and therefore am quite overjoid of yr. refusing him admittance, and at this present moment I am sure that this refusal must if known in the world prove advantageous to you, as it proves that you are not desirous to advise with a man who professes himself to be a democrate, and if the world in general was as much inclined to relate the good as to invent what is bad, the circumstance might be made a very excellent article in yr. favour in the public prints.[26]

Three days after Sheridan was rebuffed by the Prince, he took his revenge by helping to stage an extraordinary public demonstration of support for Princess Caroline, with distinct overtones of *lèse-majesté*. The polls for the Westminster election closed that day, 13 June, with Fox safely returned. When this happened, "fifty bludgeon-men" wearing Fox's cockades rushed to the hustings to acclaim their hero. There, as *The Times* reported, "they were obliged to wait until by the orders of Citizen Sheridan, the chair which had been fitted up for his Majesty when he goes to Drury Lane Theatre, was brought down to the hustings for Mr Fox." The bludgeon-men then carried Fox through the streets in the King's chair. As the procession passed Carlton House, where the Princess was living, "the mob expressed their wish to see the infant princess, in consequence of which the sash of one of the upper windows was held up, and the Royal child shown to the populace, who gave three cheers . . ."

The Prince was enraged and demanded that the King should be told that Caroline was "paying her court to Mr Fox and his mob at the time I was declining to see Sheridan." She had, he whimpered, allowed herself to be made "the tool, not only of private views, but of party, and even of the worst of parties at this moment, the democratick . . ."[27] Whether it occurred to him that the same Sheridan might intend to make himself a tool of the democrats is not at all clear.

Chapter 29

MEN, WOMEN, AND OGLES

Through all of this Sheridan's personal life had been as unsettled as ever. After the deaths of Eliza and Mary he suffered another loss when his brother-in-law and one of his closest friends, the witty and playful Richard Tickell, committed suicide. A playwright, dabbler in verses, and enthusiastic ally in Sheridan's practical jokes, Tickell had been married to Eliza's sister Mary before her death in 1787, and had then remarried. On 6 November 1793 Tickell "threw himself out of a window of the attick storey in the Fount Court of Hampton Court, and dashed the back part of his head to pieces. His carriage was waiting for him at the time to bring him to the Stamp Office, where he had a place, and Mrs Tickel[l], a beautiful woman, was in the room. Distressed circumstances and an apprehension of being arrested, it is said, is the cause of this momentary phrenzy."[1] He was the same age as Sheridan.

As soon as he received news of his friend's death, Sheridan dropped everything and rushed to Hampton Court, where he stayed for some days. He brought all his considerable force of persuasion to bear on the task of keeping Tickell's suicide out of the newspapers. He arranged that the evidence before the inquest would be merely that Tickell was in the habit of getting out onto the roof to tend his window boxes, with the inference that he had slipped and fallen to his death. The verdict was therefore one of accidental death. Having achieved his first aim, Sheridan organised for Mrs. Tickell and her children to stay at his house in Wanstead, treating them with striking courtesy and patience. He subsequently fixed up one of the sons in the navy and another in the East India Company.[2]

With so much death around him, and none of his own siblings now living in England (Charles, Betsy, and Alicia were all now settled in Dublin), his son, Tom, was his only family. He had three houses—one in Grosvenor Street in London, the Wanstead house, and his country retreat in Isleworth—but no home. Since Eliza's death, he could not bear to be in the Grosvenor Street house and, when in London, slept in a hotel.[3] When in Isleworth, he tended to fret over his son so much that Charles Grey urged him to have a glass case made for Tom. The boy's tutor, William Smyth, found Sheridan's nervousness about his son incomprehensible. He complained that once, when there was ice on the pond, Sheridan badgered him not to let the boy go skating: "He would certainly be drowned." Smyth objected that he was himself a good skater, that he would have a servant stationed on the bank with a rope and a ladder, and that the ice was thick enough to bear a waggon. Sheridan at last relented and set off for Drury Lane. Half an hour later, Smyth heard a violent ringing at the gate, and there was Sheridan in his carriage: " 'Now do not laugh at me Smyth,' he said, 'but I cannot rest or think about anything but this damned ice and this skaiting, and you must promise me that there shall be none more of it.' I said what may be supposed; and in short was at last obliged to thrust my hand through the bars, which he shook violently, in token that his wishes should be obeyed."

He was, in 1794, still only forty-three, and with such evident loneliness it was inevitable that he should remarry. He was still in love with Harriet Duncannon, as would become obvious, but she had turned her attentions to a younger man, Lord Granville Leveson Gower. In his melancholy state it was not surprising that he should be attracted to a young and vibrant woman like Esther Jane Ogle (whom he always called Hecca), the eighteen-year-old daughter of the Dean of Winchester. In spite of his position, her father was a radical and held, according to Fanny Burney, "dreadful republican views." It is likely, therefore, that they met in political circles—almost certainly, as William Smyth maintained, at Devonshire House.

Hecca was tall, green-eyed, and slightly gawky, but full of the kind of high-spirited vivacity that Sheridan needed in his life. According to Smyth, when she first met him she told him to go away, calling him a "fright" and a "terrible creature," and so arousing Sheridan's interest in her.

> After some little contrivance, he obtained a more civil word from her; at the next party a little conversation; then she proclaimed that, though quite a monster, he was very clever; then that, though to be sure ugly enough, he was very agreeable. It then occurred to her more forcibly than at first, that he was one of the most celebrated men in the kingdom; and that, to make a conquest of such a man, and to have every company observe his attention to her, was not at all unpleasant; and in this manner she went on till at last she voted that she could not live without him.[4]

By the autumn of 1794 Hecca was utterly in love with Sheridan. In a letter written some time before their marriage, she confessed to him, "I thought women in general were shy of expressing their love to Men, if so I am peculiarly brazen and impudent, for I can't help telling Sheridan everything that comes into my mind, and certainly love comes a little into it." He evidently encouraged such freedom of expression by sending her his mother's epistolary novel of sentiment, *Memoirs of Miss Sidney Biddulph*: "I think ye 3rd Vol. of S.B. very pretty indeed, some things beautiful, everybody likes it and my mother is in raptures." She was clearly excited, too, by his political connections: "Tell me whether your friend Fox knows anything about me and whether he thinks I am to be yours. I want to know him more than anybody." There is a hint, too, of a previous romance that ended bitterly: "I should be perfectly happy now were it not for the recollection of my poor friend, but I cannot help fancying, (however strange such a fancy may seem) that he is in a state where he is inform'd about me, and that it is painful to him to see me give myself to another." Something of her wildness comes through in her reply to an offer of Sheridan's to buy her a horse: "If I *must* have a horse of your choosing, let it be excessively hot and fiery, and not too tall, with a fine crest, and be sure no lady ever rode it."

Hecca acknowledged that some members of her family were less than happy at the prospect of her marriage, even remarking on "the face my maid put on this morning when she gave me your letter." It is clear that her brother, the Reverend John Saville Ogle, was hostile: "John had a letter from you this morning but did not speak of it to me. I think his letter to [her sister] Sukey a very unjust one and I must own rather impertinent, but when you come to know him better you will not repent your generosity in looking over these things." Her other sister, Kate, however, "really adores you." And, she added, "I fear not their all adoring you in time. I shall set so good an example."[5]

By Christmas, their marriage was "in contemplation . . . and wants nothing but the old man's consent to confirm it."[6] Not unreasonably, her father's concerns centred on money, and a marriage settlement had to be negotiated. It eventually involved the establishment of a trust for her, comprised of her £5,000 dowry and "£15,000 in the 3 per cents"[7] raised by Sheridan, a monetary complication that added a new layer of chaos to his finances.

Tom, informed that he was to have a new step-mother, wrote to Smyth to tell him that the bride to be was "about my own age; better me to marry her, you will say,—I am not of that opinion. My father talked to me two hours last night, and made out to me that it was the most sensible thing he could do. Was not this very clever of him? Well, my dear Mr. S., you should have been tutor to him, you see. I am incomparably the most rational of the two . . ."[8]

The wedding took place on 27 April 1795 at Winchester Collegiate Church, and was followed by a honeymoon in Southampton, much of it spent sailing. George Canning was introduced to Hecca at the opera on their return to London the following month:

> She is not very pretty, I think, but wilder and more strange in her air, dress and manners than anything human, or at least anything female that I ever saw. I am told indeed that she is nothing to what she was on the first night of her appearance, and I daresay in proportion as she humanises more and more, she will be more pleasing, for there is something interesting and animated in her countenance, and her friskiness and vivacity if [they] were not carried to such an excess as to look like impudence, would have an air of innocence not unpleasing.[9]

By the end of the year Hecca's refusal to conform to the model of a great man's wife was already being worked into the satires on her husband:

> The shackles of a wayward bride he wore;
> For since divine Cecilia was no more,

> He deem'd, inclined to ogle and to toy,
> Husbands have pains, but bachelors no joy.[10]

But to Sheridan, Hecca's originality of character was a delight. She told him that she was a novice and that her mind was a blank sheet of paper, but he assured her that he admired her astuteness and judgement of character. He transferred his superstitious worries from Tom to her, tormenting himself with visions of her being killed in a riding accident.[11] He considered her family "a most extraordinary Breed," and told her that "the World consists of Three Descriptions of Inhabitants—*Men, Women*, and *Ogles*" who, he assured her, surpassed the first two.[12] She, in turn, could hardly bear to be parted from him and told him during one brief separation while he was on business in London, "[You are] never to leave me again, you have promised it. I dreamt of you all night, and kept dreaming on till eleven this morning."[13] So invigorated was he by her presence that he was even confident he could begin to write plays again. On 17 December he bet Henry Holland that he would write and produce at Drury Lane two "dramatic pieces or three or five acts before December 30th 1799."[14]

Hecca was pregnant very soon after the wedding, and on 14 January 1796 gave birth to their son Charles, who had Fox and Grey for his godfathers. And by the summer, after he had been re-elected unopposed for Stafford, Sheridan was full of blissful visions. They had decided to use the money held in trust for Hecca to purchase for £12,384 Polesden Lacey, a 340-acre country estate in Surrey, with a seventeenth-century manor house. They would, he assured her, have

> . . . the nicest Place within a prudent distance from Town in England. And sweet Hecca shall have a House after her own Fancy and it shall be the Seat of Health and Happiness—where she shall chirp like a bird, bound like a Fawn, and grow fat as [a] little pig, and we will get rid of all the nasty Servants and have all good and do all good round us. The thought and Plan of this is my Hope and Happiness, and puts all dismal thoughts from me . . . But you my Angel you, and you only could have done it, have brought Peace and chearfulness to a restless and harrass'd Heart. —You are its resting place and Delight—every hour more and more.[15]

At one level, the expense of the estate was the last thing Sheridan needed. He was "worried to Death" about the need to get "all the monies in the world for Polesden and Hecca and Tom and Robin [his pet-name for baby Charles]." In September 1796 he had to make over his "household furniture etc." as collateral for a loan of £6,000. According to the topographical artist Joseph Farington, he even managed to borrow £80 from the lawyer acting for the seller of Polesden, Sir William Geary. The high hopes he had cherished in April for making money from Henry Ireland's sensational discovery of a new Shakespeare play, *Vortigern*—actually a crude forgery—had been dashed. He had hoped that argument over the play's authenticity—which he must have known to be be non-existent—would ensure a long run. John Philip Kemble made his contempt for the piece obvious in his playing of his part, however, and it collapsed into farce. Shortly afterwards Kemble finally acted on his regular threats to resign, and had to be replaced as acting manager by Richard Wroughton.

At another level, however, the idea of establishing his own little kingdom of peace, happiness, and justice was irresistibly alluring. Polesden conformed to the ideal of Romantic retreat into nature. The portrait painter John Hoppner and Joseph Farington went to see it, and although they found the house marked by "characteristic neglect . . . everything manifesting disorder," they were enthralled by the surroundings: as Farington reported, "The terrace . . . is fine, overlooking a steep and richly wooded bank, at the end of which is a peep of beautiful distance.—From hence we descended and in a vale below passed through a wood what had an effect that enraptured Hoppner who compared it to the inside of a fine old Gothic cathedral."[16]

This was a suitable setting for utopian fantasies, and Sheridan had good reason to dream of withdrawing from an increasingly savage political world into an idyll of bounty and bliss. Pitt had, after 1795, succeeded in driving most of the democratic opposition underground, and in spite of all the resistance of Sheridan and others, the assault on civil liberties and progressive ideas was continuing unabated. This was, as Sydney Smith recalled in old age, "an awful period for those who had the misfortune to entertain liberal opinions, and who were too honest to sell them for the ermine of the judge, or the lawn of the prelate." There was "no more hope of Whig administration than of a thaw in Zembla." Contrary opinions were barely tolerated:

> It is always considered as a piece of impertinence in England, if a man of less than two or three thousand a year has any opinions at all upon important subjects; and in addition he was sure at that time to be assailed with all the Billingsgate of the French Revolution—Jacobin, Leveller, Atheist, Deist, Socinian, Incendiary, Regicide, were the gentlest appelations used: and the man who breathed a syllable against the senseless bigotry of the two Georges, or hinted at the abominable tyranny and persecution exercised upon Catholic Ireland was shunned as unfit for the relations of social life.[17]

In this climate, life on the farm with his new baby and his new wife, "doing all good round us," represented Sheridan's fantasy of a benign political order. He had, since his early years, attacked absentee Irish landlords and been passionately devoted to the notion of great benevolence descending on the tenant farmers. Polesden was an opportunity to play out this role and to be himself, in his own small way, the ruler of a rustic Arcadia. Towards the end of his life Hecca's nephew Nathaniel Ogle stayed with them at Polesden and left a description of Sheridan's relations with the local cottagers. On a walk they approached a farmhouse and Sheridan told him that "the inhabitant of that house is a man whose bread has been dipped in the tears, but I trust the assistance I have given him, united with his own industry, will extricate him from his difficulties and enable him to provide for his family." The family had been evicted from a nearby farm, and Sheridan, believing that they had been dealt with unjustly, had made them his tenants, advanced them money, and charged them no rent for the first year.

> On entering the wicket near which several children were at play, he was recognised by them, and they shouted with one voice as they ran towards their home, "Here's Mr Sheridan." Immediately a venerable-looking old man, his son, a man about fifty (the father of the numerous offspring before mentioned) and his wife came to the door and, with looks of joy, saluted him. We entered the dwelling. Mr Sheridan, being seated, kindly inquired after the health of the family, the state of the crops on the farm, and the probability he had of success. From the answers of the man I easily discovered that Mr Sheridan was well acquainted with his affairs . . .[18]

He was also active in trying to protect the interests of the cottagers, as well as his own, in the continuing process of enclosing the commons, open land which had traditionally been used by the poorer farmers for keeping their animals. In 1804, when there was a move to enclose open land in nearby Great Bookham, he was at odds with the local landlord, George Holme Sumner. At a meeting on the enclosures, as he wrote to Hecca, "I was called to the Chair to resist Sumner's unpopularity, the poorer Claimants putting their cases entirely into my hands . . ."[19]

The attractions of retiring into such a private domain of benevolence were immense. And by 1797 they were much more than a private fantasy, for rustic retreat became in effect the official policy of his party. Despairing of change, both Grey and Fox began early that year to contemplate the option of withdrawing altogether from the fray by a secession from Parliament. On 26 May Grey proposed his second, very modest motion for parliamentary reform, which Sheridan voted for but privately condemned as an empty gesture. When it was defeated, Fox and Grey led the remaining Whigs out of the House. Sheridan now had the perfect excuse to fulfil his own fantasies and shrug off the burden of bitter resistance to a government which had assumed the powers of a virtual military dictatorship. That he chose not to do so was, once again, due to events in Ireland.

Chapter 30

THE WOODEN WALLS

In a James Gillray cartoon of 1796, "Promis'd Horrors of the French Invasion, or Forcible Reasons for Negociating a Regicide PEACE," French troops are marching up St. James's Street in London, between White's club on the one side and Brooks's on the other. The royal dukes are being tossed from the balcony of White's. The guillotine, on the balcony opposite, is dripping with blood. William Pitt, tied to a liberty tree, is being scourged by Fox. Behind them, London is in flames. Corpses hang from the lamp-posts. Sheridan is skulking into the door of Brooks's with a sack marked "Remains of the Treasury" on his head and one marked "Requisitions from the Bank of England" under his arm. It is a surreal and satiric vision, but not a completely fantastic one. For the possibility of a French invasion of Britain or Ireland or both was very real.

For a short period in 1794 and 1795 there had seemed to be a possibility of avoiding disaster in Ireland. After the split in the Whig party provoked by Burke and Sheridan, its old leader, the Duke of Portland, began to move towards an alliance with Pitt. When the marriage was consummated at the end of 1794, Portland was made Home Secretary and the Irish viceroyalty was allotted to the intelligent and liberal-minded Earl Fitzwilliam, nephew and heir of the Marquis of Rockingham. His appointment raised Catholic expectations to such a point that, unless they were fulfilled, a rebellion of some sort would become inevitable. Sheridan evidently shared the optimism that the appointment provoked (as we have seen, he employed at least one radical journalist to write in support of Fitzwilliam). Moreover, his acquaintance the Reverend Mr. O'Beirne, the cleric for whom he had written the satiric sermon on the abuse of riches, was Fitzwilliam's secretary.

Fitzwilliam, on his arrival in Ireland in January 1795, had peremptorily removed from office all the senior members of the Irish administration opposed to Catholic emancipation. He then permitted Henry Grattan to introduce an emancipation bill. On doing so, however, he was almost immediately sacked by Lord Portland, who cited the feelings of Whigs "for the established Church." He had been in office for less than two months. It was a disastrous moment in Irish history, convincing the majority of politically active Catholics that their rights could not be secured by peaceful means. The Catholic leaders announced that henceforth they would "merge their cause with that of the Nation"—in other words, that they would support the United Irishmen. And the United Irishmen themselves became more explicitly revolutionary: after May 1795 they became a clandestine oath-bound conspiracy, actively working towards a revolution, with French assistance. They also began to ally themselves with the Catholic conspirators called the Defenders.

To make matters worse, sectarian tension between Catholic and Protestant secret societies—the Defenders and the Peep O'Day Boys—reached boiling point in County Armagh. The Orange Order was founded, and quickly acquired at least tacit support from many upper-class Protestants in carrying out pogroms against Catholics. Sheridan was probably in touch with these events. A surviving copy of a pamphlet on the Armagh disturbances written by a Catholic priest and United Irishman, James Coigley, is inscribed to him by the author.

But Sheridan almost certainly learned much more. Two men whom he knew well were among those radicalised by the débâcle of the Fitzwilliam administration. One was Edward Fitzgerald, who ceased to be a mere fellow-traveller and instead approached the United Irish leadership with a direct offer to use his connections in France to open negotiations for French assistance in a revolution. The other was Arthur O'Connor, a charismatic but idiosyncratic United Irishman. (Born as Arthur Conner in County Cork into a family descended from London merchants, he had changed his name and convinced himself that he was descended from the high kings of Ireland.) In 1795 he had abandoned Irish politics in disgust and despair and moved to London, where he became friendly with Sheridan.

In April 1796 Fitzgerald joined O'Connor in London, and recruited him into his scheme for negotiations with France. Richard Madden, the first authoritative historian of the United Irishmen, who interviewed many of the survivors of its rebellion, including Fitzgerald's wife, Pamela, who was with him on the mission to France, wrote:

> When Lord Edward and O'Connor proceeded on their perilous and momentous mission to the continent in May 1796, they passed through London and Lord Edward is known to have enjoyed the society of his Whig friends, Charles Fox, Sheridan, and several other distinguished public men. O'Connor was then intimately acquainted with Fox and it may be reasonably presumed he did not pass through London without visiting Fox, though we have no account of his having done so.[1]

Madden adds that O'Connor and Fitzgerald must have told Fox the purpose of their mission.

One of Fitzgerald's biographers, Patrick Byrne, claimed that Fitzgerald did in fact dine with Fox and Sheridan and told them what he was about. It is very likely in any case that if Fitzgerald did not tell them, Arthur O'Connor did. On Christmas Eve, 1796, O'Connor wrote to Charles Fox in terms that left little room for doubt about the revolutionary intentions of the United Irishmen. What he told Fox is what he almost certainly believed at the time—that revolutionary change would come with or without French assistance.

> It has seemed to me after the best consideration that a new order of Things would force its way into the World and that so far from any civilised Nation standing in need of what's called revolutionary or French Principles from France, they each of them containing [sic] full enough of this purpose of revolution at home of native growth. Circumstances have brought them forward in France but I have no doubt of this being more ripe or indeed so ripe as some other Countries in Europe.

The United Irishmen, he told Fox, avoided breaking the law at the moment because "they are waiting patiently until they find a good opportunity to speak their sentiments but they do not think themselves authorised to do so until they have a decided majority of the Nation with them."[2] O'Connor's meaning was unmistakable: as soon the United Irishmen judged that they had majority support, there would be a revolution in Ireland. And if he was telling this to Fox, there can be little doubt that he was saying the same thing to Sheridan, whose Irish patriotism had since the early 1780s been an innate aspect of his fame. Sheridan and Sir Francis Burdett, O'Connor's closest friend amongst the opposition in England, were at this time strong allies. O'Connor was, besides, closer to Sheridan personally than he was to Fox. Harriet Duncannon afterwards told Granville Leveson Gower, "Mr Fox never liked [O'Connor] and always thought him a fool and disagreeable."[3] Sheridan, on the other hand, clearly admired him.

In any case, Sheridan would have been extraordinarily dim-witted had he failed to understand the purpose of O'Connor's and Fitzgerald's mission after 16 December, when a French fleet, led by the great general Louis Lazare Hoche, and with the United Irish leader Theobald Wolfe Tone and 14,450 French troops on board, set sail from Brest. By 21 December it had arrived at Bantry Bay on the south-west coast of Ireland. Had it landed, the invasion might very well have succeeded, for the country was poorly defended. But appalling weather intervened, and the rebellion had to be postponed.

Sheridan's family in Dublin could not understand his continuing sympathy for those who, after such an event, could continue to ally themselves with the French. On 16 February 1797 Lissy wrote to Sheridan from Dublin, berating him for making light of the French invasion.

> My dear Brother, I have so rooted a prejudice in your favour that I cannot suppose you have entirely forgotten a person who has been so long attached to you as I have been. I speak not of the ties of blood, for tho' I hold them sacred I do not suppose everyone is to be of my way of thinking . . . Did you think and know that we were really and truly upon the point of being invaded or did you like Mr Pitt suppose the Irish invasion to be an idle report? Be it as it may we were left it seems to the care of Providence,

> having no thanks to return to the English Ministry for their protection. We have today made acknowledgements where they are due—in Church. I could tell you many things, if you wish'd to know them and if the true situation of this Kingdom was at all interesting to you . . .[4]

Sheridan already knew a great deal, however, and his willingness to keep what he knew to himself is all the more remarkable in the light of the real possibility that he could quickly have entered government again. In May and June proposals emerged for the establishment of a "third party," independent of both Fox and Pitt. Before Easter, some independent Members of Parliament had approached the liberal Lord Moira to say that they "saw with excessive alarm the difficulties into which the country had been plunged"[5] and would support a change of government to bring in an administration which excluded those figures on both sides who aroused passionate objections from the public.

This putative administration would be headed by Moira and include, if he had his way, "many of those who had been acting in concert with Mr Fox." Fox himself offered to stand aside, and on 24 May sought a meeting with the King to tell him so. His intention, as Moira understood it, was to leave Sheridan, Grey, and others "at liberty to join as unconnected individuals in a new Administration." The aim of the new government would be threefold: to secure immediate peace with France and a "just and lenient system of Government" in Ireland, and to introduce measures to redress the disastrous state of the exchequer. One of those with whom Moira discussed this plan was Sheridan, who supported it and argued within the Foxite group that they should agree to prop up a broadly based administration. His support, however, was immediately interpreted as a dark scheme to gain power for himself at Fox's expense. As the Prince's secretary, Colonel McMahon, wrote to Moira, Sheridan was "traduced as wishing to abandon Mr Fox and to promote a new Administration." Moira had in mind that Sheridan would join the new government in the lucrative position of joint paymaster. To Sheridan's critics, it was inconceivable that he would not be manoeuvring his way towards this prize. These suspicions were, however, completely unfounded. Moira, writing after the scheme collapsed, vehemently defended Sheridan's conduct and insisted that he had never at any time sought advantage, let alone office, for himself. On the contrary, he had resisted Moira's pleas that he and others of Fox's friends should join the putative government:

> I had accidentally a conversation with [Sheridan] at the House of Lords. I remonstrated strongly with him against a principle I heard that Mr Fox's friends intended to lay down; namely, that they would support a new Administration but that not any of them would take part in it. I solemnly declare upon my honour that I could not shake Mr Sheridan's assertion of the propriety of that determination. He said that he and Mr Fox's other friends as well as Mr Fox himself would give the most energetic support to such an Administration as was in contemplation, but that their acceptance of office would appear an acquiescence under the injustice of the interdict supposed to be fixed upon Mr Fox. I did not, and never can, admit the fairness of that argument, but I gained nothing upon Mr Sheridan; to whose uprightness in that respect I can therefore bear the most decisive testimony. Indeed, I am ashamed of offering a testimony where suspicion ought not to be conceived.[6]

Grey, though he found Sheridan's arguments for supporting a Moira administration "not altogether without plausibility," was nevertheless convinced that such a government would be too weak to do "anything effectual for the people," and he refused to take part.[7] Nothing in the end came of it, but it did provide the context in which Sheridan's actions at this time have to be understood. His overwhelming political priority was to get rid of Pitt and to install a government that would act reasonably in Ireland.

At the same time, a new crisis sprang up in the most dangerous part of the realm—on board the ships of the British naval fleet anchored at Spithead. In attempting to crush the Defenders and the United Irishmen, the authorities had dispatched many of their members to the fleet. There they had found large-scale disaffection among sailors who were poorly fed and largely unpaid. The combination of skilled organisers and deep anger produced predictable results. On 13 April Admiral Bridport ordered the ships at Portsmouth to sail against the French, but they refused to do so until a petition outlining their demands for better conditions was answered. A fortnight later the mutiny spread to the ships at Plymouth. The "wooden walls" which had protected England against all previous attempts at invasion were crumbling.

The petition had been addressed to the Admiralty and, significantly, to Fox. Alarmed, the government tried to vote through an increase in naval pay to buy off the revolt, but the Foxites used the opportunity to raise the issue of the mutinies directly. Sheridan blamed Pitt and supported a motion of censure on the government. He stated his "disapprobation of the mode in which these demands were insisted upon" but added that to grant them would be "no more than justice"—a carefully equivocal position which stopped short of treason while supporting the sailors. He went on to propose the appointment of a special committee of both Houses of Parliament to inquire into the grievances of the sailors.[8] When a statement was produced by the sailors to the effect that Sheridan had libelled them by saying they were disloyal, he passionately denied having done so: "They could not have selected any individual on whom to make a charge of such a nature who so little deserved it." There is some evidence that the sailors themselves were subsequently convinced of his good faith towards them. When, after an act had been passed to meet some of their demands and the initial mutiny was ended, *The Times* reported that the sailors had been more impressed by Fox's and Sheridan's attacks on ministerial delay and duplicity than by the Act of Parliament.[9]

Not only did the mutiny reassert itself, however, and spread from the Spithead to the Nore, but Sheridan was left isolated by the secession of Fox, Grey, and others of his allies in May. With the real possibility that the mutineers might sail up the Thames and try to encourage disorder in London itself, Sheridan was being depicted as their ally in treason. In a cartoon by Isaac Cruikshank of the mutineer leader Richard Parker in negotiation with Admiral Buckner, Sheridan and Fox are under the table. Fox is saying to him, "Aye, Aye, we are at the bottom of it."

On 1 June the King asked Parliament to pass stricter laws against mutiny, and the next day Pitt introduced an act making communication with a person on a mutinous ship punishable by death. When it was agreed to limit the duration of this provision to a month, the support for the measure was unanimous. Sheridan, under enormous pressure, withdrew his motion calling for an inquiry into the grievances of the seamen and announced that since they had gone too far in pursuing them the House must unite against them. In common with most of the radical intellectual opposition, which failed to support the seamen, he decided that there was little point in being martyred for a cause that was almost certain to be lost. With typical opportunism, however, he chose to make a virtue of necessity and to embellish what was really a capitulation to Pitt with a few patriotic phrases: "If there is a rot in the wooden walls of old England, her decay cannot be very distant." He deplored Pitt's failure to agree to his earlier demand for a commission of inquiry, which would, he claimed, have said to the seamen: "We have gone thus far in agreeing to your demands, and will go no further; any more concessions we conceive to be both dangerous and unjust." But he admitted that things had gone beyond that point and that the question was not that of concessions but of "whether the country should be laid prostrate at the feet of France." He could not, however, bring himself to vote for yet another measure of repression, which would merely "increase the evil intended to be remedied," and he therefore abstained on the motion.[10] Two days later, deprived of their last hope of parliamentary support, the mutineers surrendered.

However equivocal his support for Pitt, this was the one time in his political career when he took the side of a repressive government against a rebellion. Several factors contributed to his decision to do so. The most obvious was that he was genuinely not in favour of a French invasion of Britain (Ireland, of course, was a very different matter), especially since France itself was moving steadily towards a new kind of dictatorship. He was, secondly, still hoping to bring down Pitt, a prospect that would be definitively destroyed if the cartoons showing him as one of the manipulators behind the mutiny could be given substance by his own actions. His belief was that Pitt could be brought down by the crisis in the public finances alone, and that it made sense, therefore, to deprive him of the accusations of sedition on which he had thrived for so long. Granville Leveson Gower reported to his mother that just before the New Year of 1798 he had heard "Sheridan lamenting in the strongest terms that Fox should talk such nonsense about reform etc., at a moment when the unpopularity attending the imposition of heavy taxes might give him an opportunity of displacing Pitt, if it were not for dread of those doctrines being practised which Fox has of late so openly supported."[11] Since Fox and Grey had seceded and the London Corresponding Society was all but crushed, there was little in the way of a reform movement either inside or outside Parliament to which he could look for assistance.

And thirdly, he was afraid. It had probably already occurred to him that if the French did land large numbers of troops in England, martial law would be declared, in which case he himself would almost certainly be arrested and, if a reactionary mob could be whipped up as it was in the Gordon Riots, possibly killed. Certainly by February 1798, but probably by the summer of 1797, he was contemplating what might happen in the event of an attempted invasion and considering ways to protect himself from arrest. On 5 February the Prince of Wales told the Duke of Northumberland that Sheridan was to speak to Fox the next day about getting up a statement pledging loyalty to the constitution established at the time of the Glorious Revolution of 1688, which would be signed by all of Fox's circle and given by the Prince to the King. "HRH said it would prevent the possibility of any man's being taken up (if Martial Law was declared) after he had signed such a declaration without some specifick charge being alledged against him, which he otherwise thought very likely to happen merely upon surmise of disaffection."[12]

These fears, which were by no means fanciful, shaped Sheridan's behaviour in the latter part of 1797 and the early months of 1798. His young wife, his baby son, and his dream of an idyllic new life in Polesden gave him reason for caution. Yet such hopes and anxieties make it all the more remarkable that he was still, where Ireland was concerned, willing to risk everything by flirting with treason.

Chapter 31

TREASON ON TRIAL

Early in 1798, at precisely the time that Sheridan was laying plans to avoid arrest, Arthur O'Connor was back in London, again preparing to go to Paris to seek French help. Large-scale and savage repression by government forces under General Gerard Lake and by Orange militias was pushing not just the United Irishmen but substantial sections of the peasantry towards rebellion. O'Connor and Edward Fitzgerald had decided that the time had come to strike, and believed that even a modest French force could make an immense difference to the chances of success.

In London, O'Connor again spent time with Sheridan and Fox. Madden, the well-informed historian of the United Irishmen, wrote:

> In February 1798, Arthur O'Connor was in London about to proceed to France on a mission to the French government from the Leinster Directory of the United Irishmen, the object of which was to press on the French authorities the urgent necessity of hastening the despatch of the promised expedition to Ireland. While O'Connor remained in London, he was constantly in the company of Fox and the leaders of the Whig Party, frequently a guest of Fox, and in close and confidential communication with him on the state of Ireland, the organisation, there is good reason to believe, and the views of the society of United Irishmen.[1]

One of the United Irishmen most closely involved in negotiations with the French, Edward Lewins, subsequently wrote that Fox did not know the details of the approach to the French but asked Edward Fitzgerald if they concerned Irish independence. Told that they did, he replied, "Good God, do nothing without being certain."[2]

As well as meeting O'Connor with Fox, however, Sheridan also met him in the company of a less respectable radical, the philosopher William Godwin. Sheridan had, in spite of his fears, remained friendly with Godwin, who, in December 1797, invited him to his marriage to Mary Jane Clairmont.[3] Godwin had long had contacts with members of the United Irishmen through his first wife, Mary Wollstonecraft, whose mother was Irish and who was in touch with Archibald Hamilton Rowan in Paris. His journals contain numerous references to his meeting "Morris," the pseudonym of O'Connor. One of these occasions was while dining at John Philip Kemble's house with Sheridan.[4]

At this point O'Connor was not merely in league with France but part of an alliance between the United Irishmen and the rump of the London Corresponding Society, now dedicated to militant republicanism. On 9 February, moreover, he was arraigned to appear before the court of the King's Bench in Dublin on a charge of seditious libel, almost certainly intended as a prelude to more serious charges.[5] On his own evidence at O'Connor's subsequent trial, Sheridan met him in London after these charges were laid, and urged him to flee England. This in itself suggests that he knew that O'Connor was probably guilty of very serious offences.

A short while later, on 24 February, O'Connor and his servant Arthur O'Leary left London with James Coigley and John Allen, a young friend of Edward Fitzgerald's who had been sent to join O'Connor after falling foul of the authorities in Dublin, intending to sail to France. On the 27th, at the King's Head in Margate, they met up with John Binns, a veteran republican conspirator. The following morning all five were arrested by two Bow Street runners who had been following Coigley since his arrival in London.

Besides knowing O'Connor well, Sheridan had also had some contact with the two other main figures, Binns and Coigley. In cross-examination by prosecuting counsel at their trial, Sheridan said that "he believed he might have met the prisoner Binns at some political meeting, but had no acquaintance with him." Almost certainly the political meetings he would have met Binns at were organised by the London Corresponding Society, which Binns and his brother Benjamin had joined in 1794, when they arrived from Dublin, where they had worked as tailor's apprentices. As we have seen, Sheridan also had some kind of contact with Coigley, who had inscribed his pamphlet on the Armagh disturbances for him. Sheridan said in evidence that he had known O'Connor for "these three years past, and have frequently seen him since." He continued:

> I never met him in any company but that of the respectable gentlemen with whom I associated; and from the opinion I had of his principles, I always conversed with him on political subjects without any reserve. His character was remarkable for its openness; he conversed on the politics relating to both England and Ireland with great frankness. But he oftener spoke about Ireland. He concerned himself so much about the grievances of that country that he wondered how the people of England could complain of any. My regard for him continued to the very last time he was with me. I then advised him not to remain in this country . . .[6]

Sheridan stood by this evidence even after O'Connor's confession later in the year that he was indeed conspiring with the French Directory to overthrow English rule in Ireland. He explained it in the House of Commons by claiming that "Mr O'Connor never had made him his confidant"[7] because he knew that Sheridan was opposed to French interference in England. He repeated his assertion that Ireland was the main topic of their conversations, and "Mr O'Connor always spoke in strong terms of any interference of foreign force in the affairs of England, and his mind seemed so much impressed by the superior grievances of Ireland that he would not admit that on the comparison England had any cause whatever to complain."

But this, of course, avoided the central issue—that of armed revolution in Ireland. Sheridan pointed out that he had not been asked any questions by the prosecution at the trial about revolution in Ireland "because it had nothing to do with the particular charge at Maidstone." "He might have differed from Mr O'Connor respecting the remedy that was to be applied to the situation of Ireland; but upon that point he was not called upon to say anything." And, significantly, he refused to say anything now:

> With respect to the provocation of Ireland to pursue any particular mode of resistance, I should say nothing; it is enough to say, that

> I never could permit Ireland to be seized on as a post from which this country could be attacked. I might pity the hardships of Ireland, but as an Englishman I could never suffer the enemy to obtain such a favourable point from which to direct their attack against our existence as a nation.

This is the only significant occasion on which Sheridan ever referred to himself as an Englishman—a mark of the strain he was under. What is most striking in his self-defence, though, is his scrupulous refusal to deny that O'Connor had told him at least something about the intention of the United Irishmen to stage an armed rising in Ireland. He denied two things—that he had ever discussed a French invasion of England with O'Connor and that he himself would have supported a French invasion of Ireland. He did not at all deny that O'Connor made him aware in some terms that the United Irishmen after 1795 felt provoked into what he had called a "particular mode of resistance."

Arthur O'Connor and his co-accused were indicted at Maidstone on Wednesday, 11 April. In his opening remarks, the judge, Sir Francis Buller, placed the proceedings firmly in the context of the aftermath of the French Revolution:

> It was the happiness of this country, for a series of years, to be almost strangers to the crime of treason, until new principles and opinions were adopted in France, and which have unfortunately misled the minds of unthinking people, and which were broached by the discontented in this country, who have pursued some means which tend to the introduction of the same kind of anarchy and confusion which have lately prevailed in France.[8]

It is interesting to note that on the day of the indictment, the Prince of Wales was trying to arrange a meeting at Carlton House between Sheridan and Pitt's Secretary of War, Henry Dundas, on some business so important that Dundas left the cabinet meeting to discuss it with him. Sheridan communicated with Dundas through George Canning, who assured him of "Mr Sheridan's good intentions." Dundas then informed the Prince, "I am perfectly satisfied that any meeting at Carlton House between Mr Sheridan and me would at this moment be productive of no good and probably would produce disagreeable consequences. Mr Sheridan is of the same opinion."[9] From the threatening tone of these comments, and in the light of subsequent events, it may be that the intention of Sheridan's approaches was to try to secure O'Connor's release.

After the indictments, the trial proper did not begin until Monday, 21 May. The delay resulted from the government's desperate search for direct evidence against O'Connor which would not blow the cover of its own spies within the London Corresponding Society and the United Irish movement. In the interval, Sheridan took the opportunity to declare in the House of Commons that he regretted the delay in the start of the trial, "because I am convinced that Mr Arthur O'Connor is not a traitor, and is incapable of acting hostilely against this country or its constitution."[10]

The most important piece of evidence against all the accused was an address found in the pocket of Coigley's great-coat, from "the Secret Committee of England to the Executive Directory of France." It had been drawn up by an Englishman, Thomas Crossfield, a radical member of the London Corresponding Society who was in league with Binns and Coigley. It suggested that the English revolutionaries were entirely alienated from the parliamentary opposition:

> Parliamentary declaimers have been the bane of the people. They have wished to raise themselves on our shoulders and want only their share of the national plunder. It is therefore the interest, both of them and the government, to continue the delusion: but they have at length pulled off the disguise: and the very men who under the semblance of moderate reform only wished to climb into power, are now willing to fall into the ranks of the People. Yes! they have fallen into the ranks; and there they must forever remain—for Englishmen can never more place confidence in them.
>
> . . . Some few of the opulent, indeed, have by speeches professed themselves the friends of Democracy; but they have done nothing to promote it—they have considered themselves as distinct from the People. The People will in return regard their claims to patriotism as unjust and frivolous. They would place us in the front of the battle, that unsupported with the wealth they enjoy, we may perish, while they endeavour to rise themselves on our ruin: but let them know that, though we may be oppressed, they can never enslave us; and that Englishmen, once free, will know how to reward these political imposters.[11]

This attack on the opposition was an important protection for Sheridan and Fox. O'Connor's defence counsel, Plumer, presented it almost as if it were intended as an active discouragement to a French invasion: "He pointed out that the letter found on Quigley [Coigley] did not hold out a hope that the French would be received by anyone of rank or consideration in this country. If ever France could harbour a hope that one of the Opposition should co-operate with them, that paper would show that their hopes had been delusive, for the paper declared open war against all men of Opposition."[12]

When it subsequently emerged that O'Connor was indeed plotting violent revolution in Ireland with French assistance, Sheridan himself relied on this address as proof of his own distance from the conspiracy. It proved, he told the House of Commons in February 1799, "that the persons who gave evidence to [O'Connor's] character were those least likely to favour the designs of France."[13] But it really proved nothing of the sort. In fact, all the address really showed was that the English working-class and lower-middle-class radicals were thoroughly disillusioned with the parliamentary reformers, as they had been for many years. Sheridan had known this, and regretted it openly since at least 1794. The address was silent, however, on the continuing relationship between the Irish revolutionaries, particularly the aristocratic radicals like Edward Fitzgerald and Arthur O'Connor, and Sheridan's political circle. It is quite likely that O'Connor never saw the address itself. Certainly, the court never saw O'Connor's own papers, which were the ones that actually dealt with the plans for revolution in Ireland rather than England. Perhaps fortunately for Sheridan, O'Connor's servant O'Leary had disposed of them down a toilet at the King's Head while Bow Street officers waited outside. The absence of those papers allowed Sheridan and Fox to maintain that they themselves would have been victims of the revolutionary conspiracy.

The government, though, hoped that the address from the Secret Committee of England would colour Sheridan, Fox, and their circle with the indelible ink of treachery. On the morning the trial opened an official writing from Maidstone to Dublin Castle with the latest news could barely contain his excitement at the prospect of a brilliant propaganda coup: "What will Fox, Sheridan, Sir Francis Burdett, Tierney, and Grattan say when the Address from the Secret Council [sic] of England to the French Directory should come to be printed?"[14] The trial at Maidstone thus became a test of wills between the government and the radicals. The government had deliberately built up tension with ostentatious security measures, including the removal of Irish regiments stationed in the vicinity of the town. At the same time, at least some of those who filled the public benches in the court were members of the London Corresponding Society down from London, and the judges had been warned by the government "that there was a very disaffected party in the town."

Sheridan gave evidence for O'Connor on Tuesday, 22 May, having attended part of the proceedings on the Monday evening at which a letter was produced from the Reverend Arthur Young, son of the famous agriculturalist of the same name, in which he said that he had tried to persuade three of the jurymen that "the felons should swing."[15] This blatant attempt to interfere with the jury may, ironically, have saved O'Connor's life by raising doubts about the government's good faith. William Wickham, co-ordinator of the government's campaign against the Irish revolutionaries, wrote to Lord Castlereagh that the acquittal of all the prisoners except the unfortunate Coigley was "entirely due to a certain letter . . . written by a clergyman of the name of Arthur Young."[16] O'Connor, however, still had to face charges in Ireland. The government suspected, though, that O'Connor's supporters were plotting his escape. As early as the middle of April, Wickham had written to Edward Cooke, one of the under-secretaries at Dublin Castle, that O'Connor's "friends are moving heaven and earth to save him, and seem no way suspicious of the means provided their ends can be obtained." He suggested that their designs could be foiled only by adopting "some very vigorous and extraordinary measures."[17]

Wickham was right. There was a plot to free O'Connor, and Sheridan was part of it. In court, Sheridan learned from Sir Francis Burdett that the state had another warrant for the arrest of O'Connor, issued by the Secretary of State, the Duke of Portland, which in the event of an acquittal could be used to make sure that he did not escape. In fact, the judges had already given leave to Portland's agent for this warrant to be executed. Sheridan and some of the others knew that there was a strong likelihood that O'Connor would be acquitted after a remarkably favourable summing up by Mr. Justice Buller. Sheridan also knew that it was equally likely that an attempt would be made to re-arrest his friend.

After the evidence of O'Connor's radical friends—including Fox, Lord Thanet, and Samuel Whitbread—and the final pleas, the jury retired for half an hour. Sheridan was sitting beside Sir Francis Burdett in the witness area, directly opposite the jury. The prisoners were in the dock, a little behind the bench where the defence counsel sat, and Sheridan's intimate friend Dennis O'Brien, who had been standing beside him in the witness area, went to stand near them. This detail is important because it supports suggestions that Sheridan and O'Brien were the instigators of the series of events that were about to take place.

When the jury returned, it delivered a verdict of guilty against Coigley, the only one against whom there was direct evidence, and not guilty against all the others. Immediately, two Bow Street runners began "pressing very violently towards the box where Mr O'Connor was," to serve him with Portland's new warrant. Robert Fergusson, one of the defence counsel, objected loudly and called out to O'Connor, "You are discharged."[18] Mr. Justice Buller told Fergusson to be quiet, stopped the Bow Street runners in their tracks, and put on the black cap to pass the sentence of hanging, drawing, and quartering on Coigley. (Subsequently, the King graciously agreed that he should be neither disembowelled nor mutilated, but he was hanged a fortnight later.) While Buller was pronouncing sentence, O'Brien, who had placed himself opposite the prisoners, looked at O'Connor, then inclined his head downwards, signalling that he was to get over the bar of the dock. The instant Buller finished the sentencing, O'Connor made to put his foot on the bar. The jailer, who was near him, grabbed his coat, but the coat either tore or slipped off and O'Connor, putting one hand on O'Brien's shoulder and another on Lord Thanet's, got over the bar and made for a door that led directly out of the court and onto a side street.

This was the signal for a riot. Someone in the court knocked down the candles, plunging much of the room into semi-darkness. An "immense number of peace officers" rushed in, as Sheridan wrote to Hecca, and started to lay about them. Some of the radicals in the court fought back. O'Connor was blocked at the door and dragged back to the dock. But the riot continued for about another five minutes.[19] A clerk of the court, called Stafford, had grabbed O'Connor's sword, one of the exhibits in the trial, and was standing on the table in front of the judges, waving it around.

Sheridan sat still while there was a possibility that O'Connor might get away. When his friend had been recaptured, though, he climbed out of his seat onto the table and confronted Stafford, told him that he was making "half the riot himself," and got him to put the sword away. He then went into the body of the court and confronted the Bow Street runners, who were holding O'Connor, insisting that "there was no such thing as an attempt to rescue O'Connor." One of them shouted back that there was and that the rioters were "come down from London; they are Corresponding Society people, and they are come down on purpose to rescue him."[20] Another called to his colleagues not to believe Sheridan, who "laid hold of him, and said he should go with me to Mr Justice Buller: I insisted upon his name and address, and he would not give it me. I then turned to the judges and he ran away."

Sheridan and Fergusson continued to remonstrate with those who were holding O'Connor, urging them not to manhandle him. Sheridan also went to the judges, to ask them why O'Connor was still being held, even though he had been found not guilty. One of them, Mr. Justice Lawrence, told him that it "would be an act of kindness in Mr O'Connor's friends to advise him to go quietly to the prison, lest some mischief should happen." Sheridan answered "with great civility" either that he had done so or meant to do it. For this, when order was finally restored, Mr. Justice Buller thanked Sheridan.

This public expression of judicial gratitude almost certainly saved Sheridan from the prosecution for causing a riot that was taken against Fergusson, Lord Thanet, and Dennis O'Brien in April 1799, even though it is obvious from the evidence that all Sheridan's actions had been directed against the Bow Street runners and not against O'Connor's supporters. His cool and controlled behaviour after it became clear that O'Connor's attempt to escape had failed deflected questions about his own role in the affair.

Sheridan's letters to Hecca, written at the time, imply that although he felt "indignation at this horrible persecution" of O'Connor, he regarded the attempt to free him as "injudicious." Lady Holland, who was intimate in Whig social circles, believed, however, that "those who were really the stimulators of the enterprise were Sheridan himself and Dennis O'Brien." She noted in her private journal at the time of the trial of Fergusson, Thanet, and O'Brien, "Just before the scuffle F[ergusson] leaned across the table to whisper [to] O'Connor. The truth of the whisper was an endeavour to deliver unseen a note from Sheridan to O'Connor, the words of which were as follows: 'As soon as the sentence is passed, leap over the bar, run to the right, and we will manage the rest.' "[21] She claimed that Fergusson had honourably kept this information to himself at his trial so as not "to involve an unsuspected person."

This version of events seems to have been given to Lady Holland by Thanet, and it is supported by the speech of the defence counsel Thomas Erskine at the trial of Fergusson, Thanet, and O'Brien. Erskine was close to Sheridan, and Sheridan was his main defence witness. Yet a part of his case was that it was impossible to distinguish Thanet's role in the riot from Sheridan's:

> Mr Justice Buller is proved to have said that Mr Sheridan conducted himself in a manner greatly to his satisfaction. But the very contrast which this evidence is introduced to furnish, instead of operating against Lord Thanet is an additional argument in his favour. Lord Thanet and Mr Sheridan are as one man in every thing which relates to public opinions, and friends in private life. Upon what principle, then, can it be made out that Mr Sheridan should be assisting the judge, whilst Lord Thanet, who had no connections with Mr O'Connor which did not equally belong to the other, should be behaving like a madman, unsupported by any of his friends or acquaintances, who were attending as witnesses upon the trial?[22]

Erskine's logic is impeccable: if Thanet was part of a conspiracy to free O'Connor—and he almost certainly was—then it is almost impossible that Sheridan was not. As Erskine put it, "It is impossible to ascribe a criminal motive, either from public opinion or from acquaintance with the prisoner, that did not apply as much to the one as to the other."

Fergusson, for his part, said nothing about the note passed to him by Sheridan—he pleaded not guilty and denied any part in the riot—but he did hint broadly that Sheridan certainly wanted O'Connor to escape. Under cross-examination, Sheridan was asked whether he believed that Thanet and Fergusson "meant to favour O'Connor's escape." He said that he had no doubt that "they *wished* he might escape." Fergusson, commenting on this after he had been found guilty, noted, "Mr Sheridan, no doubt judging of the feelings of others by his own, believed that those who might think Mr O'Connor an innocent and persecuted man, would have been *glad that he had escaped.* This is the belief of Mr Sheridan as to the supposed existence of a certain *sensation in our minds*."[23]

The belief that Sheridan had tried to free O'Connor is also supported by the fact that once back in jail, O'Connor pleaded to be allowed to see Sheridan. Sheridan, with Buller's assistance, got authority to see him alone for an hour, and he seems to have been allowed to see him again the following morning. Sheridan then went to London to meet Fox and Erskine to "settle something to be done in the House of Commons tomorrow."[24] What he in fact did was to get Henry St. John, a member of the Holland House circle, to call on Wickham and offer a deal which he must have discussed with O'Connor: If the government allowed O'Connor and his brother Roger, who had also been arrested, to go into exile in America, Fox and Sheridan would guarantee that neither of the brothers would "meddle again with either English or Irish politics." If this deal was not accepted, they would raise the matter in the House of Commons.[25] Wickham, however, believing that Sheridan and his friends might try again to free the O'Connors, either by bringing a writ of habeas corpus or by "more active measures," had already dispatched them to Dublin.[26]

In spite of all his efforts, Sheridan was blamed at Holland House because he had taken a leading part in the plot to free O'Connor but had not had the grace to get himself arrested. His answers under cross-examination at the trial of Thanet, O'Brien, and Fergusson were considered evidence of untrustworthiness. His hesitation in saying under oath that Thanet and Fergusson did not wish O'Connor to escape was identified as the main reason for their conviction, resulting in Fergusson's being sentenced to a year in prison and Thanet's being fined heavily and clapped in the Tower of London for a year. (O'Brien was found not guilty—even in the 1790s looking meaningfully at a prisoner was not proof of treason.) According to Lady Holland, if Sheridan had owned up to his part in the riot, Fergusson in particular "might have escaped." And Sheridan's reputation was not helped by the fact that, in sentencing Fergusson, the judge referred specifically to the fact that Sheridan "did not dare to affirm he believed you innocent."

The imputation, however, was unjust. In the first place, Sheridan went so far as to perjure himself in defence of his friends. He told the court that all the accused were innocent of any attempt to free O'Connor, and "There was no friend of Mr O'Connor's, I believe, but saw with regret any attempt on his part to leave the court." This was a straightforward lie, for even leaving aside his own involvement, he had written to Hecca at the time that three or four of O'Connor's friends had "endeavoured to hustle him out of Court." Second, far from helping Fergusson, a confession by Sheridan as well as destroying himself would have provided the prosecution with the direct evidence of a conspiracy, and of Fergusson's role in it, that it so obviously lacked at that time. And third, Fergusson himself pointed out that what the judge had said about Sheridan's evidence was patently wrong: "Either I mistake the evidence of Mr Sheridan, or that gentleman did say upon his oath not only that he *believed us to be* but that we *positively were* innocent of everything with which we were charged."[27]

Sheridan, therefore, took extraordinary risks for O'Connor. The charge levelled against Thanet, Fergusson, and O'Brien for their parts in the affair was described by the attorney-general as "one of the most heinous the consideration of which has been offered in the history of our law, to the decision of a jury." Sheridan had run the same risk of financial ruin and political disaster. But he had survived, yet again, by exploiting with extraordinary presence of mind the gap between appearance and reality, between performance and intention. Before a very select audience, comprised of Buller and his fellow judges watching the riot from their elevated bench, he had acted out a role as a pacifier, a bastion of civility and order in the midst of chaos. He had drawn from that audience the expressions of approval and admiration that made it impossible to prosecute him. Yet all the while he had been an instigator of the chaos. For the literal minds at Holland House and in the government, this dark game of controlled ambivalence could not but look shifty. In the public mind he had linked himself with a notorious traitor, both through his repeated and deliberate denial of the truth about O'Connor and through his part in a conspiracy to rescue him from the clutches of the government.

The full significance of these links became clear a few days after the end of the Maidstone trial, when news reached London that O'Connor's associates in the United Irishmen had risen in open rebellion. Just before the trial had opened, Lord Edward Fitzgerald, whose connections to Sheridan were more intimate than O'Connor's, was arrested in Dublin, receiving in the process what would prove to be a fatal gunshot wound. Within days, United Irishmen in Dublin, Meath, and Kildare staged a disorganised rising, and 20,000 rebels, mostly peasants armed with pikes and pitchforks, had joined battle in Wexford. Scenes that had not been witnessed since the days of Donnchadh O Sioradain and William Bedell were being re-enacted.

Even at this moment of danger, however, Sheridan's behaviour strongly suggests that he had, at best, turned a blind eye to treason. For he was planning to return to Ireland for the first time in his adult life to support Edward Fitzgerald, the man now known to be the leader of an armed revolution against the British state. On 28 May, when the rebellion was in full cry, Sheridan visited Fitzgerald's mother—Emily, Duchess of Leinster—in London. He offered his advice and "promised to go over to Ireland at the time" of her son's trial for high treason, set for 11 June.[28] Before the trial could take place, however, Lord Edward died of his wounds.

Even if Sheridan was denied the opportunity to take a public stand with Fitzgerald, he was not to be spared the mark of treachery. In July, O'Connor and the other United leaders held in Dublin made full confessions of their involvement in the United Irishmen since 1791 in return for pardons and exile. One of the main motives behind the government's acceptance of this deal lay in the blow it struck those who had given sworn evidence of O'Connor's innocence. This is obvious from a letter from the Earl of Clare, anticipating "the reversal to all the Foxs, Sheridans etc." which would follow the revelations. The government-sponsored propaganda magazine, the *Anti-Jacobin*, made the most of the opportunity, showing Sheridan giving his evidence in O'Connor's favour with a Bible in his hand and a "List of Irish Directory" sticking out of his pocket, and juxtaposing it with O'Connor's confession. The pro-government newspaper, *The Sun*, declared in September that Sheridan and his friends "are now proved to have countenanced and supported men who have confessed themselves Traitors."[29] For once, the worst thing that his enemies could think of saying about Sheridan was the truth.

Chapter 32

WICKED MEN

The rebellion had broken out at a time when Sheridan was trying to establish himself as a patriotic opponent of France. In April he supported the King's address to Parliament calling for resistance to the threat of French invasion, but again opposed the suspension of habeas corpus. Pitt wrote in some excitement to King George III to tell him that on the motion on the King's address recommending further measures to protect against a French invasion, Sheridan had made "the strongest declarations of the necessity of exertion and unanimity in the present crisis." He noted that although Sheridan had maintained his objections to the suspension of habeas corpus, he did not do so "with much vehemence or any effect." (He was in fact almost alone—just four other MPs voted with him.) The King, however, was sceptical. He was, he replied, much pleased with the conduct of the House and "not less so that when Mr Sheridan supported the address of the necessity of exertion and unanimity at the present crisis, he so far threw off the mask as not to abandon his former opinions, and consequently greatly destroy any merit his present conduct might otherwise appear to deserve by also objecting to the suspension of the Habeas Corpus Act."[1]

That scepticism would prove to be more than justified. For much as he believed in the need for a pragmatic realignment of radicalism against the French, Sheridan could not disguise the fact that he was on the side of an open rebellion in Ireland. As early as 28 February, the Prince of Wales's secretary, McMahon, informed him that "Sheridan intends . . . to bring on the affairs of Ireland in the H. of

Commons."[2] But he did not manage to do so until the rebellion had broken out. After a small and chaotic rising in Carlow in the south-east, military reprisals—floggings, torture, the murder of prisoners and the burning of the houses suspected of harbouring escaping rebels—sent hordes of people in neighbouring Wexford into insurgency. An untrained army of 20,000 men was fostered by terror, and both Catholic priests and sympathetic Protestant landlords were beseeched to provide leadership. Major towns such as Enniscorthy and Wexford were captured, and on 5 June a well-armed and disciplined militia barely held off a ferocious assault, raising the prospect that even without French help the rebels could seriously threaten English rule. Two days later a force of rebels, mostly Presbyterians, rose in Ulster.

Sheridan raised the subject on 14 June, but the gallery of the House of Commons was cleared and his remarks went unreported. Five days later, though, he returned to the attack. Portland told Pitt: "I am told from a quarter that may be depended upon that Sheridan does not attempt to conceal that his object in making the Motion he has announced for Thursday is to do all the mischief he possibly can . . ."[3]

When he did speak, it was to make an astonishing defence of the rebels and to oppose a motion to send English volunteer militias to put down the rebellion. The mask that the King had suspected him of wearing slipped away, and his true feelings poured out. When he was accused of being unwilling to assist in the crushing of the United Irishmen, he effectively accepted the accusation. He asked whether "in every case this House is bound to side with a King of Ireland and an Irish house of commons, against the people of Ireland?" If, he asked, knowing that the question was a rhetorical one, the Parliament of Ireland were

> . . . to enact torture by law, if it were to state as necessary, and establish in practice, bastilles, arbitrary imprisonments, ignominious punishment without conviction, transportation without trial, and a series of oppression too degrading, too tyrannical for human nature to endure, would the British house of commons be bound to support the Irish legislature against the resentment which such proceedings have provoked? Merely because the men who resist such oppression are called rebels, and those who oppose them are

> called the king's troops, must this house, at all hazards, support the Irish legislature?[4]

He openly distinguished between his opposition to a French invasion of Britain on the one hand and his attitude to events in Ireland on the other: "I am ready to declare that every effort ought to be exerted to prevent Ireland from falling under the power of France; but this is a point totally different from the merit of the struggle to which we are required to become parties." In reply to a government speech which asserted that the rebellion was unprovoked, he gave the ferocity of his anger free rein. Describing the use of torture and arbitrary punishment by General Lake in his campaign against disaffection he asked, "Is this conciliation? Is this lenity?" And in his favourite rhetorical manoeuvre of appropriating the language of his enemies, he picked up on the accusation in an address from the King that the rebellion resulted from the "machinations of wicked men." He had, he said, intended to move for the removal of this phrase, but on second thoughts he realised its truth:

> It is indeed to the measures of wicked men that the deplorable state of Ireland is to be imputed. It is to those wicked ministers who have broken the promises they held out; who betrayed the party they seduced into their views [the Portland Whigs] to be instruments of the foulest treachery that ever was practised against any people. It is to those wicked ministers who have given up that devoted country to plunder; resigned it a prey to this faction, by which it has so long been trampled upon, and abandoned it to every species of insult and oppression by which a country was ever overwhelmed, or the spirit of a people insulted, that we owe the miseries into which Ireland is plunged . . . These evils are the doings of wicked ministers, and applied to them, the language of the address records a fatal and melancholy truth.[5]

The rebellion, he insisted, was the war of a nation against a government.

> To keep Ireland against the will of the people is a vain expectation. With eighty thousand troops with arms and discipline against an unarmed and undisciplined multitude! . . . The struggle is one,

> not of local discontent and partial disaffection, but it is a contest between the people and the government. In such a state of things, without entering into a particular enquiry, the fair presumption is, that the government is to blame.

Before making this speech, Sheridan visted Fox in his rustic retreat, St. Anne's Hill, and persuaded him to attend Parliament on 22 June for a debate on a series of motions calling for an end to repression in Ireland. (Sir John Macpherson wrote to Sheridan on 21 June, noting that "you have induced Mr Fox to appear among us."[6]) He also succeeded in mustering most of the rest of the seceders.[7] *The Times* reported that "almost every one of the seceders returned to their posts" for the privately held debate. It seems likely that Sheridan even attempted to involve the Prince of Wales in opposition to the government's attempts to crush the rebels. On 24 June the Earl of Moira felt it necessary to warn the Prince against making an "avowal of your sentiments."[8] Neither the army nor the Irish Parliament, he said, would pay any heed to such a statement. They would, on the contrary, "perceive nothing but your opposition to them, and they would regard it with the extreme of intolerance." From this it is clear that someone had been urging the Prince to take the extraordinary step of publicly opposing the methods being used to crush a rebellion of his father's subjects. There is no direct evidence that it was Sheridan, but it would be surprising if he did not at least have a hand in it.

The Prince, in any case, took fright and issued no statement. Even with Fox again by his side, Sheridan's efforts in Parliament were fruitless—Pitt easily won the vote. The rebels were, by the beginning of July, destroyed and dispersed. When the French finally did manage to land a force of 6,000 men in the west of Ireland near the end of August, it was already too late, and the force succeeded only in further deepening the abyss of bloodshed and atrocity. The great hope that had animated Sheridan's public life, that of an independent, non-sectarian Ireland, had been obliterated. Never again would Catholic, Protestant, and Dissenter be united in pursuit of a single vision for the island's future. Neither speeches nor political manoeuvrings could change that fact.

Sheridan had only one resource to fall back on—the theatre. The dreadful events in Ireland, and his own hopelessly compromised position in relation to them, forced him into his most sustained theatrical enterprise since *The School for Scandal*. By the end of 1798 he was believed to be at work on a play inspired by a German drama. Early in 1799, it was widely known that the source of Sheridan's new play was to be *Die Spanier in Peru* (*The Spaniards in Peru*) by Friedrich von Kotzebue. The play had almost certainly been drawn to his attention by Matthew Gregory Lewis, author of *The Monk* and other tales of the grotesque, whom he commissioned to prepare a literal translation. Lewis, however, dropped out of the project because, as he wrote to Walter Scott on 6 January, "as to the German Play, Sheridan is so vexatious and uncertain that I want to give up the bargain and have nothing to do with it."[9] Sheridan instead used at least two other translations.

Some of Sheridan's motives in turning to the work of this prolific producer of dramatic sensations were undoubtedly commercial. Drury Lane had already had a success in 1798 with *The Stranger*, a version by Benjamin Thompson of Kotzebue's *Menschenhaas und Reue*, which Sheridan himself had certainly worked on and "improved."[10] Likewise, Covent Garden had, around the same time, produced *Lover's Vows*, an adaptation of Kotzebue's *Das Kind der Liebe*. Since both the theatre and Sheridan himself were in urgent need of money, cashing in on the latest vogue was an obvious move.

But if the initial motivation to stage a Kotzebue play was commercial, it also had political significance. The *Anti-Jacobin Review and Magazine* complained in October 1798 that German dramatists like Kotzebue were trying "to render the upper classes of society objects of indignation or contempt; and to confine all virtue, and every noble quality, to the lower classes of the community; and, at the same time, to propagate and diffuse the principles of the *new philosophism*." Adapting Kotzebue could thus be seen as a subversive act, and the King himself was warned of the dangers. In January 1799, while Sheridan was working on *Pizarro*, the Duchess of Württemberg wrote from Stuttgart to King George III:

> Much mischief is done at present by the Theatre, as Kotzebue, who is the favourite author of the public, tries to render vice plausible and virtue insignificant, in addition to which he weakens every principle. I regret very much to see by the papers that many of his plays are translated into English but trust their total mischievious tendency may, when acted, offend a British audience and compleatly prevent any body encouraging them.[11]

Sheridan's decision to appropriate *The Spaniards in Peru*, then, was not merely a commercial enterprise. He worked on it for six months, with the kind of painstaking effort that he would never have devoted to a straightforward piece of hack work. The effort was very considerable, for his former facility was long gone. By March he was cursing "this damned Town," where "there is not getting half an hour without interruption," but expecting nevertheless to finish his text by the end of the month.[12] By the middle of April he was ordering plans for the production to be set in train and reportedly declaring that "he had written every word of it himself."[13] He promised to deliver a final script by 10 May, when the theatre advertised "a new play called *Pizarro*" to be premiered twelve days later.

But in fact, by then the fourth act had not yet been delivered, and, as Thomas King complained, "there is not, as yet, one part written out for a performer and there are to be eleven pieces of complicated music, not one of which is yet composed."[14] Michael Kelly, who had been chosen to prepare the music, pestered Sheridan for texts, only to be told, " 'Depend upon it, my dear Mic, you shall have plenty of matter to go on with to-morrow'; but that morrow came not, which, as my name was advertised as the composer of the music, drove me half crazy."[15] The delays were extreme even by Sheridan's standards. The text was not submitted to the Lord Chamberlain until twenty-four hours before the first performance. What is more, Sheridan continued to revise it even after the first performance, lasting an intolerable five hours, had begun. Neither Mrs. Siddons nor John Philip Kemble, who played the central roles, had their lines for "the last scenes of the last act . . . while the beginning of the piece was being performed."[16] The play, in fact, was not really completed until the fourth performance, undergoing drastic editing in the meantime.

Some of the delay was due to Sheridan's usual dilatoriness. But what he was attempting was not easy. *Pizarro* is closer to being an original play than a mere adaptation. Most of the play's plot and much of its melodramatic form, were taken directly from Kotzebue: Pizarro's depradations against the Indians have been revealed by the monk las Casas. As a result, his lover, Elvira, is coming to despise him, and his lieutenant, Alonzo, has changed sides and is helping to lead the Incas. On the Peruvian side, Cora, beloved of the hero Rolla, has married Alonzo. In the battle that follows, Rolla selflessly rescues

Alonzo and his infant child at the cost of his own life. Good and evil are at war, and good wins through.

But Sheridan commandeered Kotzebue's play as a vehicle for his own purposes. The huge financial investment in the production—what Thomas King called "wonderful expense"—was matched by Sheridan's emotional investment. Even Hecca was reported, a fortnight before the opening, to be suffering "agonies of mind about this Play."[17] When, on the opening night, the audience was clearly unhappy with the under-rehearsed playing of the last act and the intolerable length of the piece as a whole, Sheridan "retreated to the Piazza Coffee House, greatly annoyed and discomfited."[18] On the third night, he was to be seen counting out the rhythms of the speeches on his fingers, stamping his feet in anger at what he regarded as mistakes by the actress Dorothea Jordan, repeating speeches to himself, clapping his hands in childish delight at John Philip Kemble's declamations as Rolla.[19] Lady Holland was, when he came into her box as she watched the play, "surprised at his eagerness."[20] Clearly, he cared very deeply about this play.

And he had good reasons for doing so. As a work of art the finally delivered version of *Pizarro* was no masterpiece, but as a political act it was astonishing. It was no accident that Sheridan included a passage of his Warren Hastings speech in the play, for *Pizarro* was really an attempt to re-create the emotional conditions of that great triumph, to conjure up a public event that would not so much appeal to the public mind as conquer public sensibilities. He had concluded, in fact, that in the current intellectual climate rational argument led nowhere. "The whole world knows," he told the House of Commons in January, "that never was there a period when fine speeches more powerfully affected the public; and never a time when, from fancied security or habitual indifference, the public appeared less eager profoundly to examine any question." He wished that public men might "begin to free themselves, by a collected vigorous effort, from the chains imposed by beauty, or the seductive allurements of amorous sportive imagination."[21] But in fact he recognised that no amount of argument was going to win the day on the subject closest to his heart—Ireland—and that if the political contest had to be fought out with recourse to imaginative allurements, he was not without weapons of his own.

In fact, Sheridan had good reason to seek to bypass rational political argument. His political position at the time was, in a sense, irrational. It was made up of elements that did not cohere. Opposition to a French invasion but support for the United Irish rebellion staged with French help; a passionate British patriotism and a belief that the British government was an organised tyranny; republican instincts and dependence on the Prince—these contradictory parts could not add up to a recognisable political whole. Sheridan tried instead to stage a kind of emotional coup, to gain the high ground of imaginative sympathy so that the failure of his powers of reasoned persuasion might be overlooked. He tried, in fact, to dramatise his own public career. What is most extraordinary about the enterprise is the degree to which it succeeded.

Pizarro was much more about Sheridan than it was about either Spaniards or Peruvians. For all the controversies associated with him, Sheridan's name still carried immense weight with the public, and the news that he was to present a virtually new play created huge excitement. His sister-in-law, Jane Linley, feared on the day of the opening that "the public expectation is at such a pitch that I doubt if *Sheridan's self* will answer it or not."[22] All the boxes were sold in advance, and at three o'clock the doors of Drury Lane were besieged by a crowd "equal to any that ever happened" at the theatre. Thousands of people turned up without tickets and the ensuing chaos was reminiscent of the scenes outside Westminster Hall a decade earlier when Sheridan gave his speech at the Hastings trial: "Ladies of the first fashion, in full dress, were fainting; some lost a shoe, others a hat; the stair-case windows were broken; the door-keepers could not resist the torrent, and many went in without paying; the outside of the doors were surrounded by hundreds who dared not enter, and many went away who had places, rather than encounter the crowd."[23]

The play itself was pitched at the same high note. Sheridan set out to seize control of public feeling by assaulting the senses. *Pizarro* is much more a spectacle than a drama, intended to overwhelm rather than to dismantle the audience's defensive scepticism. Mrs. Larpent, wife of the Lord Chamberlain's examiner of plays and one of the very first readers of the text, understood this exactly when she went to see it on stage. She described it in her diary as "a flash of language, which, when examined, is more Sound than Sense—forced violent Situations, and everything brought forward to seize the imagination—Judgement has nothing to do in the business . . ."[24]

For these effects, Sheridan drew on the full resources of the new Drury Lane. If the new arena could not really accommodate subtlety, Sheridan moved in the opposite direction, putting the emphasis on large-scale visual effects, on stirring music, and especially on Loutherbourg's designs. One part of the play—the Inca ceremony at the Temple of the Sun—was virtually an opera. For a contemporary audience this would have been sensational. And the acting, by a stellar cast including the Kembles, Sarah Siddons, and Dorothea Jordan, was at the highest pitch of heroic declamation. Sheridan hoped to confound political logic with an appeal to the heart and the senses, just as he had done in 1788, when he had brought tears to the House of Commons.

The reprise of the Hastings trial was made more or less explicit in the play itself. The subject of the play—native resistance to European exploitation—is, of course, the same as that of the Hastings speeches. One of the central figures in the drama is the great Dominican monk Bartolomeo de las Casas, whose attacks on abuses of the Indians led to the appointment of a royal commission of inquiry in Spain in the 1550s. Whereas in Kotzebue's original play las Casas dreams of "visionary worlds, like Plato" and is a somewhat unworldly character, Sheridan makes him unequivocally heroic. The reason is obvious: the echo of Sheridan's own denunciations of British abuses of another set of Indians in the 1780s, which also led to the appointment of a great national inquiry, was entirely intentional. To make sure that the parallels were not lost, Sheridan included key images from his Hastings speech within the body of the play. The most notable borrowing, almost certainly recognisable to much of the audience, was in the speech that the Inca hero, Rolla, gives to his troops preparing to face Pizarro's Spaniards in battle. In the Hastings speech, Sheridan had compared the British to vultures and the Indians to lambs: "Like a vulture with her harpy talons grappled in the vitals of the . . . lamb, they flap away the lesser kites, and then they call it protection! It is the protection of the vulture to the lamb." In *Pizarro*, Rolla says, "They offer us their protection—Yes, such protection as vultures give to lambs—covering and devouring them!"[25]

Likewise, in his changes to Kotzebue's text, Sheridan drew attention to parallels between the Peruvian women hidden away for safety during the battle and the begums of Oudh. In the original, their refuge is merely an "open space in a forest." In *Pizarro*, Sheridan makes it "the sacred caverns, the unprofan'd recess, whither, after this day's sacrifice, our matrons, and e'en the Virgins of the Sun, retire."[26] In these sacred places, the Peruvian treasures are hidden. Again, to an audience that remembered the rhetoric of the Hastings speech, describing the sacrilegious defilement of the women's quarters, these holy places could not but bring to mind the zenana of the begums of Oudh. Similarly, a scene in which Pizarro threatens a Peruvian captive with torture to make him reveal the "the secret path that leads to your strong-hold among the rocks" recalls the torture of the eunuchs in Oudh.

Finally, *Pizarro* was underpinned with the same borrowings from Rousseau as the begums speech had been. Just as the speech depended on a contrast between natural feelings and sophisticated savagery, so the play dramatised this contrast in the figures of Rolla and Pizarro. Rolla is, explicitly, a "romantic savage!"[27] Pizarro, a European adventurer like Hastings spurred by "insatiate avarice," is the very image of the corruption of innocent human nature by greed. By reviving the notion of the Noble Savage and restating his belief in the natural innocence of humanity, Sheridan was defending philosophical principles that had come under attack in the climate of reaction of the 1790s. Hannah More, in her popular moral tracts, had warned: "It is a fundamental error to consider children as innocent . . . rather than as beings who bring into the world a corrupt nature and evil dispositions."[28] In *Pizarro*, Sheridan flaunts his continued adherence to this "fundamental error." Cora's question "Are not all men brethren?"[29] is a decidedly rhetorical one.

Through these parallels, Sheridan pitched the play on territory where he was least vulnerable in the public mind: he drew on the last great moment when his powers of persuasion had been unequivocally successful. And under these auspices, he dramatised his own dilemmas. For as well as containing an allegory of England and India, the play also presented a version of England and France and one of England and Ireland. The irreconcilables of Sheridan's politics—opposition to a French invasion, support for the United Irishmen—could be reconciled at least in the imagination.

No one has ever doubted that at one level the allegory refers to England and France, and it was certainly intended to reclaim for Sheridan some of the patriotic high ground lost by his support for the Irish rebellion. Some contemporary commentators noted the political significance of this manoeuvre. The *Monthly Magazine* remarked, "Considering the political obloquy with which he has lately been overwhelmed, we admire the dexterity with which he has engrafted his loyal *clap traps*."[30] Sheridan did make a very deliberate appeal to patriotic sentiment, and it worked. But instead of surrendering his radical principles in the process, he instead sought to claim the force of patriotic and loyalist sentiment for the same radical causes he had always espoused. The more perceptive of the Tories understood this perfectly well.

King George himself was induced to attend a performance on 5 June, his first visit to Drury Lane in four years. And much was made both at the time and afterwards of the visit as a symbolic acceptance of Sheridan's recantation of his former principles. But King George did not actually like *Pizarro*, telling Lord Harcourt that it was "a poor composition."[31] This is not very surprising, for the play's apparently monarchist sentiments are decidedly ambivalent. They are set, significantly, in the speech of Rolla's in which the vulture-lamb metaphor from the begums' oration is repeated. In it, Rolla says that the Spanish

> . . . call on us to barter all of good we have inherited and proved, for the desperate chance of something better which they promise.—Be our plain answer this: The throne WE honour is THE PEOPLE'S CHOICE—the laws we reverence are our brave Father's legacy—the faith we follow teaches us to live in bonds of charity with all mankind, and die with hope of bliss beyond the grave. Tell your invaders this, and tell them too, we seek no change; and, least of all, such change as they would bring us.[32]

That this is intended to be heard as a rallying-call against French invasion would be obvious even if Sheridan had not written the word "Nelson" at this point in the margin of one of the literal translations with which he was working. Lady Elizabeth Foster described the confusion Sheridan had sown in the political sphere: "The violent Ministerialists are angry that Sheridan should have such applause; the violent oppositionists are as angry at the loyalty of the Play; and the rigid and censorious are suspicious of such pure morality and mild religion from the pen of a person esteemed profligate."[33] Among those unimpressed by the play's "loyalty" was Fox, who described it as "the worst thing possible."[34]

Yet it is important to remember that, in Sheridan's view, the real attack on the "laws we reverence" was coming not from French or English Jacobins but from Pitt and the court. For five years he had been defending the "traditional" English liberties guaranteed by the settlement of 1688—habeas corpus, freedom of the press, freedom of association—against the government. He had consistently argued that the constitution was most seriously endangered by reaction. The denunciation of "change" in Rolla's speech was undoubtedly aimed at France, but it was not meant to give comfort to the government. When Pitt remarked of *Pizarro* that "there is nothing new in it," he was right.[35]

William Cobbett, then still a Tory propagandist, picked up its echoes of radical rhetoric and heard in Rolla's words the doctrines of Arthur O'Connor and Tom Paine. The words capitalised in Sheridan's printed text—THE PEOPLE'S CHOICE—are strikingly reminiscent of the toast "The People, our Sovereign," first uttered by the Duke of Norfolk and repeated by Fox at a Whig Club dinner in May 1798. For doing so, Fox had been removed from the Privy Council by King George, on Pitt's suggestion, and the government had considered a prosecution, rejecting the idea only because it feared the consequences of an acquittal. The words also repeat those used by Sheridan himself in 1795 in his speech calling for the restoration of the Habeas Corpus Act, where he referred to the King as "owing his title to the people's choice." Cobbett spotted in the speech a theology that "prefers deism before christianity," and a political "doctrine of *cashiering Kings*, and choosing others in their stead."[36] Apostrophizing Sheridan a few years later, he seized on the phrase about the people's choice and asked:

> What shall we say when your "truly English" play-vamping loyalty has enlightened Rolla, so long before the poor fellow's time, with the most brilliant illumination of the republican societies here, affiliated and unaffiliated, of which you yourself were a member? You use the very phrases of their favourite maxim, that the *throne* . . . is the "choice of the people." This, everyone must remember, is the corner stone of the creed of Price, Paine, O'Connor, and all their disciples . . .

Sheridan's principles as enunciated in the speech, said Cobbett, would "compel his Majesty's successors to ascend the throne, if they ascended it at all, from the hustings of Covent Garden, or of some other place where "the *choice of the people*" might be made known."[37] Shortly after the play's first production, the *Anti-Jacobin Review and Magazine* also complained that the implicit political message in the portrayal of Pizarro himself was not the simple patriotism that appeared on the surface: "In *Pizarro*, we have a chief, or general, painted in the most infamous characters, being only meant as a malevolent portrait of men in high stations, although it is disguised with the cloak of history."[38]

Not only is the allegory of England and France ambivalent, however, but the play also dramatises aspects of the Irish rebellion and, more specifically, of Sheridan's own implication in treason. While much attention has been paid to the anti-French sentiments in *Pizarro*, the ringing justification of treason in the figure of Alonzo has received almost none. Yet every significant speech that Sheridan made in Parliament while he was working on *Pizarro* was about Ireland and the rebellion.

One of the main additions that Sheridan made to Kotzebue's original text is a speech in which Alonzo, who has deserted the Spanish to fight for the Peruvians, defends himself against Pizarro's accusation that he is an "audacious rebel," a "renegado from thy country and thy God" who has "warred against thy native land." Alonzo's response is strikingly reminiscent of Sheridan's speech on the Irish rebellion the previous June. In that speech, he had declared that it was not treason to resist inhumane laws. He had asked whether, merely because those who resist torture and oppression are called rebels, and those who support them are called the King's troops, it was treachery not to side with the King. The same ideas and rhetorical reversals are at the heart of Alonzo's response to Pizarro's accusation of betrayal. Alonzo says, as Sheridan had said less than a year earlier, that treason is the betrayal of human ideals, not of a country. He locates treachery not in disobedience but in the act of breaking human bonds of trust:

> No! Deserter I am none! I was not born among robbers! pirates! murderers!—When those legions, lured by abhorred lust of gold, and by thy foul ambition urged, forgot the honour of Castilians, and forsook the duties of humanity, THEY deserted ME. I have not warred against my native land, but against those who have usurped its power. The banners of my country, when first I followed arms beneath them, were Justice, Faith and Mercy. If these

are beaten down and trampled under foot—I have no country, nor exists the power entitled to reproach me with revolt.[39]

This redefinition of treason recalled the ideals of the Hastings trial, but placed them in the much more dangerous context of the Irish rebellion. And just after this speech, Sheridan inserted in the play a utopian vision of religious conversion that conjured up the mission of William Bedell and Sheridan's own ancestors. Alonzo evokes a vision of "the lovely fields of Quito" turned by native labour and Spanish benevolence into a garden of holy delights. The natives have been turned away from "superstitions strange and sullen" to true religion. Now there is "many an eye, and many a hand, by gentleness from error won, raised in pure devotion to the true and only God!"[40] This is a vision, not of France or England, but of an idealised Ireland in which, instead of sectarian warfare, there is a blending of Protestant and native virtues.

Pizarro, then, functioned as a kind of imaginative *apologia* for Sheridan's public career. Threaded through it were textual references to the high points of his oratory: the begums of Oudh speech, the attacks on Pitt's repressive measures, the rallying-cry against French invasion, and the defence of Irish traitors. And at its heart was an audacious defence of treason. Its three heroes—las Casas, the denouncer of imperial exploitation; Alonzo, the man who knows that loyalty to humanity must take precedence over loyalty to country; and Rolla, the vigorous opponent of foreign invasion—are all aspects of Sheridan's idealised self. He himself is the real hero of a play whose primary purpose was to re-establish his own fame.

And it worked. In spite of a dreadful opening night, reminiscent of the first performance of *The Rivals*, *Pizarro* became the most successful play of its time. By the fourth night a whole character and eighty minutes of playing time had been excised, and in this more manageable form it became a huge commercial success. It played straight through until the end of the season on 29 June, thirty-one nights in all, grossing £14,000, and then became a great stand-by at Drury Lane until the middle of the nineteenth century. A month after the first performance, Sheridan published his text, and it went through twenty-one editions, amounting to 30,000 copies, in 1799 alone. In written form, of course, the allusions to his own political speeches were more obvious to his audience.

Sheridan was overjoyed. By the end of May, Jane Linley was reporting that his "vanity is not a little gratified by the popularity this play has gained."[41] At dinner with Lord Holland, he was "so delighted with *Pizarro* that his allusions are taken from it in everything he says."[42] Since the play itself was full of so many allusions to things he *had* said, a kind of circle was now complete.

Chapter 33

AN UNPURCHASABLE MIND

In the fantasy world of *Pizarro* the Indians defeat the conquistadors and live happily ever after, but in the real world the success of the play could do nothing to prevent the reversal of all Sheridan's hopes for Ireland. In January 1799, even before it opened, the first moves were made to have the Irish Parliament give up its hard-won legislative independence and accept the principle of union with Great Britain. The motion was defeated by 111 votes to 106, but the narrowness of the margin made it certain that the government would try again.

When at the same time the House of Commons in London received an address from King George calling for a "complete and final adjustment" of relations between Ireland and Britain, Sheridan did his best to oppose it. And he did so in a manner that was unusually personal. He knew, as he put it, that

> . . . the grounds I stand on are at once ticklish and dangerous; that my motives are liable both to misrepresentation and misapprehension; that a licentious few and an ignorant many will distort or not perceive the grounds of my arguments and the use I am desirous to make of them. But there are topics, on the discussion of which a man must not wholly consult the degree of safety to his reputation among the unfeeling portions of mankind—on which he must forget what he owes to his own dignity, if fearful of the insidious misrepresentation of his sentiments, or the more insidious misrepresentation of his motives, he shrink from the sub-

> ject and fail to do that which is peremptorily his duty. I feel that to be silent on the present occasion were to act from terror in a way unworthy of the majesty of truth . . . My country has claims upon me which I am not more proud to acknowledge than ready to liquidate, to the full measure of my ability.[1]

That Ireland was the country that had claims on him was a significant confession, for just a year earlier, under the pressure of the mutinies, he had felt the need to describe himself as an Englishman. Now he not only campaigned relentlessly against the Act of Union (he spoke on the subject five times during 1799), but he also took up the cause of Colonel Edward Despard, a distinguished soldier of Irish landed stock who had joined the London Corresponding Society and conspired with Edward Fitzgerald. Despard had been arrested in a government sweep of militant republicans that followed the Maidstone trial of Arthur O'Connor and the rest, and held in terrible conditions at Cold Bath Fields prison.

When an inadequate report into conditions in the prison was produced, Sir Francis Burdett called for a fresh inquiry, and Sheridan seconded his motion before the House of Commons. Those who carried out the inquiry had refused to take evidence from Despard on the grounds that he had petitioned for the report in the first place. Sheridan was scathing: "If Colonel Despard had stated in his petition that he had lost the use of any of his limbs, deprived of his arm, or that his hand was taken off, the house, by this rule of evidence, was to say—O. no; we will not hear Colonel Despard himself, for he is a petitioner . . . we will examine the surgeon and other persons who were concerned in the taking off [of] his hand."[2]

Such an abuse of the law, he maintained, would "lead inevitably to torture and the train of horrors that accompanied such cruelties." He also challenged the legality of the warrants under which Despard and the other state prisoners had been arrested. The challenge was, of course, largely symbolic. Besides himself and Burdett, only four other MPs could be persuaded to oppose the mistreatment of those charged with high treason. And treason was an easy crime to commit: Sheridan cited the case of a Manchester shopkeeper called Patterson who inscribed the name "Pitt and Patterson" over his cart. Asked why he had done so when he was known to have no partner in his business he replied, "Ah, if he has no share in the business, he has a large share in the profit of it." For this he was arrested and held for a period in Cold Bath Fields prison. In such a climate the chances of securing decent treatment for someone like Despard—who really was a traitor—were very small indeed.

Sheridan's opposition to the Act of Union was equally futile, and by the end of 1800 the Act was law. He nevertheless remained determined to pursue the claims of his country. In order to do so effectively, however, he had to complete his escape from the clutches of treason, to disguise the almost naked sedition of 1798 in the protective colours of patriotism. This was not an entirely cynical exercise, though. Like much of the radical intelligentsia of Europe, Sheridan was becoming disillusioned with France. He could not see Napoleonic France as a beacon of liberty from which the rest of Europe might draw light, though he was still inclined to excuse Napoleon's dictatorship as a necessity of war. In June 1800, Sheridan called Napoleon a "great man":

> That Bonaparte may justly be denominated an usurper, I admit; that he is a self-appointed dictator in France, I admit; but it must not be forgotten that the situation of the country required the vigorous hand of such a dictator as he is. That Bonaparte possesses more power than is compatible with the liberties of France, I admit; but that he possesses more power than is necessary to protect the Republic, and to enable it to resist those enemies seeking to destroy it, is what I will not admit.[3]

In spite of the restrictions on "true liberty" in France, Sheridan still regarded Napoleon as a ruler under whom "the sufferings of humanity have been alleviated," a protector of the arts and science, a man who had acted with "moderation, humanity and magnanimity" in his dealings with England. He held out the hope that once the war was over and France secure, Napoleon would be able to turn his energies inwards and give France real freedom.

By the end of the year, there were signs of a change of tone. When Pitt's government disavowed the Treaty of El-Arish, which had been signed by the British commodore Sir Sidney Smith and which allowed the French to withdraw honourably from Egypt, Sheridan moved a motion calling for a separate peace with France. He condemned the disavowal of the treaty and spoke as passionately as ever for peace. But at the same time, he condemned the ministers "for ever once entertaining an overture for a maritime truce" with France. While "there was nothing too exorbitant for the French to ask as a compensation for suspending hostilities on the continent," any limitation on the naval power of Britain was unthinkable.[4] It would, indeed, be a "legitimate cause of war."

The contradiction, envisaging as it did the possibility of all-out war at sea and complete peace on land, was flat. The disjunction between Sheridan's rhetoric of patriotism and his ideals of pacifism and liberty was beginning to show. Though still willing to talk of Bonaparte in terms of high praise, and still a tireless opponent of the war, Sheridan was under severe strain. And as it became ever more clear that Napoleon's dictatorship was no temporary exigency of war, Sheridan was forced into a volte-face.

The Peace of Amiens, signed in April 1802, brought about the conditions for which Sheridan had pleaded. France was now secure, and according to his own predictions, Napoleon should now be able to turn his energies inwards and give the French people their freedom. What actually happened was the precise opposite: Napoleon used the opportunity of peace to have himself declared Consul for Life, with virtually complete dictatorial power. He became, in effect, a monarch in all but title and outward show, and these he would add in 1804, when he became hereditary emperor. From the summer of 1802, therefore, France had lost the last of its revolutionary veneer. Not just to Sheridan, but to even the most hardened of the English Jacobins, France now appeared "simply in the guise of a commercial and imperial rival, the oppressor of the Spanish and Italian peoples."[5] Napoleon could no longer appear as the embodiment of popular rights. Jacobin republicanism as a movement deriving its inspiration from and placing its hopes in France was dead.

And Sheridan knew who had killed it. In December 1802 he declared:

> Jacobinism is killed and gone, and by whom? By him who can no longer be called the child and champion of Jacobinism—by Bonaparte . . . he gave it a fraternal hug and strangled it. Did the French annex Piedmont, did they enter Switzerland, with *The Rights of Man*? Did they talk of those rights when Bonaparte told the people of Italy they were a set of dolts and drivellers, and were unfit to govern themselves?[6]

If Sheridan now shifted ground, it was because the ground he had been standing on had been taken from under his feet. After the collapse of the Peace of Amiens in May 1803, war began once more, and this time all the former Jacobins became patriots. John Bone, the former secretary of the London Corresponding Society, began to write in support of the war. After the Battle of Trafalgar, the London Corresponding Society veteran John Thelwall wrote a *Poem and Oration on the Death of Lord Nelson*. From now on, as E. P. Thompson has put it, "if the Tree of Liberty was to grow, it must be grafted to English stock."[7] Sheridan was merely the first of the radicals fully to understand this necessity.

He made his new position completely clear on 8 December 1802, when he spoke in support of government proposals to keep the army and navy in a state of preparation for war during 1803. He spoke about Napoleon's annexation of Piedmont and his occupation of Switzerland and concluded, "Look at that map of Europe now and see nothing but France."[8] He then went into a tirade against Napoleon which caused the "First Consul" great offence:

> My humble apprehension is that, though in the tablet of his mind there may be some marginal note about cashiering the King of Etruria, yet that the whole text is occupied with the destruction of this country. This is the first vision that breaks upon him through the gleam of the morning; this is his last prayer at night, to whatever Deity he addresses it, whether to Jupiter or to Mahomet, to the goddess of battles or to the goddess of Reason. But, sir, the only consolation is that he is a great philosopher and philanthropist.

Sheridan's change of attitude was significant enough to be of direct concern to Napoleon himself. In November 1802, seven months after the signing of the Peace of Amiens, Napoleon had sent General Antoine-François Andréossy to England as his plenipotentiary ambassador. At the end of December, Andréossy had a six-hour dinner with the Prince of Wales and Sheridan. As the ambassador reported to Napoleon, the purpose of the dinner, aside from the consumption of copious quantities of food and wine, was to allow Sheridan to "make excuses for the personal abuse [of Napoleon] he had allowed himself in his speech in the House of Commons."[9]

In spite of the closing compliment in Sheridan's speech, Napoleon had been furious at these barbed utterances. Sheridan's much more complimentary speech on Napoleon of June 1800 had been published twice that year in France itself and had been something of a sensation.[10] The subtitle of one of the editions—*Our victories and our armies treated as they deserve by the English parliament . . . An energetic speech in favour of a general peace spoken by Sheridan in the English parliament . . .* —suggested its appeal to the first consul. Sheridan's change of tack was therefore all the more annoying to Napoleon. He had his foreign minister, Talleyrand, write to Andréossy to express outrage at "libels directed against the present administration of France." It is clear that Andréossy had made his master's anger known to Sheridan and that the dinner was arranged to attempt a reconciliation.

The meeting is remarkable as evidence both of the state of the relationship between Sheridan and the Prince of Wales and of Sheridan's remaining private ambivalence about Napoleon. Since Sheridan spoke no French and Andréossy little English, the Prince "served as interpreter, and supported and enlarged on Sheridan's chief points." In spite of the bottles going round, "as is the custom of the country," Andréossy had little difficulty remembering the Prince's words, because they were repeated time and again: "Sheridan was forced to speak strongly against the First Consul [Napoleon] in order that he might be able in the end to keep peace. It was only possible to attain that object by supporting the proposals made by the ministers in favour of an efficient army and navy."

Sheridan told Andréossy through the Prince that he "was unwilling for us to have the left bank of the Rhine, for he said we could then send troops down the river to make an attack on England." The Prince laughed at Sheridan and told the ambassador: "You must know, Sheridan is not a man; he is the most extraordinary creature alive; with all his vices he is endowed with the rarest talents." At the end of the dinner Sheridan, "after making himself very charming," told Andréossy "how delighted he was at the good fortune that had enabled him to get to know me personally, and added, 'When we meet in the future we shall know just where we stand.' "

Interwoven with this change of attitude to France was the slow collapse of his adherence to the Foxite Whigs. He had always made clear his disagreement with Fox's decision to secede from Parliament, and in his speech on the union with Ireland in January 1799, he made that disagreement public, declaring that "though at present the banners of opposition be furled in secession, they will again be displayed and that its members will come forward and . . . prove worthy of their principles, and of that liberty they value dear."

By November 1800, though, Sheridan and Grey, the one Foxite most inclined to join him in active parliamentary opposition, were openly in conflict. Sheridan opposed Grey's amendment to the King's address, which proposed to omit references to the government's disposition towards peace with France. Sheridan said, as Pitt reported to the King, that the House should "avoid anything which could prevent unanimity."[11] Fox wrote to Dennis O'Brien:

> There is some ill blood between them upon private accounts relative to money matters, and . . . S[heridan] very foolishly let it out upon this occasion, for I understand he was quite hostile to G[rey] in his second speech. These things cannot be helped, but they are additional reasons to make me satisfied with secession as far as relates to myself. I have said all I could to soften Grey in regard to Sheridan, and know him enough to think that, if occasions call for their acting together, it will not be his fault if they do not . . . S[heridan] will never do anything quite wrong in politics, but whether he will ever go on very steadily and straightforward I doubt.[12]

These tensions became all the more pertinent when three months later their arch-enemy, William Pitt, suddenly fell from office. Pitt believed himself under a moral obligation to deliver Catholic emancipation, which he had all but guaranteed in the course of the debates on the union of England and Ireland. But he did not have the support of his own cabinet—only Grenville, Dundas, and Windham were fully behind him, while Lord Loughborough was bitterly opposed, Portland and Westmoreland were tending towards opposition, and even Pitt's brother, Chatham, was discreetly absent from discussions.

More importantly, King George was imperiously and implacably determined not to tolerate Catholic emancipation. The views of those who favoured the measure were, he informed Grenville, only "the opinion of expediency." His views, by contrast, were "grounded on a solemn oath taken and the uniform conduct of this kingdom and I think most wisely since the exclusion of the House of Stuart."[13]

Pitt had no option but to resign, leaving the dull Speaker of the House, Henry Addington, to try to form an administration. This he had to do without any of Pitt's most talented supporters—Grenville, Dundas, Windham, Canning, or Spencer—causing Sheridan reportedly to remark, "When the crew of a vessel is preparing for action it is usual to clear the decks by throwing overboard the lumber, but he had never heard of such a manœuvre as that of throwing their great guns overboard."[14]

And in any case, Addington's authority was weak. He had, as Philip Ziegler has put it, three disadvantages: "He was not an aristocrat, he was not an orator, and he was not William Pitt."[15] In Canning's famous put-down, Pitt was to Addington as London was to Paddington. His weakness, moreover, raised what was for the conservatives the terrible prospect of Sheridan and his ilk coming to power. As George Rose told Pitt, "I could not consider his abilities in any degree equal to his situation, and that the consequence of Mr Addington being obliged to retire would be either that a *Jacobin* Government must take place or that Mr Pitt must return to office."[16] Philip Yorke, the new Secretary of War in Addington's cabinet, wrote to his mother on 11 February, explaining that his tenure of office might be as short as six weeks because "a great and terrible conflict" was to be expected. He acknowledged the weakness of the new administration but told her that "it *must* be formed as it is, or Messrs Sheridan, Grey and Tierney sent for."[17]

At precisely this moment of vulnerability, the King, having stated his mind, promptly lost it. On Friday the 13th, the physical symptoms that had accompanied his illness in 1788 returned, and at an evening party the following Thursday signs of mental disturbance became apparent, with his "conversation and conduct" observed to be "very extravagant."[18] By Sunday he was "evidently deranged" and his old "mad doctors" of 1788, the Willises, were sent for. The King himself blamed Pitt for his illness, provoking the latter into an extravagant declaration that he would never again in the King's lifetime, in or out of office, raise the subject of Catholic emancipation.

The Prince of Wales was, at least temporarily, in the position of regent, but the political circumstances were especially confused. Pitt had resigned on 5 February, but Henry Addington had not yet received his seal of office. The old cabinet was still the only one competent to perform any official act, but Pitt warned the Prince that he would help him only on condition that he should not continue to take advice from Sheridan and the other Foxites. The opposition was itself in some disarray. When, for instance, Addington proposed that the attorney-general, Sir John Mitford, should replace him as Speaker of the House, Sheridan attempted to nominate the Whig Charles Dundas instead, and claimed that Dundas had taken the required oaths. When this was challenged, however, he backed off, implying, as the King gloated, that he had been guilty of "the extreme folly of having proposed [a] person not eligible."[19]

There was, nevertheless, a real chance that Sheridan might come to power. Within a fortnight of the King's becoming ill, the Prince was consulting widely about a putative cabinet. Lord Moira would be Prime Minister, with Sheridan as Chancellor of the Exchequer, Fox as Home Secretary, and Grey as Secretary of War. In dealing with the King's illness, Sheridan was anxious to avoid the mistakes of 1788, especially as there was a real prospect of the King's death. He had learned that George III was never more popular than when he was thought to be on the point of death. And he had exploited to the full a heaven-sent opportunity to restore himself in the eyes of monarchists when, on a visit to Drury Lane the year before, in May 1800, the King had been fired at as he entered the royal box. Sheridan, with his usual presence of mind, had ushered the Queen and the princesses away with the excuse that there was a pickpocket in the pit, and kept them in a side-room until the fuss had died down. At the end of the play, when the audience demanded "God Save the King," he had it sung with an impromptu verse of his own composition:

> From every latent foe,
> From the assassin's blow,
> God save the King.

As an excuse for a public enactment of his own loyalty, the assassination attempt might almost itself have been an improvised play of his own devising.

He was careful not to lose the credit he had gained, and on 27 February 1801, when an examination of the physicians on the 1788 model was called for in Parliament, he successfully opposed the demand, receiving in the process some rare praise from Pitt. Not all the Tories were convinced, however, and as Lady Stafford noted, "His Enemies say it was dictated by his Head, allowing the last to be equal to anybody's but his poor Heart, they say, was well described by his Father,"[20] who had reputedly said that Sheridan contained both Charles and Joseph Surface within himself.

By the beginning of the second week in March, though, the King was on the road to recovery, and the Prince of Wales and the Duke of Kent were permitted to see him. The Prince told his father that "everybody had been to the Queen's House" to show concern for his health. The King replied to the effect that "Mr Fox had not been, but that Mr Sheridan had, who he verily thought had a respect and regard for him; particularly dwelling on his conduct at Drury Lane Theatre when the attempt was made on his Majesty's life by the madman."[21]

The prospect of attaining power through the Prince had, nevertheless, been raised again in Sheridan's mind. He therefore tried to achieve three things. One was to keep the hated Pitt out of office. The second was to preserve a distinctive Foxite position by preventing the formation of new political alliances. And the third was to maintain his hold over the Prince of Wales. These aims together required a careful balance between keeping Addington, who had made peace with Napoleon, in office on the one hand and preventing defections to him from the Foxite ranks on the other.

In January 1802 Addington was hoping that the Foxite Whigs might be persuaded to join him. "Sheep as he is," wrote Canning, "he is calling in the wolves to his assistance . . ." Sheridan was personally well disposed to Addington, but determined that any arrangement would have to be a matter of much more than the securing of a few lucrative offices. George Tierney, however, was manoeuvring for a place in Addington's cabinet and hoping to bring some of the more lukewarm Foxites—Lord Moira, Thomas Erskine, Lord Bedford, and Charles Grey—with him.

At a banquet of the Whig Club at which Grey, who had once belonged to the Friends of the People, was present, Sheridan spoke of "those persons who, thrown by accident in the outset of life into situations for which they are not fitted, become Friends of the People for a time, and afterwards, finding their mistake, desert the popular cause."[22] Grey, "full of wrath," wrote afterwards to his brother-in-law Samuel Whitbread, remarking that "Sheridan must have been drunk." The Duchess of Devonshire believed the attack was actually aimed at Tierney, who had been present, and Fox tried to assure Grey that this was indeed the case. But Sheridan knew that Grey had been in discussion with Tierney too, and the vagueness of his attack, however greatly influenced by alcohol, was probably deliberate. Tierney commented to Grey that although Sheridan's speech was partly levelled at himself, it was in "part I think at other people."[23] The Whig grande dame, Lady Melbourne, too, believed that Sheridan was casting his aspersions widely, remarking that the speech "seemed more like addressing the Plural than an individual such as Tierney . . . I am myself furious with Sheridan."

But the attack had the desired effect, effectively stopping any large-scale desertion to Addington. This did not prevent Sheridan from cementing good relations with the Prime Minister, whom he genuinely liked and who had, for him, the enormous virtue of not being Pitt. He did not share Fox's aristocratic contempt for Addington's bourgeois dullness. Addington alone could keep the peace with France, lift the repression of the radicals, and keep Pitt out of office. Sheridan could have had almost any sinecure he wanted from Addington, who desperately needed his authority and oratorical talents, and he later claimed to have rejected the offer of a peerage. Instead he gave critical and fiercely independent support. Dining at Addington's home towards the end of the year, he told him, "My visits to you may possibly be misconstrued by my friends, but I hope you know, Mr Addington, that I have an unpurchaseable mind."[24]

He knew that although Pitt had effectively passed his office to Addington, attacks on the administration and especially on the peace treaty with France were aimed at bringing Pitt back. In December, in a speech on the army estimates, effectively a debate on the peace with France, Sheridan attacked Addington's critics by comparing their criticism to that in the rhyme "I do not like thee, Doctor Fell"—they did not like him but could not reveal the true reason, which was the fact that he was not Pitt. Addington, he said, had been a fine Speaker of the House, but what did the war party expect him to do?

> Did they expect that when he was Minister he was to stand up and call Europe to order? Was he to send . . . the Serjeant at Arms to the Baltic, and order the Northern powers to the bar of the House? Was he to see the powers of Germany scrambling like members over the benches, and say "Gentlemen must take their places"? Was he expected to cast his eye to the Tuscan gallery, and exclaim that strangers must withdraw? Was he to stand across

> the Rhine and say "the Germans to the right, and the French to the left"?

The rhetoric was cleverly double-edged, at once defending Addington and implicitly acknowledging his weakness. He then launched an attack on the hidden agenda of Addington's critics—the desire to restore Pitt to office. "Why are we told that there is but one man alone who can save the country? . . . Mr Pitt the only man to save the country! No single man can save the country. If a nation depends only upon one man, it cannot, and, I will add, it does not deserve to be saved; it can only be done by the parliament and the people."[25]

This attack was aimed, however, as much at his own side as at Pitt's supporters. For Sheridan was becoming increasingly convinced that now that Napoleon had narrowed the great divide between reformers and reactionaries, there was a real danger that Fox might be tempted to repeat the dreadful mistake he had made by coalescing with Lord North twenty years before. Fox, for all their disagreements, was still his friend. Pitt was still his enemy. The thought that the two might end up in the same government was more than he could bear.

Chapter 34

UNLIMITED OFFERS

Early in September 1803 Charles Greenwood, an army agent and treasurer to the Prince of Wales's brother, the Duke of York, called on Sheridan to tell him that Sheridan's son Tom had been appointed aide-de-camp to the duke with a place in the duke's household. It was an offer calculated to appeal to Sheridan's most vulnerable spot: his affection for his eldest son and sense of guilt that he had not done more to secure his future. Sheridan "expressed his surprise, as he did not think himself a favourite" with the duke. Greenwood answered that the appointment was not really the duke's idea but the King's. It was, he said, "his Majesty's express commands that Mr T[om] Sh[eridan] was to be provided for."[1] On hearing this, Sheridan refused the offer.

This was an extraordinary event. King George, whom Sheridan had opposed for thirty years, whose ministers he had harassed, whose enemies he had comforted, was suddenly anxious to do him a personal favour. And he was not the only one, for around the same time, Sheridan was being offered almost anything he wanted. "The offers to him," reported Harriet Duncannon, "were unlimited; he rejected them all." They came both from Addington and from the King, each of whom was trying to get him to join the administration. On 8 October Sheridan's nephew Charles Robert (son of his brother, Charles), who was in London, wrote to Thomas Le Fanu, his cousin in Dublin: "My father is to go to Mr Addington with him, who takes RBS' advice in every thing—the King has pressed him (RBS) to take office but in vain."[2]

Since the spring, it had been obvious that Fox, with the support of the Prince, was manoeuvring to join his faction with another. During March, the Prince gave a dinner at which the possibility of a "unity of parties" was explored, bringing together the Fox and Grenville factions. It had also been obvious since the previous year that Sheridan was bitterly opposed to any such move. To many of his old enemies, this seemed to be the time to try to detach him from Fox altogether and to bring him into their fold. In mid-May William Windham, once his personal friend, then the most zealous of the apostates who had followed Burke into Pitt's arms, "made an unexpected address" to Sheridan. Taking him by the arm, he asked, "Cannot we meet our old friends again and try to do something for the country in these difficult times."[3]

Speculation that Sheridan was about to join the government was given a further boost by his very obvious lack of warmth to Grey and Fox in the House. In the debate on the termination of peace negotiations with France, Grey moved an amendment merely saying that the war should be supported but holding out the desire and hope for peace. He noted: "I believe Sheridan is going again to play the devil."[4] On 24 May, when Fox spoke, Grey noted that "Sheridan would not attend." On 4 June, in the most important vote of the session, on a motion of censure on Addington's administration which was supported by George Canning and the Grenville faction, Fox and his closest followers left the House without voting. But Sheridan, significantly, voted with Addington.[5] The well-informed Joseph Farington heard, "It is said S[heridan] is to be Secretary of War."[6]

Sheridan denied all along that he was going to join Addington's government, however. Farington noted on 10 June: "It has been reported that Sheridan was coming into office and it has been mentioned to him, but He replied that it might as soon be expected that Whitbread and Grey would insult each other as that he should ever quit Fox."[7] Fox, however, did not see it that way and told Grey in July that although the Prince was still trying to bring the factions of the Opposition together Sheridan "goes on courting the Ministers more and more every day."[8] Sheridan's refusal to play along with Fox's manoeuvrings even turned the Prince against him. On 17 August Harriet Duncannon wrote to Granville Leveson Gower that "the Prince of Wales is very angry with Sheridan." Sheridan blamed the Duchess of Devonshire and Harriet herself for spreading stories about him and accused them of seeing politics only

> . . . thro' the eyes of one man (Mr Fox) which was always bad enough even before it was dash'd with the Grenville infection, which we caught from my Brother, Ld. Morpeth and you. That he himself (poor Innocent!) being the only good and honourable politician, was hated for this reason, and that we by way of serving our mottled party scrupled no lies against him, either as to his public or private Character. The P[rince] replied by telling him he would not hear his friends abus'd, but that neither my Sister nor I had ever mention'd his name; that he always should retain great private affection for him, but that before he could trust him as a Political adviser his conduct must be explain'd, and he must state explicitly his future intentions.[9]

The Prince rushed off to give both the duchess and Fox a full account of this row.

Sheridan's problem was, in a sense, that he was acting too honourably. It was accepted, even to those who had known him for a long time, that a man of his ambition could not be acting as he was except in pursuit of personal advantage. That his motives were entirely selfless merely made his behaviour incomprehensible. His aristocratic friends, who still believed deep down that only one of their own ilk could act independently in politics, could not imagine that he was after all following his own conscience. Sheridan could at this time have had almost anything he wanted—a hereditary peerage, a lucrative government sinecure, an appointment for Tom that would secure his future comfort—if he would join Addington's administration. Both the Prince of Wales and Fox, moreover, were telling him that he was wrong not to take up one of the offers, if not for himself, then at least for Tom. "The P[rince] told him," wrote Harriet Duncannon, "that both he and Mr Fox thought him wrong in [refusing all offers]; that Mr Fox particularly said that, as he had no doubt Sh[eridan] acted sincerely, according to his opinion, in supporting Ministers, he could see no reason why approving of them, he should not take some place of responsibility with them, and that if he, S[heridan], would not for himself, it was quite wrong to leave Tom unprovided for."

Sheridan had, besides, a strong personal reason to accept office: to put his financial worries behind him and bring some stability to his life. His marriage was in deep trouble. When he and Hecca had first married, he had convinced both her and himself that theirs would be an elegant and peaceful existence. They would live amidst the rustic beauty of Polesden, where together they would bring up their little son. Had he followed the lead of Fox and Grey and retired from a losing battle, the dream might have come at least a little true. Instead, Hecca found herself married to a man wrapped up in dark and seditious conspiracies, playing strange games. And with his devotion to political stratagems came his frantic and disordered existence of late nights, dark affairs, and deep draughts of claret.

By the summer of 1803 he was fighting with Hecca, and she was threatening to leave him. Harriet Duncannon wrote to Lord Holland that Sheridan was "never sober for a moment and his affairs worse than ever *pour comble* he has quarrelled with Mrs S. A sort of separation took place but I believe it is partly made up again, at least they live in the same house, but not very good friends."[10] By 30 June Sheridan himself was writing to Hecca, "By my Life and Soul if you talk of leaving me now you will destroy me. I am wholly unwell—I neither sleep nor eat. You are before my eyes Night and Day . . . if I live till you have mind to know me you will not cease to love me."

But, in fact, during the debates in the House he was thinking neither of his wife nor of the war with France but of Harriet Duncannon. On the night of 23 June, just after Grey had moved an important amendment, he slipped out of the House, "half famish'd and ready to sink under Noise, heat and fatigue" and, as he admitted, "half drunk," to write to her with a description of the debate.[11] And on the next night, he did what he claimed never to have done before—"Left the House while Fox was speaking," again to write to Harriet, who had replied to his letter of the previous day. Such attention suggests that he was again paying court to Harriet, though whether this was the cause or the consequence of his estrangement from Hecca is impossible to say.

The stream of offers from Addington and the King must have been all the more attractive, holding out, as well as the promise of political power, the prospect of personal rescue. Yet when the Prince and Fox urged him to accept office from Addington, Sheridan answered that "his situation was peculiar, subject to great misrepresentation, and that his receiving anything like emolument for himself or [his] family from Ministers would *contaminate the purity* of his support and dishonour him forever; and, in short, that he had refused and the whole transaction was at an end."[12] This concern for his own political purity affected not just himself and Hecca but Tom, who was already showing signs of his mother's weak health and who, though handsome, witty, and very intelligent, was never going to be able, as his father had done, to shift for himself. Efforts to fix him up in a comfortable station had been under way at least since 10 June, when the Prince wrote to the Duke of Northumberland urging him to find a parliamentary seat for Tom, a young man to whom he said he had been attached "from the moment of his birth." Northumberland replied, however, that he had already used up all his powers of electoral patronage on securing an opening for his own son.

On 2 October Pitt's friend George Rose noted that "provision is to be made for Sheridan's son as a reward for the father's services; but to avoid wounding the delicate feelings *of both*, there is an intention of giving Sir John Morshead an employment, that the Prince of Wales may appoint Thomas Sheridan to the situation Sir John now has." The position was the surveyorship of the Duchy of Cornwall. Much as he doted on Tom, however, Sheridan would not let him take this sinecure. He also during these months refused an offer of "a great place for Tom" in Malta, as well as the lucrative position of aide-de-camp in the Duke of York's household already mentioned. All Tom got in the end was a commission in the Prince's regiment, the 10th Light Dragoons, and a posting as aide-de-camp to Lord Moira, just appointed as commander-in-chief in Scotland.

Sheridan, in fact, was bitterly angry at Fox's suggestion that he should accept office because he approved of Addington's government. "On the contrary," he told the Prince, "I think them very bad, but anything is better than a junction between Mr Pitt and Fox." The Prince, however, replied, "I am afraid your fears are groundless; nothing so good for the country is likely to take place." "Good God, Sir!" burst out Sheridan. "Is it possible you should speak this of that man?" Tears came to his eyes as he pleaded with the Prince to "withstand the snare preparing for him." And he started to work on what he hoped would be the Prince's painful memory of Pitt's mistreatment of him during the regency crisis. His own interests, he warned, were about to be sacrificed to "political prostitution."

> And this Fox calls friendship for your Royal Highness, and such friendship outweighs, in your opinion, my tried *devotion*. Can you have a doubt that Pitt bears a personal enmity to your royal High-

> ness, which he has express'd by every slight (not to say insult) from the first moment of his political career to this day, and that it is only want of power, not of will, that prevents his barring you from the throne itself and assuring your legal rights to your brother?

The Prince, who had been thoroughly persuaded by Fox of the wisdom of a coalition with Pitt, acknowledged the truth of what Sheridan said, but added, "The man, whoever he may be, who rescues this kingdom from the ruin the present miserable Administration are bringing on will have Claims to my warmest gratitude, and will receive it, let his opinion of me be what it may . . ."

Sheridan's fury at the willingness of his aristocratic friends to regard him as merely a better class of hired hand broke out in more or less open spite against Fox. According to Thomas Creevey, Sheridan was from September 1803 onwards "damning Fox in the midst of his enemies, and in his drunken and unguarded moments, has not spared him even in the circles of his most devoted admirers." At the Duke of Bedford's mansion in Woburn, Sir Robert Adair, one of Fox's closest friends, challenged Sheridan to a duel over one such insult, and Sheridan accepted. Only the intervention of Samuel Whitbread, who was present, prevented the duel from taking place. Harriet reported on 11 September:

> The quarrel between Adair and Sheridan was terrible. Adair had truth and honour on his side, but alas! they were in bad hands. He is a sad arguer with anyone, and with Sheridan he had no chance. At Whitbread's, the argument was begun again with him, and became so vehement that if luckily Sheridan, who began sober, had not ended drunk and fallen asleep, it was thought impossible to prevent serious consequences. Whitbread was so angry and thump'd the table so, that they thought he was going so to strike S[heridan] who call'd out "My boisterous landlord means to silence me by the weight of his arm, as he cannot by that of his arguments."

Sheridan knew that negotiations between Pitt and Fox were being conducted through the medium of George Canning and the Duchess of Devonshire, and in his desperate search for allies in the struggle to prevent a coalition he even softened towards George Tierney, whom he had come to regard as a contemptible opportunist. At one meeting with Tierney, he raged, "I had rather see Fox dead than join'd with Pitt, and whilst I have life, I will never suffer it." To which Tierney added, "My good friend, do not bluster quite so loud. Whether such a junction is possible or likely I cannot say, but one thing I am sure of—that your living or dying, liking or disliking, will have very little to do with it."[13] It was the bitter truth: for all his eminence, and all his steadfastness, Sheridan would always be valued by the Devonshire House clique only in proportion to his usefulness.

Thomas Creevey found that, at Devonshire House, "everyone is against Sheridan," and indeed the Duchess of Devonshire wrote to the Prince towards the end of the year saying, "I think Sheridan's reasoning that every encouragement is to be given to these foolish people [Addington and his friends] merely to keep out one man [Pitt] as selfish as it is weak and unpatriotic." She accused Sheridan of pursuing "jealousies and idle dreams," but added, "I give him, as I have always done, the credit of believing he will not be entirely seduced away, but he will give constant cause thro' his vanity to be often suspected."[14] Sheridan's "vanity," of course, chiefly consisted of having the temerity to trust his own judgement and the pride to resist bribes.

In the middle of October the Prince arranged a meeting with Fox and Sheridan, hoping to bring about a reconciliation between them. Sheridan gave a long explanation of his own conduct, which was, he said, motivated entirely by his fear that Fox was about to create a coalition with Pitt. Fox replied, "That is, in plain English, that your enmity to one man is stronger than the safety or ruin of your country."[15] There had been "no intercourse" between himself and Pitt, he insisted, a denial that was somewhat qualified by his assertion that "if Mr Pitt happened to be of the same opinion with him . . . he could not see why a man of great talents agreeing with him on any point should tempt him to change his opinion; that for the good of the country he hop'd they should agree, and that the questions they differ'd on would not be broach'd." "That they shall by God!," interrupted Sheridan, "if Tierney or I can find them. But things are, I fear, gone too far when you talk of no intercourse. Can you say upon your honour that all those meetings between Mr Canning and the Duchess at Devonshire House were not purposely to carry messages backwards and forwards between you and Pitt?" Fox laughed and said he had heard nothing of any such meetings. Adding sarcastically that he was "glad there was so good a prospect of a strong opposition," he walked out, leaving Sheridan in a rage.

Things calmed down somewhat when Addington, who was still clinging to power, made overtures about an alliance with the Foxites. Fox, Sheridan, and the Prince went to Lord Moira's house in St. James's Place on 24 October to discuss how to respond. Fox was convinced that by supporting Addington as a way of keeping out Pitt, his faction had become "complete Court tools or absolute cyphers." But he agreed that Sheridan should use his friendship with Addington to try, as Fox wrote to the Duke of Northumberland, to "bring the question *immediately* to a point, whether any coalition with him and the Prince's friends is or is not practicable."

Grey was unhappy that Sheridan had been trusted with the job: "I do wish we could get rid of him and his intrigues for ever." And Fox suspected that Sheridan did not in fact approach Addington, and professed himself "glad it should be so." At this time he regarded Sheridan as "mad with vanity and folly," but retained, nonetheless, a degree of affection for him. As he wrote to Grey, "Of Tierney and Sheridan, I think worse of the former, you of the latter, but we each of us retain perhaps a little kindness for our respective favourites."[16] Fox and Grey, however, were engaged in intrigues of their own, and Sheridan had the pleasure of catching them in the act. On 27 February 1804, he went to Fox's house looking, according to Grey, "more fiery and horrible than ever." He was shown by a politically naïve servant into a room where Fox and Grey were about to begin a meeting with Lord Grenville, Pitt's former foreign secretary, to explore a coalition. Grey wrote: "I only saw him for a moment before going into the inner room with the Grenvilles, with who he is not yet quite cordial." Sheridan was delighted with this "droll Scene."

And he managed to win the Prince back to his side of the argument. By 2 April the Fox loyalist Thomas Creevey was complaining that Sheridan's "insuperable vanity has suggested to him the brilliancy of being first with the Prince, and governing his councils. He will, if he sees it practicable, try, and is now trying to alienate the Prince from Fox, and to reconcile him to the wretched Addington." Lord Melville, after meeting Lord Moira on 4 April, wrote to Pitt:

> It was as if Sheridan, whom *by some means* Mr Addington seemed to have got hold of, was playing or would play a game for the

> purpose of impressing the Prince that the easiest mode by which he could gain any object, even that of an extensive plan of Government on the footing recommended by Lord Moira, was by admitting into his friendship and confidence Mr Addington, whose interest and inclination it certainly was to cultivate the friendship of the Prince.[17]

Sheridan, however, wanted to restore relations with Fox, who told Grey on 6 April, "Sheridan has been here and as I judge is very desirous of getting right again, but you may easily believe my dependence on him is not very firm." Sheridan and Hecca had called at Fox's rustic retreat, St. Anne's Hill, on the pretext that Hecca wanted to meet Fox's wife, Elizabeth Armistead. Hecca immediately began to tell Fox how upset she was that there could ever be a quarrel "between the two greatest men in England, formed by nature to be friends, and by their union and talents to govern the world." She cajoled them both into shaking hands with each other.

Even so, Fox wanted the reconciliation to be understood as a personal, not a political one. He was, he said, "much obliged to them for calling," but "begged they might avoid all political subjects." Sheridan said that it was impossible for them to do so, "as he had something of importance to communicate." He would not speak in front of the hated Adair, who was present, and dragged Fox out into the garden. They returned after half an hour on such friendly terms that Sheridan invited himself and Hecca to stay for dinner, explaining that Polesden was under repair. But their political relationship was beyond repair. As Adair was leaving, he asked Fox whether his conversation with Sheridan had altered his political intentions. Fox said, "None in the world. What alteration could anything he can tell me make?"[18]

The friendship that had shaped all of Sheridan's political and much of his personal life would never really recover from the breach. They had been through too much together ever to really dislike each other, but equally too much had been said for trust to be restored. After May 1804, when Addington's government finally fell and Pitt came back into office without Fox at his side, the two would be able to work together in opposition. But by then Sheridan's mind was set on power not in London, but in Dublin.

Chapter 35

PUT ASIDE THE MASK OF MYSTERY

The problem of what to do with the heir to the throne while its occupant remains stubbornly alive is in Britain a perennial one. With an heir as troublesome as King George III's eldest son, it was especially acute. The Prince of Wales sought work. One option which he desperately wanted to be opened for him but which his father persistently refused was to take command of an army. The other, mooted as early as 1797, was for him to be sent to Ireland as Lord Lieutenant. He had, through Sheridan and Lord Moira, long cultivated a reputation as a friend of Ireland, and the office, which combined high ceremony with a modicum of power, greatly attracted him. More to the point, it greatly attracted Sheridan. And all through the intricate animosities of the split with Fox the idea of returning to his native land as a man with the power to put into practice the sentiments he had so stirringly expressed was taking hold of his mind.

This arose at a time when Sheridan's reputation was beginning to suffer an assault more damaging than the often grotesque caricatures of Gillray and Cruickshank. Cartoons were self-consciously satiric exaggerations, but the work of William Cobbett, the greatest polemicist of the age, addressed itself more directly to facts. Cobbett would be remembered to history as a great radical, but at this time he was a conservative, and his hatred of Sheridan was a legacy of the split between Burke and Sheridan in 1790. Burke had taken William Windham with him into the alliance with Pitt, and Cobbett was Windham's man. Ironically, just at the time when Windham was beginning to make friendly overtures towards Sheridan, the journalist he had unleashed on his old friend was beginning to bite.

Cobbett was a dangerous antagonist for Sheridan because he had the perspicuity to see the contradictions between Sheridan's claims of loyalty and his practice of treason. Sheridan's game depended on the speed of the hand deceiving the eye, but Cobbett's eye was especially sharp. And he kept it focused on Sheridan's shifting political identity. In June 1797, after Sheridan's speech on the Nore mutiny, Cobbett attacked him in *Porcupine's Gazette*, published in Philadelphia, where he was based at the time, claiming that the English public in warming to Sheridan's patriotic rhetoric was like "a terrified patient who despairing of his case, gladly accepts of the assistance of one whom he knows to be a quack."[1] In 1799, as we have seen, he spotted the seditious sentiments that lay behind the apparently loyal façade of *Pizarro*.

In 1803 he was given another opportunity to expose Sheridan as a traitor in patriot's clothing. In February Colonel Despard, whose case Sheridan had taken up four years earlier, was executed for high treason, having attempted, after his release from Cold Bath Fields prison, to organise a new armed conspiracy. Then, on 23 July, the remnants of the United Irishmen under Robert Emmet staged an abortive rising in Dublin. Though premature and confused—the most serious blow against the administration was the squalid murder of the Irish attorney-general, Lord Kilwarden, and his nephew—the attempted coup revealed a surprising persistence of radical conspiracy. And, as Cobbett was quick to realise, it also renewed, at a time when Sheridan was assumed to be on the brink of entering government, the relevance of Sheridan's entanglements in United Irish treason in 1798.

Prime Minister Addington, referring to a speech on the war with France, had praised Sheridan's use of the "language of a true patriot." Within a week of the Dublin insurrection, Cobbett reminded his readers: "With respect to Irish rebellions, indeed, Mr Sheridan has not, if our memory serves us, always been perfectly correct; and if we have much judgement of the matter, the records of the assizes at Maidstone will contribute but very little towards that historical page which the sapient Mr Addington forsees posterity will read with admiration!"[2]

Sheridan responded a few days later in the House of Commons with mocking references to Cobbett's closeness to Windham. When

Windham defended Cobbett, Sheridan described his speech as a "silly panegyric" and, on rather weak grounds, tried to impute disloyalty to Cobbett himself.[3] In a fight over loyalty and treason, of course, Cobbett had much better ammunition and proceeded to fire it with unerring aim.

Throughout the second half of 1803, Cobbett attacked Sheridan's failure to speak out against treason. If Sheridan spoke in the Commons, Cobbett would criticise his speeches. If he did not speak, Cobbett would criticise his silence. In the 16 July edition of his *Weekly Political Register*, for instance, Cobbett wrote: "It is with no small degree of surprise that we see Mr Sheridan persevere in his senatorial silence," noting that he had spoken "not a word . . . at this dangerous crisis." A week later he noted: "Mr Sheridan, to whom we have for weeks past been looking for a little 'true English feeling' has not yet broken out. He did, indeed, make a slight opening the other night; but, so imperfect was it, so far short of the sallies that he was wont to make, that, after considerable altercation, it was impossible to determine *on which side he spoke!!!*"

He also tried to thwart Sheridan's attempt to win back some patriotic credentials by moving a vote of thanks to the volunteer corps, a motion taken on 10 August. The subject was close to Sheridan's heart because of fond memories of the Irish Volunteers of the 1780s, to which he alluded in his speech, and of his own role in using them as a lever for political change. Equally, he repeated the old radical belief that "great standing armies, however disciplined and powerful, were not to be implicitly trusted" and that volunteer corps were more in keeping with "the constitutional liberties of this country."[4] On 29 August he wrote privately to Addington, protesting against proposals to limit the intake of recruits to the volunteers when the "Mass of the People" had a right to take arms.

By making himself a champion of the volunteer corps, Sheridan was trying simultaneously to be true to radical principles and to wrap himself in the flag. There is evidence that this effort was successful. In late August, for instance, the *Morning Post* reported that Sheridan was spotted in the crowd watching a parade of the volunteer corps of St. James's parish and was "invited, with the most flattering attention, into the kept ground."

Cobbett set out to remind the public of Sheridan's recent past, and to associate him again with French revolutionaries and United Irishmen. He pointed out that in France "it was *the Volunteers*, and not the regulars amongst whom the defection began. It was with the former, and not with the latter, that the disloyal, base, bloody, insolent, and cowardly Citizen Lafayette, so often eulogised by Mr Sheridan, hunted the Royal Family from place to place, led them prisoner to their capital, and finally effected their ruin together with that of the monarchy."[5] He also mocked Sheridan's call in the same speech for Windham and his colleagues to "suspend their political animosities for the moment," reminding his readers that "Mr Sheridan, who *now* calls for *perfect silence* as to the conduct of ministers, because it is a crisis of so great peril, did, during 1798, during that time of *greater peril*, keep up a *loud and incessant opposition*, in which he was joined by all the Jacobins of the country." Part of this opposition, of course, was "his eulogium on the principles of Arthur O'Connor." He then hinted that he might at some stage turn his attentions to Sheridan's turbulent private life, thanking an anonymous correspondent for "a long list of anecdotes respecting Mr Sheridan's *private* character and conduct . . ."

Cobbett was obviously trying to provoke Sheridan into either condemning or supporting Robert Emmet and the other conspirators. But Sheridan had good reasons for holding his tongue, for by August 1803 he was already plotting to give himself a role in the government of Ireland. Sheridan's scheme was that the Prince of Wales would go to Ireland but that the lord lieutenancy would be replaced by a council of which the Prince would be the president and whose other members would be Lord Moira, John Hely-Hutchinson (an Irish peer who favoured Catholic emancipation), and, of course, Sheridan himself. It was this plan that lay behind all the manoeuvrings that created such unease amongst his old allies. He told Thomas Creevey of his plan in August: "The Prince is quite heated upon the subject; nothing else is discussed by them."[6]

What Sheridan had in mind, clearly, was that he would himself move to Dublin and introduce Catholic emancipation. On 17 August Francis Horner noted that in the wake of the rebellion in Ireland, a plan had been suggested to the Prince that he, Moira, Hutchinson, and Sheridan should go to Ireland. "I really believe the humbug popularity of Sheridan and Moira might have a healing effect, especially if assisted by the more substantial measure of [Catholic] emancipation . . . The Doctor [Addington] said of this scheme . . . that it would be as much as their places were worth to hint at it."[7]

A part of Sheridan's scheme, and a key reason for his refusal to join Addington's government, was his hope of placing himself at the head of what would be in effect an Irish party at Westminster. With the passage of the Act of Union, the Irish Parliament was dissolved, and Irish constituencies now sent their representatives to London. Clearly, Sheridan's ambition was to try to establish a power base amongst these Irish MPs as a first step in the establishment of a reforming administration under the Prince in Dublin. On 11 August French Laurence, who had been speaking to Sheridan, wrote to his friend Lord Fitzwilliam, expressing the view that Sheridan

> has too much pride and ambition to accept anything which Mr Addington can or will give him. He will not, if I know him at all, submit to be subordinate to the present cabinet and placed on a level with Tierney, following too in his wake. On the other hand, he is daily losing, or rather has already lost, the regard of all his former connections; has merely confirmed himself in the favour of the newspapers, gained possibly some popularity among the Volunteer Corps who do not see through his policy; and not yet succeeded in drawing after him the following of an Irish party.[8]

It was essential to Sheridan that he should both strengthen his own hold over the Prince and weaken the position of his brother, the Duke of York, who was bitterly opposed to Catholic emancipation. He did so by stirring up animosity between the duke and Addington. General Sir Robert Wilson told Lord Hutchinson on 25 November 1803 that "at the present moment Addington and the Duke [of York] by our friend Sheridan's *tattle* are at daggers drawn, therefore of course every attempt will be made to thwart the Duke and expose him to general animadversion . . ."[9] Yet within months, Sheridan was claiming the credit for having effected a reconciliation between the royal brothers. George Rose wrote in his diary on 25 February 1804: "Mr Sheridan stated confidently this morning that a perfect reconciliation had taken place between the Prince of Wales and the Duke of York, and that it was effected by him exclusively."[10] Lord Glenbervie wrote on 1 March: "It seems a reconciliation has taken place between the Prince and the Duke of York. The newspapers ascribe this to the good offices of Sheridan." Where the royal family was concerned, he was perfectly prepared to manipulate its members to his own advantage.

It was equally critical for Sheridan that he direct the Prince's choice between his two great desires: either to be given a senior military command or to be made Lord Lieutenant of Ireland. While the first of these notions was closest to Prince George's heart, it did not of course suit Sheridan's purposes. He therefore took the brave and risky step of using his influence with Addington to oppose any military appointment for the Prince. Fox informed Northumberland that "the present Ministry . . . can no more give [the Prince] any military command or send him Lord Lieutenant to Ireland than you or I in our present situations can. I think Lord M[oira] sees this, but Sheridan either does not or *will* not see it." Around the same time, Fox was accusing Sheridan of telling lies when he maintained that the Prince did not want a public issue made of the King's refusal to give him a prominent military position. When the Prince wrote to Fox telling him that, on the contrary, he was anxious that "the topic should be revived," the latter told General Fitzpatrick, "What Sheridan said though I knew it was a lie at the time, gave me an opportunity of asking orders [from the Prince] which I did, however, without naming Sh[erida]n . . ."[11] Sheridan, however, must have remonstrated with the Prince over this, because on 16 December the Prince wrote to him with the assurance that there was "no one in the world who entertains a higher regard for you than I do, nay, I may even say entertains a sincerer affection for you than I do."[12]

Soon that affection was given tangible form. On 20 February 1804 the Prince notified Sheridan of his appointment as receiver-general of the Duchy of Cornwall "during pleasure" (meaning that the appointment could be revoked at any time by the Prince). The average yearly income was reckoned by George Rose to be £1,200, though it may have been as high as £1,400. In gratitude, Sheridan wrote a fawning letter to the Prince, promising that "to the end of my Life I will strenuously employ every Faculty of my Mind in your service."[13] The appointment was, as he immediately informed Addington, "wholly unsolicited," and indeed it came at a time when Sheridan had recently demonstrated his independence from the Prince by opposing his desire to be given a military command:

> Had it been the result of a mean and subservient Devotion to the Prince's every wish and object I could neither have respected the Gift, the Giver or myself. But when I consider how recently it was my misfortune to find myself compell'd by a sense of Duty stronger than my attachment to him wholly to risk the situation

> I held in his confidence and favour, and that upon a subject on which his Feelings were so eager and irritable I cannot but regard as a most gratifying Demonstration that he has clearness of judgment and firmness of Spirit to distinguish the real friends of his true Glory and Interests from the mean and mercenary Sycophants who fear and abhor that such Friends should be near him.[14]

As well as offering considerable financial rewards, the appointment had the advantage of making Sheridan an official member of the Prince's council, able, as he told Addington, to visit the Prince "on trying occasions openly and in the face of Day and put aside the mask of mystery and concealment." Intent as he was on pursuing the aim of moving to Dublin with the Prince, the advantage of having an official position in his household outweighed the desire for ostentatious independence that caused him to refuse offers of advancement from Addington and the King. The Duchy of Cornwall appointment, indeed, was widely seen as confirming suspicions that Sheridan was about to become a leading figure in any new administration that would be formed if, as seemed likely at the time, the King's illness led to a regency. George Rose noted in his diary on 21 February that it "strongly confirms the probability of my former conjectures respecting what may be expected from a Regency Government."[15]

Accepting the position also offered the attraction of seeing General Gerard Lake, to whom the Prince had previously promised it, deprived of it. This was the same General Lake who had operated martial law against the United Irishmen in Ulster in 1797, failing in the process to curb the excesses of his men. He was, for instance, responsible for the execution in October 1797 of William Orr, a young Presbyterian farmer in Armagh, on a discredited charge of administering oaths, an act widely seen as "judicial murder." In 1798, even the military commander-in-chief in Ireland, Abercromby, was appalled by Lake's methods, and issued a general order in February 1798 warning against "irregularities in the conduct of the troops of this kingdom." Lake's brother angrily claimed that the position had already been promised to him, and Sheridan offered to give it up. He knew, however, that Lake could not legally hold the office since he was out of the country as commander-in-chief of British forces in India. In the end a deal was struck whereby Sheridan would hold the office while Lake was abroad. In effect, the only period when

General Lake was able to hold it was in 1807–8, after which Sheridan assumed it for life.

Again, Sheridan's family connections expected preferment: his nephew Charles Robert wrote to Dublin in December: "It is a shame that Dick does not appoint H.L. [Henry Le Fanu, Betsy's husband] to a situation in Cornwall, where he has such patronage."[16]

Ironically, the scheme of moving to Dublin was derailed by the return once again of the King's illness, which, because of the likelihood that the Prince might at any moment become regent, made it necessary, for him to stay in England. By the end of February Sheridan was under great stress. He wrote to Hecca of "the worry I live in," for "there never was known before anything equal to the agitation of Peoples minds at this moment." The Prince was continually summoning him ("I must absolutely see you for two minutes *here* tonight") at all hours, seldom, as he told Hecca, letting him go home "after twelve at Night and He has often kept me till 5 in the morning not supping or with a drop of wine but in his bed-room. Then I see Fox every day—and Addington almost every evening."[17]

To Grey's despair, Sheridan was again the trusted go-between in plans for a regency government. Grey wrote on 24 February: "The Prince is in great agitation and talks all day without ceasing to Mrs Fitzherbert and McMahon. Sheridan has seen him occasionally and is the only person in politics who has done so, except Lord Thurlow. Through Sheridan, everything comes to Fox, a terrible channel, I think, tho' Fox seems at present satisfied with his conduct. Sheridan has also had communications with Addington which I distrust very much tho' Fox on this head also seems perfectly secure."[18]

Even when the King recovered and the regency again failed to materialise, Sheridan remained the Prince's main adviser. On 30 November 1804 Charles Ward wrote to his wife, Jane Linley, explaining why it was difficult for Sheridan to devote himself to theatre business:

> I am now waiting for Sheridan's appearance, we got half way thro' yesterday when a message from the Prince run away with him . . . Indeed I can well excuse him, now I see his everyday life. At this period entre nous he is really determining the fate of the Country. The King has quarrelled with the Prince & insists upon taking away the little Princess from her father & educating her himself, this the Prince resists & the arrangement of the Contest

> is confided to Sheridan, who is now fighting with his Pen both Pit[t] and the Chancellor & I lay wager if you will go halves he will prove superior. How can he devote hours to consider Scene shifting and artificial mules, Jane.[19]

Yet, in a sense, scene shifting was very much on his mind, and over the coming years he continued to wait for the opportunity to return to Ireland. As he moved towards middle age, the place he left as a small child was becoming more and more an imaginary homeland.

Chapter 36

DEPRAVED IMAGINATION

Just after the New Year of 1805, Harriet Duncannon's nineteen-year-old daughter, Caroline Ponsonby (later Lamb), received a letter which, her mother complained, was filled "with every gross, disgusting indecency that the most depraved imagination could suggest, worse indeed than anything I ever heard, saw, or read, or could imagine . . . It is what I am quite convinced you would not believe possible, even supposing it addressed to some woman in the street." What disturbed Harriet most was the signature. It was signed "Mr Hill," and the name had come up in intimate conversation a few nights previously at Devonshire House. The Duchess of Devonshire had told Caroline of a Mr. Hill who had professed himself her admirer and said she was the prettiest and cleverest girl in London. Caroline had laughed, "Dear Mr Hill, I shall set about admiring him whenever I meet him," and his name had become an in-joke with which to tease her. Whoever put his name to this obscene letter was privy to all the tattle of Devonshire House. And it was, moreover, "very well written."[1]

Two days later, Harriet herself got an obscene letter. And at the same time Sir Robert Adair, a friend of Fox, brought her the original version of an article that had been submitted to the *Morning Post* but not published. It was full of scurrilous gossip about Harriet, her husband Lord Duncannon, and Harriet Cavendish, the Duchess of Devonshire's daughter, who was to marry Harriet's lover Granville Leveson Gower. What shocked her this time was the handwriting on the manuscript and the unthinkable idea that it prompted: "I will not think the letter can be from the same person—this is bad enough." Even to Leveson Gower she could not explain the cause of her suspicions.

A few weeks later two more obscene letters, this time signed "Mr Ward," were sent to Caroline St. Jules, Lady Elizabeth Foster's daughter, and to Harriet Cavendish. Included with the letters were pornographic prints. In the meantime, the *Morning Post* had continued to receive a stream of abusive articles, attacking the duchess for her involvement with politics, sneering at Harriet Cavendish's "nymphlike figure," but mostly aimed at Harriet Duncannon. There were stories about her lovers, hints that Mr. Hill was consoling her in Leveson Gower's absence as British ambassador to Russia, and tales of "violent dissipation and gaeity."[2] "It certainly seems," she wrote to Leveson Gower, "a plan to hurt me."

The letters continued throughout February. The duchess got one "very abusive of us all," attacking Lady Elizabeth Foster and Leveson Gower's sister-in-law, but again aimed mostly at Harriet Duncannon. The duchess herself, it said, "had forbearance enough to stop short of danger, and only took money from her lovers," while Harriet was much worse. The letters to Harriet contained allegations about the infidelities of Leveson Gower. And Mr. Hill, too, received a letter, this time purporting to come from Harriet herself and containing "great advances in the same sort of language." The younger women continued to receive letters of "coarse indecency," always with "horrible Prints and drawings which it is shocking for them to see."

Almost from the start of this campaign, when she first saw the handwriting on the scurrilous manuscript submitted to the *Morning Post*, Harriet concluded that Sheridan was the author of both the letters and the articles. The writing was "dreadfully like one I know very well." The letters were clever and well written, often beginning with verses. Over time her suspicions were confirmed by some unknown evidence which she considered absolutely conclusive. She hated "being in the power of a person who could write thus." Quite apart from the handwriting, everything about the letters pointed to Sheridan: the ventriloquism, the cleverness, but, above all, the strange intermingling of politics, sex, and class that marked his obsession with Harriet. She had ceased to be his mistress after their affair had threatened a public and political scandal in 1789. She had, shortly afterwards, replaced Sheridan with the young Leveson Gower, who was both an aristocrat (he subsequently became Earl Granville) and a passionate devotee of Pitt. In the normal way of their world, the end of Sheridan's affair with her should have been no more than a natural movement from friendship to love and back again. Instead, her desertion became, for him, a crucible of insecurities. Sex with Harriet, the more beautiful sister of the Duchess of Devonshire, had been the crowning proof of his conquest of the oligarchy. It had given him an absolute assurance that, in the world of the Whig elite, he could be an equal. Her choice of a younger, richer aristocrat, and a follower of his greatest political enemy, left a void which he could not fill. He needed to torment her, to woo her, to regain possession of her.

At first, he had tried to do so by charm. In July 1797, shortly after Leveson Gower had gone abroad, Harriet found Sheridan at her door, announcing that he had come to see "the Majesty of grief." With sublime sarcasm, he teased her with assurances that her lover would be back within days, because "all the farmers in England meant to send a petition for there was no hope of any harvest now the bright beams that us'd to warm and vivify our Atmosphere were withdrawn."[3] A few days later, even though she had ordered her servants to admit no one, she again found him in her house. She received him coldly, but, as she admitted to Leveson Gower, "Demon-like, he was so abominably entertaining that I ended by being glad he came, and letting him stay till almost dinner time." This, too, was part of the pattern of their relationship—she wanted to be rid of him, but found him, when he was "gentle and amus'd," irresistible company.

In August he again called on her in the morning and announced that he would return for dinner, which to her astonishment he did. She found him "very pleasant," but he complained continually about Leveson Gower's usurping his place in her affections. "I am wasting all my efforts to entertain you," he said, "while you are grieving that you cannot change me into Lord Leveson. You would not be so grim if he was beaming on you." He began to make "fine speeches" about his love for her, and she realised with alarm that he intended to stay, not just for the evening, but for the night. She called her servant and ordered her chair to be brought, telling him that she had to go out. But realising that she probably had nowhere to go, he followed her. She called at various houses, pretending that she was going in, but hadn't the nerve to knock. He followed her all the way home.

She reached the door just ahead of him, and got inside just in time to tell the servants not to let him in. As she was running up the stairs, she could hear him "expostulating with the porter."[4]

This fruitless pursuit continued over the following years, with him too obsessed to accept that she no longer wanted him, and her finding too much pleasure in his company to cut him off completely. Over time, though, his attempts at courtship acquired an air of menace. In March 1802 he accosted her in her box at the opera, sitting beside her and filling every pause in the music with whispered abuse of Leveson Gower and lurid accounts of his infidelity to her. When she told him that she trusted her lover implicitly, he sneered, "How are the mighty fallen." In August he arrived unannounced at her door, and she told her maid to say she was out. "Tell her," he said, "I called twice this morning and want particularly to see her, for I know she is at home." When the maid repeated that her mistress was out, he said, "Then I shall walk up and down before the door till she comes in." He paced up and down outside for an hour before knocking on the door again, at which point she sent the maid out again to say that she was too unwell to see him.[5]

Elements of both fear and shame had entered their attitudes to each other. She recalled wistfully that "there was a time when I was not afraid of him," but that now she was "not in a mood to be flatter'd or abus'd, frightened or complimented, and he is in one . . . to torment me, which he can do if he pleases." But the intimidation was not entirely one-sided, for, as she confessed, "I imagine Sheridan fears me, because often when no body else could stop him, one word or look from me has done so at once, which I believ'd to be *conscience*, that knowing how much he has injur'd me made him feel something like shame in my presence; but this does not always hold good when he is in his ways."[6] Yet she, too, retained some tinge of shame about her treatment of him: "I feel the justice of some of his attacks . . ."

By August 1803, when Sheridan's relations with Fox and the Devonshire House set were at their lowest ebb, his obsession with her betrayal took on a more explicitly political dimension. He complained to the Prince about the "treachery" of the behaviour of Harriet and the Duchess of Devonshire towards him. According to Harriet, "He told the P[rince] that he must not give credit to the stories told him by us (calling us by no very gentle Epithet)." He said that the sisters, Leveson Gower, and Lord Morpeth "scrupled no lies against him, either as to his public or private Character."[7] And his allegations were not without foundation—both the duchess and Harriet had joined in the general disparagement of him by the Foxites, Harriet, for instance, complaining in familiar terms of his "duplicity and inordinate Vanity."

It was this sense of personal and political betrayal, darkened by shadows of madness and obsession, that broke out in the obscene letters. All the resentments that festered in the void between his hatred for, and attraction to, the world of the Whig oligarchs burst through in a torrent of obscenity. Under the strain of maintaining a public face at odds with his private motives, his personality collapsed. At various times over the previous quarter of a century, when the King's loosened tongue had vented dark obscenities, Sheridan had been the one to mind his words, to keep a tight rein on language and thought. In his madness the King's speech had been "blended not infrequently with indecencies." All his intimate fantasies about the Countess of Pembroke had been given utterance, for example, and, as he said himself when his sanity returned, "he must have said many very improper things, and much must have scaped him then which ought not."[8] Now Sheridan, after years of trying to exploit the King's delusions, had himself caught the malady, and very improper things escaped him.

And there was an even more ironic reversal, for such scandalous letters, written by the author of *The School for Scandal*, could hardly have been a more self-conscious exercise in hypocrisy. The opening lines of that play must now have seemed to him like a distorting mirror in which he could see a grotesque image of himself:

> *Lady Sneerwell:* The Paragraphs you say, Mr Snake, were all inserted?
>
> *Snake:* They were Madam—and as I copied them myself in a feign'd Hand there can be no suspicion whence they came.

It was Sheridan who put into Lady Sneerwell's mouth the statement that "the male-Slanderer . . . must have the cowardice of a woman before he can traduce one." It was he who made Snake's signing forged letters with someone else's name the epitome of vileness. It was he who excoriated the publication of tittle-tattle about the love affairs of the aristocracy in the newspapers. What depths of hatred and self-contempt must he have plumbed to make him ape his own most famously contemptible characters.

At the time of the obscene letters, Sheridan was both physically and mentally ill, sunk in an abyss of debilitation, depression, and self-pity. Indeed, both he and Hecca had convinced themselves that they were dying, even though neither of them seems to have been seriously ill. In an undated letter from around this time, he wrote to her that he was too depressed to go out, and was "sitting by myself most melancholy and gloomy . . . Great Pain is a very bad thing but I think a fit of very low Spirits in solitude as bad." She had evidently written to him that she was dying and accused him of not caring. He told her that "it is owing to your Letter this morning, and the constant anxious thoughts that follow me respecting your health with at times the most unreasonable apprehensions that have put my Heart so down this Night." He had "according to my usual foolish and nervous superstitions put myself down for dying yesterday morning." Whatever she thought of him, he wrote, "I would with the hand I am now writing with I would cut off the other to ensure your health and Life. Do not ask me whether I would take care of Charles were anything to happen to you—look to me with no reliance . . ."[9] The following day, he thought himself "worse than ever."

In such a low state, the contradictory attitudes to sex that he had lived with for so long could no longer be contained. A strain of sexual puritanism had been evident in his personality from his early twenties, intimately linked to his ambivalent feelings about the theatre. Both his father and he had always had to struggle to assert the propriety of the theatrical profession against the imputation that actresses were little better than whores and actors pimps. His own entry into political life was fundamentally dependent on his ability to defeat such perceptions by keeping Eliza off the stage. And yet, once he was accepted as a gentleman, he had enjoyed the sexual freedom that the aristocracy allowed itself. Instead of succeeding each other, though, this contradictory set of attitudes continued to coexist. After Sheridan's death, Lord Henry Holland said of him that what

> accounted for many of his inconsistencies was the high, ideal system he had formed of a sort of impracticable perfection in honour, virtue etc.—any thing short of which he seemed to think not worth aiming at—and thus consoled himself for the extreme laxity of his practice by the impossibility of coming up to the sublime

> theory he had formed . . . prudery and morality were always on his lips, while his actions were one series of debauchery and libertinism.[10]

It was this impossible conjunction of the puritan and the libertine that now caught up with him. The obscene letters were, from Harriet's accounts of them, both wildly pornographic and violently censorious, full of both invitations to, and condemnations of, sexual indulgence.

Sheridan was fortunate that, instead of confronting him, Harriet contented herself with snubbing him in public and composing a coded verse for the *Morning Post*, painting him as Snake and Sneerwell, herself as the victim of their spite, and making him aware that she knew who had written the letters:

> Shame to the pen whose coward poisons flow
> In secret streams with baneful malice fraught
> That emulates th' assasins Midnight blow
> By hate directed and vengeance wrought.
> Yet generous Minds the name will ne'er reveal,
> Tho' known! nor deign a stigma to impart,
> But leave the dastard miscreant to feel
> The Conscious pangs of a corrupted heart.[11]

He seems to have taken the hint. Not only did the letters stop, but he took flight and spent much of the rest of the year out of London.

Sheridan made, during all of 1805, only one substantial speech in Parliament, his long, brilliant, and vitriolic attack on Pitt on 6 March, after which he set off with the Prince of Wales for Leicestershire, where they stayed with Lord Moira. Pitt's administration had been shaken by the report of an inquiry into the conduct of the Admiralty during his first administration, which led to a defeat for the government and the resignation of Henry Dundas (now Lord Melville), who had been implicated in financial irregularities. Much of the attack on Melville was orchestrated by Earl St. Vincent, who had been First Lord of the Admiralty in Addington's administration. Sheridan was certainly conspiring with St. Vincent, who, on 4 March, wrote to a contact in the Admiralty enclosing a memorandum from Sheridan and telling him to provide him with the information he required: "Send up that you are come from me. He will turn out and see you in his Night Gown . . ."[12]

He would also have been, in normal circumstances, in a good position to take advantage of the next political event, Addington's resignation from the cabinet on 5 July. A few days earlier Addington told Sheridan of his intention, knowing that the news would be communicated to the Prince and, as Henry Temple (Viscount Palmerston) put it later in the month, "the choice of the messenger plainly pointed to the object of the communication."[13] The King, indeed, was outraged that both his son and Sheridan knew of Addington's departure before he himself did.[14] There was widespread expectation of a new administration and of Sheridan's playing a large part in it. The day after Addington's resignation, the *Morning Post* reported, "Mr Sheridan and Mr Windham, if they do not divide the *loaves* and the *fishes*, seem at last to divide the jobs between them; *each*, however appears to be somewhat jealous of the other's portion."

But in fact Sheridan had no appetite for intrigue. As well as his own shame, he was haunted by a ghostly visitation from the past. Eliza's younger sister, Jane, came to stay at Polesden. She was the same age as Eliza had been when she entered the last stages of her terminal illness. Like Eliza then, she had just had a baby daughter. And like Eliza, she was dying of tuberculosis. She had come to Polesden in the vain hope that a change of air might do her good. For Sheridan, watching her must have been like living again through the terrible days of 1792. He took flight. In August he left Polesden and headed north, staying first with Samuel Whitbread, then with William Ord in Northumberland, with Hecca's relatives in Newcastle, with Grey at Howick, and finally travelling on to Scotland, where he stayed with Lord Lauderdale and the Duke of Atholl and was fêted in Edinburgh. The main purpose of the visit was probably to meet up with Tom and his new wife, Caroline Henrietta Callander, whom Sheridan thought "lovely and engaging and interesting beyond measure, and, as far as I can judge, with a most superior understanding."[15] In the middle of October, he and Hecca returned to Howick to stay with Grey again.

Leaving Hecca behind with the Greys, he went to stay with the Prince at the Pavilion in Brighton for three weeks. He pressed the Prince with great vehemence to transfer the receivership of the Duchy of Cornwall to Tom. Thomas Creevey, who was staying near the Pavilion, saw him "cry bitterly" one night while entreating the

Prince on the subject. But the latter was unyielding, telling Sheridan that his "reputation was such that it made it not only justifiable but most honourable to him, the Prince," to have Sheridan in the office.

He was drinking heavily enough to make himself ill. One morning he told Creevey and his wife that he was so unwell that "he was in a perfect fever." Creevey felt his pulse and found it "going tremendously." After his first bottle of wine, however, it "subsided almost instantly." He then stayed with them all day, and had another bottle and a half of wine after dinner. He went back to the Pavilion to bed and, at about midnight, the Prince enquired for him. When Creevey told him that Sheridan was ill, the Prince sent up to Sheridan's room with a bottle of claret. Creevey entered the bedroom, "his great fine eyes being instantly fixed upon me and said: 'Come, I see this is some joke of the Prince, and I am not in a state for it.' "

Yet two hours later, he was out of bed, "powdered as white as snow," smartly dressed, and downstairs in the ballroom. The supper had been served already, but he went into the kitchen, joked with the servants, and charmed them sufficiently that "he was surrounded by supper of all kinds, every one waiting upon him. He ate away and drank a bottle of claret in a minute, returned to the ballroom and when I left it between three and four he was dancing."[16]

In his more sober moments, he spent his time talking to Creevey about his schooldays and early life: Harrow, Bath, the duels, Waltham Abbey, the writing of *The Rivals*, his first election for Stafford. And bizarrely, while he was trying to abandon himself in the pleasures of the moment or to lose himself in thoughts of the past, he was confronted by an apparition from his time of greatest triumph. Warren Hastings and his wife called at the Pavilion, and the Prince introduced them to Sheridan. According to Creevey, Sheridan "lost no time in attempting to cajole old Hastings, begging him to believe that any part he had taken against him was purely political, and that no one had greater respect for him than he had himself." Hastings replied coldly and superbly that it would be a great consolation to him in his declining years if Sheridan were to say in public what he had just said in private. Sheridan mumbled his excuses and left.

Shortly afterwards, when he visited the Marquis of Abercorn's house in Middlesex for a season of lavish amateur theatricals in which Tom and his wife were to take part, he was again faced with painful reminders of past glories. For the first time in his life, he sat through a full performance of *The Rivals*, but had to watch it in the painful knowledge that Harriet was also in the room. "It made me very nervous," he wrote to Hecca. "I don't mean the writing or sentiments of the Play but the recollection of the Days, when, just past twenty one, I wrote it—many years before I knew some *dear Friends!* who sat on the [parliamentary] Bench with me or their world or their system."[17]

He was still part of that system and in mid-November went to see Addington at his house, White Lodge, to try to cajole him into joining the opposition and bringing about Pitt's fall. He did so, Addington thought, "with the knowledge if not at the instigation" of the Prince, and "I told him distinctly that I would not *dabble*."[18] In any case, Sheridan's mind was probably taken up more with his political allies than with his political enemies. Hecca was still with the Greys in Northumberland, and yet again, his political relationships were becoming entangled with sexual jealousies. Grey and Sheridan had always been the least trusting of political allies, and now a further dimension was added to their rivalry. Lord Henry Holland said after Sheridan's death that "Lord Grey hated S[heridan] and for an odd reason, because he intrigued with Sheridan's last wife."[19] Hecca and Grey's wife, Mary, were cousins, and because of her own family connections with Northumberland, she had obvious reasons for staying on at Howick. She was also attracted to Grey, however, and in a letter written to Eleanor Creevey at this time she describes the "extreme charm" of his "good looks." What passed between them is not recorded, but it was certainly more than the chit-chat of distant relatives. As she confessed to Leveson Gower, "I confided my griefs to him—he pitied me . . . and in short an intimacy arose between us beyond whatever existed but not till I beheld him under the influence of passion for me did I in thought ever deviate from what was right." The thought begat the deed: she "passed those bounds which leave a woman no comfort but in the excess of her love."[20] Two years later Harriet Duncannon reproached Grey for his "from first to last abominable conduct" towards Hecca. By way of answer, he "beat his head, call'd himself by a thousand harsh names, cried out and threw himself at my feet . . . he clasp'd both my hands in his, press'd them to his forehead as he knelt before me quite sobbing aloud."[21] This display strongly suggests that the relationship between Hecca and Grey had been, at least for a while, a very serious love-affair.

Sheridan had never been so alone. Even on Christmas Day, he was sunk in loneliness and self-pity: "There is," he complained to Hecca, "no Peer, no Gentleman, no christian Sweep that does not make something social out of [Christmas], and I suppose I am the single Person not manacled who has spent it in my cell without communion with any fellow creature—but such is the fact—I have not stirr'd out of your Drawing room, indeed I had no where to go, and I am pleased to find how much better my nerves endure solitude than used to be the case."[22]

A few days later he wrote telling her that he was still alone, but his spirits had lifted enough for him to joke that he was becoming "a Hermit only that I shan't have beard enough—I know a nice spot in Ranmorwood for my cell only there is no *chrystal Spring* near it." He was, he boasted, mending his ways, getting up before dawn and breakfasting by candlelight. His melancholy, resigned mood was prompted perhaps by a third visitation from the past. After meeting Hastings and seeing *The Rivals*, he was forced to remember who he had been and who he was. Shortly after New Year's Day, and at almost exactly the same age that Eliza had been at her death, Jane Linley died. At her funeral he was tormented by memories of Eliza's awful funeral procession from Bristol to Wells Cathedral. Thinking about it, he began to imagine his own funeral and to hope that, unlike the strange year he had just passed, it would be simple and dignified.

Chapter 37

ROUGH WORK ON THE HUSTINGS

Within a matter of months that sense of isolation and those intimations of mortality ceased to be merely personal and became historic. One by one, the great entanglements and rivalries of Sheridan's life simply disappeared. On 23 January 1806 William Pitt, stunned by the news of Napoleon's monumental victories over Britain's allies at Ulm and at Austerlitz, died. He was forty-six. On 30 March the Duchess of Devonshire, at the age of forty-nine, followed him. Even before her death, she had suffered from constant headaches and partial blindness as a result of a diseased eye. Her body had become bloated, her complexion worse than Sheridan's, and her neck was immense.[1] On 24 June his brother, Charles, just fifty-six, died at Tunbridge Wells. On 13 September Charles James Fox, at fifty-seven, succumbed to corpulence and dropsy. All of them were either younger or just slightly older than Sheridan himself.

In the space of nine months, the antagonisms and friendships that had done most to shape his life had vanished. For half a century, he had striven to prove himself a better man than the more favoured Charles. For thirty years, he had orbited around Devonshire House, held in place by equal and opposite forces of attraction and repulsion. For the same period, his public life had been shaped by his complex loyalty to Fox, whom he had often disagreed with but never betrayed. And for a quarter of a century, Pitt had been the political "Other" against which he had defined himself. With none of the four had his relationship been simple, but between them they had formed the landmarks by which he mapped his world. With their disappearance he now found himself in a strange landscape where he was the most prominent curiosity. He had become, quite suddenly, a brilliant anachronism, the last of the great eighteenth-century orators.

Sheridan waited almost four months before paying a public tribute to Pitt, and when he did, it was decidedly ambivalent. He told the House of Commons that "there were many who flattered him more than I and some who feared him more; but there was no man who had a higher respect for his transcendent talents, his matchless eloquence, and the greatness of his soul; and yet it has often been my fate to have opposed his measures." Opposing Pitt's Additional Force Bill, he prayed, "Let the failure of the measure be buried in his grave, and never remembered in his epitaph."[2] Pitt's death left, as Fox put it, "a chasm, a blank that cannot be supplied," but voids have to be filled and the prospect of a new government awakened Sheridan from his morbid reflections. While Pitt was dying, he was already arranging meetings with Addington, acting as go-between for both the Prince and Fox, but helping to keep Addington's nominee, the anti-Catholic Duke of Buckinghamshire, out of the cabinet. A coalition bringing together the Foxites, the Grenville faction, and Addington's followers in a ministry of all the talents was quickly cobbled together. Of the Foxites, Erskine, Grey, Fitzwilliam, Spencer, and Fox himself—as foreign secretary—got cabinet positions. Sheridan was offered a post outside the cabinet, the office of treasurer of the navy, which he had been prepared to accept during the first regency crisis seventeen years earlier as a stepping stone to greater things. As he protested to Fox, "It is 17 years since when you professed to me that I should not be content to accept that alone."[3] To take it now was to acknowledge that he was no nearer to power than he had been then. But Grenville, who was to be Prime Minister, despised him for his role in preventing a Fox-Grenville coalition in 1803. And the office came with attractive compensations—£4,000 a year and an official residence in Somerset Place in Westminster. He was also made a member of the Privy Council. His motives for accepting it were not, however, entirely mercenary; he turned down the offer of the more lucrative but politically less important sinecure of the chancellorship of the Duchy of Lancaster, which would have given him £2,000 a year for life.

His most important concern was with arranging some post for Tom, to whom, in March, he assigned a quarter share of Drury Lane.

While his brother, Charles, was expecting that some of the blessed manna of patronage would fall on him, Sheridan made it clear to the Duke of Bedford, who had been made Lord Lieutenant of Ireland, that

> I have the greatest good will to my Brother but The Object of my heart is my Son. Having been Thirty years a Whig politician and Six and twenty years in Parliament, and having expended full £20,000 of my own money to maintain my seat there and in all the course of my Political life struggling thro' great dif[f]iculties and risking the Existence of the only Property I had, I am certain I have only to state the short preceding sentence to make your Grace understand me distinctly on this subject.[4]

The note of injured pride was an echo of his deep sense of anger and humiliation. On taking up the office of treasurer of the navy, he had to resign his seat at Stafford and stand for election again. The new administration offered to bring back into Parliament, at its own expense, some of the new office-holders—the attorney-general Arthur Piggott and the solicitor-general Samuel Romilly. The Duke of Norfolk offered Sheridan one of the seats in his control, but he refused, in the belief that Fox would arrange to pay for a campaign at Stafford. When all the available seats were given to others, however, Sheridan discovered that no arrangement had been made for him, nor had anything been done for Tom. He reminded Fox that in the spring of 1804, during the King's illness, "when perhaps I was deemed of more *use* than the present *famed* administration may estimate," he had received "a very distinct pledge from you that Tom should be taken care of." He was forced to threaten that he would refuse to take office at all unless a position was found for Tom. He did so in terms that made clear his feeling of semi-detached loyalty to the new government: "In one word if nothing can be done for my Son The *Grenville Administration* are perfectly welcome to dispose of my office."[5] In the event, he was re-elected without opposition at Stafford, and Tom was given a place in Ireland as joint muster-master general, worth about £500 a year.

If Pitt's death proved no great turning-point in his fortunes, neither did that of the Duchess of Devonshire. Shortly after her death, the Prince, visiting Harriet Duncannon at Roehampton, conveyed a message from Sheridan, asking her to forgive him for the outrages of the previous year. She returned a stern and unyielding reply: she wanted nothing to do with him, but if he would leave her alone, she would always be glad to hear good news of him.

He had passed, once and for all, outside the golden circle of the Whig oligarchs. If his treatment in the formation of the government had not been enough to make this clear to him, then the events surrounding Fox's illness and death ought to have done so. Fox became ill in May, and by the summer, confined to Stable Yard in Chiswick and unable to continue his broken journey to St. Anne's, he had begun to joke about his own death, suggesting that the various doctors who examined him should put their diagnoses in sealed envelopes to be opened at his post-mortem. Sheridan certainly anticipated his death. On the very night it happened he was writing to John Graham, a supporter of his in Westminster, on the subject of the vacancy that would be left in the most prestigious and most democratic seat in the House of Commons: with all ratepayers entitled to vote, it had 12,000 electors, many of them shopkeepers, tradesmen, and artisans.

None but the sons of lords and baronets had represented Westminster before, but for a long time Sheridan had had his eye on this prize. As early as 1790, Eliza had mentioned in a letter to him her "regret that you did not stand for Westminster with Charles [Fox], instead of Lord John [Townshend]," suggesting that the idea had been discussed between them.[6] According to Lord Holland, by 1802 Sheridan had "nearly persuaded [Fox] to retire from parliament, in order that he might himself succeed" to the Westminster seat.[7] Fox himself at that time went as far as informing his Westminster agent that Sheridan "should have my Seat, and that I would do anything I could to forward such an object."[8]

That was, however, before the falling-out of 1803, and Sheridan had now to contrive how best to assume again the borrowed mantle as Fox's trusted friend. Given the fraught state of their relationship over the previous three years, an apostolic succession, a laying-on of hands, was necessary. Whether it ever really occurred is unclear. Thomas Moore asked the Hollands whether it was true that Fox when he was dying had refused to see Sheridan, and "they answered it was true." Lord Lansdowne confirmed this.[9] Samuel Rogers, however, told Moore that he was with Fox in his room in Stable Yard when Sheridan arrived. "I must see him, I suppose," said Fox, and when Sheridan came towards the bed, he put his hand out to him.

Sheridan subsequently told Rogers that Fox whispered to him, "My dear Sheridan, I love you, you are indeed my friend . . ." But Moore reckoned that "this was excellent invention of Sheridan, who knew no one could contradict him."

As recently as 15 February, however, Fox had written to Grenville during the search for a place for Tom saying, "I am anxious for his welfare independent of my friendship for his father."[10] And just as Sheridan had reasons to play up his last meeting with the dying Fox, so the Whig oligarchs had their reasons to deny that it had happened at all. They were already planning a savage betrayal of Sheridan. During the summer, as Fox was dying, the Duke of Northumberland approached his cousin, Prime Minister Lord Grenville, with the idea that his own son, Lord Hugh Percy, should succeed Fox in Westminster. Charles Grey, Sheridan's supposed friend and ally, wrote to Northumberland offering Percy "all the assistance that I can give him." The government, while assuring Sheridan that nothing would be done about Westminster until he had declared his intentions, planted stories in the press suggesting that if he stood he might lose his position as treasurer of the navy.

Percy was an absurd candidate to put before an independent electorate with strong radical traditions. He was twenty-one, and as the Westminster radical Francis Place, a Charing Cross tailor, put it, he was "without pretension to talents of any kind."[11] But he had two advantages for the government: he was the son of a powerful Whig magnate, and he was not Sheridan. For the administration, the aggrieved and semi-detached Sheridan was already an uncomfortable presence, but with the prestige of Westminster behind him there was a risk that he might become utterly unmanageable. As Eleanor Creevey put it two days after Fox's death, "None of the present party wish . . . to quarrel with [Sheridan], yet perhaps they may all think . . . that with his present ambitious hostility he might make being the member for Westminster a most troublesome engine for mischief." A week later Lord Holland remarked that "considering his *connexions*, talents and appearance of steadiness to the mob and the public I fear there is too much disposition to set him at defiance and too great a desire to get rid of him altogether than is either prudent or perhaps right."[12]

Three days before Fox died, and while he himself was still recovering from a fever, Sheridan finally learned that "Lord Percy would with certainty be a candidate" for Westminster. Yet the "contempt and disregard" that had been shown him galvanised him into action. He managed to put himself in charge of the arrangements for Fox's funeral and, having taken control of the body, laid claim to the spirit. On the day of Fox's death, he went to a public meeting at the Whig headquarters in the Crown and Anchor Tavern, "to consider a proper person to succeed that great man in representation of the City of Westminster." Percy was proposed by Dennis O'Brien, but the show of hands was strongly in Sheridan's favour. While claiming that "I have step by step followed Mr Fox through the whole course of his political career," Sheridan acknowledged in his speech that "there have been occasions upon which I have differed from him." Fox, though, "knew that nothing on earth could separate or detach me from him." He claimed Fox's legacy as his own with the "boast that I never in my life gave one vote in Parliament that was not on the side of freedom."

Looking back over his own political career, Sheridan avowed that, given the chance to do it all again, he would rather remain by Fox's side, "an exile from power, distinction and emolument, rather than be at this moment a splendid example of successful servility, or prosperous apostasy—though clothed with power, honours, titles, and gorged with sinecures and wealth obtained from the plunder of the people." Though avoiding an attack on Percy, he made a brilliant appeal to the audience's sympathy for his own achievements as a self-made man: "To be at all capable of acting upon principle, it is necessary that a man should be independent; and to independence the next best thing to that of being very rich, is to have been used to be very poor. Independence, however, is not allied to wealth, to birth, to rank, to power, to titles, or to honours. Independence is in the mind of man or it is nowhere."

Without referring directly to the hints in the press that he would lose his office if he stood for Westminster, he defied the government to carry out the threat: "No minister can expect to find in me a servile vassal. No minister can expect from me the abandonment of any principle I have avowed, or any pledge I have given. I know not that I have hitherto shrunk in place from opinions I have maintained while in opposition." Any minister who would ask him to do so would find that "my office should be at his service to-morrow. Such a ministry might strip me of a situation, in some respects of considerable emolument, but he could not strip me of the proud conviction that I was right; he could not strip me of my own self-esteem; he could not strip me, I think, of some portion of the confidence and good opinion of the people."[13]

And then, with all his old political and theatrical skills, having shown the crowd what they might have had, he told them that they could not have it. Towards the end of the speech, he revealed, to cries of "No, no, no," that he was retiring from the contest, on the grounds that "nothing could ever have induced me to have proceeded to a disputed poll on this occasion," with Fox not yet in his grave. He urged unanimous support for Percy, ensuring, however, the passage of a motion in his own favour:

> That the long and faithful services of Mr Sheridan in Parliament, his uniform support of all the principles and measures . . . his almost unrivall'd Talents and his devoted attachment to his late departed Friend do eminently qualify him to succeed Mr Fox as Member for Westminster. At the same time, this meeting cannot but acquiesce in the motives which induce him to withdraw himself on the present occasion in the sanguine hope that upon a future opportunity they may be enabled to manifest the high sense they entertain of his merits.[14]

With Sheridan's tactical withdrawal, Percy was elected unopposed on 7 October. Just six days later, the cabinet decided to dissolve the Parliament and call new elections, and Sheridan announced his intention to stand. The Duke of Northumberland, angered that he had spent £2,500 having his son elected to a parliament that sat for just seventeen days, withdrew his son's candidacy, leaving the way open for Sheridan. He stood for Westminster, leaving Tom to contest Stafford. The government nominated an admiral, Sir Samuel Hood, seen by many as a Tory, to run with him.

Percy's earlier candidacy had, however, damaged Sheridan. Much as he was outraged by it, as far as the electorate could see, Sheridan had stood aside in Percy's favour. A lavish fête paid for by Northumberland after his son's election had infuriated the radical section; the Charing Cross tailor, Francis Place, one of the main radical organisers, never forgot the sight of the Duke of Northumberland's servants throwing bread and cheese to the crowds and ladling out beer: "I was not the only one who felt indignation. Almost every man I knew was much offended with the whole of the proceedings and with all who were concerned in them." Then, when Percy suddenly disappeared, Sheridan was wrongly tainted with the suspicion that he had engineered Percy's election as a way of holding the seat open for himself. William Cobbett, who had long attacked him from a Tory church-and-king position, now saw the opportunity to come at him from the opposite direction. Taunting the Westminster electors with the shame of being the "menial servants of a few great families," he joined forces with Place and a loosely knit but highly effective group of radical tradesmen—tailors, glass-makers, boot and shoe-makers—to try to destroy a man he had long depicted as a dangerous subversive. Together, Cobbett, Place, and their allies were the harbingers of a new kind of democratic politics, combining a relative egalitarianism with an ebulliently British identity. Their radicalism was rooted in a rage to divide the nation—which they conceived of as made up of honest, solid, hardworking Englishmen—from all that was not the nation. Much as Sheridan shared their egalitarian instincts, he could also be defined, under Cobbett's influence, as being outside the true English nation, excluded not only by his holding of a government office but by his Irishness and his theatrical connections.

Cobbett's continued vehemence against Sheridan after his own conversion to radicalism was inspired at least in part by the fact that he had attacked Sheridan on grounds on which he himself was even more vulnerable. As the title of a book he published in 1804 put it, Sheridan was a "Political Proteus," an inconsistent opportunist. But he himself had shifted his political stance even more dramatically, from fervid anti-Jacobin to populist democrat. In all his shifts, though, Cobbett kept Sheridan in sight, and remembered him principally as the traitor who had colluded with the United Irishmen and Arthur O'Connor. The man he set out to destroy was, above all else, the slippery, seditious Irishman.

On 27 October James Paull, a follower of Sir Francis Burdett and a former ally of Sheridan's in the House of Commons, was announced as an independent candidate for the seat, with Cobbett, Burdett, and Place as his most important backers. The weight of Cobbett's influence over Paull can be judged from the fact that, as late as 29 September, Paull had declared himself a fervent supporter of Sheridan's and urged him to stand against Percy. Yet Sheridan realised at once the seriousness of Cobbett's challenge. On the evening of Paull's nomination, he remarked, "I count on some rough work on the Hustings."[15]

His apprehensions were justified. He was now caught in a pincer movement between the old oligarchy and a new, incipient democracy. On the one hand, the aristocracy's control of the House of Commons had never been greater—no fewer than 234 MPs owed their seats in some way to aristocratic intervention. On the other, this control was increasingly resented, and there was no longer the bogey of the Jacobins on which to vent popular resentment. On the one hand, he was the holder of a lucrative place in a government dominated by aristocrats. On the other, his political principles had been much more consistently radical than those of many of his "democratic" opponents. Politics was becoming polarised between the aristocrats and the middle classes. The anomalous position that Sheridan, as a middle-class democrat working *within* the old elite, had occupied for so long was disappearing. He had no map of the new political landscape with which to find his way.

The very ambiguities which he exploited for so long were now turned against him. So successfully had he played his double game of loyalty and treason, insider and outsider, friend of the Prince and friend of the people, Irish revolutionary and English patriot, that he now found himself open to attack on every front and from entirely opposite directions. As the holder of a lucrative sinecure, he could be damaged by the contrast that Paull's handbills made between the "Honest Men of the *middling* Classes" who made up most of the electorate and the pampered placeman who wanted to represent them. Yet he could also be portrayed as an impecunious swindler. In a cartoon by Isaac Cruikshank, he is addressing the crowd from the hustings, saying, "Gentlemen, I am proud on this occasion to *pay* you my respects—I shall bring in a *bill* of rights—I will give your oppressors a *Check*." Members of the audience are calling out, "Damn your *respects*, pay us our own *bills*," "I have brought you a *bill* for Claret," and "You know your *Checks* are worth nothing."

He could be attacked as a false democrat who, in office, had done nothing to advance reform (even though he had been in office for a mere nine months). But he could also be attacked as a dangerous revolutionary and a friend of Irish subversion. One of Paull's handbills, signed by "A Calm Observer" but probably written by Cobbett, brilliantly elided the two accusations, conjuring up a Sheridan who was both the treasurer of the navy and the ally of Arthur O'Connor:

> If you look at his political life you will find it exhibiting equally repulsive traits:—At one time the friend and supporter of principles subversive of the Constitution and of all order; the advocate of the French Revolution and its wildest theories; the defender of an O'Connor; the systematic opposer (whether right or wrong) of all the measures of the Government; yet, when in *place*, pursuing the same measures; inconsistent, tergiversating, unpatriotic, and the Apostate of Public Liberty.[16]

He could be attacked both as an aristocrat and as a member of the lower orders. Again Cobbett managed at one and the same time to evoke middle-class resentment of the aristocracy and to revive the old prejudice that held that an actor could not be a gentleman. In the same handbill, English distrust of the Irish, puritan disdain for the loose morals of the aristocracy, and the historic link between theatre and prostitution were enlisted against him:

> Who is asking to be one of your Representatives? The Son of an obscure Irish Player, a profession formerly proscribed by our laws; and its followers by various statutes stigmatized as *incorrigible rogues and vagabonds*.—Possessed of a considerable portion of Ribaldry, disgusting obscenity, and dissoluteness of manners, this *Harlequin Son* of a *Mountebank Father* was indulged by some few of the depraved Nobility of the age with admission to their society as a kind of *hired Jester*, whose grossness of conversation was calculated to stimulate their already too luxurious debauchery.—From these beginnings he moved through all the gradations of *meanness, tricking* and *impudence* to the station he now fills; his career has been marked with every species of profligacy and extravagance; to support which, he has been compelled to resort to low cunning and vile impostures.

This disparaging use of theatrical references was a constant theme of the anti-Sheridan campaigns. James Gillray, in his cartoons on the election, showed Sheridan dressed as Harlequin. Cobbett referred to his supporters as "the base tricksters, the green-room imposters, the vile herd of diverting vagabonds,"[17] his election workers as "play-actors, scene-shifters, candle-snuffers, and Mutes of the Theatre, aided by a pretty numerous bevy of those unfortunate females who are in some sorts intimates of that mansion." And this description drew not only on traditional middle-class suspicion of theatrical types but on a more directly political metaphor forged by Edmund Burke in his attacks on the French Revolution. These words of Cobbett are, in fact, a direct echo of Burke's attack, in the fourth *Letter on a Regicide Peace*, on the revolutionary Directory in Paris, in which he had used not just the same images but many of the same words: "candle-snuffers, revolutionary scene-shifters, second and third mob, prompter, clerks, executioners . . . grinners in the pantomime, murderers in tragedies, who make ugly faces under black wigs,—in short the very scum and refuse of the theatre."

The ideal for which Thomas Sheridan had endured riots, for which his son had risked death in his duels with Mathews—that theatre people might be gentlemen, entitled to a place in the public world—was being undermined. The hustings—fifteen days of open-air speeches in Covent Garden with the cumulative poll counted at the end of each day—was a vast theatre, but a theatre in riot. Sheridan, like his father faced with Kelly, could no longer control the house. On the first day at the hustings, 3 November, when he had to be helped onto the platform by a party of men with bludgeons, his first audible words were "Gentlemen, I wish to know whether you really want a riot or an election." Each side had its own mob, armed with cudgels, and the air was thick with threats of violence.

As he left the hustings on that first day, Sheridan was subjected to what his supporters advertised as "a daring and desperate assault." His assailants, according to a handbill issued by his campaign organiser, Peter Moore, offering a reward of a hundred pounds for information on their identity, were "three ruffians, who it appears had planted themselves there for that purpose; one of whom, named Davenport, now in custody and committed for trial, aimed a stroke at Mr Sheridan's head, which by testimony of four respectable witnesses, would probably have killed him on the spot had not his weapon been arrested."

John Davenport was a butcher. He wrote to Sheridan from prison expressing "very artless and sincere contrition" and telling him that "his wife, who has lost the use of her right hand, and a large family, might perish for want, if deprived of his support." He explained that he was very drunk at the time and did not know whom he was attacking. Sheridan declared his willingness to forgive him and instructed Peter Moore to have him released from prison and "to provide that his family may not be injured by his confinement."[18]

But Sheridan had his own "cudgel-men," and an element of ethnic conflict entered into the wild disorder of the election campaign. While his running-mate, Sir Samuel Hood, donned the mantle of the recently dead Admiral Nelson, and his supporters, many of them seamen, sang "Rule Britannia," Sheridan's procession to the hustings was preceded by "a posse of Hibernians from the purlieus of St Giles" armed with cudgels and shouting "Sheridan for ever." St. Giles had a large population of Irish labourers and was one of the areas of London in which the United Irishmen had been most active a decade before. In 1797, for instance, the United Irish leaders had prepared a large number of printed addresses for distribution there, including United Irish rules and signs. In 1799 the government estimated that there were between 15,000 and 40,000 United men in London. By the time of the 1806 election they had ceased to exist as an organised force, but there can be little doubt that at least some of those anonymous Irishmen who provided Sheridan's armed bodyguard were former United men. Their presence is a warning against seeing the Westminster election as a simple struggle of the lower orders against the higher. James Paull, the radical candidate, was a wealthy man who had made his money as a nabob in the East India Company. Many of his supporters were indeed artisans and tradesmen. But one of Sheridan's disadvantages was that much of his personal following—the Irish labourers from the slums—was even lower in the class hierarchy, so low, indeed, that they had no votes.

The notion that Sheridan's candidacy was favoured by the prostitutes of Covent Garden may in fact be based on more substantial evidence than the usual assumption of the times that linked all actors to whores. The famous madame Mother Butler is mentioned by a number of sources as a Sheridan partisan. During the election campaign, the young Tory MP Lord Palmerston (subsequently Prime Minister) asked, "What would Fox have said to have seen the man who sets up as his representative coaxing *Mother Butter* [sic] from the hustings at Covent Garden and publicly thanking all the *whores of both theatres* for their assistance and support."[19] A pamphlet published the following year alleged:

> Like his son Tom, Mr Sheridan has always been a man of gallantry, though his amours have never been recorded in Westminster Hall. We have, however, his own authority, repeatedly given from the hustings in Covent Garden, that he is the favourite of

> all the pretty women in Westminster. The only one he has thought fit to particularize is Dame Butler, the Queen of Covent Garden, at whose convenient mansion he has, we believe, passed many of his morning hours.[20]

William Earle, who knew Sheridan at this time, mentioned many years later in a description of Sheridan's supporters in Westminster, "poor old Mother Butler in the field beating up for recruits, and marching at the head of her battalion to the polls."[21]

From the first day of polling, Sheridan with 178 votes was trailing Paull with 327, and was just ahead of Hood with 161. Two days later the figures were 789 for Sheridan, 1,281 for Hood, and 1,516 for Paull. On 7 November, the fifth day of polling, Harriet Duncannon noted: "Sheridan will certainly be beat. I hear he looks very ill and is terribly out of spirits."[22] He remained outwardly confident, telling Lord Holland, "My Friends have taken a little Panic—I have not." But his apprehension was sharp enough to force him into what was to prove, in the longer term, a fatal mistake. He allowed his own support committee to coalesce with Hood's. This undoubtedly gained him votes—electors were allowed to vote for two candidates, so Hood's voters could also support Sheridan—but it also aligned him much more openly with the establishment. Hood's campaign, with its sailors in uniform singing "Rule Britannia," was crudely "patriotic," and some of his supporters had been attacking Paull as a dangerous democrat and teasing him about his humble origins as the son of a tailor. By allowing himself to be associated with it, Sheridan tarnished his own democratic credentials and allowed Cobbett to work up outrage amongst the tradesmen that they had been treated as "low and insignificant men." In one sense, regardless of the outcome of the vote, Cobbett had already ensured Sheridan's defeat by forcing him into a particular mould very effectively. For the first time in his political career, Sheridan had lost command of the terms in which he would be publicly viewed.

In the short term the alliance with Hood ensured victory for Sheridan. He passed Paull on the eleventh day, and at the end of polling took the second of the two seats. Hood had 5,478 votes, Sheridan 4,758, and Paull 4,481. But almost 80 percent of Sheridan's total was made up of split votes (cast for him and one of the other candidates), and in most cases the other vote was for Hood. He would not, in other words, have been elected under his own steam. The political world in which he had been so intimately at home was dying. What ought to have been the triumphant culmination of a career in politics was, instead, the beginning of its end. Just as he had secured the mantle of Fox it had begun to fall apart at the seams. And to make matters worse, Tom was heavily defeated in the contest at Stafford, where Sheridan's defection to Westminster after twenty-six years was greatly resented.

A month after the election Paull presented to the House of Commons a petition against Sheridan's return, which alleged that it had been accomplished through intimidation and bribery. There was widespread expectation that such a petition might be upheld. By the end of December Lord Palmerston was exulting, "Sheridan is they say what you call *in for it*; he has *put his foot in* it completely. People in London talk of the pillory and Newgate, but it seems certain he will be turned out of his seat and in that case his creditors will take care of the rest. I shall be sorry for it, as we shall lose some entertaining speeches in Parliament, otherwise I shall feel great pleasure that he at length gets his dessert."[23] Even Sheridan's old friend George Canning thought that the petition might succeed and that he would be ruined.

In Westminster Hall, though, Sheridan was on home ground, and he managed to have Paull's petition laughed off the stage. Instead of dealing with the evidence, to great comic effect he treated Paull's witnesses to the kind of forensic demolition he had used on Warren Hastings and Elijah Impey. He revelled in the deliberately bathetic effect created as he, the man who had brought the governor-general of India to heel, now turned his attention to mere mortals. With one of them, a former sailor called Weatherhead, he demonstrated to his audience that the man had deserted from a number of ships in turn, and then went through his statements in various navy documents:

> It is not more difficult to fix the station of this naval officer to a certain ship than to fix his birth to a certain place; he had the singular good fortune to be born at a number of different places; he was *first* at Newcastle, he was born at Morpeth, and after some other birth he was *brought forth* at London (*A loud laugh*). But there is another slight objection to the character of this witness; in the month of September, 1803, he petitioned to be examined for a lieutenancy, and to the recommendatory certificate of the differ-

> ent captains under whom he served, there was but one objection, namely, that they were all discovered to be *forgeries*.[24]

With this flourish, he announced that his "sense of delicacy" required him to withdraw from the House while the vote was taken. The petition was then rejected as "false and scandalous."

With his position as representative for Westminster apparently secured, Sheridan was able to lend his weight to the one important reform made by the Grenville administration: the abolition of the slave trade. Typically, he urged the necessity of going beyond a prohibition of the trade in human beings to an actual emancipation of those who were already slaves in the West Indies, and conjured up in vivid rhetorical images the reality that haunted the debates:

> It was not probable that because cargoes of human misery were no longer to be landed on their shores, that because their eyes were to be no longer glutted with the sight of human suffering, or their ears pierced with the cries of human distraction in any further importation of negroes, that the slave-drivers would soon forget their fixed habits of brutality, and learn to treat the unhappy wretches in their charge with clemency and compassion.[25]

He had no time, though, to pursue such ideals and to rebuild his radical reputation. A month after the petition was rejected, the government fell over King George III's implacable opposition to its proposals to extend to Britain the mild measures of relief for Catholics that had been introduced to Ireland in 1793. On 26 March 1807 the King ordered, without much evident regret, "the usual letters of dismissal" for Sheridan, and he moved out of his splendid official residence at Somerset House. Parliament was dissolved and Sheridan had to face another election in Westminster. The organisation which had almost managed to get Paull elected was still in place and further embittered by the rejection of Paull's petition. And this time Cobbett had a much more credible candidate to support—Sheridan's old ally of the 1790s, Sir Francis Burdett. Burdett and Sheridan had long appeared as partners in political caricatures, and they worked together in dangerous causes like Arthur O'Connor's trial and the inquiry into Cold Bath Fields prison. They fell out for obscure reasons around the turn of the century, but by 1802 Burdett seems to have been anxious to show his friendship for Sheridan. Without being asked, he offered a rectory in Huntingdonshire which was in his gift, to Sheridan's old friend and teacher at Harrow, Dr. Samuel Parr. As Parr wrote to Sheridan, Burdett had informed him that "a great additional motive" for the offer was "that I believe that I cannot do anything more pleasing to . . . Mr Fox, Mr Sheridan and Mr Knight; and I desire you, sir, to consider yourself as obliged to them only."[26]

On 18 August 1802 Burdett noted in a letter to Thomas Creevey that Sheridan had been to see him the previous day and is "grown quite loving again." Hecca had been on the hustings to support Burdett and was "much delighted and entertained at being hailed as Mrs Burdett."[27] In February 1804 Sheridan spoke in the House against attempts to challenge Burdett's election for Middlesex.

And even in November 1806, when he was unsuccessfully contesting Middlesex, Burdett used Sheridan's criticisms of Cold Bath Fields prison to defend his own: "It is but lately since that subject was revived upon the hustings at Westminster, by the Treasurer of the Navy, a man . . . who holds now a lucrative place under Government. That candidate dwelt upon it as a service he had rendered his country, in supporting the exertions I made to rectify those abuses, and yet now gentlemen come upon the hustings and insist that there were no abuses."[28]

Ominously, though, Burdett said in the same speech, "I have no objection to the Treasurer of the Navy sitting in Parliament; but as he is a member of the Government, a placeman, and a sinecure Placeman, I do not wish that he should be returned for Westminster." Even though their political principles were indistinguishable, and even though they had faced the same accusations of sedition over the previous twenty years, Burdett had thought it politic to distance himself from Sheridan. Now, as a candidate himself for Westminster, he was in open competition with him.

Sheridan seems to have considered supporting Burdett himself. *The Times* reported on 29 April that he was resigning from Westminster. "If B[urdett] stands," he wrote on 2 May, "most of my Troups will support him. And with all my heart for I will have nothing to do with the Popery Lord nor the ministerial Brewer."[29] These last two references were to Lord Cochrane, an anti-Catholic naval officer who was standing for Westminster as an independent, and John Elliot, a local brewer who was the Portland candidate. Sheridan's intentions seem to have been to swing behind Burdett, to work for Tom at Stafford, and himself take a safe seat at Ilchester, which was in the Prince's pocket. Only when Tom's renewed candidacy at Stafford ran into more trouble did he decide to contest Westminster himself in the hope that, if he won, he could hand Ilchester on to Tom.

Even then, he wanted to run not against Burdett but with him against Paull, Elliot, and Cochrane. On at least three occasions over the coming days, Tom Sheridan met with Burdett's committee asking for a coalition.[30] And while Sheridan launched bitter attacks on Cochrane from the hustings, alleging that his naval career had been powered by political corruption, he could hardly attack Burdett's principles without insulting his own. But Cobbett's was the decisive influence amongst the Westminster radicals, and his crusade against Sheridan was far too deeply rooted in personal and political animosity to allow for such an alliance. Without it, and without the support of the government, which was now headed by his old enemy the Duke of Portland, Sheridan had little chance. He justified his campaign to Lord Moira partly on the grounds that "I have put down the cry of 'No Property,' " and said he was "determined to go on, and if I am supported as I think I ought to be, I shall succeed." But he trailed both Burdett and Cochrane all the way through the polling, and finished on just 2,645 votes, compared to 5,135 for Burdett and 3,708 for Cochrane. His vote was, though, very clearly a radical one: all but 700 of those who supported him cast their votes either for him alone or for him and Burdett. This suggests that if he had been able to secure an alliance with Burdett, the two of them would have won seats.

As it was, he had followed Pitt and Fox, not quite to the grave, but to a kind of political death. He had the Ilchester seat to fall back on and to keep him in Parliament, but it was not the kind of seat he wanted to fill. As Cobbett put it, without much exaggeration, "This election is the beginning of a new era of parliamentary representation." For all that he had dreamed of such a new era, Sheridan would not be part of it. While he was fighting and losing the second Westminster election, a young aristocrat just out of his old school, Harrow, sat down and drew up a list of the books he had read, the great minds he had encountered in preparing himself for a public life. He arranged them under headings: literature, history, science, geography. Under "Eloquence," Lord Byron listed "Demosthenes, Cicero, Quintilian, Sheridan . . ."[31] Enrolled with the great orators of Greece and Rome, Sheridan already seemed, to a new generation, to belong with the legendary names of a more heroic era, with the resonant but now silent voices of the past.

Chapter 38

THE EXPERIENCE OF DEFEAT

Defeat was a new experience for Sheridan: ". . . the most unfortunate occurrence of my life. It was a real misfortune which I can never get over. It was my total ruin as a public man."[1] He could not, at first, accept that he had lost, and resorted to the same kind of allegations against his opponents that they had made against him after the election of 1806. He and Tom held a public meeting that resolved to raise money by subscription to fund a petition to Parliament against Lord Cochrane's election. He asserted that he and his friends could prove that Cochrane had resorted to bribery, and claimed that in one instance he had paid an elector two guineas for his vote. According to Cobbett, "Almost every person with whom one spoke upon the subject appeared to believe that Lord Cochrane would be ousted in consequence of the petition."[2] There were even "several meetings" held to consider nominations for a putative new election.

But, in fact, Sheridan had no evidence of bribery, or at least no witnesses were prepared to testify to it. When the time came for the petition to be heard, Peter Moore, the chairman of Sheridan's campaign, had to admit that "facts existed to warrant it, but no witnesses." Eventually the petition lapsed, when neither Sheridan nor any of his agents appeared before Parliament to support it. This allowed the gleeful Cobbett to allege that the whole thing was a swindle, and that the public subscription had been "a trick whereby to get money to be pocketed" by the Sheridans, Moore, and Sheridan's agent, John Frost.

Though he was still in Parliament, Sheridan's prestige was greatly diminished. Ilchester, which he now represented, was regarded as little better than a pocket borough, and its electors had been described as "poor and corrupt, without honour, morals, or attachment to any man or party."[3] He had no power except his influence over the Prince, who, now that Fox was dead, was free to drift away from the vaguely radical principles he had once espoused. The opposition was incoherent, and had little hope of making trouble for the government, even if it knew what it wanted to be troublesome about. Although he had been in the House during the preceding days, Sheridan "did not take the oaths nor attend" the vote on the King's address to the new Parliament.[4] The government had a majority so large as to be almost without precedent.

Misfortune seemed to favour Sheridan. In June he was thrown out of his coach in an accident and injured his knee when his leg was caught between the spokes of a wheel.[5] The theatre offered no consolation. The trustees of Drury Lane were becoming increasingly impatient with Sheridan's failure to meet their financial demands. Since the previous July they had been trying to get him to hand over the income from licenses to sell fruit in the theatre and from rents of adjoining houses, and had been fobbed off by Sheridan's solicitor, Henry Burgess. Their patience snapped a fortnight after the election in mid-June, however, when Burgess informed them that "he has applied the rents received from the houses to another purpose by the express direction of Mr Sheridan." They wrote in exasperated tones demanding that Sheridan give them a straight answer about whether or not he was going to hand over the money.[6]

Throughout 1807 and 1808 the pressure was unrelenting. Having been fobbed off for a while, the trustees again reached a point of exasperation in October 1808. They wrote to Sheridan accusing him of breaking the agreement with the new renters by hiring actors for the new season at a rate "exceeding that of the last in expense" without their approval, and of failing to hold regular board meetings. They warned that Sheridan's behaviour would be examined at a meeting of the new renters on 21 November, and that "we shall naturally be called upon at that time or perhaps before by the committee to state how far you have performed the engagement we have mentioned . . . on the faith of which they discontinued their application to the Lord Chancellor."[7]

There was, too, a further source of humiliation. In July 1807 his son Tom, who had failed again in his bid to take his father's old seat in Stafford, was the defendant in an action for criminal conversation brought by Peter Campbell of Edinburgh over an incident that had taken place a year and a half before Tom's marriage to Caroline Callander. Tom had fallen in with the Campbells, a well-to-do couple with large possessions in the West Indies, when he arrived in Edinburgh in 1803 as aide-de-camp to Lord Moira, then commander-in-chief of the forces in Scotland. Though they had been married for thirteen years at that time, and had three children, Mrs. Campbell was still only twenty-nine. According to her husband, she had become flighty while he was away in the West Indies, though she continued to express her absolute devotion to him.

Sued for criminal conversation with Mrs. Campbell, Tom did not defend the action, but was called before the sheriff's court for the assessment of damages. The hearing was a disaster for him, exposing him not just to moral opprobrium and financial ruin but, perhaps more seriously for his political career, to ridicule. The most damaging witness, the housekeeper Mary Brotherton, described how Tom had arrived at their house at eight o'clock one night in February 1804, while Peter Campbell was in London. A while later he pretended to leave and Mrs. Campbell went to bed, having asked for "clean night linen." Sometime later she saw Tom, still in his military uniform, enter the bedroom. In the morning when she confronted Tom on the landing, he tried to pretend that he had just arrived and asked if her mistress was at home. She warned him that " 'if you do not quit the house immediately, or if you return again before Mr Campbell comes home, I'll shoot you.' Upon which the defendant flew down the stairs, and got out of the house."[8]

For Sheridan's enemies, the image of his son in military uniform fleeing from a housekeeper who had threatened to shoot him was irresistible. A report of the trial published in London was accompanied with a print showing Tom confronted by a wizened old nurse in a night cap brandishing a brass candle-stick, and in this exaggerated version the story seemed not just to illustrate the debauchery of the Sheridans but to satirise their weakness as a bulwark against French invasion.

The report of the trial was prefaced with a scurrilous potted biography of Sheridan himself, noting, for instance, that in *The School for Scandal* "he drew from himself both the profligacy of *Charles* and the hypocrisy of *Joseph*," and linking Tom's sexual disgrace with his father's loose morals. Tom's counsel in the Campbell case was forced to plead poverty, claiming that although his client was indeed the son of Richard Brinsley Sheridan "and that he inherited some portion of his talents, his wit, and his genius . . . that was all his inheritance." In spite of his plea that excessive damages would "be the means of shutting the defendant in a prison for the remainder of his days," Peter Campbell was awarded £1,500.

Already in debt from the second Westminster election, and with the trustees of the theatre becoming ever more restive about his evasion of his financial commitments to them, Sheridan now had to try to raise this huge sum to keep his beloved son out of jail. It seems that he had to resort to borrowing from his employees at Drury Lane. The actor Richard Wroughton told Thomas Moore in 1818 that "he and other actors had subscribed a hundred pounds each to enable Sheridan to pay Tom's damages in the crim. con. case with Mrs Campbell—they were paid some back, but I believe very little."[9]

Under all this pressure, Sheridan's mind seems to have snapped again. Earlier in the year he had been trying to make himself pleasant to Harriet and her family, hoping that her refusal to forgive him for the anonymous letters could be worn down. In January a wary Caroline Lamb reported to her, "Mr Sheridan called on me yesterday, was very pleasant and seemed to have no mysterious intents."[10] One evening, when she went to visit Caroline at Melbourne House, Harriet herself was frightened by a "ruffian-like-looking" man at the entrance who turned out to be Sheridan. He followed her up to William and Caroline Lamb's apartments on the middle floor and stayed all evening, displaying such charm that, in spite of herself, she could not help laughing.

On 28 August, though, in the midst of tending to Caroline, who was about to give birth, Harriet received an urgent summons from Hecca, begging her to come instantly. At midnight she drove to Sheridan's house and found him drunk and distracted. He began to implore her forgiveness, calling himself a wretch and saying, in front of Hecca, that he had loved her more than anyone he had ever met. When Hecca objected, he told her, "My dear Hecca, you know I love you more than anyone else." "Except *her*," she interjected; to which he responded, "Don't talk nonsense." Eventually at three o'clock in the morning, Harriet escaped, but only after having Sheridan locked into his room.

Shortly afterwards, Sheridan began to pester Harriet for an invitation to the christening of Caroline's baby. She replied that all the invitations were being issued by Lady Melbourne, Caroline's formidable mother-in-law. She, in turn, told Sheridan that all the guests would be relatives. On the evening of the christening party, however, the assembled company were awaiting the arrival of the Prince of Wales, who was to be the child's godfather. When the double doors were thrown open, Sheridan entered and announced the Prince, and himself as the gentleman attending him.

After supper they sat down to play a game in which each player was to write a verse and hand it to the guest beside them for a reply, also to be in verse. Sheridan, who had placed himself beside Harriet, passed her the following lines on the baby:

> Grant heaven, sweet Babe, thou mayest inherit
> What Heaven only can impart,
> Thy Father's manly sense and spirit,
> Thy Mother's grace and gentle heart,
> And when to manhood's hopes and duties grown,
> Be thou a prop to thy great Sponsor's throne.

Harriet's reply, outwardly bland, had a hidden barb:

> May he who wrote ye verse impart
> To the sweet baby whom he blesses
> As shrewd a head, a better heart,
> And talents he alone possesses.

Sheridan, who had to read out Harriet's verses, gave himself a few seconds to think by pretending to find the writing indistinct. He then read the last two lines in an altered, and from his own point of view, more flattering form:

> A wiser head, as pure a heart,
> And greater wealth than he possesses.

In November he pursued Harriet to the Lambs' Brocket Hall, imposed himself as a guest on them, and pestered Harriet by trailing her from room to room. In the nursery he went down on his knees to her and she, in what was surely a reference to Tom's sexual embarrassments, asked him whether he had a grandchild as pretty as hers. He flew into a terrifying rage and, muttering darkly about Leveson Gower, stormed out of the room. Later, as she was leaving, he offered to hand her into her carriage. In doing so, he crushed her hand so strongly that it became bruised and swollen, and "so *cut* where the ring goes" that she had to discontinue wearing it. Even so, her exasperation was not without a tinge of pride. "Confess," she wrote to Leveson Gower, "that the rarity of this makes it worth telling—people don't usually maim grandmothers for the sake of their *beaux yeux*. One may boast a little when it happens to one."[11]

At the same time, the leadership of the opposition became vacant with the death of Grey's father and the son's elevation to the House of Lords. Sheridan heard the news at Devonshire House. Both Harriet Duncannon and Elizabeth Foster "thought we perceived a mixture of satisfaction in his regrets" at his rival's bereavement. He remained fiercely angry with Grey, whom he accused of having prevented Tom from winning the Stafford seat,[12] but his behaviour had become so notorious, and his position so marginal, that he had no hope of taking Grey's place. As Harriet noted, "It has always been his ambition to lead the Op[position], and with talents and Eloquence to entitle him to any thing had he chose it, he has so degraded a mind and character that there is scarce any one who has sunk so low as to look up to Sheridan as his chief."[13] In any case, Grenville, who still controlled the most important faction of the opposition, placed an absolute veto on either Sheridan or Whitbread. He considered neither of sufficiently high social standing to take over from Grey.

Sheridan's drinking was now beginning to affect his performances in Parliament. On 21 January 1808, in the debate on the King's address, Sheridan made what Prime Minister Spencer Perceval described to the King as a "very violent" speech in the early hours of the morning; according to reports by Wellesley and Grey, he was drunk. Grey, however, wrote to his wife that, in spite of his intoxication, Sheridan's speech had "amongst much absurdity . . . some good things and . . . seems in general to be praised."[14] On 12 April, when he attacked Windham with "considerable vehemence and warmth," he was suspected of being under the influence. And on 16 June, Whitbread wrote to Grey: "You will see by the papers that Sheridan, in concert with Canning, and against the wishes of all his friends, has been making a Motion about Spain. He did all he could to create a cry for himself as distinguished from all of us, but he was so exceedingly drunk he could hardly articulate. A more disgraceful exhibition was seldom if ever witnessed, but it served to make mischief."[15] Even at his worst, making mischief was still his greatest talent.

Chapter 39

THE GREAT SHERIDAN

Just after Sheridan's defeat in the second Westminster election, he and his supporters held a public meeting to raise funds for their unsuccessful appeal against the outcome. It was ostensibly a meeting of an old establishment faction beaten by the rise of a new breed of nineteenth-century urban radicals. To later historians, if it was noticed at all, it was merely as the last squeal of a dying, if once magnificent, animal. Yet the presence in that gathering of two men in particular suggests that even now, as a fifty-six-year-old politician on the wrong side of the historic watershed, Sheridan was regarded as much more than a mere representative of an old regime.

In an acerbic report, William Cobbett noted that "at this meeting, the celebrated Mr John Frost was a leading man, and that his health was given as a toast, by the elder Sheridan at one time, and by the celebrated Peter Moore at another time . . ."[1] In spite of Cobbett's sarcasm, John Frost really was a celebrated man. In December 1792, while Louis XVI was on trial for his life, he and Joel Barlow had been the delegates of the London Corresponding Society to Paris, and in that capacity they had addressed the National Convention. They made no bones about their hope for an English revolution: "After the example given by France, Revolutions will become easy: Reason is about to make a rapid progress and it would not be extraordinary if, in a much less space of time than can be imagined, the French should send addresses of congratulation to a National Convention of England."[2]

Revolutions did not become easy, of course, and for John Frost, lawyer, follower of Tom Paine, and founder member of the London Corresponding Society, they had come especially hard. Frost was sentenced to the pillory and eighteen months' imprisonment in 1793 for allegedly saying, "I am for equality . . . Why, no kings!" in a Marylebone coffee house. While he was imprisoned, Sheridan had cited his case in Parliament as a trumped-up fabrication by the government, part of its "system of delusion."[3] He did so even though he was perfectly aware of Frost's address to the National Convention. Mocking the government's justification of war by condemnation of the French republican system, he asked "whether, if the French do not again receive Mr Frost with an address, and think proper to have another king, that we shall then be in a state wherein we shall have nothing to fear?"[4]

On his release from Newgate in December 1793, Frost was drawn through the streets by a crowd that stopped at Carlton House to jeer the Prince of Wales, a fact that makes his presence at Sheridan's meeting as the toast of his friends all the more remarkable.[5] Unlike some of the other persecuted radicals of the 1790s, Frost remained politically active after his release, and supported Sir Francis Burdett in the Middlesex election of 1802. But he then supported Sheridan in the Westminster elections, and acted as his agent in 1807. Nor was he just a political ally, for Frost also acted for Sheridan in the byzantine financial affairs of Drury Lane, and held some of its shares on Sheridan's behalf. Around this time Frost seems to have been arrested for debts he incurred on Sheridan's behalf; Sheridan sent him money during another short stay in Newgate. A letter written in 1839 by Frost as an old man to Sheridan's grandson, Richard Brinsley Sheridan of Frampton, makes it clear that he was on very intimate terms with both his grandfather and father: "It was a fanciful promise of your grandfather that we should sink or swim together. I smiled at the conceit and often told him he would sink me, while he swam."[6] According to Frost, he had received a letter from the tutor to Sheridan's son Charles at Richmond, informing him that he and the boy were "without food to eat, or a candle to sit by," and had gone there with £100 to rescue them. He also bought clothes for Charles, who was, "as his father observed, ragged as a clot," and redeemed Hecca's sheets and table linen from a pawn shop.

Hecca once described Frost as "the only honest and true friend [Sheridan] had about him, from whom she should know the truth of his affairs."[7] In 1814, Sheridan referred to "Citizen Frost," as he sometimes called him, as "my old and constantly respected Friend John Frost," adding that "no one is better informed with respect to the unjust political oppression he has suffer'd than myself."[8] When Sheridan himself was imprisoned for debt, it was Frost who stayed with him, organised enough money to secure his release, and walked him home to Savile Row. Why, if Sheridan was merely a political dinosaur, would such a man be so intimate a supporter?

Also at the meeting after the Westminster election was another man who had known the dubious pleasures of the pillory, this time more recently: Peter Finnerty, former editor of the United Irish newspaper the *Press*, published by the movement in Dublin in 1797, after its original organ, the *Northern Star*, had been suppressed. Owned by Sheridan's friend Arthur O'Connor, the paper had been explicitly pro-French and had cultivated contacts with the London Corresponding Society. It was itself suppressed after O'Connor's arrest in Margate.

In October 1797 Finnerty had published in the *Press* an anonymous letter attacking the Lord Lieutenant, Earl Camden, over the execution of the young Presbyterian William Orr and describing Orr's trial as "one of the most sanguinary and savage acts that have disgraced the laws." Finnerty was charged with seditious libel and held for two months, during which he experienced the "severest rigours of a jail." He was then sentenced to the pillory in Green Street in Dublin. Arthur O'Connor and an "immense concourse of people" stood with him. On his release, he announced, "I can suffer anything provided it promotes the liberty of my country."[9]

Finnerty had fled to London after the rising in 1798 and joined the United Irish network there. He was involved on the fringes of Colonel Despard's conspiracy in 1802, fled back to Dublin at the news of the latter's arrest, and took part in the preparations for Robert Emmet's attempted revolt in 1803, before making his way back to London.[10] He then became deeply involved with Sheridan. He went with Sheridan's friends Burgess and Major Downs to Stafford at the end of October 1806, to help organise Tom's campaign, and on 15 November wrote a letter explaining Sheridan's position to the *Courier*, a paper with deep connections to the United Irishmen and the London Corresponding Society.[11] During the Westminster campaign, Paull wrote to Finnerty: "I am not opposing Mr Sheridan." Finnerty not only passed the letter on to Sheridan but had it published in the *Courier*.

It should not be supposed that by the time of this very close and confidential association with Sheridan, Finnerty had given up the radicalism of 1803. Finnerty was sentenced to eighteen months' imprisonment in February 1811 for his scathing reports in the *Morning Chronicle* on a disastrous British military expedition to Walcheren in the Low Countries. One of Percy Bysshe Shelley's first poems was published the following month with the object of raising money to "maintain in Prison Mr Peter Finnerty." The fact was that even at this late stage of his life, Sheridan had the most intimate associations with a known revolutionary.

It is not unreasonable to surmise that Finnerty, with his active links with the remnants of Irish radicalism, was one of the channels through which Sheridan, at this time, developed two very striking connections. The first was with Anne Devlin. The daughter and sister of prominent United Irishmen, she had played an important part in Robert Emmet's attempted revolution by setting up as a base a farm in Rathfarnham, outside Dublin, and by acting as his housekeeper. She managed to avoid execution, but was imprisoned and tortured. In 1806, when she was finally released from prison after three years of brutal mistreatment, Sheridan tried to contact her. As she later recalled:

> Brinsley Sheridan Esq. sent a gentleman to know if I would give him a detail of my imprisonment and sufferings. He said they should be laid before the world. I then supposed it was a book he was going to write and I had no wish to make my name more public, and declined to grant his request. He came again, but my sufferings were too recent and galling, and I could not bear to go over them. The gentleman expressed his surprise and astonishment at my unwillingness. He took some notes from my father.
>
> I had no great faith then in Members of Parliament and did not know the worth of Mr Sheridan's character. Had I been aware of it, and known that it was on a parliamentary investigation, it would be far from me to refuse the information that was sought.
>
> But the gentleman certainly did not make us comprehend the nature of his message. Nor did we rightly understand it for several months afterwards when a gentleman who had been a state prisoner told and explained it to me. I then told him I would give him the information or to any person he would send to me. The

> matter died away, and I am sorry for the sake of my country, that the opportunity was lost.[12]

Finnerty seems by far the most likely "gentleman who had been a state prisoner" to be trusted as a channel of communication between Sheridan and a survivor of Emmet's rebellion. In Parliament in this period, Sheridan described himself as receiving information on Ireland "from both public and private sources."[13] At least some of those were people who were or had been on the wrong side of the treason laws.

Such contacts are all the more remarkable when it is remembered that at this very time Sheridan was in government as treasurer of the navy and was, moreover, still actively pursuing his scheme for getting into the Irish government with the Prince of Wales. In the negotiations for the formation of that administration, Sheridan, in March 1806, had considered a position for his family in Ireland more as a right than a favour. He told the Duke of Bedford, then Lord Lieutenant of Ireland:

> I feel it would be a baseness in me not to assert my confidence that no mark of *Irish* favour conferred on *me* or any of my *Family* would be unpopular in *Ireland* . . . I feel it no boast or conceit to say, adverting to the . . . manifest disposition of the Irish to look now to the Prince, that any person honoured with his confidence and understanding his purposes on this great subject, and being himself an Irishman, is not guilty of great Presumption in wishing to connect himself more manifestly with Ireland . . .[14]

That connection, moreover, was pursued even while he was in the throes of defeat in the second Westminster election. In 1807 the MP for Wexford, John Colclough, approached Sheridan to ask him to stand in the general election as his running mate. Wexford had been the crucible of the 1798 rising, and Colclough was a close relative and namesake of one of the executed rebel leaders. According to another of Colclough's relatives, the barrister Jonah Barrington, "Mr Colclough was determined to put the pride, spirit, and patriotism of the county to proof, and therefore proposed Mr Richard Brinsley Sheridan as joint candidate with himself, declaring that he was authorised by the independent freeholders of the county to say that they should feel the greatest gratification in being represented by so distinguished an ornament to the name of Irishman."[15]

At the time of the Wexford election, Sheridan was campaigning against the Irish Insurrection Bill, which authorised further measures of repression against Ireland's rural secret societies—Whiteboys, Rightboys, Hearts of Steel, Threshers. Sheridan believed that all these disturbances were an understandable reaction against the imposition of tithes on the Catholic peasantry to pay for the upkeep of the established Protestant church. In August 1807, when Sheridan visited the box at the opera occupied by Harriet Duncannon (now elevated as Lady Bessborough), he told her that "there were but two honest men in England, himself and Lord B[essborough]. I did not understand at first but he means for being the only two of our friends against the Irish Insurrection Bill. Lord B[essborough] protested and I believe will be alone [in the House of Lords]."[16]

In opposing the bill in the Commons Sheridan made his longest and one of his most forceful speeches on Ireland, which he now referred to throughout as "my country."[17] His object was, he said, "to serve the cause of justice and my country." He called for an investigation into the causes of unrest in Ireland and accused Parliament of "legislating for Ireland in the dark." And he put into a historical perspective the existence of a "French party" in Ireland. The existence of such a party could not, he insisted, be used "as a justification for the oppressive laws it was quoted to support. For what policy could be more mischievous and inhuman than a perseverance in the same persecuting measures which originally created that party?" In any case:

> When was it that such a party did not exist in that country? Since the days of Elizabeth, from the very commencement of those foul and tyrannous measures which originated in national jealousy, political prejudice, or religious dissension, but particularly the latter, which drove Catholics of high spirit from their native country, numbers of such exiles found an asylum in France, and hence a correspondence between them and their relations in Ireland, which naturally led to the creation of a French party in Ireland and an Irish party in France.

On his mind, no doubt, were his own Jacobite ancestors, who had fled to France with the Old Pretender. And it was this long view of

Irish history that he was most anxious to impress on his listeners. He attacked the ministers for complaining about Irish disaffection without considering its causes:

> When they express their surprise that the Irish are not contented, while, according to their observation, that people have so much reason to be happy; they betray a total ignorance of their actual circumstances. The fact is, that the tyranny practised upon the Irish has been throughout unremitting. There has been no change but in the manner of inflicting it. They have had nothing but variety in oppression extending to all ranks and degrees of a certain description of the people [i.e., Catholics]. If you would know what this varied oppression consisted in, I would refer you to the penal statutes you have repealed, and to some of those which still exist. There you will see the high and the low equally subjected to the lash of persecution; and still some effect to be astonished at the discontents of the Irish.

He illustrated the folly of such astonishment with the parable of an Irish drummer called on to deliver a lashing to a miscreant soldier:

> When the boy struck high, the poor soldier complained: "Lower, bless you," with which the boy complied. But soon after the soldier exclaimed: "Higher, if you please." But again he called out "A little lower," upon which the accomodating boy addressed him—"Now, upon my conscience, I see you are a discontented man; for strike where I may, there's no pleasing you." Now your complaint of the discontents of the Irish appears to me quite as rational, while you continue to strike, only altering the place of attack.

Sheridan had been reading "several valuable books and pamphlets" on the condition of the Irish tenant farmers, and it was to their plight that he addressed most of his concern. With remarkable prescience, he attacked the previous administration's proposals for the emancipation of well-to-do Catholics while leaving the mass of the Catholic tenantry disenfranchised:

> I think they began at the wrong end. They should have commenced the measure of redress in Ireland at the cottage, instead of at the park and the mansion. To have gone first to the higher

> orders of the Catholics; to have sought to make them judges and peers and commoners; I do not know that such a proceeding, had it taken place, would not rather have served to aggravate discontent, as it might have been construed into a design to divide the interests of the Catholics. Sure I am, that with a view to serve or to conciliate the Catholic population, I mean the poor, the peasantry, its effect would be nothing; indeed it would be quite a mockery. It would be like dressing or decorating the top masts of a ship when there were ten feet [of] water in the hold, or putting a laced hat on a man who had not a shoe to his foot. The place to set out to in Ireland for the relief of the people is the cottage.

He also confronted the growing tendency of defenders of the Ascendancy in Ireland to blame the poor for their own misery:

> I have always been shocked at the assertion that the Irish peasantry might be comfortable if they chose to be industrious; and that it is idle to attempt any improvement of their condition. It is abominable to hear blame laid on providence instead of laying it on man. Can any set of men, I would ask, be found who manifest so much of the qualities of which those cruel calumniators would deprive them as the Irish peasantry? But they are only calumniated by those men who would degrade them below the level of the human creation, in order to palliate their own inhumanity towards them. We are told in England that the unhappy Africans were insensible to the ordinary feelings of humanity, in order to render us indifferent to their sufferings, and to the custom of the slave-trade. On similar motives the character of the Irish peasantry is so foully misrepresented by some men in this country and in Ireland also.

In answer to those charges, he revealed a keen knowledge of the lives of Irish labourers in London:

> Can any man exhibit more of enterprise than those peasants, in coming to this country in search of employment, or more of affection for country and family, in returning home with the pittance they earn here? Is it not manifest to every one of you, that the charge of indisposition to industry cannot apply to those poor men, who, in fact, do all the hard work of this metropolis?

In pursuit of this much more explicit concern for the Irish poor, Sheridan accepted the offer to stand for Wexford. He and Colclough were opposed by two Tories, William Congreve Alcock of Wilton Castle and Abel Ram. Sheridan and Colclough, whose families were converts from Catholicism, had the support of the "Catholics and liberal Protestants," while their opponents represented the "Ascendancy party," determined to regain a seat lost to Colclough the previous year.

Sheridan's candidacy stirred the Catholic peasantry into fervour, and encouraged them to defy their landlords even though the voting was by open ballot and those who did so would be known. Jonah Barrington recalled:

> The flame of patriotism had caught the mass of the population; tenants no longer obeyed the dictates of their absent landlords nor the menaces of tyrannic agents; no man could count on the ties of his former vassals. The hustings was thronged with crowds of tenantry, constitutionally breaking away from their shackles, and voting according to their principles of free agency for Sheridan—a man known to them only by the celebrity of his talents.

There was, wrote Barrington, no doubt at all but that Sheridan, even without setting foot there, was going to be elected as MP for the most famously rebellious county in Ireland.

Problems arose, however, when many of the freeholding tenants on the estate of a Mrs. Cholmondeley, whose votes had been promised to Alcock, began to indicate openly that they would not take direction from their landlord. They declared that "at every risk they would support Colclough and 'the great Sheridan.'" Alcock challenged Colclough to "hand over the votes," an argument led to a challenge, and on the following day, the last of the poll, a duel took place between the two in the countryside outside Wexford town.

Hundreds of people went to witness the event. Both men were near-sighted, and there was argument over Alcock's insistence on wearing glasses, which Alcock's side won. Silence and immobility descended on the crowd. Alcock fired first and his shot went straight through Colclough's heart. He "spoke not, but turning on one side, his heart's blood gushed forth, his limbs quivered, he groaned and expired." His peasant supporters set up a great death yell, "so savage and continuous, so like the tone of *revenge*, that it would have appalled any stranger to the customs of the country." They collected the body on a plank, and paraded it through the streets of Wexford.

The polling, however, went ahead and, with Sheridan's and Colclough's supporters in disarray, Alcock was elected.[18] Even in the midst of all this chaos, however, Sheridan was less than 150 votes behind Alcock—polling 729 votes to the latter's 875. Alcock was charged with murder, but at his trial in March 1808 the judge, Cusack Smith, a confirmed Tory, ensured that he was acquitted. "Judge," urged Barrington, who acted as special counsel for the prosecution, "of Sheridan's feelings on receiving this intelligence."

What should have been a heroic drama turned into a gothic tragedy. Alcock, haunted by horror and remorse, went mad and sank into "irrevocable imbecility," to end his days in a strait-jacket. His sister, who had been a close friend of Colclough's, was deeply affected by his and her brother's deaths, and herself fell into insanity. Yet again, Sheridan's hopes of helping to lead his country towards a rational and enlightened future collapsed in blood and madness.

He retained his connections with Wexford after the disastrous election of 1807, even so, and in 1812 presented in Parliament a petition from the county looking for Catholic emancipation.[19] In 1805, when the Catholic Association in Ireland sent a petition to London asking for emancipation, Tom had met its delegates a number of times with his father, and after 1807 he, too, was approached about the possibility of standing for Wexford. Because of his frail health, however, nothing came of these approaches.

It needs to be remembered that Sheridan's views on Ireland were not the mere detached thoughts of an expatriate but a declaration of intent by a man who still hoped to be in a position to implement his ideas. Through all this time Sheridan watched for an opportunity to get himself appointed to the Irish government and into a position to work towards building a coalition of groups united on the Catholic question and on Ireland. In late 1810, when King George's illness entered its terminal phase and a new regency was in preparation, he was hoping to be appointed as Chief Secretary for Ireland in a ministry headed by Grey and Grenville. He even persuaded the Prince to ask both of them to give him the job. The request was, however, "peremptorily rejected by Grenville." Grey, though declaring himself willing to allow Sheridan "a place, however high, with large emoluments," said that sending Sheridan to Ireland would be like "sending a man with a lighted torch into a magazine of gunpowder."[20]

Grey at least understood that his deeply held views and continuing connections with veteran revolutionaries meant that Sheridan could still have had an explosive impact on Ireland. Far from being a spent force, he was articulating virtually all the issues that would dominate Irish politics throughout the nineteenth century. The imposition of tithes for the upkeep of the Church of Ireland on the Catholic and Presbyterian peasantry would remain as a major source of unrest for decades. The notion that the Catholic peasantry could be an independent political force would be given substance by Daniel O'Connell after Sheridan's death. The idea of forming a distinctive Irish party at Westminster would be made a reality by Isaac Butt and Charles Stewart Parnell. The belief that real reform in Ireland would have to start in the cottage rather than the manor, with the concerns of the ordinary tenantry, would animate the great movement for land reform led by Michael Davitt. And the dream that he embodied of an Irish politics beyond the sectarian divide between Protestants and Catholics would remain just about alive in the late twentieth century. If in England Sheridan belonged to the past, in Ireland he was very much a man of the future.

Chapter 40

THE BURNING DOME

Approaching midnight on 24 February 1809, George Canning was in the middle of a commanding speech on the war in Spain when, as Prime Minister Spencer Perceval later informed the King, "an event occurred in the midst of his speech which occasioned considerable confusion in the House." If the excitement of the contemporary theatre owed much to the fact that the candles remained lit, so did its danger. When the new Drury Lane was opened in 1794 an epilogue written by James Boaden had boasted that

> The very ravages of fire we scout
> For we have wherewithal to put it out.

According to William Smyth, Sheridan had once been present when the scenery caught fire and, after the blaze was extinguished, was asked by one of the actors if he should tell the audience what had happened. In response, Sheridan told him, "You fool, don't mention the word 'fire'; run and tell them that we have water enough to drown them all, and make a face."[1]

On this occasion in 1809, though, neither water nor grimaces could outface the blaze, and it took hold of the whole theatre. The treasurers managed to save the iron chest which contained the valuable patent, but little else survived. In less than a quarter of an hour after flames were noticed, a column of fire extended 450 feet across the entire façade. To onlookers, there was something almost majestic about the whole spectacle, as if it were itself the theatre's most awesome show—an impression which was heightened when the statue of Apollo which crowned the façade toppled gracefully into the flames.

The fire was so strong that an "immense blaze of light from the conflagration shone in at the windows of the House, as strongly as if it had been in the Speaker's garden." Cries of "Fire! Fire!" began to interrupt Canning's speech and, according to Hansard, Sheridan "in a low voice stated across the table that the Drury Lane Theatre was on fire." When it was suggested that Parliament should be adjourned, Sheridan declined the offer, saying that "whatever might be the extent of the individual calamity, I do not consider it of a nature worthy to interrupt our proceedings." Many members nevertheless went to look, "and a most tremendous and splendid sight it was, illuminating as it did the river, the bridge, Lambeth Palace, and all the surrounding buildings."[2] The light was so bright that it was said that people in Fulham could read the time on their watches in the open air at midnight. Lord Byron tried to capture the sensation:

> As flashing far the new Volcano shone
> And swept the skies with lightnings not their own
> While thousands thronged around the burning dome.

George Tierney wrote next day that Sheridan "stayed in the House of Commons the greater part of the time while the fire was burning, and appeared to me to be in a sort of stupid despair."[3] And by the time he had seen the utter devastation of the theatre for himself, Sheridan had adopted an attitude of stoic resignation. He sat at his favourite Piazza Coffee House and watched the building burn. When someone remarked on his composure he reportedly joked, "A man may surely take a glass of wine by his own fireside."[4]

He wrote to Hecca from the site with the news of "a great worldly calamity—as certainly the world must esteem it but as I am not greatly moved by it, and owing I am sure to high and good Principles, I mean you no ill compliment in trusting that you will bear it as I do—Drury-lane-Theatre lies in burning ashes on the Ground." He had been worried by Hecca's ill-health and he assured her, "Had I felt this blow as many would have done, so may God judge my heart if every trace of regret would not have been driven from my mind by the real Pain which your account of yourself has since given me. Only *you* be well and I will yet surmount everything but without you there is nothing I wish to struggle for."[5]

According to George Tierney, just £40,000 of the losses of £300,000 was insured. Just as seriously for Sheridan, who depended on the theatre for his day-to-day spending, there would be no cash coming in for many months. He was so short of money that he had some workmen search the debris and, when they found the remains of a peal of bells that had been used in the theatre, sold them for £90.[6] Lord Moira wrote on 17 March that the Prince had given Tom Sheridan £1,000 to relieve him of the immediate difficulties caused by the burning of the theatre.

The day after the fire Sheridan told the Drury Lane company that they must stick together and protect the most vulnerable of the ordinary workers in the theatre:

> I am aware that many of the principal performers may get profitable engagements at the different provincial theatres, but what then would become of the inferior ones, some of whom have large families? Heaven forbid that they should be deserted!—No: I most earnestly recommend and entreat, that every individual belonging to the concern should be taken care of. Let us make a long pull, a strong pull, and a pull all together; above all, make the general good our sole consideration. Elect yourselves into a committee; but keep in your remembrance even the poor sweepers of the stage, who, with their children, must starve, if not protected by our fostering care.[7]

His relative calm may have reflected a sense of relief that with the destruction of what had been a disastrously expensive and unworkable building, there was at least a chance to extricate himself from the impossible financial complications that had tormented him. Realising that no one would invest in a new theatre under his control, he persuaded his old Foxite ally and sometime adversary Samuel Whitbread, a relative of Hecca's, to take charge of consolidating the debts, raising money, and organising the construction of a new theatre, which was accomplished with remarkable efficiency: the building was completed in October 1811. He also successfully fought off an attempt to create a third theatre patent for London, which would have lowered the value of his remaining asset—the patent itself. In doing so he made ruthless use of his political position—the issue was decided by the Privy Council, of which he was a member.

It was clear, however, that neither he nor Tom could have any further role in the management of the theatre. Whitbread raised £400,000 but, as he wrote to Tom of his attempts to attract investors, "the Question asked before any Man or Woman will put down their Names is this 'Has Mr Sheridan anything to do with it?' A direct Negative suffices . . ."[8] Sheridan's own attitude to this prohibition was utterly ambiguous. On the one hand, he declared that he longed "to be fairly and honourably freed from all connection with this to me disagreeable property."[9] But on the other, he was highly insulted when Whitbread suggested that he had "no business to interfere" in the design and construction of the new theatre. He protested that even though he did not own the new building, he would be blamed if it turned out badly and that "the reproaches of disappointment thro' the great body of the subscribers would be directed against me and me alone."[10]

While logic suggested that he should simply walk away, his sensitivity to any reflection on his honour was still so great that he could not bring himself to do so. And the failure of the new committee even to consult a man who was, after all, the greatest dramatist of his time, was a blow to his pride. Resignation was one thing, exclusion quite another, and he became increasingly bitter about the severing of his family's connections with the theatre that he, his father, and his son had helped to run since the 1770s. He refused to accept the offer of the use of a box at the new theatre and eventually refused even to set foot in it when Tom's melodrama *The Russian* was playing there in 1813, telling the manager, "You know I do not enter your damned theatre."[11]

To the new management, he was already a great figure of the past. In August 1812, on the completion of the new Drury Lane, the management committee invited poets to submit an address for the opening. When none of those submitted came up to scratch, Byron was approached. He laboured over an appropriate tribute to Sheridan, deliberately working in a reference to Sheridan's *Monody on Garrick*, placing himself, by implication, in the position that Sheridan had occupied when he wrote it. Already Sheridan's death was being imagined:

Far be that hour that vainly asks in turn
Such verse for him as crown'd his o'er Garrick's urn.

Sheridan was still alive, however, and, moreover, had a financial interest in the success of the new theatre: he had agreed to defer the payment of what was owed to him for the patent until the theatre was open. Sheridan's interest in the patent was sold for £40,000, of which £24,000 was for his half-share, £12,000 for Tom's quarter-share, and £4,000 for the fruit shops. Although he had to pay the Linley family and some other claimants out of his share of the proceeds, he was confident that there would be enough left over to allow him to be "discharged from a single Debt to any one [on] earth and give what remains of my life to . . . exertions of my own . . ."[12]

For Whitbread, however, the task of sorting out the finances of the theatre was a nightmare, and he was unwilling to release Sheridan's money until he had placed the theatre on a sound footing. So long as there were outstanding claims against Sheridan—many of them unjustified—the scrupulous Whitbread would not give him what he was owed by the theatre. Whitbread proposed in 1812 that Sheridan should "take a considerable portion of your balance in bonds, leaving those bonds in trust to answer the events."[13]

Such an offer was useless to Sheridan, who needed cash. His assets undoubtedly outweighed his debts. But most of them were tied up in the trust established for Hecca, which included Polesden and all the land he had added to it. Because he had undertaken not to touch that money until the total sum in the trust exceeded £40,000, none of it could be used even to make Hecca's daily life more comfortable. With the rest of his money tied up in the complicated wranglings with Whitbread and the Drury Lane committee, he was left with little cash apart from the money he got from the Duchy of Cornwall with which to manage his household expenses and to fend off his creditors.

Even before the end of 1809 his financial situation was so bad that he was forced to issue appeals like the following to his friend and solicitor Henry Burgess:

> There is no man living who has been under embarrassments who has more carefully abstained from asking or accepting pecuniary obligations from private friends than myself. I know it is the bane and interruption of confidential intercourse, but a[n] exigence of

> so urgent and pressing a nature . . . has occur'd that I have not [a] moment's time to turn myself round to procure the means of preventing a disgraceful seizure at my country Place . . . [I] pledge myself to you never to ask a similar favor or anything of the kind.[14]

His London house at Queen's Street had a "garrison" installed to keep out the bailiffs.[15] This state of siege was to continue more or less continually for the next five years. There was a period of respite in the summer of 1810 when he received an unexpected windfall. He called in to the Charing Cross bankers that handled the account of the Duchy of Cornwall to see if a friendly clerk would advance him ten pounds on future payments. "Ten pounds!" replied the clerk, "to be sure I can, Mr Sheridan. You've got my letter, sir, have you not?" Sheridan had not received the letter because he could not afford to pay the postage. The clerk explained that £1,300 had been placed in his account as his percentage of a huge fine that had been paid for one of the Duchy estates. Thomas Creevey, with whom Sheridan and Hecca were staying at the time, wrote:

> Sheridan was, of course, very much set up with this £1,300, and, on the very next day upon leaving us, he took a house at Barnes Terrace, where he spent all his £1,300 . . . he was as full of fun during these two months as ever he could be—gave dinners perpetually and was always on the road between Barnes and Oatlands (the Duke of York's), in a large job coach upon which he would have his family arms painted . . .[16]

After two or three months, however, the money had run out, the local shopkeepers would no longer supply him without being paid, and he and Hecca were forced to move out.

On 26 July 1811 Sheridan was in the audience at the Lyceum Theatre for a performance of *The Tailors* and, in one of those moments that were strewn through his life, his private dilemmas became for an instant a public spectacle. In the prelude to the play a distressed theatre manager is assailed by a bailiff. The audience knew that Sheridan was present, and there was a kind of shifting, embarrassed silence. It hung in the air until Sheridan himself shattered it with a loud and long laugh and began to applaud heartily. The audience was startled for a moment, and then the whole theatre joined him in an explosion of laughter.[17] His situation as a great public man without the money to sustain the trappings of greatness was in truth rather laughably incongruous. And by the time of that memorable incident in the theatre, it had become even more so, for this famously impoverished man had by then a good friend who was, in all but name, the King of Britain, Ireland, and the empire.

Chapter 41

BETRAYAL

After October 1810, when he had celebrated fifty years on the throne, King George III began almost literally to live in the past. His madness struck again just at the moment of his golden jubilee, and as it took hold, it became increasingly difficult to stop him from retreating into the eighteenth century. He was not worried about his health—since he knew himself to be immortal he had nothing to fear—but he acted out scenes from his former life, reviewing troops commanded by long-dead generals, holding animated conversations with friends who were unavoidably detained in the hereafter, arranging ceremonies for occasions that had already passed into history, enjoying concerts whose music had long since died on the air. "He actually describes the dress, the conduct, and the conversation of different persons, who are thus recalled into life."[1]

Whether an imaginary Sheridan took part in any of these conversations is not recorded, but for him there was no temptation to join the King in a perpetual past. At the end of March 1809 Sheridan had become "extremely unwell . . . with a painful attack of a nature which has prevented my applying to any business";[2] there were even rumours that he was dead. But he was very much alive and, with the King slipping into a slow but terminal decline, the moment he had worked for since 1788 finally arrived: on 8 January 1811 the Prince of Wales was declared Prince Regent. His powers would be restricted for a year, but unless his father staged a recovery even more miraculous than those in the past, he would then be King in all but name.

For Sheridan, after three years of calamity, the future suddenly seemed to hold prospects. His influence with the Prince seemed strong: the Whig leaders, Grey and Grenville, had been infuriated when Sheridan had altered their draft of the Prince's reply to Perceval's offer of a limited regency. At best, Sheridan's dream of being sent to Ireland as Chief Secretary would become a reality; at worst, he would have a significant position in a new government in London.

However, by the beginning of February, when Sheridan and the other Privy Councillors dressed up in their ceremonial robes to conduct the swearing-in of the Prince as regent, he already knew that the Tory government of Spencer Perceval was, at least for the time being, to be left in office. Sheridan's warning to the Prince that "his character would be wholly gone" if he persisted with this decision was entirely ignored.[3] Gallingly, Sheridan himself had to write to Perceval in the Prince's name, informing him that he was to be retained in office. Sheridan made the letter sound as tentative and grudging as he possibly could, adverting to the Prince's "situation of unexampled embarrassment" at having to retain Perceval, and stressing that he was doing so only to avoid upsetting his father and "interfering with the Progress of his Sovereign's recovery."[4]

The Prince's behaviour was, nevertheless, deeply disturbing. It was not that Sheridan was greatly enamoured either of his opposition colleagues or of the Prince's political principles. He told Harriet Duncannon that the "struggle for pre-eminence" among the various factions "threatened to subdivide the subdivisions of Op[position] till they became like atoms known to exist but too numerous to count —and too small to be felt."[5] Sheridan had in fact been moving closer to his old protégé George Canning, whom he trusted on what was now for him by far the most important political issue, that of Catholic emancipation.

He had also been disgusted by the Prince's behaviour in April 1810, when Sir Francis Burdett was arrested for challenging the action of the House of Commons in committing a former London Corresponding Society organiser to prison for organising political debates. Burdett's rather histrionic attempt at resistance (Lord Cochrane drove up to his Piccadilly house in a hackney coach and prepared to booby-trap all the entrances with gunpowder) led to injuries among the crowd which had gathered to support him. Sheridan told Hecca that he agreed with Burdett in principle but regarded him as "barbarous" for "His cruelty and total indifference to the fate of an innocent mob, enthusiastic in his cause."[6] But he also damned the Prince of Wales and the Duke of York for putting on a show of military strength by parading seven thousand soldiers in Hyde Park. He held his tongue, though, so as to retain his personal popularity and his links with the Prince in the hope that his long wait for power would finally pay off.

In July 1810, on the occasion of Lord Grenville's accession as chancellor of Oxford University, Sheridan had been given powerful proof of his public popularity when his name was proposed for an honorary doctorate. It was an honour greater than that awarded to his father many years before. Three members of the faculty objected, however, and Sheridan would not accept the award unless it was unanimous. When he appeared at the ceremony, the undergraduates created an uproar at the failure to honour him and insisted that he be seated among the doctors. They also circulated a handbill demanding to know whether it was consistent with the spirit of the university to withhold honour from "a man whose talents have, through a long and arduous career, eminently adorned, and whose patriotism has, upon every trying occasion, stood forward to support, the general interest of his country?"[7]

Sheridan had restored his reputation for patriotism so far that the Corporation of the City of London had even invited him to write the inscription for a monument in the Guildhall to the great naval hero Horatio Nelson. Having held his tongue enough to be widely regarded as a patriot, and having swallowed his anger at the Prince's behaviour during the Burdett riots, he now hoped to reap the ultimate reward.

Sheridan, as a member of the Prince's household, greeted the two thousand guests (among them the exiled French royal family) who celebrated the Prince of Wales's accession to the regency at a fabulous fête in the grounds of Carlton House in June 1811. It was expected that "old Sheridan," as he was now habitually called, was about to be brought into the government, and that the only thing that might keep him out of office was his own punctilious refusal to serve with the anti-Catholic Spencer Perceval. Yet it was also public knowledge that Sheridan was virtually bankrupt, the only thing keeping him out of debtors' prison being his immunity from prosecution as a Member of Parliament.

In spite of his good-humoured laughter at the theatre, Sheridan was resentful of any suggestion that his private vulnerability might make him sacrifice his principles in order to gain office; he was sensitive to the humiliating disparity between his public standing and his private penury. At the Pavilion in Brighton that gap was cruelly exposed by Sir Philip Francis when Sheridan, the Prince, and their friends were joking about how they would all be elevated to the House of Lords by the regent and began thinking up appropriate titles and testimonials for each other. Sheridan became visibly upset when Francis suggested for him the title of "The Man Who Extends England's Credit."[8]

As time went on, the Prince's willingness to keep Perceval's Tory government in office began to look less like the initial caution of a regent whose powers were restricted for a year and much more like a positive choice. It became clear that he expected Sheridan and other friends like Lord Moira and Lord Hutchinson simply to join a slightly altered Perceval administration. As it became equally clear that King George was not going to recover—he was tending to "decline into some unnatural frame of thought after a sentence or two"—the Prince's reluctance to bring the Whigs into office seemed increasingly inexplicable. Most alarmingly, the Prince was beginning to move closer to his reactionary brother, the Duke of Cumberland, and to turn against the cause of Catholic emancipation. He hinted that, although he himself still favoured the measure, it might not be right to enact it while his father was still alive.

This, to Sheridan, was a betrayal of everything he stood for. Instead of hoping to strengthen his ties with the Prince Regent, he now became increasingly anxious to get out from under his influence by securing a seat in Parliament that did not fall under the Prince's patronage. His decision to do so, in the battered and vulnerable state in which he found himself, was the bravest of his life, far more courageous than any elopement, duel, or gamble. He knew that if he left the Prince's protection and then failed to win a seat for himself, he would be at the mercy of his creditors. Having avoided jail through all the turbulent flirtations with treason, he now risked the debtors' prison.

Had he been prepared to settle for a quiet life and the retention of the parliamentary immunity that protected him from prosecution for debt, he could have not only joined the government in a lucrative position and remained as the member for Ilchester but also brought Tom in with him for the same constituency. Disillusioned as he was with Grey and Grenville, the likely leaders of any Whig government, all he had to do to save himself from torment and possible disaster was to forget the Catholics of Ireland and agree to serve in a government where the subject of emancipation was forgotten. For a man of sixty-one who through his political career had refused many offers of titles and riches, and who had suffered the loss of his theatre, such a move would have been no great disgrace. Yet, as he explained to the Catholic activist Edward Jernyngham, his "ardent wish to support the catholic Claims in an *independent* seat" was "the sole political object now near my heart . . . My motive is to stand the master of my own motions in the ensuing session of Parliament, especially on the *Question of the Catholic Claims*."[9]

He was convinced that Spencer Perceval's government, which the Prince Regent was keeping in power, was doing its best to stir up anti-Catholic and anti-Irish feeling. The murders of two publicans and their families in December 1811 led to a wave of panic, and Sheridan believed that the magistrates were determined to "fasten by any means, perjury or otherwise, the late murders on *Irishmen* and to have it believed that there exists a Popish P[l]ot to massacre all the Protestant Publicans!" The police, he claimed, "have strict orders to bring no one before them who does not '*speak with an Irish brogue*' or any witnesses whose examination they cannot commence by asking if they are papists and bidding them cross themselves." One of those suspected of the murders was widely advertised as an Irishman even though, according to Sheridan, he "was no more an Irishman than he was a Laplander," while his associate, a Dane, was allowed to escape.[10]

In this context, the failure of the Prince Regent to do anything for the Catholics made Sheridan's position as the holder of a parliamentary seat in the Prince's gift increasingly untenable. The Ilchester seat had been given to Sheridan with no visible strings attached. As he had written to the Prince in 1808, when his position as receiver-general of the Duchy of Cornwall was made permanent, "I hold my seat in the house of Commons from *you*, Sir, and *you alone*." But, he had added, he was grateful for "your gracious allowance of me to follow the course which the Habits, Principles and Connexions of my past political Life exhort me not to abandon."[11] Sheridan seems not to have known that in order to get the seat for him, the Prince had stupidly given a written promise to its "owner," Sir William Manners, that he would make him a baron "whenever the opportunity may offer"—in other words, on the King's death. This unconstitutional and unfilial promise later caused serious problems for the Prince, but even at the time it almost certainly added to his belief that Sheridan was under an obligation to use the seat to further his interests.[12]

Thus, not long after he had taken the Ilchester seat, Sheridan met the Prince riding down Oxford Street and found himself being accused of having deserted him "privately and politically."[13] The Prince had apparently assured Lord Wellesley that Sheridan would neither speak nor vote on a motion of censure against him, to which Sheridan responded that he did not, for a moment, believe that his friend would ever ask him to abase himself by "betraying the unpurchaseable consistency and sincerity of my political Principles."[14] This of course was a rhetorical device—he clearly had realised that the Prince was trying to make him do exactly that. And he had expressed that realisation in the most dramatic way—by tendering his resignation as receiver-general of the Duchy of Cornwall. His resignation was refused, and shortly afterwards relations were restored sufficiently for Sheridan to give the congratulatory speech at the Prince's birthday party. But the tension between Sheridan's sense of his own independence and the Prince's assumption that he could influence Sheridan's behaviour in Parliament had become obvious. Now, with the Prince as regent, that tension would quickly surface again.

Early in February 1812, when Lord Morpeth put down a motion calling for the relief of Catholic disabilities, Sheridan came under severe pressure not to vote for it.[15] He did not give in to the pressure, of course, but he was so disgusted that he seriously considered withdrawing from Parliament. He told Hecca, "It has been a toss up whether I should not have taken the Chiltern Hundreds [i.e., resigned his seat] and been out of Parliament this Day—but I shall continue to consult nothing as a Public man but my own self-esteem." He told George Tierney that he intended to secede from Parliament and "vote no more, except for the Catholics."

His position as a public man who was also the Prince's man was indeed invidious. Sheridan was a member of the Prince's household but, as he told Tom, "while he continues [with the Ministers] array'd against the Catholic claims, they cannot have a vote in their support from me, and therefore I ought not to continue to owe my seat to their Master."[16] The Prince, for his part, wanted Sheridan to retain the Ilchester seat, and to remain constrained by his own parliamentary patronage. But Sheridan now began to think of getting out from under the Prince's influence by standing again for his old seat in Stafford. By early March 1812 he was telling Tom that "the dread of the expense only retards my declaring myself." On St. Patrick's Day he was given further reasons for making the move. At the annual dinner in the Freemason's Tavern of the Benevolent Society of St. Patrick, at which he had spoken for the last thirty years, it had been tradition to toast the health of the Prince as the great hope for Catholic emancipation. This year, though, in his address as chairman of the dinner, Lord Moira pointedly omitted the toast. Moira had refused to support Perceval because of his Irish policies, and Sheridan had conveyed his views to the Prince, leading to an acrimonious meeting. Moira's omission of the toast was understood in this context as a pointed criticism.

Although he subsequently denied being drunk, Sheridan was very probably not sober when he stood up and reportedly declared that he "knew well the principles of the Prince Regent and that so well satisfied was he that they were all that Ireland could wish, that he hoped, that as he had lived up to them, so he might die in the principles of the Prince Regent . . . He could only assure them that the Prince Regent remained unchangeably true to those principles." While Sheridan himself was applauded, every mention of the Prince was greeted with hisses and cries of "Change the subject!" To make amends for this "ungenerous conduct," the *Morning Post*, which was controlled by the Prince, then published a risible encomium on its sovereign master, whom it described as "the Glory of the People" and "an Adonis of Loveliness." When the *Examiner* was then provoked into publishing a reply in which the Prince Regent was described as, amongst other things, "a violator of his word" and "a man who has just closed half a century without one single claim on the gratitude of his country or the respect of posterity," the author and editor, Leigh Hunt, and his brother John were sentenced to two years' imprisonment. Sheridan's defence of the Prince, which he intended as a reminder to the regent of his previous commitments, had succeeded merely in proving the folly of expecting the new sovereign to be any better than the old one.

Sheridan was now caught in a political no man's land, on the side neither of the Prince nor of his Whig critics. The Whigs despised the Prince for not bringing them into office. Sheridan despised the Whigs but was also disgusted at the Prince's lack of principle. Shortly after the St. Patrick's Day débâcle, he attended a banquet at Carlton

House where the Prince launched a "furious and unmeasured attack" on his former political allies. His daughter, Princess Charlotte, who had been brought up on "the principles of Mr Fox," burst into tears, and Sheridan led her from the room.

In Parliament Sheridan made his objections to the Prince's political conduct plain, and marked Ireland as the measure by which he wanted his own to be judged. He explained:

> My objection to the present Ministry is, that they are avowedly arrayed and embodied against a principle—that of concession to the Catholics of Ireland—which I think, and must always think, essential to the safety of this empire. I will never give my vote to any administration that opposes the question of Catholic Emancipation. I will not consent to receive a furlough upon that particular question, even though a Ministry were carrying every other that I wished. In fine, I think the situation of Ireland a paramount consideration.

As if sensing that his political career might be drawing to a close, he told the Parliament of which he had been a member for thirty-two years, "If they were to be the last words I should ever utter in this House, I should say, 'Be just to Ireland, as you value your own honour;—be just to Ireland as you value your own peace.' "[17] Whether he knew it or not, it was to be his political last will and testament.

On 11 May 1812 Prime Minister Perceval was shot through the heart in the lobby of the House of Commons by a commercial agent who had been ruined and unhinged by the war. Sheridan chose this moment to make his declaration of independence. He wrote to the Prince on 21 May to say that while his zeal to serve him was unaltered, the best way of doing so was "by preserving the independence and consistency of my public character."[18] This was a clear indication of his intention to run for Stafford and get out from under the Prince's parliamentary patronage. A successful canvass of the town earlier in the month had convinced him that his prospects of returning to his old seat were very good. According to a statement later published on his behalf, only twenty of the 600-odd burgesses (electors) declined to support him.[19] On this visit, Sheridan found that many of the shoe-makers who worked in the town's principal industry were unemployed and hungry, and he distributed money and meal tickets to them. Buoyed by the warm response, he was confident of being able to put the bad years since 1807 behind him and to re-establish the political base he had held for twenty-six years.

He nevertheless became closely involved in the negotiations for a new, pro-Catholic government. Lord Liverpool had succeeded Perceval as Prime Minister, but he had so little authority that he was forced to resign within a fortnight. In the negotiations for a replacement, Sheridan spent his time shuttling between the Prince, Lord Moira, and the Duke of Wellington's brother, Lord Wellesley, who had been Perceval's foreign secretary. His intention was to help form a government on the basis that, as Wellesley later explained, "the claims of the Catholics should be taken into early consideration, with a view to a final and conciliatory adjustment."

On 28 May Thomas Creevey met Sheridan "coming from a long interview with the Prince, and going with a message to Wellesley . . . He described the Prince's state of perturbation of mind as beyond anything he had ever seen."[20] The importance of Sheridan's role is obvious from the fact that Wellesley called to his house on the morning he was authorised by the Prince to explore the possibilities of forming a new administration. Wellesley returned an hour later and offered him a position in the putative government. He received, as Sheridan later told the House of Commons, "a most disinterested denial of accepting any official situation."[21]

Sheridan's disinterestedness was proved by the fact that he risked the Prince's wrath by urging him to include Charles (now Lord) Grey, whom he had the strongest personal reasons to despise, in any new administration. On 1 June he told the Prince, "I should be insincere if I attempted to dissemble the deep regret I have felt at an apparent alteration in your manner towards me—produced solely I must believe by my expressing an opinion that a Proscription of Lord Grey in the formation of a new administration would be a proceeding equally injurious to the estimation of your Personal dignity and the maintenance of the Public Interest."[22] In a thinly disguised warning about the dangers of autocracy, Sheridan was cheeky enough to quote to the Prince Regent the Junius Letters, Philip Francis's great attacks on George III's government, which had so influenced his own youthful attitude to politics: "Junius says in a public Letter of his address'd to your Royal Father 'Fate that made you a King forbad your having a Friend.'" The Prince, however, had a friend in himself, and he was sure that "you will never require from me any proof of that attachment and devotion inconsistent with the clear and honourable independence of mind and conduct which constitute[s] my sole value as a public Man . . ."[23] Polite and carefully coded as it was, this was still a remarkably defiant statement. Sheridan was telling his sovereign in effect that his loyalty as a subject, a member of his household, and a beneficiary of his patronage in Parliament was strictly conditional on the maintenance of his freedom to think and act according to his own lights.

Sheridan's support for Grey was, however, complicated by an odd piece of intrigue. Grey refused to join a new administration unless the Prince's reactionary advisers, Lord Hertford and his son Lord Yarmouth, resigned. When they agreed to do so, Sheridan was supposed to tell him, but did not. This was subsequently used as proof that he was all the time plotting to keep Grey out of government. The reality was more mundane however: Sheridan knew, as his letter to the Prince makes clear, that the regent had no intention of bringing Grey and the Whigs into office and that his advisers' offer to resign was no more than a gesture; the Prince Regent was merely going through the motions of trying to put together a pro-Catholic administration. His real intention became clear early in June, when he decided to reappoint Lord Liverpool as head of an administration that would let the Catholic question lie.

Realising that the Prince Regent had merely used him as a decoy, and even further alienated from Grey by the acrimony that followed, in August Sheridan declared his willingness to work with George Canning in politics from then on.[24] Canning had refused to join any administration that would not support Catholic emancipation and in June had scored a great success with the passage of a motion proposed in the House of Commons to the effect that the laws discriminating against Catholics should be considered after the summer recess. Sheridan seems to have played some part in trying to get Canning to join in an alternative government with Addington. When the former two met at the Home Office and agreed to bury the hatchet, Canning noted, "I have instigated Sheridan to ask him to dinner on Friday."[25] Nothing much came of the approaches, however.

More anxious than ever to prove his independence from the Prince Regent, Sheridan offered himself for Stafford again in the general election in October. According to Charles Butler, Sheridan left London too late to carry out an effective canvas—possibly because his canvas in May had left him overly confident of success. Three days before the poll, however, he discovered that a Colonel Wilson had been invited to stand by a number of the burgesses who had previously offered him their support. Sheridan refused to stand in tandem with a second candidate, and most of those whom he had relied on deserted him.

The *Staffordshire Advertiser* claimed that there had been "groundless reports" spread to injure Sheridan's cause by "vulgar and illiterate people." Sheridan himself afterwards claimed that those who were "hastily misled to withdraw their support from me" were "either young burgesses who scarcely knew me, or newcomers who had never known me at all."[26] He blamed Whitbread's refusal to pay him £2,000 from the much larger amount he was owed by Drury Lane, calling him a "scoundrel."

He came bottom of the poll. But, according to Butler, whose source of information was Sheridan's most important Stafford supporter, Edward Jernyngham, "such was the fascination of his manner, and such the attraction of his name, that, before he left town, the electors seemed to be in despair that they had not voted for him, and a large proportion of them would escort him out of the town."[27] After the election, indeed, a delegation from Stafford called to his house in London to present him with an inscribed cup and an address signed by the mayor on behalf of the burgesses. In reply, Sheridan assured them that "if I am in the House of Commons at all, I must sit there free, unfettered, and independent, or I hold [it] no exile to be excluded."[28]

After the defeat at Stafford, the Prince Regent once again offered to help find a seat for Sheridan. Hecca was against the idea of Sheridan's taking a seat under the Prince's patronage, but Tom was in favour. He recognised that the breach between his father and Grey was "*final* and *irrevocable*." If Grey were returned to power, he told Hecca, Sheridan would not necessarily be excluded from office, but he would be given a position only as "a *Prince's man*, and without even the appearance of influence *with the party* or admission to their confidence." But neither did he think much of his father's prospects as an independent MP:

> Since Fox's death, up to the appointment of the regency nearly, my father might have been Minister of the Country any day in the year, would he but have dedicated himself to parliamentary

> duty and made but common exertion to place himself on that height. This is notorious, admitted by all parties. Tell me then if when everything that could prompt and facilitate presented itself to his ambition, when even procrastination could not destroy, nay seemed to improve the opportunity, and his prominence was increased and authority established by the delay of his appearance, when private as well as public circumstances goaded him on all sides to come forward, if then and with such advantages he abandoned the task, what is there to expect from *solitary* exertion *now*?[29]

It was a fair question. Sheridan was, as Tom pointed out, a member of the Prince's household, and his independence from the Prince was in any event curtailed by the implicit requirement of his position that "he never can appear rang'd with those who are hostile to him." Tom urged his father, therefore, to recognise that "the day of struggle and combat is past," and to make a deal with Wellesley's faction in Parliament. The Prince, he believed, would tolerate such an arrangement.

There were two seats vacant at Wootton Bassett, a notoriously rotten borough. Sheridan also received an offer from "some of the most respectable persons in the Corporation" to stand for a vacant seat in Salisbury, and seems to have considered doing so.[30] But everything depended on the Prince Regent's advancing him money, and the arrangements for this led to complications which finally severed the links between them. The precise truth of what happened is impossible to fix with any certainty, and after Sheridan's death it became the subject of bitter recriminations. It seems that Lord Moira approached the Prince to ask him to put up the money to buy Sheridan a seat at Wootton Bassett, which was effectively on sale for £3,000. The money was lodged with Sheridan's solicitor, John Cocker, for payment to the owner of the seat, and Sheridan was to go to Wootton Bassett to conduct the necessary negotiations. A few days later, however, he wrote to the Prince to explain that he had been unable to go and that he was making alternative arrangements for a seat (presumably at Salisbury). The Prince then sent his secretary, Colonel McMahon, to retrieve the £3,000 from Cocker. He, however, claimed to know nothing of any attempt to buy a parliamentary seat and said that the money had been used to pay off some of Sheridan's debts, "and particularly a debt to himself, Cocker."[31]

What probably happened was that Cocker simply decided on his own behalf to seize the money as payment for Sheridan's debts to him: this is what Sheridan himself asserted and there is no good reason to doubt it. Sheridan in the meantime changed his mind about taking a seat from the Prince, which would put him back in the awkward situation he had been in as the member for Ilchester. By the time he went to look for the money back, Cocker had impounded it. The Prince claimed afterwards that the whole thing had been a deliberate fraud on Sheridan's part and that, out of shame, Sheridan never came near him again. This is not quite true—Sheridan did continue to see the Prince for a while afterwards, and they certainly had a meeting on 9 April 1813. But their relations were undoubtedly at a very low ebb, and rumours reached Tom in Dublin in May that "my father has had a violent quarrel in public with the Prince." The chances of repairing the breach, moreover, receded considerably with the departure in April of their mutual friend Lord Moira, who had been appointed governor-general of Bengal.

The affair of the £3,000 was in any case more an excuse for than cause of the breach. The brutal truth was that now that he was in power the Prince Regent had no further use for Sheridan. Now that he had come into his own, he had abandoned his old Foxite poses and was becoming as hardened an opponent of Catholic emancipation as his father had ever been. Sheridan was no more than an awkward reminder of the political follies of his youth. The man who had rescued him when he married a Catholic, who had used his powers of persuasion as an orator and of intrigue as a political operator to get his debts paid, who had written his correspondence at moments of crisis, was now an ungovernable, old, and impudent subject. Sheridan, the most subtle of traitors, had himself been unsubtly betrayed.

To Sheridan's depression at realising that the mirage that had remained on the horizon for most of his political career had finally evaporated was added a further burden. Hecca was in the early stages of the cancer that was to kill her, and she was declining before his eyes. "Watching by a sick couch with the most gloomy apprehensions which my desponding temper always fix in my mind, was hard work to my nerves, even in my stout Days," he confessed.[32] But these were not his stout days, and his resilience was being worn away. Weighed down with worry over Hecca's illness, the increasingly desperate state of his finances, and the hopelessness of his political situation, Sheridan was even neglecting his son Tom, who had now left Scotland and was stationed in Dublin. Tom's health was itself no better, and he was "miserably thin and weak."[33] His difficulty in breathing would not allow him to walk or ride at a fast pace. But Sheridan was so depressed that he could not even bring himself to write to his beloved son. In May 1813, when Hecca wrote to Tom in Dublin, she received a sarcastic reply: "I am *very* thankful to you for your letter because we have never been such regular correspondents that I could claim such attention from you, and its contents . . . show that I owe it to an effort of good-will of which I shall not be unmindful." He complained that "since I quitted Scotland, I have not known whether you or my father were dead or alive."[34] Sheridan eventually replied in July, confessing that in his depression and disgust he had nothing pleasant to communicate: "Politics I am sick of. The Prince I know nothing of. Party is a Cheat, Stafford worse, and the Theatre and the Conduct towards me, I hate to think of." And he did not believe assurances that Hecca was on the mend. Thoughts of his own death were weighing on his mind, and he was "arranging and winding up all my affairs and accounts as if it were certain I could not outlive the next three months."[35]

But Tom's plight at least served to rouse him. Tom had mentioned in May that it would be a "God send" to get an appointment "in the Cape or elsewhere" for the sake of his health. The Cape of Good Hope had long been regarded as having the right atmosphere and climate for sufferers from respiratory complaints, and Tom, hoping that a posting there might save him, had written to ask the Prince for help in getting one. Sheridan's dispute with the Prince, with whom Tom was in even worse odour, led him to believe that he could expect nothing from that quarter. Instead, with help from Lord Sidmouth and Lord Bathurst, he applied to the Duke of York, who proved eager to help, and got him a post at the Cape. Tom came to London in September to prepare for his departure to Africa, but the sight of him threw Sheridan into even deeper despair. Here, before his eyes, was Eliza's ghost. "He so reminds me of his mother," he told Hecca, "and his feeble, gasping way of speaking affects and deprives me of all hope."[36]

Such was Sheridan's gloom that even reminders of his greatness served only to underline the change in his fortunes. In mid-December 1813, Lord Byron was discussing Sheridan with some friends and delivered his own opinion:

> Whatever Sheridan has done or chooses to do has been, *par excellence*, the *best* of its kind. He has written the best comedy (*School for Scandal*), the best drama (*The Duenna*, to my mind far beyond that St Giles lampoon, *The Beggar's Opera*), the best farce (*The Critic*—it is only too good for a farce), and the best address (Monologue on Garrick); and, to crown all, delivered the very best oration (the famous Begum speech) ever conceived or heard in this country.

When this tribute was relayed to Sheridan the next day, he burst into tears. Lord Holland told Byron what happened and he, too, was moved. "Poor Brinsley," he wrote in his journal, "if they were tears of pleasure, I would rather have said these few but most sincere words than have written the *Iliad* or made his own celebrated Philipic. Nay, his own comedy never gratified one more than to hear that he derived a moment's gratification from any praise of mine, humble as it must appear to 'my elders and my betters.' "[37] Sheridan's tears may indeed have been prompted by pleasure, but it is much more likely that they sprang from a deep sense of sorrow. Between the aspirations of the years of the great achievements listed by Byron and the reality of what, after all, it meant to be a prince's friend lay a desolate terrain of abandoned hope.

Chapter 42

A GOOD HUMOURED MISANTHROPE

When he was still young and in the ascendant, Sheridan had fun with disaster. When he wrote *The Critic*, he had Mr. Puff describe his career as a successful writer of begging letters, inventing myriad misfortunes to wring tears and money from his benefactors. Puff wrote letters as if from a debtors' prison, varying the causes of his distress. "I suppose never man went thro' such a series of calamities in the same space of time!—Sir, I was five times made a bankrupt, and reduced from a state of affluence, by a train of unavoidable misfortunes!" He made his fortune from "bankruptcies, fires, gouts, dropsies, imprisonments, and other valuable calamities."[1] Now, as he approached death, Sheridan seemed to be working his way through Puff's list. Fire, bankruptcy, and ill-health had reduced him to writing begging letters. Imprisonment was one of the few calamities that remained.

Sheridan knew that with the loss of his seat in Parliament, he was liable to be arrested for unpaid debts. In May 1814, less than two years after he had turned down Lord Wellesley's offer of a place in the government, this final humiliation had to be faced. He was taken to Tooke's Court, a sheriff's sponging house, and held there over a debt of £600. John Frost "passed a week with him night and day in Tooke's Court neglected by all."[2]

Whitbread had refused to give him £12,000 that he was owed by Drury Lane because of a dubious claim against him. Sheridan wrote to him from prison in a fury:

> Whitbread, putting all false professions of Friendship and feeling out of the Question, you have no right to keep me here. For it is in truth *your* act. If you had not forcibly with-held from me the £12,000 in consequence of a threatening Letter from a miserable swindler whose claim *you* knew to be a *lie*—I should at least have been out of the reach of *this* state of miserable insult—for that and that only cost me my seat in Parliament. And I assert that you cannot find a Lawyer in the Land, that is not either a natural born Fool or a corrupted Scoundrel who will not declare that your conduct in this respect was neither warrantable or legal . . . I shall only add that, I think, if I know myself, had our Lotts been reversed and I had seen you in my situation, and had left Lady E[lizabeth, Whitbread's wife] in that of my wife I should have risked £600 rather than have left you so altho' I had been in no way accessory in bringing you into that condition.[3]

When Whitbread came to see Sheridan in jail, Frost "urged him *in vain* to join me in relieving him." A furious row developed with "high words unpleasant" exchanged, and Sheridan ordered Whitbread to quit his sight. Sheridan claimed bitterly that Whitbread had "found the object of your humane visit satisfied by seeing me safe in Prison." He claimed that there were "still thousands and thousands due to me both legally and equitably from the Theatre," and this seems to have been true: at the end of May, after his release, the theatre paid him £4,600 and he protested that £1,000 had been deducted "under a complete misapprehension of the justice of the case."[4] He was also due to receive £1,200 left to him in the will of Edward Drakeford, a Stafford businessman who had died in March, as "a mark . . . of respect for the distinguished talents and public virtues of that enlightened Patriot and Statesman."[5]

Hecca also visited him even though she was ill. (Sheridan's grandson Brinsley noted in May 1814 that "Grandmama is very ill and she [h]as got two Doctors to attend her."[6]) She wrote to Whitbread: "Sheridan's state of mind kills me—all I can say to him seems to poison his mind then. Clarke [presumably one of her doctors] has given me leave to go and see him . . ." He was eventually released, and Frost walked him home, giving him £70 to pay "house fees etc."

Yet even when Whitbread visited him in these terrible circumstances, he found him "speculating upon Westminster."[7] Astonishingly, even at his lowest ebb, he was making plans for a spectacular re-entry into Parliament, this time not through a rotten borough but through the great seat of Westminster that had given him his greatest triumph and his worst defeat. In the spring of 1814 another Westminster by-election seemed likely. Lord Cochrane, who held one of the seats, was implicated in a stock-exchange scandal (unjustly, as it turned out) and expelled from Parliament.

As early as 8 March, Lord Byron had discussed the subject with Sheridan while drinking at Brooks's:

> Sherry means to stand for Westminster, as Cochrane (the stock-jobbing hoaxer) must vacate. [Henry] Brougham is a candidate. I fear for poor dear Sherry. Both have talents of the highest order, but the youngster has *yet* a character. We shall see, if he lives to Sherry's age, how well he will pass over the red-hot ploughshares of public life. I don't know why but I hate to see the *old* ones lose, particularly Sheridan, notwithstanding all his mechanceté.[8]

The Whigs, rather surprisingly, put Sheridan forward as their prospective candidate. In July, the *Morning Post* reported that Sheridan "has been solicited to stand for Westminster in the case of a vacancy, from such a combination of respectable quarters that, though he has very properly declined giving an answer under the present circumstances, there would be no doubt of his success."[9] The decision to support him was motivated largely by antipathy to Henry Brougham, the ambitious young lawyer who wanted the seat and whom the old Whigs regarded as an unprincipled opportunist. He had also earned the Prince Regent's enmity both by his acting as defence counsel at the trial of Leigh Hunt and by taking up the cause of his estranged wife, Princess Caroline. The old Foxite faction around Holland House, as Creevey reported, "from personal hatred [of Brougham] supports Sherry." The influential Bedford section of the Whigs, however, was resolved to desert Sheridan and support Brougham.[10]

The prospect encouraged Sheridan even to make renewed overtures to the Prince Regent. He wrote to his secretary, Colonel McMahon, to announce his decision to stand, telling him, "I have the Whig *support* made known to me thro' the Duke of Norfolk. This will enable me only to be a more powerful and efficient Friend to the Prince.—After what has passed between me and Lord Sidmouth [his old friend Addington] I cannot doubt the support of

Government. Without a Boast depend on it no man can beat Bro[u]gham, but myself, and against me I think He will yet shrink to stand."[11]

Sheridan's candidacy rendered a Whig-Radical alliance at the by-election impossible, since those who had fought two bitter campaigns against Sheridan could not now give him even their tacit support. The Tories, however, decided not to put up a candidate but to support Sheridan in an effort to break the Radical hold on the borough. Their decision ensured that the contest, if it happened, would be a close one and that Sheridan had a very real chance of resurrection.[12] He himself thought of it as a lap of honour, a suitably dignified ending to the drama of his days. As he wrote to the Duke of Norfolk, "This Crisis and last effort is the winding up of my political exertions and perhaps the last gratification remaining to my public or even private Feelings . . ."[13]

His hopes were blighted, even to the end. Brougham did not "shrink to stand," and, with the support of the Bedford faction behind him, showed every sign of putting Sheridan through a campaign almost as fierce as the great battles of 1806 and 1807. In spite of official Whig support, Sheridan suspected that Grey, Grenville, and Whitbread would come out against him and back Brougham. And as it became clear that Cochrane had been wrongly accused, public sympathy began to move in his direction. Sheridan had, finally, no money to fight a campaign. The Duke of Norfolk, his most significant backer, was "despairing of the supplies he hoped for," and Sheridan himself could not risk incurring still more debts.[14]

His despair was not quite deep enough to allow his political judgment to be entirely obscured by self-delusion, and for all these reasons he decided to withdraw. Making a virtue of necessity, he had a statement read from the hustings. Declaring that he had never held a seat in the Commons "but on the sole condition of being the master of my own vote and voice—the servant only of my conscience," he implied that this concern for parliamentary independence had led him to the conclusion that Cochrane's expulsion was unjust and that "the expelled member has a right to appeal to his Constituents."[15] He was, therefore, withdrawing in favour of Cochrane.

It was a superb execution of that most difficult of manoeuvres—the dignified retreat. It won praise even from some of the radicals—Sir Francis Burdett declared that "an act more graceful or more politic he could not have performed at the present instant."[16] And at the same time it thwarted Brougham, who came under irresistible pressure to follow Sheridan's lead and withdraw. As a result, Cochrane was reelected unopposed.

The Prince Regent, however, was unimpressed. Even after his own betrayal of all the principles he had formerly espoused, and even after the break between them, he still expected Sheridan to wage war on his enemies, the most hated of whom was Brougham. At a fête in Carlton House a few days after the Westminster poll, Sheridan was given to understand (though not directly by the Prince, who seems not to have spoken to him) "that the Prince was dissatisfied at my giving way on the Westminster election." Sheridan still had hopes of working his way back into a position of influence with the Prince, but it must have been clear to him after this episode that whatever he did or failed to do would from now on be regarded as further proof of his disloyalty. He remained a member of the Prince's household (the Duchy of Cornwall appointment had been made his for life), but he no longer had his master's ear, let alone the power to act as his voice.

Most of what he received from the Duchy of Cornwall and from the theatre was swallowed up by his debts, and soon he was unable to hold on to even his most prized possessions. Variations on the auction scene from *The School for Scandal* were played out in reality at regular intervals. The cup he had been presented with by the burgesses of Stafford was pawned for £40.[17] The same fate befell many of his books. He sold six paintings, including two or three by Gainsborough and two by George Morland, for £660. Eventually even Joshua Reynolds's famous portrait of Eliza as St. Cecilia had to be sold in November 1815. Sheridan kept a copy he had commissioned from Sir William Beechey, but selling the original was still a painful moment: "I shall part from this Picture as from Drops of my Heart's blood."[18]

He was, moreover, imprisoned for a second time, in August 1815, in Fetter Lane sponging house. Nathaniel Wraxall reported that a young friend of his was detained there "in a large apartment with Sheridan and Sir Watkin Lewes . . . They remained shut up there for three days, at the end of which Sheridan procured his liberation. He was morose, taciturn and gloomy before dinner—for they all slept in the same room; but when he had drunk nearly two bottles of wine, he became comparatively cheerful and communicative."[19] Joseph Farington recorded that Sheridan in Fetter Lane received between £400 and £500 to get him out, but that one of his old tenants in Polesden called on him "in the utmost distress" and asked for his help in preventing the seizure of his goods. "Sheridan asked Him what sum w[oul]d relieve Him. The man replied that £300 w[oul]d restore Him to His former state. Sheridan gave him the money."[20]

Those two moods—morose and expansive—became the poles of his existence. He suffered from insomnia, and the bouts of melancholy (what he called "an unaccountable dejection of Spirits without a cause") that had afflicted him all his life became more frequent. Hecca's illness and above all his certainty that Tom's life would be not much longer than his mother's made him reproach himself with "a perverse fatality in my nature which has often made me seem most negligent to those I most love."[21] In these bouts of introspection he saw himself more and more clearly as Charles Surface—a good-hearted man whose presiding virtue of generosity contains within it the vice of thoughtlessness. He suffered

> . . . self-reproach clear of anything my *Heart* ever entertain'd or suggested. I never have done a dishonest or a base act. I never have omitted to do a generous or a benevolent one where I had the Power—but sins of *omission*—Oh me—senseless credulity, destructive procrastination, unworthy indolence, all abetted by one vile habit [drinking], somewhat perhaps to be palliated by an original infirmity of constitution . . . but never to be excused.[22]

Yet Sheridan acquired, through all his disasters and disappointments, a certain air of resigned stoicism. He became, as he said, "a perfect misanthrope but a good humoured one."[23] Though he and Hecca spent much of their time apart (officially because the sea air at Cowes was judged better for her health), their separation was relatively amicable. He enjoyed angling on the river Mole, sailing at Cowes, having his grandchildren (left behind by Tom and his wife when they went to the Cape) and their aunts around him, visiting the tenants at Polesden, which had long since been rented out. He did not greatly miss the fabulous society that he had once participated in at Devonshire House and Carlton House, and enjoyed satirising the gossip that had continued to flourish in spite of *The School for Scandal*: "There is an Irish Countess brought to bed of a black child solely from looking very often at a black Servant in the Family—and there is a Duchess who has a grown up Daughter with the Head of a Pig—those I understand are the chief Topics in the fashionable world . . . I am fast turning into a Hermit and like nothing but shade and solitude."[24]

Often he ate alone at a cheap chop-house. When he was feeling sociable, he preferred old friends to new acquaintances and liked to eat and, more to the point, to drink with the playwright George Colman, the Harris brothers, who owned Covent Garden, the poet Samuel Rogers, Douglas Kinnaird, Sir Gilbert Heathcote, and Lord Byron. One night in October 1814, Byron and Kinnaird, both almost as drunk as he, had to help Sheridan down a corkscrew staircase, "which had certainly been constructed before the discovery of fermented liquors, and to which no legs, however crooked could possibly accommodate themselves." When they got him safely home, they found his manservant, "evidently used to the business," waiting for him in the hall.

He did not always have such considerate company to help him home. One night a watchman found him in the street, "fuddled and bewildered and almost insensible." "Who are you, sir?" No answer. "What's your name?" A hiccup. "What's your name?" Sheridan, in a slow, deliberate, and impassive tone, managed to dredge up the name of the most famously abstemious and righteous figure of the day: "Wilberforce." Even Sheridan's dregs, as Byron noted, were still better than most other people's flights of inspiration.[25] He could still charm the most unlikely people. Byron, beset by bailiffs himself, asked one who called with an order against him if he had nothing for Sheridan. "Oh Sheridan!," said the bailiff, "ay, I have this," and he pulled out his pocket book. "But, my lord, I have been in Sheridan's house a twelvemonth at a time—a civil gentleman—knows how to deal with *us*."[26]

He retained his interest in politics, and until the Duke of Norfolk died in December 1815 he retained the hope that his old friend would be able to get him back into Parliament. He followed with close interest the extraordinary events of 1815, when Napoleon returned from exile to attempt to retake power in France. Betraying his deepest political sympathies to Hecca, he assured her that Napoleon would not become a monarch because "he is extremely in the hands of good Republicans and Friends to real Liberty—and they have brought about and contrived this new revolution and not Buonoparte."[27]

Sheridan had now become, in common parlance, "poor old

Sherry." The association of age and decrepitude with a man who was, after all, only in his mid-sixties had as much to do with politics as with chronology. It harked back to Gillray's great caricature of William Pitt, "Uncorking Old Sherry." It expressed the notion that he was a political dinosaur, a relic of a different age. And it fed into a new strain of moralising. Sheridan's decline became a warning. Behold how moral and fiscal laxity has tarnished a once-golden boy. Behold this drunken, dissolute, and debt-ridden man and see where revolution and debauchery lead. After his death, these notions would become almost permanently fixed in his biographies.

But there was in fact another side to Sheridan's decline: he survived long enough to be seen and remembered as an old man. He had lived through an age when the burden on leading politicians had increased at an extraordinary rate. Britain had developed into a modern state while still being run by politicians who, out of office, were unpaid and, in office, lacked the support of the great bureaucratic machines that would later be taken for granted. Sheridan had been an active politician all through the period from the American war to the Battle of Waterloo, when the sheer weight of political business had put an immense strain on a system of government that was unprepared for it. He had been the opposition spokesman on financial affairs at a time when, between 1792 and 1805, the workload of the Treasury doubled because of the fiscal imperatives of the war against France. In the period of his active political life the amount of legislation passed in the House of Commons, of committees formed by it, and of late-night sittings of the House all quintupled.

The personal toll had been enormous. Very many leading politicians became alcoholics. Pitt and Fox died young. And in 1815 Sheridan's capacity for survival received a grim tribute when Samuel Whitbread, weighed down by the double burden of trying to cope with Drury Lane's byzantine finances and of carrying on a redundant career as a radical MP, cut his own throat. He became one of nineteen Members of Parliament known to have committed suicide between 1790 and 1820.[28] Six years of the kind of life that Sheridan had led for more than thirty were enough to break even a man of Whitbread's intelligence and resourcefulness. Looked at in this context, what is remarkable about Sheridan is not his decline but that, having written five extraordinary plays, run one of the two major theatres in Britain for longer than the great David Garrick had done, delivered hundreds of parliamentary speeches, slogged through endless hours of tedious committees, run in two of the most turbulent election campaigns of his times, and maintained himself as a figure of hope for many people in two different countries—Ireland and Britain—he was still alive enough in 1815 to fascinate even so impatient a young man as Byron.

It is striking that when Sheridan was on his own, he liked nothing better than to read Sir Walter Scott, especially the early *Waverley* novels, which were appearing from 1814 onwards. When *Guy Mannering* appeared in 1815, he told Hecca that he was "enchanted with the work. I class it above any book of its character and description that I ever met with in my Life—to a Highland Scotsman it must have a tenfold recommendation."[29] The spell that Scott wove for him must have been similar to the enchantment of his parents at the *Ossian* poems, conjuring up a vision of a Gaelic past in which the awkwardnesses of his own heritage—the Irish language, Jacobitism, and treason—were given the sanction of heroic romanticism. For he was himself closer than ever to his antecedents—Ulster dialect words like "clargie" for "clergyman" creep into his letters as reminders of his Cavan background. After all the humiliations, Irishness was what was left of his pride. He could find no higher praise of a servant than that he was "capable of that sort of affectionate attachment which sometimes lays quick hold of an Irish Heart."[30] Scott's depictions of a broken but still proud Gaelic civilisation, nobler even on its last legs than what was taking its place, must have helped to heal and console him in what he realised with increasing clarity were his own final days.

Chapter 43

A NICE DERANGEMENT OF EPITAPHS

On 17 August 1815 the Prince Regent was travelling to the Pavilion at Brighton from the Duke of York's estate at Oatlands, where he had been to wish his brother a happy birthday. His route took him close to Polesden and Leatherhead, where Sheridan had borrowed a house, called Randalls, from his friend Richard Ironmonger.[1] Sheridan divided his time between a house in Savile Row in London and Randalls, which, as he wrote in an invitation to Tom's sisters-in-law to bring his grandchildren there, had "every comfort with cream Pigs Hens eggs Chickens most excellent vegetables and Fruit and everything particularly comfortable for a Family with small Brats."[2] The Prince later claimed that Sheridan was at this time spending much of his time with "some low acquaintance he had made—a harness maker; I forget his name, but he had a house near Leatherhead."

As he drove through the area the Prince Regent saw Sheridan about thirty yards ahead, walking along the pathway, wearing black stockings and a blue coat with metal buttons. He turned to his companion and said, "There is Sheridan." As he spoke, Sheridan turned off into a lane and never looked behind at the royal coach. It was the nearest the ruler of England would ever come again to the man on whom he had depended so much for nearly forty years.[3]

Sheridan was taken ill in early December 1815, and between then and late March 1816 he was confined "to my bed or room" for all but three or four days.[4] He had swollen veins in his leg, an abscess in his throat, a total loss of appetite (he claimed to be "never eating four ounces of solid food altogether"), and a racking cough which he said "seems resolved to scoff at the other three maladies and carry me off his own self."[5]

From the beginning of this period of illness he knew he was dying. He gave himself about three months of remaining life, writing some letters on 15 December "not to be published till *three years* after my Death. You will have that time and about three months as I guess before you can be pleased or hurt by anything I have written . . ."[6] In this mood he wrote to Hecca:

> Never let one harsh word pass between us during the period, which may not last long, that we are in this world together, and life, however clouded in me, is mutually spared to us. I have expressed the same sentiment to my son . . . and I had his answer —a most affecting one—and, I am sure, very sincere; and have since cordially embraced him. Don't imagine that I am expressing an interesting apprehension about myself which I do not feel.[7]

He seems to have recovered enough around the beginning of February to go out to dinner parties. The Earl of Essex wrote to the actor Edmund Kean on 3 February, "I want to make you *vain* by telling you what Sheridan said last night before the Wine had taken hold of his senses."[8] Essex had persuaded him to end his boycott of Drury Lane and go with him to see Kean performing. In one of the intervals, Essex found Sheridan in the green room "with all the actors around him, welcoming him back to the old region of his glory, with a sort of filial cordiality. Wine was immediately ordered, and a bumper to the health of Mr Sheridan was drank by all present, with the expression of many a hearty wish that he would often, very often, re-appear among them."[9]

He also had dinner around this time at the house of the auctioneer Robins, at which Lord Byron saw him cry. Someone remarked on "the sturdiness of the Whigs in resisting Office, and keeping to their principles." Sheridan reportedly replied:

> "Sir, it is easy for my Lord G., or Earl G., or Marquis B., or L[or]d H., with thousands upon thousands a year—some of it either *presently* derived or *inherited* in Sinecures or acquisitions from the public money—to boast of their patriotism, and keep aloof from temptation; but they do not know from what tempta-

> tions those have kept aloof, who had equal pride—at least equal talents, and not unequal passions, and nevertheless knew not in the course of their lives what it was to have a shilling of their own." And in saying this he wept.

It was the nearest he came to writing his own epitaph.

He did, however, set about preparing a kind of memorial. He had always been very reluctant to publish an authorised edition of his works, but his friend Samuel Rogers had told him in 1814 that he could now raise £4,000 by doing so.[10] Little was done, however, until early in 1816, when Rogers and Lord Byron undertook to organise an edition of the plays and poems. An agreement with the publisher John Murray was prepared on 12 May 1816, and Sheridan seems to have drawn up a detailed plan for the publication of his plays, poems, and speeches. He became increasingly insistent on getting hold of all his manuscripts. His brother-in-law William Linley wrote that Sheridan was "exceedingly anxious to have every document and paper belonging to him collected and brought to him, and Mr Charles Sheridan applying to me, in the name of his Father, for a Chest of Papers which was then in the possession of my Mother, though containing no documents of the least consequence, I conceived that I ought, also to deliver over to his Charge, the *Manuscripts* in question."[11]

By the middle of March, however, he was again so ill that he could not, for the first time in his life as a public man, attend the St. Patrick's Day dinner in London. The Duke of Kent, who presided, wrote to tell him that he had "announced the afflicting cause of your absence to the company, who expressed, in a manner that could not be *misunderstood*, their continued affection" for him.[12] That same affection was expressed in a letter from his sister Lissy in Dublin. She tried to comfort him by telling him that her own son Tom was very like him in appearance and character of mind but, remembering their own childhood, she contrasted his fate to Sheridan's:

> At that period of existence, when the temper, morals, and propensities are formed, Tom had a mother who watched over his health, his well-being, and every part of education in which a female could be useful. *You* had lost a mother who would have cherished you, whose talents you inherited, who would have softened the asperity of our father's temper, and probably have pre-

> vented his unaccountable partialities. You have always shown a noble independence of spirit, that the pecuniary difficulties you often had to encounter could not induce you to forego. As a public man, you have been, like the motto of the Lefanu family, "*Sine macula*" [without stain]; and I am persuaded had you not too early been thrown upon the world, and alienated from your family, you would have been equally good as a private character.[13]

Such comfort was all the more necessary because, sick as he was, he was still in imminent danger of being dragged off again to a debtors' prison. Sheridan's debts were actually quite modest. After his death the highest estimate of what he owed was £8,000. This, however, was the sum *claimed*—Sheridan himself insisted that no more than £3,000 was due. And as well as being a debtor, he was also a creditor—his son Charles referred, for instance, to one sum of £1,400 owed to his father.[14] The trust which had been established for Hecca and Charles was worth about £40,000, but he could not, of course, use any of that money. And without it he was virtually destitute.

On 15 May his friend Samuel Rogers received a note from him: "I am absolutely undone and broken-hearted . . . They are going to put the carpets out of the window, and break into Mrs S's room and *take me*—for God's sake let me see you."[15] Rogers and Thomas Moore went to the house that night and were told by a servant that Sheridan was safe from arrest for the moment, but that it was intended to "paste bills over the front of the house next day." In the morning Moore went with £150 that Sheridan had requested and found Sheridan "good-natured and cordial as ever . . . his voice had not lost its fulness or strength, nor was that lustre, for which his eyes were so remarkable, diminished. He showed, too, his usual sanguineness of disposition in speaking of the price he expected for his Dramatic Works, and of the certainty he felt of being able to arrange all his affairs, if his complaint would but suffer him to leave his bed."[16]

He seems, for a short while, to have convinced himself that he would live, and even that he would be able to get back into Parliament. He ventured out for a drive in a carriage on 8 June.[17] The following day, he wrote to George Canning cadging a loan of £100, which Canning sent to him immediately, and telling him that "I think I may come among you by next Sessions."[18] He was even, at times, cheerful enough to joke about his health. According to Byron,

Sheridan was advised to have an operation, but replied that he had already had two, which was enough for any man's lifetime. Asked what they were, he replied, "Having my hair cut and sitting for my picture."[19]

Byron left England without seeing Sheridan again. Samuel Rogers wrote to Walter Scott: "Poor Sheridan! I sat very often by his bedside. Just before he finally took to his bed, and a day or two before Lord Byron left England, I prepared a little supper for us, and looked with pleasure to the meeting; but, alas, I went alone, and carried an excuse from Lord Byron."[20]

Shortly afterwards, Sheridan's condition worsened again, and behind the cheerfulness the knowledge that he was dying prompted memories of childhood. Talking with his old friend John Graham, he remembered his school-days at Harrow and how he would go out into the fields on his own with a book, a piece of bread, and a sausage, and drink "from any Brook or Pond that came in his way." He recited for Graham a ballad, "King Henry and Queen Eleanor," which he had learned by heart at Harrow from listening to an old cobbler's singing.[21]

About the middle of June, Sheridan and Fox's old friend Dennis O'Brien wrote to the *Morning Post* calling on his former political associates to relieve his distress: "Oh delay not—delay not to draw aside the curtain within which that proud spirit hides its sufferings . . . Prefer ministering in the chamber of sickness to mustering at 'The Splendid sorrows that adorn the hearse.' I say, *Life* and *Succour* against Westminster Abbey and a Funeral!"[22] But in a sense many of Sheridan's former associates had already accorded him a glorious funeral. In their minds, he already belonged to the past, and they were more comfortable with him as an adornment to a heroic age of parliamentary struggle than as a living and awkward reminder of what had succeeded it.

Not for nothing did most descriptions of Sheridan's death follow the rather exaggerated account given by King George IV nine years later. He claimed that both Sheridan and Hecca were starving, that the "whole house was in a state of filth and stench that was quite intolerable," and that Sheridan had been left for a week under a red and blue horse-blanket to wallow in his own filth. These vivid and appealingly lurid images have been retailed as fact even though the King had them at third hand: he was told by his secretary, McMahon, who was told by John Taylor Vaughan. And in any case the King had reasons of his own to promulgate a hellish vision of the consequences of Sheridan's foolish pride and stubborn independence.

What seems to have happened is that Vaughan, hearing of Sheridan's situation, approached McMahon to ask for some assistance for him. The Prince apparently offered £500, but Vaughan said that £200 would do. This, however, was refused by Sheridan's friends, who "were not willing that, under the circumstances, Mr Sheridan should lay himself under obligations to the Prince Regent."[23] This probably accorded with Sheridan's own wishes. He told his French translator, Agricole Châteauneuf, who visited him on his deathbed, "Shame on the Regent for abandoning me. No, I am dying, so I forgive him."[24] This last gesture of defiance may well have contributed to the Prince's willingness to exaggerate the squalid nature of Sheridan's death. No first-hand account is nearly so lurid. His son Charles wrote to Tom that "the reports you may have seen in the newspapers of the privations and the want of comforts which he endured are unfounded . . . he had every attention and comfort which could make a death-bed easy."[25] William Earle, who visited him a number of times in his last days, reported that he "wanted for nothing." A friend of Hecca's, Mrs. Parkhurst, wrote to Lissy in Dublin that "Mr Sheridan wanted neither medical aide . . . the consolation of Piety or the exertions of friendship. He had three of the first physicians in London every day. His wife, his son and his mother-in-law were constantly with him. The Bishop of London saw him many times. Lord Lauderdale did all he could for the regulation of his affairs."[26]

Even without the Prince's exaggerations the scene was poignant enough. It is clear that the house was beset by bailiffs and that much of the furniture had already been seized. Tom's former tutor, William Smyth, hearing that Sheridan was dying, went to see him. "Nothing," he remembered, "could be so deplorable as the appearance of every thing, wherever I turned my eyes. There were strange-looking people in the hall. The parlour seemed dismantled, into which I was shewn. On the table lay a bit of paper, thrown carelessly and neglected. I took it up and it was a prescription, if I recollect, from Sir Henry Halford; but it was only, I saw, a strong cordial."[27] Smyth spoke to Hecca, whom he found dignified and calm. Contrary to the Prince's later claim that she was herself bed-ridden and starving, it is clear that she was able to move about. Charles reported that "she attended my father to the last, though ordered not to move from a sofa; while the painful scene lasted, the anxiety of her mind gave her, in spite of the pain she was in, a degree of strength which, in her state, astonished me . . ."

On 4 July Sheridan's former lover Harriet Duncannon, now Lady Bessborough, came to see him. He asked her what she thought of his looks, and she said his eyes were brilliant still. He took her hand and gripped it hard, telling her that he did so as a token that, if he could, he would come to her after death. She became frightened and asked why, having persecuted her all his life, he would want to do so after death. "Because," he said, "I am resolved you should remember me."[28] Samuel Rogers recalled Sheridan saying on his deathbed, "Tell Lady Bessborough that my eyes will look up to the coffin-lid as brightly as ever."

His boast was not entirely idle. Two days after her visit he slipped into a peaceful unconsciousness, showing no signs of being aware of those around him. But, according to Charles, his "eyes had to the last a most beautiful and touching expression, a sort of subdued and softened brightness." For the sake of the moral that was to be drawn from his death by posterity, this look was transformed into an expression of religious awe as the Bishop of London prayed over him.[29] The bishop, who was a relative of Hecca's, did visit him on his deathbed, but when Samuel Rogers asked him what Sheridan's religious feelings were at the end, he told him, "I had no means of knowing; for when I read the prayers, he was totally insensible; Mrs Sheridan raising him up, and joining his hands together." Around noon on 7 July Sheridan slipped quietly into death. His face, so long the screen on which his oratory was projected, remained so still that no one watching him die could tell the precise moment at which he passed from life.

Mrs. Parkhurst urged his sisters in Dublin to take comfort in the fact that

> He is gone where you and all of us must follow him, that he is no longer before hard-hearted judges who could only know his actions—he is before the God who created him and who knows the temptations of his nature, who will take account of when he resisted as well as when he yielded. He has taken with him a thousand charitable actions, a heart in which there was no *hard part*, a spirit free from envy and malice—and he is gone in the undiminished brightness of (his) talent, gone before pity had withered admiration.[30]

His body was removed to the house of his friend Peter Moore, who did for him the office that Sheridan himself had done for Fox—arranging a funeral at Westminster Abbey. According to Lord Thanet, who knew him well, Sheridan would have wanted to be buried beside Fox and not, as was the case, in Poet's Corner. Not only was he defined in death as a writer rather than a politician, but he was also, with a fine touch of unintended comedy, buried beside Richard Cumberland, the playwright he had so wonderfully satirised in *The Critic*.

With Sheridan safely in his coffin, the process of transforming him into a colourful, fabulous, and essentially harmless genius could begin. Rescued by death from the bailiffs, he was seized by the aristocracy. For the first time since his birth nearly sixty-five years before, he was placed entirely in the hands of the rich and powerful. At one o'clock on Saturday, 13 July, the man who had disdained to "hide his head in a coronet" was carried from Moore's house to Westminster Abbey by the Duke of Bedford, the Earl of Lauderdale, Earl Mulgrave, the Lord Bishop of London, Lord Holland, and Lord Spencer. Following them in solemn procession were two princes, the Duke of York and the Duke of Sussex; the Duke of Argyle; the Earls of Thanet, Jersey, Harrington, Bessborough, Mexborough, Rosslyn, and Yarmouth; Lords George Cavendish and Robert Spencer; Viscounts Sidmouth, Granville, and Duncannon; Lords Rivers, Erskine, and Lynedoch; and the Lord Mayor of London. "Such a catalogue of Mourners!" wrote Samuel Rogers to Walter Scott that afternoon. "And yet he was suffered to die in the hands of the Sheriff."[31]

When the show was over and Sheridan's remains had been duly claimed by the powers that be, the radical philosopher William Godwin returned alone to the grave. To him the memory of Sheridan meant something entirely different. In the coming week he went again and again to the silent abbey to sit in front of the plain stone that marked the resting place of a man who had been one of his heroes. He remembered a man to whom he had written an open letter calling for a revolution in England. He remembered a man who had done all in his power to create a Britain that valued freedom over conquest and an Ireland that was stultified neither by Catholic tribalism nor by Protestant claims to ascendancy. He recalled to mind an evening over sixteen years before at his own house when Sheridan had sat up talking with two fellow Irishmen, the revolutionary Arthur O'Connor and the lawyer and orator John Philpot Curran, who had coined a famous phrase about the price of freedom being eternal vigilance. Sitting there, Godwin remembered how the conversation that night had taken "a most animated turn, and the subject was of Love."[32] That silent tribute of memory was, in its own way, as fitting a memorial to what might have been as the volley that rang out over the grave of William Bedell.

Notes

1: Bloody Characters

1 The details in this chapter are taken from two eyewitness accounts of events in Cavan in 1641. One, *Life and Death of William Bedell*, was written by Bedell's son, William; the other, *Speculum Episcoporum or The Apostolic Bishop*, is by his chaplain Alexander Clogie. They are published together as *Two Biographies of William Bedell, Bishop of Kilmore*, edited by E. S. Shuckburgh (Cambridge, 1902).

2 O'Sheridan is usually referred to as Dennis, and it is clear that those who spoke to him in English used this name. Alexander Clogie, who knew him well, refers to him (Shuckburgh [ed.], *Two Biographies of William Bedell*, p. 196) as "Donoch [in English Dennis] O'Sheridan." His name, therefore, was Donnchadh, which properly translates as Donagh, not Dennis. To avoid confusion, I have restored the original name.

3 Shuckburgh (ed.), *William Bedell*, pp. 58–59.

4 Roy Foster, *Modern Ireland 1600–1972* (London, 1989), p. 85.

5 Marianne Elliot, *Partners in Revolution* (New Haven and London, 1982), p. 9.

6 Sir Charles King (ed.), *Henry's Upper Lough Erne in 1739* (Dublin, 1892), p. 7.

7 Shuckburgh (ed.), *William Bedell*, p. 332.

8 Letter of Bishop of Meath, 1688, in Saxe Bannister (ed.), *Some Revelations in Irish History; or Old Elements of Creed and Class Conciliation in Ireland* (London, 1870), p. xxiii.

9 Shuckburgh (ed.), *William Bedell*, p. 134.

10 Ibid., pp. 126–29.

11 Ibid., p. 186.

12 Foster, *Modern Ireland*, p. 87.

13 Shuckburgh (ed.), *William Bedell*, p. 70.

14 Ibid., p. 204.

15 Saxe Bannister (ed.), *Some Revelations in Irish History*, p. xxiii.

16 King (ed.), *Henry's Upper Lough Erne in 1739*, p. 15.

17 Foster, *Modern Ireland*, p. 115.

18 King (ed.), *Henry's Upper Lough Erne in 1739*, p. 15. The Reverend William Henry is a good authority on the relationship of these two bishops to Dennis Sheridan, both because he wrote his account within a reasonable period of their deaths and because he was himself Rector of Killesher, Dennis Sheridan's old parish. That Bishop William Sheridan was Dennis Sheridan's son is also confirmed in the letter from the Bishop of Meath in 1688 already cited, where he says, "What relates to Mr Sheridan you may receive a more ample account of from the Bishop of Kilmore who is his son."

19 S. J. Connolly, *Religion, Law and Power: The Making of Protestant Ireland 1660–1760* (Oxford, 1992), p. 240; King (ed.), *Henry's Upper Lough Erne in 1739*, p. 15.

20 See his two letters to Sir Hans Sloane in 1708, British Library, Sloane Ms. 4041 f. 81 and Ms. 4060 f. 347.

2: The Godfather

1 Esther K. Sheldon, *Thomas Sheridan of Smock Alley* (Princeton, N.J., 1967), p. 180.

2 Harold Williams (ed.), *The Correspondence of Jonathan Swift* (Oxford, 1963), Vol. III, pp. 93–94.

3 Irvin Ehrenpreis, *Swift: The Man, His Works, and the Age* (London, 1983), Vol. III, p. 133.

4 See S. J. Connolly, *Religion, Law and Power* (Oxford, 1992), pp. 299–300.

5 Ibid., p. 301.

6 Jonathan Swift, *Gulliver's Travels* (Oxford, 1986 edition), pp. 204–5.

7 Williams (ed.), *Jonathan Swift Correspondence*, p. 93–94.

8 Ibid., p. 67.

9 See Connolly, *Religion, Law and Power*, p. 240.

10 Williams (ed.), *Jonathan Swift Correspondence*, p. 68.

11 See J. A. Downie, *Jonathan Swift, Political Writer* (London, 1984), p. 344.

12 Swift, *Gulliver's Travels*, p. 41.

13 Williams (ed.), *Jonathan Swift Correspondence*, p. 93.

14 Thomas Sheridan, *The Life of the Rev Dr. Jonathan Swift* (Dublin, 1785), p. 372.

15 The alarm in Dublin Castle is not perhaps as suprising as it might seem. There was already considerable concern in official quarters at the widespread practice on the part of clergymen with Jacobite leanings of neglecting to "mention his Majesty and their Royal Highnesses in the prayer before their sermons." A few years earlier, a clergyman in Kilkenny had chosen for the same anniversary of the Hanoverian accession, the text "Thou shalt not set a stranger over thee." See Connolly, *Religion, Law and Power*, p. 241.

16 Williams (ed.), *Jonathan Swift Correspondence*, pp. 93–94.

17 Ibid., p. 100.

3: No One Else to Love

1 Brinsley Butler, son of the Earl of Lanesborough, was the MP for Cavan, and either he or the Earl probably acted as sponsor at the baptism. A family memory of Brinsley Butler almost certainly lies behind Alicia's belief that her brother had been christened Richard Brinsley Butler.

2 Frederick A. Pottle (ed.), *Boswell's London Journal 1762–1763* (London, 1950), p. 91.

3 Benjamin Victor to Charles Lucas, quoted in Esther K. Sheldon, *Thomas Sheridan of Smock Alley* (Princeton, N.J., 1967), p. 191.

4 See ibid., pp. 197–222.

5 See Anna L. Barbauld (ed.), *The Correspondence of Samuel Richardson* (London, 1804), Vol. IV, p. 147.

6 Ibid., p. 165.

7 Alicia Sheridan to Hester Sheridan, 9 November 1816, in W. Fraser Rae, *Sheridan: A Biography* (London, 1896), Vol. I, pp. 73–75.

8 Frances Sheridan to Samuel Whyte, March 1759, quoted in John Watkins, *Memoirs of the Public and Private Life of the Right Honourable R. B. Sheridan* (London, 1817), Vol. I, p. 159.

9 Ibid., p. 161.

10 Thomas Moore, *Memoirs of the Life of the Right Honourable Richard Brinsley Sheridan* (London, 1825), Vol. I, p. 11.

11 Watkins, *Memoirs*, p. 162.

12 Pottle (ed.), *Boswell's London Journal*, p. 58.

13 Ibid., p. 151.

14 Thomas Sheridan to Samuel Whyte, 14 October 1764, in Watkins, *Memoirs*, pp. 123–24.

15 James Boswell, *The Life of Samuel Johnson* (London, 1992), pp. 245–46.

16 *The World*, 8 January 1788.

17 John Gore (ed.), *Thomas Creevey's Papers, 1793–1838* (Harmondsworth, 1985), p. 33.

18 Lord Holland, *Further Memoirs of the Whig Party* (London, 1816), p. 240.

19 Watkins, *Memoirs*, pp. 164–65.

20 Samuel Parr to Thomas Moore, 3 August 1818, in Moore, *Memoirs*, Vol. I, p. 7.

21 Cecil Price (ed.), *The Letters of Richard Brinsley Sheridan* (Oxford, 1966), Vol. I, p. 1. I have cited this edition throughout, but I have also consulted the emendations that Professor Price intended to make for a future edition. Where the texts given here differ from the published versions, the changes are in line with these emendations.

22 Gore (ed.), *Creevey's Papers*, p. 33.

23 See for instance William Smyth, *Memoir of Mr Sheridan* (Leeds, 1840).

24 *The Speeches of the Late Right Honourable Richard Brinsley Sheridan* (London, 1816), Vol. II, p. 117. The editor of these volumes of speeches is given only as "A Constitutional Friend," but is often believed to be Sir John Phillipart.

However, for clarity's sake, and in the absence of definite editorial attribution, I will refer to Sheridan himself as the author of these volumes of speeches.

25 Watkins, *Memoirs*, p. 130.

26 Thomas Sheridan to Samuel Whyte, in ibid., p. 133.

27 Price (ed.), *Sheridan Letters*, Vol. I, pp. 2–3.

28 See Yale Ms., Ms. Vaults, Sheridan Shelves, "Algebra 1769."

4: The Language of Truth

1 Alicia Sheridan to Hester Sheridan, 9 November 1818, reprinted in W. Fraser Rae, *Sheridan: A Biography* (London, 1896), Vol. I, p. 75.

2 In 1785, Mary Tickell wrote to Sheridan's wife mentioning Garrick's adaptation of *The Country Girl* and recalling that it was in this play that "a certain *Friend of Your's* was to have made an honourable and delicate entree into the *World*." Walter Sichel suggests that this is a reference to Sheridan himself, but there is no other evidence to show that this was the case. See Walter Sichel, *Sheridan* (London, 1909), Vol. I, pp. 262–63.

3 Thomas Moore, *Memoirs of the Life of the Right Honourable Richard Brinsley Sheridan* (London, 1825), Vol. I, p. 15.

4 John Gore (ed.), *Thomas Creevey's Papers, 1793–1838* (Harmondsworth, 1985), p. 33.

5 H. S. Woodfall (ed.), *The Letters of Junius* (London and New York, 1878), pp. 213–14.

6 In August 1762, Thomas Sheridan had written to his booksellers from Windsor ordering Hawkesworth's edition of Swift's works.

7 See Paul Kleber Monod, *Jacobitism and the English People 1688–1788* (Cambridge, 1989), p. 231.

8 Ibid., pp. 41–42.

9 Ibid., pp. 110–11.

10 Cecil Price (ed.), *The Letters of Richard Brinsley Sheridan* (Oxford, 1966), Vol. I, p. 4.

11 Charles Louis de Secondat Montesquieu, *De l'esprit des lois*, edited by Robert Derathe (Paris, 1973), Vol. I, p. 212 (my translation).

12 Moore and Sichel, dating the Novus letters to 1770, believe that Sheridan's object in them was to defend the ministry of Lord North. North, however, succeeded Grafton in January 1770, and the letters were written in October 1769.

13 Gore (ed.), *Creevey's Papers*, p. 33.

5: Like Sons of One Father

1 Thomas Sheridan, *An Oration pronounced before a Numerous Body of the Nobility and Gentry* (Dublin, 1757), p. 19.

2 Thomas Sheridan, *British Education: Or, The Source of the Disorders of Great Britain* (London, 1956), pp. 47–48.

3 James Boswell, *The Life of Samuel Johnson* (London, 1992), p. 159.

4 Frederick A. Pottle (ed.), William Sheridan, *Catholick Religion Asserted by St Paul, and Maintained in the Church of England* (Dublin, 1686), pp. 18–19.

5 Fredrick A. Pottle (ed.), *Boswell's London Journal 1762–1763* (London, 1950), p. 182.

6 See Hugh Trevor-Roper, "The Invention of Tradition: The Highland Tradition of Scotland," in Eric Hobsbawm and Terence Ranger (eds.), *The Invention of Tradition* (Cambridge, 1983), pp. 16–18.

7 Boswell, *Life of Johnson*, p. 284.

8 Ibid., p. 244.

9 Thomas Sheridan, *Dissertation on the causes of the Difficulties which occur in learning the English Tongue* (London, 1762), pp. 29–30.

6: The Beginning of Happiness

1 Cecil Price (ed.), *The Letters of Richard Brinsley Sheridan* (Oxford, 1966), Vol. I, pp. 18–21.

2 Halhed's original text is in the British Library, Add. Ms. 25935.

3 Thomas Moore, *Memoirs of the Life of the Right Honourable Richard Brinsley Sheridan* (London, 1825), Vol. I, p. 20.

4 Quoted in W. Benzie, *The Dublin Orator* (Leeds, 1972), p. 17.

5 John Gore (ed.), *Thomas Creevey's Papers, 1793–1838* (Harmondsworth, 1985), p. 33.

6 Quoted in W. Fraser Rae, *Sheridan: A Biography* (London, 1896), Vol. I, p. 99.

7 Yale Ms., z 1245; Moore, *Memoirs*, Vol. I, p. 26.

8 Sheridan's manuscript of *Hernan's Miscellany*, Vol. I, is reproduced most fully in Rae, *Sheridan*, Vol. I, pp. 417–20, and also in Moore, *Memoirs*, Vol. I, pp. 27–30, and Walter Sichel, *Sheridan* (London, 1909), Vol. I, pp. 302–5.

9 Quoted in Rae, *Sheridan*, Vol. I, p. 116.

10 Price (ed.), *Sheridan Letters*, Vol. I, p. 24.

7: The Language of Love

1 See Clementina Black, *The Linleys of Bath* (London, 1926), p. 15.

2 See the account written by Alicia Sheridan for Thomas Moore, and published in full in W. Fraser Rae, *Sheridan: A Biography* (London, 1896), Vol. I, pp. 162 ff.

3 Ibid., p. 149.

4 *The London Chronicle*, 30 July–1 August 1775, quoted in Cecil Price (ed.), *The Letters of Richard Brinsley Sheridan* (Oxford, 1966), Vol. 3, p. 300.

5 See Rae, *Sheridan*, Vol. 1, pp. 185–86.

6 Charles Lamb recounts the incident, with some very obvious inaccuracies, in an essay "My First Play," published in the *London Magazine* in December 1821. Sheridan repaid the favour in 1780 by giving Field free tickets to Drury Lane, unknowingly introducing the five-year-old Lamb to the theatre.

7 See John Ewart's letter to RBS of 27 March 1772, in Birmingham Public Library.

8 Some sources suggest that the ship on which Sheridan and Eliza travelled

belonged to Field, but it is obvious from the letter from Ewart to Sheridan cited above that it was Ewart's. He expresses the wish that "the captain behaved equall to my recommendation."

9 Price (ed.), *Sheridan Letters*, Vol. I, p. 240.

10 Wilfred S. Dowden (ed.), *The Journal of Thomas Moore* (Newark and London, 1984), Vol. I, pp. 65–66.

11 See the statement drawn up by Alicia Sheridan for Moore, in Rae, *Sheridan*, Vol. I, p. 168.

12 See Price (ed.), *Sheridan Letters*, Vol. I, p. 25, where, in a letter written to Charles on 15 April, RBS says that Eliza "has been entered some time" at a convent.

13 Letter from "W.B." to RBS, 22 March 1772, in the Widener Ms., included in Rae, *Sheridan*, Vol. I, pp. 171–72. Rae and others assume that "W.B." is William Brereton, a friend of both the Sheridan and Linley families, but it may well be William Bowers, landlord of the Sheridans' lodgings in Kingsmead Street, Bath, whose benevolent interest is mentioned in the account of the affair that Alicia gave to Moore.

14 Ibid.

15 In the letter to Charles of 15 April, Richard says he wrote to Mathews "above a week ago." These details are in a letter Sheridan drafted for the *Bath Chronicle* in May or June 1772, in Price (ed.), *Sheridan Letters*, Vol. I, p. 27. The narrative that follows is based on this statement, on that prepared by Alicia Sheridan for Moore, and on Sheridan's lengthy letter of July 1772 to Mathews's second, Captain Knight, ibid., pp. 30–34.

16 See Esther K. Sheldon, *Thomas Sheridan of Smock Alley* (Princeton, N.J., 1967), p. 276.

17 Rae, *Sheridan*, Vol. I, pp. 189–90, contains most of the text of this letter but omits this passage from the original in Widener Library, Harvard University.

18 Joseph Farington, *The Farington Diary* (London, 1923), Vol. II, pp. 193–94.

19 Dowden (ed.), *Moore's Journal*, Vol. II, p. 452.

20 G. G. S[igmond], *The Dramatic Works of Richard Brinsley Sheridan, with a Short Account of His Life* (London, 1902), Vol. I, pp. 50–51.

21 The account that follows is based on Alicia Sheridan's statement to Moore; on a contemporary letter of Thomas Sheridan to his brother-in-law Richard Chamberlaine, quoted in Rae, *Sheridan*, Vol. I, pp. 203–4; on a detailed statement drawn up by Mathews's second, William Barnett, in October 1772, in Moore, *Memoirs*, Vol. I, pp. 88–92; and on Sheridan's fragmentary draft of a reply, ibid., pp. 93–98 and in Price (ed.), *Sheridan Letters*, Vol. I, pp. 73–76. These accounts diverge on some details, but they agree on the essentials.

22 See Price (ed.), *Sheridan Letters*, Vol. I, p. 244.

23 Ibid.

8: Gentlemen and Players

1 In W. Fraser Rae, *Sheridan: A Biography* (London, 1896), Vol. I, p. 202.

2 For histories of duelling, see V. G. Kiernan, *The Duel in European History:*

Honour and the Reign of Aristocracy (Oxford, 1988), and James Kelly, *That Damn'd Thing Called Honour: Duelling in Ireland 1570–1860* (Cork, 1995).

3 The account that follows is drawn from Esther K. Sheldon, *Thomas Sheridan of Smock Alley* (Princeton, N.J., 1967), pp. 84 ff.

4 Quoted in Siobhan Kilfeather, "Look Who's Talking: Scandalous Memoirs and the Performance of Gender," in *Irish Review*, No. 13 (Belfast), Winter 1992/93.

5 National Library of Ireland, Le Fanu Papers, Dr. Thomas Sheridan to Thomas Carte, 21 June 1733.

6 Letter to Richard Chamberlaine, in Rae, *Sheridan*, Vol. I, pp. 203–4.

7 See Cecil Price (ed.), *The Letters of Richard Brinsley Sheridan* (Oxford, 1966), Vol. I, p. 244.

8 Quoted in Rae, *Sheridan*, Vol. I, pp. 201–2.

9: The Great Gate of Power

1 Cecil Price (ed.), *The Letters of Richard Brinsley Sheridan* (Oxford, 1966), Vol. I, p. 78.

2 Quoted in W. Fraser Rae, *Sheridan: A Biography* (London, 1896), Vol. I, pp. 252.

3 Price (ed.), *Sheridan Letters*, Vol. I, p. 61.

4 Ibid., p. 67.

5 Ibid., p. 71.

6 Ibid., p. 45.

7 Widener Ms., sheet 17.

8 Price (ed.), *Sheridan Letters*, Vol. I, pp. 40–41.

9 Ibid., p. 68.

10 *Westminster Magazine*, March 1773, p. 219.

11 Price (ed.), *Sheridan Letters*, Vol. I, pp. 47–59.

12 Ibid., p. 35.

13 Ibid., p. 77.

14 Elizabeth Linley to RBS, Widener Ms., sheet 19.

15 Price (ed.), *Sheridan Letters*, Vol. I, p. 46.

16 Widener Ms., sheet 23.

17 Quoted in Rae, *Sheridan*, Vol. I, p. 255.

18 Price (ed.), *Sheridan Letters*, Vol. I, p. 68.

19 Ibid., p. 81; Clementina Black, *The Linleys of Bath* (London, 1926), p. 104.

20 Price (ed.), *Sheridan Letters*, Vol. I, p. 83.

21 The fragmentary remains of what seems to have been a long essay on Chesterfield are given in Thomas Moore, *Memoirs of the Life of the Right Honourable Richard Brinsley Sheridan* (London, 1825), Vol. I, pp. 134 ff., and Walter Sichel, *Sheridan* (London, 1909), pp. 471 ff.

10: Beastly Pimping Actors

1 Peter Jupp (ed.), *The Letter Journal of George Canning 1793–1795* (London, 1991), pp. 230–31.

2 Cecil Price (ed.), *The Letters of Richard Brinsley Sheridan* (Oxford, 1966), Vol. I, p. 80.
3 James Boswell, *The Life of Samuel Johnson* (London, 1992), p. 556.
4 Frederick A. Pottle (ed.), *Boswell's London Journal 1762–1763* (London, 1950), pp. 136–37.
5 Price (ed.), *Sheridan Letters*, Vol. III, pp. 293–307.
6 Ibid., Vol. I, p. 85.
7 Reproduced in Thomas Moore, *Memoirs of the Life of the Right Honourable Richard Brinsley Sheridan* (London, 1825), Vol. I, pp. 137–38.
8 Sheridan, *The Rivals*, I, ii, in Cecil Price (ed.), *The Dramatic Works of Richard Brinsley Sheridan* (Oxford, 1973), Vol. I, p. 85.
9 See W. Fraser Rae (ed.), *Sheridan's Plays, first printed from his Mss* (London, 1902), p. xxxix. Frances Sheridan's *A Journey to Bath* is also printed in this volume.
10 Sheridan, *The Rivals*, I, ii, in Price (ed.), *Dramatic Works*, Vol. I, p. 86.
11 Ibid., prologue, p. 72.
12 Ibid., II, i, p. 92.
13 Ibid., V, i, p. 135.
14 Ibid., III, iii.
15 Quoted in Price (ed.), *Dramatic Works*, Vol. I, p. 40.
16 Ibid., Vol. I, p. 70.
17 George H. Nettleton, "The Books in Lydia Languish's Circulating Library," *Journal of English and German Philology*, Vol. 5, London, 1903–5, pp. 492–500.
18 Sheridan, *The Rivals*, III, iv, in Price (ed.), *Dramatic Works*, Vol. I, p. 115.
19 John Gore (ed.), *Thomas Creevey's Papers, 1793–1823* (Harmondsworth, 1985), p. 35.
20 Price (ed.), *Sheridan Letters*, Vol. III, pp. 292–93.

11: One Leg at Boston

1 The full text is published in Walter Sichel, *Sheridan* (London, 1909), Vol. I, pp. 624–29.
2 James Boswell, *The Life of Samuel Johnson* (London, 1992), p. 523.
3 Cecil Price (ed.), *The Letters of Richard Brinsley Sheridan* (Oxford, 1966), Vol. I, p. 21.
4 Sheridan, *The Rivals*, preface, in Cecil Price (ed.) *The Dramatic Works of Richard Brinsley Sheridan* (Oxford, 1973), Vol. I, p. 71.
5 Sheridan, *St Patrick's Day*, I, ii, in ibid., p. 170.
6 See Jean Dulck, *Les Comédies de R. B. Sheridan* (Paris, 1962), pp. 152–53.
7 Price (ed.), *Sheridan Letters*, Vol. I, p. 89.
8 Sheridan, *The Duenna*, III, v, in Price (ed.), *Dramatic Works*, Vol. I, p. 274.
9 Ibid., I, iii.
10 *Garrick Correspondence*, Victoria and Albert Museum, London, Vol. 22, ff. 14–15.
11 A breakdown of the various meetings involved can be worked out from the

claim for legal fees by Robert Crispin, who acted for the purchasers, BL, Add. Ms. 44919 ff. 39–43.

12 Price (ed.), *Sheridan Letters*, Vol. I, p. 100.

13 Ibid., p. 97.

14 The promissory note was sold in 1952; see Maggs catalogue, no. 809, item 259.

12: Light Entertainment

1 Oliver Goldsmith, *The Citizen of the World* (London, 1969), p. 75.

2 William Windham to Thomas Amyot, 18 December 1809, quoted in Marc Baer, *Theatre and Disorder in Late Georgian London* (Oxford, 1992), p. 39.

3 Ibid., pp. 76–77.

4 Quoted in Baer, *Theatre and Disorder*, p. 65.

5 Ibid., p. 75.

6 Goldsmith, *The Citizen of the World*, p. 75.

13: Bringing the House Down

1 Frederic Reynolds, *The Life and Times of Frederic Reynolds* (London, 1826), Vol. I, p. 110.

2 Jean-Jacques Rousseau, *Letter to M. d'Alembert*, trans. A. Bloom (Ithaca, 1968), pp. 58–59.

3 Denis Diderot, *The Paradox of Acting*, quoted in Richard Sennett, *The Fall of Public Man* (New York, 1986), p. 112. I am greatly indebted to Sennett's brilliant discussion of the public personality of the eighteenth century in this book.

4 See Eric Rump, "Sheridan, Congreve and *The School for Scandal,*" in James Morwood and David Crane (eds.), *Sheridan Studies* (Cambridge, 1995), pp. 58–70.

5 Quoted by F. W. Bateson in the introduction to his edition of *The School for Scandal* (London, 1989), p. xxi.

6 Cecil Price (ed.), *The Letters of Richard Brinsley Sheridan* (Oxford, 1966), Vol. I, p. 95.

7 Sheridan, *The School for Scandal*, I, i, in Cecil Price (ed.), *The Dramatic Works of Richard Brinsley Sheridan* (Oxford, 1973), Vol. I, pp. 359–60.

8 James Boswell, *Life of Samuel Johnson* (London, 1992), p. 246.

9 Price (ed.), *Dramatic Works*, Vol. I, pp. 302–3.

10 Richard Brinsley Sheridan, *The Speeches of the Late Right Honourable Richard Brinsley Sheridan* (London, 1816), Vol. 4, pp. 188–89.

11 William Cobbett (ed.), *The Parliamentary History of England* (London, 1818), Vol. 32, p. 441.

12 *London Evening Post*, 1–3 May 1777, quoted in Price (ed.), *Dramatic Works*, Vol. I, p. 302.

13 Sheridan, *The School for Scandal*, III, i, in Price (ed.), *Dramatic Works*, Vol. I, p. 388.

14 Ibid., p. 389.

14: All the Rage

1 George Otto Trevelyan, *The Early History of Charles James Fox* (London, 1880), p. 87.
2 Linda Colley, *Britons* (New York, 1994), pp. 61, 155.
3 Quoted in Christopher Clayton, "The Political Career of Richard Brinsley Sheridan," in Morwood and Crane (eds.), *Sheridan Studies* (Cambridge, 1995), p. 138.
4 Lord John Russell (ed.), *Memorials and Correspondence of Charles James Fox* (London, 1853–57), Vol. III, p. 67.
5 Thomas Moore, *Memoirs of the Life of the Right Honourable Richard Brinsley Sheridan* (London, 1825), Vol. I, p. 289.
6 British Library, Add. Mss. 44041, f. 30 (Gladstone Papers).
7 Theodore Zeldin, *An Intimate History of Humanity* (New York, 1995), p. 35.
8 Cecil Price (ed.), *The Letters of Richard Brinsley Sheridan* (Oxford, 1966), Vol. I p. 40.
9 Ibid., Vol. III, p. 202.
10 Quoted in R. Compton Rhodes (ed.), *An Ode to Scandal Together with a Portrait by Richard Brinsley Sheridan* (Oxford, 1927), p. 13.
11 Ibid; letters to Mrs. Canning in Walter Sichel, *Sheridan* (London, 1909), Vol. II, p. 64; Fanny Burney in C. F. Barrett (ed.), *Diary and Letters of Madame D'Arblay* (London, 1842), Vol. I, p. 182.
12 Price (ed.), *Sheridan Letters*, Vol. I, p. 84.
13 William Le Fanu (ed.), *Betsy Sheridan's Journal* (London, 1960), p. 133.
14 Leslie A. Marchand (ed.), *Byron's Letters and Journals 1821–2* (Cambridge, Mass., 1979), Vol. IX, p. 15.
15 Price (ed.), *Sheridan Letters*, Vol. I, p. 125.
16 The essay is published in Sichel, *Sheridan*, Vol. I, pp. 598–601; and in Moore, *Memoirs of Sheridan*, Vol. I, pp. 280–88.
17 Colley, *Britons*, p. 191.

15: Theatrical Politics

1 See James Boswell, *Life of Samuel Johnson* (London, 1992), p. 709.
2 Printed in W. Fraser Rae, *Sheridan: A Biography* (London, 1896), Vol. II, p. 4.
3 Quoted in Esther K. Sheldon, *Thomas Sheridan of Smock Alley* (Princeton, N.J., 1967), p. 290.
4 *The Camp*, I, i, in Cecil Price (ed.), *The Dramatic Works of Richard Brinsley Sheridan* (Oxford, 1973), Vol. II, p. 729.
5 *The Critic*, I, i, ibid., p. 497.
6 Ibid., pp. 503–4.
7 Quoted in Price (ed.), *Dramatic Works*, Vol. II, pp. 470–71.
8 *The Critic*, I, ii, ibid., p. 515.
9 Ibid.
10 Ibid., p. 483.
11 II, ii, ibid., pp. 524–25.

12 Ibid., p. 528.
13 Details from Sheldon, *Thomas Sheridan of Smock Alley*, p. 298.
14 William Le Fanu (ed.), *Betsy Sheridan's Journal* (London, 1960), p. 27.
15 National Library of Ireland, Le Fanu Papers, Thomas Sheridan to Alicia, 10 November 1784.
16 Robert D. Hume, "The Multifarious Forms of Eighteenth Century Comedy," in George Winchester Stone (ed.), *The Stage and the Page: London's "Whole Show" in the Eighteenth Century Theatre* (Berkeley, 1981), p. 24.

16: A Public Man

1 Minutes of the Westminster Committee, February–July 1780, BL, Add. Mss. 38593.
2 Quoted in Walter Sichel, *Sheridan* (London, 1909), Vol. I, p. 102.
3 Ibid.
4 Cecil Price (ed.), *The Letters of Richard Brinsley Sheridan* (Oxford, 1966), Vol. I, p. 135.
5 Christopher Hibbert (ed.), *Captain Gronow: His Reminiscences of Regency and Victorian Life 1810–60* (London, 1991), pp. 224–26.
6 John Watkins, *Memoirs of the Public and Private Life of the Right Honourable R. B. Sheridan* (London, 1817), Vol. I, p. 257.
7 William Earle, *Sheridan and His Times, by An Octogenarian, who stood by his knee in youth and sat at his table in manhood* (London, 1859), pp. 220–39. Earle's account of this event is not based on personal observation: his acquaintance with Sheridan dates from 1790. But he claims to have heard it directly from Sheridan, who was fond of recalling the details of his first political triumph.
8 *The Hibernian Journal*, 23–26 September 1780.
9 Price (ed.), *Sheridan Letters*, Vol. I, p. 134. The italics are in the original.
10 Ibid.
11 *Public Advertiser*, 5 December 1780.
12 See Richard Brinsley Sheridan, *The Speeches of the Late Right Honourable Richard Brinsley Sheridan* (London, 1816), Vol. V, pp. 335–36.
13 Ibid., Vol. I, pp. 13–14.

17: Dreams of Empty Fame

1 National Library of Ireland, Le Fanu Papers, p. 2595.
2 Ibid., Thomas to Alicia, 15 November 1783.
3 William Le Fanu (ed.), *Betsy Sheridan's Journal* (London, 1960), p. 61.
4 NLI, Le Fanu Papers, 15 November 1783.
5 Cecil Price (ed.), *The Letters of Richard Brinsley Sheridan* (Oxford, 1966), Vol. I, p. 139. "Mon Frère" is here given as "France," but the editor intended to amend the passage for later editions.
6 NLI, Le Fanu Papers, 23 June 1783.
7 Quoted in Edith M. Johnston, *Great Britain and Ireland 1760–1800* (Edinburgh and London, 1963), p. 66.
8 C. F. Sheridan, *Observations on the doctrine laid down by Sir William Blackstone*

respecting the extent of the power of the British Parliament, particularly with relation to Ireland (Dublin, 1779).

9 Quoted in Thomas Moore, *Memoirs of the Life of the Right Honourable Richard Brinsley Sheridan* (London, 1825), Vol. I, p. 372.

10 Price (ed.), *Sheridan Letters*, Vol. I, p. 140.

11 Ibid., p. 143.

12 Richard Brinsley Sheridan, *The Speeches of the Late Right Honourable Richard Brinsley Sheridan* (London, 1816), Vol. I, pp. 31–33.

13 See James Kelly, *Prelude to Union: Anglo-Irish Politics in the 1780s* (Cork, 1992), p. 37.

14 Ibid., p. 39.

15 Price (ed.), *Sheridan Letters*, Vol. I, p. 144: Sheridan to Richard Fitzpatrick.

16 Ibid.; the emphasis is Sheridan's.

17 Ibid., p. 148.

18 Ibid., p. 153.

19 *English Chronicle*, 7 December 1782; *London Courant*, 3 and 23 December 1782.

20 Wilfred S. Dowden (ed.), *The Journal of Thomas Moore* (Newark and London, 1984), Vol. II, p. 642.

21 Sheridan, *Speeches of Sheridan*, Vol. I, p. 84.

22 Ibid., p. 52.

23 Ibid., p. 53.

24 Sir N. William Wraxall, *Historical Memoirs of My Own Time* (London, 1904), p. 564.

25 Price (ed.), *Sheridan Letters*, Vol. I, p. 156.

26 Sheridan, *Speeches of Sheridan*, Vol. I, pp. 216–18.

27 E. B. Impey, *Memoirs of Sir Elijah Impey* (London, 1857), p. 356.

28 See P. J. Marshall, *The Impeachment of Warren Hastings* (Oxford, 1965), pp. 20–21; and L. G. Mitchell, *Charles James Fox and the Disintegration of the Whig Party* (Oxford, 1971), p. 65.

29 See Conor Cruise O'Brien, *The Great Melody: A Thematic Biography of Edmund Burke* (New York, 1992), p. 315.

30 Sheridan, *Speeches of Sheridan*, Vol. I, p. 72.

18: The Catholic Queen

1 "The Ms Journal of Captain E. Thompson, R.N.," *Cornhill Magazine*, XVII, 1868, p. 634.

2 A. Aspinall (ed.), *The Correspondence of George, Prince of Wales* (London, 1963), Vol. I, p. 507.

3 Cecil Price (ed.), *The Letters of Richard Brinsley Sheridan* (Oxford, 1966), Vol. I, p. 240.

4 Prince of Wales to Fox, quoted in Christopher Hibbert, *George IV* (London, 1972), Vol. I: *Prince of Wales*, p. 52.

5 See Charles Langdale, *Memoirs of Mrs Fitzherbert* (London, 1856), p. 163.

6 Ibid., p. 172.

7 Lord John Russell (ed.), *Memorials and Correspondence of Charles James Fox*

(London, 1853), Vol. II, pp. 287–90. See also the note of a conversation between Grey and Grenville in 1814, BL, Add. Ms. 58949, f. 116–21.

8 Richard Brinsley Sheridan, *The Speeches of the Late Right Honourable Richard Brinsley Sheridan* (London, 1816), Vol. I, p. 380.

9 A. Aspinall (ed.), *The Later Correspondence of George III* (Cambridge, 1961–70), Vol. I, p. 283.

10 William Le Fanu (ed.), *Betsy Sheridan's Journal* (London, 1960), pp. 162–63.

19: A Great Stir about Paddy Land

1 William Le Fanu (ed.), *Betsy Sheridan's Journal* (London, 1960), p. 58.

2 National Library of Ireland, Le Fanu Papers, Elizabeth to Alicia, undated but evidently 1784.

3 Letter of 10 March 1784, published in Thomas Moore, *Memoirs of the Life of the Right Honourable Richard Brinsley Sheridan* (London, 1825), Vol. I, pp. 409–17.

4 Ibid.

5 NLI, Le Fanu Papers, undated.

6 Cecil Price (ed.), *Letters of Richard Brinsley Sheridan* (Oxford, 1966), Vol. I, p. 164.

7 Quoted in James Kelly, *Prelude to Union: Anglo-Irish Politics in the 1780s* (Cork, 1992), p. 99.

8 No speech of Sheridan's for 12 May is recorded, but this crucial remark is recorded in the Rutland manuscripts, Vol. III, p. 206.

9 Richard Brinsley Sheridan, *The Speeches of the Late Right Honourable Richard Brinsley Sheridan* (London, 1816), Vol. I, p. 164.

10 Ibid., pp. 166–67.

11 A. Aspinall (ed.), *The Later Correspondence of George III* (Cambridge, 1961–70), Vol. I, p. 173.

12 Price (ed.), *Sheridan Letters*, Vol. I, p. 163.

13 Kelly, *Prelude to Union*, p. 163.

14 Quoted in Moore, *Memoirs of Sheridan*, Vol. I, pp. 431–32.

15 Kelly, *Prelude to Union*, p. 190.

20: A Day in the Life

1 Wilfred S. Dowden (ed.), *Thomas Moore's Journal* (Newark and London, 1984), Vol. I, p. 92.

2 National Library of Ireland, Le Fanu Papers, Elizabeth to Alicia, undated.

3 William Smyth, *Memoir of Mr Sheridan* (Leeds, 1840), p. 43.

4 James Boaden, *Memoirs of the Life of John Philip Kemble* (London, 1825), Vol. I, p. 203.

5 Smyth, *Memoir of Mr Sheridan*, p. 42.

6 Boaden, *Memoirs of Kemble*, p. 204.

7 Smyth, *Memoir of Mr Sheridan*, pp. 55–56.

8 Thomas Medwin, *Conversations of Lord Byron: Noted During a Residence with His Lordship at Pisa* (London, 1824), p. 235.

9 Joseph Farington, R. A., *The Farington Diary* (London, 1923), Vol. II, p. 81.
10 Kenneth Bourne (ed.), *The Letters of the Third Viscount Palmerston to Laurence and Elizabeth Sullivan, 1804–1863* (London, 1979), p. 67.
11 Dowden (ed.), *Thomas Moore's Journal*, Vol. I, p. 27.
12 Le Fanu (ed.), *Betsy Sheridan's Journal*, p. 111.
13 Cecil Price (ed.), *The Letters of Richard Brinsley Sheridan* (Oxford, 1966), Vol. I, p. 42; NLI, Le Fanu Papers, undated.
14 Farington, *The Farington Diary*, Vol. II, p. 193; Boaden, *Memoirs of Kemble*, Vol. 2, pp. 74–77.
15 Smyth, *Memoir of Mr Sheridan*, pp. 58–61.
16 See Mark S. Auburn, "Theatre in the Age of Garrick and Sheridan," in James Morwood and David Crane (eds.), *Sheridan Studies* (Cambridge, 1995), p. 44.
17 Percy Fitzgerald, *The Kembles* (London, 1871), Vol. I, p. 241.
18 Anon., *Sheridiana, or Anecdotes of the Life of Richard Brinsley Sheridan* (London, 1826), pp. 189–90.
19 Thomas Moore (ed.), *Letters and Journals of Lord Byron* (London, 1830), Vol. I, p. 404.
20 Sir N. William Wraxall, *Historical Memoirs of My Own Time* (London, 1904).
21 Thomas Moore, *Memoirs of the Life of the Right Honourable Richard Brinsley Sheridan* (London, 1825), Vol. II, pp. 85–86. His source for this story was O'Beirne himself.
22 Le Fanu (ed.), *Betsy Sheridan's Journal*, p. 160.
23 Price (ed.), *Sheridan Letters*, Vol. III, p. 202.
24 Wraxall, *Historical Memoirs*, p. 358.
25 On this subject, see Christopher Reid, "Foiling the Rival: Sheridan's Speeches," in Morwood and Crane (eds.), *Sheridan Studies*, pp. 114–30.
26 Richard Brinsley Sheridan, *The Speeches of the Late Right Honourable Richard Brinsley Sheridan* (London, 1816), Vol. I, p. 5.
27 Quoted in Mark S. Auburn, "Theatre in the Age of Garrick and Sheridan," in Morwood and Crane (eds.), *Sheridan Studies*, p. 30.
28 Dowden (ed.), *Thomas Moore's Journal*, Vol. I, p. 91.
29 Price (ed.), *Sheridan Letters*, Vol. II, p. 196.
30 Sheridan, *Speeches of Sheridan*, Vol. I, p. 47.
31 Ibid., p. 154.
32 Ibid., Vol. IV, p. 75.
33 John Gore (ed.), *Thomas Creevey's Papers, 1793–1823* (Harmondsworth, 1985), p. 22.
34 Henry Lord Brougham, *Historical Sketches of Statesmen Who Flourished in the Time of George III*, First Series (London, 1845), Vol. II, p. 32.
35 Lady Minto (ed.), *Life and Letters of Sir Gilbert Elliot* (London, 1874), Vol. I, p. 189.
36 National Library of Ireland, Le Fanu Papers, N 2975.
37 W. Fraser Rae, *Sheridan: A Biography* (London, 1896), Vol. II, p. 128–29.

38 Moore (ed.), *Letters and Journals of Lord Byron*, Vol. I, pp. 634–35.
39 Samuel Taylor Coleridge, *Remorse* (London, 1813), pp. 3–6.
40 George Otto Trevelyan, *The Early History of Charles James Fox* (London, 1880), p. 482.
41 Smyth, *Memoir of Mr Sheridan*, p. 44.

21: A Speaking Picture

1 E. B. Impey, *Memoirs of Sir Elijah Impey* (London, 1857), p. 354. The author, Impey's son, attributed this information to Edward Monckton, son of Sheridan's running mate.
2 Keith Feiling, *Warren Hastings* (London, 1954), p. 276.
3 Richard Brinsley Sheridan, *The Speeches of the Late Right Honourable Richard Brinsley Sheridan* (London, 1816), Vol. I, pp. 103–4. This speech is an important contradiction of Conor Cruise O'Brien's claim in *The Great Melody: A Thematic Biography of Edmund Burke* (London, 1992), p. 357, that Sheridan was not, before February 1787, "an enthusiast for the India cause."
4 Sheridan, *Speeches of Sheridan*, Vol. I, pp. 270–99.
5 Countess of Minto (ed.), *The Life and Letters of Sir Gilbert Elliot, 1st Earl of Minto, 1750–1806* (London, 1874), Vol. I, pp. 123–24.
6 Quoted in W. Fraser Rae, *Sheridan: A Biography* (London, 1896), Vol. II, pp. 60–61.
7 Ibid., pp. 58, 62.
8 R. V. Smith (ed.), *Letters Addressed to the Countess of Ossory, from the year 1769 to 1797* (London, 1848), Vol. II, pp. 298–99.
9 Pitt cited in P. J. Marshall, *The Impeachment of Warren Hastings*, p. 530; Charles Sheridan cited in Rae, *Sheridan*, Vol. II, p. 65.
10 William Le Fanu (ed.), *Betsy Sheridan's Journal* (London, 1960), p. 109.
11 Quoted in Walter Sichel, *Sheridan* (London, 1909), Vol. II, p. 122.

22: The Rights of Man

1 Fanny Burney, *The Diary and Letters of Madame D'Arblay* (London, 1842–46), Vol. IV, pp. 56–62.
2 Keith Feiling, *Warren Hastings* (London, 1954), p. 351.
3 Cecil Price (ed.), *The Letters of Richard Brinsley Sheridan* (Oxford, 1966), Vol. I, p. 180.
4 National Library of Ireland, Le Fanu Papers, Elizabeth to Alicia, undated.
5 Richard Brinsley Sheridan, *The Speeches of the Late Right Honourable Richard Brinsley Sheridan* (London, 1816), Vol. II, pp. 55–127. I have also, where the text seems less garbled or fuller, made use of the version of the speech in E. A. Bond (ed.), *Speeches of the Managers and Counsel in the Trial of Warren Hastings* (London, 1859–61), Vol. I.
6 *A Trip to Scarborough*, II, i, in Price (ed.), *The Dramatic Works of Richard Brinsley Sheridan* (Oxford, 1973), Vol. II, p. 586.
7 William Le Fanu (ed.), *Betsy Sheridan's Journal* (London, 1960), p. 106.
8 Dr. Daniel Jarvis's letter to Thomas Moore, in Moore, *Memoirs of the Life of*

the Right Honourable Richard Brinsley Sheridan (London, 1825), Vol. II, pp. 14–16.

9 Printed in W. Fraser Rae, *Sheridan: A Biography* (London, 1896), Vol. II, p. 74.

23: The Tongue Set Free

1 See C. F. Barrett (ed.), *Diary and Letters of Madame D'Arblay* (London, 1842), Vol. IV, pp. 272–73.
2 Ida Macalpine and Richard Hunter, *George III and the Mad-Business* (London, 1991), p. 20.
3 See Christopher Hibbert, *George IV* (London, 1972), Vol. I: *Prince of Wales* pp. 79–80.
4 P. H. Stanhope, *Life of the Right Honourable William Pitt* (London, 1867), Vol. I, p. 391.
5 Macalpine and Hunter, *George III and the Mad-Business*, p. 29.
6 A. Aspinall (ed.), *The Correspondence of George, Prince of Wales* (London, 1963), Vol. I, p. 382.
7 Ibid., p. 371.
8 Quoted in Cecil Price (ed.), *The Letters of Richard Brinsley Sheridan* (Oxford, 1966), Vol. I, p. 187.
9 William Le Fanu (ed.), *Betsy Sheridan's Journal* (London, 1960), pp. 130–31.
10 Payne to Sheridan, Thomas Moore (ed.), *Memoirs of the Life of the Right Honourable Richard Brinsley Sheridan* (London, 1825), Vol. II, pp. 24–27.
11 Robert H. Taylor Ms.
12 Price (ed.), *Sheridan Letters*, Vol. I, pp. 189.
13 British Library, Add. Ms. 41579, f. 12.
14 Richard Brinsley Sheridan, *The Speeches of the Late Right Honourable Richard Brinsley Sheridan* (London, 1816), Vol. II, pp. 164–66.
15 Aspinall (ed.), *Correspondence of George, Prince of Wales*, Vol. I, p. 371.
16 Sydney Ms., William L. Clements Library, Ann Arbor, Michigan, Vol. 15.
17 Price (ed.), *Sheridan Letters*, Vol. I, p. 190.
18 Ibid., p. 192.
19 Ibid., p. 196.
20 Ibid., p. 198.
21 Ibid., p. 201.
22 Sheridan, *Speeches of Sheridan*, Vol. II, p. 144.
23 Le Fanu (ed.), *Betsy Sheridan's Journal*, p. 138.
24 Portland cited in Duke of Buckingham and Chandos, *Memoirs of the Courts and Cabinets of George III* (London, 1853), Vol. I, p. 451; Duchess of Devonshire cited in Walter Sichel, *Sheridan* (London, 1909), Vol. II, p. 406.
25 Le Fanu (ed.), *Betsy Sheridan's Journal*, p. 149.
26 Ibid., p. 109.
27 Ibid., p. 156.
28 Price (ed.), *Sheridan Letters*, Vol. I, p. 210.
29 Aspinall (ed.), *Correspondence of George, Prince of Wales*, Vol. I, p. 382.

30 *Duchess of Devonshire's Diary*, in Sichel, *Sheridan*, Vol. II, p. 422.
31 O. Browning (ed.), *Political Memoranda of the 5th Duke of Leeds* (London, 1884), pp. vi–ix.
32 Le Fanu (ed.), *Betsy Sheridan's Journal*, p. 142.
33 See Macalpine and Hunter, *George III and the Mad-Business*, p. 272.
34 Le Fanu (ed.), *Betsy Sheridan's Journal*, pp. 151–52.
35 Ibid., pp. 156–57.
36 The Earl of Bessborough (ed.), *Lady Bessborough and Her Family Circle* (London, 1940), p. 48.

24: A Hero and a Harlequin

1 William Le Fanu (ed.), *Betsy Sheridan's Journal* (London, 1960), pp. 167–69.
2 John Gore (ed.), *Thomas Creevey's Papers, 1793–1828* (Harmondsworth, 1985), p. 36.
3 Wilfred S. Dowden (ed.), *The Journals of Thomas Moore* (Newark and London, 1984), Vol. I, p. 70.
4 *Recollections of the Table Talk of Samuel Rogers* (New York, 1856), pp. 63–71.
5 Cecil Price (ed.), *The Letters of Richard Brinsley Sheridan* (Oxford, 1966), Vol. I, p. 208.
6 Ibid.
7 American Philosophical Society Ms.
8 Le Fanu (ed.), *Betsy Sheridan's Journal*, p. 154.
9 Brian Fitzgerald (ed.), *Correspondence of Emily Duchess of Leinster* (Dublin, 1953), Vol. II, p. 337.
10 Journal of Lady Elizabeth Foster, Chatsworth House Mss., 5 June 1789.
11 Lord John Russell (ed.), *Memorials and Correspondence of Charles James Fox* (London, 1853–57), Vol. II, p. 361.
12 Price (ed.), *Sheridan Letters*, Vol. I, p. 226.
13 Thomas Copeland (ed.), *The Correspondence of Edmund Burke* (Cambridge, 1958–78), Vol. VI, p. 10.
14 Price (ed.), *Sheridan Letters*, Vol. I, p. 226.
15 Le Fanu (ed.), *Betsy Sheridan's Journal*, p. 156.
16 "Some Unpublished Letters of Mrs Sheridan to Mrs Canning," appendix to T. H. Sadlier (ed.), *The Political Career of Richard Brinsley Sheridan* (Oxford, 1912), pp. 81–85.
17 Le Fanu (ed.), *Betsy Sheridan's Journal*, p. 195.
18 Esther K. Sheldon believes the play was Burke's, but the *Dublin University Magazine* of April 1837 attributes it to "Brennan, Burke's friend." Either way, it is clear that Burke had a strong interest in the rejected play.
19 Esther K. Sheldon, *Thomas Sheridan of Smock Alley* (Princeton, N.J., 1967), p. 121.
20 James Boswell, *The Life of Samuel Johnson* (London, 1992), p. 794.
21 Price (ed.), *Sheridan Letters*, Vol. I, p. 211. Price dates this letter 13 April, but Thomas Copeland, editor of Burke's correspondence, give it as 30 March, which seems more likely.

22 See Albert Goodwin, *The Friends of Liberty* (London, 1979), pp. 120 and 137.
23 Quoted in Conor Cruise O'Brien, *The Great Melody: A Thematic Biography of Edmund Burke* (New York, 1992), p. 505.
24 *The Parliamentary History of England* (London, 1816), Vol. XVIII, p. 330.
25 Richard Brinsley Sheridan, *The Speeches of the Late Right Honourable Richard Brinsley Sheridan* (London, 1816), Vol. II, pp. 242 ff.
26 Countess of Minto (ed.), *The Life and Letters of Sir Gilbert Elliot, 1st Earl of Minto, 1750–1806* (London, 1874), Vol. II, p. 351.
27 Dowden (ed.), *Moore Journal*, Vol. II, p. 107.
28 In evidence at Tooke's trial in 1794, Sheridan "said that he himself objected to Mr Tooke's amendment." See Moore, *Memoirs of Sheridan*, Vol. II, p. 246.
29 Goodwin, *The Friends of Liberty*, p. 124.
30 Sheridan, *Speeches of Sheridan*, Vol. II, p. 256.

25: Night, Silence, Solitude, and the Sea

1 Thomas Moore (ed.), *Letters and Journals of Lord Byron* (London, 1830), Vol. I, p. 505.
2 Cited in Stella Tillyard, *Citizen Lord: Edward Fitzgerald 1763–1798* (New York, 1998), p. 138.
3 Cited in Clementine Black, *The Linleys of Bath* (London, 1926), pp. 151–52.
4 Ibid., p. 155.
5 Brian Fitzgerald (ed.), *Correspondence of Emily Duchess of Leinster* (Dublin, 1953), Vol. II, p. 66.
6 William Le Fanu (ed.), *Betsy Sheridan's Journal* (London, 1960), p. 140; Godwin cited in William St. Clair, *The Godwins and the Shelleys* (London, 1990), p. 50.
7 Cecil Price (ed.), *The Letters of Richard Brinsley Sheridan* (Oxford, 1966), Vol. I, p. 237.
8 Fitzgerald (ed.), *Duchess of Leinster Correspondence*, Vol. II, p. 64.
9 Ibid., p. 66.
10 Price (ed.), *Sheridan Letters*, Vol. I, p. 239.
11 Sheridan, in ibid., p. 245; Fitzgerald in Fitzgerald (ed.), *Duchess of Leinster Correspondence,* Vol. II, p. 69.
12 Wilfred S. Dowden (ed.), *The Journal of Thomas Moore* (Newark and London, 1984), Vol. II, p. 807.
13 Lady Sarah Napier to William Ogilvie, 11 July 1792, in Fitzgerald (ed.), *Duchess of Leinster Correspondence*, Vol. II, p. 337.
14 Price (ed.), *Sheridan Letters*, Vol. II, p. 257.
15 Fitzgerald (ed.), *Duchess of Leinster Correspondence*, Vol. II, p. 71. Fitzgerald expressed his regret that Sheridan felt that he had been indiscreet, but added, "I think the story being known is his fault and not mine."
16 Ibid., pp. 69–71.
17 Ibid., pp. 68–69.
18 William Smyth, *Memoir of Mr Sheridan* (Leeds, 1840), p. 28.

19 Cited in Wellek and Ribeiro (eds.), *Evidence in Literary Scholarship* (London, 1979), p. 318.
20 See Tillyard, *Citizen Lord*, p. 149.

26: Hercules and the Hydra

1 The painting is in the National Portrait Gallery in London.
2 J. B. Morritt to Walter Scott, 1 July 1811, in Wilfred Partington (ed.), *The Private Letter-Books of Sir Walter Scott* (London, 1930), p. 20.
3 Quoted in William St. Clair, *The Godwins and the Shelleys* (London, 1989), p. 51.
4 Joseph Farington (ed.), *The Farington Diary* (London, 1923), Vol. I, p. 36.
5 Richard Brinsley Sheridan, *The Speeches of the Late Right Honourable Richard Brinsley Sheridan* (London, 1816), Vol. II, p. 245.
6 See Simon Schama, *Citizens: A Chronicle of the French Revolution* (New York, 1989), p. 560.
7 Quoted in John Brims, "Scottish Radicalism and the United Irishmen," in Dickson, Keogh, and Whelan (eds.), *The United Irishmen* (Dublin, 1993), p. 338.
8 Sheridan, *Speeches of Sheridan*, Vol. III, pp. 208–9.
9 John Norris, *Shelburne and Reform* (London, 1963), p. 278.
10 *Proceedings of the Society of Friends of the People in the Year 1792* (London, 1793), p. 4.
11 Dated 20 March (from the watermark almost certainly 1792), this letter is in the Robert H. Taylor collection.
12 *Proceedings of the Society of Friends of the People*, pp. 16–17.
13 A. Aspinall (ed.), *The Later Correspondence of George III* (Cambridge, 1961–70), Vol. I, p. 591.
14 Sheridan, *Speeches of Sheridan*, Vol. III, p. 12.
15 This and following quotations from *Proceedings of the Society of Friends of the People*, pp. 58–65.
16 *A Letter from Lord George Gordon in Newgate, to Baron de Alvensleben, Minister from Hanover* (London, 1792), p. 5.
17 *Collection of Addresses Transmitted by Certain English Clubs and Societies to the National Convention of France* (London, 1793), pp. 93–94.
18 Sheridan, *Speeches of Sheridan*, Vol. III, p. 53.
19 National Library of Ireland, Handbill in NLI, p. 101.
20 Sheridan, *Speeches of Sheridan*, Vol. II, p. 215.
21 Ibid., pp. 88–89.
22 See Blanchard Jerrold (ed.), *Thomas Walker, The Original* (London, 1874), Vol. I, pp. 82–83.
23 Sheridan, *Speeches of Sheridan*, Vol. III, pp. 35–36.
24 Jerrold (ed.), *Thomas Walker*, Vol. I, p. 90.
25 Ibid., p. 75.

26 See John Brims, "Scottish Radicalism and the United Irishmen," in Dickson, Keogh, and Whelen (eds.), *The United Irishmen*, pp. 151 ff.
27 Sheridan, *Speeches of Sheridan*, Vol. III, p. 255.
28 C. Kegan Paul, *William Godwin, His Friends and Contemporaries* (London, 1876), Vol. I, p. 121.
29 Sheridan, *Speeches of Sheridan*, Vol. III, p. 255.
30 Irish National Archives, 620/21/8.
31 Dickson, Keogh, and Whelan (eds.), *The United Irishmen*, p. 199.
32 INA, 620/21/8.
33 Sheridan, *Speeches of Sheridan*, Vol. III, pp. 381–82.

27: A Snake in the Grass

1 See R. Compton Rhodes, *Harlequin Sheridan* (Oxford, 1933), pp. 71–72.
2 See Marianne Elliot, *Partners in Revolution* (Newhaven and London, 1982), pp. 60–67.
3 Examination of Benjamin Vaughan, Irish National Archives, 260/21/19.
4 Examination of William Stone, 9 May 1794. INA, 620/21/19.
5 Examination of Richard Wilson, INA, 620/21/19.
6 Examination of Benjamin Vaughan, INA, 260/21/19.
7 Examination of Richard Wilson, INA, 620/21/19.
8 Peter Jupp (ed.), *The Letter Journal of George Canning 1793–1795* (London, 1991), p. 96.
9 Elliot, *Partners in Revolution*, p. 67.
10 Lord Holland told Thomas Moore this story. Widener Ms.
11 Sheridan's statement is in INA, 620/21/19, and in Cecil Price (ed.), *The Letters of Richard Brinsley Sheridan* (Oxford, 1966), Vol. II, pp. 5–12.
12 Informer's report, INA, 620/21/39.
13 See Compton Rhodes, *Harlequin Sheridan*, p. 158.
14 Thomas Moore, *Memoirs of the Life of the Right Honourable Richard Brinsley Sheridan* (London, 1825), Vol. II, pp. 187–89.

28: Citizen Sheridan

1 Peter Jupp (ed.), *The Letter Journal of George Canning 1793–1795* (London, 1991), p. 180.
2 Richard Brinsley Sheridan, *The Speeches of the Late Right Honourable Richard Brinsley Sheridan* (London, 1816), Vol. IV, p. 21.
3 Jupp (ed.), *Letter Journal of Canning*, p. 149.
4 See Cecil Price (ed.), *The Letters of Richard Brinsley Sheridan* (Oxford, 1966), Vol. I, p. 205.
5 A transcription of this part of Sheridan's evidence is given in Thomas Moore, *Memoirs of the Life of the Right Honourable Richard Brinsley Sheridan* (London, 1825), Vol. II, pp. 246–47.
6 See James Dugan, *The Great Mutiny* (New York, 1965), pp. 26–27.

7 E. P. Thompson, *The Making of the English Working Class* (Harmondsworth, 1991), p. 150.
8 Cited in A. Goodwin, *The Friends of Liberty* (London, 1979), p. 373.
9 Canning in Jupp (ed.), *Letter Journal of Canning*, p. 84.
10 Sheridan cited in Goodwin, *Friends of Liberty*, p. 23.
11 Quoted in James Morwood and David Crane (eds.), *Sheridan Studies* (Cambridge, 1995), p. 145.
12 See Sheridan, *Speeches of Sheridan*, Vol. III, p. 177.
13 Jupp (ed.), *Letter Journal of Canning*, p. 100.
14 William Smyth, *Memoir of Mr Sheridan* (Leeds, 1840), pp. 31–35.
15 P. J. Marshall, *The Impeachment of Warren Hastings* (Oxford, 1965), p. 85.
16 Sheridan, *Speeches of Sheridan*, Vol. IV, pp. 79 and 84.
17 Jupp (ed.), *Letter Journal of Canning*, p. 265.
18 A. Aspinall (ed.), *The Later Correspondence of George III* (Cambridge, 1961–70), Vol. II, p. 416.
19 Sheridan, *Speeches of Sheridan*, Vol. V, p. 103.
20 Ibid., pp. 112, 115.
21 Joseph Farington, *The Farington Diary* (London, 1923), Vol. I, p. 109.
22 Sheridan, *Speeches of Sheridan*, Vol. V, p. 136.
23 Irish National Archives, 620/23/142.
24 Price (ed.), *Sheridan Letters*, Vol. II, pp. 39–40.
25 Aspinall (ed.), *Correspondence of Prince of Wales*, Vol. III, p. 221.
26 Ibid., p. 223.
27 Ibid., pp. 232–33.

29: Men, Women, and Ogles

1 Joseph Farington, *The Farington Diary* (London, 1923), Vol. I, p. 13.
2 William Smyth, *Memoir of Mr Sheridan* (Leeds, 1840), p. 54.
3 Ibid., p. 17.
4 Ibid., pp. 56–57.
5 Widener Library ms.
6 Peter Jupp (ed.), *The Letter Journal of George Canning 1793–1795* (London, 1991), p. 171.
7 Farington, *Diary*, Vol. I, p. 99.
8 Smyth, *Memoir of Mr Sheridan*, pp. 47–48.
9 Jupp (ed.), *Letter Journal of Canning*, p. 260.
10 "The Political Dramatist in November," quoted in R. Compton Rhodes, *Harlequin Sheridan* (Oxford, 1933), p. 171.
11 See, for example, Cecil Price (ed.), *The Letters of Richard Brinsley Sheridan* (Oxford, 1966), Vol. II, pp. 44 and 47.
12 Ibid., pp. 22–24.
13 Widener Library ms.
14 Harvard ms. M 344.
15 Price (ed.), *Sheridan Letters*, Vol. II, p. 44.

16 Farington, *Diary*, Vol. II, p. 118.
17 *The Works of the Rev. Sydney Smith* (London, 1865), Vol. I, p. vii.
18 Nathaniel Ogle to Thomas Moore, 17 February 1819, reproduced in W. Fraser Rae, *Sheridan: A Biography* (London, 1896), Vol. II, pp. 206–7.
19 Price (ed.), *Sheridan Letters*, Vol. II, p. 228.

30: The Wooden Walls

1 Richard Madden, *The United Irishmen, Their Lives and Times* (Dublin, 1858), pp. 378–79.
2 Irish National Archives, 620/15/3/7.
3 Castalia, Countess Granville (ed.), *Private Correspondence of Granville Leveson Gower* (London, 1916), Vol. I, p. 360.
4 Le Fanu Papers, National Library of Ireland, p. 2594.
5 The Earl of Moira to Colonel J. McMahon, 15 June 1797, in A. Aspinall (ed.), *The Correspondence of George, Prince of Wales* (London, 1969), Vol. III, pp. 349–54.
6 Thomas Moore, *Memoirs of the Life of the Right Honourable Richard Brinsley Sheridan* (London, 1825), Vol. II, p. 274.
7 See E. A. Smith, *Lord Grey 1764–1845* (Oxford, 1990), p. 69.
8 Richard Brinsley Sheridan, *The Speeches of the Late Right Honourable Richard Brinsley Sheridan* (London, 1816), Vol. IV, p. 401.
9 James Dugan, *The Great Mutiny* (New York, 1965), p. 160.
10 Sheridan, *Speeches of Sheridan*, Vol. IV, pp. 426–28.
11 Castalia (ed.), *Leveson Gower Correspondence*, Vol. I, p. 194.
12 Aspinall (ed.), *Correspondence of Prince of Wales*, Vol. III, p. 410.

31: Treason on Trial

1 Richard Madden, *The United Irishmen, Their Lives and Times* (Dublin, 1858), p. 297.
2 Quoted in Marianne Elliot, *Partners in Revolution: The United Irishmen and France* (New Haven and London, 1989), p. 212.
3 William St. Clair, *The Godwins and the Shelleys* (London, 1989), p. 241.
4 Ibid., p. 539.
5 Elliot, *Partners in Revolution*, p. 181.
6 *The Trial at Large of Arthur O'Connor Esq., Johns Binns, John Allen, Jeremiah Leary and James O'Coigley for High Treason, before Judge Buller etc. under a special commission at Maidstone in the County of Kent, taken in short hand* (Dublin, 1798), p. 81.
7 Richard Brinsley Sheridan, *The Speeches of the Late Right Honourable Richard Brinsley Sheridan* (London, 1816), Vol. V, p. 89.
8 *The Trial at Large of Arthur O'Connor* . . . , p. 3.
9 A. Aspinall (ed.), *The Correspondence of George, Prince of Wales* (London, 1969), Vol. III, p. 422.
10 Sheridan, *Speeches of Sheridan*, Vol. V, p. 9.
11 *The Trial at Large of Arthur O'Connor*, p. 51.

12 Ibid., p. 73.
13 Sheridan, *Speeches of Sheridan*, Vol. V, p. 88.
14 J. Pollock to Edward Cooke, Irish National Archives, 620/18A/4.
15 Cecil Price (ed.), *The Letters of Richard Brinsley Sheridan* (Oxford, 1966), Vol. II, pp. 92–93.
16 William Wickham to Lord Castlereagh, 23 May 1798, INA, 620/18A/11.
17 William Wickham to Edward Cooke, 15 April 1798, INA, 620/18A/11.
18 *The Whole Proceedings upon an Information Exhibited ex officio by the King's Attorney-general against the Right Hon. Sackville Earl of Thanet, Robert Fergusson, Esquire, and others for a Riot and Other Misdemeanours, tried at the bar of the Court of King's bench, April 25, 1799 . . . to which are added Some Observations by Robert Fergusson on his own Case* (London, 1799), p. 26.
19 Ibid., p. 29: Evidence of Mr. Justice Heath.
20 Ibid., p. 117: Sheridan's evidence.
21 Walter Sichel, *Sheridan* (London, 1909), Vol. II, p. 291.
22 Ibid., pp. 65–66.
23 Ibid., p. 146.
24 Price (ed.), *Sheridan Letters*, Vol. II, pp. 94–95.
25 William Wickham to Edward Cooke, 26 May 1798, INA, 620/18A/11.
26 William Wickham to Lord Castlereagh, 24 May 1798, INA, 620/18A/11.
27 *The Whole Proceedings* . . . , p. 146.
28 Brian Fitzgerald, *Emily Duchess of Leinster* (London and New York, 1949), p. 249.
29 Elliot, *Partners in Revolution*, p. 210.

32: Wicked Men

1 A. Aspinall (ed.), *The Later Correspondence of George III* (Cambridge, 1961–70), Vol. III, p. 49.
2 A. Aspinall (ed.), *The Correspondence of George, Prince of Wales* (London, 1969), Vol. III, p. 412.
3 Aspinall (ed.), *Later Correspondence of George III*, Vol. III, p. 77.
4 Richard Brinsley Sheridan, *The Speeches of the Late Right Honourable Richard Brinsley Sheridan* (London, 1816), Vol. V, p. 16.
5 Ibid., p. 18.
6 Quoted in Walter Sichel, *Sheridan* (London, 1909), Vol. II, p. 281.
7 See Cecil Price (ed.), *The Letters of Richard Brinsley Sheridan* (Oxford, 1966), Vol. II, p. 96.
8 Aspinall (ed.), *Correspondence of Prince of Wales*, Vol. III, pp. 440 ff.
9 See Wilfred Partington (ed.), *The Private Letter-Books of Sir Walter Scott* (London, 1930), p. 218.
10 See Thomas Moore, *Memoirs of the Life of the Right Honourable Richard Brinsley Sheridan* (London, 1825), Vol. II, p. 275.
11 Aspinall (ed.), *Later Correspondence of George III*, Vol. III, pp. 175–76.
12 Price (ed.), *Sheridan Letters*, Vol. II, pp. 109–10, 111.
13 See letters of Jane Linley dated 15 April and 22 April, BL, Add. Ms. 52615.

14 Osborne Ms.
15 *Reminiscences of Michael Kelly* (London, 1826), Vol. III, p. 143.
16 Fanny Kemble, *Record of a Girlhood* (London, 1878), Vol. I, pp. 283–84.
17 Mrs. Bouverie, quoted in Cecil Price (ed.), *The Dramatic Works of Richard Brinsley Sheridan* (Oxford, 1973), Vol. II, p. 628.
18 *The Life and Times of Frederic Reynolds Written by Himself* (London, 1827), Vol. II, p. 262.
19 James Boaden, *The Life of Mrs Jordan* (London, 1831), Vol. II, p. 3.
20 The Earl of Ilchester (ed.), *The Journal of Elizabeth, Lady Holland* (London, 1908), Vol. II, p. 80–81.
21 Speech of 31 January 1799, in Sheridan, *Speeches of Sheridan*, Vol. V, p. 46.
22 BL, Add. Ms. 52615.
23 *Morning Post*, 25 May 1799; quoted in Price (ed.), *Dramatic Works*, Vol. II, p. 632.
24 Mrs. Larpent's diary, 14 January 1800; quoted in ibid., Vol. II, p. 631.
25 *Pizarro*, ibid. Vol. II, p. 669.
26 *Pizarro*, II, i, in ibid., p. 667.
27 *Pizarro*, I, i, in ibid., p. 664.
28 Quoted in Roy Porter, *English Society in the Eighteenth Century* (Harmondsworth, 1982), p. 372.
29 Price (ed.), *Dramatic Works*, Vol. II, p. 666.
30 The *Monthly Magazine*, Part II, 1799 (London, 1800), p. 1050.
31 Joseph Farington, *The Farington Diary* (London, 1923), Vol. I, p. 286.
32 Price (ed.), *Dramatic Works*, Vol. II, p. 669.
33 Letter of 27 December 1799, quoted in ibid., p. 635.
34 A. Dyce (ed.), *Recollections of the Table-Talk of Samuel Rogers* (London, 1856), p. 97.
35 W. Oxberry, Introduction to *Pizarro* (London, 1824), p. viii.
36 *Cobbett's Weekly Political Register*, 17 September 1803, p. 390.
37 William Cobbett, *The Political Proteus, A View of the Public Character and Conduct of R. B. Sheridan Esq*. (London, 1804), pp. 84–85.
38 *Anti-Jacobin Review and Magazine* (June, 1799), Vol. III, p. 208.
39 *Pizarro*, III, iii, in Price (ed.), *Dramatic Works*, Vol. II, p. 682.
40 Ibid.
41 British Library, Add. Ms. 52615.
42 Earl of Ilchester (ed.), *The Journal of Elizabeth, Lady Holland*, Vol. II, pp. 80–81.

33: An Unpurchasable Mind

1 Richard Brinsley Sheridan, *The Speeches of the Late Right Honourable Richard Brinsley Sheridan* (London, 1816), Vol. IV, pp. 27–28.
2 Ibid., Vol. V, p. 95.
3 Ibid., pp. 163–64.
4 Ibid., p. 186.

5 E. P. Thompson, *The Making of the English Working Class* (Harmondsworth, 1986), p. 495.
6 Sheridan, *Speeches of Sheridan*, Vol. V, p. 223.
7 Thompson, *The Making of the English Working Class*, p. 495.
8 Hansard, Vol. 36, col. 1062 ff.
9 Andréossy's letter to Napoleon is cited in full in P. Coquelle, *Napoleon and England 1803–1813* (London, 1904), pp. 9–11.
10 See Françoise Chatel de Brancion, *R. B. Sheridan, personnalité, carrière politique* (Paris, 1974), pp. 270, 477.
11 Sheridan, *Speeches of Sheridan*, Vol. V, p. 41; Pitt in A. Aspinall (ed.), *The Later Correspondence of George III* (Cambridge, 1961–70), Vol. III, p. 437.
12 Ibid.
13 Ibid., pp. 486–87.
14 House of Commons, 16 February 1801, quoted in Philip Ziegler, *Addington* (London, 1965), p. 97.
15 Ziegler, *Addington*, p. 110.
16 Aspinall (ed.), *Later Correspondence of George III*, Vol. III, p. 507.
17 Ibid., p. 525.
18 George Rose, quoted in ibid., p. 507.
19 Ibid., p. 496.
20 Castalia, Countess Granville (ed.), *Private Correspondence of Granville Leveson Gower* (London, 1916), Vol. I, p. 301.
21 Cited in Ida Macalpine and Richard Hunter, *George III and the Mad-Business* (London, 1991), p. 126.
22 Mabell, Countess of Airlie, *In Whig Society* (London, 1921), pp. 24–27.
23 E. A. Smith, *Lord Grey 1764–1845* (Oxford, 1990), pp. 80–81.
24 Ziegler, *Addington*, p. 170.
25 Sheridan, *Speeches of Sheridan*, Vol. V, pp. 218–22.

34: Unlimited Offers

1 Castalia, Countess Granville (ed.), *Private Correspondence of Granville Leveson Gower* (London, 1916), Vol. I, pp. 430–32.
2 Le Fanu Papers, National Library of Ireland, p. 2595.
3 Joseph Farington, *The Farington Diary* (London, 1923), Vol. II, p. 101.
4 A. Aspinall (ed.), *The Later Correspondence of George III* (Cambridge, 1961–70), Vol. IV, p. 99.
5 Ibid., p. 104.
6 Farington, *Diary*, Vol. II, p. 105.
7 Ibid., p. 107.
8 A. Aspinall (ed.), *The Correspondence of George, Prince of Wales* (London, 1967), Vol. IV, p. 350.
9 Castalia (ed.), *Leveson Gower Correspondence*, Vol. I, p. 427.
10 Holland House Ms.; cf. Walter Sichel, *Sheridan* (London, 1909), Vol. II, p. 70.
11 Cecil Price (ed.), *The Letters of Richard Brinsley Sheridan* (Oxford, 1966), Vol. II, pp. 196, 198–99.

12 Castain (ed.), *Leveson Gower Correspondence*, Vol. I, pp. 430ff.
13 Ibid, p. 437.
14 Creevey in Gore (ed.), *Thomas Creevey's Papers, 1793-1823*, p. 15. Aspinall (ed.), *Correspondence of Prince of Wales*, Vol. IV, p. 553.
15 Castalia (ed.), *Leveson Gower Correspondence*, Vol. I, p. 437.
16 Aspinall (ed.), *Correspondence of Prince of Wales*, Vol. IV, pp. 350–51.
17 Ibid., p. 531.
18 Castalia (ed.), *Leveson Gower Correspondence*, Vol. I, p. 456.

35: Put Aside the Mask of Mystery

1 Cobbett quoted this article in *Cobbett's Weekly Political Register*, 17 September 1803, p. 385.
2 Ibid., 30 July 1803, pp. 159–60.
3 Richard Brinsley Sheridan, *The Speeches of the Late Right Honourable Richard Brinsley Sheridan* (London, 1816), Vol. V, p. 240.
4 Ibid., pp. 248, 247.
5 *Cobbett's Weekly Political Register*, 13 August 1803, p. 212.
6 John Gore (ed.), *Thomas Creevey's Papers, 1793–1838* (Harmondsworth, 1985), p. 11.
7 *Memoirs and Correspondence of Francis Horner* (Edinburgh, 1849), p. 134.
8 A. Aspinall (ed.), *The Correspondence of George, Prince of Wales* (London, 1967), Vol. IV, p. 470.
9 Ibid., p. 453.
10 Ibid., p. 493.
11 Ibid., p. 456.
12 Ibid., p. 469.
13 Cecil Price (ed.), *The Letters of Richard Brinsley Sheridan* (Oxford, 1966), Vol. II, p. 211.
14 Ibid., p. 212.
15 Aspinall (ed.), *Correspondence of Prince of Wales*, Vol. IV, p. 507.
16 Le Fanu Papers, National Library of Ireland, p. 2596.
17 Price (ed.), *Sheridan Letters*, Vol. II, p. 216.
18 Aspinall (ed.), *Correspondence of Prince of Wales*, Vol. IV, p. 519.
19 Clementina Black, *The Linleys of Bath* (London, 1926), p. 270.

36: Depraved Imagination

1 Castalia, Countess Granville (ed.), *Private Correspondence of Granville Leveson Gower* (London, 1916), Vol. II, p. 3.
2 Ibid., p. 8.
3 Ibid., Vol. I, p. 160.
4 Ibid., p. 216.
5 Ibid., p. 351.
6 Ibid., p. 352.
7 Ibid., p. 427.

8 Ida Macalpine and Michael Hunter, *George III and the Mad-Business* (London, 1991), p. 70.
9 Cecil Price (ed.), *The Letters of Richard Brinsley Sheridan* (Oxford, 1966), Vol. II, p. 243.
10 Wilfred S. Dowden, *The Journal of Thomas Moore* (Newark and London, 1984), Vol. I, p. 60.
11 Castalia (ed.), *Leveson Gower Correspondence*, Vol. II, pp. 17–18.
12 Earl St. Vincent to Benjamin Tucker, Sotheby's catalogue, 28 March 1972, lot 473.
13 Kenneth Bourne (ed.), *The Letters of the Third Viscount Palmerston to Laurence and Elizabeth Sullivan* (London, 1979), p. 43.
14 Philip Ziegler, *Addington* (London, 1965), p. 242.
15 Price (ed.), *Sheridan Letters*, Vol. II, p. 249.
16 John Gore (ed.), *Thomas Creevey's Papers, 1793–1838* (Harmondsworth, 1985), p. 37.
17 Price (ed.), *Sheridan Letters*, Vol. II, p. 251.
18 Ziegler, *Addington*, p. 247.
19 Dowden (ed.), *Thomas Moore's Journal*, Vol. I, p. 61.
20 PRO, Granville Papers, 30/29/6/2, quoted in Linda Kelly, *Richard Brinsley Sheridan: A Life* (London, 1997), pp. 248–49.
21 E. A. Smith, *Lord Grey 1764–1845* (Oxford, 1990), pp. 146–47.
22 Price (ed.), *Sheridan Letters*, Vol. II, p. 250.

37: Rough Work on the Hustings

1 E. A. Smith, *Lord Grey 1764–1845* (Oxford, 1990), p. 15.
2 Richard Brinsley Sheridan, *The Speeches of the Late Right Honourable Richard Brinsley Sheridan* (London, 1816), Vol. I, pp. 318–19.
3 Cecil Price (ed.), *The Letters of Richard Brinsley Sheridan* (Oxford, 1966), Vol. II, p. 263.
4 Ibid., p. 260.
5 Ibid., p. 263.
6 Thomas Moore, *Memoirs of the Life of the Right Honourable Richard Brinsley Sheridan* (London, 1825), Vol. II, p. 121.
7 Wilfred S. Dowden (ed.), *The Journal of Thomas Moore* (Newark and London, 1984), Vol. I, p. 61.
8 Fox Mss. British Library, Add. Mss. 47566, f. 118.
9 Dowden (ed.), *Moore Journal*, Vol. I, p. 68.
10 A. Aspinall (ed.), *The Later Correspondence of George III* (Cambridge, 1961–70), Vol. IV, p. 427.
11 Francis Place Papers, BL, Add. Mss. 27850, f. 12.
12 These two statements are quoted in Marc Baer, "The ruin of a public man: Richard Brinsley Sheridan as a political reformer," in James Morwood and David Crane (eds.), *Sheridan Studies* (Cambridge, 1995), p. 160.
13 Quoted in R. Compton Rhodes, *Harlequin Sheridan* (Oxford, 1933), pp. 209–10.

14 Price (ed.), *Sheridan Letters*, Vol. II, p. 278.
15 Ibid., p. 291.
16 *The History of the Westminster and Middlesex Elections in the Month of November 1806* (London, 1807), pp. 129–31.
17 *Cobbett's Weekly Political Register*, 2 April 1808, pp. 513–18.
18 Price (ed.), *Sheridan Letters*, Vol. II, p. 302.
19 Kenneth Bourne (ed.), *Palmerston–Sullivan Letters, 1804–1863* (London, 1979), p. 72.
20 *The Trial of Thomas Sheridan Esq. for Criminal Conversation with the Lady of Peter Campbell Esq. in the Sheriff's Court on July 7th 1807. Damages Fifteen-Hundred Pounds!!!* (London, 1807), p. 11.
21 William Earle, *Sheridan and his Times* (London, 1859), Vol. II, p. 218.
22 Castalia, Countess Granville (ed.), *Private Correspondence of Granville Leveson Gower* (London, 1916), Vol. II, p. 227.
23 Bourne (ed.), *Palmerston–Sullivan Letters*, p. 77.
24 Sheridan, *Speeches of Sheridan*, Vol. V, p. 333.
25 Ibid., p. 329.
26 Moore, *Memoirs of Sheridan*, Vol. II, p. 302.
27 John Gore (ed.), *Thomas Creevey's Papers, 1793–1838* (Harmondsworth, 1985), p. 3.
28 *The Times*, 11 November 1806.
29 Price (ed.), *Sheridan Letters*, Vol. IV, pp. 7–8.
30 See Francis Place Papers, BL, Add. Mss. 27850, f. 20.
31 Thomas Moore (ed.), *Letters and Journals of Lord Byron* (London, 1830), Vol. I, p. 97.

38: The Experience of Defeat

1 A. Aspinall (ed.), *The Correspondence of George, Prince of Wales* (London, 1969), Vol. VI, p. 68.
2 *Cobbett's Weekly Political Register*, 2 April 1808, pp. 513–18.
3 John Brooke, *The House of Commons 1754–1790: Introductory Survey* (Oxford, 1964), p. 13.
4 A. Aspinall (ed.), *The Later Correspondence of George III* (Cambridge, 1961–70), Vol. IV, p. 596.
5 Cecil Price (ed.), *The Letters of Richard Brinsley Sheridan* (Oxford, 1966), Vol. III, p. 12.
6 The Trustees of Drury Lane to Richard Brinsley Sheridan, 26 June 1807, BL, Add. Ms. 42720, f. 66 and f. 69.
7 BL, Add. Ms. 42720, ff. 145–46.
8 *The Trial of Thomas Sheridan Esq. for Criminal Conversation with the lady of Peter Campbell Esq. in the Sheriff's Court on July 7th 1807. Damages Fifteen-Hundred Pounds!!!* (London, 1807), p. 12.
9 Wilfred S. Dowden (ed.), *The Journal of Thomas Moore* (Newark and London, 1984), Vol. I, p. 28.

10 The Earl of Bessborough (ed.), *Lady Bessborough and her Family Circle* (London, 1940), p. 156.
11 Castalia, Countess Granville (ed.), *The Private Correspondence of Granville Leveson Gower* (London, 1916), Vol. II, pp. 308–9.
12 Price (ed.), *Sheridan Letters*, Vol. III, pp. 4–5.
13 Castalia (ed.), *Leveson Gower Correspondence*, Vol. II, p. 307.
14 Aspinall (ed.), *The Later Correspondence of George III*, Vol. IV, p. 12.
15 Ibid., p. 63.

39: The Great Sheridan

1 *Cobbett's Weekly Political Register*, 2 April 1808, pp. 51–58.
2 *Collection of Addresses Transmitted by Certain English Clubs and Societies to the National Convention of France* (London, 1793), p. 25.
3 Richard Brinsley Sheridan, *The Speeches of the Late Right Honourable Richard Brinsley Sheridan* (London, 1816), Vol. III, p. 89.
4 Ibid., p. 120.
5 See E. P. Thompson, *The Making of the English Working Class* (Harmondsworth, 1968), pp. 120–21, 141.
6 Letter of John Frost to Richard Brinsley Sheridan of Frampton (Sheridan's grandson), 7 February 1839. Sotheby's catalogue, 29–30 November 1972, lot 368. A full transcript is in the papers of Cecil Price.
7 Ibid.
8 Cecil Price (ed.), *The Letters of Richard Brinsley Sheridan* (Oxford, 1966), Vol. III, p. 181.
9 *Trial of Mr Peter Finnerty, late printer of The Press, for a libel against his Excellency Earl Camden, Lord Lieutenant of Ireland* (Dublin, 1798).
10 See Marianne Elliot, *Partners in Revolution* (London and New Haven, 1982), p. 96.
11 Price (ed.), *Sheridan Letters*, Vol. II, pp. 292, 293.
12 John Finegan (ed.), *The Anne Devlin Jail Journal* (Cork, 1968), pp. 115–16.
13 Sheridan, *Speeches of Sheridan*, Vol. V, p. 346.
14 Price (ed.), *Sheridan Letters*, Vol. II, p. 269.
15 *Recollections of Jonah Barrington* (Dublin and London, 1919), pp. 187–94.
16 Castalia, Countess Granville (ed.), *The Private Correspondence of Granville Leveson Gower* (London, 1916), Vol. II, p. 271.
17 Sheridan, *Speeches of Sheridan*, Vol. V, pp. 341–67.
18 *James Kelly, That Damn'd Thing Called Honour: Duelling in Ireland 1570–1860* (Cork, 1995), pp. 237–38; Michael Barry, *An Affair of Honour: Irish Duels and Duelists* (Fermoy, 1981), pp. 63–65.
19 Price (ed.), *Sheridan Letters*, Vol. III, p. 151.
20 A. Aspinall (ed.), *The Correspondence of George, Prince of Wales* (London, 1969), Vol. VII, p. 189.

40: The Burning Dome

1 William Smyth, *Memoir of Mr Sheridan* (Leeds, 1840), p. 38.
2 A. Aspinall (ed.), *The Later Correspondence of George III* (Cambridge, 1961–70), Vol. V, p. 210.
3 Ibid.
4 Thomas Moore, *Memoirs of the Life of the Right Honourable Richard Brinsley Sheridan* (London, 1825), Vol. II, p. 368.
5 Cecil Price (ed.), *The Letters of Richard Brinsley Sheridan* (Oxford, 1966), Vol. III, p. 52.
6 Ibid.
7 *Reminiscences of Michael Kelly* (London, 1826), Vol. II, pp. 255–56; see also Anon., *Sheridiana; or Anecdotes of the Life of Richard Brinsley Sheridan* (London, 1826), pp. 216–17.
8 Price (ed.), *Sheridan Letters*, Vol. III, p. 131.
9 Ibid., p. 127.
10 Ibid., p. 132.
11 Ibid., p. 174.
12 Ibid., p. 128.
13 Reproduced in Moore, *Memoirs of Sheridan*, Vol. II, p. 434.
14 Robert H. Taylor Ms. docked "R. B. Sheridan to Mr Burgess."
15 Price (ed.), *Sheridan Letters*, Vol. III, p. 69.
16 John Gore (ed.), *Thomas Creevey's Papers, 1793–1838* (Harmondsworth, 1985), p. 33.
17 Basil Francis, *Fanny Kelly of Drury Lane* (London, 1950), pp. 30–31.

41: Betrayal

1 Ida Macalpine and Michael Hunter, *George III and the Mad-Business* (London, 1991), pp. 159–70.
2 Richard Brinsley Sheridan to John Hosier, 7 April 1809, Robert H. Taylor Ms.
3 Christopher Hibbert, *George IV: Prince of Wales* (Harmondsworth, 1972), p. 280.
4 Cecil Price (ed.), *The Letters of Richard Brinsley Sheridan* (Oxford, 1966), Vol. III, pp. 286–87.
5 Castalia, Countess Granville (ed.), *The Private Correspondence of Granville Leveson Gower* (London, 1916), Vol. II, p. 353.
6 Price (ed.), *Sheridan Letters*, Vol. III, p. 75.
7 Reproduced in John Watkins, *Memoirs of the Public and Private Life of the Right Honourable R. B. Sheridan* (London, 1817), Vol. II, p. 507.
8 Christopher Hibbert, *George IV: Regent and King* (Harmondsworth, 1975), p. 79.
9 Price (ed.), *Sheridan Letters*, Vol. II, p. 135.
10 Ibid., p. 146.
11 Ibid., p. 28.
12 Ibid., pp. 230–33.

13 Ibid., p. 37.
14 Ibid., p. 38.
15 Ibid., p. 147.
16 Ibid., p. 149.
17 Reproduced in Thomas Moore, *Memoirs of the Life of the Right Honourable Richard Brinsley Sheridan* (London, 1825), Vol. II, p. 430.
18 Price (ed.), *Sheridan Letters*, Vol. III, p. 156.
19 The statement, from the Salt Library Ms. in Stafford, is reproduced in W. Compton Rhodes, *Harlequin Sheridan* (Oxford, 1933), pp. 232–34.
20 John Gore (ed.), *Thomas Creevey's Papers, 1793–1838* (Harmondsworth, 1985), p. 100.
21 Price (ed.), *Sheridan Letters*, Vol. III, p. 158.
22 Ibid.
23 Ibid., p. 159.
24 Castalia, Countess Granville (ed.), *The Private Correspondence of Granville Leveson Gower* (London, 1916), Vol. II, p. 444.
25 Philip Ziegler, *Addington* (London, 1965), p. 331.
26 Price (ed.), *Sheridan Letters*, Vol. III, p. 172.
27 Charles Butler, *Reminiscences* (Boston, 1827), pp. 86–97.
28 Price (ed.), *Sheridan Letters*, Vol. III, p. 172.
29 Tom Sheridan to Hecca, 16 November 1812, National Library of Ireland ms. 7373. Price (ed.), *Sheridan Letters*, Vol. III, p. 175, dates this letter as 1813, but it is in fact dated "Nov. 16. 12" and sent from Scotland, where Tom was living at that time.
30 Price (ed.), *Sheridan Letters*, Vol. III, p. 169.
31 Louis J. Jennings (ed.), *The Croker Papers: The Correspondence and Diaries of the Late John Wilson Croker* (London and New York, 1884), pp. 279–88. This is George IV's own account of the transaction, dictated to Croker late in life.
32 Price (ed.), *Sheridan Letters*, Vol. III, p. 175.
33 Tom Sheridan to Hecca, 25 May 1813, NLI, Ms. 7373.
34 Ibid.
35 Price (ed.), *Sheridan Letters*, Vol. III, p. 173.
36 Ibid., p. 177.
37 Thomas Moore (ed.), *Letters and Journals of Lord Byron* (London, 1830), Vol. I, pp. 469–70.

42: A Good Humoured Misanthrope

1 *The Critic*, I, ii, in Cecil Price (ed.), *The Dramatic Works of Richard Brinsley Sheridan* (Oxford, 1973), Vol. II, pp. 513–14.
2 Frost's account is in the letter of 7 February 1839 to Sheridan's grandson R. B. Sheridan of Frampton, Sotheby's catalogue, 29–30 November 1972, lot 368. A full transcript is in the papers of Cecil Price.
3 Cecil Price (ed.), *The Letters of Richard Brinsley Sheridan* (Oxford, 1966), Vol. III, p. 188.

4 Osborn Ms., Richard Brinsley Sheridan to C. W. Ward, 30 May 1814.
5 *Staffordshire Advertiser*, 19 March 1814, quoted in Price (ed.), *Sheridan Letters*, Vol. III, p. 201.
6 5 May 1814, Sotheby's catalogue, 29 November 1973, lot 373.
7 Wilfred S. Dowden (ed.), *Thomas Moore's Journal* (Newark and London, 1984), Vol. II, p. 818.
8 Thomas Moore (ed.), *Letters and Journals of Lord Byron* (London, 1830), Vol. I, p. 505.
9 *Morning Post*, 6 July 1814.
10 See Robert Stewart, *Henry Brougham, His Public Career 1778–1868* (London, 1985), pp. 89–91.
11 Price (ed.), *Sheridan Letters*, Vol. III, p. 190.
12 See A. Aspinall, "The Westminster Election of 1814," *English Historical Review* (October, 1925), pp. 57–58.
13 Price (ed.), *Sheridan Letters*, Vol. III, p. 191.
14 Ibid., p. 194.
15 Ibid., p. 192.
16 *Morning Chronicle*, 12 July 1814.
17 John Frost's letter to R. B. Sheridan of Frampton (see n. 2 above).
18 Sheridan to "My Dear Sir," 23 November 1815, reproduced in René Wellek and Ribeiro, *Evidence in Literary Scholarship* (London, 1979), p. 319.
19 H. B. Wheatley (ed.), *The Historical and Posthumous Memoirs of N. W. Wraxall* (London, 1884), p. 53.
20 Joseph Farington, *The Farington Diary* (London, 1923), quoted in James Morwood, *The Life and Works of Richard Brinsley Sheridan* (Edinburgh, 1985), p. 69.
21 Price (ed.), *Sheridan Letters*, Vol. III, p. 175.
22 Ibid., pp. 205–7.
23 Ibid., p. 212.
24 Ibid., p. 217.
25 Moore (ed.), *Letters and Journals of Lord Byron*, Vol. I, pp. 634–35.
26 Ibid., p. 650.
27 Price (ed.), *Sheridan Letters*, Vol. III, p. 224.
28 See Linda Colley, *Britons: Forging the Nation 1707–1837* (New York, 1994), p. 151.
29 Price (ed.), *Sheridan Letters*, Vol. III, p. 223.
30 Ibid., pp. 216, 238.

43: A Nice Derangement of Epitaphs

1 Cecil Price (ed.), *Letters of Richard Brinsley Sheridan* (Oxford, 1966), Vol. III, pp. 214–15.
2 Ibid., p. 215.
3 This account was dictated by George IV to the Tory John Wilson Croker in November 1825, and published in Louis J. Jennings (ed.), *The Croker Papers:*

The Correspondence and Diaries of the Late John Wilson Croker (London, 1884), Vol. I.

4 Price (ed.), *Sheridan Letters*, Vol. III, p. 245.
5 Ibid., p. 240.
6 Sotheby's catalogue, 23 July 1982, lot 619.
7 Price (ed.), *Sheridan Letters*, Vol. III, p. 242.
8 Folger Ms., R 193.
9 Thomas Moore, *Memoirs of the Life of the Right Honourable Richard Brinsley Sheridan* (London, 1825), Vol. II, p. 446. Moore says that on this occasion Sheridan assured the Earl of Essex that the Duke of Norfolk was about to bring him into Parliament. This is, however, impossible—the duke died in December 1815 and it is clear from the earl's letter to Kean that the visit to Drury Lane took place in February 1816.
10 Price (ed.), *Sheridan Letters*, Vol. III, p. 202.
11 British Library, Add. Ms. 29764, ff. 26–27.
12 Reproduced in Moore, *Memoirs of Sheridan*, Vol. II, p. 450.
13 Ibid., pp. 452–53.
14 See Charles Sheridan's letter of 20 December 1823, published in Cecil Price (ed.), *The Dramatic Works of Richard Brinsley Sheridan* (Oxford, 1973), Vol. I, pp. 15–16.
15 Price (ed.), *Sheridan Letters*, Vol. III, p. 246.
16 Moore, *Memoirs of Sheridan*, Vol. II, pp. 455–56.
17 William Earle, *Sheridan and His Times* (London, 1859), p. 292.
18 Price (ed.), *Sheridan Letters*, Vol. III, p. 343.
19 Thomas Moore (ed.), *Letters and Journals of Lord Byron* (London, 1830), Vol. I, p. 400.
20 Wilfred Partington (ed.), *The Private Letter-Books of Sir Walter Scott* (London, 1930), p. 185.
21 R. Compton Rhodes, *Harlequin Sheridan* (Oxford, 1933), p. 10.
22 Moore, *Memoirs of Sheridan*, Vol. II, pp. 458–59.
23 *New Times*, 19 November 1825, reprinted in *Sheridiana; or Anecdotes of the Life of Richard Brinsley Sheridan* (London, 1986), pp. 246–47. This newspaper was under official control, and it is almost certain that this report was planted by the Prince in reply to accusations that he had neglected the dying Sheridan.
24 Price (ed.), *Sheridan Letters*, Vol. III, p. 248.
25 W. Fraser Rae, *Sheridan: A Biography* (London, 1896), Vol. II, p. 286.
26 Le Fanu Papers, National Library of Ireland, p. 2596.
27 William Smyth, *Memoir of Mr Sheridan* (Leeds, 1840), pp. 67–68.
28 Lord Broughton, *Recollections of a Long Life* (London, 1909), Vol. II, p. 102.
29 Smyth, *Memoir of Mr Sheridan*, pp. 68–69.
30 Le Fanu Papers, NLI, p. 2596.
31 Partington (ed.), *The Private Letter-Books of Sir Walter Scott*, p. 186.
32 William St. Clair, *The Godwins and the Shelleys* (London, 1990), pp. 407–8.

Index